Venetian Inscriptions
Vernacular Writing for Public Display in
Medieval and Renaissance Venice

LEGENDA

LEGENDA is the Modern Humanities Research Association's book imprint for new research in the Humanities. Founded in 1995 by Malcolm Bowie and others within the University of Oxford, Legenda has always been a collaborative publishing enterprise, directly governed by scholars. The Modern Humanities Research Association (MHRA) joined this collaboration in 1998, became half-owner in 2004, in partnership with Maney Publishing and then Routledge, and has since 2016 been sole owner. Titles range from medieval texts to contemporary cinema and form a widely comparative view of the modern humanities, including works on Arabic, Catalan, English, French, German, Greek, Italian, Portuguese, Russian, Spanish, and Yiddish literature. Editorial boards and committees of more than 60 leading academic specialists work in collaboration with bodies such as the Society for French Studies, the British Comparative Literature Association and the Association of Hispanists of Great Britain & Ireland.

The MHRA encourages and promotes advanced study and research in the field of the modern humanities, especially modern European languages and literature, including English, and also cinema. It aims to break down the barriers between scholars working in different disciplines and to maintain the unity of humanistic scholarship. The Association fulfils this purpose through the publication of journals, bibliographies, monographs, critical editions, and the MHRA Style Guide, and by making grants in support of research. Membership is open to all who work in the Humanities, whether independent or in a University post, and the participation of younger colleagues entering the field is especially welcomed.

ALSO PUBLISHED BY THE ASSOCIATION

Critical Texts
Tudor and Stuart Translations • New Translations • European Translations
MHRA Library of Medieval Welsh Literature

MHRA Bibliographies
Publications of the Modern Humanities Research Association

The Annual Bibliography of English Language & Literature
Austrian Studies
Modern Language Review
Portuguese Studies
The Slavonic and East European Review
Working Papers in the Humanities
The Yearbook of English Studies

www.mhra.org.uk
www.legendabooks.com

ITALIAN PERSPECTIVES

Editorial Committee
Professor Simon Gilson, University of Oxford (General Editor)
Dr Francesca Billiani, University of Manchester
Professor Manuele Gragnolati, Université Paris-Sorbonne
Dr Catherine Keen, University College London
Professor Martin McLaughlin, Magdalen College, Oxford

Founding Editors
Professor Zygmunt Barański and Professor Anna Laura Lepschy

In the light of growing academic interest in Italy and the reorganization of many university courses in Italian along interdisciplinary lines, this book series, founded by Maney Publishing under the imprint of the Northern Universities Press and now continuing under the Legenda imprint, aims to bring together different scholarly perspectives on Italy and its culture. *Italian Perspectives* publishes books and collections of essays on any period of Italian literature, language, history, culture, politics, art, and media, as well as studies which take an interdisciplinary approach and are methodologically innovative.

APPEARING IN THIS SERIES

20. *Ugo Foscolo and English Culture*, by Sandra Parmegiani
21. *The Printed Media in Fin-de-siècle Italy: Publishers, Writers, and Readers*, ed. by Ann Hallamore Caesar, Gabriella Romani, and Jennifer Burns
22. *Giraffes in the Garden of Italian Literature: Modernist Embodiment in Italo Svevo, Federigo Tozzi and Carlo Emilio Gadda*, by Deborah Amberson
23. *Remembering Aldo Moro: The Cultural Legacy of the 1978 Kidnapping and Murder*, ed. by Ruth Glynn and Giancarlo Lombardi
24. *Disrupted Narratives: Illness, Silence and Identity in Svevo, Pressburger and Morandini*, by Emma Bond
25. *Dante and Epicurus: A Dualistic Vision of Secular and Spiritual Fulfilment*, by George Corbett
26. *Edoardo Sanguineti: Literature, Ideology and the Avant-Garde*, ed. by Paolo Chirumbolo and John Picchione
27. *The Tradition of the Actor-Author in Italian Theatre*, ed. by Donatella Fischer
28. *Leopardi's Nymphs: Grace, Melancholy, and the Uncanny*, by Fabio A. Camilletti
29. *Gadda and Beckett: Storytelling, Subjectivity and Fracture*, by Katrin Wehling-Giorgi
30. *Caravaggio in Film and Literature: Popular Culture's Appropriation of a Baroque Genius*, by Laura Rorato
31. *The Italian Academies 1525-1700: Networks of Culture, Innovation and Dissent*, ed. by Jane E. Everson, Denis V. Reidy and Lisa Sampson
32. *Rome Eternal: The City As Fatherland*, by Guy Lanoue
33. *The Somali Within: Language, Race and Belonging in 'Minor' Italian Literature*, by Simone Brioni
34. *Laughter from Realism to Modernism: Misfits and Humorists in Pirandello, Svevo, Palazzeschi, and Gadda*, by Alberto Godioli
35. *Pasolini after Dante: The 'Divine Mimesis' and the Politics of Representation*, by Emanuela Patti

Managing Editor
Dr Graham Nelson, 41 Wellington Square, Oxford OX1 2JF, UK
www.legendabooks.com

Venetian Inscriptions

Vernacular Writing for Public Display in Medieval and Renaissance Venice

RONNIE FERGUSON

Italian Perspectives 50
Modern Humanities Research Association
2021

Published by Legenda
an imprint of the Modern Humanities Research Association
Salisbury House, Station Road, Cambridge CB1 2LA

ISBN 978-1-78188-638-0 (HB)
ISBN 978-1-78188-642-7 (PB)

First published 2021
Corrected and expanded edition 2023

All rights reserved. No part of this publication may be reproduced or disseminated or transmitted in any form or by any means, electronic, mechanical, photocopying, recording or otherwise, or stored in any retrieval system, or otherwise used in any manner whatsoever without written permission of the copyright owner, except in accordance with the provisions of the Copyright, Designs and Patents Act 1988, or under the terms of a licence permitting restricted copying issued in the UK by the Copyright Licensing Agency Ltd, Saffron House, 6–10 Kirby Street, London EC1N 8TS, England, or in the USA by the Copyright Clearance Center, 222 Rosewood Drive, Danvers MA 01923. Application for the written permission of the copyright owner to reproduce any part of this publication must be made by email to legenda@mhra.org.uk.

Disclaimer: Statements of fact and opinion contained in this book are those of the author and not of the editors or the Modern Humanities Research Association. The publisher makes no representation, express or implied, in respect of the accuracy of the material in this book and cannot accept any legal responsibility or liability for any errors or omissions that may be made.

Trademark notice: Product or corporate names may be trademarks or registered trademarks, and are used only for identification and explanation without intent to infringe.

© Modern Humanities Research Association 2023

Copy-Editor: Dr Amanda Wrigley

CONTENTS

❖

	Acknowledgements	ix
	Abbreviations	x
1	A Body of Venetian Public Texts *c.* 1300–*c.* 1525	1
	1. Defining the vernacular epigraphic corpus	1
	2. The critical background	8
	3. Ordering and categorising	17
	4. The analytical framework	20
2	The Medium and the Message	33
	1. Evidence of inscriptional processes	33
	2. Trajectories of script use	41
	3. Language	50
3	Corpus: Edition, Translation and Commentary	65
	Index of Inscriptional Persons	387
	Index of Inscriptions by Present Location	391
	Index of Commented Words, Constructions and Linguistic Features	393
	Bibliography	412

To Annie,
who made it possible

ACKNOWLEDGEMENTS

This book has seen the light of day thanks above all to the support of my family. The deepest debt of gratitude goes to my wife Annie. She has been the constant companion of my field trips to Venice, helping me to locate, measure and transcribe the city's medieval and Renaissance inscriptions and providing me with unfailingly sound advice. The vast majority of the photographs in the volume are hers. Our son, Dr Stefan Ferguson of the Bildungszentrum Markdorf in Baden-Württemberg, read the introductory sections. His criticisms and observations were invaluable for clarifying my ideas and sharpening up their expression.

I am indebted to the British and Commonwealth Committee of the Gladys Krieble Delmas Foundation of New York who awarded me a grant of £3000 to carry out archival research and fieldwork for the present volume. My sincere thanks go to Giulio Lepschy and to Brian Richardson who generously supported my application. My grateful thanks, also, to Simon Gilson and Graham Nelson of Legenda, the former for recognising the value of the inscriptional project, the latter for seeing it through to completion with skill, taste and patience. Amanda Wrigley was a thoughtful and sharp-eyed editor.

Many people in Venice facilitated my research. These include the staff of the Museo Correr, the Biblioteca del Museo Correr, the Archivio di Stato, the Museo Archeologico Nazionale, the Frari church, St Mark's Basilica, the Doge's Palace and the Arsenal. In particular, Andrea Bellieni, the Director of the Museo Correr, took the time to discuss and firm up my intuitions about the likely origins and provenance of the inscribed fourteenth-century baptismal font in the Correr. Commander Luca Pegoraro spent a morning giving my wife and me a personal tour of the Arsenal, locating the fifteenth-century epigraphs in the complex and allowing us to photograph them. His help was invaluable as was that of the Arsenal's Assistente Linguistico Patrizia Rigo. On both the practical and human side a warm thank you to our friends Anna Linguerri and Nico Nordio for their companionship and hospitality and to the staff of the Hotel agli Alboretti.

Finally, I wish to acknowledge my debt to the pioneering work of my predecessors in the field of Venetian epigraphy, especially that of the peerless Emmanuele Antonio Cicogna.

R.F., St Andrews, January 2021

This second printing appends one further item, CI 110, a significant find which may be the latest-dated Gothic inscription to survive in Venice. I am grateful to Dr Franco Benucci for bringing this discovery to my attention. The Corpus presented here, and the numbering of its items, is otherwise unchanged.

R.F., August 2023

ABBREVIATIONS

AIRE   Archivio delle Istituzioni di Ricovero e di Educazione
ASV   Archivio di Stato di Venezia
BMC   Biblioteca del Museo Correr
BNM   Biblioteca Nazionale Marciana
CEMP   *Corpus delle Epigrafi Medievali di Padova* <http://cem.dissgea.unipd.it>
CI   Corpus Inscription
CIFM   *Corpus des inscriptions de la France médiévale* <https:www.persee.fr/collection/cifm>
CIL   *Corpus Inscriptionum Latinarum* <https://cil.bbaw.de>
DIO   *Deutsche Inschriften Online* <http://www.inschriften.net>
OED   *Oxford English Dictionary* <http://www.oed.com>
OVI   *Corpus dell'Opera del Vocabolario Italiano dell'italiano antico* <http://gattoweb.ovi.cnr.it>

PART I

A Body of Venetian Public Texts
c. 1300–c. 1525

1. Defining the Vernacular Epigraphic Corpus

The core of the present volume is a substantial and fully illustrated corpus of vernacular writing for public display produced in Venice and its lagoon between *c.* 1300 and *c.* 1525. The collection of 109 inscriptions, the largest of its type ever published for any Italian city, is edited, translated and explicated. Each transcribed epigraph is examined in detail in terms of its dating, location, type, material support, appearance, dimensions, present physical state, inscriptional ensemble, historical background, lettering, language and critical history. The individual entries are integrated with one another, as far as possible, through comment and cross-referencing. In this way the reader is directed to traditions, innovations and recurrences in both medium and message. The corpus as a whole is defined, described, evaluated and contextualised in the present introductory section of the book (I. A body of Venetian public texts *c.* 1300–*c.* 1525), while in the second introductory section (II. The medium and the message) the evidence of the collection provides the concrete basis for wider reflection on inscriptional processes, script use and language choice.

A consideration of the key terminology employed here and elsewhere for the corpus is helpful for bringing into focus the nature and significance of the collection. 'Inscription' and 'epigraph' (in Italian, *iscrizione* and *epigrafe*) are used as synonyms throughout the study.[1] These terms, as they have traditionally been understood, are defined as follows by the *Oxford English Dictionary* (OED), *s.vv.* 'inscription' and 'epigraph':

> That which is inscribed; a piece of writing or lettering upon something; a set of characters or words written, engraved or otherwise traced upon a surface; *esp.* a legend, description, or record traced upon some hard substance for the sake of durability, as on a monument, building, stone, tablet, medal, coin, vase, etc.

Such a definition, with its emphasis on the hardness and durability of the inscription surface, is an accurate statement of the scope of the terms as they have been applied, from the early modern period and into the present, to classical epigraphy both Roman and Greek. It is straightforwardly appropriate to around 70% of the epigraphs in our corpus which are on stone or, in four cases, on metal. It is probably flexible enough to accommodate less immediately orthodox items in the collection such as the palimpsestic painted names of months on the second portal arch of St Mark's Basilica (CI 79), the inked woodblock captions on paper of Jacopo de' Barbari's bird's eye view of Venice (CI 82-CI 91) and the legends inscribed on parchment upon Fra Mauro's great *mappa mundi* (CI 62-CI 66). It could even include the ribbon dedication on the maiolica dish (CI 109) which brings the corpus to a close. It is a less comfortable fit, however, for the range of writing painted in egg tempera, oil or fresco on wooden panel, canvas and plaster found on sixteen corpus entries, including the picturesque guild boards in the Museo Correr (CI 96-CI 99).[2] More seriously still, while the OED definition includes coins and medals, which do not figure directly in our corpus, it ignores embroidered script on fabric such as that found on both sides of a confraternity banner from Torcello (CI 33, CI 34).

A more complete (if still not materially comprehensive) definition of inscription or epigraph, where the length and tenor of the inscribed message, its physical location and its reception are also addressed, was proposed by Armando Petrucci, arguably the founding theorist of medieval epigraphy in Italy. This definition has come to underlie the assumptions of most contemporary epigraphers working in the medieval period:

> un testo di natura commemorativa, enunciativa o designativa, di solito di non lunga estensione, inciso (ma a volte anche dipinto o eseguito a mosaico) con propositi di accuratezza ed intenzioni di solennità su un supporto di materiale duro (marmo, arredi, oreficerie, e così via), ed esposto alla pubblica visione in un luogo chiuso (chiesa, cappella, palazzo), o all'aperto (piazza, via, cimitero).
> (A. PETRUCCI 1992: 38)

Petrucci's consistent deployment of the cover term *scritture esposte*, useful in emphasizing that inscriptions are not exclusively lapidary, has gained wide currency in recent years. It has generated the pithy expression *volgare esposto*, translatable as 'vernacular writing for public display', for vernacular inscriptions as a category.[3] I have deliberately co-opted this phrase into the title of the present volume in order to underline that it is not only the hardness or supposed durability of its material support that turns a piece of writing into an epigraph, but equally its function as, or as part of, a displayed artefact in the widest sense. I take issue slightly here with Petrucci whose restriction of indoor public display to church, chapel, palace and the like excludes more private settings where an inscribed object was plausibly meant to be seen by friends, acquaintances and strangers.[4] There are two intriguing examples in the corpus: the legends on a series of allegorical frescoes from the walls of a private house in the heart of Venice (CI 5, CI 6, CI 7) were undoubtedly conceived to be seen and read by others. The inscribed plate dedicated to a woman by an admirer (CI 109) is more marginal. I have included it, nonetheless, as it appears to straddle the boundary between private gift and object of display — richly decorated maiolica dishes were often shown off in public areas of the household — and to bear a message that is simultaneously personal and conventional.[5]

The timeframe of the corpus is not arbitrary. While the *terminus a quo* largely chose itself, for the *terminus ad quem* I deliberately applied a cut-off point based on cultural-cum-linguistic factors. As it happens, there are no surviving vernacular inscriptions in or from Venice before 1300.[6] The earliest dated epigraphs in the corpus are the commemorative text painted on to the *ancona* of St Donatus of 1310 from Murano (CI 2) and, from the historic centre of Venice itself, the funerary inscription of 1311 carved on a stone sarcophagus in the burial ground of the Scuola Grande di S. Giovanni Evangelista (CI 3). The collection begins, however, with a well-known but undated epigraph: the enigmatic dictum cut on to the sculpted frieze running round the bottom of the remarkable outside wall of St Mark's Treasury, in the passageway into the Doge's Palace. Its dating has attracted intense critical speculation, with hypotheses ranging from the twelfth to the fifteenth centuries. I assign it to *c*. 1300 in an extended example of the type of epigraphic philology that informs my treatment of the corpus as a whole.

Establishing an end date for the collection was more problematic, inasmuch as vernacular inscriptions continued to be produced in Venice throughout the sixteenth century, if at a much reduced volume, in more restricted contexts and registers, and employing an increasingly Tuscanised language. 1525, the year of the publication of Pietro Bembo's *Prose [...] nelle quali si ragiona della volgar lingua* in Venice, symbolically marked the moment when the archaising Trecento variety of Tuscan, modelled on Petrarch and Boccaccio in particular, became the basis of the standardised written 'Italian' rapidly adopted by elites throughout the peninsula. The Venetian which had been the vernacular of inscriptions from all social milieux in the city and lagoon in the fourteenth and fifteenth centuries was thereby soon reduced to the status of a 'dialect',[7] in writing at least, although it remained until the modern period the spoken language of the city and its overseas possessions at all societal levels (FERGUSON 2007: 209–17). In 1523 Andrea Gritti was elected Doge. During his autocratic reign the elitist, classicising tendencies present in Venice since the mid-fifteenth century were definitively entrenched. These were inimical to the vernacular epigraphy which flourished in our period. I use *c*. 1525 for these combined reasons. The final inscribed object in the collection is in actual fact dateable to between 1520 and 1530.

The use of the adjectives 'medieval' and 'Renaissance' in the title of the book is linked to the above observations. The Middle Ages and the Renaissance remain critically useful markers, although no one is in any doubt as to their conceptual and chronological fluidity or to their variable applicability by discipline, city and country. The cultural turn to which I have alluded, manifest in painting and architecture in Venice from the mid-Quattrocento, is a commonplace in art-historical period segmentation.[8] For the epigrapher there can also be no doubt of its reality. The almost total rejection of the vernacular in favour of Latin in high-register inscriptions, combined with the simultaneous abandonment in epigraphy of Gothic majuscules in favour of monumental Roman capitals, suggests that a major paradigm shift took place in the city at around that point. It is convenient to think of it as a watershed between 'medieval' assumptions, attitudes and forms and the new cultural outlook of the Renaissance, although the evidence of the corpus suggests that in Venice, with its conservative native traditions, such a process did not happen overnight and that epigraphic residues from the past persisted or resurfaced. It is worth noting in this context that studies on vernacular epigraphy in Italy invariably define themselves as 'medieval', sometimes stretching that elastic adjective to include the fifteenth century as a whole. The reason for the avoidance of 'Renaissance' is essentially a practical one: vernacular inscriptions tailed off more markedly elsewhere in Italy in the Quattrocento than they did in Venice, and are virtually non-existent in the Cinquecento outside of Venice. For the sake of convenience I therefore confine myself largely to the term 'medieval' when discussing vernacular epigraphy in the section below on the critical background to the discipline in Italy.

The geographical boundaries of the corpus are the city of Venice and its lagoon islands. The majority of the inscriptions (100 of the total number) are, or were originally, sited in the *centro storico* itself, with the islands providing the remaining nine. Murano contributes four entries: CI 2, CI 8, CI 38 and CI 51. Torcello is also home to four, with CI 33, CI 34, CI 46 and CI 56. A solitary inscription, still in situ, comes from Mazzorbo (CI 35). At an early stage I took the decision to limit the corpus to Venice and the islands, with the proviso that I include not only those surviving Venetian epigraphs still found there, in situ or not, but also those few now housed or displayed elsewhere. I exclude inscriptions originating in Venice's hinterland — whether from urban centres such as Padua, Treviso, Vicenza, Verona and Belluno or from more rural locations — where different script and language traditions operated, even under Venetian rule, and where the use of Latin was in any case overwhelming. Although they are surprisingly few in number, the vernacular inscriptions from the Veneto mainland require a study of their own.[9] In order to safeguard the coherence of the collection I also excluded anything from the coastal *Ducatus Venetus*, the *Dogado* running from Cavarzere in the south west to Grado in the north east, even if it was Venetian in language, and anything from Venice's overseas territories.[10]

On the same basis I also decided, reluctantly, to rule out vernacular inscriptions of the period executed by Venetians themselves for centres outside Venice, even for a Venetian sponsor. For this reason the two painted inscriptions in Venetian on the vivid series of tempera panels illustrating the life of St Sebastian, painted in 1367 by Nicoletto Semitecolo for the sacristy of the Basilica del Santo in Padua and now in the Museo Diocesano of that city, do not figure.[11] The same applies to the painted Gothic signature statement on the triptych of the *Madonna, Child and Saints* of 1382 by Guglielmo Veneziano in Recanati,[12] as well as to the authorial epigraph carved on a wooden *cartiglio* at the foot of the extraordinary early-Quattrocento polychrome crucifix, standing 194 cm high, in the church of SS. Apollinare e Cristoforo at Casteldimezzo near Pesaro. It was an entirely Venetian creation, painted by Iacobello del Fiore (Early Venetian, Iacomelo de Flor or de Fior) and carved by Antonio de Bonvesin, the finest *intaiador* of sculpted crucifixes of his day in Venice.[13] Also excluded for this reason is Alvise Vivarini's vernacular signature statement on the *Enthroned Madonna and Child* (1483) in the church of S. Andrea in Barletta.[14] On the other hand, I have included the signature statement by

Lorenzo Veneziano on the panel of the *Mystic Marriage of St Catherine* (1360) in the Accademia. Although there is a suspicion that the painting may have been executed for a mainland commissioner we have no certainty in this matter. I also omitted any painted authorship inscriptions whose authenticity seemed to me dubious for linguistic or palaeographic reasons.[15] Equally, any inscription on a painting whose Venetian provenance seemed debatable was rejected.[16] Inscriptions no longer in existence but recorded in the past, even by experienced observers such as Cicogna, are not part of the corpus.[17] Finally, I excluded the Venetian food captions on the hundreds of porcelain slipware fragments or intact items found in the lagoon. These plates and bowls are generally dated to the post-1550 period, or even later. Some of them seem to me, on grounds of script and language, to come within the later part of our period. However, the absence of dating records, and of a secure stylistic tradition within which to place them, made their inclusion too hazardous.[18]

An additional limitation on the size of the body of texts has been imposed by the conspicuous epigraphic losses sustained by the city and its islands since the sixteenth century. These were partly caused by the inevitable ravages of time. They were exacerbated by the corrosion of the salt air of the lagoon and, in the modern period, by air-borne pollution from household oil heating and especially, in the twentieth century, by sulphur dioxide from the refineries at Mestre-Marghera on the immediate mainland. A different man-made contributor to the impoverishment of the city's epigraphic legacy came about through the destruction of churches, monasteries and confraternity buildings in the wake of the Napoleonic suppression of religious establishments and guilds in the early nineteenth century.[19] The sudden catastrophic abolition of these key centres of epigraphic production and protection, and the subsequent lamentable sell-off of important artefacts from Venice's cultural heritage, were only attenuated in the epigraphic field by the preservation efforts of a handful of patriotic local scholars and enthusiasts.[20] One only has to read through the inscriptions recorded in Cicogna's six published volumes and in his manuscript notebooks in the Biblioteca del Museo Correr (BMC) to realise just how much has been lost since the mid-nineteenth century.[21] Judging by Cicogna's copies of inscriptions he had come across in earlier unpublished manuscripts, but which had not survived, it is also apparent that much had disappeared before his time.

Within all these constraints the corpus is as complete as it was possible for me to make it. In the nine years since the project began I have personally sought out and recorded every vernacular inscription whose potential whereabouts I knew of (or suspected) from all relevant published and manuscript sources and from my own field trips. During this process I uncovered others that had been completely forgotten or neglected, notably the earliest dated inscription in the historic centre of Venice (CI 3), a sole surviving gravestone from our period in the cloisters of S. Francesco della Vigna (CI 78), and an overlooked tomb slab in S. Zanipolo commissioned by the German warehouse packers of the Fontego dei Todeschi (CI 73). Nevertheless, there were potential inscriptional locations to which, despite my efforts, I was unable to obtain access — the church and cloisters of S. Giobbe in Cannaregio which have been off limits for a number of years because of restoration work, and the inside of the former confraternity-guild house of the chest-makers (Venetian, *casseleri*) at S. Maria Formosa — and so it is just possible that a handful of inscriptions still remain to be recorded properly and contextualised.

The essentially Venetian nature of the vernacular that is the privileged medium of the corpus, as well as the few but fascinating examples of code mixing and Tuscanising tendencies present, are considered in the second introductory section ('The medium and the message') and analysed in detail within individual entries. Suffice it to say at this point that the paucity of *volgare* inscriptions from the mainland Veneto in our period already suggests how exceptional Venice is with regard to the weight of vernacular presence. In an Italian landscape where Latin dominated epigraphy throughout the Middle Ages and Renaissance, and indeed even up to the early nineteenth century, no region or city — not Pisa, Florence, Siena, Bologna, Padua, Milan or Rome — came anywhere near to generating the volume of vernacular inscriptions, relative to Latin ones, produced in Venice.[22] The limited statistics available are eloquent. For Venice and the islands I have counted, on the basis of Cicogna's published and unpublished transcriptions, 313 fourteenth-century lapidary inscriptions, with 218 in Latin and 95 in the vernacular (in other words, 30.35% of the total). For the fifteenth century I found 537 lapidary inscriptions, with 434 in Latin and 103 in the vernacular (in other words, 19.18% of the total). Although precise figures for other major centres are lacking, these vernacular percentages are without question the highest by far of any Italian centre, and remarkable when one considers the universal dominance of Latin as the epigraphic medium in Italy. The possible reasons for the unusual prominence of the vernacular in Venice are considered in the context of our reflection on language in the corpus.

Finally, a word about the importance of the corpus, bearing in mind that it is the most coherent and comprehensive record yet published of the surviving vernacular epigraphic legacy of Venice from the Middle Ages and Renaissance, in other words from the very period when Venice — following a remarkable process of immigration, reclamation, coalescence, urbanisation and maritime then mainland expansion — emerged as a dynamic and fabulously wealthy commercial metropolis: at the apogee of its political stability, territorial outreach, and cultural influence. The philosopher, archaeologist and epigrapher R. G. Collingwood famously stated that:

> Inscriptions can enhance the narrative derived from works of history and other sources preserved through the manuscript tradition in three ways: they may reveal events otherwise unknown; they may supplement the information offered by the manuscript tradition; or they can enhance the details known elsewhere by revealing elements of process that might otherwise be hidden from us. Because inscriptions are very different in type, their use in conjunction with, or in constructing, a historical narrative must follow the basic rule of all epigraphic analysis: each text must be read in light of related literary and documentary texts, its physical location, and the process by which it was created. (COLLINGWOOD 1930: 162)

The rhetorical conventions of many of the Latin inscriptions from the Middle Ages and, especially, the Renaissance in Venice tend to bleach their message of time and place. Our vernacular epigraphs, on the other hand, are firmly rooted in everyday realities, humble or exalted, of individuals and collectivities in Venice, providing precise names, dates and places, and recording events and attitudes. They therefore make available to the epigrapher, and to the historian of society and culture, exactly that fine-grained enhancement and supplementation of information, as well as those revelations evoked by Collingwood.

No Latin inscription in Venice has the combined power of information and feeling of the great lunette inscription in Early Venetian at S. Maria della Carità (CI 14). Sculpted in raised, gilded letters on a surface measuring 230 x 100 cm, in eighteen lines of 332 words and 1392 characters, it describes the effects of the earthquake and plague of 1348 on Venice, on Venetian society and on the confraternity itself. We learn from its vivid narrative what buildings were destroyed, what percentage of the population is thought to have died, what the exact plague symptoms were, what the decimation of the *scuola grande* felt like, how many of the confraternity board died, what the names of its chief officers were and how society reacted to the catastrophe.[23] There is no Latin confraternity inscription in the city or islands to compare with the concrete information provided by the plaque of the *scuola piccola* dedicated to St Thomas at the side of the church of S. Tomà (CI 23). It gives us the organisation's offices and officers, with surname-cum-tradenames which reveal the artisan base — cloth shearer, haberdasher, dyer, goldsmith and shoemaker among them — of the confraternity. It includes the names of the alderwoman and the female dean, as well as the date of the original statute and membership book, the *mariegola* (< MATRICŬLA). No lofty laudatory inscription for the famous dead has the touching impact of the one-line epitaph in Venetian on the sarcophagus of the nobleman Simon Dandolo in the Frari which informs us simply that he loved justice and wished to improve the common good (CI 25).

Nowhere is the Latin-vernacular contrast in form and content starker than on the multiple inscriptions in and around the atrium of the Scuola Grande di S. Giovanni Evangelista. There the eye is immediately drawn to a few highly visible Latin proclamations, especially to the dedicatory declaration on the exquisite septum by Pietro Lombardo under which one passes to enter the confraternity precinct. The impeccable Latin, carved in elegant monumental capitals punctuated with Roman *hedera* leaves, reads: *Divo Ioanni apostolo et evangelistae / protectori* ❧ *et sanctissimae crvci* ❧. Outside and inside the main buildings, however, there are no such grand public relations messages. Instead, the down-to-earth details of the confraternity's history are recorded in a series of fourteenth- and fifteenth-century Gothic inscriptions in Venetian: the burial arrangements for its members (CI 3); the stages in the completion of the fabric of the *scuola*, including who paid for them and who gave permission (CI 17, CI 18); how and when a new almshouse built to lodge poor women came about (CI 48); and the date, installation and sponsor of a new organ and pulpit (CI 45).

2. The Critical Background

It is a critical commonplace that medieval Italian epigraphy is a discipline still to some extent in its infancy and, in particular, that the study of vernacular inscriptions of the Middle Ages (and *a fortiori* of the Renaissance) in Italy is the poor relation of Latin epigraphy.[24] There are several overlapping reasons for its relative neglect, patchy coverage and uncertain status.[25] Surprisingly, at first sight, the subject has been overshadowed rather than sustained by the intense attention and respect traditionally accorded to the ubiquitous inscriptions of the ancient, and especially the Roman, world. Those epigraphs, visible, legible and numerous, were cut into stone in prestigious and relatively homogeneous inscriptional capital lettering in public spaces throughout the highly literate Roman Empire, from Britain to the Middle East, with Rome as its epicentre. They have long been regarded as an essential tool in classical studies, and have consequently been extensively collected, edited, analysed and integrated into historical and archaeological work.[26] Even the scholarly interest in the neo-Roman inscriptional revival of Latin in the Renaissance period, fostered by Italian Humanism and of which the Veneto was a centre of experimentation and diffusion, has had few if any positive repercussions for medieval epigraphy in Italy, and especially not for its severely neglected vernacular branch.[27]

The settled state of classical epigraphy as a discipline — based on the high level of typological, material, linguistic and palaeographic homogeneity of its source material, on its physical and documentary accessibility,[28] and on its centuries-long research tradition — have stacked the odds against medieval epigraphy and, even more so, against its vernacular subdivision. The medieval epigraphist in Italy faces daunting challenges in precisely these areas. At the most basic level, the process of locating, documenting, photographing, editing and explicating Italy's legacy of medieval inscriptions is still at a relatively early stage: more advanced in some centres than in others, but nowhere complete. It is especially the case for those inscriptions, the overwhelming majority, dating from 1100 onwards. Vernacular epigraphy in particular has had to wait until very recently for the first tentative nationwide survey of critical activity in the field.[29] Whereas classical inscriptions are available in large public and private collections, most medieval lapidary inscriptions — especially the vernacular ones — tend still to be in situ or close to their original locations, unprotected and largely not censused. This very much holds true in Venice where only a minority are safeguarded and labelled. Most of the few that are protected are housed and displayed in the finest collection of medieval stone epigraphs in the city, in the cloisters and on the stairs of the Seminario Patriarcale complex at the Salute.[30]

It is worth pointing out, in this context, a reality that is too seldom considered. Compared to the artefacts of classical epigraphy — overwhelmingly confined to lapidary inscriptions — the range of medieval inscriptional types and material supports across the peninsula and within individual centres is considerably more diverse.[31] In Venice alone a single church, the Basilica of St Mark, contains hundreds of lines of medieval epigraphic text in mosaic, as well as inscriptions of many sorts and techniques on a wide range of liturgical objects, reliquaries and plaques. As for script itself, the classical epigrapher deals almost exclusively with Roman monumental capitals and their occasional related variant, the *scriptura actuaria* often called 'rustic capitals'. The medieval Italian epigraphist faces a bewildering array of letter types — mainly majuscules but occasionally minuscules or with minuscule intrusions — which are rarely identical from centre to centre and whose chronology of appearance is variable and overlapping.[32]

While the period from around 1300 to 1500 was unquestionably the high point in vernacular epigraphy in Italy until the nineteenth century, we remain to a large extent in the dark about the quantitative distribution of such inscriptions across the peninsula. In fact, apart from Venice, we know little yet about the precise or even approximate ratio within each city and region of vernacular to Latin inscriptions. The lack of a national inscriptional corpus for the pre-modern period, of the kind long underway in other major countries, is often and justifiably held up as both cause and symptom.[33] That such an Italian database remains highly desirable, indeed a *sine qua non* for the full development of the subject, is beyond dispute. It would allow cross-regional evaluations of Italo-Romance inscriptions, on a quantitative and qualitative basis, revealing urban and regional similarities, divergences and peculiarities. It would disclose, too, how they cluster by chronology and category.[34] Finally, such a resource would facilitate the meaningful cross-national screening that has hitherto not been feasible. What has been present on the ground in Italy is some excellent work by gifted and dedicated epigraphists in specific locations. The result is that we have relatively extensive knowledge of a few cities such as Pisa, Bologna and Modena thanks, in the first case, to Ottavio Banti, in the second to Bruno Breveglieri and Giancarlo Roversi, and in the third to Augusto Campana.[35] On the other hand, there remain significant gaps in our appreciation of the medieval epigraphic production, especially in the vernacular, of great cultural centres like Milan, Genoa, Florence and Naples.[36]

Until very recently, the epigraphic history of Venice has been a paradoxical one, consisting of starts and stops. Venetian recording and collecting of classical inscriptions began promisingly with Marin Sanudo's trip in 1483 to the Veneto *terraferma* where he transcribed twenty-five Roman inscriptions around Lake Garda (BUONOPANE 2014) and, in the sixteenth century, with the Grimani family's formidable and much-admired collection of antiquities, including Latin and Greek epigraphs, which — left to the state by Domenico Grimani in 1523 and Giovanni Grimani in 1587 — went on to form the basis of the Museo Archeologico Nazionale off St Mark's Square. By the late Cinquecento a start had also been made to recording the city's own medieval and Renaissance epigraphic heritage. The impetus came, unsurprisingly, from quality guidebooks dedicated to Venice. The pioneer in this domain was Francesco Sansovino. His well-informed, attractively laid out and beautifully printed best-seller, *Venetia città nobilissima* (SANSOVINO 1581), was studded with inscriptions — some in italics, others in capitals of various sizes and in different fonts — principally from churches across the city and from the Doge's Palace. Obviously responding to a fashion for Latin epigraphic testimony of famous men, Sansovino recorded many of the major inscriptions, mainly epitaphs, of this type in the city. To his credit — and this was groundbreaking — he also included two fourteenth-century vernacular inscriptions whose importance did not elude him, copying them out with a good degree of accuracy using an interpretative transcription. The first was the splendid foundation epigraph of 1346, from the now demolished church of S. Antonio Abate in Castello, which is at present in the Seminario Patriarcale cloisters. It is one of the outstanding pieces in our corpus (CI 13). He also recorded the now destroyed column inscription of 1376 commemorating in Venetian the foundation of the Oratorio del Volto Santo which still stands in Cannaregio.[37] That inscription was commissioned by the economically significant Lucchese merchant community in the city which crops up more than once in the corpus.

In the much expanded and rather chaotically laid out second edition of *Venetia città nobilissima* (SANSOVINO and STRINGA 1604), Giovanni Stringa, the canon of St Mark's, packed the revised text with extra inscriptions, leaving Sansovino's original ones as they were. He was the first, as far as I am aware, to record the raised commemorative inscription of 1344–45 from the *scuola grande* of S. Maria della Carità (CI 9) which initiated the peak period of vernacular epigraphy in medieval Venice. He also recorded the self-publicising vernacular inscription of *c.* 1385, in effect the 'calling-card', of the Venetian sculptor Polo Chataiapiera beneath the monument to the *condottiere* Iacopo Cavalli in S. Zanipolo (CI 44). While both of the above appear to have been eye-witness transcriptions, Stringa's record of the famous *damnatio memoriae* of the patrician traitor Baiamonte Tiepolo — carved on a column standing near the church of S. Agostin (CI 32) — seems to be based on popular hearsay. Nonetheless he accurately preserved for posterity a fascinating lapidary inscription from the Cappella del Rosario, situated to the left of the main altar in S. Zanipolo. This epigraph perished in the fire that destroyed that chapel in 1867.[38] Sansovino and Stringa's example was replicated in the later seventeenth century by Domenico Martinelli's *Ritratto di Venezia* (MARTINELLI 1684) which, like their guidebook, was crammed with Latin epitaphs from across the city. Following their example, he too recorded a few vernacular inscriptions. The S. Maria della Carità and S. Antonio Abate epigraphs (CI 9, CI 13), as well as the dedicatory epitaph in the Oratorio del Volto Santo, were repeated. Less expectedly, two more humble commemorative inscriptions appeared: the epigraph of the devotional confraternity of S. Tomà (CI 23) and the plaque on the outside of the almshouse of *ser* Natichlier Cristian at S. Ternita (CI 4) carrying the first fully Gothic vernacular inscription in the city.

In their high-class guides to the city, Sansovino and Stringa, followed by Martinelli, had built a modest foundation upon which a properly structured history, or at least record, of Venetian vernacular epigraphy could have been built. It did not happen. In fact, vernacular inscriptional studies in Venice can be said to have marked time between the early seventeenth and early nineteenth centuries. This statement can be verified concretely by checking how little had changed in terms of inscriptional recording between Sansovino, Stringa and Martinelli, on the one hand, and Giannantonio Moschini's important two-volume *Guida per la città di Venezia* (MOSCHINI 1815) on the other. Moschini's topographical scope was, on the face of it, more wide-ranging than theirs, with sections on the lagoon islands and on a range of palaces and institutions in the city. Culturally well informed and interested in epigraphy, Moschini in fact included a host of Latin inscriptions in the 1,000 or so pages of his two volumes. However, the continuing bias in his work in favour of Latin, *uomini famosi* and *monumenta insigna* meant that he only found space for a meagre four fully transcribed vernacular inscriptions. These are, in order, the Polo Chataiapiera plaque (CI 44), the Treasury dictum (CI 1), the niello inscription from 1375 on the *Column of the Flagellation of Christ* (CI 39), and the writing painted on to the *ancona* of St Donatus on Murano (CI 2).[39] He saw the Simon Dandolo tomb in the Frari but ignored its epitaph in Venetian (CI 25), and he transcribed the first line of the 1344–45 foundation inscription in the ex-Scuola di S. Maria della Carità (CI 9), finishing it with an 'etc.', whereas if it had been in Latin he would have spared no effort to record it in its entirety. The reasons for his few, seemingly random, inclusions are obvious. The Chataiapiera message is set under a hugely prestigious tomb; the Treasury dictum is embedded on the outer wall of St Mark's in the corridor leading to the Doge's Palace; the *Column* inscription is an exceptional work of art, one of the finest in the Basilica Treasury, commissioned by two Procurators of St Mark; the historical importance of the ancient devotional image in SS. Maria e Donato was self-evident. Another factor militating against vernacular epigraphs, and not only in Moschini, was Gothic script which by this time seemed to present some difficulty for the transcriber. One notices that on the Treasury inscription (CI 1) Moschini misread the Gothic <u/v> for an <l>.

Although 1600–1800 was largely a period of stasis as far as vernacular inscriptions were concerned, there were sporadic signs of interest in the subject. In antiquarian publications a few epigraphs found themselves transcribed as historical testimony. This was usually, but not always, in the context of ecclesiastical history in such publications as Flaminio Corner's multi-volume survey of Venetian churches, Gianfrancesco Pivati's ten-volume encyclopaedia and Giannantonio Meschinello's three-volume study of St Mark's Basilica. Corner's teeming work in Latin is particularly useful. Although the transcriptions in it are on occasion inaccurate, CORNER (1749) is valuable for the following precocious recordings: the great plague epigraph on the lunette at the entrance to the confraternity of S. Maria della Carità (CI 14); the 1349 inscription from the *scuola* of S. Giovanni Evangelista (CI 17); the Pietà appeal inscription (CI 20); the plaque in Corte S. Andrea (CI 21) whose relief and inscription he rendered in a fine line drawing; and the S. Polo *campanile* inscription (CI 28). In the opening volume of his survey of the epigraphs in San Marco, Meschinello was the first to record the Treasury dictum (CI 1) that begins our corpus (MESCHINELLO 1753, I: 29). Otherwise, inscriptional studies in Venice went underground in the period, confined largely to manuscript collections commissioned by wealthy patrician connoisseurs for their private libraries. Although not always accurate in their transcriptions, such antiquarian compilations were useful and were much consulted by Cicogna (who recognised their limitations) when he was given access to them in the nineteenth century.[40] However, in the eighteenth century there was one outstanding advance in inscriptional recording within its hitherto neglected monumental context. This was the great undertaking of the Venetian-Flemish artist Giovanni (or Jan) Grevembroch (c. 1731–1807) who, under the enlightened patronage of the patrician Pietro Gradenigo (1695–1776), illustrated a large number of monuments in Venice. His meticulously drawn and beautifully coloured pictures, with their written comments, are of immense historical value. Without them we would not, for example, be able to appreciate in their original state the two great inscriptions at S. Giovanni Evangelista which have been largely devastated by time and pollution (CI 17, CI 18). In addition, his drawings are the first to record the 1345 inscription and relief of the *Madonna and Child* on the façade of the Accademia (CI 10) and the 1505 inscription over the entrance to the Corte Nova almshouses in Cannaregio (CI 93). The four volumes of Grevembroch's illustrations (GREVEMBROCH 1754), invaluable though they are to historians, have never been published and can still only be consulted directly in the Correr library.

The first qualitative leap in Venetian epigraphic studies, particularly from the point of view of the vernacular, occurred in the early 1820s with the separate publications of Giannantonio Soravia and Emmanuele Cicogna. Although Soravia's modest three-volume work — devoted, one per volume, to the church of S. Zanipolo, to the Frari and associated churches, and to S. Rocco — cannot be compared in terms of size and scope to Cicogna's great *œuvre*, its significance should not be underestimated. In the first place he recorded nine vernacular inscriptions, including those at S. Giovanni Evangelista (CI 17, CI 18, CI 48), S. Polo (CI 28), S. Tomà (CI 23) and the Frari (CI 25, CI 49). Some, like those of the Scuola dei Milanesi in the Frari (CI 49) and the almshouse in Calle de la Laca (CI 48), were transcribed for the first time. Secondly, Soravia is one of the first observers to show genuine interest in epigraphic script itself. Like Sansovino before him, he had his inscriptions printed in an interesting and varied way. He went further, though, in seeking to record their original layout as faithfully as possible, showing among other things where letters or words were run together, and to transcribe diplomatically using special signs for suspension bars, abbreviations and interpuncts. Although he did not go into the specifics of palaeographic description when treating an individual epigraph, he occasionally indicated if the script was in Gothic majuscules or Roman monumental capitals, employing the terms 'caratteri moderni' and 'caratteri antichi' respectively. Last but not least, Soravia provided some cultural context for his chosen inscriptions.

Almost immediately after the appearance of Soravia's volumes, Venice had the benefit of having virtually its entire inscriptional legacy on stone transcribed, and in part historically contextualised, by one of Italy's greatest antiquarian scholars of the nineteenth century, Emmanuele Antonio Cicogna (1789–1868).[41] In addition to his admirable work in protecting and collecting inscriptions threatened by the edicts and actions of the Napoleonic, Austrian and Italian governments of Venice, Cicogna copied out some 11,000 lapidary inscriptions, Latin and vernacular, in

Venice and on the islands, beginning his immense task of locating and transcribing in January 1817. His ambition was to cover all Venetian epigraphy, from post-classical to contemporary, irrespective of location, with the important exception of St Mark's Basilica. He more or less achieved this, with the major proviso that around 9,000 of the transcriptions actually remained unpublished at his death, preserved in his manuscript inscriptional notebooks which he left to the Biblioteca del Museo Correr.[42] The remainder were published in his lifetime in six tightly-packed volumes (CICOGNA 1824–53) where, in the introduction to the first volume, he provided a detailed and reliable account of Venetian epigraphic scholarship as a whole from the Renaissance to the nineteenth century.[43] Cicogna's obsession with completeness, covering almost 1,000 years of epigraphic production in Venice, was both his strength and his weakness. It had been suggested to him that he operate a selection based on importance and quality of inscription but he explicitly, and rightly, ruled this out in his introduction on the grounds that it was impossible to know for sure, at that moment and in the future, what constitutes major or minor significance. Nevertheless, the criticism can be laid at his door that if he had concentrated on the Middle Ages and Renaissance alone — where the most vulnerable and arguably most culturally interesting part of the city's epigraphic heritage lay — it is likely that most of what had fortuitously survived from those periods would have been published. As it is, basically only those inscriptions from our period which happened to be in and around the churches covered in the six volumes were published, while very little of the public vernacular writing scattered throughout the city outside of churches appeared in print.

Cicogna's approach was totally new and his achievement, dedicated explicitly to his native Venice, is magnificent. It remains not only the starting point but the constant point of reference for any serious study of Venetian inscriptions, Latin or vernacular. With him epigraphy became for the first time the centre of a major scholar's attention. In addition, he was the first, apart arguably from Grevembroch whose focus was different, to treat Latin and vernacular epigraphs with equal attention and respect. His organising principle was to concentrate one by one on the churches of Venice and their immediate surroundings, providing historical background in each case, before systematically tackling every inscription from every period within range.[44] With his historical interests to the fore he was himself clear that his principal concern was the content rather than the form of the inscriptions. Nevertheless he paid close attention to reproducing form, rather in the manner of Soravia. His method involved, first, the transcription of each epigraph in capital letters. He copied as diplomatically as possible, with the aim of presenting appearance and layout as faithfully as he could. He recognised the practical limits of this approach, though, by explicitly opting not to set out his transcriptions like the originals but instead to condense them on the page homogeneously, using vertical lines to indicate line endings. He left abbreviations as they were, signalling them with overbars. He did not attempt to reproduce internal abbreviation strokes, such as the Tironian 7 slashed through <d> for *de*, using instead a short line above the letter to indicate these. He did, however, always reproduce the Tironian 9 for *con-* or *com-*. Where raised or miniaturised letters were part of the original he had recourse to superscript, and if a suitable font was available he reproduced word-end abbreviations such as the combined 2 and 4 symbol, common in Latin inscriptions for *-rum* endings. Gaps or illegible passages were indicated by a sequence of dots, usually three, without square brackets. Interpuncts were indicated with full stops.

Cicogna's typical procedure was, immediately after his transcription, to provide brief information about where and how he transcribed the epigraph, sometimes supplying details about its state and including references to other scholars who had mentioned it. Since he deliberately chose not to devote time to describing the inscriptional whole, the monumental context of an epigraph is usually omitted or only briefly sketched in. Measurements are not provided. This procedure can be appreciated by considering the start of his commentary on a vernacular inscription of 1374 (now lost) commemorating the finding of the bones of 200 presumed child martyrs under the church of S. Stefano on Murano where the plaque itself was originally affixed.[45] With many Latin inscriptions he would leave out such preliminaries, proceeding immediately to his historical strengths. His accompanying indices are exemplary in their completeness.

Comparison between his published and manuscript transcriptions (copied out in his neat hand in lined notebooks) and those inscriptions which have survived shows Cicogna to have been a thorough transcriber who achieved a high degree of accuracy. As an educated Venetian and antiquarian, his handling of Early and Middle Venetian is generally sound, although as a non-palaeographer his reading of script in the vernacular, when the state of the inscription made comprehension tricky, sometimes let him down. One of his main palaeographic weaknesses was the failure to indicate the <ç>, widespread in Early Venetian and an important indicator whenever dating is an issue. He transcribed it as a <z>, as did Soravia who also sometimes used <c>. He unfortunately only mentioned script, as such, sporadically and was clearly more at home in his comments on names, places and protagonists where his expertise is invaluable and where his vast historical knowledge, packed into footnotes, was deployed. Fortunately, his text is punctuated with line drawings of epigraphs which were particularly curious or striking.

The exceptional groundwork carried out by Cicogna, and also by Soravia and Moschini on a lesser scale, did not fall completely on deaf ears. The outlook of Romanticism, followed by the archival positivism underpinning new journals like the proceedings of the *Istituto Veneto di Scienze, Lettere ed Arti* (from 1843) and the *Archivio Veneto* (from 1871), found an ideal subject in the fabric and history of Venice. The fall of the 1,000-year Republic and the subsequent economic decline and cultural despoliation of the city opened up a period of intense concern for recovering and recording its past whose best-known voices were Ruskin and Pompeo Molmenti.[46] The time was finally ripe in this climate for an interest, scholarly or amateur, in Venice's written vernacular records of all kinds — archival, literary and even epigraphic — and in its language itself which was felt to be already under siege from Italian and from modernity. This impetus produced the two editions of Giuseppe Boerio's unsurpassed *Dizionario del dialetto veneziano* (BOERIO

1829 and 1865). It was at this moment that vernacular inscriptions were first grouped and considered together, albeit modestly, above all as tangible examples of Venice's linguistic heritage. Seen from a distance, the opening pages of Bartolomeo Gamba's booklet on Venetian dialect texts (B. GAMBA 1832) — which reproduce from Cicogna, Moschini and BETTIO (1829), rather than from personal fieldwork, twelve vernacular inscriptions, eight of them extant in Venice — are indeed modest. However, the potential impact of Gamba's work should not be underestimated. He revealed to a wider public with an appetite for dialect heritage a virtually unknown part of Venice's written past, most of it still visible to the curious within the city. He reproduced, with brief but useful references to location and to previous transcribers, the great letter from Urban V on the loggia of the Doge's Palace (CI 30); the Treasury dictum (CI 1); the inscriptions on the nearby Justice capital (CI 54) and Fruit capital (CI 53) of the Palazzo Ducale; the painted writing on the St Donatus devotional image on Murano (CI 2); the Baiamonte Tiepolo column condemnation (CI 32); the confraternity inscription at S. Marcilian (CI 50); the epitaph of Simon Dandolo (CI 25); the plaque from 1358 commemorating new houses at the Calle del Paradiso (CI 22); and the epigraph from the merchants' confraternity recording the legacy to them of a house by the politician Antonio Tron (CI 107).[47]

In spite of this start it took another sixty years for the first article purely on Venetian vernacular inscriptions to appear in a scholarly journal. Giovanni Ferro's short piece in *Il Propugnatore* (FERRO 1889) was modestly innovative.[48] Limiting himself to early inscriptions which were explicitly dated, Ferro grouped eleven fourteenth-century epigraphs, ten of them extant, transcribing mostly but not exclusively from direct observation. Six had already appeared in print but Ferro distinguished himself by publishing together the three inscriptions on the outside wall of the S. Maria della Carità complex (CI 10, CI 11, CI 12) and the great lunette inscription there describing the 1348 plague (CI 14), as well as an epigraph from the confraternity of S. Matia which was in the Seminario Patriarcale (CI 27). Above all he appreciated that the original layout of the inscribed plaquettes on the already published *Column of the Flagellation of Christ* inscription (CI 39) had become jumbled at some point in the past, and he restored the correct word order. His transcriptions themselves are of variable quality and accuracy and, like Moschini and Cicogna, he rendered <ç> as <z>. Nevertheless, Ferro contributed to raising the low profile of Venetian vernacular epigraphs by treating them as a worthy, if minor, object of study and by sketching in a critical background for individual items.

That critical framework was further filled in by Enrico Bertanza and Vittorio Lazzarini's miscellany of early Venetian documents (BERTANZA and LAZZARINI 1891). They considered the Treasury dictum (CI 1), the St Donatus inscription (CI 2), the Baiamonte Tiepolo column epigraph (CI 32), and the two inscriptions on capitals of the Doge's Palace (CI 53, CI 54). Unfortunately they chose not to reproduce any of these epigraphs themselves from direct observation. Perhaps more significant for the future of the discipline, in terms of method, tone and coherence, was the essay devoted by Giuseppe Tassini to all the inscriptions in the church, monastery and confraternity of S. Maria della Carità, where he transcribed diplomatically, provided some sound contextual comments, and created name indices (TASSINI 1876). Most importantly, in the second part of his essay, focused specifically on the confraternity, he recorded together the surviving vernacular inscriptions of the *scuola grande*: the three under the façade reliefs (CI 10, CI 11, CI 12), the raised epigraph of 1344–45 (CI 9), and the magnificent plague inscription of 1348 (CI 14). As Tassini made clear, he was perfectly acquainted with Cicogna's work and had consulted his manuscript notebooks.

In spite of Cicogna's labours and the nascent interest shown subsequently in Venetian epigraphy, the fact remains that by the end of the nineteenth century little more than two dozen inscriptions from Venice's surviving vernacular epigraphic legacy had actually been published in any form, a disappointing total which remained unaltered until the end of the twentieth century.

For most of the twentieth century, vernacular epigraphy in Venice and elsewhere in Italy made few advances. The reasons were multiple and overlapping. There was the absence of a solid and widespread philological base in Italian universities such as that which existed in Germany and France. Medieval epigraphics lacked an academic home, and those few interested in inscriptions would have faced a climate of indifference, or worse, to the study of inscribed dialect writing. The belated coming of age of Venetian vernacular epigraphy only began towards the end of the century. Not surprisingly it arose from within two closely related areas of increasing academic strength in Italy: textual philology and history of the language. These had generated an exceptional concentration of interests and strengths in the study of the language, literature and archival documents of Venice and the Veneto, from their origins to the Renaissance, not only in the universities of Venice and Padua but in centres as far apart as Udine and the Scuola Normale Superiore in Pisa. It was from this renewal — which produced figures of the stature of Gianfranco Folena, Manlio Cortelazzo, Ivano Paccagnella, Furio Brugnolo, Alfredo Stussi and Giorgio Padoan — and from the gradual formation of a solid academic hinterland of research and teaching in epigraphics in Venice and Padua,[49] that the conditions finally arose in which the scientific work of editing and analysing Venice's surviving vernacular epigraphs could be undertaken. Three scholars have mainly been involved until now: Alfredo Stussi, Lorenzo Tomasin and the present author. All three were trained in history of the language, dialectology and textual exegesis, with a special interest in Venice and the Veneto. It is no surprise, then, that the main strengths of their approach have been in the textual, linguistic and, to some extent, historical elucidation of Venetian vernacular inscriptions. Script in their methodology has had a generally lower profile, as has been the case in most medieval epigraphic work in Italy, vernacular or otherwise, where it tends to be described in isolation and is rarely considered historically or comparatively.[50] In the pathfinding stage the focus of all three was on publishing philologically sound editions of individual or small groups of Venetian epigraphs. This branched gradually into an exploration of wider dimensions of vernacular epigraphy.[51] I, in the meantime, published the first substantial edited and commented compilation dedicated to fourteenth-century Venetian inscriptions and then the first volume devoted to the epigraphic legacy of the Venetian confraternities of the Trecento and Quattrocento.[52] Only now, with the present volume, is the city's exceptional production of vernacular inscriptions from the Middle Ages and Renaissance finally gathered, censused and fully explicated. What had long been suspected is at last becoming clear: in terms of quantity, quality and the socio-cultural importance of its vernacular epigraphic inheritance, Venice is unrivalled in the peninsula. The best recent examples of medieval epigraphics from Venice, the Veneto and elsewhere suggest a turning point in both the recognition of the specificity and importance of vernacular epigraphy and in the methodological development of the discipline itself.[53]

3. Ordering and Categorising

For the ordering of the 109 corpus entries I adopt a broadly chronological approach. This progressive structuring of the material self-evidently allows for a better appreciation of developments in script and language. It also brings out peaks and troughs in inscriptional activity and the evolution of epigraphic types and norms. Structuring by time is facilitated by the high number of inscriptions which carry explicit dates, around 70% of the total. A significant number of the undated epigraphs can also be placed with a fair degree of precision. Among these are the charitable endowment of an almshouse by Natichlier Cristian (CI 4) at S. Ternita. I date it *c.* 1312 because the wording of Cristian's endowment legacy from 1312 suggests that building work on the *hospedal* was already underway or completed at that point. The *damnatio memoriae* of Baiamonte Tiepolo (CI 32) is likely to be from *c.* 1364, the year in which the Senate decree for its erection was voted through. The papal bull in stone inscribed on the loggia of the Palazzo Ducale (CI 30) is assigned to *c.* 1362, as the original was issued in Avignon soon after Urban V's accession that year. The undated relief plaque of the German shoemaking workers in Calle de le Boteghe at S. Stefano (CI 42) is ascribable to 1384, the year the shoemakers' confraternity was licensed by the authorities. The vernacular 'calling card' plaque of the sculptor Polo Chataiapiera, below the tomb of Iacopo Cavalli in S. Zanipolo, can reasonably be assigned to *c.* 1385 since Cavalli died in 1384 and documentary evidence suggests that work began soon afterwards. Other inscriptions can be dated with a reasonable degree of accuracy on stylistic grounds, sometimes combined with script and/or language criteria. This is the case with the Treasury inscription (CI 1) which opens the corpus *c.* 1300 and with the painted maiolica plate (CI 109) that brings it to a close *c.* 1525. It is also true of Çuane da Bologna's signature on his panel of *Our Lady of Humility* (CI 43), originally painted for the Scuola Grande di S. Giovanni Evangelista. Knowledge of the painter's career suggests the 1380s for the execution of the picture. Others still can be located within a discrete time range based on documentary evidence. This applies to the Pietà charitable appeal plaque which I cautiously place between 1343, when Clement VI issued the indulgence mentioned in the inscription, and 1352, when he died. The vernacular captions on the Justice capital (CI 54) and Fruit capital (CI 53) on the arcade of the Doge's Palace are both dateable to between 1422 and 1442, when work on the section of the palace concerned was carried out. Strong circumstantial evidence suggests that the earliest and latest dates for the legends on Fra Mauro's *mappa mundi* (CI 62–66) are likely to be *c.* 1448 and *c.* 1460. The remainder of the inscriptions have had, of necessity, to be assigned a broader dating based either on style, script or language, or on a combination of these, and to be inserted within the corpus order with some degree of uncertainty. In this group are the Da Lezze coat of arms (CI 61) on a house-front in Cannaregio, attributed to the mid-fifteenth century, and the inscribed ownership cartouches of the S. Marcilian neighbourhood association which are probably from the second half of the fifteenth century. Interesting connected cases are the pairs of inscriptions on the *barbacane* corbel (CI 101, CI 102) and on the street divider (CI 103, CI 104), located in parallel alleyways at the Rialto. On script and language alone they would have to be ascribed broadly to the late fifteenth or early sixteenth centuries. However, our knowledge of the great Rialto fire of 1514 suggests that they may well have been erected shortly after this date in a rebuilding campaign.

I have modified my chronological approach on five occasions. In two cases I grouped inscriptions executed at different dates because they formed a deliberately coherent ensemble, monumental or thematic, which had to be considered as an entity. This is the case with the inscriptions beneath the three reliefs set on the façade of the former Scuola Grande di S. Maria della Carità at the Accademia (CI 10, CI 11, CI 12) which are dated, respectively, 1345, 1377 and 1384. It also explains why I grouped the two great inscriptions formerly embedded one beneath the other in the atrium of the Scuola Grande di S. Giovanni Evangelista (CI 17, CI 18) in spite of their dates (1349 and 1453) being widely separated. Slightly different is the case of the two inscribed ledgerstones of the German warehouse packers, the *ligadori de Fontego*, in S. Zanipolo (CI 73, CI 74), which were set into the floor of the church at an interval of a few years (1472 and 1478). Their identical function and sponsorship, as well as their closely matching aesthetic, made it compelling to consider them together. Similar reasons led to the grouping of the four vividly painted guild boards now in the Museo Correr but originally in the Palazzo dei Camerlenghi at the Rialto (CI 96–99). Although neither of the two cartouche inscriptions of the S. Marcilian housing association (CI 71, CI 72) is dated, similarity of style, identity of purpose and proximity of display made their grouping persuasive.

The information to be gleaned from a multi-layered approach to categorising our inscriptions is useful for understanding patterns in the corpus that are invisible at the level of the individual epigraph. The most abstract categorisation is by type. It discloses that approximately 50% of our inscriptions can be classed, in the broad sense, as commemorative. The next largest grouping, with around 20% of occurrences, comprises captions, legends and toponyms. This is followed at around 10% by moralising or didactic epigraphs, 8% by authorship statements (of painters or sculptors), 5% by funerary writing (epitaphs and tomb ownership) and 4% by charity-related inscriptions (appeals, legacies, almshouses).

Another broad category of analysis is by sponsorship.[54] This is particularly revealing of the role of Venice's confraternities, great, small or national. Almost half the artefacts in the collection, some 48%, were commissioned by the *scuole*. Mapping this figure on to the typological classification, it is clear that most of the commemorative category is occupied by the confraternities, although their sponsorship also extends into the funerary and authorship groups. Approximately 20% of artefact commissions are from individuals not directly connected with the Venetian government, while a further 12% can be linked either to the authorities or to state officials. Roughly 18% of artefacts are attributable to ecclesiastical sponsorship (church or religious house). The remaining few are linked to patrician families or to associations (charity, neighbourhood residents, Arsenal workers). When one carries out a count by support material employed, the dominance of lapidary inscriptions (around 68%) maps fairly neatly on to the commemorative-confraternity intersection, although it also spills over into the charity, didactic, authorship and, of course, funerary categories. Painting support materials — wall plaster, wooden panel, canvas or maiolica, corresponding to the medium of fresco, egg tempera, oil paint or pigment — make up approximately 13% of epigraphs. A similar figure applies to ink support materials (parchment or paper). Metalwork (gilded silver, niello, appliqué, bronze) and fabric account for some 3% and 1.5 % of inscriptions respectively.

Two further important refinements can be made to the large lapidary category, where the majority (51 out of 71) are in Istrian limestone — and, in one case, a re-used Roman artefact, in Aurisina limestone from near Trieste — alongside a surprisingly substantial contingent in marble (18 out of 71) and a single tomb in trachite. Marble is employed, as expected, for some of the most prestigious commissions in the corpus, such as the magnificent CI 14 and CI 30, but it supports more apparently modest inscriptions such as CI 4 on the Natichlier Cristian almshouse, the Piarini will in stone on Murano (CI 8), and several *scuola piccola* reliefs (CI 19, CI 108).[55] In each of these cases the sponsor, whether individual or confraternity, evidently had the means to opt for the more expensive stone.

One further category of analysis, by date, helps us to grasp distribution trends in the corpus chronology which are easily lost within the volume of inscriptions. The first trend is more general; the second focuses on confraternities. The tally of inscriptions from the first four decades of the fourteenth century is a meagre eight (with five securely dated). At that point there is the most remarkable explosion of vernacular inscriptional production ever seen in Venice. Fully twenty-two inscriptions are located in the thirty-year period between 1341 and 1370. Subsequently the fever of epigraphic activity subsides to more sedate levels, with around two to four examples per decade on average. The higher end of this average is achieved between 1421 and 1450 and again between 1491 and 1520. Scholars working on Venetian vernacular epigraphy had long suspected that the mid-fourteenth century was the high point of the vernacular moment. The figures yielded by the corpus not only confirm this intuition but show a truly exceptional intensification of activity that was never repeated. There is no obvious single explanation for the phenomenon and the vagaries of time and chance cannot be discounted. However, the conjunction of factors we touch on below in the section on language choice — intense economic activity, the flowering of confraternities with, at that point, relatively broad-based governance structures, and the powerful penetration of the vernacular into the written sphere even at official levels — are likely to come into it. In addition, vernacular influences from Tuscan were as yet absent, while the return to Latin promoted by Humanism was still distant. Be that as it may, it is not only the quantitative upsurge in inscriptional numbers that is striking. It is also the quality and substantiality of the epigraphic texts themselves and the range of sponsorship involved, reaching right up to the highest levels of the state. Epigraphs such as the great narrative of the plague in the lunette at S. Maria della Carità, with its raised and gilded letters, and the Venetian translation of the papal bull in the Doge's Palace, again with raised and probably gilded letters, would never be equalled in terms of physical excellence and linguistic sweep.

The distribution of confraternity types also tells its own interesting story, one that partly intersects with the overall chronological distribution pattern. Most telling is the timescale of inscriptions from the *scuole grandi*, the spiritual and originally flagellant brotherhoods each with many hundreds of members, which became increasingly rich and influential in the course of our period. The high point of their vernacular epigraphic production, between 1345 and 1375, overlaps significantly with the overall peak in vernacular inscriptions in Venice. It then drops off markedly. In the 125 years between 1400 and 1525 there are only three surviving vernacular inscriptions from the *scuole grandi* compared to the ten for the sixty-year period between 1340 and 1400.[56] On the other hand, the vernacular inscriptional activity of the more modest *scuole piccole* — whether of the purely spiritual type or else combining guild and confraternity functions — is shown by the statistics to be on a steady rise within a constrastively later timescale. From a zero base between 1300 and 1350, and three attestations between 1351 and 1400, they rise steadily to four in the first half of the Quattrocento, with four again in the second half of the century. They peak between 1501 and 1525 with a surprising six attestations. The confraternity-guilds with a national basis, in our cases German and Dalmatian, have a spread that is all their own. From a very low baseline of two occurrences in the century between 1350 and 1450, they rise to prominence in the 1451–1525 period with six examples which, if our corpus end-date were extended just a little, would be augmented by those from the Scuola degli Albanesi at S. Maurizio.[57]

4. The Analytical Framework

As a multi-dimensional artefact a vernacular inscription can only be properly understood within a balanced contextualisation that reflects this complexity. We have already applied different layers of categorisation to the corpus as a whole in order to enhance our understanding of the collection, thereby uncovering crosscurrents and trends, peaks and troughs, patterns and clustering in Venetian vernacular epigraphy over two and a quarter centuries. A similar approach, with multiple and intersecting angles of attack, can be equally productive at explicating the individual inscriptions from the period. While such a critical desideratum appears to be self-evident, it is too seldom applied systematically. The traditional reference corpus for epigraphy, the CIL, is rather notorious in this respect. Conceived in the nineteenth century and dealing with a truly imposing mass of material, its guiding preoccupation appears to have been to make available to scholars in a rigorous and pithy way the vast body of Roman epigraphs, treating them primarily as texts. This manifestly textual focus explains why, until recently, it eschewed photography. Other features of its presentational and critical approach follow logically from its text-based stance. Transcriptions are rarely interpretative and, except in a few cases, the comments on individual epigraphs are brief in the extreme, with little information provided on the physical location of the inscription within its monumental context. Commentary on history, script and language (mainly but not always impeccable Classical Latin) tends equally to be minimal. The bibliographical information provided is voluminous although so synthetic that it is not always easy to unpack.

Medieval epigraphic corpora have inevitably been conditioned, at least in part, by the overwhelmingly prestigious example of the CIL. This may explain why the scholar or other interested party consulting them sometimes comes away with a feeling of incompleteness, disappointed that only particular facets of the epigraph have been given real explicative prominence. This important point was recently picked up and made explicit by Vincent Debiais:

> L'ensemble des entreprises d'édition des inscriptions médiévales en Europe ont traditionnellement privilégié l'une ou l'autre composante du système 'inscription'. Le *Corpus des inscriptions de la France médiévale* s'attache ainsi plus particulièrement au contenu de l'inscription, à sa dimension textuelle; le plus récent corpus des inscriptions médiévales italiennes est focalisé sur les questions paléographiques et sur le nombre et les formes des signes sculptés ou peints; l'entreprise espagnole du *Corpus Inscriptionum Mediae Aevii Hispaniae* se consacre quant à elle à la dimension diplomatique des textes épigraphiques. Aussi justifiables et fécondes soient-elles, ces différentes approches ont une tendance à extraire l'inscription de son environnement — iconique, architectural ou archéologique — pour produire un texte brut et indépendant, sans relation formelle ou sémantique avec ce qui l'entoure. (DEBIAIS 2015: 55)

In addition to Debiais's justified criticism of approaches that isolate an inscription from its surroundings, it is not difficult to point to other problematic areas where the tendency to abstract the inscription from its 'environment' could fruitfully be rectified in the framing grid of medieval epigraphic corpora. One would suggest, first of all, a more layered approach to representing the epigraph itself. This ought ideally to incorporate the following: photographic representation of the text and, where appropriate or possible, its material or iconographic surroundings; a semi-interpretative transcription followed by a fully interpretative one; and, lastly, a translation of the inscription into the language of the study or into English. Such multi-layering, with photographs as the initial visual reference, obviates the need for fully diplomatic transcription. In any case, attempting to reproduce most medieval script diplomatically is a thankless task that tends to generate visually clumsy and misleading results. This is because, as things stand, the fonts at our disposal, even those allegedly tailor-made to replicate certain script types, are too generic to render the sheer profusion and subtlety of letter variants and abbreviation signs. The history of the object itself and of its dating, if the latter is not explicit, should then be sketched in or, in particularly complex cases, tackled at length. As complete a description as possible of the physical location and context of the inscription should be provided. Up to a point most of these aspects are indeed incorporated into the explicative frameworks of medieval epigraphic corpora nowadays, but seldom as fully as one would like.[58] However, the most glaring lacunae are at present located in the treatment of script and language, the technical aspects most in need of contextualised explication in that they carry, conjointly, the form and content of the written epigraphic message.[59] As such they urgently require historicisation that, wherever possible, should go beyond pure description of what is in front of the editor, no matter how accurate and useful that description may be. This is especially the case in vernacular epigraphy where the language involved is almost never standardised and therefore 'transparent' and where script type is rarely a given, as it is in Latin epigraphy, but instead only becomes fully meaningful when considered as part of a localised system with its own traditions.

I have structured my own analytical grid, identical for each inscription, in order to try and fulfil the criteria and desiderata outlined above.[60] Inscriptions are represented photographically, transcribed in two ways and translated.[61] They are then contextualised and explicated by a framework articulated by date, location, type, material support, appearance, dimensions, present physical state, inscriptional ensemble, historical background, lettering, language and critical history. The descriptions of script and language strive to be sensitive to the diachronic or historical dimension, with particularities, continuities and innovations flagged up both within and between inscriptions by consistent cross-referencing. Each inscription ends with bibliographical references to all editions or studies of it published since 1900. If the earliest edition appeared before 1900 this is signalled and referenced, as are particularly significant studies dedicated to the epigraph before that date. It hardly needs to be underlined that this analytical approach operates most effectively when taken in conjunction with the introductory sections of the book. These offer the wider-ranging critical and historical background at the macro level within which the inscriptions, individually and collectively, can best be assessed on the micro level. The three indices at the end of the book aim to further enrich the reader's experience. The first gathers together the name — followed by the role, profession or status — of persons appearing within the corpus inscriptions. The second allows the present location of each inscription to be pinpointed while revealing the overall distribution of surviving vernacular inscriptions both within and outside the city. The third provides a systematic directory of words, constructions and linguistic features commented on in the corpus.

Finally, a word about the transcription conventions I have adopted for the inscriptions dissected in the corpus. Transcription practice in medieval epigraphic corpora is not fully standardised. Many of its conventions are held in common by all of them, notably the indication of missing letters within square brackets or the opening out of abbreviations within round brackets. Others, such as the use of capitals or lower-case italics as the transcription medium, or the use of the slash or vertical line to indicate line divisions, vary from study to study. Still other variations are down to the judgement made by an editor in terms of the linguistic and scriptural nature of a particular collection. In the present corpus I adopt the following semi-interpretative system for the head transcription.

The text is transcribed in small capital font, irrespective of whether the original is in Gothic majuscules, monumental capitals, or even in a combination of script types with Romanesque elements. No initial capitalisation is used, except on the few occasions where it actually occurs in the inscription itself: CI 48 and CI 57 on stone, and CI 62–64 on Fra Mauro's *mappa mundi*. As in the originals no capitalisation is applied to proper names, animate or inanimate, except once, on CI 107. I do not attempt to mimic the original layout. Instead, line endings are indicated conventionally by means of a single vertical line between spaces.[62] The vertical line is inserted between letters, with spacing, when there is a word-split at line end on the inscription itself. A double vertical line indicates a deliberate and more substantial separation between the sections of text concerned, as on the blocks of writing in CI 95, CI 96, CI 100, CI 105 or between the caption categories in CI 82–91. The separation of discontinuous captions on the joined panels of CI 37 is signalled by blank square brackets in the text. Line numbers are always inserted in subscript at the line ends unless these coincide with the splitting of a word. Reduced-size line(s) inserted at the end of an inscription (as on CI 13 and CI 95) are transcribed in smaller font.

Ligatures are indicated by a double inverted breve over the letters concerned, as on A͡R. Raised or lowered letters are rendered by superscript and subscript. Inserted or nested letters are shown by means of left-facing or right-facing curly brackets, as appropriate, so D E{ indicates that a miniaturised E is nested within the preceding D (as on CI 71), while }EN^T{ indicates that miniaturised E and T are inserted, at the heights indicated, within the N (as on CI 75). The forms of the letters <u> and <v>, used interchangeably for the /u/ or /v/ sounds in the epigraphs, are respected in transcription. Punctuation in the originals is generally limited to interpuncts of varying shapes and sizes, commonly mid-high, less commonly on the baseline. I reproduce these in a form approximating to the shape and proportional size of the originals. The same applies to the various other division marks, such as triple vertical dots and other punctuating or decorative marks and shapes used to finish off the epigraph. I indicate the *signum crucis*, plain or decorated with interdots, when it is present at the beginning or end of an inscription. When a mark in the guise of an asterisk has been used in the original to indicate text insertion, I replicate it in superscript. I transcribe without apostrophes and accents, none of which are present in the corpus. On CI 61, though, an interpunct is inserted, as on the original, between definite article and noun in *l·homo* 'the man' to separate them, and on CI 30 (l. 34) where a similar interpunct again avoids the hanging article in *l·ano* 'the year'. In both cases I transcribe *tel quel*. On CI 79 I use arrows to indicate the transition from an earlier palimpsestic state to a later one.

None of the numerous abbreviation signs in the corpus, mainly but not exclusively on Gothic script, are rendered diplomatically. I open them all out within round brackets in the transcriptions. The only problems arise with some fourteenth- and early fifteenth-century epigraphs where there may be uncertainty over how to interpret the abbreviation (overbar or slash) of 'saint', masculine and feminine. Since *san* or *sen* and *santa* or *senta* are possible I opt for caution, transcribing *s(-n)* and *s(-)nta* or *s(-nta)* unless there is persuasive evidence elsewhere in the same inscription to indicate the greater likelihood of one or the other form. A similar procedure is adopted for the overbarred or slashed abbreviations of *ser* or *sier* 'Mr' and *miser* or *misier* 'Sir, Mr'. In the absence of persuasive evidence I transcribe *s(r)* and *mis(r)*. Portions of an inscription that are illegible but can be reconstructed with a high degree of certainty — either from the context or from earlier photographs, illustrations, transcriptions or other reliable sources — are integrated into the transcription within square brackets. A short section of text which is illegible and cannot be reconstructed with certainty is indicated by three dots within square brackets. A longer section of epigraph that is irreparably damaged and cannot be reconstructed with certainty is represented by a continuous dotted line within square brackets. The length of the dotted line is approximately proportional to that of the missing section. Letters which are difficult to read are indicated by an underdot, while a letter that the stonecutter has inadvertently missed out is restored in italics. When the wrong letter has been sculpted by mistake it is replaced in the transcription by the correct letter within angle quotation marks, so the partitive d‹e›la for dcla (CI 9, l. 11) and ‹q›ueste 'these' for the erroneous oueste (CI 30, ll. 29–30). The emendation is flagged up in the inscription commentary.

The head transcription is followed in every case by a fully interpretative one, in lower case within square brackets, where capitalisation, punctuation and accents follow modern practice and where Latin insertions are italicised. Within the present introduction, whether in the body of the text or in footnotes, a modified form of the head transcription system is used for the sake of convenience. The inscription is transcribed in lower-case italics, with dates and numerals in small capitals. Slashes indicate line divisions and there is no line numbering.

Notes to Chapter 1

1. Inscription and *iscrizione* are from the Latin accusative INSCRIPTIŌNEM (nominative INSCRIPTĬO) 'inscription', itself from the verb INSCRĪBĔRE 'to inscribe' (literally 'to write into or on'). Epigraph and *epigrafe* are from Greek ἐπιγραφή 'inscription' from ἐπιγράφειν 'to write upon' < ἐπί 'upon' + γράφειν 'to write'. The derivative terms for the practitioner of the discipline are epigrapher or epigraphist (Italian: *epigrafista*). The object of study is epigraphy and the discipline is either epigraphy or epigraphics, with the Italian *epigrafia* covering all of these. A glance at the chronology of this terminology is instructive. Epigraph and epigraphy are seventeenth-century coinages in English, while *epigrafia* and *epigrafe* were very uncommon in Italian until the nineteenth century. All are learned terms originally applied, unsurprisingly, to classical epigraphy which was until relatively recently epigraphy *tout court*. The terms inscription and *i(n)scrizione* could, for their part, be described as semi-learned and they have a longer history in both languages. Inscription goes back in English to the sixteenth century, appearing memorably in the casket scene of the *Merchant of Venice* (II. vii. 14). It gradually replaced the earlier *scripture*. The Italian (or rather Tuscan) equivalent, sporadic in the Middle Ages, started to appear commonly in the mid-sixteenth century, spelled *inscrizione*. The normal term for an

inscription in Italy in the medieval period was *titulo/titolo* (from TĬTŬLUM, nominative TĬTŬLUS, the most frequently used word for 'inscription' or 'superscription' in ancient Rome) and it was, in particular, associated with epitaphs and with the *titulus crucis*. It is also used for the numerous imaginary inscriptions in the *Hypnerotomachia Poliphili* (COLONNA 1499).

2. On the traditional dominance in epigraphic studies of lapidary inscriptions, with the concomitant neglect of painted ones, see DEBIAIS (2015: 49).
3. See in particular A. PETRUCCI (1985) and (1997).
4. On the extent to which an inscription is for public display, see L. PETRUCCI (2010: 25–29) and GEYMONAT (2014: 57–60). The fluidity of the concept of inscription is underlined by KOCH (1995: 267–70).
5. On the display of large dishes on sideboards in the *portego* area of Venetian palaces, see SANSOVINO (1581: 263v) and FORTINI BROWN (2006: 54–55).
6. A vernacular inscription, allegedly dated 1269, was recorded for Murano by Giannantonio MOSCHINI in the early nineteenth century (1808: 47 n. 1), although his account is ambiguous about whether this tomb epitaph was actually still visible in his day or whether, more probably, he was reporting it from an unacknowledged manuscript source. Moschini's transcription was then reproduced by B. GAMBA (1832: 12) with the comment: 'È questa la più antica iscrizione sepolcrale in veneziano, in cui si vegga scolpito l'anno. Leggesi nel pavimento della chiesa di S. Stefano di Murano come venne riportata dal Moschini'. It is also recorded in MONACI (1912: 41). The inscription itself had long disappeared when it was reproduced by Cicogna in the mid-nineteenth century in a slightly different form from Moschini's, thus certainly reflecting another manuscript source consulted: *MCCLXIX. sep. de s Michiel Amadi / franca per lv e per i soi heredi* ('1269. Burial plot of Mr Michiel Amadi, held in perpetuity for himself and his heirs'). In his comments on the inscription, CICOGNA (1824–53, VI: 378, 465) was sceptical about the 1269 date which he believed was more likely to have read 1369. The whole muddled issue was well reviewed by FERRO (1889: 444–47) who came down on Cicogna's side. I too am convinced that Cicogna's prudence was justified and that the tomb owner in question was in fact Michiel or Michele Amadi, prosperous dyer and sometime warden of the Scuola di S. Giovanni Battista on the island, who is mentioned in CI 26 of 1361.
7. In the pejorative sense of a substandard form of a national language the term dialect has no place in scientific linguistics. Venetian, like the other so-called dialects of Italian, is in fact a dialect of Latin, descended from it through processes of language change. It can also be described geo-historically as a dialect of Italy. In its loaded sense, 'dialect' reflects a socio-political value judgement linked to the formation of national languages and to the consequent downgrading of other varieties spoken within a national territory.
8. For a balanced discussion of period segmentation in Italian art history, see PREVITALI (1979).
9. How surprisingly slim the vernacular epigraphic pickings are from the mainland Veneto is evident from GRAZIANI (2013), although its corpus is not comprehensive. The two main epigraphic centres on the Veneto mainland in our period were Padua and Verona. I have surveyed both centres personally. The surviving inscriptions from Padua are almost exclusively in Latin. The picture for Verona is more nuanced, with a small but not insignificant body of vernacular inscriptions produced during the *signoria* of the della Scala family in the fourteenth century. The majority are now held in the Castelvecchio museum. A selection of these is examined in GIOVÈ MARCHIOLI (1994: 278–80).
10. The best-known example from the *Dogado* is the seven-line inscription reverse-punched on to a metal plaque at the foot of the gilded-silver altar screen known as the *paliotto* in the early Christian basilica of S. Eufemia in Grado. In stiff Gothic majuscules, with some omissions and infelicities occasioned by the reverse-writing technique, it carries the name of the Venetian Donado Macalorsa (i.e. Maçalorsa, literally 'she-bear killer') the silversmith, or perhaps (although it is less likely) the commissioner, of the screen: + *M·C·C·C·LXXII · de septenbrio · in lo tenpo de/l nobele · miser Andrea · (Con)tarini · doxe de V/eniesia · e mis(er) Fran·cescin · (Con)tarini / · (con)te d/e Grado fo f/ata qvesta pala / e Donado Macalorsa · / de Veniesia me fexee* [sic]. On the few surviving vernacular inscriptions on Venice's coastal strip see TOMASIN (2012a). Little is known about the presence of Venetian vernacular inscriptions on the Adriatic coast or *de là da mar*. The

only indisputably authentic one I am aware of is the brief motto carved over a coat of arms on the so-called Venetian House in the main square, Piazza Tartini, of the Istrian town of Piran (Pirano) just down the coast from Trieste. The crenellated escutcheon, embedded towards the top of the Gothic façade, is from the second half of the fifteenth century, and the inscription in Roman capitals reads: *Lasa pvr dir* ('Let them talk', in the sense of 'Don't listen to them'). Now in Slovenia, Pirano was Venetian for 500 years. Possibly genuine (although *Lugio* for *Luio* 'July' is surprising at this early date) is the red graffiti on a column at the south entrance of the church of the Holy Sepulchre in Jerusalem: *1384 a Lugio / Piero Vendramin*. The two lines, in a minuscule hand, are bisected by a merchant mark. Oliver Rackham reported a line of facetious fifteenth-century graffiti from Crete, scrawled by a priest in Venetian and Latin in the little thirteenth-century hilltop church of Agia Anna at Nefs Amari (RACKHAM and MOODY 1996: 181). I interpret his transcription of it as: *1450 a di 8 avosto hic fvit p(res)b(yte)r Petrvs Bvffvs*. The most remarkable surviving Venetian vernacular inscription executed outside Italy is in England. Dated 1491 it is on the ledgerstone (203 x 112 cm) of the mariners of the Venetian confraternity (founded 1451) of St George and St Tryphon of the Dalmatians on the floor of the church of St Nicholas in North Stoneham near Southampton, where the crewmen of the Venetian Flanders galleys had a burial place. Carved in eclectic capitals, still strongly influenced by Gothic, it runs around the edge-strip of a bluish limestone slab featuring a foliated imperial-eagle shield in low relief in the centre and the four evangelists in corner roundels. Its lettering (*c.* 5 cm tall) reads: *An(n)o d(omi)ni / M · CCCC · LXXXXI · sepvltvra / de la / schola de Sclavoni*.

11. The artist's authorship inscription, at the foot of the *Judgement of St Sebastian*, is painted in black cursive Gothic minuscules: *Nicholeto · Simitecholo · da Veniexia · inpe(n)se ·*. The series is dated at the bottom of the *Entombment of St Sebastian* as follows: MCCCLXVII adi xv d(e) decembre. On Semitecolo, the Padua panels and their inscriptions, see TESTI (1909: 307–14).

12. Now in the Museo Diocesano of Recanati it was originally in the local church of S. Maria Assunta di Castelnuovo. Commissioned by a Venetian citizen, Andrea C(h)oluço, it reads: ·M·C·C·C·L·X·X·X·I·I · del · mexe · de março · adi · VI · fe fa · s(ier) · Andrea · Cholvço · çitadin · de · Veniexia · qvesto · lavorier ·:~ // Gvielmus pinxit.

13. The inscription carved by Bonvesin in vigorous Gothic majuscules on the crucifix scroll, and now damaged in its middle part, reads: *Antvonio de Bonv/esin · intaia mo qvest/o lavori[er] [...] Veniex/ia · Iacomelo de Fior. p.* The verb *intaia* (i.e. *intaià*) is the 3rd person singular past historic of *intaiar* 'to carve'. See MARKHAM SCHULZ (2004) for the context of this outstanding artefact, with an illustration on p. 294.

14. Painted on a cartellino at the foot of the throne it is signed: *Alvixe Vivari(n) M· CCCC· LXXXIII· p.* When signing in Latin, Alvise called himself ALOVISIVS VIVARINVS.

15. Notably the authorial signature inscription of Stefanus Plebanus on the sumptuous *Madonna and Child* panel, dated 1369, in the Museo Correr. TESTI (1909: 304–05) also called its authenticity into question for well-argued palaeographic and historical reasons.

16. In particular, the brief vernacular inscription, to the effect that anybody not entered in the book of life will be damned, in the volume held open by Christ on one of the panels of the unsigned *Polyptych of the Apocalypse* in the Accademia. Generally dated to the later fourteenth century, the series of tempera and gold panels came from the monastery church of S. Giovanni Evangelista on Torcello. Although they are now usually assigned to Jacobello Albaregno I am not fully convinced of this Venetian attribution. The inscription itself has nothing to mark it off as specifically Venetian.

17. The unpublished vernacular inscriptions seen personally by Cicogna are re-transcribed, with the abbreviations employed by him opened out, in FERGUSON (2013c: 116–26).

18. These incised and glazed slipware artefacts (*ceramica graffita*) are held in two locations. The great majority are in the ceramics collection of the Galleria Franchetti at the Ca' d'Oro. They are part of the trove of some 13,000 pottery fragments from various sites in the lagoon collected between the wars by the school teacher and amateur archaeologist Luigi Conton. The collection was acquired by the Italian state in 1978 and has since been kept in the Giorgio Franchetti Gallery, although only a small number of the vernacular captioned articles are displayed at any one time. The second much smaller group features finds gathered over the years from the

Borgognoni district of Torcello, some of which are undoubtedly connected with the former abbey complex of S. Tommaso dei Borgognoni. They are stored or displayed in the medieval section of the Museo Provinciale on Torcello. Some captions, such as *fritole* 'doughnuts, fritters' in the Galleria Franchetti, are on an isolated sherd. A few others, such as *salata* 'salad, lettuce' in the Ca' d'Oro, are on a fully intact dish. Most, featuring *rosto* 'roast', *figà* or *figado* 'liver', *tripe* 'tripe', *puine* 'ricotta cheeses', *brodo* 'broth', *fromaio* 'cheese', *risi* 'rice', *bisi* 'peas', pasta dishes like *macaroni*, *bigoli*, *lasagne*, *rafioi* 'ravioli', and a range of stews, fish, shellfish, fruit and vegetables, are on fragments large or small. They belong to a Venetian Renaissance fashion for scratching legends with the names of foods and dishes on to tableware. The strongly serifed *capitalis* script employed is generally, though not always, casually applied. Occasionally its appearance tends to the Gothic. Altogether, a hundred or so of these pieces with vernacular captions survive.

19. For the background and details of the suppressions see BERTOLI (2002). For their effects see ZORZI (1984).
20. See DI LENARDO (2014: 23–28).
21. It is sufficient to read Cicogna's transcriptions of the 217 epigraphs in the church of S. Maria dei Servi in Cannaregio, demolished in the early nineteenth century, to appreciate what has been lost (CICOGNA 1824–53, I: 33–98).
22. A recent attempt to survey the vernacular epigraphic landscape of Italy between the eleventh and fifteenth centuries (CACCHIOLI and TIBURZI 2014) gave a provisional total of eighty for Florence and Siena combined, of which almost two thirds were on paintings. Rome had twenty-four all told, Lazio outside of Rome had thirteen, and southern Italy as a whole only twenty. Numbers from the north-west of the country were negligible. Given the brevity of the majority of the epigraphs surveyed, and the substantial nature of many in the present corpus, it is likely that the textual dominance of Venice in vernacular epigraphy is even more striking than that suggested by the raw numbers.
23. FERRO (1889: 452) rightly described it as 'importantissima non solo come monumento del dialetto Veneziano di quel tempo, ma ancora per le cose che ricorda'.
24. Armando Petrucci notoriously declared that 'In Italia [...] un'epigrafia medievale praticamente non esiste, e tanto meno ne esiste una che si occupi specificamente di epigrafi medievali in lingua volgare' (A. PETRUCCI 1997: 47).
25. It should be emphasised that medieval epigraphy, although more developed in some European countries (notably Germany and France) than in others, still suffers generally from the parcelisation of research coverage that characterises Italy, with islands of expertise alongside large areas of neglect.
26. 'È cosa ben nota che le iscrizioni romane, nate dalla volontà di trasmettere ai posteri informazioni e dati precisi, sono *ab immemorabili* riconosciute come fonti storico-culturali di indiscutibile valore e che l'epigrafia classica è sempre stata ed è tuttora coltivata' (ROVERSI 1982: 5). On the importance of Latin inscriptions in supplying information for various historical fields see REYNOLDS (1960).
27. On the Renaissance revival of classical capitals in fifteenth-century epigraphy see MARDERSTEIG (1959), MEISS (1960) and MORISON (1972: 264–314). On the central role of the Veneto in this process see ZAMPONI (2006) and PINCUS (2017).
28. The obvious example is the fundamental, vast and ongoing *Corpus Inscriptionum Latinarum* (CIL), with its *c.* 180,000 inscriptions, seventeen volumes, thirteen supplements including indices and illustrations, and an online database. Initiated by the German classicist and epigrapher Theodor Mommsen, the CIL has since the mid-nineteenth century been the essential reference point for classical epigraphic studies.
29. CACCHIOLI and TIBURZI (2014); CACCHIOLI, CANNATA and TIBURZI (2016). One is reminded by the recentness of this first survey that a few scholars in the past were almost wistfully aware of the potential of a comprehensive knowledge of Italy's vernacular epigraphy, but also of how far off it was. As early as the mid-nineteenth century Giambattista Giuliani wrote: 'Sarebbe pur bellissima ed utile impresa quella di scrivere la storia della volgare epigrafia dal secolo XIII a tutto il XV' (GIULIANI 1865: 66–67).
30. On the Seminario collection, see the excellent volume by DI LENARDO which includes his

editions of three significant fourteenth-century vernacular inscriptions (2014: 92–97, 104–15).
31. On the types and material supports of medieval inscriptions see CIOCIOLA (1995).
32. Augusto Campana put it succinctly: 'Nel campo medioevale la varietà delle forme grafiche è immensamente maggiore che per le iscrizioni antiche' (CAMPANA 1968: 16). Majuscule script (usually but not necessarily capital) is written between two notional bounding lines. Minuscule, with ascenders and descenders, spans an imaginary four-line stave.
33. The point was made in BANTI (2000: 61). It was reiterated more recently by GRAMIGNI (2012: 6–7): 'L'Italia [...] non è che agli albori di questo tipo di studi [...]. I contributi di epigrafia medievale, per quanto ben articolati e validamente argomentati, si devono per forza di cose basare su *corpora* disponibili. Se questi *corpora* sono sporadici, disarticolati, non uniformi, interrotti e ripresi dopo anni di sviluppo della disciplina, come può un paleografo, uno storico dell'arte, uno storico in senso stretto servirsi delle testimonianze incise in modo corretto? [...] La disponibilità di *corpora* maggiormente coerenti e sufficientemente ampi è il presupposto essenziale per un reale avanzamento degli studi di epigrafia medievale.' DEBIAIS, FAVREAU and TREFFORT (2007: 102) have extended such criticisms to medieval epigraphics as a whole: 'Cet état d'avancement de la recherche est tributaire de l'émergence récente de la discipline épigraphique dans les études médiévales et du caractère incomplet des corpus de référence.' Although now a little dated, GIOVÈ MARCHIOLI (1994) offers a thorough review of this patchy coverage, with a selective bibliography of the work published up to that point in individual Italian centres.
34. The obvious models are, for France, the twenty-six volumes (to date) of the *Corpus des inscriptions de la France médiévale* (CIFM), edited by Robert Favreau and others; and, for Germany, the around 100 volumes (to date) of the *Deutsche Inschriften des Mittelalters und der frühen Neuzeit*, founded by Friedrich Panzer in the 1930s and available online as the *Deutsche Inschriften Online* (DIO). Italy now has the ongoing *Inscriptiones Medii Ævi Italiæ*, of which three volumes have been published including the latest on the Veneto (DE RUBEIS 2010). Unfortunately, for our purposes, this project only covers the early Middle Ages. However, an ambitious database project of Italian vernacular inscriptions, involving a cross-departmental team at La Sapienza university in Rome, has been announced. See CACCHIOLI, CANNATA and TIBURZIO (2016).
35. BANTI (1996) and (2000); BREVEGLIERI (1997); ROVERSI (1982); CAMPANA (1984).
36. As recently as 2012 Tommaso Gramigni made the remarkable observation that 'il numero di testimonianze epigrafiche fiorentine del secolo XIV in lingua volgare non è noto: il tema meriterebbe un approfondimento specifico' (GRAMIGNI 2012: 88 n. 47).
37. This inscription was recorded while it was still intact (CICOGNA 1824–53, I: 94).
38. Stringa's accuracy is confirmed by Cicogna's unpublished transcription of the epigraph. I published the inscription, with Cicogna's abbreviations expanded and with contextual comments, in FERGUSON (2013c: 124).
39. MOSCHINI (1815, I: 151, 235, 381 and II: 439). In his earlier guidebook of Murano, Moschini was the first to record the St Donatus inscription (1808: 105–06).
40. The best known of them is the seventeenth-century *Memorabilia Venetiarum monumenta antiqui recentioribus lapidibus inscripta* by Giovanni Giorgio Palfero, held in the Marciana at BNM, mss. lat. Cl. X, 144 (=3657). Elsewhere in the Venetian state, the collecting and displaying of classical inscriptions was given an exceptional boost by the opening in the first half of the eighteenth century of Scipione Maffei's lapidary collection in Verona, probably the first museum of inscriptions in Europe. Originally called the Museum Veronense and now known as the Museo Lapidario Maffeiano, it contains at present over 500 pieces, mainly Roman but also Greek, Etruscan, palaeo-Venetan and Arabic. Originally it also housed a small group of medieval vernacular inscriptions from Verona itself, mainly from the Scaliger period. These are at present displayed in the Castelvecchio museum in the city.
41. All the unpublished inscriptions appeared, without critical comment on script and language and without criteria of reproduction, in PAZZI (2001).
42. They are consultable among his *Inedite*, in seventeen *buste*, at BMC, 2007–2023.
43. CICOGNA (1824–53, I: 11–18). An accurate summary of the criticism of this period can also be found in DI LENARDO (2014: 15–22).
44. 'Entro poscia nel tempio, e cominciando per lo più sulle pareti a dritta, indi seguendo a sinistra,

e poi sul pavimento scorrendo, registro con progressiva numerazione le lapidi che ritrovo, il numero stesso delle righe tenendo, e le stesse abbreviature, affinché più materialmente fedele, che possibile sia, sottopongasi la epigrafe agli occhi del leggitore' (CICOGNA 1824–53, I: 25).

45. 'Ho copiata sulla pietra colla possibile diligenza questa lapide, la quale vidi affissa sul muro dell'atrio detto da noi *el portego* della Chiesa tra una porta e l'altra. Ove sono i punti non potei leggere per la corrosione. Tengo quindi essere più fedele alla pietra la mia copia di quella del Coleti nell'Italia Sacra dell'Ughelli (T. V. 1401.), del Cornaro (l. e p. 145) e del Cappelletti (Chiese d'Italia T. IX. 589). // Questa pietra, dopo che io l'aveva veduta sopralluogo fu trasportata nel Chiostro del Seminario patriarcale, e leggesi a p. 79 del libro: *La Chiesa ed il Seminario di S.Maria della Salute* (Venezia 1842 8.), ma pure infedelmente. Il salino, che regna in tutto quel Chiostro, ha vieppiù corroso la detta lapide, a tale che oggidì riesce presso che impossibile il rilevarne parola' (CICOGNA 1824–53, VI: 459). The S. Stefano inscription is transcribed from Cicogna, with a commentary, in DI LENARDO (2014: 203–05).

46. Ruskin actually transcribed in his notebooks a few Venetian vernacular inscriptions and commented on their monumental context. See in particular CI 44 and CI 54.

47. He commented presciently in his introduction to the inscriptions that 'Non poche sono le Iscrizioni tanto sepolcrali che d'altra spezie, che ne' secoli XIII a XV si scolpirono e si esposero alla pubblica vista a Venezia, dettate in rozzo italiano, o nel Dialetto nazionale' (B. GAMBA 1832: 11).

48. In 1870 Bartolomeo Cecchetti had published a fundamental article on early Venetian documents in which he mentioned the Treasury inscription (CI 1), criticising both Gamba and Cicogna for the very early dating they had assigned to it (CECCHETTI 1869–70: 1590). In an unusually confident palaeographic statement for the period he asserted that 'i caratteri sono quelli comunissimi nelle iscrizioni del 1300, e nella mollezza dei segni accennano al ripristono del tipo romano'. The first part of that statement is largely correct; the second is not.

49. Notably with Nicoletta Giovè Marchioli and Franco Benucci in Padua and Flavia De Rubeis and Lorenzo Calvelli in Venice.

50. An outstanding exception is found in the work on Pisan inscriptions of Ottavio Banti.

51. Alfredo Stussi, the pioneer in the field, published a series of groundbreaking vernacular epigraphic studies between 1980 and 1997: see STUSSI (1980a, 1980b, 1995a, 1995b and, with wider reflection on Tuscan and northern Italian epigraphs, 1997a). He was followed by Lorenzo Tomasin, his former student at the Scuola Normale Superiore in Pisa: see TOMASIN (2001a, 2012a, 2012b and, with broader geographical and philological contextualisations, 2014 and 2016). The present author has published FERGUSON (2015a, 2015b and, with a focus on the use of script and language as dating tools in epigraphic philology, 2017).

52. FERGUSON (2013c) and (2015c), respectively.

53. At the present time the most methodologically impressive medieval epigraphics project centred on an Italian city is the *Corpus delle Epigrafi Medievali di Padova* (CEMP), based at the University of Padua and co-ordinated by Franco Benucci. Encouraging for the continued revival of interest in medieval Veneto vernacular inscriptions are two recent *tesi di laurea* from Ca' Foscari: GRAZIANI (2013) and MOCELLIN (2016). More recently still, the graffiti of Venice from the twelfth to the twentieth centuries have become the object of a cataloguing initiative at Ca' Foscari (in the context of the Venice Time Machine project) led by Flavia De Rubeis. In addition, Francesca Malagnini has just published a volume on the graffiti of Venice's quarantine island, the Lazzaretto Nuovo (MALAGNINI 2017), and another on the inscriptions — both Latin and vernacular, from the mid-sixteenth century onwards — of its plague hospital island, the Lazzaretto Vecchio (MALAGNINI 2018). The re-employed Roman epigraphic *spolia* in Venice and the lagoon are now being intensively studied within the aegis of the Laboratorio di Epigrafia Latina at Ca' Foscari. See CALVELLI (2015) and (2016). At the wider Romance level it is heartening that the first work to attempt to collect, document and study all the extant medieval vernacular Romance inscriptions up to 1275 has been published: L. PETRUCCI (2010).

54. The percentages given in the sponsorship category are necessarily approximate. In the case of some paintings we cannot be sure if they were commissioned by religious establishments or by confraternities. With a number of inscriptions there may well be commissioning overlap:

for example, between church and government on CI 30, between charitable organisation and church on CI 20, and between confraternity and individual on CI 41 and CI 107. I have counted by artefact rather than by inscription in establishing percentages in order to avoid the statistical distortion that would be caused by itemising the 10 de' Barbari toponym groups (CI 82–91) and the 5 *mappa mundi* legends (CI 62–66).

55. White Greek marble appears to be used throughout, although it is not possible to be absolutely sure in all cases. The Venetian terminology in our period is *marmoro* or *malmoro* 'marble' as opposed to *piera (viva) de/da P(u)ola, Parenço/Parenzo* or *Rovigno/Ruigno* 'Istrian stone'.

56. Their abandonment of the vernacular coincides with the cultural turn in the second half of the fifteenth century in Venice that we have already touched on. It is reflected in the *scuole grandi* by, among other things, the increasing elimination of the tradesman element from the executive boards. Richard Mackenny has pointed out that this period of 'more magnificent and ostentatious artistic patronage [...] also institutionalized a division between lesser and greater confraternities. The distinction between *scuole piccole* and *scuole grandi* dates clearly from the second half of the fifteenth century, the first signs of a lengthening hierarchy of institutions that was alien to their first principles' (MACKENNY 2018: 14–15).

57. Although the *scuola* building is now a private residence, its façade is still intact on the narrow Calle del Piovan at S. Maurizio. It forms one of the most picturesque, if flawed, inscriptional ensembles in the city. On the long lintel running over the entrance door and ground floor windows there is carved in Roman capitals, but with the <a> in forked form, a single-line vernacular inscription on Istrian stone announcing the confraternity's presence: *Scola ⊥ S ⊥a Maria ⊥ San ⊥ Gallo ⊥ di ⊥ Albanesi*. Above it on a fascia row are elegant relief sculptures in the Lombardo style depicting St Gall, the Virgin and Child, and St Maurice. This inscription and these reliefs are undated, but in my opinion the epigraph is from around the turn of the century, probably a few years before Carpaccio's *Annunciation* (1504), and may therefore just possibly be within the timescale of our corpus. A *scuola* keen to advertise its presence and embellish its interior with outstanding paintings, as the Albanians were, would likely have stamped its ownership mark over the entrance as a priority. The rest of the frontage decoration, however, is undoubtedly from *c.* 1530. Midway up the façade between the two first-floor windows is a large rectangular plaque, unique of its kind in Venice, whose relief shows in synoptic form the assaults on Scutari in the 1470s. The overwhelming Ottoman forces are represented on the sculpture by what is probably meant to be Mehmet II, with his turban and huge scimitar, and with his Vizir behind him. Sharply cut on the body of the plaque itself in monumental capitals is the Latin inscription dedicating it as an eternal memorial from the people of Scutari to its heroes faithful to Venice, and in gratitude for the generosity of the city and its authorities: *Scodrenses ⊥ egregiae ⊥ svae ⊥ in ⊥ vene/tam ⊥ rem ⊥ p ⊥ ꝓidei ⊥ et ⊥ Senatvs ⊥ in ēte / veneti ⊥ beneficenciae ⊥ singvlaris / aeternv(m) ⊥ hoc ⊥ monimentvm ⊥ p ⊥*. Carved on the massive upper frame of the relief is a vernacular inscription: *Asedio / segondo / MCCCC/LXXIIII* ('Second siege, 1474'). Neither insignia nor wording are laid out properly, the former being off centre, the latter with awkward separations, the date in reverse order and a badly inserted <o> on *segondo*. The Latin of the plaque inscription itself has the unfortunately conspicuous *eidei* for *fidei* and is unclear at the end of the first line. Finally, running along the cornice under the eaves of the building is a commemorative vernacular epigraph dated 1531, with large, deeply cut and strongly contrastive *capitalis* letters still bearing traces of black infilling: MDXXXI *in tempo de Tomaso Mamoli gastaldo e Nicolo Cuci baretaro vichario e compagni*: 'In the time (in office) of the alderman Tomaso Mamoli and of the deputy Nicolò Cuci, hatmaker, and their colleagues'. I have had to reconstruct the correct wording as the plaques comprising the inscription are laid out in jumbled order. The similarity of letter forms and ductus of all the inscriptions on the middle and upper sections of the façade suggests that only one stonemason and his team were involved. Why their work was so chaotic is unclear.

58. The best recent examples from Italy, especially strong in terms of their contextual and historical commentary sections, are the volume of the *Inscriptiones Medii Ævi Italiæ*, edited by Flavia De Rubeis, dedicated to the Veneto (DE RUBEIS 2010), and the first volume of the CEMP edited by Franco Benucci (BENUCCI 2015).

59. As Augusto Campana put it: 'Ogni iscrizione è un monumento complesso, che presenta sempre

almeno tre aspetti: quello del *testo* scritto, quello della *scrittura* (forme grafiche), e quello del *monumento* (materia e forma di supporto, elementi artistici di corredo, inserimento in un contesto architettonico e artistico)' (CAMPANA 1968: 7).

60. The topics treated in my grid are more or less standard nowadays in medieval epigraphic corpora but, of course, with different emphases and methodologies of treatment in each. The grid adopted by the CIFM, called there the *Schéma d'étude des inscriptions*, is ordered as follows for each inscriptional entry: A — *Fonction de l'inscription*. B — *Lieu de conservation*. C — *Support et dimensions*. D — *Transcription*. E — *Traduction*. F — *Remarques paléographiques*. G — *Remarques linguistiques*. H — *Sources (bibliques, littéraires, liturgiques ou profanes) et formules*. I — *Commentaire historique et datation*. For a detailed consideration of the content and compilation of inscriptional grids, in the context of Latin epigraphy, see DI STEFANO MANZELLA (1987).

61. Apart from two instances, all the corpus inscriptions are translated into English. These are the months on the portal of St Mark's (CI 79), where a translation is unnecessary, and the Venetian place-name captions on de' Barbari's view of the city (CI 82–91) where it is inappropriate. No interpretative transcription is provided for the de' Barbari toponyms as it is not called for.

62. On two inscriptions, CI 53 and CI 79, the single-word nature of the 'lines' (fruit or vegetables in the case of the former, months of the year in the latter) made numbering unnecessary.

PART II

The Medium and the Message

1. Evidence of inscriptional processes

Thanks to its size, geographical homogeneity, typological variety and extended timescale the vernacular corpus is rich in information about largely neglected inscriptional issues and practicalities. It reveals, first of all, that there is little in our period to distinguish vernacular from Latin inscriptions apart from their language choice. The great script watershed in the mid-fifteenth century affected both, as did experimentation with revival lettering of various sorts in the later Quattrocento. Even at the hands-on level their practice is largely indistinguishable. Inscriptional guide-lines are rare in both, as was generally the case in Italy,[1] in contrast with France where stonemasons' bounding lines for header and footer were not only frequently present but often became a highlighted decorative feature.[2] The employment of lead-based black infilling in the grooving of V-cut letters was also a common feature in both Latin and vernacular epigraphy in Venice, as was that of colour on crenellated frames and sometimes on the background of the inscription plaque.[3] The use and evolution of interpuncts and finishing touches were also shared, with the former moving from simple mid-high dots prevalent throughout the fourteenth century to more varied decorative and calligraphic forms in later Gothic.[4] Even in the area of abbreviation signs, where some conventions were necessarily linked to specific Latin or vernacular forms, there was widespread parallel continuity, with differences only becoming perceptible after the onset of revival Roman lettering.[5] Unsurprisingly there was an increasing tendency on late-fifteenth and early-sixteenth century Latin epigraphic script to avoid the abbreviation signs typical of Gothic, a trend also replicated on particularly careful vernacular inscriptions of the time (CI 93, CI 106). One is occasionally surprised, though, by the persistence of essentially Gothic conventions well into the sixteenth century on some impeccably Roman monumental vernacular inscriptions such as CI 107.

Conspicuous evidence that vernacular and Latin epigraphic conventions moved forward in a synchronised way was the sudden joint tendency, in the mid-Trecento, to choose raised rather than incised lettering for particularly prestigious commissions. Raising is a difficult, expensive and unforgiving technique requiring exceptional skill on the stonemason's part, especially in Gothic majuscular epigraphy with its intricacies of line and stroke thickness. There are four outstanding examples of this Venetian speciality, probably borrowed from the Byzantines, in the corpus (CI 9, CI

14, CI 17, CI 30).[6] If proof were needed that workshops in Venice, or at least some of them, were comfortable with both Latin and vernacular commissions this is it.[7] Even the proportion of marble to Istrian stone used for inscription tablets is similar in both groups. In fact the only striking divergence between Latin and vernacular epigraphy is the occurrence of double-sided inscriptions. This is a particularly Venetian development, applying only to vernacular epigraphs, dictated by the need for all-round visibility of the inscription. There are four examples in the corpus: one on a well from 1349 at the Anzolo Rafael (CI 15, CI 16); one on a confraternity banner from Torcello dated 1366 (CI 33, CI 34); one on the stone *barbacane* at the Rialto, probably from the early sixteenth century (CI 101, CI 102); and one on the yardstick in Calle Toscana (CI 103, CI 104) from the same period.

In addition, the corpus allows us privileged access to behind-the-scenes actions, processes and negotiations which are normally invisible, or were meant to be. Thus uncorrected mistakes by the stonemason are revealed to our scrutiny. Most are probably down to slips of the chisel or to momentary inattention but occasionally they may suggest that the level of literacy of a particular craftsman was shaky or that he copied slavishly from an imperfect or partly illegible master text from the *scriptor* (CI 20, CI 25, CI 35, CI 48). Sometimes the act of correction, with letter insertions, is less than aesthetically ideal and also raises questions about margins of tolerance (CI 108). On other occasions it appears that an oversight was down to the commissioner and it is the stonecutter who has had to do his best to come to terms with it, inserting whole lines or blocks of text in cramped subscript like a footnote or even slotted in as an addendum on a contiguous surface (CI 13, CI 95). In one instance (the frescoes featuring CI 5, CI 6, CI 7) it looks as if an artist may have had to deal with a commissioner's re-think, painting out inscriptions originally drafted in Latin and replacing them with vernacular equivalents.

When it comes to the sequence of higher-level processes involved in the realisation of an inscription in the Middle Ages and Renaissance we know precious little. Indeed the conceptual frame within which such practical stages are discussed, or rather touched on, in the discipline still largely refers back to Roman epigraphy, and is based on some evidence and considerable assumption. I have therefore occasionally used terms such as *scriptor* and *ordinatio* within my corpus commentaries to refer to the writer of the inscriptional text, on the one hand, and to its layout on the other, as if they had a solidly definable medieval reality.[8] In truth, the line of command and execution leading in our period from the commissioning of the epigraphic text, via its drafting, to its *mise-en-page* then final inscribing on to the epigraphic surface, is still clouded in uncertainty. Since the formal documentation for process of this kind is largely non-existent, or at best allusive, our assumptions remain largely that.[9] Even our knowledge of how lapidary inscriptions, the most numerous, familiar and best studied of all, found their way on to stone is to a great extent conjectural. Among the basic questions that remain for the most part unanswered in the lapidary context — but which are also, *mutatis mutandis*, applicable to other inscriptional mediums — are the following. To what extent was the stonemason responsible for the form and content of an epigraph? Did he decide on layout, punctuation and letter forms? Were these, instead, dictated to him, or discussed with him, and if so how and by whom? Was he always provided with a text to copy from? What leeway was he allowed when it came to language forms in a vernacular inscription? Were all masons literate? Was there a distinction between a stonemason or stonecutter and a sculptor? Were there masons, perhaps within workshops, who specialised in inscription work? Even such obvious technical queries as how the text was lined up on the surface or how letter forms were regularised with consistency are not straightforward to deal with.[10] The present collection contains an unusual wealth of materials which touch, often indirectly but sometimes directly, on these fundamental questions within the Venetian context. While seldom bringing definitive answers they shed light in some cases and provide intriguing clues in others. A few particularly salient groupings and conclusions are highlighted below, while individual cases are considered in the corpus commentaries.

A useful starting point for assessing evidence of inscriptional process in the corpus, and particularly the extent of control exercised over it by commissioner and craftsman respectively, is provided by one of the few surviving legal sources from our period to mention such matters, albeit fleetingly. This exceptional document is a contract dated 5 April 1400. Drawn up in Venice by a notary public, it involved Francesco I Gonzaga, ruler of Mantua, and the Venetian stonemason called in the contract *Piero Polo taiapiera da Venexia*.[11] The commission was for Piero Polo to construct an elaborate wall tomb, for a fee of 625 ducats, to commemorate Francesco's recently deceased wife Margherita Malatesta. One is struck above all in the agreement by the minute precision of the instructions given to the stonemason in terms of the types of stone to be used (Carrara marble, white and pink Istrian stone, red Verona limestone, black stone), measurements to be applied and motifs to be sculpted. On the other hand there seems to be much less micro-management of the inscription process. Only the positioning of the epitaph plaque is mentioned and the type of lettering required (raised rather than incised): *nel meço deno eser lo patafio de letere relevade* 'in the middle [of the plaque] there should be the epitaph in raised letters'. Everything else regarding the epitaph is left unsaid, as if it were simply understood. As it happens, the tomb, formerly in the Gonzaga chapel in the church of S. Francesco in Mantua, was dismantled and dispersed in the eighteenth century, so we cannot judge how far Gonzaga's instructions for the monument were followed to the letter. Fortunately the inscription itself — eleven lines of raised Gothic majuscules on an imitation scroll — has survived and is displayed in the Palazzo Ducale in Mantua. One can surmise that the master text, in rhetorical Latin, must have been drafted by a functionary or scholar at the Gonzaga court and provided to Piero Polo. It was evidently felt that a competent stonemason could be entrusted to take things from there. The evidence of the corpus — in conjunction with that of a Venetian vernacular will from 1474 where, alongside precise tomb type and detailed Latin epitaph verses, specific lettering instructions are confined to 'large and legible' (PAOLETTI 1893–97, I: 76) — suggests that the moderate epigraphic control exercised by Francesco Gonzaga, with the craftsman given a written text and basic specifications and then left to get on with the job, may well have been fairly common. However, with its profusion of varied and sometimes complex cases the corpus also provides a salutary warning against generalising too confidently about the dynamics of inscriptional processes, especially when the vernacular was involved. One further possible lesson to be drawn from the Gonzaga contract is reinforced by everything we know about stonecutters in Venice in our period. While there were of course masters, assistants and apprentices in the trade, and while some operators and their workshops obviously had more prestige than others, it seems reasonable to conclude that there was as yet no formal distinction between a stonemason and a sculptor.[12]

Understanding the inscriptional chain from start to finish is probably least problematic in the case of authorial statements on a completed artefact (itself the object of the commission) where the sequence of stages is in part short-circuited. On the face of it, textual commissioning in such cases seems to be removed from the equation, with the epigraphic message — its tenor, location, layout, script and language — apparently down to the craftsman or artist alone who thus became *scriptor, ordinator* and, in the broadest sense, *sculptor*. A perfectly straightforward example would appear to be the two white lines of Gothic majuscule writing in Venetian against a dark green ground at the foot of the *Mystic Marriage of St Catherine*, painted by Lorenzo Veneziano in 1360 and now in the Accademia (CI 24). In those lines Lorenzo recorded the year, month and day of the work's completion, his own name and where the panel was executed. Our assumption about Lorenzo's autonomy of decision-making in this respect appears to be confirmed by the very similar script deployed on other surviving and signed paintings of his such as the panels of *St Mark*, of *St Peter*, and of the *Annunciation with Saints* in the Accademia. What is more, the generous size of the epigraph on the *Mystic Marriage* and the way the viewer's eye is impudently drawn to its presence by the elegant red shoe of an angel pointing directly at it and, on the other side, by dangling red tassels falling towards it, suggest that Lorenzo may indeed have been the sole decision maker involved in extent and placement.[13] Our certainty is disturbed, though, by one awkward fact that needs explaining: the authorial statements he painted elsewhere in his surviving *œuvre* are in Latin. Another example, simpler still one would think, is the brief undated statement in the vernacular painted in Gothic majuscules by Giovanni da Bologna, probably in the 1380s, at the bottom of his strikingly red and blue panel of *Our Lady of Humility* now in the Accademia (CI 43). It is noticeable, again, that on his signature statements on other works the script is similar but the language chosen is Latin. One cannot help but wonder who took the decision on which language to employ. Was it simply the painter using his own judgement about what was appropriate at that particular time and place for that particular commissioner, or was he in fact given explicit instructions by the sponsor of the painting? A series of commissions involving Antonio Vivarini and Giovanni d'Alemagna suggests that the latter cannot be ruled out.

The authorial statement at the foot of Vivarini and d'Alemagna's towering tempera panel of the *Coronation of the Virgin* in S. Pantalon (CI 59) is painted in black *littera textualis*. It is dated 1444 and is entirely in Venetian. The inscription is partly replicated by its Latin equivalent carved on wood by Ludovico da Forlì — again in *littera textualis* — at the bottom of the devotional image of the *Redeemer*, in the chapel of St Tarasius in the church of S. Zaccaria, painted by Vivarini and d'Alemagna the previous year. It reads: *Iohanes et Antuonius d(e) Muranio pi(n)xeru(n)t*. That phrasing is repeated almost word for word in the same chapel under the polyptych of St Sabina: *Iohanes et Antonius de Muranio pinxerunt*. On the other hand, when the ebonist Cristoforo da Ferrara collaborated with them on another commission it was the vernacular that was again preferred. This message is inscribed and gilded on the frame at the foot of the central panel (*Virgin and Child*) of the polyptych, now in the National Gallery in Prague, which they executed for the Lion chapel in the church of S. Francesco Grande in Padua. It reads: *MCCCCXLVII Cristoph d(e) Ferara intaia Antonio d(e) M(u)ra(n) e Zoha(ne) Alaman p(ense)*. This time the epigraph is in Roman capitals. It is not without interest to note, in summary, that in a parish church in Venice and even in a Franciscan church in the heart of Padua the Vivarini team of craftsmen signed in the Venetian vernacular. For the patrician nuns of the richly endowed S. Zaccaria in Venice they reverted to Latin. In Padua, a centre of Humanist-inspired antiquarian experimentation with handwriting in the mid-fifteenth century, they abandoned the traditional Gothic bookhand. These choices are unlikely to be random. The balance of probability within such a complex sequence of shifts is that in each case the artists consulted their commissioners about preferences in terms of script and language. They may even have been told what was preferred (or demanded) at the contractual stage. The same may well apply to Lorenzo Veneziano's *Mystic Marriage* and Giovanni da Bologna's *Our Lady of Humility*. We do not know who sponsored the former, so our conclusion remains speculative. The latter, though, was commissioned by the *scuola grande* of S. Giovanni Evangelista in the heart of the period when it was a conspicuous sponsor of vernacular epigraphy in Venice. If the above case studies have anything to teach us it is that in considering a commissioned artefact we need to be wary of assuming that the *sculptor* who signed off on it was as fully autonomous in his epigraphic options as one might initially assume.

There are nevertheless important examples in the corpus where control of the inscriptional process does genuinely appear to have been in the hands of the executor himself. In two instances in particular we have something close to certainty about this. The first is the signature plaque in marble (CI 44) appended by the Venetian sculptor Polo Chataiapiera at the foot of his splendid funerary monument to the *condottiere* Iacopo Cavalli in S. Zanipolo (c. 1385).[14] Everything about this self-confident piece of personal publicity suggests that it is entirely autonomous and unconditioned by the tomb sponsors. Polo's white marble plaque sits just below the larger laudatory plaque to Cavalli which he inscribed in Latin in raised lettering, presumably following a text which he was commissioned to execute. His own plaque differs from it in size, decoration, language and script and was clearly conceived independently as a sort of trademark. By great good fortune these conclusions are removed from the realm of speculation by the survival of a later signature plaque of Polo's at the foot of another sarcophagus. This is the tomb of the *condottiere* Prendiparte Pico in Mirandola. There, a decade later, Polo had gone a stage further, actually placing his own very similar oblong plaque above the Latin praise to Pico. Thanks to this tablet we know the extent to which Polo's marketing strategy was both autonomous and sophisticated. The smart Gothic majuscular script is identical to that in S. Zanipolo as is the wording of the passe-partout advertising message in a Tuscan-based vernacular. In Mirandola, though, the language of the three lines was tweaked to incorporate local Emilian features. In Venice it had been partly modulated into *venexian* for its local audience. On his own inscription, then, Polo seems to have assumed, with some bravado, the role of *scriptor*, *ordinator* and *sculptor*, deciding even on script and language choice. It can hardly be a coincidence that he is the first sculptor in the corpus to name himself. It would be fascinating to know if Polo was allowed by contract, or simply verbally, to insert his calling-card inscriptions. It could be argued that he had independence in this domain because his inscriptions were not part of the commissioned work, but this would be disingenuous. In both cases the plaque is clearly integrated.

The second instance of such independence on the part of the executor or executors can be found on the two commemorative plaques from 1456 embedded on piers in the oldest section of the Arsenal by the workmen who erected the great brick supporting structures in the newly built dockyard sheds (CI 67, CI 68). These remarkable rough-and-ready examples of 'popular' inscriptions in Venetian, featuring a jumble of majuscule and minuscule letters, have all the appearance of having been planned, carved and put in place by the *Arsenalotti* themselves — presumably amateurs at inscriptional stonecutting — without commissioning or mediation of any kind.

In two other less clear-cut cases the evidence points in the direction of relative executor independence. The first is the series of inscriptions on the Justice capital of the Doge's Palace with their unexpected vernacular mingling Tuscan and Venetian elements, their *sui generis* archaic script and their unique abbreviation system. As I argue in CI 54, the two anonymous Tuscan craftsmen who appear to have sculpted the beautiful figurations of justice around the capital were presumably instructed in detail by the commissioning agent regarding the precise subjects of the scenes to be carved. One suspects, though, that when it came to the accompanying captions they were given greater leeway. What we now have in front of us suggests general instructions about the legend for each scene, with the sculptors allowed to express them in their own words. It may well be that the only limitations on their choice were that a Venetian public should have no problem with understanding them and that the lettering should look somewhat old-fashioned. The second is the single line inscription on the sarcophagus of Simon Dandolo (CI 25). The sculptor of that fine tomb is likely to have been given a master text with the preamble of the epitaph in Latin, followed by the longer vernacular section. In spite of this the latter displays some linguistic forms, including a north lagoon infinitive type, which are substandard and must be down to the stonemason himself. Equally interesting is the fact that Dandolo, who commissioned the job and was still alive five months later (when he made his will), did not intervene after the event to have the infinitive corrected, even though there was enough space for it to be rectified seamlessly.

The loop that all epigraphers hope to close, linking the actual named commissioner and patron of the artefact and its inscription to its named executor in a documentable way — in which all intermediate stages and choices are visible — comes closest to realisation for a lapidary inscription in one truly unique case. This is the authorial epigraph (CI 47) cut boldly on to an altarpiece from 1408, formerly in the church of S. Beneto in the *sestiere* of S. Marco and now held in the Metropolitan Museum in New York. The altar dedicated to St Peter was built and offered to the church by a prosperous master stonemason from the local parish, Girardo Taiapiera, whose profession and surname had become one. Integral to the offering was the bright polychrome altarpiece, with a vigorous relief of St Peter flanked by St Paul and John the Baptist, planned and sculpted by Girardo and featuring himself and his wife in miniature kneeling in prayer at the foot of the scene. Girardo also decided on the wording of the inscriptional text carved in Gothic majuscules in Venetian. It records his full name and the date of execution and is dedicated to God, the Virgin Mary and the celestial court. The choice of language, script, abbreviations and layout of the inscription was also entirely his. Determined to include a relatively lengthy epigraph, he inscribed it in a radically unorthodox but highly effective location on the artefact: in thirty short and sharply-cut lines running all the way down the right-hand side (approximately 11 cm wide) of the massive object which stands some 1 m 70 cm tall. In this way Girardo married practicality to advantage in that worshippers approaching the altar from the right could not miss his highly visible message. We have proof here of what and how an able stonemason chose to carve when he was sponsor and sole epigraphic decision-maker, and was determined that his commemorative inscription would be read by his fellow parishioners. By so doing he also contributed some clarity to two key queries: whether the sculptor was likely also to be the carver of inscriptions, and how literate stonecutters were. Girardo was a prosperous master mason, literate in the vernacular, who carried out his own inscriptional work.[15]

Two counter examples, different in kind but similar in effect, show just how far a commissioner could dominate the inscriptional transaction, imposing his own desiderata and thereby limiting the craftsman's freedom of action. It is unlikely to be a coincidence that both inscriptions represent legally binding documents transferred on to stone. The first is Angelo Piarini's will, originally embedded on the front of his house on Murano so that his precise testamentary wishes would be publicly known and could not be traduced (CI 8). The second is the translation into Venetian of the papal bull issued from Avignon by Urban V — with charitable appeal complemented by concessionary indulgence — which is in full view on the first-floor loggia of the Doge's Palace (CI 30). Piarini's almost manic desire to eliminate ambiguity by fixing his own words in stone, without the intermediary of a notary, means that the stonemason had to reproduce word for word the fascinating mixture of Muranese Venetian and Tuscan of his everyday speech. To enhance the legibility of his detailed and tightly-packed wishes he seems to have insisted, for the first and only time in the corpus, that the mason employ preparatory lining, some of which is still just detectable. The sculptor of the papal bull was certainly equally constrained. Everything on the thirty-five lines of raised lettering on the plaque suggests that precise instructions were the order of the day. The chancery functionary who translated the original Latin into Venetian provided the mason with a master text in minuscule in which some of the original punctuation of the document was intact. The mason's job was to reproduce this in stone in raised Gothic majuscules while preserving, again uniquely in the corpus, punctuation marks that represented breathing pauses.[16] That he had to follow the text to the letter is confirmed by his consistent and highly eccentric use of double <l>, following common minuscule longhand practice. The sculptor's strenuous efforts to justify his inscription on both sides of the plaque, including the use of a squiggle to avoid an end space, suggest that in this respect too he was under instruction from the commissioner.

Finally, the evidence from a range of inscriptions suggests that the processes which produced them involved varying degrees of intelligent collaboration between sponsor and executor. When Giovanni Mansueti was, we presume, told by the board of the silk weavers' guild-confraternity that they wished not only the date of execution of his *Arrest of St Mark in the Synagogue* (1499) to appear but also the names of all ten commissioning officials and their rank, this must have seemed something of a problem. The *Arrest* takes the viewer into a dramatic and exotic world in which the insertion of a bald list of officials on the oil painting would have sounded a jarring note. Mansueti solved the issue, apparently to the satisfaction of all concerned, sacrificing nothing of the painting's aesthetics. He employed the familiar cartellino device, enlarged and unfolded to create the illusion of a letter, 'attaching' it to a dais step where it was readable. Wedged between the foot of a Mamluk dignitary directly above it on the step and a prowling leopard just below, it drew the eye in naturally (CI 81). On the cartellino Mansueti placed the board officials' names, not in epigraphic script but in the normal Venetian *mercantesca* longhand. Just above it he continued the amusing illusion by 'printing' in capitals his own signature in Latin on what looked like the front of another smaller unfolded letter.

Arguably the most complex and satisfying case of collaboration in the corpus is found on the magnificent lunette inscription at S. Maria della Carità, with its narrative of the plague of 1348 (CI 14). This impressive and complex artefact could not have been realised without co-operation bordering on partnership between the board of the confraternity and the craftsmen who carried out their wishes. The *scuola grande* produced a substantial text for inscribing, one of the finest surviving pieces of dramatic prose in Early Venetian. The master mason rose to the challenge of transferring the unusually long eighteen lines on to a cropped semi-circular surface measuring 230 x 100 cm in large raised Gothic majuscules. In spite of all the lines being of different lengths he even achieved justification on both sides, regularity in letter and word spacing and exceptional legibility. The laying out of a major text, employing the most demanding inscriptional technique, on such an awkward expanse of surface can only have been achieved by careful forethought and planning. It is hard to imagine that chiselling work was carried out without prior experimentation. This may have involved a mock-up or else a design on a soft-plaster tracing floor of the type used by the master masons of medieval cathedrals.[17] The words would then have been painted or drawn in charcoal directly on to the lunette within some kind of erasable lining, possibly applied with chalked twine, to mark headers and footers. The stone would have been carved in the mason's yard before being transported to the Carità and hauled up into place above the entrance door. It is inconceivable that a project of this scope, involving building, painting, gilding and enamel work too, was done without teamwork and close co-ordination between commissioners and tradesmen. That the confraternity were happy with the result is clear from their subsequent publication and distribution of the inscription text.

2. Trajectories of script use

Venice *c.* 1300 was heir to multiple epigraphic script traditions, none of which had achieved exclusivity in the city by the time our corpus opens. Generalising about trends in script choice across a highly variegated Venetian environment over the more than three centuries before 1300 for which dateable evidence exists, although only sporadically pre-1100, is hazardous. However, a broad dynamic — one which is a useful template for assessing the complex situation on the ground in the period of the corpus and for appreciating the trends, innovations and anachronisms revealed by it — can be discerned.[18]

For lapidary inscriptions the evidence suggests that post-Carolingian Roman capitals — sober, tendentially square in module and monoline in cut — became gradually inflected in the tenth and, especially, eleventh centuries by uncial letter forms. By *c.* 1100 epigraphic script in Venice remained essentially capital but with numerous uncial intrusions. It was also marked by the surprising presence of irregular capitals of various types. These included some angular-cut letters, notably <c> and <g>, alongside archaisms such as the <n> with a low middle stroke and the lambda-type <a>. Ligatures as well as miniaturised, overlapping and nested letters sometimes appeared as well.[19] One has the distinct impression that in the twelfth century these co-existing but rather contradictory tendencies cluster at two poles. The most clearly characterised of the two is the type strongly associated across Europe with the Romanesque designation.[20] It is compressed in its module, largely unserifed and decidedly monoline. It favours a narrow capital type although it can occasionally incorporate uncials. Most noticeably, it specialises in the sort of serial ligaturing, miniaturising and nesting that was prevalent in France in the eleventh century: not only for space-saving reasons but as an aesthetic principle. At its best there is a severe, impressive elegance in its thin-cut look.[21] At its extreme it fetishises illegibility, suggesting that the message is a deliberate, perhaps playful, rebus. This strand, probably deriving its characteristics from the display scripts of Romanesque manuscripts, petered out in the early thirteenth century, softened at the close by

Fig. 1.1. Tomb inscription of Dogaressa Felicita Michiel, c. 1100. © A. S. Ferguson.

Fig. 1.2. Detail of twelfth-century Romanesque inscription, church of S. Giacomo di Rialto. © A. S. Ferguson

the increasing input of uncials. At the other pole, typical of the twelfth and the first half of the thirteenth century in Venice, were inscriptions featuring a squarer and more generously spaced majuscular script, still largely monoline and only modestly serifed. In it, capitals and uncials were combined in varying proportions, as they later would be in Gothic, although this precurser majuscular script generally lacks the stylistic unity either of Gothic or of the quintessentially Romanesque script. It is fair to say, though, that such mixed, more-or-less uncial alphabets — tending increasingly in the thirteenth century to what could be called a kind of proto-Gothic in their sinuosity of ductus, contrastive stroking and serifing — prepared the ground for the decisive mental shift to the Gothic aesthetic in Venice in the late thirteenth and early fourteenth centuries.[22]

The influences on Venetian Gothic, when it made its belated appearance, would inevitably have been multiple. The style was established throughout western Europe, and the great university cities close to Venice, Padua and Bologna, were centres where Gothic was already deeply, indeed almost exclusively, embedded.[23] Inevitably, therefore, there were similarities between the Gothic which eventually took root in Venice after 1300 and that of other Italian centres. Nevertheless one is struck by the often quite strong differences in temper between fourteenth-century inscriptions in Venice and those in Padua and in areas close to the university city

Fig. 1.3. Mixed capital-uncial inscription, 1219, from the church of S. Giustina.
© A. S. Ferguson

Fig. 1.4. Inscription by Master Bertucius on bronze door of St Mark's Basilica, 1300.
© A. S. Ferguson

where the influence of its inscriptional workshops was strong.[24] The lettering in Paduan Gothic epigraphy, from the second half of the thirteenth century and through the fourteenth is, by and large, much more consciously sophisticated, sometimes even fussy, in its carving, with an emphasis on calligraphic finesse and decorativeness — recalling, and often surpassing, French, German and Iberian examples — that is rarely seen in Venice. Indeed the evidence from the transition to Gothic in Venice suggests the specifically local influence of two initially separate sources on Venetian outcomes.

The first of these is the stylistically unified capital-uncial majuscule alphabet familiar to contemporaries above all as the official state script stamped on Venice's coinage in the last third of the Duecento. By the end of the thirteenth century this script was appearing in outstanding metalwork inscriptions in and on the Basilica.[25] It had evolved into a *sui generis* type of Gothic where capitals and uncials with strong stroke contrast and open aspect were combined in a spiky, powerfully serifed and muscular way and where the capital forms featured sturdily emphatic stems.[26] Its influence can be detected on a lapidary inscription of 1299 sculpted for the coopers' guild in Cannaregio,[27] as well as on the two earliest stone inscriptions in the corpus (CI 1 and CI 3). It remains very obvious on the powerfully cut inscription of the confraternity of the *Dodexe Apostoli* (CI 19) of 1351. The other source, more decorative and calligraphic, was the pervasive influence of Gothic manuscript titling capitals, ubiquitous in the visual imagination of all those who could read, or even just see, books in Venice and elsewhere.[28] It was particularly familiar to thousands of Venetians from the initials in the *mariegole* statute books of the city's confraternities and guilds which were major sponsors of epigraphy in Venice and the lagoon.[29] Its influence is palpable on the modest CI 4 of *c*. 1312 from the almshouse sponsored by Natichlier Cristian and on the outstanding CI 13 of 1346 from the church of S. Antonio Abate in Castello. Among the city's Trecento Latin inscriptions manuscript influence underlies the beautiful epigraph dated February 1317 (*more veneto*) and signed by the enigmatic sculptor 'Marcus Romanus', on a plaque above the sarcophagus with its magnificent reclining figure of St Simeon the Prophet, in the church of S. Sim(i)on Grando: arguably the finest early Gothic inscription in Venice (WOLTERS 1976: cat. 12 and ill. 34). It is also the reference point for the script of the sophisticated commemorative plaque of 1344 from the church of S. Giovanni Evangelista on Torcello which is now in the Seminario Patriarcale (DI LENARDO 2014: 98–102). It is plausible that the conjugation in various proportions of these two feeder sources contributed to conferring on the Venetian Gothic of the corpus its own rather open flavour.[30] The restrained traditions established thereby may explain why the refined and sometimes mannered ornateness that is not unusual in the mature Gothic of Padua, Verona and France only occasionally came to the fore in Venice and never dominated the city's epigraphic production.[31]

The complex trajectory of lapidary inscriptions up to 1300 and beyond is further complicated by some unexpectedly archaic outliers. These need to be noted if one is to appreciate the long-term eclecticism of epigraphic choices in Venice within the timescale of the corpus. Six examples are particularly revealing. The gilded eleventh-century inscription in St Mark's running below the balustrade of the matroneum beneath a series of Byzantine-type plaques strikes one immediately as remarkable. This epigraph was obviously of the highest official importance in its celebration of the Basilica, and for it the authorities had recourse to beautiful, amply spaced Roman capitals of the Carolingian type, without ligatures or uncials.[32] The second case, possibly from the eleventh century and also from St Mark's, is the touching epitaph plaque embedded in the chapel of St Isidore and dedicated to a baby who died aged eight days (PINCUS 2017: 47–48). It features a highly stylised, self-consciously mixed script combining sometimes square, sometimes partly compressed, monoline capitals with a selection of uncial forms, notably an <m> with billowing curves topped by decorative top loop, a lambda <a> and a left-curved <u/v>. The lettering shows unpredictable height variations, and the eye is drawn by a sprinkling of inserted, miniaturised, raised and ligatured forms. The third example is the epitaph plaque of *c.* 1290, in S. Zanipolo, dedicated to doge Çane Dandolo. This inscription reverts to a by then dated Romanesque manner, combining thin-cut monoline capitals with occasional uncials.

Perhaps the most notorious example of inscriptional archaism in Venice is the pair of epigraphs on the side of the sarcophagus of the two thirteenth-century Tiepolo doges set against the façade of S. Zanipolo. The longer of the two inscriptions, on the central plaque, features an antiquarian-looking Romanesque script with a very particular type of Greek mu employed repeatedly. The shorter one-line statement running along the bottom strip is, by contrast, carved in Gothic majuscules. PINCUS (2000: 14–35, 171–75) dates the longer inscription to the first half of the fifteenth century and the shorter, Gothic one, to the fourteenth century. DE RUBEIS (2008: 39–40), on the other hand, considers both to have been executed immediately post-1279 and, despite the radically different types of script, to have been carved by the same stonemason. Whatever the truth of the matter, the almost incongruous juxtaposition on such a prestigious sarcophagus of widely varying letter styles is astonishing. One cannot help noting that a similar antiquarian script to that on the upper plaque of the Tiepolo tomb recurs in the fifteenth century on the three-line tomb inscription, again in S. Zanipolo, of Nicolò Vitturi who died in 1423. On the tomb slab of Faustino Miani (died 1435) in the Frari, the epitaph running round the edges is also carved in an exquisite antiquarian script, compressed and tendentially monoline. It features Romanesque raising and ligaturing, the Greek-style mu, uncial <e>, an open-top <a>, and an archaic <n> with a low middle stroke.[33] The final extreme example of antiquarian eclecticism is the four-line epitaph to Cardinal Antonio Correr (died 1445) originally from the church of S. Giorgio in Al(e)ga on the lagoon island of that name. It is now displayed in the cloisters of the Seminario Patriarcale. The elegant, mannered, deliberately archaic script is monoline, unserifed and partly compressed. Its sources are to be found in various Romanesque traditions but it recalls, above all, the alphabet used in the mosaics of the twelfth-century dome of the Pentecost in St Mark's. Its unique <o> forms, pinched in the middle to form almost an 8, are exactly as on the cupola.

One cannot ignore, in fact, the compelling influence on the eclectic hinterland that we have just explored of the prestigious mosaic traditions of the lagoon and

THE MEDIUM AND THE MESSAGE   47

FIG. 1.5. Detail of Faustino Miani epitaph (1435) in the Frari. © A. S. Ferguson

FIG. 1.6. Late twelfth-century inscription with Byzantine ligatures
on the Ascension dome of St Mark's Basilica:
Dicite quid statis quid i(n) aethere co(n)sideratis. © A. S. Ferguson

their epigraphy: from the solemn eleventh-century apses in Torcello and Murano through to the dazzling array of western and Byzantine scripts that adorn the walls and domes of St Mark's at the religious heart of the city-state.[34] From our epigraphic perspective perhaps their most influential effect was the creation of beautiful novel alphabets in which native Romanesque forms were moulded in different ways by Byzantine teams of mosaicists. The resulting multiplicity of scripts, featuring exotic ligaturing and modelling, made familiar Greek-influenced letter forms such as the minuscule <q> treated as a majuscule and, most obviously, the <m> in the form of a capital mu which persisted in Venice into the Renaissance period and which crops up periodically in the corpus.[35] Equally, their sumptuous and authoritative diversity can be said to have sanctioned the eclectic freedom which informed Venetian epigraphic choices right into the sixteenth century.[36]

The corpus throws up many examples of such inscriptional creativity. Prominent is the experimental archaic script carved by the sculptors of the Justice capital on the Palazzo Ducale in the early fourteenth century (CI 54). More surprising still, and with wider implications, is the rather precocious reception of monumental capitals in Venice. They appear in a vernacular inscription as early as 1446 (CI 60), and fourteen years before this in a Latin one.[37] These largely overlooked attestations bring forward by several decades the introduction of revival Roman square capitals in the Veneto which is usually assigned to 1450–60.[38] The recourse to Romanesque traits on a vernacular inscription as late as 1479, with miniaturising, raising, nesting and thin strokes on large-scale letters, is worthy of reflection. The inscription is carved and laid out idiosyncratically below the attractive, originally coloured, lunette relief of St Mark healing the cobbler Anianus on the shoemakers' confraternity-guild house at S. Tomà (CI 75). The stonemason working for the S. Marcilian housing association, or possibly his commissioners themselves, also opted for an odd monoline script, full of trickery, for the two building ownership plaques in the neighbourhood (CI 71, CI 72). In the context of such receptivity to eccentric options one should perhaps be less taken aback than one is at the appearance of the great epigraphs, highlighted in black, cut on the first prestigious Renaissance monument in Venice, the classical gateway from 1460 at the entrance to the Arsenal. These are, of course, sculpted in revival Roman script, but their square capitals feature a breathtaking medley of rebus letters in overlapping, miniaturising and nesting patterns in the characteristic twelfth-century Romanesque manner. One strongly suspects that space constraints are not the whole story here and that the mason and his commissioner delighted in what is nothing less than a bravura display of eclectic letter cutting.[39] In fact, it can be said that the carved or painted monumental capitals in our corpus — even in the late fifteenth and early sixteenth centuries when Trajanic capital script was dominant — retain the quirks and adaptable variability that typify Venetian vernacular epigraphy in the Middle Ages and Renaissance: from directly documented imitation of a known classical model (CI 106), via the persistence of medieval abbreviation insertions (CI 107), to an eccentric or flourished *capitalis* (CI 96, CI 97, CI 109).

Very much in line with these miscellaneous choices are the multiple appearances of non-majuscular epigraphic scripts in the corpus. Perhaps most surprisingly

Fig. 1.7. Inscription in rebus Roman capitals on right-side entablature of Arsenal gateway, 1460. © A. S. Ferguson

unorthodox are the two 'home made' commemorative inscriptions sculpted by the craftsmen of the Arsenal on boat-shed piers there (CI 67, CI 68), where a melée of casual majuscules, minuscules and cursive insertions jostle for position. On the other hand, lapidary epigraphs in minuscule script, which flooded inscriptional production in Spain and France in the fifteenth century and were sometimes present before this, are rare in Venice. The only case in the corpus is a motto inscribed on the coat of arms displayed on a house front in Cannaregio (CI 61). It is carved in *fere textura*, a luxury offshoot of the standard *littera textualis* book hand. This highly stylised and decorative northern European minuscule also appears on a painted banderole (CI 55) as early as 1429, while *littera textualis* itself features in 1444 at the bottom of the great tempera panel of the *Coronation of the Virgin* painted by Antonio Vivarini and Giovanni d'Alemagna in S. Pantalon (CI 59). Cursive minuscule is prominent on the Fra Mauro *mappa mundi* and on de' Barbari's cityscape, in both cases alongside *capitalis* script of various sorts. It also appears on the *trompe l'œil* letter painted by Giovanni Mansueti on his canvas of the *Arrest of St Mark in the Synagogue*, where the writing commissioned by the guild of silk weavers is laid out in *mercantesca*, the everyday longhand of Venice (CI 81). Finally, an attractive display minuscule, in effect a high-grade version of *mercantesca*, is deployed by Carpaccio on the inscription at the foot of his *Annunciation* (CI 92) painted for the Albanian confraternity.

3. Language

According to Armando Petrucci, inscriptions are invariably the highest level of writing in any literate society:

> Non dimentichiamo che la scrittura esposta, con le sue evidenti caratteristiche di solennità e di formalità esecutiva, che ne comprovano la particolare dignità e l'importanza del messaggio trasmesso, ha costituito e costituisce in ogni società di scrittura il grado più alto di espressione scritta. (A. PETRUCCI 1997: 45–46)

This generalisation seems unexceptionable when applied to classical epigraphy, both Latin and Greek. It is convincing, by and large, as an explanation for why Latin remained the dominant inscriptional medium throughout Italy and elsewhere in the medieval period as a whole. The lower quality or functional restriction of the few vernacular inscriptions produced in Italy up to the thirteenth century confirm rather than contradict Petrucci's point.[40] Its explanatory force is equally valid, but less immediately obvious, when applied to the epigraphic production — mainly in Latin but also, to different degrees, in the vernacular — in some of the great merchant cities of northern and central Italy between 1300 and 1500. In these complex polities a nexus of factors had come into play which complicated the definition of what exactly 'il grado più alto di espressione scritta' might be, and which rendered increasingly porous and less predictable the boundaries of the formerly entrenched bilingualism separating Latin in writing from vernacular in speech. One of the visible consequences of this shift was the emergence of a new modulation of epigraphic language where Latin and the vernacular became distributed, albeit unevenly in quantitative terms, according to situation, function and commissioner of the message conveyed.[41] The factors underlying this change can be summarised as: the increasing presence in official domains of a written form of the local vernacular; the parallel growth in prestige and perceived communicative effectiveness of this *scripta*;[42] and complex forms of economic activity requiring the ability to read and write. Together they fostered an increase in secular literacy and, therefore, a potentially wider audience for vernacular inscriptions. In the Trecento these interconnected developments peaked in Venice. The city had become one of the world's great mercantile hubs, poised between East and West. It had exceptional levels of literacy.[43] It had a *scripta* with growing prestige.[44]

However, there is one further factor which in Venice undoubtedly acted as the catalyst for a truly exceptional flowering of inscriptions in the vernacular: the presence of the *scolae magnae* (or *scuole grandi*) and the *scolae comunes* (or *scuole piccole*).[45] To a greater extent than other Italian mercantile city states Venice was a stable polity where exceptionally dense and widespread networks of social and spiritual participation — embedded at the neighbourhood level but with members drawn from across the city — provided a key stimulant for epigraphic expression. Encouraged and controlled by the authorities, yet autonomous in the day-to-day running of their collectivities, the guild-confraternities and spiritual brotherhoods, great and small, permeated the fabric of the city with their religious and civic activities even though they had no formal political role. The huge memberships of these lay sodalities, drawn almost exclusively from the citizen and artisan classes, and in some cases including women,[46] exercised complex activities of individual and collective salvation, mutual self-help and charitable largesse, as well as labour organisation and regulation within the trade guilds. These activities were channelled through executive boards of elected officers where reading and writing were, as a matter of course, essential everyday skills for the drawing up of agendas, the drafting of minutes, and the reading and issuing of decisions and communications. The pride and identity of the *scuole* were expressed through programmes of building and artistic commissioning centred on the enlarging, furnishing, refurbishing and embellishing of their buildings and meeting halls. They were enshrined in their precious and constantly updated statute-and-membership book, the *mariegola* — beautifully illuminated and, by 1300, invariably written in Venetian — which they saw, venerated, read and had read out to them. It was essential that the *mariegola* be in the universally understood vernacular, not only because the statutes, updated and periodically communicated in assembly, had to be clear to all, but first and foremost because the salvation of each brother's (or sister's) soul might be at stake.[47] The corporate solidarity and pride of the confraternities were expressed publicly on feast days when they paraded through the city bearing banners and sometimes relics, as can most famously be visualised from Gentile Bellini's *Procession in Piazza San Marco* (c. 1496). They expressed them for themselves, for contemporaries and for posterity in their abundant vernacular epigraphy where the written word of these practical people, from civil servants and bankers to humble craftsmen, was enshrined in stone, and occasionally in other mediums, in the native language familiar to all. It is not surprising that forty-five of our 109 inscriptions (fully 41% of the corpus, equal to some 48% of inscriptional artefacts themselves) are linked to the *scuole*.[48]

Our survey of inscriptions in Venice in the Middle Ages and Renaissance has revealed the surprisingly weighty epigraphic presence of the vernacular alongside Latin throughout most of that period, and particularly from the mid-fourteenth to the mid-fifteenth centuries.[49] It has also shown that except for the latter part of our timespan the vernacular occupied the full range of inscriptional types and sponsorship, with the partial (but only partial) exception of patrician epitaphs. Latin epigraphs were, of course, perfectly comprehensible to a small elite and remained strongly present, although far from exclusive, in ecclesiastical inscriptions which, like epitaphs, were a type whose traditions were associated with Latin. Nevertheless it is worth underlining that the occupation by the vernacular of even the higher end of the spectrum of epigraphic writing in Venice in our period is truly remarkable.

It is self-evident that, unlike Latin inscriptions, vernacular ones were available for all literate persons to read directly and that, if need be, they could also be read out to those who were illiterate or only partially literate. As we have noted, this obvious observation accounts in large measure for the attraction vernacular epigraphy had for the *scuole* of Venice. It also explains why individuals, great or more modest, making an endowment or benefaction or else involved in a work of public utility and commemorating it in stone, favoured the vernacular to advertise their generosity. Similarly, sculptors or painters signing their work would often employ the Venetian *volgar* in order to advertise their expertise as widely as possible. The vernacular was equally the logical choice for urgent charitable appeals to the general population or for notices about construction limits to be respected in narrow streets or about ownership rights. In such cases immediate comprehensibility was of the essence. However, it is particularly significant for our understanding of the new prestige and attractiveness of vernacular epigraphy that it was also deemed appropriate for commissions of the highest level. Examples in the corpus are too numerous to require the case to be laboured. It is sufficient to point to the most prestigious epigraphic locus in the city in St Mark's Square, on the one hand, and, on the other, to two inscribed artefacts which had international resonance: Fra Mauro's *mappa mundi* and the de' Barbari view of Venice.

When the authorities wished an important inscriptional message to be conveyed unequivocally within the religious and political hub of the city, around the Doge's Palace and St Mark's, they too had recourse as often as not to the transparency of the vernacular. The monitory dictum about acts and their consequences (CI 1) on the spectacular outside wall of the Treasury confronted, on their left, those entering the Palazzo Ducale where political power was wielded and justice dispensed. The *exempla* carved on the Justice capital and captioned in the vernacular faced them on their right (CI 54). On the loggia of the first floor of the palace they could read the Venetian translation of Urban V's bull carved in raised and probably gilded letters on the wall overlooking the courtyard (CI 30), with its charitable appeal and concessionary indulgence. Inside the Treasury next door they could appreciate in the vernacular the largesse of two Procurators of St Mark who had paid for arguably the most striking example of the goldsmith's craft produced in Venice in the period, the *Column of the Flagellation of Christ* (CI 39). The Procurators, one of them shortly to become doge, advertised their sponsorship of it in Venetian on niello plaques. On a wider scale still, Fra Mauro, anxious for his *mappa mundi*, dedicated to Venice, to achieve maximum impact opted to inscribe his hundreds of topographical legends in the vernacular (CI 62–66) because, as he put it on one of them: 'In questa opera per necessità ho convenuto usar nomi moderni e vulgar perché al vero se io havesse fato altramente pochi me haveria inteso salvo qualche literato'. In this way his unrivalled map of the known world, along with the documentary evidence of Venice in 1500 bequeathed by Jacopo de' Barbari in the inscribed topography of his breathtaking cityscape (CI 82–91), have come down to posterity fully mediated by their authors' civic identity as expressed through the vernacular from which it was indissociable.

The vernacular medium of the overwhelming majority of the 109 inscriptions in the collection is Venetian, the written form of the everyday spoken language of all classes in the Venetian state in the period 1300–1525 and into modern times. A handful, while not fully Venetian, have *venexian* as their starting point or point of reference, including the three moralising fresco legends (CI 5, CI 6, CI 7) which appear to show traces of 'colonial' Venetian from the eastern Adriatic coast. A very few are consciously inflected by elements of Tuscan or else are involved, in varying degrees, in code mixing between Venetian and Tuscan. As for Latin, it is occasionally present in our inscriptions in the type of limited and well-defined role typically found in the set formulae of vernacular documents and statutes of the period, including the *mariegole*.[50]

As a language employed by every stratum of a densely populated society, richly articulated at neighbourhood level, *venexian* had both unity and diversity.[51] In other words it was not only a system recognised as such, and identified with, by all speakers. It was also a layered diasystem with social, local and age diversification, both within the lagoon and within the city itself. At the top of the diasystem it possessed what could be termed informal norms for judging and regulating more-or-less appropriate variants within grammar, vocabulary and pronunciation, although in Venice these were slower than expected to bed in as a result of the complex and intertwined way in which the city and its spoken language were forged. Such evolving norms, retarded by the likely origins of Venetian as a koine variety,[52] would eventually be transferred to the written domain. In its textual form Early Venetian is attested from *c.* 1200. The evolving dynamic of its status from then until the later stages of our period can be conceived of as a parabola. For analytical convenience the parabola can be split into three segments. The rising phase of the curve started in the thirteenth century as Venetian, hegemonic in every spoken context, was transferred on to the page and gradually extended its contexts and registers of use. The apex of the curve was reached in the fourteenth century and coincided, as we have noted, with the greatest burst of vernacular inscriptional activity ever seen in the history of Venice. Written Venetian in the Trecento continued, well into the century, to display in its middle and lower registers the expected levels of structural variability and norm variation predicted by its koine origins. However, in its highest textual registers — in the vernacular versions of the regulations of government offices, in the statutes of guilds and confraternities, in legal documents and in historical chronicles — it had reached by the mid-fourteenth century a degree of stability that one is tempted to call an informal codification, almost indeed a prelude to the status of 'language' in the modern sense. Spoken Venetian, in the meantime, was already exerting the kind of linguistic influence on its maritime possessions and outposts that would irresistibly affect its mainland empire in the fifteenth century. One of the most significant features of the Venetian employed in our corpus, and a further confirmation of Petrucci's claim about the exceptional status of inscriptional writing, is that it conspicuously displays, from the early to mid-fourteenth century, the substantial structural stabilisation of high-register written Venetian and the virtually complete removal of diatopic and diastratic variants from within it.

The declining phase of the curve occurred in the course of the fifteenth century as the narrow gap between omnipresent spoken Venetian and its written *scripta* began to widen again. Paradoxically, this occurred just at the point where the *scripta* had more or less reached parity in status with Latin in Venetian chancery practice. In its most official registers textual Venetian was coming to be increasingly diluted by external influences, mainly but not exclusively exerted by the rising prestige of Tuscan on its elites (as on those of other Italian cities).[53] This partial dilution in the direction of Tuscan in the later fifteenth and early sixteenth centuries can occasionally be detected in the corpus, for instance in the phonology and morphology of Fra Mauro (CI 62–66). However, on only one epigraph from the early Cinquecento (CI 93) is there a conscious, although not entirely successful, attempt to fully Tuscanise the inscriptional vernacular. On the contrary, more than other types of high-register documentation of the time the inscriptional Venetian of the corpus remained substantially itself until the end of our period. This is not one of the least significant linguistic revelations of the collection.

This large corpus of mostly high-register texts is a reservoir of information, spanning roughly two and a quarter centuries, about Early Venetian and the initial decades of Middle Venetian.[54] We can trace through it the stabilisation of important structural norms which came from the contending feeder streams in the koineisation process. In this category is the definitive settling of infinitives around the form in -r, such as *far* 'to make, to do' (CI 1, CI 21, CI 29), *eser* 'to be' (CI 14), *aver* 'to have' (CI 6), *inpensar* 'to think, to reflect' (CI 1), *inchontrar* 'to befall' (CI 1), *levar* 'to raise' (CI 13), *tremar* 'to tremble' (CI 14), *morir* 'to die' (CI 14) and *mostrar* 'to show' (CI 32), with only a single residue of competing variants surviving from among our inscriptions.[55] The -r infinitive paradigm would become absolutely dominant in the subsequent history of Venetian. Similarly, the apocope on noun and adjective endings, which was bewilderingly variable in the earliest stages of Venetian, is seen in the corpus to crystallise substantially round the compromise system between final vowel deletion and retention that was still in operation in Modern and Contemporary Venetian.[56] However, other dominant variants in the fourteenth century — such as /ol/ alongside the minority segment /al/ (*Riolto* rather than *Rialto*) and /en/ rather than /an/ (*sen, senta* 'saint' rather than *san, santa*) — are shown as giving way quickly post-1400 to the originally minority variant.[57] It may well be, in both cases, that proximity of the minority variants in /al/ and /an/ to their equivalents in Tuscan and in northern Italian *scripta* practice facilitated their eventual victory. The same reason probably explains the demise of the formerly dominant and quirky Early Venetian adverbial ending -mentre in favour of the originally minority variant -mente, as in Italian. We find *comunamentre* 'commonly' in CI 14 (c. 1348) but, by 1362, CI 30 has *grandemente* 'greatly', *continuamente* 'continually', *ubertosamente* 'fruitfully' and *devotamente* 'devoutly'.

Conservative tendencies appear strongly in the preservation of the consciously careful -ado, -ada past participle endings (< -ātum, -ātam), as against the outcomes in -ao and -à which are often found in texts of more modest register and which were presumably closer to the spoken language. Voicing tendencies on intervocalic consonants follow this pattern too, halting at a conservative /d/ and /v/ and only very occasionally, in the latter, disappearing to /Ø/.[58] Noun endings from -ātem are generally, therefore, in -ade, but occasionally the more 'modern' form in -à appears, so that twice *podestà* 'mayor' shows up instead of the usual *podestade*.[59] The outcome of Latin L followed by yod preserves the original /j/ throughout the corpus (with *conseio* 'council' < consĭlĭum and *luio* 'July' < *lulius), and thus contrasts with the characteristic reflex in /ʤ/ (giving *consegio* and *lugio*) which dominated from Middle Venetian onwards.

We are provided by the corpus with fine-grained detail about one of the most complex and long-lasting phenomena in the history of Venetian phonology, the diphthongisation or otherwise of reflexes of stressed mid vowels Ĕ and Ŏ into <e> or <ie> and <o> or <uo> respectively. It can be traced particularly conspicuously in the corpus in constantly recurring doublets like *miser* ~ *misier* 'Sir, Mr', *lavorer* ~ *lavorier* 'work, piece of work, artefact' and *sc(h)ola* ~ *sc(h)uola* 'confraternity, confraternity building'. The data reveal a complex situation over the period, with diphthong innovations staggered by lexical diffusion through individual words and with pockets of resistance, particularly in lexemes like *(h)omo* 'man', *(h)omeni* 'men' and *bon* 'good'. Here the process may have been inhibited by the presence of a following nasal (BAGLIONI 2016: 365), although forms such as *Antuoni(i)o* (Anthony) in CI 15 (1349), CI 16 (1349), and CI 76 (1482), alongside eight instances of *Ant(h)onio* ranging from 1348 to 1507, remain awkward to account for by internal factors. The general drift is confirmed to be in the direction of the diphthongisation of both vowels in the course of the fourteenth century, in line with the evidence of other types of Venetian texts of the period. It is followed, though, by a slow, uneven return to non-diphthongised forms in the course of the fifteenth century.[60] On a less turbulent scale we are enabled to trace the evolving, but still unresolved, pattern of masculine possessive pronouns in Venetian. The corpus evidence also provides the occasional surprise, forcing philologists to revise their perspective. Perhaps the most striking example is found in the configuration of the passive, a construction which is richly represented in the epigraphs. Contrary to what was believed to be the majority case in Early Venetian texts, the predominant (although not exclusive) pattern in the corpus is of complete agreement in gender and number between noun(s) and past participle, irrespective of whether the participle precedes or follows.

Both geographic and class variants in the corpus are few and far between.[61] This, as we have seen, tells its own story about the stability achieved by the Venetian *scripta* at the epigraphic level. However, stylistic variation is particularly strong in the collection and fills a gap in our understanding of the potentialities of written Venetian of the period. This can be appreciated tellingly by comparing, on the one hand, the extreme hypotactic sentence structure of the bull from Urban V (CI 30) with the equally extreme parataxis of the narrative of the plague in the lunette at S. Maria della Carità (CI 14). Equally, the pugnacious legalese of Angelo Piarini's will (CI 8) jars with the sustained commemorative solemnity of the elegant S. Antonio Abate plaque (CI 13).

Notes to Chapter 2

1. Probably the best-known Italian example is the epitaph plaque from 1259 of the Lercari brother and sister, with its double guidelines infilled in black, from the church of S. Giovanni di Pré in Genoa and now in the Museo di S. Agostino in that city. The proximity of the Genoese Republic to Provençal, Burgundian and French territory is unlikely to be coincidental. The inscription is mostly in Latin but the last line is in the vernacular. See L. PETRUCCI (2010: 135–37, ill. 31).
2. For a good example of this French tradition going back to the Romanesque period, see CIFM, vol. 22, ill. 76.

3. Traces of black infilling are still present on numerous vernacular and Latin inscriptions of our period. Time has taken a greater toll of epigraphic pigment, but colour can be made out on a number of the inscriptional plaques in the corpus, particularly those which have always been kept indoors. Notable are the traces of a chequered green and pink pattern on the crenellated frame of CI 45, the faded black and gold chequering surrounding CI 44, the black lettering on gold ground on CI 49, and the gold script on black ground of CI 14.
4. Notable examples of this trend are the elegant spiral interpuncts on CI 57, the unique knotted-rope dividers on CI 69 and the rosettes on CI 80. For a theoretical perspective on the decoratively intrusive interpuncts typical of medieval French epigraphy see INGRAND-VARENNE (2016).
5. On the manuscript background of epigraphic abbreviation conventions see CAPPELLI (1928) and BISCHOFF (1990: 150–68). On the transition between the heavy use of abbreviations on Gothic inscriptions and the lighter-touch practice on revival Roman capitals see NYBERG (1978). An interesting example of abbreviation crossover is visible on the *damnatio memoriae* inscription of Baiamonte Tiepolo (CI 32) where the 3 symbol used in manuscripts and epigraphs for the Latin accusative -*m* is employed to render the nasal sound in the vernacular. Fascinating and unique in its overall preservation on stone of manuscript abbreviation practice is the translated papal bull of Urban V on the Doge's Palace (CI 30).
6. Raised-letter inscriptions were rare in Roman times. They became a Greek speciality in the Byzantine Empire and almost certainly passed from there to Venice. See STUSSI (1997a: 171–72). Interestingly, the Byzantines may themselves have been influenced by letter raising in the Islamic world where this inscriptional technique was not uncommon on prestige epigraphs.
7. For possible evidence of the same stonemason being involved in two different commissions where raised lettering was used, one in Latin, one in the vernacular, see CI 9.
8. Terminology such as *scriptor, ordinatio, ordinator* and *sculptor* is lifted from Latin sources of various kinds, as are the label *officina* for the stonemason's workshop and the designations *lapicida* or *lapidarius* for the stonecutter or mason himself. On these terms and on a reconstruction of the processes involved in ordering and executing a Roman lapidary inscription see EDMONDSON (2014).
9. There is tantalising contractual evidence in two cases in the corpus. A 1349 legacy of 300 ducats for the commissioning and inscribing of two well heads at the Angelo Rafael in Dorsoduro by the wealthy merchant Marco Arian is the best surviving example. Two inscriptional details are stipulated in his will. On one of the wells it is to be made clear in writing that the *pozzi* are for commoners and gentlemen alike. On both wells Arian's merchant mark is to figure. The first of the two wells disappeared before the modern period so we cannot ascertain how far his first interesting stipulation was carried out. The second well still survives and bears Arian's merchant mark as well as an almost identical commemorative inscription on both sides (CI 15, CI 16). We do not know if it was Marco or his family who commissioned the text. The second example is vaguer still. Found in the written accounts of Pacifica, abbess of the Ognissanti complex in Dorsoduro, it mentions the transport of an already inscribed Roman funerary urn to the Buora stonemasons' workshop at S. Stefano for conversion into a well head, and the subsequent payment to a well-maker for installing the well at the convent. Unfortunately, no reference is made to the actual commissioning which led to the beautifully carved vernacular epigraph on it dated 28 June 1518 (CI 106). This is a great pity since the Buora family of sculptors ran a quality stonecutting business that was much in demand for important commissions in the city and beyond (MARKHAM SCHULZ 1983).
10. Critical interest in the regularisation of inscriptional lettering is usually confined to experiments in the Renaissance with the geometrical construction of Roman monumental capitals. Curiously there has been no interest, as far as I know, in establishing how regularity was achieved on Gothic majuscular lettering in its many guises where the stonemason did not have the luxury of working only with horizontal and vertical lines and with segments of a circle. Study of the many examples in the corpus suggests that with their set squares, T-squares, rulers and compasses, and operating within temporary guide-lines, masons could efficiently mark out key points of each letter on the stone. They then seem to have worked freehand with chisels and mallet, tolerating

slight and often pleasing diversities in the shape of the same letter and relying on know-how and experience. In the case of some particularly skilled masters the degree of regularity obtained by this method was quite remarkable.

11. Archivio di Stato, Mantova, archivio Gonzaga, *D.V.*, 1, *busta* 323.
12. In Early Venetian a stonemason, stonecutter or sculptor was simply called a *taiapiera* or occasionally a *scarpelin*. *Taiapiera* was gradually replaced by the variant *tagiapiera* in late Early Venetian and in Middle Venetian and continued in that form into Modern Venetian. The Latin *mariegola* of the stonemasons, with extensive extracts from its Venetian redaction, is in MONTICOLO (1896–1914, III: 249–62). Unfortunately, there is nothing about the cutting of inscriptions in the statute which is concerned mainly with working regulations. These regulations, like all contemporaneous documentation on the subject, confirm that the stonecutting profession was a male preserve. On the names, tools and materials of Venetian stonecutters in our period see SAGREDO (1856), CECCHETTI (1887b), CONNELL (1988) and (1993). On stonemasons and their workshops in Renaissance Venice see GOY (2006: 67–77). The best-known pictorial representation of a stonemason's workshop in the city is in Canaletto's oil painting *Campo S. Vidal and S. Maria della Carità* (c. 1725), also known as *The Stonemason's Yard*. There is, rather surprisingly, no surviving inscription from our period produced by the confraternity-guild of stonemasons, the *Sc(u)ola d(e)i Tagiapiera*. Their meeting house can still be seen in Campo S. Aponal (*sestiere* of S. Polo) just as it opens into Calle del Campaniel. On the frontage is a seventeenth-century Istrian stone tablet (approximately 70 x 70 cm), under a relief of the four crowned saints who were the *scuola*'s patrons, with the inscription: MDCLII / Scola di / Tagiapiera. For splendid medieval depictions of Venetian stonemasons at work, see the capitals of the *Mestieri* and of the *Santi e discepoli lapicidi* on the Doge's Palace (MANNO 1999: 106–08, 111–13). However, the earliest depiction known to me of a stonemason actually carving an inscription is from 1557 on the etching of the *Fountain of Roaig* in the Auvergne by Bernard Salamon. It shows a stonemason, sitting on a rise with chisel and mallet in hand, as he sculpts a large Latin inscription in monumental capitals on to a rock face. Below him two gentlemen, either commissioners or Humanists, point to and comment on the scene. A fine reproduction of the etching is in BENESCH (1969: 211).
13. It is not impossible, of course, that Lorenzo was asked to sign — and told how — because his name was considered prestigious. On the placement of inscriptions on medieval Italian paintings see GARDNER (2010).
14. Polo is usually known in modern art-historical literature as Paolo di Jacomello (delle/dalle Masegne). He may well have been a relative of the Piero Polo who carved the Margherita Malatesta tomb inscription for Francesco I Gonzaga.
15. It is worth pointing out that there is no evidence in the corpus to suggest that some stonemasons in a *bottega* specialised in inscription cutting alone.
16. It goes without saying that any stonemason capable of converting the minuscule of the fair copy of the inscription text which he was given into epigraphic majuscules had to be literate. However, it cannot be discounted that in some cases somebody else 'converted' the text for him which he then merely copied. This might explain why errors sometimes seem hard to account for as mere slips of the chisel.
17. Such floors, which were spread with plaster of Paris, survive at York Minster and at Wells Cathedral.
18. For local details of this dynamic and its variations see DE RUBEIS (2008). De Rubeis's overall analysis of the complex development of Italian medieval epigraphic script coincides substantially with my own and with that outlined by DI LENARDO (2014: 34–35). On the still problematic terminology of Italian medieval lapidary lettering and on its evolution, with an up-to-date bibliography of contrasting critical viewpoints, see GIOVÈ MARCHIOLI (2015: 25–26 n. 2). For a European contextualisation of my synthesis see KLOOS (1980).
19. These trends can be seen on the beautiful twenty-line Latin epitaph of the Dogaressa Felicita Michiel (c. 1100) in the narthex of St Mark's, on the wall just inside the main entrance to the Basilica.
20. Romanesque is an essential, if potentially slippery, term, hovering between chronological

and stylistic designation and including a variety of script tendencies. As such, it is more heterogeneous and less clearly definable than Gothic which itself has struggled to achieve a unified definition applicable to script across time and place.

21. A well-known example in the centre of Venice is the twelfth-century monitory-cum-exhortative inscription addressed to the merchants of the Rialto marketplace. It is carved on a large Istrian stone cross, with long horizontal strip beneath, set into the rear exterior of the church of S. Giacomo di Rialto. Unpacked, its rebus lettering reads: *Sit crvx tva vera salvs hvic Christe loco // Hoc circa templvm sit ivs mercantibvs aeqvvm : pondera nec vergant nec sit conventio prava* ('May your cross, Christ, be the real salvation of this place. Around this temple may the law be equal for merchants, (and) let there be no false weights or bad contracts').

22. Probably the best known and best preserved inscription in this style is the dedication epigraph of 1219 from the church of S. Giustina now held in the Seminario Patriarcale at the Salute. A fine but little known example is the four-line Latin verse inscription on the outside wall of the presbytery of the church of the Anzolo Rafael in the *sestiere* of Dorsoduro, above a plaque showing a relief of the Archangel Raphael with Tobias and his dog. It commemorates the re-consecration of the church in 1193 and offers a year's pardon to penitents visiting the church. Its elegant, airily spaced monoline majuscular script combines capitals and uncials with disconcertingly little consistency, so that a Romanesque capital <t> coexists with the highly calligraphic curved form of the letter, as do a narrow capital <e> and its rounded uncial equivalent. One <u/v> is straight-sided, the others are uncialesque. There is a modicum of ligaturing, letter raising and nesting. It reads: + *Septenis dep(osi)tis annis de mille ducentis ·/ cum fuit vndena madii lux ac duodena ·/ hec est sacrata dom(us) a Tobioluce notata ·/ si penitens uadit anno penam r[eleua]bit :~.* The best surviving late example of this script type is the S. Fosca inscription of *c.* 1247 (considered at CI 33, CI 34). A concrete pointer that such precursor capital-uncial alphabets did not lead directly to Gothic in Venice is the fact that the highly distinctive semi-uncial <t> with its stem curved back sinuously on itself, typical of French Gothic, is in fact one of their most characteristic letter forms. Significantly, this feature was only very rarely incorporated into mature Gothic in Venice and is absent from our corpus.

23. An early example of Gothic in Venice which seems to have remained isolated is the single line of script running along the front of the sarcophagus of doge Marin Morosini in the narthex of St Mark's. Morosini died in 1253 so it is not unreasonable to suppose that the inscription dates from the 1250s. Containing the surprising vulgarism *reqviesit* for *reqviescit* (presumably a pronunciation spelling), it reads: + *Hic · reqviesit (in) p(ace) · d(omi)n(v)s · Marinvs · Morocen(vs) · dvx* ≈. Its anachronistic appearance within the Basilica may well be down to Morosini's reworked early-Christian *spolia* sarcophagus having been inscribed on the mainland before being conveyed by waterway to Venice.

24. See the CEMP and G. GAMBA (2015).

25. Its influence is tangible on the authorship inscription of the goldsmith Master Bertucius, inscribed along one of the bronze front doors of the Basilica, which is explicitly signed and dated 1300: + MCCC : *magister* : *Bertvcius* : *avrifex* : *venetvs* : *me fecit* :. The script can be seen archetypally on the long band of legends running over the scenes from the life of St Mark on the splendid *Altar Frontal of St Mark* (*c.* 1300) displayed in the Basilica Treasury (no. 83). In painted form, from the same period, it figures on the captions accompanying the painted figures of S. Cataldo, S. Biagio and the Blessed Giuliana on the underside of the lid of Giuliana's wooden burial chest, formerly in the church of SS. Biagio e Cataldo on the Giudecca and now in the Museo Correr. On the powerful Gothic of this type stamped on the coinage of Venice in the later thirteenth century see DAY, MATZKE and SACCOCCI (2016: 1006–1010).

26. This impressive majuscular alphabet may derive ultimately from the imperial display script of early eleventh-century psalters and lectionaries, from centres in the German-speaking lands, such as the magnificent *Psalterium Egberti* held at Cividale del Friuli (see BARBERI 2000). The immediate models for it on metalwork are very much in the form of the German imperial *gotische Majuskel* script on goldsmithery. The most prestigious and influential manifestations of the script were engraved memorably and at length on the silver-gilt arches (*c.* 1200) of the *Karlsschrein* — the shrine containing the remains of Charlemagne — in the choir area of the cathedral at

Aachen. On the nature of the precocious Gothic majuscule developed by German goldsmithery, see BORNSCHLEGEL (2010: 209–11).
27. The *scuola* building of the coopers, originally bearing the twelve-line Latin inscription dated 1299 (*more veneto*), was located beside what was the Crosechieri (subsequently the Gesuiti) church. The building was demolished in the nineteenth century and the inscription is now embedded on a house wall at Cannaregio 4902 — above the doorway and beneath two eighteenth-century epigraphs from the same confraternity-guild — opposite the church of the Gesuiti. On the *Arte dei Buteri* or *Boteri* see CI 98.
28. A. PETRUCCI (1997: 48–49) insisted that epigraphic Gothic throughout Europe was entirely based on display script: 'In essa [scil. *la maiuscola gotica*] la dipendenza dal modello librario è totale, in quanto si tratta del medesimo tipo di maiuscola che nei codici è adoperato per i titoli, per gli *incipit*, per le iniziali, per i titoli correnti, insomma per tutte le parti di apparato'. While this is undoubtedly true as a general statement, the sources of Venetian Gothic are less straightforward.
29. See HUMPHREY (2007 and 2015) for a wide range of examples.
30. Height-to-width letter ratios in Venetian Gothic tend to a modest 1.3:1 module when measured on the letter <o>. Paduan Gothic tends to a slightly more compressed 1.5:1 on the same letter. French ratios on <o> oscillate between 2:1 and 3:1. The open aspect of fourteenth-century Venetian Gothic revealed by such comparisons is perceptible even on the engraved writing in Latin on the twin golden plaquettes at the foot of the Pala d'Oro altar screen in St Mark's. On those highly visible and prestigious epigraphs from 1345, commissioned by the doge Andrea Dandolo, calligraphic elegance and structural strength are held in perfect balance. In fact, on the letter <o> the height-to-width ratio barely exceeds 1:1. See PINCUS (2019: 320–22) for transcriptions and translations of the dedicatory Pala d'Oro texts. A prestigious and even more conspicuous inscription in the Basilica, the dedicatory black-on-white mosaic epigraph in Latin of 1355 over the altar in the chapel of St Isodore, is unusually mannered stylistically in the context of Venetian Gothic (as well as featuring a Greek-style <m>). Nevertheless, even its ratio on <o> does not exceed 1.5:1. The St Isodore inscription is transcribed and discussed in DE FRANCESCHI (2005: 25–26) and GEREVINI (2019).
31. It is of more than passing interest to note that the presence of multiple script traditions in Venice was undoubtedly instrumental in retarding the onset of Gothic in the city and lagoon. The great northern fashion became established there almost a century later than in France and Germany, and more than half a century after Florence, Padua and Verona. The distinctive features of epigraphic Gothic in Venice in the period of its almost absolute dominance between the mid-fourteenth and mid-fifteenth centuries can be said to lie on a continuum of greater-to-lesser intensity. They are: contrastive strokes; integration into a majuscule script of capitals with letters of uncial provenance; 'uncialesque' appearance involving overall roundedness; the tendency to close <c>, <e>, <f>, and sometimes <u/v>, with hairstrokes; pronounced serifing; (limited) module compression; and aesthetic decorativeness in the ductus. Walter Koch's analysis of the transition from Romanesque to Gothic script on the European level yielded broadly similar overall character traits, but with a markedly earlier timescale than in Venice and with greater intensity in these tendencies (KOCH 1999). On the use of Gothic as a descriptor see MARTÍN LÓPEZ and GARCÍA LOBO (2010).
32. Its praise of the Basilica, for the mosaics, marbles and gold which make it the honour of churches, reads: + *Historiis* ✥ *auro* ✥ *forma* ✥ *specie* ✥ *tabularum* ✥ *hoc* ✥ *templum* ✥ *Marci* ✥ *fore* ✥ *decus* ✥ *ecclesiarum*. The only letter which is slightly unorthodox is <a> with forked crossbar.
33. The inscription reads: *Sepvltvra · spectabilis · d(omi)ni · Favstini · Emiliani · nobili · veneti · (con)d(am) · d(om)in(i) · Petri · s(an)c(t)i · Cassiani · et · svorvm · heredvm · MCCCCXXXV ·* ('Burial plot of the distinguished gentleman Faustino Miani, Venetian nobleman, son of the late sir Peter, of S. Cassian, and of their heirs. 1435').
34. On Byzantine cultural influence on Venice, see PERTUSI (1990) and RIZZARDI (2005). On the mosaic inscriptions in St Mark's see E. VIO (1999); KLOOS (1984); and DA VILLA URBANI (1991) where all the inscriptions are collected.
35. Both were already present in 1299 on the otherwise fully Gothic inscription of the coopers' guild in Cannaregio (see CI 1 and n. 27 above). On the occasional use in the corpus of the Greek capital upsilon for <u/v> see CI 37.

36. On the influence of Byzantine Greek lettering in Venice and elsewhere in Italy in the fifteenth century see A. PETRUCCI (1991).
37. The earliest inscription in monumental capitals that I have found in Venice is the plaque (60 x 30 cm) from 1432 in Istrian stone, uniquely surmounted by a fortified tower in high relief, at Fondamenta Bragadin 587 (Dorsoduro), marking the Ospizio delle Pizzocchere (Venetian, *pizzocare* 'pious lay women, tertiaries') di S. Agnese. The script is beautifully cut in *capitalis*, but with Byzantine <m> used in both occurrences in a striking example of the continuing eclecticism of Venetian epigraphy: Iesvs // Mvlieribvs / piae legata / anno / MCCCCXXXII. The earliest vernacular inscription in Venice in the 'new' script is found carved (less expertly) into the Istrian stone left-side pillar of the shoemakers' confraternity-guildhouse, the Scuola dei Calegheri, in Campo S. Tomà (CI 60). It is dated 1446. On the similar timescale for Bologna, see BREVEGLIERI (1997: 89–90). For Pisa, where Roman capitals appeared a few decades earlier, see BANTI (2000: 90–96).
38. See ZAMPONI (2006). In her palaeographic comments on the collection of Paduan medieval and Renaissance inscriptions published in the first volume of the CEMP, GIOVÈ MARCHIOLI (2015: 31) remarked on the surprising fact — given that Padua was a centre of experimentation with classical script — that epigraphically the introduction of antiquarian monumental capitals in Padua 'si afferma definitivamente a partire dalla metà, meglio ancora dal terzo quarto del secolo'. She also noted the attendant persistence of Gothic inscriptions there into the second half of the fifteenth century. On the other hand, Verona — which was not a university city and which came under Venetian rule from 1405 — saw classical epigraphic lettering appear on a similar timescale to Venice.
39. When teased out the Arsenal gateway inscriptions from 1460 read as follows. Left entablature: Dvce · in·clito · Pascali / Maripetro ('In the time of the illustrious Doge Pasquale Malipiero'). Right entablature: Leo · de Molino · M(arcvs) · Contareno / Al(oysivs) · Capelo · provedadori · ordinari · censere ('Decreed by the *Provedadori Ordinari* Lio de Molin, Marco Contarini (and) Alvise Capello'). Left column base: Ab vrbe · con(dita) · $M^O XXXVIIII^O$ ('In the 1309th year from the foundation of the city'). Right column base: · (Christi) · incarn(atione) · $M^O CCCC^O LX^O$ ('In the 1460th year from Christ's incarnation'). It is not insignificant that on a Latin inscription the patrician officials chose to have their Arsenal function as *Provedadori Ordinari* expressed in the vernacular instead of in the usual Latin form *Provisores*.
40. This idea is elaborated upon by Livio Petrucci in his analysis of pre-1275 vernacular inscriptions (L. PETRUCCI 2010: 41–68).
41. Armando Petrucci himself illustrated this modulation by examining the complex alternation and layout of Latin and vernacular inscriptions on three paintings in Siena from the first half of the fourteenth century: the *Maestà* fresco (1315) by Simone Martini in the Sala del Mappamondo in the Palazzo Pubblico; the fresco of the *Buono e cattivo governo* (1338) by Ambrogio Lorenzetti, also in the Palazzo Pubblico in the Sala dei Nove; and the *Annunciation* panel (1343) by Lorenzetti, now in the Pinacoteca Nazionale di Siena (A. PETRUCCI 1997: 52–53).
42. By *scripta* (pl. *scriptae*) I mean the local scriptorial practices, whether literary or not, which developed in the Veneto and elsewhere in Italy before the more-or-less gradual adoption of written Tuscan *c.* 1500. Tullio De Mauro described a *scripta* as the 'insieme degli usi scrittori, per una determinata area o regione e in un determinato periodo, della lingua volgare medievale, spec. con riferimento alle lingue romanze' (DE MAURO 2000, *s.v. scripta*). A simple working definition of the term for the medieval period is 'una tradizione scritta della lingua materna' (FORMENTIN 2014: 6). For a wider discussion of the concept — coined by Louis Remacle in the context of medieval Walloon (REMACLE 1948) — see VIDESOTT (2009: 9–12).
43. Although statistics for literacy in Venice in our period are not available, all the circumstantial evidence suggests that it was high, going well beyond the educated patrician, chancery, notarial, banking and ecclesiastical strata to reach even modestly well-off merchants, grocers and traders, and even penetrating down to the higher and medium level of artisans and their wives. Already in the mid-nineteenth century, Samuele Romanin in his *Storia documentata di Venezia* had noted that the profusion of personally signed documents in the medieval Venetian records was significant in this respect: 'Le molte sottoscrizioni dichiarate di proprio pugno nei documenti

mostrano che il sapere scrivere non era, come altrove, cosa rarissima, ed infatti leggere, scrivere e far di conto sono essenzialissime cose ad un popolo dato a mercatura' (ROMANIN 1853–61, II: 400). More recently, BARTOLI LANGELI (2000: 47) considered that the high number of vernacular inscriptions in a city like Venice in our period was eloquent testimony in itself of vernacular literacy rates, in as much as they were 'la più spiccata evidenza materiale di un rapporto collettivo, condiviso con l'alfabeto'.

44. Lorenzo Tomasin has underlined the exceptional nature of the transfer of Venetian to official written domains in this period: '[...] la progressiva espansione del volgare nella cancelleria dogale. Un fenomeno che a Venezia è possibile osservare meglio che in qualsiasi altro comune (o corte) dell'Italia coeva per via dell'ampiezza e della varietà della documentazione, quasi integralmente pervenuta: ampiezza e varietà che dunque vanno riguardate come causa ed effetto insieme del prender piede della scrittura in volgare'. He saw particularly important underlying factors for this expansion as the presence of a vibrant economy with unusually high literacy levels: '[...] a favorire l'impiego della nuova lingua furono, tuttavia, anche vari fattori esterni, cioè un contesto sociale e culturale come quello della Venezia tardomedievale, nella quale un'alfabetizzazione ben più diffusa si accompagna a una straordinaria vivacità economica' (TOMASIN 2007: 69–70).

45. 'La parola greca σχολή con cui Aristotile aveva disegnato un "gremio" di studiosi indicava nella sua forma latinizzata *schola*, prima qualunque associazione di persone che esercitavano la stessa professione, di chierici addetti ad una chiesa determinata, di laici consociati per uno scopo profano o religioso, poi anche la sede dei rispettivi sodalizi' (MEERSSEMAN 1977, I: 6). On the many facets of the lay confraternity phenomenon in Venice in the Middle Ages and Renaissance, see: SBRIZIOLO (1967, 1967–68 and 1970: 715–63); PULLAN (1971 and 1981: 9–26); PIGNATTI (1981); MASCHIO (1981); GRAMIGNA and PERISSA (1981 and 2008); MACKENNY (1987, 1997, 2000 and 2018); WURTHMANN (1989); CANIATO and DAL BORGO (1990); MANNO (1995); FORTINI BROWN (1996a); PAMATO (1999 and 2001); ORTALLI (2001); GUZZETTI and ZIEMANN (2002); GLIXON (2003); G. VIO (2004); D'ANDREA (2013). On sponsorship in the *scuole grandi*, see SOHM (1982); WURTHMANN (1989); HUMPHREY (2007); KÖSTER (2008). On sponsorship in the *scuole piccole*, see HUMFREY and MACKENNY (1986); HUMFREY (1988); MANNO (1995). On the epigraphy of the *scuole*, large and small, see FERGUSON (2015c).

46. On female membership of the Venetian confraternities, see PAMATO (2001) and GUZZETTI and ZIEMANN (2002). Examples of women board officials are found on CI 23.

47. This point is made abundantly clear in the *mariegola* of the Scuola Grande di S. Giovanni Evangelista. The statute stipulated that when a brother died the ordinances on what precise practical measures were to be taken for his soul should be read out by the warden and his colleagues to the membership: 'Et aço che le aneme de diti nostri fradeli che de questo siegolo passa, algun deffecto no padischa, volemo e ordenemo ch'el nostro Vardian con li suo compagni sia tegnudi de leçer, o farse tra lor spesse fiade leçer, li dicti privilegii, la copia de quali se scriti distintamente in volgar [i.e. in the vernacular] su lo libro che se scriti i nomi de nostri fradeli. Açoche per lor se possa far tuto quello che far se die per rifrigerio de le dite aneme pasade' (SIMEONE 2003: 83).

48. The dominant presence, numerically and textually, of the Venetian confraternities great and small is unmistakable in the corpus. Alfredo Stussi outlined the psycho-linguistic reasons for the epigraphic prevalence of the vernacular in this context: 'ben si capisce che in scritture esposte celebrative venisse usato non il latino ma il volgare locale, più familiare sia ai mercanti e banchieri, sia agli artigiani (tintori, orafi, calzolai, sarti, ecc.) che le avrebbero lette, o se le sarebbero fatte leggere: il contatto linguistico li avrebbe gratificati e confermati nell'adesione fedele e operosa a un'organizzazione pia, ricca e soccorrevole' (STUSSI 2005: 59).

49. Possibly the only partly comparable case to that of Venice in terms of the high percentage of vernacular epigraphic use (within the context of the overall dominance of Latin) is found in thirteenth-century France. From a sample, A. PETRUCCI (1997: 55–56) counted eighty-nine cases of the vernacular in the period 1230–1300. The social provenance of the persons concerned was strikingly different from Venice, with feudal lords most frequent, followed by women (largely noblewomen), and then male bourgeois. There were only three cases of vernacular epitaphs

of men of religion, all of them from noble families. The transition to the vernacular in late medieval inscriptions from western France is explored in INGRAND-VARENNE (2017: 317–496).

50. On the functional distribution of Latin within vernacular inscriptions, see STUSSI (1997a: 152–54) and CANNATA (2020).

51. *Venexian* (Italian, *veneziano*) is historically the most common native spelling of Venetian, with the historic variants *venezian* and *venes(s)ian*. It is currently pronounced [veneˈsjaŋ] in the International Phonetics Association (IPA) transcription. The city has called itself *Venexia* (with Early Venetian variants *Venecia*, *Veniexia* and *Ven(i)esia*) since the later medieval period, the current pronunciation being [veˈnɛsja].'

52. On the settlement of Venice from the Veneto mainland, and on how this population dynamic plausibly generated the formation of Venetian as a new koine variety, see FERGUSON (2003, 2005, 2007 and 2013b).

53. See TOMASIN (2001b: 59–123) for a detailed tracking of this process. Written Venetian of the period was also sometimes affected by the prestigious compromise *scripta* of the northern Italian chanceries. The best-known example of such conjoined influence is to be found in the language employed by Marin Sanudo in his *Diarii*, covering the late fifteenth and early sixteenth centuries. The extraordinary impasto of Venetian, Tuscan and northern Italian *scripta* forms that he employed is studied in LEPSCHY (1996).

54. Here and elsewhere in the study I adopt a periodisation that reflects sociolinguistic factors in the history of Venetian. My classification is: Early Venetian (c. 1200-c. 1500), Middle Venetian (c. 1500-c. 1800), Modern Venetian (c. 1800-c. 1950), Contemporary Venetian (c. 1950-the present). Each boundary signals a watershed moment where societal or cultural events with linguistic repercussions altered the status and/or structure of Venetian. Conventionally, 1200 indicates the appearance of Venetian in written texts. 1500 stands for the moment when Tuscan was achieving consensus status among Italy's elites and interfering with unmarked written Venetian of all registers. The grammatical codification of Tuscan/Italian represented by the 1525 boundary of the corpus was also imminent at that point. 1800 coincides approximately with a linguistic turning point in the fortunes of Venice and Venetian, consolidated and accelerated half a century later by unification with Italy. It marks the end of Venetian political and institutional independence, the Napoleonic and Austrian interludes with the awakening of Italian patriotism in the middle classes, and the removal of even spoken *venexian* from the official public sphere. 1950 is roughly the point at which middle-class Venetian-speaking parents began increasingly to employ Italian with their children. It marks the beginning of the new and unusual Venetian-Italian diglossia that since then has grown to become the typical mode of spoken exchange among Venetians.

55. See the infinitive *acrese* 'to increase', with absence of final /r/, for the expected *acreser* in CI 25. Deletion of final /r/ on the infinitive was typical of the northern lagoon area. Another infinitive type, not found in the corpus but very common in the earliest Venetian texts and in lower-register writing from the fourteenth century, involved the loss of the post-tonic vowel, as in *vendre* 'to sell'. This form was typical of the north-eastern Veneto varieties which were one of the two main feeder streams for Venetian. Also absent from the corpus (except for examples that are down to Tuscan input) is the type retaining the final /e/ as in *vendere*, typical of the other main feeder stream, from the south-western Veneto mainland. This full form was common in the earliest Venetian texts and persisted, even in some regulatory statutes, well into the fourteenth century.

56. On singular nouns and adjectives this system predominates in the corpus. It appears as a compromise between radical northern Veneto apocope and overall southern Veneto vowel retention, and tendentially involves the deletion of final /e/ and /o/ after /n/ and /l/, and of /e/ after /r/ on original paroxytones (words stressed on the penultimate syllable), but not on derivatives of original geminates ('double' consonants) or after a *muta cum liquida*. At the mid-point in the fourteenth century we already find epigraphic sequences such as: *avril* 'April', *posesion* 'property', *onor* 'honour', *Bisuol*, *Vidal*, *vardian* 'warden' (CI 9, 1344–45); *incarnacion* 'incarnation', *conversion* 'conversion', *nasion* 'nation(s)', *mal* 'illness', *carbon* 'coal', *pare* 'father', *vardian*, *Piero*, *Trivisan*, *Bon*, *fiol* 'son' (CI 14, c. 1348); *lavorier* 'work, piece of work, artefact',

vardian, Çane (John), nobele 'noble', Albertin, Marin, Çanin, Badoer, omo 'man', frar 'brother', prior 'prior' (CI 17, 1349); honor, apostolo 'apostle', remixion 'remission', pecator 'sinner', Nadal, scrivan 'secretary', degan 'dean', Piero, Fero, çimador 'cloth-shearer', tentor 'dyer', nonçolo 'undertaker', avril (CI 23, 1359).

57. Nevertheless /ol/ survived until the end of the fifteenth century in a few isolated but much used words such as gastoldo (alongside gastaldo), the alderman of a guild-confraternity.
58. The exception is CI 14 (c. 1348) where there is uncertainty with third conjugation imperfects (but not with first and second conjugation ones). Thus moria '(they) died' is found alongside vegnia 'came' but also vegniva.
59. That such innovative forms in -à, destined to prevail long-term, were not necessarily lower diastratically in the diasystem is suggested by the fact that the two examples of podestà in the corpus — one from 1311 (CI 2) and one from 1374 (CI 38) — were probably drafted on the orders of two different mayors of Murano, in both cases a Venetian patrician.
60. After the eighteenth century diphthongisation of stressed mid vowels ceased to be productive in Venetian. However, some forms survived, fossilised in their diphthongised form, into Modern and Contemporary Venetian. This has produced uneven patterns in reflexes of mid vowels, with the current outcome on any given word not simple to predict on the basis of its etymology. For the detail of this variegated picture and for a discussion of patterns of fluctuation in diphthongisation in diachronic perspective, from Early to Contemporary Venetian, see FERGUSON (2007: 86–90).
61. The most visible examples are to be found on two inscriptions from the lagoon islands, one from Murano, the other from Mazzorbo. On the unique will in stone drafted by the Tuscan exile Angelo Piarini (CI 8, 1340) not only do we find arguably the most remarkable instance of code mixing in any Venetian medieval document but, within the unmediated spoken character of his legal stipulations, a series of possible Muranese provincialisms. On the inscription from Mazzorbo (CI 35, 1368) two apparent anachronisms are perceptible: lavoriero 'work, piece of work, artefact', without the usual apocope of final /o/ after /r/, and logo 'place' where the diphthongised luogo would have been expected at that date.

PART III

Corpus: Edition, Translation and Commentary

Corpus Inscription 1

LOM PO FAR E ₁| DIE INPENSAR ₂|
E UEGA QUEL|O CHE LI PO IN|CHONTRAR ₅

[L'om pò far, e die inpensar, e vega quelo che li pò inchontrar.]

TRANSLATION: Man can act, so must reflect and consider what may befall him.

DATE: Undated, but probably *c.* 1300. The inscription has previously been dated, in the main impressionistically, to various points between the twelfth and fifteenth centuries (FERGUSON 2017: 230–31). However, the stylistic evidence of the accompanying carvings points to the ensemble having been sculpted in the second half of the thirteenth century (PERRY 1977: 40 n. 51; NIERO 1993: 140; TIGLER 1995a: 221–22; AGAZZI 2019) or, at the latest, in the early fourteenth century (DORIGO 2003, I: 540–41; SCHREINER 2019: 93; TIGLER 2019: 145 n. 13). The palaeographic and linguistic evidence of the inscription itself, presented below, suggests a date around 1300. This would make it the oldest inscription in the corpus.

LOCATION: On the skirting frieze running along the external wall of the Treasury of St Mark's Basilica, on the south façade of the church near the main Porta della Carta entrance to the Doge's Palace (*sestiere* of S. Marco). The inscription is located just above ground level, over the step and under the marble bench immediately to the left of the group of four late-antique porphyry figures known as the 'Tetrarchs' — probably brought to Venice in the thirteenth century after the sack of Constantinople — embedded in the corner of the Treasury. Lying at the foot of the magnificent wall of the Treasury with its exotic assemblage of Byzantine-type marble plaques, the inscription passes unremarked by all but a few of the thousands of tourists who rest on the bench each year.

TYPE AND DESCRIPTION: Didactic. A moralising five-line inscription with a popular proverbial flavour. Rhyming and roughly metrical, the carved dictum points out that one should think of the consequences to oneself before acting. It seems to reproduce, down to its tripartite structure, the Latin proverb: *Quidquid agis, prudenter agas et respice finem* ('Whatever you do, do it prudently and think of the consequences'). The inscription cartouche, like the accompanying frieze and bench, is in Istrian stone. It measures 31 × 24 cm and is slightly convex, representing as it does an unfolded parchment whose end-scrolls are held by two flying *putti*, each pursued by a dragon with its jaws round one of its feet. The *putti* look round, dismayed but too late, to see what is happening. The frieze itself is 5 m 85 cm long overall and is divided into a series of six oblong boxed compartments. The first and longest, taking up almost half the total length, has the inscription at its centre. It is followed by a row of five smaller compartments carved with bas-relief animals, seemingly in a chase. The eye of the observer is strongly drawn to the inscription by the serried leftward motion of the sculpted animals and the left-side *putto*; it is brought to a halt at the plaque by the motion in the opposite direction of the right-side *putto* and by the impressive mass of the Tetrarchs.

Fig. 3.1. CI 1 (bottom left) and its immediate surroundings in the 1960s. © A. Scarpa.
Fig. 3.2. CI 1. © A. S. Ferguson.

The sense of the inscription and the iconography of its sculptural context have generated an extensive critical literature, summarised first in BERTANZA and LAZZARINI (1891: 3) then in TIGLER (1995a: 221–22). The scene may well, in my view, be a figurative enactment of the prudential message of the inscription. More specifically, Giovanni Saccardo argued that since the Doge's Palace once acted as a palace of justice-cum-prison (see CI 30) the epigraph was admonitory, with the hunting scene of the frieze an allegory of vice and its punishment (SACCARDO 1888–92, II: 261). Although we know nothing of the circumstances surrounding the commissioning of the frieze and the inscription, their central position and public visibility in a ceremonial passageway in the heart of Venice — between the great centres of religious and political authority of the Venetian state — strongly suggest government sponsorship via the *Procuratores Sancti Marci*, the Procurators of St Mark (see CI 39).

LETTERING: Gothic majuscules but incorporating several rare or unique letter forms. The only lapidary inscription in the corpus to be cut entirely on to a curved surface. The text, carved in V-section, tends towards an unbroken or irregular spacing that requires a little teasing out. The grooving is unevenly worn down with occasional damage to the letters, especially the <m> of *lom* (l. 1), and the inscription tablet has been notably roughened, particularly at the top. In spite of its deterioration which, as revealed by photographs taken in the 1950s and 1960s (DEMUS 1960: ill. 25), seems to be relatively recent, the inscription remains legible with care. The chiselling looks heavy, with strong wedges on the base of the shafts of the letters (which at around 3 cm high and ranging from 2 to 3 cm wide are large in relation to the inscription surface), but the earlier images reveal a finer contrast in stroke width. The message, justified on the left and with regular interlinear spacing, must originally have been easy to decipher for the passer-by. This is especially the case as it is apparent from the oldest images — and particularly from a mid-nineteenth-century daguerreotype probably taken by Ruskin (UNRAU 1984: 21) and from the late nineteenth-century photographs taken for Ferdinando ONGANIA (1881–85: port. 5.3, ill. 200, 201) — that the writing was picked out with black infilling to resemble inked letters on a manuscript. If this were the case it might explain the apparently limited groove depth.

The uncialesque lettering looks at first sight like the familiar inscriptional Gothic that came to dominate Venetian vernacular epigraphy in the fourteenth century. Characteristic of that system are the diagonal terminal spurs on the <s> in *inpensar* (l. 2); the wedge serifs on head and foot of <l> and <i>; the billowing lateral strokes of the <m> in *lom* (l. 1), with the left loop closed; the <d> in *die* (l. 3) with ascender curled straight to the left and splay-serifed; the well-developed parallel upstroke on the arm of <l>; <c>, <e> and <f> closed by hairstrokes throughout; enlarged minuscule <h>; downward-pointing spikes on the topstroke of <t>; and ligatured <ar> in *inchontrar* (ll. 4–5). In addition, the limb of <h>, the upstroke on <l> and the right stem of <u/v> are finely curved and tapered. The overall effect is one of rounded but muscular Gothic decorativeness. It is worth pointing out, however, that the drift towards such outcomes was already palpable on thirteenth- and very early fourteenth-century uncialesque lettering in Venice on mosaic, metal and stone.

Indeed CI 4, cut with mature stroke modulation and aesthetic panache around 1312, replicates many of the forms of the present inscription in a uniformly Gothic script derived from manuscript titling capitals. In other words, the appearance of well developed, stone-carved Gothic epigraphic lettering in Venice around 1300 is more than plausible. It is no coincidence that the epigraph on the magnificent bronze door, known as the Porta San Pietro, to the left of the main entrance portal to St Mark's — explicitly dated 1300 and signed by the Venetian goldsmith Magister Bertucius — is in a muscular type of Gothic lettering with some similarity to ours. An early date for our inscription would be compelling if its lettering also betrayed archaic features.

Perhaps the most striking letter on the inscription is the unusual and splendidly cut rounded capital <g> in *vega* (l. 3). The commoner rounded epigraphic <g> was derived ultimately from Roman rustic capitals. It was elongated in aspect, low-set and modest in swirl. It was regular alongside the square <g> in post-classical and post-Carolingian inscriptions in Italy up to the tenth century. It occurs repeatedly in the present corpus having become the standard form of the letter in Romanesque and then Gothic inscriptions not only in Venice, Padua and the Veneto generally, but throughout Romance Europe. However, the sort of curled <g> found in our inscription is a *unicum* in Venetian epigraphy, Latin or vernacular. Its square proportions and calligraphic finesse, comprising tapering triple spirals and elongated backswept arm mirroring these, mark it out as the most perfect surviving example of a rarer tradition of capital <g> probably derived from manuscript majuscules. Some of its characteristic features are detectable, hybridised with the commoner rounded <g>, in tenth-century inscriptions from Rome (GRAY 1948: 140) and in Romanesque and Gothic inscriptions in Venice and elsewhere in the thirteenth and fourteenth centuries. It is most closely matched in aspect and ductus by the capital <g> on the early twelfth-century inscription on the tomb of the *dogaressa* Felicita Michiel in the narthex of St Mark's, and by the forms of the letter on a series of Venetian commemorative ecclesiastical inscriptions on marble, dated 1188, 1219 and 1220 (DI LENARDO 2014: ill. VII, X, XII). The clearest realisation of its archetypal forms — with arm upswept or splay-serifed — can be seen in book display capitals in Beneventan script from southern Italy, particularly in a series of manuscripts from around 1200 (TRONCARELLI 1991: 353–55). The former variant is best represented in stone by our inscription. The latter makes its finest and last appearance in Venetian vernacular epigraphy in an inscription from 1363 of northern lagoon provenance (CI 31).

A feature occurring regularly on Venetian Romanesque epigraphs of the 1200s — alongside the predominant straight-stemmed form — is the curved <u/v> seen in *vega* (l. 3) and *quelo* (ll. 3–4). In the fourteenth-century Gothic inscriptions in the corpus this trait is very much in the minority. When it does appear it usually displays left-sided curvature. It may not be a coincidence that right-stem curvature on <u/v> is present in the mosaics inside St Mark's and happens to be especially prominent on the splendid inscription (1260–70), combining capital, uncial and Byzantine features (on its *ab initio* left half), on the St Alypius portal of the Basilica, over the mosaic depicting the ceremonial arrival of Mark's body in Venice.

Strikingly archaic, and unique within the corpus, is the lowercase <q> of *quelo* (ll. 3–4) with its straight tail standing on the baseline: a feature alien to mature Gothic inscriptional practice. Ultimately derived from uncial alphabets the epigraphic use in Venice (and, occasionally, pre-1300 on the Veneto mainland) of the *q* treated as majuscule probably emerged via Byzantine influence. Coinciding with the *koppa* letter, sometimes used as a symbol in earlier Greek for the numeral 90, it was deployed on titling script by the Byzantines for the sigma-tau ligature and came to be used by them for <q> when writing Latin (MORISON 1972: 71, 220). It is a feature that appears in Venice alongside the curved <u/v> on Byzantine Romanesque mosaics on ceiling and wall inside St Mark's and on the archaic, essentially Romanesque, inscription with uncial elements on the tomb (*c.* 1290) of the doge Çuane Dandolo in S. Zanipolo. It is also visible on the capital-uncial inscription, *c.* 1247, embedded on the side of the church of S. Fosca on Torcello, commemorating the exhumation of the bones of the virgin saint from Ravenna (see CI 33, CI 34). Most pertinently, for our dating purposes, it features on the 1299 inscription in Latin from the coopers' guild (the *Scuola de(l)i Buteri* or *Boteri*) now on a housefront in Cannaregio (no. 4902) opposite the church of the Gesuiti (see CI 98). This epigraph, too, is already vigorously Gothic as a whole but with some features extraneous to that system: not only the lowercase <q> but also the Greek-style <m> in the form of a mu. One has to wonder if the <q> and the other striking script features of the Treasury epigraph were suggested to the stonemason by the paper or parchment draft of the text given to him by the commissioner of the inscription, or whether these particular forms are down to his own initiative. Be that as it may, the last case known to me of minuscule <q> used in this way in a fully Gothic inscription in or near Venice is its occurrence, three times, on a one-line epitaph (*c.* 1325) carved on the tomb of Pileo I da Prata. The sarcophagus is affixed to an inside wall of the out-of-the way provincial church of S. Giovanni dei Cavalieri in Prata di Pordenone (now in Friuli-Venezia Giulia) and is ascribed by WOLTERS (1976: cat. 16, ill. 53) to a Venetian stonemason. Also from 1325 is its single appearance on a Gothic inscription, commissioned by Cangrande della Scala to commemorate the building of a section of the Verona city walls, now displayed in that city's Castelvecchio museum.

Very distinctive, and strongly linked to the thirteenth-century mosaic decoration in St Mark's, is the short medial crossbar on the <i> of *die* (l. 2), *inpensar* (l. 2), *li* (l. 4) and *inchontrar* (ll. 4–5), as well as on the shaft of the <t> in *inchontrar*. This rather rare trait — to be seen sporadically on fourteenth-century French Gothic inscriptions, notably on the vernacular captions carved on the north-porch columns of Chartres cathedral, and occasionally on thirteenth-century Paduan inscriptions — occurs nowhere else in our corpus in the fourteenth century. In St Mark's, though, it is prominent on the surround inscription on the mosaics of the thirteenth-century Dome of the Creation, and shows up in the company of lowercase <q> and right-curved <u/v> on the mosaics of the late-thirteenth century Moses cupola. It also features on the St Alypius portal inscription, as well as on the engraved Gothic running titles — reminiscent in their lettering of the metalwork door inscription by Magister Bertucius — on the silver-gilt *Altar Frontal of St Mark* (*c.* 1300) in the Basilica Treasury (no. 38).

Taken as a whole, the palaeographic evidence suggests a date around 1300. It may not be a coincidence that, according to Francesco Sansovino, the south façade of St Mark's was embellished by doge Pietro Gradenigo with plundered pieces in the last decade of the thirteenth century (SANSOVINO 1581: 119r). This was the culmination of the restructuring and beautifying of Piazza San Marco initiated in the late twelfth century under doge Sebastian Çiani or Ziani (AGAZZI 1991: 155).

LANGUAGE: The brevity of the text means that it can provide only limited evidence to confirm our dating. Diphthongisation in Early Venetian of original stressed vowels Ŏ and Ĕ in a free syllable (and even, occasionally, of Ē: see below and CI 56) occurred along a definitely traceable but complex timeline. It was almost non-existent in the thirteenth century and very limited in the early fourteenth — with most instances confined to derivatives of Ĕ — before becoming overwhelming later in the century. The employment then, twice, of the undiphthongised modal *po* 'can' (ll. 1 and 4) < PŎTE(S)T rather than the later diphthongised variant *può* is consistent with a late thirteenth- or early fourteenth-century date. This is confirmed by the attestations in the *Opera del Vocabolario Italiano* (OVI) database which show *po* 'can' in Early Venetian confined in writing to the period *c.* 1200–1335 (OVI, *s.v. po*), with *può* appearing post-1310. The other modal, *die* or *die'* 'must' (l. 2) < DĒBET (with stressed Ē), appears to be a diphthongised variant of *de'* which had predominated until *c.* 1300. After a period of overlap *die* went on in the following decades to overwhelm *de'*. It is recorded in 1304 in a mercantile decree (TOMASIN 2013: 25) and appears, actually juxtaposed with *po*, in another official Venetian document of *c.* 1330 (OVI, *s.v. die'*). It recurs in the Corpus at CI 27. It would be tempting to read much into the occurrence of *lom* (in other words, *l'om* 'man') in l. 1, rather than the expected *(h)omo* found without exception elsewhere in our corpus. It could be construed as an example of the much more extensive apocope of final vowels on nouns in Early Venetian pre-1300, although *omo* invariably appears with *om* in the earliest texts. It is more likely that the apocopated form is dictated here by the metrics of the saying or, given the 'spoken' paratactic syntax of the proverb, that it is a relic popular variant. The three verb infinitives show the apocopated form in -r which prevailed in high-register Early Venetian texts and went on to become the norm throughout the history of *venexian*: *far* 'to do, to make, to act' (l. 1); *inpensar* 'to think, to reflect' (l. 2), with the typical Venetian verbal prefix *in-* (see *inlumina* 'illuminates' CI 30, ll. 4–5); and *inchontrar* 'to meet, to encounter' and here 'to befall' (ll. 4–5). *Li* '(to) him' (l. 4) is the normal Early Venetian 3rd singular masculine indirect object pronoun, indicating that *inchontrar* in the sense of 'to befall' is intransitive. *Vega* 'let him see/consider' (l. 3), from the infinitive *veder* (stressed on the first syllable), is an exhortative present subjunctive (like Italian *veda*) and is paralleled by *vaga* 'let him go', *staga* 'let him stay', *daga* 'let him give'.

RECENT STUDIES: PERRY (1977: 40 n. 51); HEMPEL and JULIER (1979: 55); STUSSI (1980a: 91 n. 11); MURARO (1985: 29); NIERO (1993: 140); TIGLER (1995a: 221–22); STUSSI (1997a: 157–58); STUSSI (1997b: 916); DORIGO (2003, I: 540–41); FERGUSON (2013c: 81–83); TOMASIN (2014: 176); PINCUS (2016: 249–50); FERGUSON (2017). The inscription was first published in MESCHINELLO (1753, I: 29).

Corpus Inscription 2

CORANDO :' | M CCC X INDI|CION VIII :' | IN TE(M)PO DE LO $_4$|
NOBELE HOMO $_5$| MISER DONATO $_6$| MEMO HONORA|DO PODESTA DE |
MVRAN FACTA :' | FO QVESTA AN|CONA DE MISER $_{11}$| SAN DONADO :'

[Corando Mcccx, indicion vIII, in tempo de lo nobele homo miser Donato Memo, honorado podestà de Muran, facta fo questa ancona de miser San Donado.]

TRANSLATION: In 1310, indiction 8, during the term of office of the gentleman Sir Donado Memo (as) right-honourable mayor of Murano, this holy image of St Donatus was made.

DATE: 1310. The oldest explicitly dated inscription in our collection. For the first and only time in the corpus, the text employs the medieval Venetian chancery practice of indicating the year Venetian style (*more veneto*) starting on the 1 March, alongside the indiction, Byzantine style, which functioned on a fifteen-year cycle changing every first of September.

LOCATION: For some 700 years the image hung in the twelfth-century Basilica dei SS. Maria e Donato (Modern Venetian, Basilica de San Donà de Muran) on Murano, latterly on the wall of the north nave. In the first half of the nineteenth century Cicogna saw it behind the main altar as did MOSCHINI (1808: 105–06 and 1815, II: 439) where he recorded its inscription on both occasions. Moschini, in fact, appears to have been the first to transcribe it, rendering it accurately apart from *honorando* instead of *honorado* (ll. 7–8). According to CORNER (1758: 614), however, the *ancona* was previously venerated in a chapel to the right of the main altar. The artefact was restored c. 2000 and is now exhibited in Venice in the Museo Diocesano above the cloister complex of S. Apollonia.

TYPE AND DESCRIPTION: Commemorative of the commission and commissioner of the artefact. The text is painted on the bottom left-hand side of the gilded and tempera-painted wooden carved devotional panel (*ancona* in Venetian), measuring 201 × 143 cm, depicting the fourth-century St Donatus of Evorea sculpted in low relief. The written text itself covers a rectangular area roughly 20 × 10 cm. The careful layout of the inscription and its formal wording, with formulae following documentary manuscript practice, suggest close collaboration between painter and sponsor. As such it contrasts with the more painter-centred CI 24.

The original location of the panel within the church is not known but the writing — which is still in good condition and perfectly legible — would probably have been directly at the worshipper's eye level. The object was commissioned by the then mayor of Murano, the Venetian patrician Donado (or Donato) Memo who appears in miniature, kneeling and praying with his wife to the saint, at the foot of the image. The bones of St Donatus — whose name is shared by the sponsor — were brought to Murano from Cephalonia, in Byzantine territory, by Venetian crusaders in 1125. A rebuilding campaign began immediately after the arrival of the holy

FIG. 3.3. CI 2. © A. S. Ferguson.

relics and the church was rededicated jointly to the Virgin and Donatus. Featuring marked elements of Byzantine style in its architecture and mosaic decoration it was completed in 1141, indiction 5, as is attested by a mixed capital-uncial Romanesque inscription still legible on the magnificent mosaic floor decoration of the aisle. It is not surprising that the *ancona* itself is Greek influenced in both its iconography and inscription.

The unsigned panel may originally have been freestanding or could possibly have been the centrepiece of an altar triptych. It is often associated with the workshop of the important Venetian painter who signed himself Paulus de Veneciis or Paulus Venetus and is known in Italian as Paolo Veneziano (born before 1333, died after 1358), in which case it must be one of his earliest commissions. See GUARNIERI (2015: 159–60). The image is titled variously 'Icon of St Donatus', 'St Donatus with Mayor Mem(m)o and his wife', or 'St Donatus with two kneeling donors'. The bearded bishop-saint, clutching a crosier in his right hand and a closed book in his left, imposingly fills the panel which imitates an archway with spiral columns on either side. The vernacular inscription is wedged between column and crosier.

Against a shimmering gold ground, the saint's rich episcopal vestments stand out in vivid and sumptuous colours: a brilliant red pectoral cross embroidered in gold on a royal blue chasuble with exquisitely sculpted cascading folds, over green alb and pale-blue cassock. On his haloed head he wears a golden mitre studded with gems. He is explicitly named S(an)c[tv]s / [Do]natv(s) / epi(scopv)s ('St Donatus, Bishop'), with the looped abbreviation normally expressing <us> on the forename, in the partly obliterated red-painted Latin inscription, whose letters measure some 4 cm, at his shoulders. The two tiny kneeling figures beneath him are charmingly realistic in execution. For another representation of St Donatus, this time on a stone inscriptional plaque from Murano, see CI 38.

Otto DEMUS (1960: 187) noted that 'The wooden relief of St Donatus in Murano, dated 1310, shows the application of a Byzantine drapery design to a western ecclesiastical costume. It is certainly the work of a Venetian who had studied Byzantine models'.

LETTERING: Moderately uncialesque Gothic majuscules with some Byzantine inflexions. The well-spaced, slightly elongated, elegant red lettering averages around 0.7 cm in height — tallest on the first two lines and the last — and is justified on the left. The unjustified spaces on the right are filled by punctuation which has no actual syntactic function, consisting each time of a colon followed by a mid-high comma. This mark is typical of manuscript practice where it signalled the end of a block of text. The Gothic of the inscription is, in fact, influenced less by epigraphic precedent than by manuscript titling capitals. This is most obvious on the calligraphic backstroke of the eleven examples of capital <a> curving markedly below the baseline. In two cases this extended stroke loops back up to form a join with the leg of the preceding consonant: the <r> on *Muran* (l. 9) and the <n> on *Donado* (l. 12). On only two other calligraphic inscriptions in the corpus, one on stone (CI 57) the other in paint (CI 55), is such letter joining seen. The Murano epigraph contrasts with most of our other fourteenth- and early fifteenth-century Gothic inscriptions in terms of the alternation on it of uncial- and capital-derived forms for the same letter: in this case <d> and <m>. Apart from the single uncial <d> on *corando* (l. 1), it favours in all remaining eight cases the capital <d> type. Similarly, the strongly uncial <m> in the date (l. 2) and on the surname *Memo* (l. 7), with billowing closed left bow, contrasts markedly with the remaining five examples of the letter. Here, as in CI 1, deliberate Greek influence — via titling-script features used in the Eastern Empire and deployed in Byzantine Romanesque mosaic inscriptions in Latin — is evident. On the <m> on *miser* (ll. 6 and 11), on the third letter of *Memo* (l. 7) and on *Muran* (Murano), l. 9, the fork, starting down the stems, forms a mid-high shallow V that descends to the baseline in a perpendicular line. This is in effect the Greek square capital mu. It is a form that also figures in the large-scale lettering *Virgo Maria* 'Virgin Mary' above CI 10. The considerable prestige and influence on Venetian epigraphy of this Greek type of <m> can reasonably be ascribed to the writing traditions brought by the Byzantine mosaicists who decorated, or influenced the decoration of, the great early basilicas in the lagoon of Venice. It is unmistakably present on some mosaics within St Mark's, for instance on the running legends in the baptistery cupola depicting Christ dispatching the Apostles to the Gentiles. It also strikes the spectator forcefully on the towering gold-backed mosaics of the Virgin Mary in both the Cathedral of S. Maria Assunta on Torcello (in Latin) and, more pertinently still, in SS. Maria e Donato on Murano (in Greek). The undulating horizontal tail on the capital <q>, pointing left rather than right, is a feature that occurs only sporadically in fourteenth-century Venetian epigraphy and only twice in surviving vernacular inscription of our period (CI 39, CI 48). The legs of <h> and <n> exhibit the expected sinuosity typical of Gothic. On the other hand, downstroking on <t> is limited or barely suggested, the parallel upstroke on <l> is short, and hairstroking on <c>, <e> and <f> is moderate. The two examples of <u/v>, on *Muran* (l. 9) and *questa* (l. 10), are straight-sided. Overall, the ductus of the painted script is restrained, with clarity to the fore rather than decorativeness. The rather conservative, Byzantine feel of the inscription is very much in keeping with the style of the *ancona* itself.

LANGUAGE: The regularising tendency of all gerund endings in Early Venetian, of whatever conjugation, to converge analogically on the *-ando* type of 1st conjugation -ARE verbs is seen in *corando*, l. 1 (from *corer* = [ˈkorer] 'to run' but here meaning 'during, in the course of'), as well as in the same verb in CI 3 (l. 4). *Miser* 'Sir, Mr' (ll. 6, 11 and elsewhere in the corpus) is from Old Provençal *meser* 'my Lord'. It shows raising of pre-tonic vowel /e/ to /i/ and, as expected at this date, an undiphthongised second syllable. I have resolved the nasal suspension bar over *tepo* 'time' (l. 4) as *tempo* since that form is closer to the original Latin than *tenpo* which occurs frequently in the collection. My choice is conditioned by other Latinising tendencies in the inscription such as *Donato* (l. 6), alongside the normal vernacular *Donado* (l. 12), *homo* (l. 5) and *honorado* 'honoured' (ll. 7–8) with redundant <h>, and the Latinate spelling and word order of *facta fo* 'was made' (ll. 9–10), clearly modelled on the conventional formula FACTA FUIT (= FACTA EST) found in contemporary Latin inscriptions and documents. The agreement between *facta* and *ancona* (ll. 9–11) is the first of many examples of perfect alignment of gender and number between past participle and noun in the dozens of passive constructions in the corpus (see CI 9). *Ancona* 'icon, devotional image', ultimately from Greek εἰκών 'sacred image' or its accusative form εἰκώνα (MUSSAFIA 1873, *s.v. ancona*; CORTELAZZO 1970: 11–14), is also present in CI 24 (l. 2). *Indicion* (ll. 2–3) and *Muran* (l. 9) show the normal Venetian vowel apocope of /e/ or /o/ after -*n* on original paroxytones. In this conservative linguistic context the construction *honorado podesta* (ll. 7–8) stands out as 'modern'. *Podesta* 'mayor' (l. 8) < PŎTESTĀTEM 'power, authority', accented on the final <a>, appears in this form here and on another inscription from Murano, CI 38, dated 1374. In both cases it is somewhat surprising to find the apocopated variant of this word, rather than the expected, and at this stage commoner, *podestade*, although it may have been favoured by similarity with the nominative Latin *potestas* familiar from official decrees. Early Venetian documentation very much leans towards the preservation of intervocalic /d/, and even occasionally /t/, on endings derived from -ĀTEM and -ĀTUM (FERGUSON 2007: 177–86). Both conservative outcomes are attested on the present inscription with *Donato*, *Donado* (but not *Donà* as in sixteenth-century texts) and *honorado*. One notes, too, that *podestade de Muran* appears on a third Muranese inscription (CI 51) from more than a century later. Interesting, also, is the masculine adjective *honorado* applied to what was an originally feminine noun. Indecision on whether to follow *ad sensum* or grammatical gender with *podestà*, *podestade* was in fact common in the Italo-Romance vernaculars. As in his choice of the vernacular over Latin, the commissioner of the epigraph, presumably Donado himself, preferred the innovative language option. The mayorship (Venetian, *podestaria*) of Murano was instituted by Venice in 1275. In the fourteenth century the term of office was one year. On the mayor of Murano and his role see FORMENTIN (2017: 48–55).

RECENT STUDIES: TESTI (1909: 146–50); WOLTERS (1976, II: 149); STUSSI (1980a: 90–91); STUSSI (1997a: 158); FERGUSON (2013c: 83–84). The first review of early critical literature on the *ancona* inscription was published in BERTANZA and LAZZARINI (1891: 33)

Corpus Inscription 3

+ SEPULTURA DELI $_1$ | FRARI BATUDI D(E)LA $_2$ | SCOLA DE · S(-N) · IOH(AN)E · EUA(N) | G(E)L(IST)A FATA CORA(N)DO ·M^o | ·CCC^o · XI · SOTO · SER $_5$ | ÇANE DA TRESSAGA $_6$ | GUARDIA(N) · (E) LI SOI · OFICIA[LI] $_7$

[+ Sepultura deli frari batudi dela Scola de S. Iohane Evangelista, fata corando MCCCXI soto ser Çane da Tressaga, guardian, e li soi oficiali.]

TRANSLATION: Burial place of the flagellant brothers of the Confraternity of Saint John the Evangelist. Made in 1311 under (the leadership of) Mr Çane da Tressaga, warden, and his officials.

DATE: 1311. The oldest explicitly dated vernacular inscription surviving in the historic centre of Venice itself.

LOCATION: In situ. Carved on a sarcophagus on the floor of the so-called Spazio Badoer, beside the church and in front of the meeting house of the confraternity of S. Giovanni Evangelista, in the picturesque Campiello S. Zuane or *de la Scuola* (*sestiere* of S. Polo). This pillared hall has preserved the remains of the confraternity's ancient burial site. The *scuole*, large and small, possessed burial grounds either in the confraternity precincts or by/in the church where they worshipped. This is the only surviving medieval one in Venice or the lagoon. The Spazio Badoer is generally used by this now revived brotherhood as an exhibition centre. For the importance of the patrician Badoer family to the confraternity of S. Giovanni Evangelista see CI 17, CI 18.

Our present epigraph is the first of the five vernacular inscriptions in the corpus connected to this ancient and culturally important *scuola grande*. The flagellant *Scuola dei battuti* (Early Venetian, *Sc(u)ola d(el)i batudi*) of S. Giovanni Evangelista was founded in 1261 and subsequently designated as a *scola magna* by the Council of Ten. The lay brotherhood's original seat was in the church of S. Aponal in the *sestiere* of S. Polo but in 1301 it moved, with the permission of the Badoer, to the site of the church and hospital of S. Giovanni Evangelista not far from the Frari. On the history, architecture and patronage of the *scuola* see VAZZOLER (2005). For an inventory of the confraternity's manuscript statutes (*mariegole*) see LEVANTINO (2011: 31–34). Its oldest *mariegole* are located in the ASV, *Scuola Grande di S. Giovanni Evangelista*, reg. 7 (early fourteenth century, in Latin), and reg. 3 (fourteenth century, in Venetian). An edition of the *mariegola* in reg. 8 (early fifteenth century, in Venetian) is in SIMEONE (2003). On the vernacular and Latin inscriptions of the confraternity see CICOGNA (1855).

TYPE AND DESCRIPTION: Funerary inscription on a plaque on the front side of a wide sarcophagus (237 × 141 × c. 50 cm) used for burying the brothers of the confraternity. The inscription plaque measures 30 × 30 cm and, like the rest of the sarcophagus, is hewn from what appears to be igneous trachite stone, grey and rough to the touch. Wear and tear affect the immediate legibility of only a few letters on the bottom right-hand side of the plaque. The slightly raised edges

Fig. 3.4. CI 3. © A. S. Ferguson.

of the inscription tablet are plain but it is lobed at the corners. It is flanked on the sarcophagus by two large trilobe crosses, each in a roundel. The text of the inscription itself is preceded by a small carved cross. To the left of the sarcophagus is another common grave of the brothers, of similar dimensions, in Istrian stone with an inscription in Latin dated 10 October 1302.

LETTERING: Tendentially Gothic majuscules but with a stiff, unadorned feel to them. The chiselling favours a more angular, unyielding ductus than is usual in Gothic script, giving a somewhat compressed aspect to the thick, substantially monoline, letters. These are cut deeply in V-section and range in height from 2.5 cm on the first line to 1.5 cm on the last. The <a> throughout typifies the stonecutter's approach, with its rigid stems and short, straight topstroke angled down sharply on the left. The angular serifs on the <c>, <e>, <f> and <s>; the sharp downstroke on the <t> and on the ascender of uncial <d>; the short spiked upstroke on <l>;

the decisively chiselled cedilla on *Çane* (l. 6); the straight <n> of capital origin; the abbreviation bars with angled ends in imitation of the end flicks of a pen seen on manuscript stroking; and the unadorned chevron or tilted 7 in l. 7 (signifying 'and') reinforce this effect. Uncialesque, though, are the <u/v>, with left curvature throughout, the <m> on the date, and the <h> on *Iohane* (l. 3) where the leg turns back on to the stem to form a bow, albeit a rather square one. On the hooked abbreviation strokes on *Iohane* and *Evangelista* (ll. 3–4), frequent in manuscripts but uncommon in our corpus, see CI 23. The text — commissioned, of course, by the board of the *scuola* and probably drafted by the warden himself — is justified both left and right and displays fairly regular and generous spacing between words and lines. Word separation is further emphasized by mid-high interpuncts, although some of these seem to have been worn away.

The pattern of tomb decoration and style of epitaph on a raised lobed plaque seen on our sarcophagus appear to have been common in Venice in the late-thirteenth and early-fourteenth centuries, with examples still visible on the sepulchres attached to the external wall of the church of S. Zanipolo and present sporadically elsewhere in the city's churches. The origins of this type of tomb in Venice are complex and not fully understood (DORIGO 2003, I: 516–21). The superficially Gothic script used on almost all of them has strikingly similar qualities to ours, in terms of plainness, uprightness and thickness of cut. Notable, in particular, for its strong iconographic and script affinity to the burial chest in the Spazio Badoer is the undated tomb at S. Zanipolo of Marin Contarini of S. Paternian and his heirs. This carries a Latin inscription whose lettering — which includes the Greek mu for <m>, discussed in CI 1 and CI 2, and un uncial <p> with tail extending well below the baseline — suggests a date before 1300: + *Sepultura d(omi)ni / Marini (Con)tareno / · s(ancti) · Pat(er)niani fillio / (con)da(m) · d(omi)ni · Iacobi (Con)/tareno s(an)c(t)o(rum) apo·stolo(rum) et eo(rum) / eredum* ▲. The impression conveyed by this series of sarcophagus inscriptions is of a conservative stonecutting tradition perpetuated by Venetian workshops specialising in tomb epitaphs, a tradition about to be superseded by the Gothic fashion. The distinctive type of lettering they employ — apparently little affected by the Romanesque interlude — last appears, to my knowledge, on the sarcophagus of Andrea Signolo of S. Pantalon, dated 1321, now visible outside the Frari in campo S. Rocco within the fenced-off patch of greenery along the church wall: $M^o CCC^o$ · XXII · / *mense · ienvarii / die · XVIII · exsev/nte hobiit · d(omi)n(u)s / Andreas · Signolo / de co(n)finio · s(an)c(t)i · / Pantaleonis · o/rate pro eo*.

It is not impossible that this archaic-looking script, of which the above are the final vestiges, could be the late phase of a style of funerary lettering — based originally on aspectually strong, austere block capitals but gradually absorbing uncial features — that was traditional in the lagoon. The chain of evidence is too fragmented to allow for certainty here, but the testimony of the best preserved sarcophagus from Torcello, dating from before the turn of the first millennium, lends some support to the hypothesis. This is the re-used Roman sarcophagus of the priest Dominicus, discovered in what is now the sacristy of Torcello cathedral in 1909 and affixed to the wall there. It is the sole survivor of the many medieval sarcophagi in the Torcello cathedral cemeteries which have been destroyed or re-employed in building works over the centuries (AGAZZI 2005; BOTTAZZI 2012: 101–02). The emphatic stroking of the epitaph on the front panel, dated 980, and its unadorned capital characters, occasionally inflected with uncial <d> and <e> but also with <p> of uncial origin dropping below the baseline, bring our later Venetian examples to mind: + *In n(omine) · D(omi)ni : ann(o) : ab inc(arnatione) D(omi)ni DCCCC/LXXX : i(n) hvc tvmvlv req(v)esit / Dominicvs p(res)b(yte)r mase[...] / q(vi) legitis orate D(ev)m p(ro) me peccatore.* This Torcellan script itself may possibly be related to the style of square, unserifed, thickly monoline Roman capitals that characterises the unrivalled range of votive and funerary writing on the floor of the remarkable palaeo-Christian basilica (formerly cathedral) of St Euphemia in Grado. Since Grado cathedral was the mother church of all the churches on the north Adriatic coast in the early Middle Ages its influence on S. Maria Assunta of Torcello and on the nascent Venice was profound. Most convincingly like Dominicus's epitaph is the mosaic inscription from about AD 600 in S. Eufemia dedicated to Bishop Marcianus (ZOVATTO 1971: 47, ill. 66).

In stark contrast to this funerary script tradition is the peculiar lettering in Latin on the plaque on the side of the other surviving confraternity tomb alongside ours in the Spazio Badoer. It is a highly uncialesque, almost cursive Gothic, with hairstrokes closing <e> and <c>, spikes on the topstroke of <t>, genuine semi-uncial <l> forms, and strongly serifed heads and feet of perpendiculars: *S(epultura) scole fr(atru)m ver/beratorum s(an)c(ti) Iho/h(an)e Ev(angelist)e fact[a] mi(llesim)o / CCCII mensis oc/tobris die X.* ('Burial place of the confraternity of flagellant brothers of St John the Evangelist made in 1302 on October 10th'). The carving of the inscription on this older tombstone is less regular, less accurate (the first <h> in *Ihohane* is a mistake), more tightly packed and less neatly paginated.

LANGUAGE: Among the surviving sarcophagi with a similar funerary script, ours is the only one to employ Venetian. It is no coincidence that it was commissioned by a lay confraternity on its way to becoming one of Venice's great *scuole*: one of those socially mixed institutions with large memberships drawn from across Venice which over the next century and a half would be important patrons of vernacular epigraphy in the city.

Iohane John (l. 3) < IOHANNES is a semi-learned form contrasting with the usual Venetian *Çane* (later *Çuane*) employed here in l. 6 (see CI 17, CI 18). For *frari* 'brothers' (l. 2) see CI 9, CI 17, CI 18. The *frari batudi* (l. 2) are literally the 'beaten brothers', with reference to their practice of self-flagellation (Early Venetian, *disciplina*), *batudi* (Italian, *battuti*) being the regular Venetian masculine plural past participle of *bater* 'to beat'. Diphthongisation of stressed Ŏ and Ĕ is, as expected at this early date, absent in *scola* (l. 3) and *ser* 'Mr' (l. 5). *Scola* itself is literally 'school' < SCHOLA 'corporation', but here as elsewhere in the collection it has the specifically Venetian meaning of 'confraternity'. *Guardian* 'warden, confraternity head' (l. 7), instead of the more usual Venetian form *vardian* (*vardian grando* in full) employed commonly in the corpus, is a minority variant that also appears occasionally in the *scuola*'s statutes. Both are ultimately from the Germanic root **war(d)-* 'watch, guard'. Çane da Tres(s)aga or Tresega is confirmed in the statutes as warden for the year 1311 (SIMEONE 2003: 124–25) and is also recorded as being re-elected in 1316. The *vardian grando* was the chief executive officer of a *scuola grande*, elected for one year and supported by a deputy (*vic(h)ario*). He chaired, and introduced proposals to, the confraternity chapter, the *capitolo*, and was responsible for the day-to-day running of the *scuola*. His *oficiali* 'board officials, officers' (l. 7), a term used here and in CI 38, constituted the elected governing board or executive, known as the *banca* 'bench', of a Venetian confraternity. They are often referred to in the corpus, though, as the *conpagni* or *compagni* 'peers, colleagues, companions' of the *vardian*. These officials, also elected for one year, were the *vardian da ma(i)tin* (literally the 'morning warden' as the flagellant processions were originally held on Sunday mornings), who was the master of ceremonies and finance officer; the *scrivan* 'clerk, scrivener' who was the secretary and accountant; and twelve *degani* 'deans, deacons, counsellors', two from each *sestiere* of the city. In addition, one or two caretaker-cum-undertakers (*nonçoli*) were elected. For the corresponding officers of a *scuola piccola* see CI 23. *Li soi* 'his' (l. 7) is the first in a long series of unstressed 3rd singular possessive adjectives, with or without the definite article, in the corpus. For the forms and pattern of these possessives across the corpus and into Modern Venetian see CI 94.

RECENT STUDIES: FERGUSON (2013c: 84–85), the first published edition of the inscription; TOMASIN (2014: 175); FERGUSON (2015c: 39–40). Recorded, but not published, by Cicogna.

Corpus Inscription 4

HOSPEDA | L · DE SER · N | ATICHLI | ER · DA CHA · | CRIṢTIAN 5
[Hospedal de ser Natichlier da cha' Cristian.]

TRANSLATION: Hospital of Mr Natichlier of the house of Cristian.

DATE: 1312 or very soon thereafter. The inscription is undated, but in 1312 one Natichlier Cristian donated to the Procurators of St Mark *de Citra* — who had responsibility for bequests in the *sestieri* of S. Marco, Castello and Cannaregio — a hospital, endowed by legacy, dedicated to the care of twenty poor or infirm women. The original testamentary documentation from July 1312, setting up the almshouse and stipulating the appointment of a prior and prioress, preferably man and wife, to manage it, has survived (AIRE, b Patrimonio 1 A46, 3 July 1312) and is reproduced in SEMI (1983: 98–100) along with plans of the building. The wording of the will ('ordino quod hospitalis et domus quod fieri feci pro anima mea in contrata Sanctae Trinitatis [...]') implies that by July 1312 the building was completed or well underway. The foundation remained a women's hospice until it was closed down in 1887. After a period as a night shelter it has been taken over in recent years by an activist collective.

LOCATION: Calle del Morion no. 2951 in the *sestiere* of Castello. The inscription plaque is embedded in situ on the wall to the left of the building entrance, about 275 cm above pavement level. The medieval hospice building is substantially intact on the outside but the interior has been completely restructured. It is located in an out-of-the-way eastern part of the city in the parish of S. Ternita (Italian, S. Trinità), just south of the church of S. Francesco della Vigna, and forms the corner between Calle del Morion and Ramo al ponte S. Francesco. Just round the corner, on the Ramo side and at the same height, is a rectangular plaque in Istrian stone. It carries a damaged and worn Latin inscription in Roman capitals, dated 1 August 1479, which records the restoration of the almshouse by the Procurators of St Mark and, by implication, the transfer of jurisdiction to them: *[...]icto Venerio Antonio e/[...] rnardo Ivstiniano divi M/[arci] procvratoribus hospitale / Natichlieri Cristiani pie restav[...] / MCCCCLXXVIIII die p^o avg[...]*. Neither inscription has, fortunately, been defaced by the colourful murals that now cover the walls of the social centre. The hospital is visible on de' Barbari's great woodcut cityscape of 1500 (CI 82–91). It can be seen, with its pitched roof and large oculus window on the gable end, just opposite the courtyard wall of Palazzo Contarini *della porta di ferro*.

TYPE AND DESCRIPTION: Commemorative and documentary. The inscription, recording a charitable donation by an individual, is carved on a crenellated white marble wall plaque. The inscription surface measures 42 × 38 cm. This is the first appearance in the corpus of marble as an inscriptional support and of the characteristic Venetian crenellated frame which recurs so commonly in fourteenth- and fifteenth-century epigraphy. Natichlier Cristian was a member of the ancient Venetian Cristian (or Cristiano) family, already householders in the city in the

Fig. 3.5. CI 4. © A. S. Ferguson.

eleventh and twelfth centuries. They are recorded in 1312 as possessing eight properties for rent in the S. Ternita parish where the hospice was built (DORIGO 2003, I: 337). Natichlier's wealth is indicated by the foundation of a private hospital, by its long-term endowment lasting some 150 years, and by the quality support material, frame and carving of the inscription.

LETTERING: Gothic majuscules, delicately uncialesque throughout, carved in V-section. Although this is a modest artefact with a brief message, it is not without epigraphic importance. The first fully Gothic epigraph in the corpus, it is unaffected — unlike CI 1, CI 2 and CI 3 — by other script traditions. It is markedly indebted in its calligraphic finesse to manuscript titling capitals. The inscription tablet has worn well, as is often the case with marble in Venice, and has only sustained serious roughing on the bottom line of writing where the middle letters -is- in *Cristian* (l. 5) are damaged. The lettering averages 3.25 cm in height and is clear and legible. The inscriptional space itself is surprisingly generous. The lines are well separated as are the words which are also marked off, in most cases, by interpuncts. The epigraph is justified on the left. The script is expertly and sharply cut, with a very conscious use of thick and thin strokes and variable angles of attack within individual letters for clarity and aesthetic effect. Admirable are the chiselling, contrasting widths and delicately bracketed splay-serifs on <a>, <h>, <l> and <n>, the tapering and looping terminal flourishes on the foot of <h>, <n> and

<r>, and the elegant swash on the head of <n> and <p>. The letters <c> and <e> are closed with fine hairstrokes.

LANGUAGE: It befits the practical, social nature of the Cristian charitable initiative — embedded in its local neighbourhood — that it should advertise and memorialise itself not in Latin but in the vernacular, thereby reaching the widest audience in parish, *sestiere* and city.

Hospedal 'almshouse, hospital, hospice', with the Latinising initial <h>, is from < HOSPITALEM 'relative to guests'. It shows the characteristic Early Venetian voicing of intervocalic T > /d/. The eventual complete lenition of /d/ has led to the Modern/ Contemporary Venetian form *ospeal*. *Ser* (l. 2) 'Mr' remains undiphthongised at this early date in the fourteenth century. The <h>, commonly used with <c> to express velar /k/ in Early Venetian and also in Early Tuscan, is seen in *cha* 'house, family, palace' (l. 4) — pronounced [ka] —, an abbreviation of *casa* or *caxa*. *Cha*, written Ca', is used nowadays before the names of many Venetian palaces. *Natichlier* (ll. 2–4) was originally a surname. The nexus -*chl*- may have been pronounced either [tʃ] or [dʒ] in Early Venetian. The second of the two, the voiced palatal, is more likely here on the basis of the Latin origin of the name, NATIGERIUS, and of spelling evidence such as the recorded contemporaneous Venetian name Damia(n) Natigiir (STUSSI 1965: 60).

RECENT STUDIES: TOMASIN (2012a: 23–24); FERGUSON (2013c: 85–86). Transcribed first, but with some errors, in MARTINELLI (1684: 202).

Corpus Inscriptions 5, 6, 7

SPERA(N) | ÇA [...] | TVTE LE ₃ | CHOSE ₄ | CHE LE ₅ | SIRA ₆ | SPER[..|.]A DIO ₈
[Sperança [...] tute le chose che le sirà sper[...] a Dio.]

CHO(N)S | TA(N)CIA ₂ | NON S | [...] ÇO TI CO ₄ | AVER S | TABILIT | ATE ₇
[Chonstancia non s[...] co' ti co' aver stabilitate.]

TE(M)PER | A(N)ÇA ₂ | TEMPRA(RA) ₃ | LA TOA F | ORTEÇ | A ₆
[Temperança temprarà la toa forteça.]

TRANSLATIONS: Hope [...] all things hoped of her to God.

Constancy is not [...] with you like having stability.

Temperance will temper your fortitude.

DATE: Undated but probably executed in the first half of the fourteenth century. Although the frescoes were initially assigned to the later Trecento, the arguments put forward by LONGHI (1978: 40), MARIACHER (1957: 159–61) and DORIGO (2003, I: 565) for a pre-1350 date are now the art-historical consensus, officially accepted by the Museo Correr itself. The palaeographic and linguistic evidence from the inscriptions, presented below for the first time, tends to confirm this dating.

LOCATION: Discovered in 1913 on the walls of a room in a house in the S. Zulian district (*sestiere* of S. Marco) belonging to Don Emilio Antonelli. The frescoes were detached, framed with a gesso backing and purchased by the Museo Correr. They are now displayed in the museum's picture gallery.

TYPE AND DESCRIPTION: Moralising, didactic messages. These are painted on illusionistic scrolls held by allegorical Virtue figures on what survives of a unique decorative fresco cycle originally from a private Venetian interior of the period. The framed remnants are unsigned and the artist is not known. The damaged fragment of fresco with the figure of Temperance is 219 × 221 cm while the section with the allegory of Charity, Constancy and Hope is 192 × 124 cm. The scroll held by Charity is completely destroyed. The frescoes depict(ed):

> a cycle of personified virtues and other allegories painted around the walls of a room. Silhouetted against a black background, the Virtues are seated on thrones beneath an arcade that features gabled arches surmounted by tiny nude figures alternating with aedicules crowned with open cupolas. Flame-like trees behind the arcade imply a garden setting. (FORTINI BROWN 1996b: 64)

Temperance, pointing downwards towards an object beyond the edge of the fragment, has her traditional two ewers: one of water, one of wine. Charity holds a basket of bread and feeds a loaf to a pauper. Constancy, a young woman whose face is now largely damaged by paint flaking, contemplates a reflected image of herself as an old woman (or perhaps an image of the inconstant moon). Hope, with arms

Fig. 3.6. CI 6. © A. S. Ferguson.

outstretched, is about to receive what looks like a ring from a small, flying, haloed figure — possibly a saint — above her. One is struck by the lively Virtues and by the remarkably impudent little classical nudes in the background. While the aphorisms on the scrolls are, of course, conventional their wording and emphasis are quirky. The whole work is densely allusive and iconographically rich, with Humanist overtones. Its motifs and Gothic aesthetic suggest a mainland centre. Given the location of these frescoes, which ostentatiously decorated a private residence, we are in the unusual presence here of displayed writing at the interface of private and public.

LETTERING: Painted Gothic majuscules. Vigorously uncialesque with strong stroke contrast within individual letters, the black script — averaging 2 cm in height and clearly legible where undamaged — mimics ink writing and obviously owes more to manuscript calligraphy than to stone epigraphy. Sometimes, as in the <h> of *che* (CI 5, l. 5) with its arm tucked under the stem and ending in extravagant swirls, and in the contrastive double stroking on <a>, <c> and <n> — found nowhere else in the corpus but prominent on the famous tomb inscription of Antenor in Padua dateable to 1284 —, the influence of titling capitals is obvious. The irregularity of letter heights and the casual layout, in line with the tilted perspective of the banderoles, are part of an illusionistic game. It suggests to the spectator that fluttering written texts are being glimpsed. The surprise is that the lettering is majuscule, rather than the minuscule that would actually have been used on a real scroll and which is often employed when a 'book' or 'scroll', with a written message meant to be legible, is represented in paint or stone (see CI 59).

Particularly striking are the flared serifs on <c> and <e>, the tapering spikes on <t>, and the consistently stylish Gothic <a> with its downcurved left stem. Also notable are the confident and prominent cedillas on *sperança* (CI 5, ll. 1–2), *temperança* (CI 7, ll. 1–2) and *forteça* (CI 7, ll. 4–6). Unique is the use of the abbreviation after *tempra* (CI 7, l. 3), presumably to indicate the future ending *-ra* (in other words, *-rà*). This symbol, resembling the fusion of a 2 and a 4, was normally employed on medieval Latin manuscripts and inscriptions for the *-rum* ending, and I know of its use in no other vernacular epigraph in Venice. The three reversed <n>s, one on CI 5 and two on CI 6, are a whimsical touch found nowhere else in the corpus. The unexpected uncial <d> of *dio* (CI 5, l. 8), with its horizontal then upswept ascender — characteristic of earlier Gothic practice and prominent on the inscriptions of Giotto's paired virtues and vices in the Arena Chapel in Padua (AMMANNATI 2017) — might possibly evoke a date early in the Trecento. However, such evidence is inconclusive in isolation, and our ignorance of the cultural milieu and provenance of the artefact suggest that extreme prudence is required here. The deciphering and interpretation of these texts is complicated by their palimpsestic nature. They are affected by partial obliteration and damage to what remains, but also display tantalising fragments of underwritten text showing through in parts. The <m> visible at the end of *stabilitate* (CI 6, ll. 5–7) and the inverted <n> (CI 5, l. 5) suggest that each vernacular message may originally have been underlain by a Latin version. For the only other palimpsestic inscription in the corpus see CI 79.

LANGUAGE: It is not without significance for the evidence it provides of the growing status of the vernacular in this period that such sophisticated, culturally complex artefacts as these allegorical frescoes employ it in preference to Latin. Uniquely in the corpus the vernacular of the inscriptions carries subtle signs pointing to the 'colonial' Venetian of the eastern Adriatic coast.

The most marked of these signs is the 3rd singular future tense of *eser* 'to be' in *sira* (in other words, *sirà*) 'will be' (CI 5, l. 6). Such raising of pretonic /e/ to /i/ in the future and conditional is typical of texts written in the Venetian-based *scriptae* used in the early to mid-fourteenth century between Istria (LUCIANI 1876) and Ragusa (DOTTO 2008: 177–78). Less distinct from Early Venetian practice but nonetheless suggestive of Adriatic origins is *-ar-* in the future stem of *temprara* (accented on the final <a>) where *-er-* was increasingly preferred in Venice itself in the course of the Trecento (see CI 30). The Latinising form *stabilitate* (CI 6, ll. 5–7) for the abstract noun 'stability' was the rule in Early Venetian. Interestingly, though, there are no Veneto occurrences of it in the OVI after 1332. As for *temprar* 'to temper' (CI 7), no Veneto instances of it are found in the OVI after 1315. *Chonstancia* 'constancy' (CI 6, ll. 1–2) is normal fourteenth-century Venetian and, like the equivalent northern Italian vernacular forms of the word, carries no cedilla. One notes, otherwise, the consistent use of cedillas for the presumed affricate sound /ts/ and the presence of the digram <ch> for the velar /k/, in line with Early Venetian and 'colonial'

Venetian texts. The 2nd singular feminine possessive adjective *la toa* 'your' (CI 7, l. 4) is perfectly regular but is the only occurrence among our public texts where the 3rd person is inevitably the norm. Similarly, *ti* (CI 6, l. 4), regular in form throughout the history of Venetian, is the only 2nd singular emphatic pronoun found in them. The passive construction in CI 5, with a future perfect verb, is also unique in the corpus. *Le* 'in her' (CI 5, l. 5) is an indirect object pronoun and is normal in Early Venetian. The overall sense of the dictum suggests that the missing verb in l. 2 is *da* (= *dà*) 'gives' or *dara* (= *darà*) 'will give'. The two instances of *co* (CI 6, l. 4), almost chiasmic in their juxtaposition, are particularly interesting: reflecting, literally, the fine but important distinction made on the scroll between constancy and stability. The first is an Early Venetian variant of *c(h)on* 'with' < CŬM; the second is an apocopated form of *c(h)omo* 'like' < QUŌMODO. Both shortened forms survived into Modern Venetian. The only other inscription in our collection to contain such a high percentage of abstract nouns is CI 30.

RECENT STUDIES: LONGHI (1978: 5, 40); MARIACHER (1957: 159–61); FORTINI BROWN (1996b: 64); DORIGO (2003, I: 565); FERGUSON (2013c: 102–03).

Corpus Inscription 8

MCCC · XL · A DI · XIII · DI · OTO[BR]IO · IO ANGELO [PIARI]NI DI [M]URANO VOIO E [ORD]INO ₁| (C)HE SE(N)PRE LE MI[E] POSESIONE SIA TE[GNUE] I(N) CO[L]MO (E) FITO [...] ₂ | R[...] I[...] CO(N)[--] ₃| [...]LA CO(N)TRADA DI S(AN)C(T)O [STEFANO DI MURA(N) TRAGA(N)DO FORA DI QVELA P(AR)]| TE OGNO AN(N)O $[....] [...] [I QVALI VADA AL C]O(N)ÇERO D(E) LA GL[EX]IA DI S(AN)C(T)O ₅|STEFANO DI MURANO L[----------------] SIA [DA]TA ALI POVERI DI [MURA(N)] [..] ₆| TUT[...] TRAG[A](N)DO [...] P· II DI [...] [...]TE OGNO AN(N)O $·II· [...] D(E) GR(OSSI) [...] D(E) [...] ₇| LO CO(N)ÇERO DELA GL[EX]IA DI S(AN)C(T)O MARTINO DI BURAN DA MAR E LA TERÇA PARTE ₈| SIA D(E)STRIBUIDA P(ER) [M]ANO D[ELA MIA M]UIERE TUNINA E ORDINO (C)HE DRIO LA ₉| MORTE D(E)LA MIA COMESARIA [...] P(ER) LEGA⟨L⟩LI PROCORATORI ₁₀| L[A] GLEXIA DI S(AN)[C](T)O STEFA[NO] D(E) MURA(N) (C)HE P(ER) LO TE(N)PO (C)HE SERA E VERA [CO]| [...] D(E)LO MIO BUONO P(RO)PONIME(N)TO SIA SE(N)PRE CO(N)PLIO DE| [...] I DITI P(RO)CORATORI P(ER) ÇIASCHUNO AN(N)O $ ·XX·P(IÇOLI)·[...]· [(C)HE SI TRA[GA] ₁₃ || DITA $·XX·P(IÇOLI) · DI SUL MO(N)TE DELE SOVRADITE ·III· PARTE [...]| VIA DITA [TUNINA] MUIERE E COMESARIA E LA SIA SE(N)PRE DONA ₁₅| E DOMI(N)A DI TUTO LO MIO STABELE E MOBELE NO(N) POSA(N)DO ALGUNA P(ER)SONA ₁₆| FARE I(N)CONTRA QVESTO MIO TESTAME(N)TO [...] (C)HE SIA PONTUALM[E](N)TE ₁₇| FERMO S⟨E⟩ ALGUNA P(ER)SONA ÇERCHERA DI RO(N)PERE O DI SPEÇA(R) O P(ER) ALG|UNO MODO E POSI VENIRE [...]LA IRA D(E) DIO E DELI SUOI S(AN)C(T)I E I(N) SOURA| TUTO DE ACCO(N)PI⟨R⟩ CO(N) LI SOI ERED[I] E SOCIESORI E ALA SOURADITA MIA CO|MESARIA O ALI SOI SOCIESORI · V · LIB(RE) · E NIE(N)TEMENO LA CARTA DI QVESTO ₂₁| TESTAME(N)TO P(ER)MA(N)GA E DURI I(N) LA SUA FERMEÇA SE(N)PRE :→

[Mcccxl, a di xiii di otobrio. Io Angelo Piarini di Murano voio e ordino che senpre le mie posesione sia tegnue in colmo e fito [...]r[...] i[...] con[---------
---] [...]la contrada di Sancto Stefano di Muran, tragando fora di quela parte ogno anno soldi [...] [...], i quali vada al conçero de la glexia di Sancto Stefano di Murano, l[----------------------] sia data ali poveri di Muran [...], tut[...] tragando [...] piçoli II di [...] [...]te ogno anno soldi II [...] de grossi [...] de [...] lo conçero dela glexia di Sancto Martino di Buran da mar. E la terça parte sia destribuida per mano dela mia muiere Tunina. E ordino che drio la morte dela mia comesaria [...] per legalli procoratori la glexia di Sancto Stefano de Muran, che per lo tenpo che serà e verà co[...] delo mio buono proponimento sia senpre conplio de[...] i diti procoratori per çiaschuno anno soldi XX piçoli [...], che si traga dita soldi XX piçoli di sul monte delle sovradite III parte [...] via dita Tunina muiere e comesaria. E la sia senpre dona e domina di tuto lo mio stabele e mobele, non posando alguna persona fare incontra questo mio testamento [...] che sia pontualmente fermo se alguna persona çercherà di ronpere o di speçar, o per alguno modo, e posi venire [...]la ira de Dio e deli suoi sancti. E in sovratuto de acconpir con li soi eredi e sociesori. E ala sovradita mia comesaria o ali soi sociesori v libre e nientemeno. La carta di questo testamento permanga e duri in la sua fermeça senpre.]

Fig. 3.7. CI 8 (lines 14–22). © A. S. Ferguson.

TRANSLATION: 1340, on the 13th day of October. I, Angelo Piarini of Murano, wish and order that my properties in the district of [....] should always be kept owned and rented out and [---] [...] district of S. Stefano in Murano, extracting from that share every year $[...] [...] which should go towards the upkeep of the church of S. Stefano on Murano [---------------------] which should go to the poor of Murano [...] all [...] deducting 2 *piçoli* of [...] [...] every year 2 *soldi* [...] *de grossi* [...] of [...] for the upkeep of the church of S. Martino on Burano *da mar*. And let it be distributed in person by my wife Tunina. And I order that after the death of my executor the church of S. Stefano on Murano should be appointed my legal administrator, so that come what may in the future [...] my good proposal shall always be carried out [...] the said administrators each year 20 *soldi*, [...] *piçoli*, and that the said 20 *soldi* [...] be drawn from the sum total of the aforementioned three shares [...] by the said Tunina, my wife and executor. And let her always be lady and mistress of all I possess, fixed and moveable, so that nobody can contradict this will of mine [...] that it be promptly put on hold if any person tries to break or split (it), or (impede it), in any way whatever, and may they (face) the wrath of God. And, above all, to be carried out by her heirs and successors. And to my above-mentioned executor, or to her successors, (I leave) 5 pounds no less. May the letter of this will survive and endure intact for ever.

DATE: October 1340 or shortly thereafter.

LOCATION: Until 1865 the inscription was embedded, probably in situ, on the outside wall of a house in the S. Stefano district of Murano, on what is now the Fondamenta S. Giovanni dei Battuti quayside, where Cicogna saw and transcribed it. 'L'ho letta sul muro di alcune case alli numeri 48 49 50 [later no. 31] sulla fondamenta di S. Giovanni, parrocchia di S. Stefano, or di Pietro Martire' (CICOGNA 1824–53, VI: 501–02). It was removed in 1865 when the group of houses, possibly those originally owned and mentioned by the commissioner of the epigraph Angelo Piarini, was renovated. At present, divided into two plaques, it is mounted and displayed on a wall of the courtyard cloister of the Museo del Vetro on Murano, not far from its original location, along with other sculpted artefacts. The museum, founded in the 1860s, was dedicated to the history of the island, principally its glass production, and our inscription has been housed there since the nineteenth century. In 1881 it was recorded by the director of the museum as being on the wall around the landing of the building's staircase: 'intorno al pianerottolo delle scale' (ZANETTI 1881: 24).

TYPE AND DESCRIPTION: Testamentary declaration with precise instructions and exhortations concerning a charitable financial legacy. The 22-line epigraph is inscribed on two rectangular marble plaques. The first one measures 89 × 45 cm, with 13 lines of script. The second is 89 × 34 cm, and holds 9 lines. It is not known when the split occurred but it is likely to be *ab initio* given the marked difference of thickness between the two tablets. Exposed to the lagoon air for over half a millennium, the plaques are much discoloured and the script of the epigraph has suffered serious deterioration, even though marble in Venetian conditions is generally hard wearing. The groove depth of the letters has been severely worn down throughout, with some words and sections now illegible, especially on the upper part of the first tablet, but also sporadically elsewhere. The inscription was already badly worn in the early nineteenth century, with sections indecipherable to Cicogna, but there has undoubtedly been subsequent deterioration. The most severe corrosion affects ll. 1–6. To salvage what is possible from these lines and from other compromised passages I have employed computer-enhanced high resolution photographs, backed up cautiously by Cicogna's transcriptions of what was still legible to him. The substantial sections of ll. 3 and 6 which are irrecoverably obliterated are indicated by a continuous line between square brackets.

The inscription is unique in the corpus in being a written legacy transferred on to stone for public view. It records the last will and testament of one Angelo Piarini, whose name is also Venetianised to Ançolo Piarin in the fourteenth-century records, concerning the future disposal of the annual rental income derived from his properties on Murano. The recipients of the endowment income are designated as the nearby church of S. Stefano (founded in the eleventh century and now no longer in existence), partly for its own upkeep and partly for the care of the poor of Murano, and the church of S. Martin on Burano (which is still operational). These are the 'three shares' referred to in the epigraph. Tunina, Piarini's wife, is appointed sole executor of his estate, and in this capacity is to receive the tidy lump sum of £5. One is struck by the man's hard-headed financial precision and foresight, by his utter trust in his wife and, above all, by his passionate determination (note the repeated use of *senpre* 'always' and the concluding fulminations) to ensure that his wishes are carried out in perpetuity. In fact, his largesse turns out to have had lasting effects on the lagoon community that he undoubtedly cared about. It is a remarkable testament to his tenacity and foresight that money from the Piarini legacy — given, as initially stipulated, to the church of S. Stefano, whose parochial functions were taken over in the nineteenth century by the nearby church of S. Pietro Martire — was the basis of a charitable foundation still named after him (the *Comunità per anziani Angelo Piarin*) on Murano at Fondamenta Colleoni 4 and 5, just along the embankment from where Piarini's properties were originally located. How quickly the estate moved initially on the matter can be judged by the fact that a Piarini-endowed hospice on Murano (*C(h)a Piarìn* as it is called in the documentation) was already recorded by the authorities as early as 1340 itself (AIRE, b Patrimonio 71, 1340). To this day the organisation provides accommodation and support for seven impoverished older women.

Although we know little or nothing of Angelo Piarini, his name, the nature of the language employed in his will, and his modest wealth point to his having been a political-cum-economic migrant to Venice from Tuscany. The surname Piarini is, however, not recorded anywhere in Italy. One can reasonably conjecture, instead, that it would originally have been Pierini, and that the form Piarin(i) is derived from a local Muranese pronunciation of his name involving the typical Veneto raising of <er> to <ar> and vowel apocope after final /n/. The concentration of the name Pierini around Lucca, even today, suggests that Angelo may have operated in the silk industry and moved to Venice with the exodus of Guelph-supporting Lucchese silk craftsmen and merchants from 1314 onwards, provoked by the severe political turmoil following the takeover of the city by the Ghibellines under Uguccione della Faggiuola (MOLÀ 1994). Piarini's origins, prosperity and residence in the S. Stefano district of Murano also suggest links with the business interests of the great Lucchese exile Michele Amadi — silk dyer, future head of the confraternity of St John the Baptist on the island, and resident at this time of S. Stefano too — who figures on another inscription in our corpus (CI 26). That epigraph may also show Tuscan linguistic intrusion. Other examples of possible Tuscan-Venetian intermingling are analysed in CI 54 and CI 93.

LETTERING: Gothic majuscules cut in V-section. Although much weathered, what remains shows the letters as having been finely carved, with good stroke contrast, in a vigorous uncialesque. Their module is relatively compressed and the ductus is sinuous, with strong flaring at the end of perpendicular strokes. These characteristics can be seen strikingly on the <i>, the <n> and the oval <o>. The <s> and <t> have elongated spike serifs, and hairstrokes are used throughout on <c> and <e>. The <g> is attractive in its balanced shape, generous swirl and splayed serif. Two types of <u/v> are employed: the majority show right-side curvature, with the straight-sided form linked exclusively to preceding <q>. The <m> is always of the uncial sort. Remarkable is the regular use of <h>, with kinked leg and following <e>, to represent <ch> in the relative pronoun *che*. A clear distinction is made between the abbreviations for *per(-)*, with the stem of <p> barred, and *pro(-)* featuring a curved hook on the back of the stem of <p>. There are a few mistakes: the first <l> on *legalli* (l. 10) is cut like a right-curved <u>; *fermo es* (l. 18) is a lapse for *fermo se* 'put on hold if' which I have corrected; the <r> of *acconpir* 'carry out' (l. 20), carved as an <a>, has also been corrected, as has the <r> in *carta* 'paper, charter' (l. 21) which had been omitted. Ligatured <ar> and <an> are frequent, with *anno* 'year' consisting of abbreviated <n> and ligatured <an> run together, followed by <o>. This is the first epigraph in the corpus to ligature <al>. No other inscription carries, as here, the currency symbols found in account books, including the $gr followed by superscript <ō> for *soldo de grosso*; $p followed by superscript <ō> for *soldo* or *dener de piçolo*; and the abbreviation *lib* for *libra*, *livra* or *lira*. On these Venetian coins and their relationship see DAY, MATZKE and SACCOCCI (2016: 642–44, 1014–15). The inscription is rounded off with three vertical dots and a wavy line with a looped decoration on the end.

Our epigraph was undoubtedly based on a master text drawn up by Piarini in his own hand. Minuscule practice lies behind the mid-high dots around numerals and the double <ll> of *legalli* 'legal', l. 10 (on this feature of Venetian writing see CI 30). It also explains the survival of the extraordinary linguistic impasto of the will itself which, one suspects, would have been ironed out by a notary. Another unique feature of this vernacular epigraph is the evidence of preparatory lining of the inscription surface, still just visible in places. The resulting regularity is a boon in that the serried lines of writing, around 2.5 cm high on both tablets, show only limited gaps between letters and words. These are further restricted in the latter part of the text, suggesting space constraint. The overall effect is one of dense *scriptio continua*.

LANGUAGE: The inscription stands out immediately in the corpus for its currency symbols and its concentration of legal and financial terms: *parte* 'share' (ll. 4–5 and 8); *comesaria* 'executor' (ll. 10, 15, 20–21); *procoratori* 'administrators' (ll. 10, 13); *monte* 'bank account, government bonds' (l. 14); *sociesori* 'successors' (ll. 20, 21); *eredi* 'heirs' (l. 20); *testamento* 'will' (ll. 17, 22). It is also set apart by its idiosyncratic tone and vocabulary. Most notable is a succession of idiomatic expressions involving juxtaposed terms. These create a solemn, almost incantatory, effect: *voio e ordino* 'I wish and order' (l. 1); *colmo e fito* 'owned and rented out', lit. 'roof and rent' (l. 2); *sera e vera* 'will be and will come' (l. 11); *dona e domina* 'lady and mistress' (ll. 15–16); *stabele e mobele* 'fixed and moveable' (l. 16); *ronpere o speçar* 'break or split' (l. 18); *permanga e duri* 'survive and endure' (l. 22). Of these I have only ever come across *voio e ordino*, *stabele e mobele* and *dona e domina* in medieval Venetian wills. Interestingly, another rare surviving vernacular will (of 1325) from the *contrada* of S. Stefano on Murano has something of the pugnacious emphasis of Piarini's (FORMENTIN 2017: 125–33).

Above all Piarini's will is a remarkable example of apparently unselfconscious code mixing, involving the writer-commissioner's native Early Tuscan and the Early Venetian of his adopted Murano. One is struck immediately by the disconcerting alternation and blending of Tuscan and Venetian forms in his text. *Otobrio* October (l. 1) with the *-brio* ending (Early Tuscan, *ot(t)obre*) is a specifically Venetian form (see CI 79) although one might have expected *otubrio*, with the raising of the second /o/ to /u/ as in CI 38, CI 47. *Io Angelo Piarini voio e ordino* (l. 1) would seem pure Tuscan but for *voio* 'I wish, want' with Venetian /j/ < L + yod rather than the Tuscan palatal lateral /λ/ of *voglio*. *Ordino* looks Tuscan but was also possible in Early Venetian, although very much in the minority compared to *ordeno*. The interpenetration of the two codes is also exemplified by the alternation throughout of *di* ~ *de* 'of' and of *Murano* ~ *Muran*. *Senpre* 'always' (l. 2 passim) and *tenpo* 'time' (l. 11) are shared by Tuscan and Venetian. *Le mie posesione* 'my properties, possessions'

(l. 2) leans towards Tuscan, with contemporaneous Venetian texts showing *posesion* for this feminine plural form (see CI 21). Also leaning towards Tuscan are: *i quali* 'which', l. 5 (rather than *i qual*); *per mano* 'by the hand' (l. 9); *buono* 'good' (l. 12); *eredi* 'heirs', l. 20 (with Venetian sometimes preferring *redi*); and *nientemeno* 'no less', l. 21 (compared to Early Venetian *nientemen*). *Contrada* 'district' (l. 4 passim) is both Tuscan and Venetian, as are *quela parte* 'that part, share' (ll. 4–5); *poveri* '(the) poor' (l. 6); *la morte* 'death' (l. 10); *legalli* 'legal' (l. 10); *proponimento* 'proposal' (l. 12); *testamento* 'will' (ll. 17 and 22); *monte*; *carta* 'paper' (l. 21) and *fermeça* 'firmness' (l. 22). While *domina* 'mistress, lady' (l. 16) is both Tuscan and Venetian, *dona e domina* 'lady and mistress' is a tautological Venetian expression, with both terms derived from DŎMĬNA, and with *dona* (Tuscan, *donna*) showing the usual Venetian aversion to geminated consonants. However, *anno* 'year' (l. 5 passim), shared by both varieties, is always employed in the preferred Tuscan pronunciation form with double <n>, although the metaplasmic *ogno* 'each, every' (ll. 5, 7), which precedes it, is clearly Venetian. *Glexia* 'church' (ll. 5, 8, 11) is also utterly Venetian, with its retention of consonant + L and with the presence of <x> for the voiced sibilant /z/. *Colmo e fito*; *fora* 'out', l. 4 (Tuscan, *fuora* ~ *fuori*); *alguna* 'any' (Tuscan, *alcuna*), l. 18; *dita* 'said' (Tuscan, *detta*), ll. 14, 15; *sovratuto* 'above all' (Tuscan, *soprat(t)utto*), ll. 19–20; *stabele e mobele* (Tuscan, *stabile e mobile*); and *in la* 'in the', l. 22 (Tuscan, *nella*) are all characteristically Venetian. *Procoratori* exists in Early Venetian but was uncommon. Piarini's choice may have been influenced by Tuscan *procuratori*.

The same extraordinary *Sprachmischung* is obvious in the verb forms used by Piarini. We have already observed the juxtaposition of *voio* and *ordino* at the outset. *Posi* (= *possi*) 'may' (l. 19) is a 3rd singular present subjunctive Tuscan outcome (contrasting with *possa* shared by Venetian and Tuscan). The 3rd singular present subjunctive endings in *permanga e duri* 'survive and endure' and the past participle *data* 'given' (l. 6) are also fully Tuscan. However, while *ronpere* (l. 18) has the Tuscan form of the infinitive *speçar* (l. 18), paired with it, has the apocopated Venetian infinitive type. *Venire* 'to come' (l. 19), which like *anno* may also be influenced by Latin, contrasts with Venetian *vegnir*, but the prefix and lenition in past participle *destribuida* (Tuscan, *distribuita*), l. 9, are typically Venetian. Also unmistakably Venetian are the 1st conjugation *-ando* gerund endings extended to other conjugations in *tragando* 'drawing' (ll. 4 and 7) — versus Tuscan *traendo* — and *posando* 'being able' (Tuscan, *potendo*). The future tense form *sera* (= *serà*) 'will be' (l. 11) spans both varieties, although *sarà* was the dominant Early Tuscan variant. *Vera* (= *verà*) 'will come' (l. 11) is incontrovertibly Tuscan (although it normally required the <r> to be doubled), contrasting strongly with Early Venetian *vegnirà* ~ *vegnerà*. Finally, *çerchera* 'will seek' (l. 18) mirrors Tuscan *cercherà*, but the cedilla indicating an affricate pronunciation, like that on *çiaschuno* 'each' (l. 13), confirms it to be Venetian. Piarini's immersion in his lagoon environment comes out strongly in his designation of Burano (l. 8). The island was indeed referred to as *Buran da mar* (occasionally *de mar*) — in other words, Burano-on-Sea — in medieval and early modern Venetian writing.

A number of features of this unique will in stone are intriguing for the potential insight they provide into the Venetian spoken on Murano in the fourteenth century.

Tunina, the name of the testator's wife, shows a case of provincial or lower-register Veneto raising of pre-tonic /o/ to /u/ (the regular Venetian diminutive of Antonia was Tonina). Very interesting is *muiere* 'wife' (l. 9). This is a Venetian variant, confined in the documentation to the thirteenth and early fourteenth centuries, which was subsequently supplanted by the dominant form *muier* (later still *muger*). Piarini's use of it suggests a Muranese archaism. *Drio* 'behind, after', l. 9 (Tuscan, *dietro* ~ *drieto*) < DE RĒTRŌ seems unproblematic at first glance. As the normal term in Modern/Contemporary Venetian it is familiar to all Venetianists. However, in the Trecento *drio* is actually restricted to texts from the Veneto mainland, with *driedo* ~ *dredo* being the standard term in Venetian writing (see CI 14, l. 6; CI 63, l. 13). Again, we are likely to be in the presence of a specific Muranese preference. Venetian *conplio* (l. 12), the masculine singular past participle of *conplir* 'to carry out, accomplish, complete' (but note *acconpir* in l. 20), catches the eye with its total lenition of the Venetian -*ido* ending (< -ĪTUM) which was dominant in medieval Venetian writing and is universal in our corpus. Similar lenition of intervocalic /d/ in a past participle affects the feminine plural *tegnue* 'held', l. 2 (= Tuscan, *tenute*), whereas Venetian texts of the period prefer *tegnude*. That lenition affected the /d/ in everyday Venetian speech is indicated by the <dh> spelling sometimes present in manuscipt wills, but the complete voicing recorded by Piarini on these three participles is only rarely attested, and never features in writing for public display. Particularly fascinating is the hapax *conçero* (ll. 5, 8), with the meaning here of 'upkeep, maintenance', contrasting with *(a)conçamento* found in fourteenth-century texts from Venice itself. Vulgar Latin *COMPTIARE from CŌMERE 'to sort out, decorate' is the origin of Venetian *conçar* 'to arrange, settle, set right, maintain, repair, season' (Italian, *acconciare*). As for its noun derivatives, PRATI (1968, *s.v. conzar(e)*) cited *conza*, *conziero* and *conziér* for the Veneto, while Boerio recorded *conza* and *conzada* in Modern Venetian (BOERIO 1865, *s.vv.*). Piarini's *conçero* is probably, therefore, an undiphthongised and unattested form of *conziero* and was plausibly a Muranese variant, although another variant, *cunçer*, is also recorded on Murano in this period (FORMENTIN 2017: 132).

RECENT STUDIES: None. The only previous edition is in CICOGNA (1824–53, VI: 501–02).

Corpus Inscription 9

+ MCCCXLIIII DIE XII DE AVRIL QVESTA POSE|
SION FO CHOMENÇADA AL ONOR DEL OLTISIMO ₂|
DIO E DELA SOA DOLCE MARE BIATISIMA MADONA ₃|
S(AN)C(T)A MARIA DELA CHARITADE E P(ER) BEN E ONOR E DE|
STRO DE TVTI LI NOSTRI FRARI DELA SCVOLA DELI ₅|
BATVDI E FO (CHON)PLIDA DEL MESE DE ÇENER E TVTA ₆| LA POSESION FO
SCOMENÇADA E (CHON)PLIDA I(N) TENPO ₇|
DE MIS(R) MAFIO BISVOL DE SE(N) VIDAL VARDIAN DELA ₈|
DITA SCVOLA E (CON) TVTI LI SVO CHO(N)PAGNI FO CHON|
PLIDA E ROBORADA E DEL SACHO DE S(-NT)A MARIA E DELE ₁₀|
BORSE DELI BONI OMENI D‹E›LA SCVOLA FO PAGADA ₁₁

[+ Mcccxliiii, *die* xii de avril, questa posesion fo chomençada a l'onor del oltisimo Dio e dela soa dolce mare biatisima madona Sancta Maria dela Charitade, e per ben e onor e destro de tuti li nostri frari dela Scuola deli Batudi. E fo chonplida del mese de çener. E tuta la posesion fo scomençada e chonplida in tenpo de mis. Mafio Bisuol de Sen Vidal, vardian dela dita Scuola, e con tuti li suò chonpagni fo chonplida e roborada, e del sacho de S. Maria e dele borse deli boni omeni dela Scuola fo pagada.]

TRANSLATION: On the 12th *day* of April 1344 this property was begun in honour of God most high and of His sweet mother, the most blessed St Mary of Charity, and for the honour and benefit of all our brothers of the Flagellant Confraternity. It was completed in the month of January. The whole property was begun and completed during the time (in office) of Mr Mafio Bisuol of San Vidal, warden of the said Confraternity, and with all his colleagues it was completed and supported. It was paid for out of the fund of St Mary and out of the pockets of the good men of the Confraternity.

DATE: April 1344-January 1345 (January 1344, *more veneto*).

LOCATION: Displayed since the early nineteenth century in the cloisters of the Seminario Patriarcale near the Salute church in the *sestiere* of Dorsoduro. Originally it was hung in, or on the outside of, the Scuola Grande di S. Maria della Carità (now home to the Accademia galleries) in the same *sestiere*. The plaque is recorded twice in the seventeenth century as being on a wall inside the *scuola* at the top of the main staircase (SANSOVINO and STRINGA 1604: 195; MARTINELLI 1684: 404). Tassini located the inscription in the Seminario Patriarcale cloisters (TASSINI 1876: 115).

TYPE AND DESCRIPTION: Dedicatory and commemorative. The plaque measuring *c.* 62 × *c.* 38 cm is in Istrian stone with a simple, narrow strip frame. Its inscription in raised letters commemorates the building of the *scuola*'s original meeting hall (called its *albergo grande* in ASV, Scuola Grande di S. Maria della Carità, reg. 311, fol. 3) and its sponsors from within the brotherhood.

The flagellant confraternity of S. Maria della Carità, founded in 1260, was the

FIG. 3.8. CI 9. © A. S. Ferguson.

earliest of the Venetian penitential lay brotherhoods known later as *scolae magnae*. It seems to have started life in the church of S. Lunardo in the *sestiere* of Cannaregio, transferring subsequently to the oratory of S. Giacomo Apostolo on the Giudecca. Eventually it moved, via a series of acquisitions and concessions, to the monastery of the Augustinian canons in Dorsoduro beside the church of S. Maria della Carità where the brotherhood already had burial plots in the thirteenth century (CORNER 1758: 448–49) as well as provisional spaces for its activities. Here in 1344, as attested by the inscription, it built on land ceded to it by the monastery — in the area of the Campo della Carità looking towards the Rio San Trovaso — the original meeting hall of what was to become the splendid confraternity complex that is still in part intact today. After the Napoleonic suppressions in the early nineteenth century the former confraternity properties housed the Accademia di Belle Arti and, eventually, the Accademia art galleries. They are now home to the galleries alone, with the entrance hall and first gallery preserving the original *scuola* nucleus. The oldest *mariegole* of the confraternity can be consulted in the ASV at: Scuola Grande di S. Maria della Carità, reg. 233 (late thirteenth and early fourteenth centuries, in Latin), reg. 233 *bis* (fourteenth century, with parts which may be earlier, in Venetian), and reg. 243 (later fourteenth century, in Venetian). On this *scuola*, significant for its rich artistic sponsorship and for its vernacular inscriptional culture, see TASSINI (1876), PIGNATTI (1981: 27–40), GOY (2006: 118–25), GRAMIGNA and PERISSA (2008: 75–78), as well as CI 10, CI 11, CI 12, CI 14.

This is the first stone-cut inscription in the corpus from the *centro storico* of Venice for some thirty years (CI 4 was from *c*. 1312 and CI 8 of 1340 originated in Murano) and inaugurates the peak period of vernacular epigraphy in Venice in the central decades of the fourteenth century. There followed in rapid succession a series of high quality inscriptions with substantial texts emanating, above all, from the city's lay confraternities, great and small, and from the ecclesiastical authorities.

LETTERING: Gothic majuscules, 2.4 cm high, densely packed, vigorously uncialesque in aspect and elevated by around 0.3 cm from the plaque surface. This is the first example in the corpus of an inscription in raised lettering. To reveal the letters in relief involves a difficult, more labour-intensive and costly technique compared to incising them into the stone. That raising was a marker of prestige is attested by its earliest use in Venice, in the fourth decade of the Trecento, on the epitaphs of two ducal tombs: that of doge Francesco Dandolo (died 1339) in the chapter room of the Frari, and that on the tomb (*c.* 1342) of doge Bortolamio Gradenigo in the narthex of St Mark's. The closeness of dates between the Gradenigo relief epigraph and that at the Carità is unlikely to be a coincidence. Our vernacular inscription follows the aspect and carving of the letters on that ducal tomb, and even the strip framing, with such striking fidelity that we may actually be in the presence of the same stonecutter. On the inscriptional importance of the Gradenigo tomb see PINCUS (2019: 320–21).

The 11 lines of the text are neatly and tightly carved on the inscription tablet. There is a strenuous attempt to achieve justification on both sides, leading to some right-side overlap on to the frame. Although gaps between words are generally provided, the textual density — with interlinear spacing only around a third of the average height of the lettering, and with limited gaps between words — is an impediment to immediate legibility, in spite of being aesthetically attractive. This problem is compounded by the manner in which the raising of the letters has made them more full bodied than would otherwise have been the case. There are no interpuncts or other punctuation marks in the text. The inscription block is largely undamaged, probably thanks to centuries spent indoors.

In themselves the letters remain perfectly clear and the stonecutter has made only one mistake: the <e> in *dela* (l. 11) appears as <c> because the lateral stroke which would have identified the former from the latter has been omitted by oversight. Especially prominent are the heavy closing hairstrokes on <c> and <e> extending below the baseline; the long tapering downstrokes on <t>; the vertical pointed serifs on <s>; the two-thirds-high parallel upstrokes on <l>; and the almond-shaped <o>. The <a> features a bulging left stem, a short diagonal crossbar and a left-inclined, generally rising, topstroke. Noticeable is the particular cutting of the cedilla on *chomençada* (l. 2) and *scomençada* (l. 7), with a tapering understroke on the <c> intersected at a diagonal. This unusual cedilla form reappears on CI 14 from the same confraternity. The <u/v> is always straight-stemmed, with strong flaring on the terminals. Ligatures are used for <al>, <an> and <ar>, while the <chon> in *chonplida* (ll. 6, 7) is abbreviated with the Tironian 9 symbol. The inscription is preceded by a partly effaced *signum crucis*. The symbol of the confraternity, the circle within a circle intersected by a Greek cross, is sculpted in relief at the bottom corners of the plaque, with representations of the flagellation paddle and whip inserted between them along the bottom.

LANGUAGE: A terminologically interesting inscription. On *posesion* 'property' (ll. 1–2, 7) see CI 8, CI 21. *Scuola* 'confraternity' (ll. 5, 11) is diphthongised here for the first time in the corpus. *Frari* (l. 5) 'brothers' (l. 5) < FRATRES — singular *frar* 'brother' < FRATREM (see CI 13, l. 10) — shows the normal Venetian lenition of intervocalic -TR- to /r/, as does *mare* 'mother' (l. 3) < MATREM. *Frari* and *fradeli* 'brothers or brethren' coexist in Early Venetian in both senses of the word. *Frari* only survives in Contemporary Venetian as the designation of the city's great Franciscan church. *Vardian* (or *vardian grando*), l. 8, used here and in other inscriptions apart from CI 3 and CI 108 which have *guardian*, was the warden, the highest official in a *scuola grande*. It shows the regular Early Venetian outcome in /v/ of Germanic /w/. *Sacho*, literally 'sack' (l. 10), was the common fund of the confraternity and contrasts with *borse* (l. 11), literally 'bags', in other words 'purses', of the individual members. *Sen* 'saint' (l. 8), rather than *san*, is the first explicit appearance in the corpus of the variant in <en> that predominated in fourteenth-century Venetian. The female equivalent appears here in two abbreviated guises. The first (l. 4) indicates the presence of a <c> so I have opened it out as *sancta*. The second omits the <c> and is probably in the vernacular form. I have left a gap in my transcription to indicate that it may be *santa* or *senta*. Two terms appearing nowhere else in the corpus are: *destro* 'opportunity, advantage' (ll. 4–5) < DEXTERUM 'propitious', and *roborada* (l. 10), from the infinitive *roborar* 'to support, strengthen, firm up, confirm' < RŌBŎRARE, a semi-learned form attested in other Italo-Romance varieties and corresponding to Early Modern English *corroborate* which had the same meanings.

Syntactically noteworthy is the succession of passives with past historic *fo* 'was' (ll. 2, 6, 7, 9–10, 11) showing consistent feminine singular agreement of the past participle with preceding *posesion*. Full agreement in the passive construction is the usual, but not exclusive, situation in the corpus and appears to occur irrespective of whether the noun precedes the past participle as here or follows it, as is the case in the majority of instances. On the complex issues involved in determining passive agreement in the early Italo-Romance vernaculars, including the relative position of the noun involved, see BENUCCI (2009a). *Questa* 'this' (l. 1) is the first of a long series of deictics or pointing words in the corpus (*questo* ~ *sto* ~ *(s)sta* ~ *la presente*), inevitable in the inscriptional context. A series of characteristic Venetian phonological traits are exemplified in the inscription. *Avril* April (l. 1) < APRĪLIS, with the normal Venetian voicing of intervocalic -PR- > /vr/, is the native form of the month which dominated most of Early Venetian (see also CI 23, CI 27, CI 29) but was gradually replaced towards the end of the period and in Middle Venetian by the more Latinising and Italianate *april* (as in CI 79, CI 92). *Chomençada* (l. 2) and *scomençada* (l. 7) 'begun' (the second variant with the Venetian reinforcing *s-*) have, as expected, the <ç> which in Early Venetian was, we assume, an unvoiced (as here) or a voiced dental affricate of the /ts/ or /dz/ type (ALINEI 1984: 242–45). Sometimes the expected cedilla under the <c> is missing in the corpus. Occasionally this may be down to a lapse by the stonecutter, but more often it appears (as in *dolce*, l. 3) to be motivated by a Latinising spelling. *Charitade* 'charity' (l. 4) < CĀRĬTATEM shows the conservative noun ending in *-ade* < -ĀTEM that dominates the corpus (see CI 2). *Oltisimo* 'most high' (l. 2) is the first example in the collection of the strong Early Venetian tendency to raise /al/ to /ol/ before a dental consonant. *Biatisima* 'most blessed' (l. 3), compared to Italian *beatissima*, shows the raising of pre-tonic /e/ to /i/. Mafio Bisuol (l. 8) from the parish of S. Vidal (Italian, S. Vitale) was, according to TASSINI (1876: 115), from an ancient citizen family.

RECENT STUDIES: STUSSI (1997a: 169); FERGUSON (2013c: 86–87); DI LENARDO (2014: 92–97); FERGUSON (2015c: 41–42). One of the first inscriptions in the corpus to appear in a printed book (SANSOVINO and STRINGA 1604: 195), this prestigious epigraph has been regularly recorded ever since.

Corpus Inscriptions 10, 11, 12

·M·C·C·C·XLV · I(N) LO TENPO DE · MIS(R) · MARCHO · ÇVLIA(N) · FO FATO ·
QVESTO · LAVORER

[MCCCXLV, in lo tenpo de mis. Marcho Çulian, fo fato questo lavorer.]

M°· CCC° · LXXVII° · FO FATO · QVESTO · LAVORIER · ₁| AL ONOR · DE DIO · E DELAVERGENE · MARIA· E D(E)L GLORI|OXO · CHONFESOR · MIS(R) · SEN · LVNARDO · E IN · MEMVO|RIA · DE TVTI · CHE · IN LO SO · SANTO DI · FO · CHOMEN|ÇADA · E CREADA · QVESTA · SANTA · FRATIRNITA|DE · E SCHVOLA :· 6

[MCCCLXXVII fo fato questo lavorier al onor de Dio e dela Vergene Maria e del glorioxo chonfesor mis. Sen Lunardo, e in memuoria de tuti che in lo so santo dì fo chomençada e creada questa santa fratirnitade e schuola.]

M° CC[C]LXXX IIII · DEL·MEXE · DE [ÇE]NER [F]O FATO · STO · LAVORIER

[MCCCLXXXIIII, del mexe de çener, fo fato sto lavorier.]

TRANSLATIONS: CI 10: This piece of work was made in 1345 when Mr Marcho Çulian was in office.

CI 11: This piece of work was made in 1377 to honour God, the Virgin Mary and the glorious confessor my Lord St Leonard, and to remember all those who were around on his holy day when this holy brotherhood and *scuola* was begun and created.

CI 12: This piece of work was made in January 1384.

DATES: 1345, 1377 and 1384 (January 1385 by modern reckoning).

LOCATION: Campo de la Carità, no. 1050 (*sestiere* of Dorsoduro), on the façade of the Accademia.

TYPE AND DESCRIPTION: Declarative and commemorative. The three inscriptions are located, separately, along the bottom of a trio of fourteenth-century devotional relief shrines in Istrian stone. These sculptures, installed over an extended period, form an attractive and artistically important ensemble on the façade of the former Scuola di S. Maria della Carità, now part of the Accademia galleries, over the main entrance between the *scuola* and the converted Carità church immediately to its left. The oldest and most elaborate shrine, the aedicule with CI 10, is sculpted in high relief and measures *c.* 250 × *c.* 140 cm. The earliest recorded devotional relief commissioned by a *scuola grande*, it is placed high up on the building frontage above the entrance door. It consists of a large niche with pitched canopy on spiral columns containing an enthroned Madonna and Child sitting within a gilded frame and surrounded by gold stars: the whole is enclosed in a castellated frame. Two angels on pedestals each bear a candlestick while two other flying angels crown the Virgin who cradles the lively Child on her knee. Confraternity brothers kneel at her feet in prayer. Under the apex is the gilded symbol of the *scuola* and a large-scale gilded

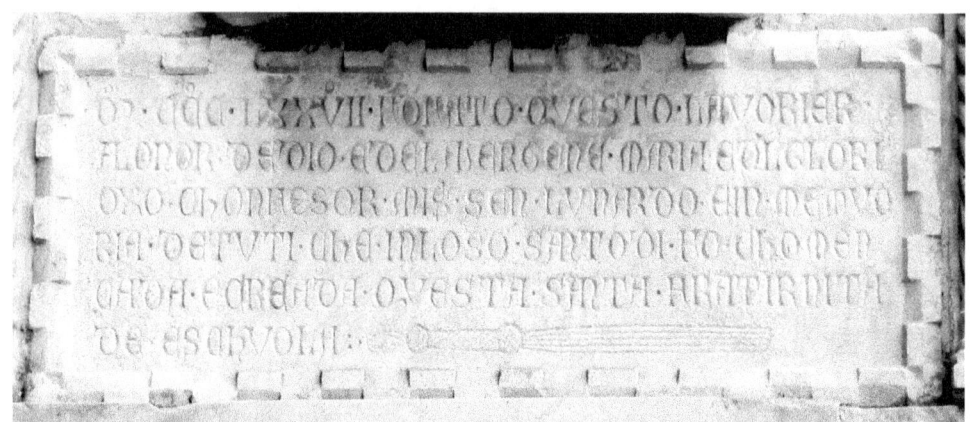

FIG. 3.9. CI 11. © A. S. Ferguson.

relief inscription, *Virgo Maria*, denoting the dedication of shrine and confraternity to the Virgin Mary. This impressive and highly visible epigraph is cut in massive, sober Gothic majuscules featuring a remarkable Greek-style <m>. CI 10 is carved in a single line along the narrow concave lower rim of the niche. This aedicule is almost certainly not exactly in situ. Commissioned in 1345 during the first major expansion of the *scuola* (see CI 9) it may have been relocated to its present site, high over the entrance, after the addition of an upper floor to the confraternity meeting house post-1384.

This shrine is flanked, lower down the façade, by the other two which are more likely to be in situ. These are *c.* 260 cm above ground level, *c.* 250 cm high and *c.* 110 cm along the base. Both consist of niches, similar in format, with spiral columns and lobed ogival canopies decorated with two symbols of the *scuola* and, at the apex, a sculpted face which may be a representation of the Holy Visage. Each niche houses the standing figure of a saint. On the left is the shrine to St Leonard, in low relief. The haloed saint, dressed in a friar's habit, clutches in one hand what appears to be a papal cross and, in the other, ankle fetters symbolising his dedication to the freeing of prisoners. Two tiny confraternity brothers kneel at his feet. CI 11 is cut within a rectangular plaque, with crenellated frame (100 × 42 cm), below the ledge on which the saint stands. On the right, a low relief depicts St Christopher with staff in hand ferrying the Christ Child across the river on his shoulders. CI 12 is cut into the narrow lower edge of this niche which is chipped in several places. Part of the date was already illegible when the inscription was transcribed by Cicogna in his notebooks (BMC, mss Cicogna, *Inedite* 2008, *busta* 499, no. 10). There is critical agreement that all three of the façade reliefs are fourteenth century and that CI 12 is dateable to 1384 (DORIGO 2003, I: 547; RIZZI 1987: 465) when the confraternity's *albergo* room was originally constructed. The parallel upstroke on the arm of an <l> (= 50), just visible before the three <x>s in enlarged high-resolution photographs of the inscription, confirms the 1384 date. The long-running restoration work on the complex, which closed off the façade to public view, was completed in 2014.

Fig. 3.10. CI 11 in context. © A. S. Ferguson.

Fig. 3.11. CI 10 in context. © A. S. Ferguson.

Fig. 3.12. CI 10. © A. S. Ferguson.

LETTERING: CI 10: Gothic majuscules cut in V-section. Worn overall and damaged on several letters (the abbreviated <s> of *mis(r)* and the <q> of *questo*) the script, around 2.5 cm high and tendentially similar in ductus to that of the 1377 and 1384 inscriptions below, is still fairly legible. CI 11: Gothic majuscules cut in V-section. Neat, soberly elegant, well-spaced, finely chiselled uncialesque script averaging 3 cm in height. The text is justified on the left, with interpuncts separating words or syntagms. It is slightly worn overall, but undamaged and perfectly legible. Particularly attractive are the sinuous ligatures involving <a> with following <r> or <n>, and the very unusual combination of <a> fused with following <u/v> — showing right-sided curvature — in *dela Vergene* (l. 2), with articulated preposition and noun run together. All other examples of <u/v> in the inscription are straight-stemmed. The sinuosity of the digraphs is picked up by the limb of the three examples of <h>, curling below the baseline, by the fine flared hairstrokes on <e> and <f>, and by the undulating tail on the <q> of *questo* (l. 1) and *questa* (l. 5). The cedilla in *chomençada* (ll. 4–5) has an unusual kinked left tilt like that of *Çulian* in the 1345 inscription. The three superscript ordinal <o>s on the date are actually cut above the digits. The end of the inscription is punctuated by a period consisting of three dots — in other words, a raised colon followed by a centred bullet point. The remaining space on the final line is completed by a horizontal relief of a whip used for flagellation, with the bunched thongs and textured handle neatly and realistically delineated. One senses the commissioner's collaboration in the pagination and regularity of this inscription. CI 12: Gothic majuscules cut in V-section. The writing, averaging 2.5 cm in height, is worn and the inscription rim is badly damaged in places, with some letters missing altogether. It can only be read fully, with care, in close up.

LANGUAGE: *Lavorer* or *lavorier* 'work, piece of work, artefact', a much used term in our collection, appears in all three inscriptions, with the still undiphthongised form in CI 10 unique in the corpus. It is the vernacular equivalent of the Venetian medieval Latin LABORERIUM 'building work(s), building site, (piece of) work' which is frequently employed in legal and administrative documents. In the case of all three epigraphs the term almost certainly refers, in part at least, to the accompanying sculpture, although the dates of CI 10 and CI 12 also coincide with the *scuola*'s major building campaigns in the Trecento. *Sen* in CI 11 (l. 3) contrasts interestingly with the <a> variants *santo* ~ *santa* in CI 11 (ll. 4 and 5). *Lunardo* in CI 11 (l. 3) is the normal Venetian form of Leonard (Italian, Leonardo). With *memuoria* (ll. 3–4) and *schuola* (l. 6) CI 11 illustrates the diphthongisation of stressed mid-high vowels that swept through Venetian in the second half of the fourteenth century. *Çener* (January) in CI 12 is the normal Early Venetian form with final vowel apocope and initial voiced affricate. For *fratirnitade* in CI 11 (ll. 5–6), rather than the more usual *fraternitade*, see CI 14 where *mortilitade* and *mortalitade* 'death rate' coexist in the same text, and also CI 42. All three of the present inscriptions have passive constructions with past historic *fo*. These show full agreement, as one would expect, between past participle and a masculine singular noun.

RECENT STUDIES: Rizzi (1987: 465–66); Ferguson (2013c: 87–88); Ferguson (2015b: 43–44). The three inscriptions were recorded but not published by Cicogna. They were first published as a group in Ferro (1889). CI 10 and the relief above were first recorded by Grevembroch (1754, I: fol. 19).

Corpus Inscription 13

:+: ANO D(OMI)NI · M·CCC·XLVI · I(N) LA FES |
TA · DE OGNASA(N)TI · I(N) LO TE(N)PO · DEL · ₂|
I(N)CLITO · SIGNOR · MIS(R) · ANDREA · DA(N)DO |
LO · DOXE · D(E) · VENIEXIA · E DEL · REVE |
RE(N)DO · I(N) CH(RIST)O · PARE · MIS(R) · NICOLO MORE |
XINI · VESCOVO · D(E) VENEXIA · FO METV |
DA · LA · PRIMA · PIERA · DE Q(VE)STA · B(E)N(E)DETA ₇|
GLIEXIA · DE · MIS(R) · S(AN)C(T)O · ANTONIO · D(E) · VIENA ₈|
E CHANTADA · LA · PRIMA · MESA · E FO DADO ₉|
LO DITO · LVOGO · P(ER) LO · ONESTO RELIGI |
OSO · MIS(R) · FRAR · GIOTO · DELI ABATI · DE FL |
ORE(N)CIA · DEL ORDENE · DE MIS(-R) · S(AN)C(T)O · AN |
TONIO · DE VIENA · PRIMO · PRIOR · E FO(N)DA |
DORE · DEL DITO · LVOGO · SIA(N)DO · LI NO |
| BELI E SAVII · SIGNORI · MIS(R) LORE/VCIO · MIN |
IO E MIS(R) · CHR(IST)OFALO · ISTRIGO⁺ E MIS(R) · ÇA |
NE BECI(N) · E MIS(R) · GIRARDO DELI NEVODI ₁₇|
E MIS(R) · NICHOLO · MAGNO · P(ER)CHURADORI |
DELO · DITO · LVOGO · P(ER) LIQVAL · SIA · SE(N) |
P(RE) FATA · ORACIO(N) · E P(ER) TVTI · QVELI LIQV |
AL · A DADO · E · CHE · DARA · DELI SVO · BE |
NI · P(ER) LEVAR · QVESTA · BENEDETA · GLIEXIA |
+ E MIS(R) · MARCHO CHATAPAN · E MIS(R) VIELMO · STRACAROL ₂₃

[+ Ano Domini Mcccxlvi in la festa de Ognasanti, in lo tenpo del inclito signor mis. Andrea Dandolo, Doxe de Veniexia, e del reverendo in Christo pare mis. Nicolò Morexini, vescovo de Venexia, fo metuda la prima piera de questa benedeta gliexia de mis. Sancto Antonio de Viena e chantada la prima mesa. E fo dado lo dito luogo per lo onesto religioso mis. frar Gioto deli Abati de Florencia de l'ordene de mis. Sancto Antonio de Viena, primo prior e fondadore del dito luogo, siando li nobeli e savii signori mis. Lorencio Minio e mis. Christofalo Istrigo⁺ e mis. Çane Becin e mis. Girardo deli Nevodi e mis. Nicholò Magno perchuradori delo dito luogo. Per liqual sia senpre fata oracion e per tuti queli liqual a dado e che darà deli suò beni per levar questa benedeta gliexia. + e mis. Marcho Chatapan e mis. Vielmo Stracarol.]

TRANSLATION: In the year of Our Lord 1346, on All Saints' day, in the time (in office) of the illustrious nobleman Sir Andrea Dandolo, Doge of Venice, and of the reverend in Christ Father Sir Nicolò Morexini, Bishop of Venice, the first stone was laid of this blessed church of my Lord St Anthony of Vienne, and the first mass was said. And the said site was given over to that honest man of God Friar Giotto degli Abati of Florence of the order of St Anthony of Vienne. He was first prior and founder of the said site whose proctors at the time were the noble and

FIG. 3.13. CI 13. © A. S. Ferguson.

wise gentlemen Mr Lorencio Minio, Mr Christofalo Istrigo[+], Mr Çane Becin and Mr Nicholò Magno. May prayers always be offered to these men and to all others who contributed, or will contribute, from their own funds to raising this blessed church. + as well as Mr Marcho Chatapan and Mr Vielmo Straçarol.

DATE: 1346.

LOCATION: Since the early nineteenth century the artefact has been in the cloister of the Seminario Patriarcale at the Salute (*sestiere* of Dorsoduro). Originally it was displayed at the church of S. Antonio Abate, also known as S. Antonio di Castello (Venetian, S. Antonio de Castelo), on the far edge of the *sestiere* of Castello. CICOGNA (1824–53, I: 159–60) located it on a wall near the sacristy of the church. Giovanni Francesco PIVATI (1746–51, X: 116) placed it near the door of the sacristy, as did SANSOVINO (1581: 6v).

TYPE AND DESCRIPTION: Dedicatory and commemorative. The 23-line inscription is on two large, white conjoined marble slabs with no frame. Together the two plaques measure 145 × 96 cm. The line dividing the marble, at around two thirds of the total length of the artefact, is clearly man-made but we do not know if it was there *ab initio* or if it was cut later. When Cicogna transcribed the inscription in the early nineteenth century it was already split. The object is exceptionally well preserved, with little deterioration either of the plaque or the text, and the magnificent epigraph is perfectly legible.

The existence of the church, with its monastery, was down originally to the Marc(h)o C(h)atapan and Christofalo Istrigo mentioned in the inscription. Having obtained from the authorities in 1334 a plot of marshland facing the island of S. Elena (Venetian, S. Lena) on the far eastern side of Venice they reclaimed it (ASV, Grazie, reg. 6, fol. 18). Istrigo went on to build a house there with official permission. He later offered the plot to Giotto degli Abati for him to found a church and monastery on it dedicated to S. Antonio Abate (CARACCIOLO ARICÒ 2007–09, II: 23–24). The first stone was laid in 1346 and Giotto was made prior of the monastery. The complex was completed around 1360 and is clearly delineated and labelled on de' Barbari's woodcut view of Venice (CI 85, l. 8). The inside of the church is depicted in Carpaccio's painting of *Prior Ottobon's vision of the ten thousand Christian martyrs at S. Antonio di Castello* (*c.* 1515) now at the Accademia in Venice. The people thanked in the inscription all contributed to the realisation of the project. They are probably the five laymen seen kneeling in bas relief before St Anthony on a plaque originally displayed in the church and now kept in the Pinacoteca Manfrediana at the Seminario Patriarcale. In 1471 the Augustinian canons regular withdrew from the monastery to be replaced by the canons regular of S. Salvatore in Bologna, and in 1476–1503 the hospital of St Anthony (or of *Miser Iesu Christo*) for indigent naval servicemen was founded at the instigation of the state. The subsequent history of the complex is outlined in CICOGNA (1824–53, I: 159–60) and in TASSINI (1863: 31–32).

This is the first inscription in the corpus to have appeared in a printed book, being one of the very few vernacular epigraphs, among numerous Latin ones, transcribed by Francesco SANSOVINO (1581: 6v-7r) in his influential guidebook of Venice.

Remarkably, it was published in Lorenz SCHRADER's *Monumentorum Italiæ* (1592: 302r), the only vernacular inscription from Venice that he included. It was also copied by MARTINELLI (1684: 89–90) in his guidebook of Venice, and by PIVATI in his ten-volume encyclopaedia (1746–51, X: 116). The first correct, diplomatic, reading was Cicogna's.

LETTERING: Gothic majuscules engraved in V-section. The lettering is exceptionally large, averaging 5 × 4 cm so almost square in scale, and very striking. It is rigorously laid out within the notional baselines and headlines. The cut of the letters is deep and the groove thickness is expertly modulated. The effect of the contrasted strokes is to create subtle variations of light and shade, giving each letter an attractive variety and unusual sharpness. In fact the script stands out so well against the white background of the marble that it seems almost to be infilled in black. This clarity, allied to the large size of the lettering and to the discrete interpuncts, is important for the overall legibility of the text. It compensates in some measure for the negligible space between letters, which occasionally encroach on their neighbours, and for the highly sophisticated calligraphic aspect of the lettering. Venetian Gothic epigraphic script is here at its most decoratively uncialesque. This is arguably the most aesthetically pleasing, if not the most immediately readable, incised inscription in the corpus.

The text, which is preceded by a *signum crucis* lightly studded with four single interpuncts between the arms of the cross (as in CI 30, another ecclesiastical epigraph), is justified on both sides and fully fills the inscription surface. The exemplary *ordinatio* of the plaque is marginally disturbed at the bottom. Here the writing looks a little cramped because the final line, slightly smaller in font size, was clearly added as an afterthought at the instigation of the commissioner(s) when it was realised that two of the sponsors' names had been overlooked, and when there was minimal space remaining. A plain cross was therefore added in superscript, like an asterisk, after the name *Istrigo* (l. 16). A similar normal-sized cross was then inserted, followed by the missing text, at the foot of the second slab. This type of insertion or footnote procedure is found on only one other stone inscription in the corpus (CI 95).

A number of recurring features stand out. Ligatures involving <a> and a following consonant are common, while the systematic use of abbreviations is particularly noticeable. The horizontal suspension bar is employed for nasals and, more rarely, <e> and the <u> of <qu>; the barred <p> stands for *per(-)*. The suspension bar appears to be missing on *Lorencio* (l. 15) although it may simply have been obliterated when the plaque was cut in two. I have restored the missing <n> in italics. Very distinctive is the elegant wavy diagonal 7 indicating abbreviated *-er* or *-ier* on *miser* or *misier* ' Sir, Mr'. I use *mis(r)* in my transcription as there is no evidence to settle the matter either way. The <ch> digram for velar /k/ predominates although *Nicholo* (l. 18) alternates with *Nicolo* (l. 5). The cedilla for the affricate sound is present in *Çane* (ll. 16–17) but not in *oracion* (l. 20) and *Stracarol* (l. 23). The first omission is unsurprising in a learned word, while the second may be due to the constraints of space at the bottom of the plaque. The letters <c> and <e> are closed with delicate outward-curving hairstrokes. The hairstroke on the <f> flares out and reaches two thirds of the way down, while the downstrokes on the <t> are long and spiky. The left stem of the <a> is so inclined that its foot is lifted clear of the baseline. The looped ascender of the uncial <d> is stylishly kinked before descending vertically almost to the baseline. Outstandingly beautiful are the splayed filigree serifs on <g> and <s>, and the <m> with billowing, closed left loop in the date and on *mis(r)* (l. 3).

LANGUAGE: The solemn, official nature of the plaque is underlined by a trio of invocations: Andrea Dandolo doge of Venice, Nicolò Morexini bishop of Castello — called here, as he probably was in common parlance, bishop of Venice — and St Anthony of Vienne to whom the church is dedicated. The elevated tone is also conveyed by the citing of the noble Florentine, Giotto degli Abati, prior of the Augustinian canons regular of St Antoine de Vienne in the Dauphinois, to whom the complex of buildings is given over, and by the listing of the patrons, designated as *nobeli e savii* 'noble and wise', who were the proctors of the site: *perchuradori* (l. 18). This recurring term in the corpus shows metathesis on the first syllable and, regular lenition of intervocal T > /d/. In keeping is the religious vocabulary: *festa de Ognasanti* 'All Saint's Day', *reverendo* 'reverend', *benedeta gliexia* 'blessed church', *chantada la prima mesa* 'the first mass [was] sung', *onesto religioso* 'honest man of religion', *oracion* 'prayer'.

The drift in fourteenth-century Venetian towards diphthongisation of stressed mid-high vowels can be seen in *luogo* 'place' (ll. 10, 14) and *piera* 'stone' (l. 7), but *Venexia* (l. 6) stands alongside *Veniexia* Venice (l. 4). *Ordene* 'order' (l. 12) and *nobeli* 'noble' (ll. 14–15) show normal Venetian lowering of the post-tonic vowel compared to Tuscan/Italian. *Pare* 'father' (l. 5) and *piera* (l. 7), with the usual reduction of -TR- to /r/, remain normal in Venetian today. *Metuda*, ll. 6–7 (Italian, *messa*) is the regular Early Venetian past participle of *meter* 'to put'. On the normal gerund form *siando* (l. 14) of *eser* 'to be' see CI 2, CI 3, CI 28. Noteworthy is the complete agreement in gender and number in the passive construction (*fo metuda la prima piera*, ll. 6–7) which is not always the case in Early Venetian texts. See FERGUSON (2015c: 66) and, for the wider early Italo-Romance context of the passive, BENUCCI (2009a). It is noticeable that in the overwhelming majority of passives in the corpus the word order, as here, is participle followed by noun (see CI 9). *Levar* (l. 22) is 'to raise' in the sense of 'to build'. It is likely that Early Venetian *gliexia* 'church' (ll. 8 and 22) < ECCLĒSĬAM was pronounced either with an unvoiced palatal as [tʃezja] or with a voiced palatal as [dʒezja]. Other Early Venetian spellings are *glesia* (CI 14, l. 4), *glexia* (CI 8, ll. 5, 8, 11), *clesia*, *giesia* and *chiexia*. The Modern/Contemporary Venetian pronunciation, influenced by Italian *chiesa*, is [tʃeza]. *Doxe* 'doge' (l. 4) has the familiar Venetian <x> for the voiced sibilant /z/ (see CI 19). The relatives *liqual* 'who(m)' (ll. 19–21) are the first examples of syntactic recurrence in the corpus (see CI 23, CI 30, CI 63, CI 64). Interesting is the attempt to maintain the original Tuscan phonology — minus the double consonants which are un-Venetian — in the name *Gioto deli Abati* (l. 11). It may be this Tuscan influence that led to the unexpected spelling *fondadore* 'founder' (ll. 13–14), without the normal Venetian apocope of the final <e>. However, on the prior's tomb cited below he is, as expected, called *fondador*, while *Gioto* has been further Venetianised to *Çoto*, with a voiced affricate. The surname *Istrigo* means 'from Istria' and was particularly concentrated in the parish of S. Barnaba (*sestiere* of Dorsoduro). *Vielmo* William (l. 23), from Germanic *Willihelm*, is an Early Venetian equivalent of Italian Guglielmo. *Morexini* (ll. 5–6) is the commonest Early Venetian spelling of Morosini (see CI 39). The Venetian surname *Straçarol* (l. 23), from *straça* 'rag', means a dealer in second-hand goods or a rag-and-bone man. The stressed /o/, here, has yet to be affected by diphthongisation. Equally colourful is *Chatapan* (l. 23), from Venetian *c(h)atar* 'to get, to grab, to earn' and *pan* 'bread'. CICOGNA (1824–53, I: 159–60) provides useful information about all the characters mentioned in the inscription.

Giotto degli Abati died in 1381. His tombstone, originally on the floor of the sacristy in the church but now lost, was carved with a relief of him holding a church in one hand and a book in the other. The frame strip carried a vernacular inscription, not seen at first hand by Cicogna, but recorded by PIVATI (1746–51, X: 117). I transcribe it from him, with due caution, removing the capitals and punctuation which cannot have been on the original, changing the <z> on Giotto's name to <ç> (on the basis of his transcription of the other epigraph), and altering *il qual* to *el qual*: MCCCLXXXI *adi 11 de avril qui e sepeli misier fra Çoto de li Abati [...] el qual fo fondador primo prior e governador de questo monestier del ordene de sancto Antonio de Viena cujus anima requiescat in paxe preca per eum amen.*

RECENT STUDIES: NIERO (1965); FERGUSON (2013c: 89–91); DI LENARDO (2014: 104–09); PINCUS (2016: 243–45). First published in SANSOVINO (1581: 6v-7r).

Corpus Inscription 14

INOME · DE · DIO · ETERNO · E DELABIADA · VERGENE · MARIA IN LANO · DELA INCARNACION ₁| DEL NOSTRO · SIGNOR · MISER IH(ESV)M CR(IST)O · M · CCC · XLVII · ADI · XXV · DE · ÇENER · LO ₂| DI · DELA CO(N)VERSIO(N) D(E) S(EN) · POLO · CERCA · ORA · D(E) BESPERO FO · GRAN · TARAMOTO · I(N) · VENIEXIA · E Q ₃| VASI P(ER) TVTO · EL · MO(N)DO · E CAÇE · MOLTE · CIME · DE · CANPANILI · E CASE · E CAMINI · E LA · GLESIA · DE ₄| SE(N) BASEIO · E FO · SI GRAN · SPAVE(N)TO · CHE · QVAXI · TVTA · LA · ÇE(N)TE · PENSAVA · D(E) · MORIR · E NO ST(E)TE ₅| LA TERA · DE · TREMAR · CERCA · DI · XL · E PVO · DRIEDO · QVESTO · COME(N)ÇA · UNA · GRAN · MORTILITAD(E) ₆| E MORIA · LA ÇE(N)TE · D(E) · DIVERSE · MALATIE · E NASIO(N) · ALGVNI · SPVDAVA · SANGVE · P(ER) · LABOCA · E ALGVNI ·₇| VEGNIVA · GLANDVXE · SOTO · LI SCAII · E ALE LENÇENE · E ALGVNI VEGNIA · LO MAL · DEL CARBO(N) · P(ER) · LE CARNE · E PA | REVA · CHE · Q(VE)STI · MALI · SE PIASE · LVN · DALOLTRO · ÇOE · LI SANI · DALINFERMI · (E) · ERA LA ÇE(N)TE · I(N) · TANTO · SPAV | E(N)TO · CHEL · PARE · NO UOLEVA · ANDAR · DAL · FIO · NEL FIO · DAL · PARE · E DURA · Q(VE)STA MORTALITA‹D›E · CERCA · MEXI ₁₀| UI · E SI SE DISEVA · COMVNA · ME(N)TRE · CHE LIERA MORTO · BE(N) LE · DO PARTE · D(E)LA ÇE(N)TE · D(E) VENIEXIA · ET · I(N) · Q(VE)STO · TE(N) | PO · SE TROUA · ESER · UARDIA(N) D(E) Q(VE)STA · SCOLA · MISER · PIERO · TRIUISA(N) · D(E) BARBARIA · E UIUE · CERCA · MEXI · II E MORI ₁₂| ELLO · E CERCA · X · DI SOI · (CON)PAGNI · E CO(N) PLU · DE · CCC DE Q(VE)LI · D(E) Q(VE)STA · SCOLA · E FO LA SCOLA · IN · GRAN · DEROTA E ₁₃| PVO · ADI · XX · D(E) · ÇVGNO · FO FATO · UARDIAN · MISER · IACOMO · BON · DALA ÇVDECHA · ANCORA · IN · QVESTO AÑO ₁₄| AVE · LI FEDEL · CRISTIANI · VNA · GRANDISIMA · GARCIA · DA · MISER · LO PAPA · CHE · IN · ÇASCADVNA · PARTE · ₁₅| CHE · LI MORIA · CONTRITI · DE · LI SOI · PECADI · DAL DI · DELA · ASENSION · DE · CRISTO · IN · FINA · AL DI · DE ₁₆| SENTA · MARIA · MADALENA · SENÇA · PENA · ANDESE · ALA · GLORIA · DE · VITA · ETERNA · ALAQVAL SI NDE ₁₇| CON[DV]GA · LO · ONIPOTE(N)TE · DIO · PARE · E FIOL · SP(I)RI(T)O · S(AN)C(T)O · LOQVAL · VIUE · E REGNA · IN · S(E)C(V)LA · S(E)C(V)LO(R)U(M) · AMEN ₁₈

[Inome de Dio eterno e dela biada Vergene Maria, in l'ano dela incarnacion del nostro signor miser Ihesum Cristo MCCCXLVII, adì xxv de çener — lo dì dela conversion de Sen Polo — cerca ora de besporo fo gran taramoto in Veniexia e quasi per tuto el mondo. E caçé molte cime de canpanili, e case e camini, e la glesia de sen Baseio. E fo sì gran spavento che quaxi tuta la çente pensava de morir. E no stete la tera de tremar cerca dì XL. E può, driedo questo, començà una gran mortilitade. E moria la çente de diverse malatie e nasion. Alguni spudava sangue per la boca; e alguni vegniva glanduxe soto li scaii e ale lençene; e alguni vegnia lo mal del carbon per le carne. E pareva che questi mali se piase l'un da l'oltro, çoè li sani da l'infermi. E era la çente in tanto spavento ch'el pare no voleva andar dal fio né 'l fio dal pare. E durà questa mortalitade cerca mesi VI, e sì se diseva comunamentre che l'iera morto ben le do parte dela çente de Veniexia. Et in questo tenpo se trovà eser vardian de questa scola miser Piero Trivisan de Barbaria. E vivé cerca mesi II, e morì ello e cerca X di soi conpagni e con plu de CCC de queli de questa scola. E fo la scola in gran derota. E può, adì XX de çugno, fo fato vardian

FIG. 3.14. CI 14 in context. © Ronnie Ferguson.

miser Iacomo Bon dala Çudecha. Ancora in questo ano ave li fedel cristiani una grandisima garcia da miser lo Papa: che in çascaduna parte che li moria contriti deli soi pecadi dal dì dela asension de Cristo in fina al dì de Senta Maria Madalena sença pena andese ala gloria de vita eterna. Ala qual sì nde conduga lo onipotente Dio — Pare e Fiol, Spirito Sancto — lo qual vive e regna *in secula seculorum*. Amen.]

TRANSLATION: In the name of God everlasting and of the blessed Virgin Mary, in the year of the incarnation of our Lord Jesus Christ 1347, on the 25th of January — the day of Saint Paul's conversion — around evening time there was a great earthquake in Venice and almost the world over. And many tops of belltowers fell, as did houses and chimneys and the church of San Baseio. And such was the fright that everybody thought they would die. And the earth did not stop shaking for 40 days. And then, after this, people began to die in great numbers. And people from all over died of all sorts of illnesses. Some spat up blood; some got swollen lymph nodes in their armpits and groin; and some got carbuncles on their flesh. And it looked like these diseases were caught from one person to the next, that is from the sick to the healthy. And people were so frightened that the father did not want to go to the son, nor the son to the father. And this wave of deaths lasted about 6 months, and it was said commonly that a good two thirds of the people of Venice had died. And at this time it happened that the warden of this *scuola* was Mr Piero Trivisan from Barbaria. And he survived around 2 months and he died with around 10 of his colleagues and with around 300 members of this confraternity. And the confraternity was in a sorry state. Then on the 20th of June Mr Iacomo Bon from the Giudecca was made warden. In that same year, too, faithful Christians received a most great grace from his lordship the Pope, saying that anybody, wherever they were, who died contrite of their sins from Ascension day until Saint Mary Magdalene's day should go unpunished to the glory of eternal life. And may God all powerful — Father, Son and Holy Ghost —, who lives *for time without end*, lead us to it also. Amen.

DATE: Post 1348. The events related are dated as starting in January 1347 (*more veneto*), that is January 1348 by modern reckoning. The chaos and death affecting the *scuola* itself would seem to rule out the elaboration and sculpting of such a sophisticated artefact in the immediate aftermath. The inscription is therefore likely to have been executed sometime in the following few years when the memory of the traumatic events was still fresh.

LOCATION: In situ on the lunette over an archway entrance in the portico area of the first courtyard of the former Scuola Grande di S. Maria della Carità (at present the Accademia galleries), *sestiere* of Dorsoduro. Now bricked up, this was originally the portal which led from the portico to the ground floor hall of the *scuola*.

TYPE AND DESCRIPTION: Large commemorative inscription in raised and gilded letters that fills around three quarters of the archway lunette. The remaining top section of the lunette is decorated by a low-relief sculpture. Overall, the artefact is 165 cm high, while the inscription itself occupies a surface area of 230 cm at the base by 100 cm at its highest point. The magnificent epigraph, carved on what is likely to be a marble plaque, stands out strikingly against its black background of pitch mastic. The relief above depicts two kneeling angels, with golden robes and wings, on a pale turquoise ground. They hold aloft the symbol of the *scuola* with its two golden concentric circles intersected by a gold cross. The spaces inside the symbol are painted in red and dark green. The inscription and accompanying relief are surrounded by a double-crenellated ogival frame inlaid in marble. Both relief and inscription are glazed. This may explain, at least in part, the exceptionally well preserved state of the whole object, effectively protected from atmospheric pollution. The text — one of the most important pieces of medieval public writing to survive in Venice — is a fascinating document. It calls up in a dramatic, moving and dignified tone the great earthquake that struck Venice in 1348. The epicentre was in Friuli and the tremors were felt hundreds of miles around. According to Tassini, the printed text of the inscription was at later periods regularly distributed by the *scuola* (TASSINI 1876: 116–17). I have discovered one of these early flyers, undated but in Gothic script, appended by Cicogna to his unpublished manuscript diary dedicated to the inscriptions at S. Maria della Carità. It is in the Correr library at BMC, *Inedite* 2008, *busta* 499, no. 11. It is likely that this exceptional epigraph was therefore the first Venetian vernacular inscription to be printed. Subsequently it appeared in publications of various types in the eighteenth and nineteenth centuries, starting with Flaminio Corner (CORNER 1749, V: 207–08) and ending with FERRO (1889: 452).

It is instructive to compare the description of the earthquake in the inscription with that given around 1400 by the chronicler Antonio Morosini (NANETTI 2010, I: 64). One wonders if his account was influenced by our text:

A dì xxv de zener, in l'ora de vesporo, in lo tenpo del prexente doxie, in lo dì de misier sam Polo, hocorse in Veniexia, e anchora fo in molte parte, el mazior taramoto che mai persona vivese e sentise al mondo e che mai aldida se dixese, e durà per plu' dì e note, che tuta la tera a hora a hora se moveva, honde grandisimo spavento fexe a tute persone. E da puo' da quel ziorno in avanti fo muorìa grandisima de persone, e altri con glandusie che vegniva in diversi luogi de le persone, e altri del mal dito charbom, e questa non zesà per spacio de mexi VIIII. E cesada adoncha quela, atrovase largisima mente eser de morti el terzo de li abitanti de Veniexia, e questo fo chusì quaxi per tute le parte del mondo, ed è vero che la tera pareva quaxi dexabitada per la pestilencia predita, e sì per caxon che la plui parte de la zente schanpava fuora de Veniexia per schivar la morte, ma pur dentro e de fuora infinita zente morì.

LETTERING: Gothic majuscules sculpted in raised lettering. The text, which is admirably measured, regular and clear in layout, is set out in 18 lines of different lengths, some of them exceptionally long for an inscription. It is almost perfectly justified on both sides: a remarkable feat of pagination given the length involved, the awkward shape of the plaque and the complexity of carving in relief. Form marries with content supremely well in this outstanding collaboration between commissioner(s), *scriptor* and stonemason which must have required careful forward planning and a detailed blueprint. Although the format and ductus of the letters are strikingly similar to those on raised inscription CI 9 of 1344–45, commissioned by the same confraternity, our epigraph avoids the legibility problems of its cramped predecessor. The individual letters, standing around 4 cm high and 0.5 cm off the plaque surface, are well detached as are the words — or occasionally syntagms, involving article or articulated preposition plus noun — which are separated by clear interpuncts. Legibility is further enhanced by the letter gilding and the contrasting dark ground. The epigraph has sustained only minimal damage, with the ascender of the <d> in *mortalitade* (l. 10) and the <dv> of *conduga* (l. 18) missing. A very few errors are apparent: the <d> for *de* (l. 1) with no abbreviation stroke through it; missing <s> in *questo* (l. 6); and <l> omitted in *gloria* (l. 17). The *e* 'and' in l. 18 should probably have followed rather than preceded *fiol*, but as a precaution I have left it as it is. Straight-stemmed <u/v> is in the majority, although from l. 9 onwards it is increasingly in competition with instances displaying left-sided curvature. Apart from *Çudecha* (l. 14) there is an unusual absence of the common digram <ch> to express the velar /k/. Cedillas are prominently shown on <c> for affricate sounds. Abbreviation overbars have a central kink and are slightly flared at the ends. At the outset of the text the expected *in nome* 'In the name of ' (l. 1) has been rendered by the syntagm *inome*, presumably a pronunciation spelling. An exceptionally wide range of ligatures is used, involving <an> and <ar> but also <al> and even <ab>.

LANGUAGE: An outstanding example of fourteenth-century Venetian prose, appropriate to its subject matter and to the elegant monumentality of the artefact. The longest and largest stone-cut inscription in the corpus, it is exceptional in developing an extended narrative of the events commemorated. The language is dignified, solemn and articulate but simultaneously concrete. The syntax, with its paratactic sequence of statements beginning with *e* 'and' is effective in conveying the relentless succession of calamities. The apocalyptic tone is reinforced by the reference to *di* XL (l. 6) 'forty days', with biblical echoes also evoked by *el pare no voleva andar dal fio nel fio dal pare* (l. 10), where *nel* = 'né 'l' — in other words, 'neither the'.

The vocabulary itself is exceptionally rich and interesting. Some noteworthy medical terms are featured: *glanduxe* 'lymph nodes, bubos' (l. 8) < *GLANDUCULAM 'small gland' (Modern Venetian singular *giandussa*), and *mal del carbon* 'carbuncles' (l. 8). *Scaii*, l. 8 (Modern Venetian *scagi*, singular *scagio* < Gk μασχάλιον, a diminutive of μασχάλη 'palm frond, armpit') are the armpits, while the plural *lençene* (l. 8) is the groin — from INGUINEM with the definite article incorporated into the noun. *Besporo* 'evening', l. 3 (< VESPERUM) shows the characteristic Venetian tendency to betacise initial /v/. It alternated in Early Venetian with *vesporo* (cf. English *vesper*). *Taramoto* 'earthquake' (l. 3) survived into Modern Venetian, with the first <a> echoing the second. The spelling of *canpanili* 'bell towers' (l. 4) reflects the syllable-final nasal velarisation which has persisted into Contemporary Venetian (see CI 28). Enlarged high-definition photographs confirm *nasion* 'nation(s)' rather than *rasion* 'reasons' in l. 7. In *alguni* 'some (people)' (ll. 7, 8) the preceding preposition *a* is understood. The seldom attested *derota* 'rout' (l. 13) may be an independent formation via Latin DE + RŬMPERE 'to break'. It is undoubtedly cognate with Old French *deroute* and the rare Trecento Tuscan *dirotta*, both with the same meaning. *Çener* (l. 2) was the dominant form for January in most of the Early Venetian period but was gradually supplanted by *zener*, with <z> rather than <ç>, in the fifteenth century (as in CI 67, CI 99). *Garcia* (l. 15) for *gracia* 'grace' is a surprising case of metathesis not otherwise recorded in the OVI (the regular form is found in CI 20 and CI 41). *Nde* 'thence, to it' (l. 17) < INDE was normal in Early Venetian and in many medieval Italo-Romance varieties, before evolving into *ne*. *Fiol* 'figlio' (l. 18) < *FILIOLUS contrasts with *fio* (2), l. 10, and with *fio* ~ *fiio* (CI 15, CI 16) < FĪLĬUS. Both traditions survived and overlapped in Venetian, as can be seen in Modern Venetian *fio* (singular), *fioli* ~ *fioi* (plural) 'son, sons'. The text refers to a number of specific locations within Venice: the church of *sen Baseio* (l. 5) (Modern Venetian, San Basegio) in the *sestiere* of Dorsoduro, *Çudecha*, l. 14 (the island of the Giudecca) and *Barbaria* (l. 12). The latter almost certainly refers to the area between Campo S. Zanipolo e Campo S. Giustina, still known as *Barbaria de le Tole*, where — as can be seen in the de' Barbari cityscape of 1500 — planks of wood (*tole*, Italian *tavole*) were stocked and dressed from the Middle Ages onwards.

The raised variants *sen* and *senta* 'saint', in <e> rather than <a>, for *san* and *santa* 'saint', are the only forms used. *Oltro* (l. 9) 'other' for *altro* shows the frequent raising of /al/ to /ol/ in Early Venetian if followed by a dental consonant. The keywords *scola* 'confraternity' and *miser* 'Sir, Mr' are still unaffected here by diphthongisation of tonic mid-high vowels. The surname *Trivisan* (l. 12), common alongside *Trevixan*, shows the frequent Early Venetian raising of pre-tonic /e/ to /i/. The *vardian* Trevisan would have been from the citizen branch of this well-known family, as patricians were not eligible to hold office in the *scuole grandi*. Variation in the pre-tonic vowel seen in *mortilitade* (l. 6) ~ *mortalitade* (l. 10) 'death rate' is paralleled elsewhere in the corpus by *fratirnitade* (CI 10) and *fradelitade* (CI 42). Imperfect *liera* 'was' (l. 11) should be analysed as *l'iera*, with the <l> particle grammaticalised to the diphthongised variant of *era* which predominated in Early Venetian post-1300. *Liera* or *iera* (see CI 45, CI 48) would gradually and regularly develop into the form *g(i)era* which is exclusive nowadays. The imperfects *vegniva* ~ *vegnia* 'came' (l. 8) show the preservation and lenition of intervocal /v/ which have alternated in the history of Venetian. Exceptional within our collection is, in fact, the sequence of imperfects and, even more so, of past historics, a tense still very much alive in Early Venetian writing but which petered out in Middle Venetian: *caçe* (in other words, *caçé*) '(they) fell' (l. 4), from the infinitive *caçer* 'to fall', *fo* '(there) was' (l. 5), *stete* '(it) ceased, stopped ' (l. 5), *començsa* '(it) began' (l. 6), *dura* '(it) lasted' (l. 10), *se trova* 'found himself' (l. 12) — all three verbs stressed on final <a> –, *vive* (in other words, *vivé*) '(he) lived' (l. 12), *mori* (in other words, *morì*) '(they) died' (l. 12), *ave* '(they) had' (l. 15). *Se piase* (l. 9) 'were caught' is the reflexive 3rd plural imperfect of the Early Venetian verb *piar* 'to catch, to take' (Italian, *pigliare*). It is often spelled *piiar*, with <ii>, in Early Venetian to reflect the palatal approximant yod sound, as is probably also the case in *scaii* (l. 8). A full array of Early Venetian definite articles are on display: masculine singular *lo* ~ *l'* ~ *el*, masculine plural *li*; feminine singular *la*, plural *le*. Although the singular *el* has made its appearance, the plural in *i* only became predominant in the fifteenth century. *Comuna mentre* 'commonly' (l. 11) is a splendid example of the original majority adverb type in Early Venetian, consisting of the feminine adjective followed (often detached, as here) by the *-mentre* (rather than *-mente*) morph (see CI 30 and FERGUSON 2007: 125).

RECENT STUDIES: MIGLIORINI and FOLENA (1952: 36–37); STUSSI (1980a: 93–94); STUSSI (1997a: 166–68); STUSSI (1997b: 917–18); REDON (2002: 168–70); FERGUSON (2013c: 91–94); FERGUSON (2015b: 45–47); D'ACHILLE (2017).

Corpus Inscriptions 15, 16

M·CCC·XL·VIIII · D(E) · LVIO · (SR) M̂AR | CHO · ARIA(N) · FIO · CHE FO · D(E) · (SR) · ÂN | TVONIIO ·₃ | ARIAN · D(E) · S(-N) · | RAFIEL · ₅ | ME FE· | ÇIT ₇

[Mcccxlviiii, de luio, sr Marcho Arian, fio che fo de sr Antuoniio Arian de S. Rafiel, *me feçit*.]

M·CCC·XL·VIIII ADI XV D(E) LVIO ₁ | (SR) M̂ARCHO ÂRIAN FIIO CHE FO D(E) ₂ | (SR) ÂNTVONIO ₃ | ÂRIAN D(E) S(-N) ₄ | RAFI⟨E⟩L ₅ | ME FEÇI(T) ₆

[Mcccxlviiii, adì xv de luio, sr Marcho Arian, fiio che fo de sr Antuonio Arian de S. Rafiel, *me feçit*.]

TRANSLATIONS: CI 15: In July 1349 Mr Marcho Arian, son of the late Mr Antuoniio Arian from St Raphael, *made me*.

CI 16: On July 15th 1349 Mr Marcho Arian, son of the late Mr Antuonio Arian from St Raphael, *made me*.

DATE: 1349.

LOCATION: In situ. Carved on opposites sides of the well head in the small square in front of the church of the Anzolo Rafael (Italian, Angelo Raffaele) in the Campo del Anzolo Rafael at the western end of the *sestiere* of Dorsoduro. CI 15 is on the side facing the church while CI 16 faces the square.

TYPE AND DESCRIPTION: Dedicatory and commemorative, the epigraphs record and celebrate the construction of a well for public use by a wealthy private sponsor. The well head in Istrian stone is 91 cm high and 109 cm at its widest, while the inscription surface covers roughly 64 × 48 × 19 cm on both sides.

The sponsor of this public utility was, as is stated in the inscription, Marc(h)o Arian, a member of a well-to-do local citizen family of merchants whose splendid thirteenth-century palace, Ca' Arian, can be admired on Fondamenta Briati just across the canal from the church and well head. The palace is remarkable for its unique triple-light window on the *piano nobile* carved with beautiful Gothic tracery: see Tassini (1879: 121–25). The well was Arian's legacy to his local community. He died during the great plague of 1348 — the subject of CI 14 — leaving 300 ducats in his will of 28 May 1348 for the building of two wells in the square fronting the church of St Raphael ('in s. Raffiel sul campo') for all the inhabitants of the neighbourhood. The will, published by Cecchetti (1887a: 272 n. 1), is a remarkable document for our purposes. It provides the only direct evidence in the corpus for the commissioning process of an inscription and its surrounding decoration. Arian insisted that one of the well heads only should carry a written message specifying that the wells were for the use of the general public as well as for the gentlemen of the district: 'e scrito su(n) sol pozo che se chomuni al povolo e a(i) boni homeni dela contrada'. He also requested that his arms and merchant sign ('larma e lo segno mio') — which would have been stamped on his bales of merchandise — be displayed, and these have in fact survived prominently on both sides of the well

Fig. 3.15. CI 15 in context. © A. S. Ferguson.

head. The second medieval well head on the *campo* no longer exists, having been replaced at a later date.

Excluding the inscribed well head from the Ognissanti (CI 106), fashioned from a re-used Roman artefact, this is one of only two medieval or Renaissance well heads with vernacular inscriptions surviving in Venice and the lagoon islands (the other, on Murano, displays CI 51). It is also one of the four examples in the corpus of 'mirror' inscriptions on a two-sided artefact, and one of only three cut in stone (the remaining two are CI 101, CI 102, and CI 103, CI 104). The other instance is the back-to-back embroidered messages on the banner of Santa Fosca from Torcello (CI 33, CI 34). It is interesting that in only one case (CI 103, CI 104) is the public message, visible from both sides, entirely identical.

LETTERING: Gothic majuscules carved in V-section. The writing on both sides of the well, averaging 3 cm in height, is worn down but remains legible. The shallow grooving shows clear traces of black infilling which would have made the messages perfectly clear in the past. The cutting of the texts is competent though not of the highest quality. A certain sloppiness is evident in the occasionally variable letter heights — excused in part by the tricky unevenness of the surface of the well — and in the slightly untidy Latin tags at the end of the inscriptions. Haste is suggested by the divergent wording and spelling of the two texts, and by the unfinished <e> on

Rafiel (CI 16, l. 5). Probably in line with these observations is the high density of abbreviations and ligatures on such short texts, with an awkward and unusual <af> in CI 15 (l. 5). Indeed, the double ligature on three of the four instances of the name *Arian* (CI5, l. 4; CI 16, ll. 2 and 4) is extreme in its compression. Striking are the triple <c>s on the date on CI 15 (l. 1), with their bowed and extended hairlines. These flourishes are not repeated on the date in CI 16 (l. 1). Also flourished are the arms of <h> and <r> on both sides descending quite extravagantly below the baseline, although this is only clear where the infilling has survived. The abbreviation of *s(i)er* on both inscriptions is unusual in the context of the corpus. Rather than the expected epigraphic diagonal s-bar or the narrow Tironian 7, the abbreviation used here is taken directly from Venetian manuscript practice: the Latin *pro* symbol resembling a P with the lower part of the bowl snaking down through, then behind, the stem. The stonemason is likely to have copied this directly from the manuscript text he was provided with. This abbreviation for *sier* is also found once on CI 38 (l. 6). Unusual, too, is the form of the <ç> on *fecit* on both inscriptions.

LANGUAGE: These inscriptions contain tantalising written traces of some pronunciation tendencies. *Fio* (CI 15, l. 2) contrasts interestingly with *fiio* (CI 16, l. 2). Both are common in Early Venetian, the second suggesting a survival of a palatal approximant yod pronunciation of the vowel. The unexpected spelling of *Antuoni(i)o* (CI 15, ll. 2–3; CI 16, l.3) with <uo> is evidence of the strong diphthongising tendencies increasingly affecting Early Venetian: so extreme in this case — on an /o/ derived from Ō rather than Ŏ — as to be reminiscent of contemporaneous Paduan texts. The <ii> in *Antuoniio* (CI 15, ll. 2–3) may be an attempt to render a popular pronunciation of N + yod as [ɲ] rather than [nj]. The form *Rafiel* for Raphael confirms the common pronunciation of the name which appears in Marco Arian's will as *Raffiel* ~ *Raphyel* and in the *mariegola* of the Scuola Grande di S. Giovanni Evangelista as *Rafiel* ~ *Raphiel* (SIMEONE 2003: 160). The Latin *me feçit* (CI 15, ll. 6–7; CI 16, l. 6) was a stock self-attribution phrase employed on works of art, but the highly unusual presence of <ç> in both instances is strongly suggestive of a vernacular affricate pronunciation. *Luio* (CI 15, l. 1; CI 16, l. 1) for July is the dominant Early Venetian derivative of IULIUS (via *LULIUS), used here and elsewhere in the corpus (CI 19, CI 26, CI 50, CI 78, CI 79).

RECENT STUDIES: RIZZI (1976: 97); STUSSI (1980a: 92); TOMASIN (2012b: 2 n. 6); FERGUSON (2013c: 94–95); FERGUSON (2015c: 45–47). CI 16 was first recorded by Cicogna and first published diplomatically by TASSINI (1879: 125 n. 1).

Corpus Inscriptions 17, 18

CI 17

M · CCC · [XLVI]III · F[O FATO · QVES]TO · LAVORIER · P(ER) · MISIER · LO VARDIAN [DELA SCOLA · DE MISER · SEN · ÇANE VANGELIS]TA · [E PER LI SOI] ₁| CONPA[GN]I · E DELI · [BENI] DELA SCOLA · E CON LAIDA · D(E)LI NOSTRI · FRARI · E FO FA[TO · CON VOLE(N)TA · DEL NOBELE OMO · MISIER · IACOMO · BADOER] ₂| DITO · [DA]PERAGA · P(RI)OR · DEL · DITO · LOGO · E CON CO(N)SE(N)TIMENTO · DEI NOBILI · OM[ENI] · [MISIE]R [MARIN BA]DOER · DE SEN · IACOMO DE LORIO E MISE[R MARI(N)] ₃| BADOER] · DE SENTO · STINA · E MISER · ÇAN(IN) · BADO[E]R · DIT[O DAPER]AGA · E MISER · FELIPO [BADOER] ₄| [E MI]SER A[LBE](R)TIN · SO [F]RAR · TVTI · CAVI · E PATRO(NI) · DEL [D]ITO · LOGO · E P(ER) S(R) · BO(R)TOLAMIO · DIT(O) · [MAÇVCO] · P(ER)C[OLAT]OR · [DEL] SO[VRA]DIT(O) MIS · [LO · PRIOR] ₅

> [MCCCXLVIIII. Fo fato questo lavorier per misier lo vardian dela Scola de miser Sen Çane Vangelista e per li soi conpagni, e deli beni dela Scola e con l'aida deli nostri frari. E fo fato con volentà del nobele omo misier Iacomo Badoer dito 'da Peraga', prior del dito logo, e con consentimento dei nobili omeni misier Marin Badoer de Sen Iacomo de Lorio, e miser Marin Badoer de Sento Stina, e miser Çanin Badoer dito 'da Peraga', e miser Felipo Badoer, e miser Albertin so frar, tuti cavi e patroni del dito logo, e per sr Bortolamio dito 'Maçuco', percolator del sovradito mis. lo prior.]

CI 18

[M]CCCC·LIII · ADI VIII · MARÇO · FO (CON)PIDO ₁| [LA] PRESE(N)TE FABRICHA · DE QVESTO · A[L]|BERGO · FATO · TUTO DA NUOUO · DI BENI ₃| [D]E NOSTRI · FRADELI · BATUDI · DE · MI[S](R) ₄| [S]AN ÇVANE · EVANÇELISTA · IN · TE(N)PO · [DEL] ₅| [N]OBELE · HOMO · MIS(R) · MARCHO · BADO[ER] ₆| [F]O DE · MIS(R) · NICHOLO · PRIOR · DEL [DI]TO · [LU|OGO] E DEL PROUIDO · E DISCRETO · [OMO] ₈| MIS(R) · IACHOMO · TATARO · V[ARDIA(N)] | GRANDO · DELA · DIT[A] S[CHVOLA] ₁₀| CON · SVO · CONP[AGNI] ₁₁

> [MCCCCLIII, adì VIII março, fo conpido la presente fabricha de questo albergo, fato tuto da nuovo de beni de nostri fradeli batudi de mis. San Çuane Evançelista, in tenpo del nobele homo mis. Marcho Badoer fo de mis. Nicholò, prior del dito luogo, e del provido e discreto omo mis. Iachomo Tataro, vardian grando dela dita Scuola, con suò conpagni.]

TRANSLATIONS: CI 17: 1349. The present work was commissioned by the Warden of the Confraternity of St John the Evangelist and by his fellow executives, both out of the funds of the Confraternity and with the help of our brothers. It was authorised by the nobleman Sir Iachomo Badoer called 'da Peraga', prior of the said site, with the consent of the noblemen Sir Marin Badoer of St Giacomo dell'Orio, Sir Marin Badoer of St Stina, Sir Çanin Badoer called 'da Peraga', Sir Felipo Badoer and Sir Albertin his brother, all owners and patrons of the said location, and with the support of Mr Bortolamio, known as 'Maçuco', deputy of the above-mentioned prior.

Fig. 3.16. CI 17 and CI 18 in situ in the 1920s. © Alinari.

Fig. 3.17. CI 17 (detail of left side). © A. S. Ferguson.

CI 18: On the 8th of March 1453 the present structure of this meeting hall was completed, entirely anew, from funds provided by our flagellant brothers of St John the Evangelist. This was in the time of the nobleman Sir Marcho Badoer (son of the late Sir Nicholò), prior of the said site, and of the most prudent and discerning man, Mr Iachomo Tataro — warden of the said *scuola* — and his colleagues.

DATE: 1349 and 1453.

Fig. 3.18. CI 18. © A. S. Ferguson.

LOCATION: Originally the two inscriptions were located one above the other, the oldest on top, on the lower part of the external wall of the *Scuola* of S. Giovanni Evangelista, in the confraternity atrium (now the picturesque Campiello S. Zuane or *de la Scuola*) to the left of the main entrance into the *scuola* building. On account of their fragile condition both artefacts were removed from their original location in the late 1920s and transferred to the inside of the confraternity building where they are now displayed. The inscriptions visible at present on the outside wall are high quality early twentieth-century copies, themselves now corroded by pollution and partly illegible. For details of the *mariegole* of the confraternity see CI 3.

TYPE AND DESCRIPTION: Declarative and commemorative. Spanning a full century, emanating from one of the oldest and most prestigious lay brotherhoods in the history of Venice, and integrated into a unique sculptural ensemble, these two inscriptions — recording historically significant refurbishments of an exquisite architectural complex — constituted one of the major epigraphic sites in Venice. The proximity of the originals and the quality of their replacements mean that the location remains impressive and retains its inscriptional importance.

Substantial sections of the originals of both inscriptions are still legible with care, although damage to the text is particularly severe in the concluding lines of CI 18, where some passages are obliterated, and on the far right of CI 17. The inscription block of CI 17 is now split twice, once near the left-hand extremity and once in the middle of the stone. To resolve doubts when transcribing the text of the originals I have had recourse to an early photograph of these originals (Alinari, ACA-F-032101–0000), which shows them when they were still in situ, as well as to the accurate copies on the outside of the *scuola*.

Although executed a century apart, the two Gothic inscriptions — CI 18 situated directly at eye level and CI 17 slightly higher — formed a deliberate iconographic whole with the impressive sculptures above them. The earlier epigraph, with its accompanying sculptural group, was cut immediately after the devastating plague that decimated Venetian society in 1348 (see CI 14). The reference to the *lavorier* commemorated (CI 17, l. 1) may include the sculpture and accompanying inscription, but it undoubtedly alludes principally to the completion of the building works on the confraternity's chapter hall (Early Venetian, *sala capitolar* or just *sala*) on the first floor of the building which had been authorised by the Badoer. The imposing artefact immediately above CI 17 is in Istrian stone (271 × 124 cm) and depicts in high relief a double line of twelve brothers kneeling penitentially before St John the Evangelist in the act of blessing. The saint, clutching the confraternity's ceremonial banner (the upper part of which is now missing), hands it solemnly to the thirteenth brother, the *vardian grando*. The framed, inset rectangular relief group is flanked by spiral columns and is surmounted by a semicircular lunette with a charming Madonna and Child relief on plain ground. It is not known when this early sculpture was placed in its present location but its appearance and frame are not Venetian in style. CI 17 is on a thick elongated slab of Istrian stone (280 × 38 cm). The inscription surface is fashioned to mimic a roll of parchment held at either end by two kneeling and hooded brothers, and is therefore curved outwards at the extremities. Above the writing are three relief crosiers, one of the symbols of the confraternity.

The second plaque (100 × 80 cm), carrying CI 18, was positioned immediately below the first, at 155 cm above ground level. It is also in Istrian stone but has a crenellated frame. Its inscription surface measures 90 × 70 cm. Near the bottom of the plaque two crosiers stand out in relief, one on either side, causing a narrowing in width of the last three lines of script. This later epigraph commemorates a renovation of the confraternity's premises completed in the mid-fifteenth century. The *albergo* (ll. 2–3) or meeting room of the *banca* (executive) on the first floor is mentioned explicitly but the chapter hall on the same floor was also refurbished at that time. The term *albergo* is also found in CI 38, again in the context of a flagellant *scuola*. *Albergo* < Gothic **haribergo* 'military shelter' — with dissimilation of the first /r/ and loss of post-tonic /i/ — could mean 'hostel, lodging(s), residence, quarters, dwelling, shelter (often for pilgrims or the poor)' or even 'storeroom' in the early Italo-Romance vernaculars, including Venetian where the form *arbergo* occasionally occurs. Only in Early and Middle Venetian, though, does it seem to have the specialised sense of 'confraternity meeting room or hall'. For the history of the confraternity of S. Giovanni Evangelista's rebuilding of its house in the fourteenth and fifteenth centuries, with groundplans, see PARTRIDGE (2015: 58–61).

The date on both the original and the copy of CI 18 are so badly worn as to be partly illegible. Given the conservative nature of the artefact in terms of palaeography, aesthetics and choice of the vernacular over Latin, recent scholarship assumed that it read 1353 (PEDROCCO 1981: 48; STUSSI 1995b; TOMASIN 2012b: 9 n. 21; FERGUSON 2015c: 51–52). However, in preparing the present volume I have reviewed all the direct and indirect evidence relating to the inscription, and this date has become untenable. My re-evaluation is based on a minute examination of the damaged original; the evidence of the early photograph of the original inscriptions; early photographic images of the replicas showing the epigraph intact; the mid-eighteenth century illustration of the epigraph made by Jan Grevembroch when it was still entirely legible (GREVEMBROCH 1754, reproduced in RIZZI 1987: 641); and the fact that the Iachomo Tataro mentioned in the inscription as head of the confraternity was indeed its warden, not only in 1453 but in 1458 (SPINAZZI 2003: 65, n. 31). His name crops up, as a wealthy citizen, in mid-fifteenth century documents (MUELLER 1997: 539–40; CLARKE, BARILE and NORDIO 2006: 223). Finally, there is the presence of Nicholò Badoer as prior in another fifteenth-century inscription from the *scuola* (CI 48), and the subtle but insistent linguistic, and to a lesser extent palaeographic, evidence outlined below. The facts, therefore, overwhelmingly confirm 1453 — when the rebuilding of the fabric of the confraternity's halls and their Gothic façade was indeed completed (ASV, *Scuola Grande di S. Giovanni Evangelista*, reg. 2, fol. 18, 8 March 1453) — as the correct dating. This was, in fact, the date transmitted in the nineteenth century by SORAVIA (1822–24, II: 216) and CICOGNA (1855: 4, 12).

Both epigraphs refer repeatedly to the Badoer family who were the great landowners in the S. Stin area, who had founded the church of S. Giovanni Evangelista in the tenth century, and who were the long-term patrons of the *scuola* itself. This patrician family also had important branches in the area of S. Giacomo dell'Orio, just to the north of S. Giovanni Evangelista in the *sestiere* of S. Crose, and also at S. Giustina on the far north-eastern side of the city in the *sestiere* of Castello: *rami* which are evoked in CI 17. On the family dispersions and interconnections of the Badoer in our period see CROUZET-PAVAN (2015: 298–301).

LETTERING: On CI 17 Gothic majuscules, averaging 2.5 cm in height, sculpted in relief. On CI 18 incised Gothic majuscules averaging 3.7 cm. The text on both plaques is elegantly paginated and justified on left and right, with some small gaps visible on the right in CI 17. The weathering suffered by the originals of both epigraphs means that statements about lettering have to be made very cautiously. What is clear is that these inscriptions, commissioned by one of the great *scuole grandi* of medieval and Renaissance Venice, are both classic examples of Venetian Gothic epigraphy, cut in its heyday in the case of CI 17, and at the close of its period of dominance in the city in the case of CI 18. The earlier of the two is sculpted in relief with great skill, revealing admirable volumetric modulation within each letter and a certain lightness of touch and attractive sinuousity not often associated with the raising technique. Prominent are the closing hairstrokes on <c> and <e>, the flourished serifs on <s>, and the overarched dipping ascender on uncial <d>. CI 18 is cut in V-section and is more spaciously laid out, with noticeably larger lettering than CI 17. The aspect of its script is not dissimilar although it is more compressed. Significantly there are few ligatures and abbreviations, and word-dividing interpuncts are consistently used. However, one notices on the later inscription the longer downward-pointing arms on <t>, the overarching ascender on <d> now touching the baseline, and the longer, outward-curving, parallel upstroke on <l>. Compared to the earlier epigraph, the left stem of <a> is now raised and tilted, and <u/v> is conveyed in both forms, with the uncial sort right-curved. This latter type had gone out of fashion in the fourteenth century but returned to favour in early fifteenth-century Gothic inscriptional lettering in Venice. One is also struck on CI 18 by the large cedilla on the <c> of *março* (l. 1) and *Evançelista* (l. 5) and by the Tironian 9 for *con* in *conpido* (l. 1). Both the general appearance of the later inscription and its lettering are conservative, however, and the palaeographic evidence alone would not have allowed the dating question to be settled.

CI 18 is a landmark piece of public writing which signals the end of an epigraphic era. It is the last inscription from the Scuola di S. Giovanni Evangelista, or indeed from any of the *scuole grandi*, that is Gothic in script and Venetian in language. In effect, it is striking that all the remaining epigraphs in the atrium of S. Giovanni Evangelista, from the later fifteenth century — more-or-less coinciding in date with the beautiful marble screen by Pietro Lombardo (1478–81) through which one enters the courtyard — and from the early sixteenth century, are in Latin. They are cut in Roman square capital lettering.

LANGUAGE: Although not in themselves decisive, a number of contrastive linguistic features suggest strongly that there is a considerable time lapse between the two inscriptions. In particular, *sen* 'saint' (CI 17, l. 1 and l. 3) and *sento* (CI 17, l. 4) versus *san* (CI 18, l. 5); *frari* 'brother' (CI 17, l. 2) — with singular *frar* (CI 17, l. 5) — replaced by the generally later form *fradeli* (CI 18, l. 4); and an increase in diphthongisation of stressed mid-high vowels, shown in the contrast between *logo* 'place' (CI 17, l. 3) and *luogo* (CI 18, ll. 7–8), as well as between *scola* (CI 17, l. 2) and *schuola* (CI 18, l. 10). However, particular caution is needed here in that CI 17 manifests variable levels of diphthongisation with, for example, the forms *misier* and *miser* 'Sir, Mr' alternating in an apparently random way (at a transitional point in time where both traditional and innovative variants would have co-existed within the speech community). Comparison here with CI 18 is not possible as the latter only has abbreviated forms of the word. *Conpido* 'completed' (CI 18, l. 1), rather than the commoner fourteenth-century form *conplido* (see CI 19, l. 3), suggests the gradual development in Early Venetian away from clusters preserving consonant + L reflexes. The masculine plural partitive article appears in three guises: the older, more conservative form *deli* (twice in CI 17, 1.2) alongside the rarer, at that stage, variant *dei* (CI 17, l. 3) which makes its first appearance here in Venetian epigraphy. The third variant, *di*, a contracted form of *de(l)i*, was probably a rapid-speech innovation. It is recorded in CI 18 (l. 3) and became increasingly common in writing in the course of the fifteenth century.

More generally, there is an interesting contrast between *Çane vangelista* (CI 17, l. 1) and *Çuane evançelista* (CI 18, l. 5). The use of the cedilla in CI 18 appears to reflect a more 'popular' spoken pronunciation than the <g> of CI 17 although, paradoxically, the apocope of the initial <e> in *Vangelista* seems more 'Venetian'. One finds another popularising form, *Çane Vagnelista*, in fifteenth-century documents. *Çane* is the overwhelmingly common form of the name John in fourteenth-century Venice, with *Çuane* or *Çoane* making inroads from the early fifteenth century. *Nobele* (CI 17, l. 2; CI 18, l. 6) shows the lowering of the post-tonic vowel in Early Venetian as compared to Tuscan/Italian. *Aida* 'help' (CI 17, l. 2) is from the common Early Venetian infinitive *aidar*. *Sen Iacomo de Lorio* (CI 17, l. 3) is S. Giacomo dell'Orio in the *sestiere* of S. Crose. The name derives from the ancient district name Lorio (< Lovrio < Luprio) whose ultimate etymology is unresolved. *Peraga* (CI 17, ll. 3, 4) is a locality north east of Padua. The patrician Badoer family had become lords of Peraga in the fourteenth century via marriage alliance with the family of that name, and possessed considerable lands on the Veneto mainland (POZZA 1982). The curious form *sento Stina* (CI 17, l. 4) is plausibly explained by STUSSI (1995b) as an affectionate diminutive of Giustina, with the masculine *sento* 'saint' form attracted by analogy to common Venetian masculine saints' names ending in -*a*, such as Barnaba, Luca, Zaccaria and Marcuola. The confraternity's *mariegola* records the expected full form in the feminine, *senta Iustina*. *Cavi* 'heads' (CI 17, l. 5) is cognate with Italian *capi*. It shows the typical lenition in Venetian of intervocalic P > /b/ > /v/. *Cavi* alternated in Early/Middle Venetian with the variant *cai* which shows complete voicing of the intervocalic. *Patroni* 'patrons' (CI 17, l. 5) is a conservative form which resisted, alongside the more regular spoken and written variant *paroni*, until the Modern Venetian period. *Percolator* 'proctor, procurator' (CI 17, l. 5) < PRŌCŪRĀTŌREM, one of the highest ranking Venetian state officials, is in this instance a 'stand-in' or 'deputy'. Appearing in the corpus in a variety of vernacular forms it commonly displays, as here, metathesis of the first syllable in Early Venetian and the dissimilation to <l> of the second <r>. See SALLACH (1993, s.v. *procurador, procurator (di S. Marco)*). *Prior* (CI 17, ll. 3, 5; CI 18, l. 7) is the prior or director of the whole complex of institutions on the site, including the hospice for women (see CI 48), who was elected by the Badoer. On *conpagni* 'colleagues, fellow executives' (CI 17, l. 2; CI 18, l. 11) see CI 3. It once more suggests the presence of syllable-final nasalisation in Early Venetian. The lack of agreement is notable in the passive construction *fo conpido la presente fabricha* (CI 18, ll. 1–2). This is the first of only a handful of agreement mismatches between past participle and noun among the dozens of examples of the passive construction in the corpus (see CI 9), a result which contrasts with the findings of STUSSI's Early Venetian texts (1965: lxxv), even allowing for the generally later dating of our collection. *Março* March (CI 18, l. 1) is the regular outcome of MARTIUS in Early Venetian (see CI 40, CI 58), although it was gradually replaced by the spelling *marzo* in the fifteenth century (CI 79, CI 96, CI 98). *Tataro* (CI 18, l. 9) 'Tartar' is a nickname connected with the Levantine trade (STUSSI 1965: 258). The change of adjective declension in *grando* 'big' (CI 18, l. 10) — rather than *grande* — remains normal even in Modern/Contemporary Venetian.

One is struck, finally, by the contrast between the down-to-earth practical language of these vernacular Gothic inscriptions and the abstract rhetoric of the Renaissance Latin epigraphs that surround them in the atrium of the *scuola*.

RECENT STUDIES: WOLTERS (1976, I: 188–89); STUSSI (1995b); FERGUSON (2013c: 97–99); FERGUSON (2015c: 51–52). Both CI 17 and CI 18 were fully transcribed, diplomatically, in SORAVIA (1822–24, II: 215–16) where CI 18 was published for the first time. CI 17 had first been recorded by CORNER (1749, VI: 333).

Corpus Inscription 19

·M ·CCC ·LI · DEL | MEXE · DE · LVIO · ₂| FO CONPLIDA · SSTA CH|
AXA · DELA SCVOLA · DELI ₄| DODEXE · APOSTOLI ₅

[Mcccli, del mexe de luio, fo conplida ssta chaxa dela Scuola deli Dodexe Apostoli.]

TRANSLATION: In the month of July 1351 this (meeting) house of the Confraternity of the Twelve Apostles was completed.

DATE: July 1351.

LOCATION: Embedded at first-floor level on the external wall of the small building immediately to one's left when exiting the church of the Santi Apostoli (*sestiere* of Cannaregio) in Campo dei SS. Apostoli. The plaque is *c.* 4 m above ground level over a shop front. The building concerned, wedged up against the base of the church's belltower, may just possibly be a remnant of the demolished medieval meeting house of the *scuola*, where the inscription plaque would have been sited *ab initio*. The artefact is likely to have been displaced from its original location on or in the meeting house after the substantial demolition of the latter in the Cinquecento. Cicogna described it as being on the wall of the bell tower (a *campanile* that dates, in its present form, from the seventeenth century) facing the *campo*.

TYPE AND DESCRIPTION: Declarative and commemorative. The brief inscription is carved on an unframed marble plaque (*c.* 50 × *c.* 25 cm) inserted into the wall but standing out slightly from it. It celebrates the completion in 1351 of the original meeting house (*chaxa*, ll. 3–4) of the confraternity of the Twelve Apostles adjacent to the church of the Santi Apostoli. The upper part of the inscription text is flanked by the enlarged symbol of the *scuola*, the initials *AP* (= Apostoli), carved in flamboyant majuscules. The plaque has become roughened and partly chipped along the edges, especially on the right-side corners, but the text itself is undamaged and eminently legible.

The *Scuola de(l)i Dodexe Apostoli* was one of the most active, successful and long-lived of the Venetian *scuole piccole* devotional brotherhoods. Its location was and is highly central, at the confluence of what is now the eastern end of the bustling Strada Nova and the Salizzada San Zuane Grisostomo, the key artery between Campo SS. Apostoli and the Rialto, always packed with commuters, shoppers and tourists. After the clearance of its original meeting house in the sixteenth century to allow for enlargement of the church, the confraternity was given a locale, still surviving, in the adjoining Campiello *drio la chiesa*, just behind the church. On the façade of this construction can be seen a plaque with an inscription in heavily Venetianised Italian. It is carved in Roman capitals, is dated 1591 and carries the same *AP* emblem as our medieval epigraph. On the stair inside the building there is yet another inscription, dated 1706, in Italian but with Venetian influenced hypercorrections. This inscription confirms the date of the foundation of the *scuola* (1350), its original location at the front of the church (*avanti la facciatta* [sic] *di* /

Fig. 3.19. CI 19. © A. S. Ferguson.

questa chiesa), the date of its transfer to the new building (1548) and of its restoration (1706). G. Vio (2004: 570–75) noted that in the period 1350–54, coinciding with our inscription, there is compelling documentary evidence of the favour in which the church authorities held the confraternity and of its many charitable initiatives. Unsurprisingly, the brotherhood appears to have owned property in the SS. Apostoli area (see CI 58).

LETTERING: Gothic majuscules sharply cut in V-section. As is usually the case in Venice, the marble plaque has weathered well, and the now darkened letters stand out exceptionally clearly against a grey ground. In addition, legibility is enhanced by the good height of the letters (averaging 3 cm), the clarity and precision of the cut, the generous spacing, the consistent use of mid-high interpuncts between words, and the absence of abbreviations and ligatures. The ductus of the text is aesthetically restrained in terms of letter modulation and curvature, giving an impression of measured self-confidence. There is some sinuosity, seen in particular in the billowing left-side bow of the <m> in the date, on <s>, <h>, and on the oversized framing initials, but overall the writing emphasizes uprights and horizontals rather than the uncialesque. This is particularly evident on the ascender of <d> which remains parallel with the baseline, on the straight topstroke of <a>, on the substantially vertical end-spiking on <c> and <t>, and on the straight parallel upstroke of <l>. This muscularity is underlined by the prominent wedge serifs on <i>, <v> and <x>.

LANGUAGE: A striking feature of the brief inscription is the treatment of sibilants. There was some hesitation in the graphic representation of these in Early Venetian, with <s>, <ss> and <x> potentially applicable to both unvoiced /s/ and voiced /z/. The most consistent of the three was <x>, mainly confined to representing /z/ and destined to become an emblematic feature of Venetian writing. There are three examples here: *mexe* 'month' (l. 2), *chaxa* '(meeting) house' (ll. 3–4) — with the digram <ch> for velar /k/ — and *dodexe* 'twelve' (l. 5). Word-initial <ss> to represent <s> is not rare in Early Venetian and is usually seen on short words such as *sse* 'if' and *ssia* 'be'. I have come across no other example, though, of *ssta* 'this' (l. 3). A shortened, originally spoken, form of *questa*, *(s)sta* coexisted commonly in Early Venetian writing with the full variant of the demonstrative adjective which predominates in the corpus. *Conplida* 'completed' (l. 3) shows the expected fourteenth-century retention, at least in writing, of the <pl> group. As a rule, other clusters involving a consonant + L were also maintained in writing through much of the Early Venetian period. In this respect *conplida* contrasts tellingly with the mid-fifteenth century *conpido* in CI 18 (l. 1). The passive construction *fo conplida ssta chaxa* (ll. 3–4) shows agreement between past participle and subject (see CI 9, CI 18). *Scuola* (l. 4) is the second appearance in the collection of the diphthongised form of this key noun which would predominate post-1350. On *luio* July (l. 2), see CI 16.

RECENT STUDIES: FERGUSON (2013c: 95); FERGUSON (2015c: 49). Cicogna recorded, but did not publish, the inscription.

Corpus Inscription 20

. + . PAPA · CLIMENTO · SEXSTO . DI . VNO · ₁| · ANNO ·XL . DI. DE ·
PERDON . (A) ÇASCHVNO ·₂| · CHE · PORCE · LEMVSENA · ALI · FANTOLI|
NI . DELAPIETATE · MISER · LO PATRIACHA ₄| DE · GRADO · MISER · LO
VESCODO · DE · ₅| · CASTELO · XL · DI ··☐ ༄ | |
· SVMA · LO P(ER)DON · DE · LAPIA|TADE . VNO · ANNO · Cº · XX · DI · ₈|
E DA(L)TRE · GRACIE · MOLTE · ༄

[Papa Climento Sexsto di' uno anno XL dì de perdon a çaschuno che porce lemusena ali fantolini dela Pietate. Miser lo patriacha de Grado, miser lo vescodo de Castelo XL dì. Suma lo perdon de la Piatade: uno anno CXX dì, e d'altre gracie molte.]

TRANSLATION: Pope Clement the Sixth has given 1 year and 40 days of indulgence to anybody who donates alms to the little children of La Pietà. The Patriarch of Grado and the Bishop of Castelo (have given) 40 days (each). Sum total of the Pietà indulgence: 1 year 120 days, and many other graces.

DATE: Undated, but localisable between 1343 and 1352. The epigraph may have been carved at any time after 1343, when Pope Clement VI issued his bull from Avignon granting the indulgence to benefactors of La Pietà (ASV, *Ospedali e luoghi pii, busta* 630, *processo* 1). Clement died in 1352. It is worth bearing in mind when considering the likely date of the inscription, as well as the modest quality of the lettering and language, that it was issued near the outset of the Pietà foundation's activities when funds would have been low and needs pressing. Since the authorities sanctioned the charity's fundraising activities in 1343, giving it some public funding, one imagines that the papal indulgence in the same year would have been speedily publicised by inscription. However, it cannot be ruled out that it was in fact promulgated to coincide with the Jubilee of 1350 in order, thereby, to have maximum impact in a city which had been shaken to its foundations since 1348 by the earthquakes and plague described vividly in CI 14. This too might explain the unprepossessing nature of the artefact. As a precaution I have therefore placed the inscription a little further forward in the corpus.

LOCATION: Embedded in the wall of the building that flanks the Ponte dei Frati bridge. The bridge links Campo S. Angelo to Calle dei Frati (*sestiere* of S. Marco) which itself leads to Campo S. Stefano. The inscription plaque is 189 cm off the ground. It faces the grandiose fifteenth-century Gothic doorway — with painted bas relief of St Augustine with friars — leading into the cloisters of the former monastery of the Augustinian hermit friars attached to the church of Santo Stefano (Venetian, San Stefano). The epigraph was in its present position when CICOGNA (1824–53, III: 187) transcribed it, although he was convinced that it must originally have been sited near the Pietà foundling hospital itself. However Flaminio Corner, who described and transcribed it with a fair degree of accuracy in the mid-eighteenth century, said that the inscription could be seen 'still affixed' ('adhuc [...] affixa') to the outside wall of the parish church rectory of S. Michele Arcangelo (CORNER 1749, VIII: 74):

FIG. 3.20. CI 20. © A. S. Ferguson

Horum unum [*scilicet* papal documents supporting the Pietà hospital] marmorea inscriptio est, quae adhuc parieti Parochialis domus S. Mich. Archang. affixa visitur, antiquis characteribus indulgentias significans, tum a Clemente VI. Pont. Max. tum a Patriarcha gradense, et Episcopo Castellano eis concessus, qui Pietatis infantibus eleemosinae subsidia largirentur.

The church of San Michele Archangelo, commonly known as S. Angelo (Venetian, S. Anzolo), was already in existence well before the fourteenth century. It was closed in 1810 following the Napoleonic suppressions, then demolished in 1837 (ZORZI 1984: 206–07). It was located at the north-eastern corner of Campo S. Angelo, near the Ponte dei Frati, and is depicted there in Canaletto's oil painting *Campo S. Anzolo*. It is quite possible, therefore, that our inscription is indeed on a remnant of the original outside wall of the parochial house which can be seen backing on to the bridge in the Caneletto oil and which subsequently became the parochial house of the nearby S. Stefano (as a modern inscription on the wall of the contiguous Oratorio dell'Annunziata attests) when the four medieval parishes of the area were amalgamated under S. Stefano post 1810. Whether the Pietà inscription was here *ab initio*, though, remains a moot point, and unfortunately de' Barbari's cityscape of 1500 provides inconclusive evidence of what the earlier building layout of the area was like. It would not, however, be at all surprising if this location had been deliberately chosen for maximum exposure. It lay on the axis linking the church and *scuola* of S. Maria della Carità at one end and the Rialto and S. Marco at the other, while it was surrounded by the churches of S. Stefano and S. Angelo and the powerful monastery of the Augustinian friars. The inscription was sensitively cleaned during the recent refurbishment of the building on the Ponte dei Frati.

TYPE AND DESCRIPTION: Charitable appeal with concessionary indulgence. The plaque in Istrian stone measures 60 × 40 cm and is unframed. The layout of the text itself is unique in the corpus. The first six lines cover the full width of the inscription surface and are justified on both sides. The remaining three, which summarise the indulgence 'offer', are separated off by a considerable gap and centred towards the bottom of the plaque. This suggests a conscious attempt by the commissioner of the text to make the message more readable and punchy.

The inscription appeals for alms to be donated to the orphans and foundlings of La Pietà hopital in Venice, the *fantolini dela Pietate* (ll. 3–4). In return, all donors are to be granted cumulative indulgences for remission of sins, computed to the day, by the Pope, the Patriarch of Grado (Andrea Dotto, 1337-?) and the Bishop of Venice (the Nicolò Morexini, 1336–67, mentioned in CI 13, ll. 5–6). The story of the Pietà orphanage and hospital, still very much operational to this day — and now officially known as Santa Maria della Pietà — is a remarkable one spanning more than 750 years. As such it may be the oldest surviving charitable foundation in Venice and one of the oldest in the world. It was officially founded in 1346 by the Franciscan Fra' Pietro of Assisi (known as Fra P(i)e(t)ruzzo), moved to pity by the sight of so many abandoned infants in the city. In 1340 he had commandeered a number of properties in the area of S. Francesco della Vigna (*sestiere* of Castello) and with the newly founded devotional confraternity of S. Francesco della Vigna set up the original nucleus of the *Ospedal dela Pietade*, supported by Senate decree in 1343 (CORNER 1749, VIII: 17–80). The name is said to originate in Pietruzzo's cry of 'Pity!' as he toured the streets begging for funds. Upon his death in 1354 responsibility for the orphans and foundlings passed, with Venetian government support, to a confraternity of pious women, the *Done de Sancta Maria de humiltà dela Celestia*, operating out of the nearby church of the Celestia. Supported by the Signoria and by charitable endowments — from the mid-fifteenth century notaries were obliged to remind testators of the institution's existence — the foundation with its hospital, orphanage and convent eventually expanded into the parish of S. Giovanni in Bragora where in the eighteenth century its modest church would be rebuilt by Giorgio Massari, taking on the familiar grand neo-classical outline that now dominates the western part of the Riva dei Schiavoni. It was here that Vivaldi, who became the Pietà's *maestro di cappella*, trained his famous choirs and orchestras of orphan girls.

LETTERING: No nonsense Gothic majuscules cut in V-section. As befits a naked appeal for funds to save desperate children the writing is without frills and makes minimal concessions to the Gothic spirit. For this reason Cicogna was not wrong to call the script 'semi gotico'. Letter height averages 3 cm although there is a good deal of variation, as can be seen on the <clim> of *Climento* (l. 1) and on *miser* (l. 5). Ligatures are employed throughout on <al>, <an> and, unexpectedly, <ap>. The abbreviations are sometimes disconcerting. The bar above the <a> on *datre* (l. 9) 'of other' would normally indicate an abbreviated <n> but here it must stand for an <l>. Similarly the bar above the <a> of çaschuno (l. 2) 'each one, anyone, everybody' is highly unlikely to represent an <n>. I give the benefit of the doubt by suggesting that it indicates the (missing) preposition *a* 'to' before *çaschuno* (frequently *çasc(h)adun(o)* in Early Venetian texts: see CI 30, l. 29). On *p(er)do* (l. 7) the final <n> has been left out altogether. It is not clear why the ordinal superscript <o> over the 100 symbol (l. 8) has been deployed. Interpuncts are present fairly consistently, although at variable heights. The inscription opens with a dotted *signum crucis* and both blocks of text end with a tailed bow, the first one preceded by three dots in the form of a triangle. This type of punctuation, confirming a paragraph or text-block ending, was familiar from manuscript practice and from the *mariegole* of the Venetian confraternities.

LANGUAGE: The shakiness of the lettering is replicated by the spelling of the inscription. *Sexsto* (l. 1) 'sixth' is a curious hybrid between Latin *Sextus* and vernacular *Sesto*. The <c> of *porce* 'offers, profers' (l. 3) should take a cedilla. *Patriacha* (l. 4) 'patriarch' ought to read *patriarcha*. *Vescodo* 'bishop' (l. 5) is a howler for *vescovo*. For the institution itself *la Piatade* (ll. 7–8) is an attested Venetian form — Sanudo uses *Piatae* alongside *Pietae*: CARACCIOLO ARICÒ (2011: 50, 162) — sitting alongside the more usual, although Latinised, *la Pietate* (l. 4). The somewhat puzzling verb *di* (l. 1) is either a shortened form of, or a mistake for, *die* (in other words, *dié*) 'gave' < DĒDIT.

The text nevertheless contains a number of interesting linguistic features. *Uno* 'one' (ll. 1, 8) is given its full form to distinguish it from *un* 'a'. *Climento* (Clement) shows Venetian raising of pre-tonic /e/ > /i/. *Perdon* (ll. 2, 7) is literally 'pardon' < Old French *perdon*, but here it is a papal or ecclesiastical indulgence for remission of sins (as in Chaucer's *The Pardoner's Tale*). *Fantolini* 'little children, infants, babies' is originally a diminutive of (IN)FANTEM 'infant'. In Modern/Contemporary Venetian it has the meaning of 'poor little children'. *Lemusena* 'alms' (l. 3) is a popular pronunciation spelling of the more usual Early Venetian *elem(u)osena* (see CI 30). It shows the raising of stressed /o/ to /u/ and rapid-speech deletion of the initial vowel. The term is from Greek ἐλεημοσύνη 'pity, mercy, charity, alms' via late Latin ELEEMOSYNA ~ ELEMOSINA ~ ELIMOSINA. A popular north-eastern term — deriving directly from the Greek as can be seen by its accentuation — that still thrived in Modern Venetian was *musina* [muˈzina] 'money box, piggy bank'. *Suma*, l. 7 (occasionally spelled *soma*) < Latin SŬMMA is the usual Early Venetian for 'sum (total)'. It also displays tonic /o/ raised to /u/. *Miser* (ll. 4, 5) remains unaffected by diphthongisation. *Castelo* is the easternmost *sestiere* of Venice. The bishop of Castel(l)o in his cathedral of S. Pietro di Castello was effectively the bishop of Venice (see CI 13), and his support for a charitable foundation in his own district is particularly appropriate.

RECENT STUDIES: STUSSI (1997a: 164); FERGUSON (2013c: 96–97). The inscription was first recorded in CORNER (1749, VIII: 74).

Corpus Inscription 21

+ M^o . CCC^o . LVI . DEL MEXE . DE ÇVGNO . FR̂AR . MAR̂CHO . MINOTO . ₁|
. PRIOR . DE . S(-N) . AN̂DREA . DE LIDO . FE FAR̂ . QVESTO . LAVORIER .
MADONA . ALÎXE . ₂| . DA PONTE . SI LASA . QVESTE . POSESION . AL DITO .
MONESTIERO . ₃

[Mccclvi, del mexe de çugno, frar Marcho Minoto, prior de S. Andrea de Lido, fe' far questo lavorier. Madona Alixe Da Ponte sì lasà queste posesion al dito monestiero.]

TRANSLATION: In the month of June 1356 Brother Marcho Minoto, prior of S. Andrea de Lido, had this piece of work made. It was Lady Alixe Da Ponte who left these properties to the said monastery.

DATE: June 1356.

LOCATION: Corte S. Andrea (*sestiere* of S. Marco no. 3981). The inscription plaque is at present affixed at eye level to the wall of this small, secluded courtyard, located midway between the churches of S. Beneto and S. Luca. It was already there in the early nineteenth century when Cicogna examined it. Like Cicogna, Tassini saw it in the courtyard itself (TASSINI 1863: 20–21). However, in the mid-eighteenth century Flaminio Corner viewed it in its original location over the entrance to the hostel and hospice, in Calle S. Andrea, of the monastery of S. Andrea del Lido (or *dela Certosa*) which owned a string of properties in the neighbourhood of the *corte* (CORNER 1758: 61). Jan GREVEMBROCH who drew the relief in situ and transcribed its epigraph made it clear that the artefact was actually located 'sopra la porta dela Corte di S. Andrea' which must have been walled off as 'appartenente a' Padri Eremitani dal 1336, dimoranti sull'isola di S. Andrea' (1754, I: fol. 8).

TYPE AND DESCRIPTION: Commemorative of the completion of a building project or, possibly, of the sculpted artefact itself. It also records the original donation of properties in this location to the monastery of S. Andrea del Lido. The inscription is carved on to the inclined bottom lip of an imposing plaque of Istrian stone with a crenallated frame measuring 102 × 77 cm. The plaque is now attached to a wall, around 1 m 80 cm off the ground, in the picturesque and little frequented courtyard, facing a charming and slightly dilapidated Gothic well head. In the centre of its striking bas-relief stands the imposing figure of the apostle Andrew, patron saint of the monastery of S. Andrea del Lido, flanked by two small kneeling figures. On one side is probably Marcho Minoto, prior of the monastery and commissioner of the *lavorier* (l. 2), with the Minot(t)o coat of arms. On the other is the monastery's benefactress, also mentioned in the epigraph, Alixe da Ponte. That the plaque was originally placed above eye level is confirmed by the inscription tablet itself (102 × 10 cm) which consists of a sturdy wedge — into which the plaque is slotted — tilted in such a way as to be easily read only from below. A similar bottom-wedge arrangement is found on CI 26. The whole work, in surprisingly good condition, is a rare and attractive survivor of its type.

Fig. 3.21. CI 21 in context. © A. S. Ferguson.

Fig. 3.22. CI 21. © A. S. Ferguson.

The Augustinians had their church and monastery on the small island of S. Andrea de(l) Lido — later called *S. Andrea del(l)a Certosa* from a charterhouse of Carthusian monks there, and now known as the *isola della Certosa* — situated midway between the main Lido itself and S. Pietro di Castello off the eastern end of Venice. In 1269 the Augustinians were left a series of houses by Dame Alixe Da Ponte (CORNER 1758: 60–64) and shortly afterwards converted them into a hostel-cum-hospice. The Da Ponte family are recorded as having extensive properties across Venice in the eleventh and twelfth centuries, of which the largest nucleus was precisely in the S. Beneto parish where the almshouse with the present commemorative inscription would be set up (DORIGO 2003, I: 58, 63, 64). On the S. Andrea hospice see SEMI (1983: 159). The church and monastery were razed to the ground after the Napoleonic suppressions, and the monastery's properties round Corte S. Andrea sold off.

LETTERING: Gothic majuscules cut in V-section. While the lettering has been worn down so that the original grooving is reduced in depth, it remains substantially undamaged. The three expertly cut lines of text are tightly packed on to the narrow inscription surface but word spacing, the consistent use of baseline interpuncts, and the height of the letters themselves (averaging just under 3 cm) ensure(d) the legibility of the text. The script itself is consciously and attractively sinuous in ductus within its limited spacing, but the consistency of line heights is thereby somewhat compromised. This slightly distracting variability is visible on the elongated hairstrokes on <c> and <e>, the curved upstroke on <l>, and the wavy arms snaking below the baseline of <a>, <h>, <r> and <x>. The eye is drawn in particular to the prominent splay serifs on the arm of <g> and on the feet of perpendiculars. Ligatures are present on <al>, <an> and <ar>.

LANGUAGE: *Çugno* (l. 1) < IŪNIUS is the normal form for June in Early Venetian. It is found without the cedilla in CI 22 and was gradually replaced by the spelling *zugno* in the fifteenth century (CI 49, CI 79). In *fe far* 'had made' (l. 2) *fe* (Italian, *fece*) is the 3rd singular past historic of *far* 'to make, to do'. This shortened Early Venetian verb form, originating in constructions like *fe far* where it was pre-tonic, occurs regularly in the corpus alongside *fexe* or *fese*. I have opened out the abbreviated S. *Andrea* (l. 2) as *s(-n) Andrea* because there is no indication in the inscription of whether we are in the presence of *san* or *sen*. *Lido* is from LĪTUS 'shore'. It was applied by antonomasia to Venice's great lagoon sandspit, but could also be used for smaller emerging islands and spits as in the present case. In Early/Middle Venetian *lido* alternated with the form *lio* showing complete lenition of T > /d/ > /Ø/. *Si* (l. 3) is an affirmative particle used for emphasis while *lasa* = [laˈsa], with unvoiced /s/ and stressed final <a>, is the 3rd singular past historic of *lasar* 'to leave' (Italian, *lasciare*). On *frar* 'brother' see CI 17, CI 18. *Posesion* 'properties' (l. 3), already used twice in the singular in CI 9, is here employed in its identical plural form. Identical singular-plural endings in *-n* are normal in Early Venetian when nouns, particularly feminines of the third declension, had had their original singular vowel-ending eroded. *Monestiero* 'monastery' (l. 3) < MONASTERIUM 'monk's cell, monastery' from Greek μοναστήριον alternates in Early Venetian with *monestier, monastier* and, less commonly, *monastiero*. *Dito* '(afore)said' (l. 3), the past participle of *dir*, is the origin of the English *ditto* which entered the language in the Renaissance period from Venetian commercial inventories.

RECENT STUDIES: RIZZI (1987: 136–37); TOMASIN (2001a: 175–76 n. 5); FERGUSON (2013c: 101–01). The inscription was accurately published with its relief in CORNER (1758: between 60 and 61). It was recorded in GREVEMBROCH (1754, I: fol. 8).

Corpus Inscription 22

+ M · CCC · LVIII · DIE · VIII · DE · CVGNO · FO · COMENCADO · ₁|
QVESTE · CAXE · SOTO · MISIER · DON · ANDREA · ABADO · DE ₂|
PONPOXA · CASTOLDO · SIER · ÇANE · DE · CONTERIB(VS) · FATO[R] ₃|
DE · QVESTE · CAXE ∴ ~

[+ Mccclviii, *die* viii de cugno fo comencado queste caxe soto misier don Andrea, abado de Ponpoxa. Castoldo sier Çane de Conteribus, fator de queste caxe.]

TRANSLATION: *On the 8th day of June 1358 these houses were begun under my Lord Don Andrea, Abbot of Pomposa. (The) steward (was) Mr Çane de Conteribus, factor of these houses.*

DATE: June 1358.

LOCATION: Salizzada S. Lio, *sestiere* of Castello. The in situ inscription stone is embedded around 4 m up on the wall of house no. 5764A. The Istrian stone slab (*c.* 100 × *c.* 25 cm) is adjacent to the well-known Gothic *arco del Paradiso* archway, roughly contemporaneous with our inscription, that looks on to the bustling thoroughfare and spans the entrance to the picturesque Calle del Paradiso.

TYPE AND DESCRIPTION: Commemorative and informative. The plaque, which is in effect a house building block, is unframed and part of the wall that forms the corner of the Salizzada as it turns into the narrow medieval alleyway known as the Calle del Paradiso. The stone has been substantially encrusted and darkened by atmospheric pollution. The text which covers less than half the area of the oblong slab is therefore now very difficult to read from ground level and goes totally unnoticed by the constant flow of passers-by in the Salizzada. Nevertheless the lettering is largely undamaged except for part of the extreme right-hand side where the ending of *fator* (l. 3) in particular is effaced. Any difficulties in deciphering the inscription can be resolved with the help of photographs. The adjacent and much admired Calle del Paradiso has two rows of terraced houses with characteristic timber jetties (Venetian, *barbacani*: see CI 101, CI 102) running the length of the street. It is the construction of these houses in the mid-fourteenth century, for renting out, by the powerful abbot Andrea of the great Benedictine monastery at Pomposa south of Ferrara in the Po delta that is the subject of the inscription. The epigraph records the date of the commencement of building works, the commissioner of these and the steward-cum-rent collector. The houses were later ceded to and exploited by the Foscari and Mocenigo patrician families who built the memorable Istrian stone arches, with *madonna della misericordia* reliefs and family coats of arms, over both entrances to the street. The bridge-side arch at the bottom of the alley is probably late Quattrocento. Although part of the *calle* towards the Salizzada was modified in the sixteenth century, this important and fascinating nucleus of everyday medieval houses remains substantially and surprisingly intact. On the terraces and their history see MARETTO (1992: 345–48).

Fig. 3.23. CI 22 in context. © A. S. Ferguson.

LETTERING: Gothic majuscules cut in V-section. The handsome script is a high quality example of Venetian Gothic stonecutting. The letters, around 3 cm high, are perfectly aligned and spaced, with mid-high interpuncts between each word. The ductus is admirably modulated, with subtle gradations of thick and thin strokes. There are no ligatures, and only one abbreviation, the curved line through the <b> of *Conteribus* (l. 3) indicating the *-us* Latin ending. Overall, the uncialesque writing is pleasing to the eye but without excess, and would have been eminently legible. Striking are the delicate hairstrokes on <c>, <e> and <f>, with the latter upcurled, the tapering curve on <n>, the fine tall upstroke on <l>, and the exquisite swirl on the <g> of *cugno* (l. 1).The <t> on *Conteribus* is very unusual in that its topstroke consists of two conjoined arches, almost suggesting an <m>. Straight-sided <u/v> is employed throughout. The cedilla is used as expected on *Çane* (l. 3) but not, surprisingly, on the <c> of *cugno* (l. 1) or *comencado* (l. 1). It cannot be excluded that these cedillas were once present but have been obliterated. The inscription ends with a triangle of dots and a long wavy line, although the presence of this end-of-text punctuation is now largely obscured by surface blackening.

LANGUAGE: The brief inscription deploys an interesting range of titles. The ecclesiastical honorific *don* 'Sir, Lord' (l. 2), for the abbot of Pomposa, is derived from DŎMĬNUS 'lord, master'. *Abado* 'abbot' in l. 2 (compare Tuscan/Italian *abate*) shows that late Latin ABATEM had undergone a metaplasmic change of declension in Venetian. The abbot Andrea, a feudal lord, can be seen kneeling before Jesus in the fresco of *Christ in Glory* — which he himself commissioned from Vitale da Bologna in 1351 — in the absidal vault of the abbey church of Pomposa, the Benedictine house at Codigoro in the Po delta. *Misier* (l. 2), here meaning 'Sir', is clearly contrasted with *sier* 'Mr' (l. 3), both now affected by the wave of diphthongisation which had not yet reached CI 20. The absence of the cedilla should not be taken to mean that the <c> in *cugno* (l. 1) and *comencado* (l. 1) was not, like *Çane* (l. 3), pronounced as an affricate. *Castoldo* 'steward, alderman' (l. 3) is a minority variant of Early Venetian *gastoldo* or *gastaldo* (see CI 23). The form with initial /k/ reappears on CI 97 from 1518 as *chastaldo*. It is probably an example of a long-term Venetian tendency to de-voice initial /g/, as in *confalon* 'banner' (Italian, *gonfalone*). The letter <x> has the usual voiced sibilant value /z/ in *Ponpoxa* (l. 3) and *caxe* (l. 4). *Ponpoxa* for Pomposa suggests characteristic Venetian nasalisation at the end of a syllable. *Die* (l. 1) 'on the day of' is an intrusive Latinism, habitually found in written documents of the period, for the normal vernacular *adi* of our inscriptions. The passive construction *fo comencado queste caxe* 'these houses were begun' (ll. 1–2) is the second example in the corpus (see CI 18) of absence of agreement between past participle and noun, a common occurrence in Early Venetian texts but in the minority in our collection.

RECENT STUDIES: STUSSI (1997a: 173); FERGUSON (2013c: 101–02). First published in B. GAMBA (1832: 17–18) based on a transcription provided to him by Cicogna who recorded the inscription (with inaccuracies) but did not publish it.

Corpus Inscription 23

A̅ NOME DE CHR(IST)O AMEN AD HONOR (E) STADO D̪EL BI | ADO A̅P(OSTO)LO
MIS(R) SE(N) ṬOMADO A̅REMIXIO(N) D(E) OGNI P̪ECATOR ₂ | M° CCC° LVIIII
D(E)L MESE̪ D(E) MAÇO FO FATA E COME(N)ÇAD̪A ₃ | Q(VE)STA B(E)N(E)DETA
SCOLA D(E) MIS(R) SE(N) TOMA A̅P(OSTO)LO GASTOL | DO S(R) MAFIO NADAL
S(O) VICA̪RIO S(R) NICOLETO DA̅LE STORE SC | RIVA̅N S(R) FELIPO NADAL
D(E)GA̅N S(R) PIERO BON DA̅L FERO E S(R) FR | A̅NCESC° VERIER E S(R) PIERO
ÇIMADOR E S(R) NICOLO BERETER E ₇ | S(R) PIERO GA̅LEDER E S(R) LORE(N)ÇO
TENTOR E S(R) A̅NTONIO ÇA[L]ED | ER E S(R) A̅NDREA OREXE IACOMELO
CA̅LEGER NO(N)ÇOLO GA | STOLDA DONA NICOLOTA E DEGA̅NA DONA
(C)H(A)TARINA DAL | A SOSA LAQVAL SCOLA FO TRATA DVNA MA̅RIEGOLA CH | E
CO(N)PARSE̪ IN M°CLXXXVII DEL MESE DAVRIL:~ ₁₂

[A nome de Christo amen. Ad honor e stado del biado apostolo mis. Sen Tomado, a remixion de ogni pecator, Mccclviiii del mese de maço, fo fata e començada questa benedeta Scola de mis. Sen Tomà apostolo. Gastoldo sr Mafio Nadal. So vicario sr Nicoleto dale Store. Scrivan sr Felipo Nadal. Degan: sr Piero Bon dal Fero, e sr Francesco Verier, e sr Piero Çimador, e sr Nicolò Bereter, e sr Piero Galeder, e sr Lorenço Tentor, e sr Antonio Galeder, e sr Andrea Orexe. Iacomelo Caleger nonçolo. Gastolda dona Nicolota, e degana dona Chatarina dala Sosa. Laqual Scola fo trata d'una mariegola che conparse in Mclxxxvii del mese d'avril.]

TRANSLATION: In the name of Christ, amen. For the honour and prestige of the blessed Apostle St Thomas, and for the remission of all sinners, this blessed Confraternity of my Lord Thomas the Apostle was set up and begun in the month of May 1359. (The) alderman (was) Mr Mafio Nadal. His deputy (was) Mr Nicoleto dale Store. (The) clerk (was) Mr Felipo Nadal. (The) dean(s) (were): Mr Piero Bon dal Fero and Mr Francesco Verier and Mr Piero Çimador and Mr Nicolò Bereter and Mr Piero Galeder and Mr Lorenço Tentor and Mr Antonio Galeder and Mr Andrea Orexe. Iacomelo Caleger (was) the undertaker. (The) alderwoman (was) Mrs Nicolota and (the) dean Mrs Chatarina dala Sosa. This Confraternity derived from a statute book which came into being in 1187 in the month of April.

DATE: May 1359.

LOCATION: In Campiello del Piovan, a small offshoot of Campo S. Tomà (*sestiere* of S. Polo), at house no. 2870. The inscription plaque is embedded in the wall, around 350 cm off the ground, above a house door — formerly the door of a sacristy — and under a first-floor window at the far end of the little square. It faces the well head in the centre of the courtyard. Just to its left is the side wall of the church of S. Tomà with the striking affixed sarcophagus — dated 1375 on its Latin epitaph in raised Gothic majuscules — of the senator and soldier Çane Priuli. Our inscription has been in its present position, where it is hard to read, since some point early in the nineteenth century. Originally it was situated at a lower level on the now demolished wall which once closed off the *campiello* when it was, as its name indicates, the courtyard of the parish priest (*piovan*) of S. Tomà. In Luca

FIG. 3.24. CI 23. © A. S. Ferguson.

CARLEVARIJS's early eighteenth-century etching of the church of S. Tomà (1703: fol. 28) our inscription can be seen on the outside of the courtyard wall, facing Campo S. Tomà, placed in public view just above eye-level. This location is confirmed by Johann Georg GRAEVIUS (1722, V, 1: 191): 'In pariete extra Templum lapis adest, in quo sequens memoraria vernacula olim lingua conscripta, ac antiquitate venerabilis'.

TYPE AND DESCRIPTION: Dedicatory and commemorative. The inscription plaque in Istrian stone with its crenellated frame measures some 75 × 50 cm, while the inscription surface itself is *c*. 71 × *c*. 46 cm. An integral part of the artefact is the relief bust of St Thomas (or perhaps an angel), around 30 cm high, atop the frame and cut from the same stone block as the inscription plaque. The figure holds a book and points down to the epigraph. The inscription celebrated the new meeting house of one of the oldest *scuole piccole* devotional confraternities in Venice, that of St Thomas. The confraternity, whose first altar and meeting place were within the church itself, had had its original *mariegola* drawn up in 1187 — as the inscription confirms — and redrawn in 1358 (G. VIO 2004: 616). The epigraph itself is a priceless public document for the explicit information about the organisational structures and membership of the many modest devotional confraternities of Venice. For an analogous inscription from a flagellant confraternity on Murano see CI 38.

LETTERING: Gothic majuscules carved in V-section. Letter grooving has been worn away somewhat by the action of time but damage is limited and the inscription remains in good shape. The left- and right-hand sides of the two top lines are partly encrusted with black from atmospheric pollution, making them tricky to read. A crack on the right-hand side starting in line 7 and snaking into line 8 obscures the <gal> in *Galeder* (l. 8). Overall, this is a highly competent piece of inscriptional sculpting. The unfussy Gothic script is attractive and elegant, and layout and pagination have been carefully thought through by commissioner, *scriptor* and stonemason, probably with a preliminary mock-up. The twelve lines of text are justified on both sides and fit the inscriptional area almost to perfection, with only a small space at the end covered by triple vertical dots and a wavy line. Given how relatively tightly packed the text is, legibility remains high. This is down to the sheer neatness and consistency of the script which averages just over 2 cm in height and, while quintessentially Gothic, is aspectually balanced in the proportion between letter height and width. Readability is also enhanced by the regular spacing between lines and by the clear gaps between words and letters themselves, with interpuncts absent. Just occasionally the stonecutter is obliged to encroach slightly on to the rim of the right-side frame: at the end of lines 5 and 6 (the <c> of *scrivan* and, especially, the <r> of *Francesco*). He seems to have been so knocked off his stride by the overrun that he proceeded to miss out the subsequent <n>, the expected cedilla on <c> and the final <o> on the word, restoring the latter in superscript. The standard ligatures involving <al>, <an> and <ar> are present.

Abbreviations are mainly limited to the Chi-Rho, the vertical overbar for <n> and the sinuous diagonal stroke through <s> for *ser* or *sier*. On l. 5, following *Nadal*, an <s> with an abbreviation or insertion hook seems to indicate the possessive adjective *so* 'his'. Most interesting and unusual of the abbreviations is the similar hooked stroke on the <h> of *Chatarina* (l. 10). Others have interpreted the <h> as a <k>, something that would be unique in the corpus. Instead, close inspection suggests that we are in the presence of an <h>, hooked high on its stem (and not near the shoulder) and ending in a wedge serif, to express *(C)h(a)*. This type of hooked and wedged sign expressing several letters — commonly employed in manuscripts (CAPPELLI 1928: xxx-xxxiii) — can be seen clearly on CI 3, on an <h> as it happens, and also on an <l>. It is perhaps most strikingly present on a Gothic inscription in Venice on the second-line <h> of the consummate Latin epigraph of 1317 carved on the tomb of St Simeon the Prophet in the presbytery of the church of S. Sim(i)on Grando. The stonemason there has emphasized that an abbreviation is involved by elegantly intersecting the leg of the <h> and the downstroke of the following <t>. Surprisingly, this sign is still found in our corpus on CI 100 of 1511, where it is used on the initial <s> to abbreviate *sanctus* and *sancta* 'saint', although that inscription is in Roman capitals.

LANGUAGE: The inscription contains a remarkable range of terminology linked to the officialdom and membership of the Venetian *scuole piccole* devotional confraternities and to Venetian crafts. *Gastoldo* (ll. 4–5) ~ *gastolda* 'alderman, alderwoman' (ll. 9–10) < Longobardic *gastald 'court dignitary' both show characteristic Early Venetian raising of /al/ to /ol/ before a dental consonant. The *gastoldo* or *gastaldo*, the variant that would predominate in the fifteenth century and beyond, was the chief officer of a *scuola piccola*, elected for one year and therefore the equivalent of the *vardian (grando)* of the *scuole grandi* (see CI 3). It could also mean 'steward' (see CI 22). The female form *gastolda* appears here for the first and only time in the corpus. Along with *degan* 'dean, deacon, counsellor' (l. 6) < DĔCĀNUS, and its female equivalent *degana* (l. 10), we have exceptional public proof here of the mixed nature of some at least of the Venetian confraternities that is attested to in their statute books. Other elected officials mentioned are the *vicario* 'deputy' (l. 5), sometimes spelled *avic(h)ario*, and *scrivan* 'clerk, secretary, scrivener' (ll. 5–6) < medieval Latin SCRIBANUS. The *nonçolo* (l. 9), a diminutive from late Latin NUNCIUS 'reporter, messenger, envoy', looked after the material objects of the confraternity and acted as its undertaker (BOERIO 1865, *s.v. nonzolo*). The inscription also provides a rich bank of what appear to be, on the one hand, settled surnames (Nadal, Bon dal Fero, dale Store, dala Sosa) and, on the other, proto-surnames. The latter are occupational surnames all linked to traditional crafts. At this point in time they appear to hover between professional designations and fixed *cognomina* and I hesitated, therefore, before capitalising them (although they are listed pell-mell, like here, with proper surnames in the confraternity *mariegole*). They are, in order: *verier* 'glazier' (< VĬTRĀRĬUS), *çimador* 'cloth shearer ' (medieval Latin CIMATOR, from CIMAM 'top part'), *bereter* 'hatter' (< late Latin BIRRETUM 'cap'), *galeder* 'wooden pail or bucket cooper' (< medieval Latin GALIDA, GALEDA or GAL(L)ETA 'vessel, wine measure), *tentor* 'dyer' (< TINCTOR), *orexe* = [oˈreze] (< AURĬFICEM) 'goldsmith' and *caleger* 'shoemaker, cobbler' (< CĂLĬGĀRĬUS). The majority show the characteristic Venetian agentive ending in *-er* < -ĀRIUS. As is common in Early Venetian, the <g> in *caleger* (l. 9) represents velar /g/, even before a front vowel. *Mariegola* 'confraternity statute and membership book' (l. 11) is the phonologically regular outcome of MĀTRĪCŬLA 'index, catalogue, list, register'. It is the only appearance in the corpus of this key term of the Venetian brotherhoods.

A number of Christian names are worthy of note. The inscription aligns characteristic Venetian forms of Thomas: *Tomado* (l. 2) ~ *Tomà* (l. 4). With a third form, *Tomao*, common in Early/Middle Venetian, the trio contrasts strikingly with Italian *Tom(m)aso*. All three, of which *Tomà* was the most innovative and the longest lasting, show the same variation as past participles of the -ĀTUM > *-ado* type in Venetian. On *Mafio* (l. 5) Matthew see CI 37, CI 41. *Nadal* (ll. 5 and 6) 'Christmas' was originally a Christian name. The name of the alderwoman *Dona Nicolota* (l. 10) is a feminine diminutive form of Nicolò (Nicholas) that appears not uncommonly in the Venetian documentation of the time.

Stado (l. 1) is literally 'state' and, like *biado* 'blessed' (ll. 1–2), shows characteristic Venetian voicing of T > /d/. *Avril* April (l. 12) displays normal Early Venetian voicing of -PR- to /vr/. *Maço* (l. 3) < MĀIUS is the regular form for May (see CI 45, CI 56, CI 96), although it was gradually replaced in the fifteenth century by the spelling *mazo* (see CI 79, CI 81, CI 98). *Mese* 'month' (ll. 3 and 12) is spelled with an <s>, unlike in CI 19 and CI 21 which have <x> for the voiced sibilant /z/. Here the <x> is reserved for the unvoiced sibilant /s/, as in *remixion* 'remission' (l. 2). The relative *laqual* 'which' (l. 11), referring to *scola*, is the second example of syntactic recurrence in the corpus (see CI 13, CI 30, CI 63, CI 64). *Conparse* (or *comparse*) 'appeared' (l. 12) is the Early Venetian 3rd singular past historic form of *conparer*. *Fo fata e comencada* (l. 3), agreeing in gender and number with *scola* (l. 4), is the majority passive pattern in the corpus. Rare in the collection are the two examples of vowel elision: *duna* (= *d'una*) 'of a', l. 11 and *davril* (= *d'avril*) 'of April', with the latter replicated in the *dapril* (= *d'april*) of CI 92.

RECENT STUDIES: RIZZI (1987: 398–99); FERGUSON (2013c: 103–05); FERGUSON (2015c: 53–54). The inscription was recorded in MARTINELLI (1684: 362). It was transcribed diplomatically by SORAVIA (1822–24, II: 187).

Corpus Inscription 24

M^O · CCC · LVIIII° A[DI] X̣X[...] D[E] FEVRARO FO FATA ₁ |
S^{TA} A͡NCONA P(ER) MA͡N (DE) LORE(N)CO PENTOR ·.· IN VENEXIA :~

[MCCCLVIIII, adì xx[...] de fevraro, fo fata sta ancona per man de Lorenco pentor — in Venexia.]

TRANSLATION: 1359, on the 2[...] of February, this holy image was made in Venice by the hand of the painter Lorenço.

DATE: February 1359 (February 1360 by modern reckoning).

LOCATION: The panel of the *Mystic Marriage of St Catherine* on which the inscription is painted is at present on display in the Accademia galleries in Venice (*sestiere* of Dorsoduro), inventory number 944. According to GUARNIERI (2006: 185–86):

> La tavola appartenne alla collezione Manin di Venezia, venne poi acquistata da Jacopo Danieli e successivamente dal conte Pellegrini di Zara. Nel 1855 Lazari (1859) vide l'opera nella collezione del conte Cernazai di Udine che alla sua morte la lasciò probabilmente in legato al Seminario Arcivescovile della stessa città [...]. Nel 1900, infine, fu donata alle Gallerie.

The whereabouts of the panel before the nineteenth century are not known. Although Lorenço is considered the most important Venetian artist of the second half of the fourteenth century, we possess only a handful of paintings securely attributable to him, with very little known about his life, commissions and artistic development. The mixture of Byzantine and Gothic elements in his work has led art historians to see the influence on him of contemporaneous artists such as Tommaso da Modena, Vitale da Bologna and Guariento da Arpo, and to link him to commissions on the Veneto mainland (RIGONI and SCARDELLATO 2011; GUARNIERI and DE MARCHI 2016). While our inscription is silent on the intended location of the panel it may, if correctly interpreted, provide clues as to whether the *Mystic Marriage* was painted in Venice. Key is the punctuation mark — consisting of an upturned triangle of dots — used after *pentor* 'painter' (l. 2). This mark represents a clear pause, breathing or syntactic. As such, it renders the reading 'Lorenço painter in Venice' problematic. It suggests, instead, that 'in Venice' is an adverbial phrase of place qualifying *fo fata sta ancona* (ll. 1–2). In other words, 'this holy image was made in Venice by the hand of the painter Lorenço' is the likelier interpretation.

TYPE AND DESCRIPTION: Statement of authorship and date. The inscription consists of two lines of white-painted writing on a dark green ground confirming the authorship of the painting by the Venetian artist Lorenço — who also signed in Latin as *Laurencius de Veneciis* or *de Venetis*, or simply *Laure(n)cius pictor*, and who is known in Italian as Lorenzo Veneziano (active 1356–72) — and its date of execution. The message runs along the bottom of the tempera painted wooden panel (87 × 58 cm). The inscription surface itself is roughly 30 × 3 cm.

Fig. 3.25. CI 24. © A. S. Ferguson.

The painting was probably the central panel of a triptych. It depicts within a gold-leaf *mandorla*, surrounded by musician angels, the Virgin Mary in pink dress and gold-trimmed azure mantle holding a lively baby Jesus who looks up at her affectionately. He is in the act of handing a ring to St Catherine, who stands by His side. This act symbolises her mystic union with the divinity (see CI 35). At the Virgin's feet are figurations of the sun and moon. Directly below the *mandorla* is our inscription.

LETTERING: Painted Gothic majuscules. The conspicuous lettering is spaced rather unevenly and the letter heights are a little variable, averaging 1.8 cm. There has been some damage to parts of the painted surface of the epigraph so that elements of the date, in particular, are unclear. The viewer's eye is impudently drawn to the presence of the inscription by the elegant red shoe of an angel pointing directly at it and, on the other side, by dangling red tassels falling towards it. Lorenço mimics inscriptional majuscules but, with the added freedom of the paint medium, he deliberately gives exaggerated filigree finesse and elongation to hairstrokes on <c> and <e>, and tapers the arms of <a>, <n> and <r> with curlicues. He even includes a full range of inscriptional abbreviations where these are not strictly called for in the space available. We find the suspension bar indicating a missing <n> in *Lorenco* (l. 2), barred <d> for *de* (l. 1), the lone Tironian 7 for *de* (l. 2), and <p> barred horizontally on its stem for *per* (l. 2). Even the <an> ligature is present twice. The painter's name appears as *Lorenco* but surface abrasion beneath the <c>, which has removed the hairstroking on that letter, may well have also erased the cedilla. Since there is no other extant work by him signed in the vernacular we have no way of knowing what his practice was in this matter. The script is strikingly similar to that on other signed paintings by Lorenço in Latin, such as the red lettering at the foot of the panels of *St Mark* and *St Peter* and the black lettering at the foot of the *Annunciation with Saints*, all in the Accademia. Our epigraph concludes with an end-of-text punctuation mark consisting of a colon followed by a short wavy line.

LANGUAGE: *Fevraro* February (l. 1) < FEBR(U)ĀRIUS is a well-documented variant in Early Venetian, alongside the commoner *fevrer* (see CI 41). *Fevraro*, though, was by far the most frequently used form on the Veneto mainland and may just possibly suggest — along with the explicit mention that the panel was executed in Venice — that the painting was commissioned on the *terraferma* (GUARNIERI 2011: 23). On *ancona* 'icon, devotional image' (l. 2) see CI 2. *Sta* 'this' (l. 2) is commented on in CI 19. Following an error whereby the <s> of *sta* was attached to *ancona*, Lorenço or his assistant covered up the mistake, not particularly felicitously, by adding <ta> in superscript. *Pentor* 'painter' (l. 2) from PICTOR 'painter', subsequently contaminated by the <n> of PINGERE 'to paint', is a regular Early Venetian variant alongside *depentor*. In Modern Venetian they were both replaced by the Italianism *pitor*. The passive *fo fata sta ancona* (ll. 1–2) is another example of perfect agreement in gender and number in the corpus between past participle and noun. In *Venexia* (l. 2) diphthongisation has yet to affect the name of the city.

RECENT STUDIES: TESTI (1909: 216–18); VAN MARLE (1924: 50); STUSSI (1980a: 91–92); FERGUSON (2013c: 102–03); RICCIONI (2017: 67).

Corpus Inscription 25

ANNO · M · CCC · LX · PRIMA · DIE · IVLII · I |
SEPVLTVRA · DOMINI · SIMON · DANDOLO · AMADOR · DE · IVSTISIA · E
DISIROSO · DE ACRESE · EL · BEN · CHOMVM · +

[*Anno* MCCCLX, *prima die iulii*. Sepultura *domini* Simon Dandolo, amador de iustisia e disiroso de acrese el ben chomum +.]

TRANSLATION: *In the year 1360, on the first day of July. Tomb of Sir* Simon Dandolo, lover of justice and desirous of increasing the common good.

DATE: July 1360. This is the date on which the sarcophagus and its inscription were completed rather than the date of Simon Dandolo's actual death or burial. In fact Bartolomeo Cecchetti found the will of Simon Dandolo of S. Silvestro in the ASV archives, dated 30 December 1360. In it Dandolo confirmed that he wished to be buried honourably within his own chapel in the Frari, and that he was leaving 200 *libre* for the painting of his chapel and tomb: 'dimitto libras ducentas pro pictura mee capelle et mee arche' (CECCHETTI 1887b: 51 n. 6).

LOCATION: Basilica of the Frari, *sestiere* of S. Polo. The inscription is on the sarcophagus of Simon Dandolo which is affixed around 10 m up on the western wall at the end of the north aisle, to the left as one enters the church through the main door. The epigraph is now impossible to read from that distance with the naked eye. However, it was eminently legible when it was in what one presumes to have been its *ab initio* location in the basilica. According to Soravia, who copied out the inscription accurately, the tomb was originally in the chapel known as S. Giuseppe (to the right of the presbytery) before being transferred, where he saw it, next to the massive baroque tomb of doge Giovanni Pesaro (SORAVIA 1822–24, II: 143).

TYPE AND DESCRIPTION: Epitaph and statement of tomb ownership. The inscription is engraved along the Istrian stone base plinth of the sarcophagus. I have not been able to precisely measure the sarcophagus, which is in *pietra d'Istria* inlaid at the front with porphyry panels, but I estimate that it is around 230 cm along the front base. The vernacular section of the epitaph, always meant to be the most visible, runs along the length of that front base. The initial Latin section with the date is mostly tucked away on the left side. The sculpted decoration on the front of the sarcophagus, which Ruskin greatly admired, has at its centre an enthroned Madonna and Child in high relief. She holds open a bible while He points with his finger to a passage in it. On the left edge is the relief figure of an Annunciation Madonna; on the right edge is the Annunciation angel. The top of the sarcophagus is decorated with a flower plinth. The two corbels supporting the tomb bear the engraved Dandolo coat of arms. In terms of form, materials and iconography the Dandolo sarcophagus in the Frari resembles several patrician tombs in S. Zanipolo: that of Andrea Morosini (*c.* 1348) and, in particular, that of Marco Giustinian (*c.* 1347) with its unusually short, matter-of-fact, Latin inscription along the bottom edge.

Fig. 3.26. CI 25 in context. © A. S. Ferguson.

Simon Dandolo was the brother of the doge Andrea (in office 1343–54). We know little about him other than a few isolated facts. He was twice mayor of Treviso, and in 1345 was one of the electors of the doge Marin Falier. In 1346 he was one of the officials sent to quell the rebellion in Zara (CARACCIOLO ARICÒ 2007–09, II: 24). The following year, on the eve of the plague crisis in the city (see CI 14), he was one of the two *Savi* dealing with the Flanders galleys (ASV, Senato, *Miste*, reg. XXIV, 17 April 1347). He was also one of the judges who in 1355 condemned the traitor doge Falier to death. His desire for justice mentioned on the epitaph may relate to this fact, although its scope and tone seem wider. The Dandolo sarcophagus stands out among the many grand fourteenth- and fifteenth-century tomb monuments with inscriptions in the major Venetian churches. Those inscriptions are always in Latin and their eulogies tend to the wordy and rhetorical. That Dandolo wished for this restrained and poignant epitaph is therefore remarkable in itself. That he should have ordered it to be expressed in the vernacular is unique.

LETTERING: Gothic majuscules carved in V-section. Measured and elegant, the script combines finesse with strength. The ductus does not emphasize the contrast between thick and thin strokes, nor is it particularly compressed. It reserves its decorativeness, instead, for the splay serifs in <d> and <s>, the curved hairstrokes on <c> and <e> and, most strikingly, for the tapering leg of <h> (which is unusually raised), <n> and particularly <r>. There are no abbreviations or ligatures and the space between letters and words, with mid-high interpuncts consistently used, further increases legibility. The writing, which fully fills the interlinear space on the plinth, is itself relatively large. On the negative side, the overall planning of the inscriptional layout leaves something to be desired. There is unnecessary space between the end of *acrese* and the following *el* and, above all, a sizeable section of the surface of the base plinth is left blank between the end of the epitaph and the final *signum crucis*.

LANGUAGE: It can reasonably be assumed that the mason who cut the inscription was the skilled craftsman who sculpted the decoration on the sarcophagus. We have already mentioned how remarkable it is that most of the epitaph was in the vernacular. The procedure whereby the formulae for date, time and place were in Latin, with the main part of the text in the vernacular, seems to be have been copied from fourteenth-century notarial practice in the city for the drafting of wills. What is equally surprising is the nature of the vernacular on display here. Although the message is a brief one, there is enough to suggest that the Venetian employed is of a somewhat lower social register than that generally on view in our collection. A number of its 'non-standard' features show up, as it happens, in fourteenth-century texts of a more modest nature than our public writing. They are probably residues of the koineisation process which culminated in the substantial elimination in the Trecento of the marked linguistic variation that characterised Early Venetian in its remotest recorded stages (FERGUSON 2007: 161–92). The most eye-catching irregular feature is the infinitive *acrese* 'to increase' (l. 2) for the expected *acreser*. No other Venetian vernacular inscription carries this final consonant apocope on an infinitive. It was a spoken trait typical of the input from the northern Venetian lagoon into the diverse mix that was Early Venetian. It survived in certain areas and social strata of the city into the nineteenth century (as well as on Burano), and was deployed in dialect literature until Goldoni and beyond in order to give class and district colour to the speech of marginal characters.There are two other clues in the epitaph that may point in the same direction. *Disiroso* 'desirous' (l. 2), with its extreme raising of pre-tonic /e/ to /i/ on a semi-learned word, is very much a minority variant among the Venetian texts in the OVI compared to *desiroso*. The same goes for the slightly surprising final <m> on *chomum* 'common' (l. 2), where *c(h)omun* is the dominant Venetian form in the OVI and in our corpus. Any doubts about the genuineness of the form *acrese* are dispelled by Marco Barbaro's sixteenth-century holograph transcription of the epitaph in his manuscript genealogy of the Dandolo family whereas, significantly, *disiroso* and *chomum* are corrected there to *desiroso* and *chomun* (SCHULZ 1993: 409). It is likely that these forms, especially the clipping of the infinitive, originate not directly from the *ordinator* of the text but from the sculptor. It is not without interest, therefore, that the sponsor of the monument tolerated such deviations from the linguistic norm from the stonemason, to the extent that he did not insist on the restoration of the final -*r* on *acrese*, even though space would have allowed for it. For another example of such apparent tolerance see CI 35. *Sepultura* 'burial place, tomb' (l. 1), followed as it is by the honorific genitive *domini* 'of (the) lord', hovers between Latin and the vernacular: see CI 78. One notes the presence of the dominant Early Venetian variant *iustisia* 'justice' rather than the more Latinising *iustitia* found on CI 54.

RECENT STUDIES: STUSSI (1997a: 153); STUSSI (1997b: 926); FERGUSON (2013c: 105–06). The inscription was first published in SORAVIA (1822–24, II: 143).

Corpus Inscription 26

M CCC LXI A DI XXV DE LVIO FO FATO QVESTO LAVORIER IN LO TENPO DE SIER MICHIEL DE LI AMADI TINTORE ₁ | VARDIAN DE LA SCVOLA DE SEN ÇANE BATISTA CON LI SVOI CON[PAGNI] ₂

[MCCCLXI, a dì xxv de luio, fo fato questo lavorier in lo tenpo de sier Michiel de li Amadi tintore, vardian de la Scuola de Sen Çane Batista, con li suoi conpagni.]

TRANSLATION: On the 25th of July 1361 this piece of work was made, in the time of Mr Michiel de li Amadi, dyer (and) warden of the Confraternity of St John the Baptist, with his colleagues.

DATE: July 1361.

LOCATION: When Cicogna saw the inscription the plaque was affixed to an outside wall beside the meeting house of the confraternity of John the Baptist on the island of Murano (CICOGNA 1824–53, VI, 1: 376). When the *scuola* buildings were demolished in 1837 the artefact was taken to the Seminario Patriarcale at the Salute in Venice for safekeeping. It remained there until the late twentieth century, but is now back in Murano displayed on a wall in the cloister of the Museo del Vetro.

TYPE AND DESCRIPTION: Commemorative. The inscription records the completion of a piece of work for the brotherhood. It is likely that the *lavorier* (l. 1) in question refers specifically to the artefact itself. This is an impressive sculpted high relief plaque, in Istrian stone with a crenellated frame, measuring 172 × 93 cm. Our inscription runs along the bottom half-rim of the plaque and along half of the surface beneath it which is deliberately angled so as to be legible from below. In both cases the tilted inscription surfaces are 172 × 5 cm.

The relief on the plaque depicts the bearded and haloed figure of St John the Baptist, patron saint of the confraternity, with his biblical animal skin clothing still showing underneath a dignified toga. He stands and blesses a row of four pairs of kneeling confraternity brothers. In front of them is the warden *Michiel de li Amadi* (l. 1) to whom the saint hands the confraternity's ceremonial banner. The two brothers behind him hold large processional candles. The iconography of this relief is strikingly similar to the one above the 1349 inscription (CI 17) in the atrium of another flagellant brotherhood, the immensely influential Scuola Grande di S. Giovanni Evangelista in Venice. On the flagellant *Scuola de S. Ç(u)ane Batista* on Murano see CI 38. The *vardian* Michiel (Italian, Michele) Amadi was a dyer (*tintore*, l. 1) and a powerful figure in the community of silk merchants who had fled Lucca in 1314 and in the following years because of the political turmoil in that city (MOLÀ 1994: 122, 280). Dyeing was, of course, an integral part of the silk production process. Amadi resided in the S. Stefano district of Murano and possibly had connections with another immigrant Tuscan businessman resident there whose inscription, blending Venetian and Tuscan features, is examined in CI 8. On the Amadi see CROUZET-PAVAN (2015: 489–95).

Fig. 3.27. CI 26 (detail) as it was in the 1970s. © A. Scarpa.

The present artefact is now in a sorry state and appears to be rapidly deteriorating. It is affected all over by exfoliation and flakes to the touch. When I examined it most recently in the summer of 2018 it had undoubtedly been cleaned and tidied up. However, the contours of relief and lettering are in an advanced state of decomposition and have become irremediably blurred. This is all the more shocking in that photographs taken in the 1970s show both epigraph and sculpture substantially intact (WOLTERS 1976, I: ill. XX). Parts of the inscription can still be deciphered with care but a full reading is only possible with the aid of earlier images.

LETTERING: Gothic majuscules cut in V-section. The script is elegantly and spaciously laid out on the two inclined rims, a system used on no other inscription in the corpus. Interpuncts may for this reason have been deemed unnecessary, although the extreme wear and tear affecting the inscription surface makes it hard to be sure. Legibility was further enhanced by the absence of abbreviations and by the height of the letters which, at around 4 cm, is generous. The ductus is well balanced with nothing exaggerated and with a number of subtle touches, most notably the tapering curved upstroke on the <l> and the very shallow curve on the straight-sided <u/v>. The <q>, with its right-sided undulating tail, is particularly attractive. *Fo* and *fato* (l. 1) are bunched together as they are clearly felt to be a single syntagm. The <ar> on *vardian* (l. 2) and the <an> on *Çane* (l. 2) are ligatured.

LANGUAGE: The language of the inscription is of particular interest as it is one of only a handful in the corpus commissioned on Murano, in this case by a Muranese corporation. One is immediately struck by *sen* 'saint' (l. 2), rather than *san*, a rare but not unique confirmation that this common Early Venetian form, with <an> raised to <en>, was also present on Murano. The epigraph confirms, too, that the wave of diphthongisation of mid-high vowels affecting Venetian was present here, with *sier* 'Mr' (l. 1), *scuola* 'confraternity' (l. 2) and even *suoi* 'his' (l. 2), the latter a genuine Early Venetian variant for *soi* (FERGUSON 2007: 132). Most interesting is *tintore* 'dyer' (l. 1), a reading I have selected in preference to *tintor*. Since an interpunct is not present, and the spacing after the word is ambiguous, it is not clear if one should read *tintor e vardian* 'dyer and warden' or else *tintore vardian* 'dyer, warden'. The latter reading has the authority of the transcriptions of the epigraph transmitted by MOSCHINI (1842: 68) and CICOGNA (1824–53, VI : 376). It would imply that the anomalous form *tintore* is down either to Tuscan influence or else is a native Muranese variant with no final vowel apocope after *-r*. The latter is a supposition for which we have no evidence and which is contradicted by the occurrence of *pistor* 'baker' and *sartor* 'tailor' in Muranese inscription CI 38 from the same confraternity. An additional potential complication is that *tintor* itself was not common in Early Venetian where *tentor* dominated (see CI 23, l. 8). However, variability between /e/ and /i/ in the pre-tonic position was very common in Early Venetian: for example, *preson* ~ *prison* 'prison' and *spiçier* ~ *speçier* 'grocer'. The fact that Michiel Amadi was a silk dyer whose family migrated to Venice from Lucca raises the distinct possibility that *tintore* is indeed a genuine Tuscan form and that, as with the inscription-will of Angelo Piarini (CI 8), we are in the presence of linguistic code mixing. See also CI 54 and CI 93 for the presence of Tuscan linguistic features.

RECENT STUDIES: TOMASIN (2012b: 3 n. 8); FERGUSON (2015c: 55). First published in MOSCHINI (1842: 68).

Corpus Inscription 27

₁| M · III · LXI · DI · XV · D(E) · A͡URIL · FO TOLTA · LA S̩CV̩O̩L̩[A ·DEL]
| GLORIOSO · A͡POSTOLO · MIS̩IER · S(AN)C(T)O · MATIA̩ · DE · S̩EN̩ ₂|
SA̩LVADOR · E FO · RE[DV]T[A] · IN · G̩L̩IES̩IA̩ · DE · SEN · BORT[OLA | M]IO̩ ·
D[OVE] S̩ENP̩(RE) · DIE · D[VRAR CO]MO̩ P̩(ER) [CARTE APAR] ₄

[MIIILXI, dì XV de avril, fo tolta la scuola del glorioso apostolo misier Sancto Matia de Sen Salvador, e fo reduta in gliesia de Sen Bortolamio dove senpre die durar, como per carte apar.]

TRANSLATION: On the 15th of April 1361 the confraternity of the glorious apostle Saint Matthias was removed from S. Salvador and was returned to the church of S. Bortolamio where it must always remain as is stated in (legal) documents.

DATE: April 1361.

LOCATION: Originally from the church of S. Bortolamio (*sestiere* of S. Marco) or from a building belonging to the devotional brotherhood of S. Mat(t)ia in the Rialto district. Cicogna saw the artefact in 1834 in the parish of S. Geremia (*sestiere* of Cannaregio) where the confraternity had properties (BMC, mss Cicogna, *Inedite* 2008, *busta* 499, nos. 490, 601). Shortly afterwards it was moved to the Seminario Patriarcale at the Salute where it is now displayed on a wall in the corridor of the *piano nobile*.

TYPE AND DESCRIPTION: Commemorative. The inscription records a fundamental event in the life of the confraternity of S. Matia: its transfer on 15 April 1361 from the church of S. Salvador back to that of S. Bortolomio, both in the Rialto district. Behind this seemingly anodyne fact lay a heated conflict between the brothers and the clergy of S. Salvador (G. VIO 2004: 405–08). The *scuola* — one of the earliest recorded in Venice — was originally housed in the Camaldolese church of S. Matia on Murano in the early thirteenth century but subsequently moved to the Rialto area in Venice, first to S. Bortolamio in 1248 and then to S. Salvador in 1352. The confraternity eventually found itself at loggerheads with the clerics of S. Salvador and decided in April 1361 to return to S. Bortolamio, enshrining its decision legally. Hence the expression *como per carte apar* 'as per legal document' at the end of the inscription. That punctilious legal agreement, recorded in the *scuola*'s statutes, is published in ORTALLI (2001: 202–05). On the peculiarities and long-term combativeness of this rather unusual brotherhood see SAPIENZA (2013). On its curious relationship with the Nuremberg merchants of the Fontego dei Todeschi who also worshipped in S. Bortolamio, and on a surviving fragment of its *mariegola*, see HUMPHREY (2015: 317–21).

The large scale high-relief statue of St Matthias with halo and toga, holding the gospel and in the act of blessing, dominates the plaque. At his feet kneel the diminutive figures of six brothers in the act of worship. The relief in Istrian stone measures 90 × 56 cm and has a crenellated frame. Enough space was provided on an angled and slotted wedge (56.5 × 7.5 cm) at the bottom of the object to hold the four-line inscription.

FIG. 3.28. CI 27. © A. S. Ferguson.

LETTERING: Gothic majuscules cut in V-section. Both statue and lettering have been worn down by the salt air, with roughening and chipping of the stone, but they are still substantially intact and now appear to be stabilised. There is some damage to the upper right side of the inscription plaque, obliterating the end of the first line. Since the grooving of the letters, which average 1.7 cm in height, has been worn down the epigraph is no longer easy to read in places. The final line in particular is a major problem, with only a few letters still decipherable because of a layer of plaster smeared on the bottom of the inscription wedge. Fortunately the epigraph was recorded by Cicogna who transcribed the illegible section of the fourth line as: *ove senp(re) die durar como p(er) carte apar*. This reading is consistent with the letter fragments which can still be made out, so I have integrated it into my transcription, modifying *ove* to *dove* as the <d> is actually detectable on high-resolution photographs. The script itself is competent, neat, well-spaced and justified on both sides, with the stonecutter making the best use of the limited surface available to him. This, in conjunction with the angle of the inscription tablet and with the use of black infilling — traces of which were still visible until the very recent cleaning of the artefact —, would have ensured a high degree of visibility. In spite of letter fading a few features of the script still stand out. The choice of <III> for 300 in the date, instead of the usual Roman CCC, is unusual. The <u/v> is straight-sided, but in *avril* (l. 1) it is right-curved and ligatured with the preceding <a>. Ligaturing is also present on the <ap> of *apostolo* (l. 2). While the <a> is broad based the <o> is markedly almond shaped. The uncial <d> displays strong splay serifs, while the <t> has long tapering downstrokes and the <e> shows curved hairstroking. Most noticeable is the <l> with a particularly long, sinuous upstroke.

LANGUAGE: Diphthongisation is consistently present with *scuola* (l. 1) and *misier* (l. 2), as are the raised forms *sen* 'saint' in *sen Salvador* St Salvator (ll. 2–3) and *sen Bortolamio* St Bartholomew (ll. 3–4). *Salvador* (Italian, *Salvatore*) shows the expected Venetian voicing of intervocalic T > /d/ and the loss of the final /e/ after /r/ on an original paroxytone. *Reduta* 'brought back' (l. 3) is the past participle of Early Venetian *redur* 'to restore, return, bring back, draw up'. *Fo tolta* (l. 1) and *fo reduta* (l. 3) are further examples of the surprising number of agreements in gender and number between past participle and noun in the corpus. *Avril* (l. 1) April < APRĪLIS is the native Early Venetian form of the month. It was gradually supplanted in writing in late Early Venetian and in Middle Venetian by *april*, closer to both Tuscan and Latin (see CI 79, CI 92). On *gliesia* 'church' (l. 3) and its pronunciation see CI 13. On *die* 'must' (l. 4) see CI 1. *Durar* (l. 4) is literally 'to last, endure'.

RECENT STUDIES: WOLTERS (1976, I: 192–93); DI LENARDO (2014: 110–14). First published in MOSCHINI (1842: 91). Recorded, but not published, by Cicogna.

Corpus Inscription 28

+ · M⁰ · CCC⁰ · LXII · DI · XXII · DE · DECENBRIO · FO · ₁|
FATO · QVESTO · CHANPANIL · SIANDO ·PERCHVR|
ADOR · LO · NOBELE · HOMO · MISER · FELIPO · ₃|
DANDOLO ·∴· ≫

[+ MCCCLXII, dì XXII de decenbrio, fo fato questo chanpanil, siando perchurador lo nobele homo miser Felipo Dandolo.]

TRANSLATION: On the 22nd of December 1362 this bell tower was completed, when the nobleman Sir Felipo Dandolo was Procurator.

DATE: December 1362.

LOCATION: The base of the bell tower of the church of S. Polo (*sestiere* of S. Polo), on the lintel over the low door giving access, at street level, to the tower.

TYPE AND DESCRIPTION: Dedicatory and commemorative. The in situ epigraph records the completion just before Christmas 1362 of the picturesque brick bell tower, with pine-cone shaped spire, of the church of S. Polo. It is not without interest that the *campanile* of the nearby Frari church — the highest bell tower in Venice after St Mark's — was begun in 1361 just as ours was being completed. We do not know how long the S. Polo tower took to raise, or who built it, but the Frari bell tower took thirty-five years (1361–96) from start to finish. We learn this from a 14-line Latin inscription in a highly-stylised uncialesque Gothic — of a type not seen in our corpus — embedded in the wall at the base of the Frari tower and ending with the dots-and-acanthus-leaf punctuation that concludes the S. Polo inscription. We also know from the Frari plaque and from the Frari's own documentation (SARTORI, 1983–89, II: 1745) who the architects were (Jacopo Çelega and his son *Petrus Paulus* = Piero Polo). One wonders if the Franciscans of the Frari and/or the financial sponsors of their tower were spurred into action by the more modest works at S. Polo just down the road.

Situated as it is at the narrowest point on the much-frequented Salizzada S. Polo that links the Frari to Campo S. Polo, just where the base of the *campanile* faces the entrance to the S. Polo church, the inscription is passed by an incessant flux of locals and tourists. The eye of those who look in its direction tends to be attracted to the two anonymous but remarkable Romanesque lions, sculpted in Aurisina limestone, flanking the epigraph on the ledge above. The inscription is carved 158 cm above pavement level on the Istrian stone architrave (142 cm wide) just above the low entrance door to the tower. The writing itself covers an area of roughly 89 × 21 cm. Lintel and epigraph have suffered inevitable wear and tear but the writing, while no longer sharp, is perfectly legible with a little care. The two fantastical crouching lions that flank it are each about a metre long. The one on the left holds a human head between its paws; the one on the right struggles with a serpent whose jaws are round its neck. According to DORIGO (2003, I: 504) they may be of mainland origin and could have been executed to decorate a pulpit.

Fig. 3.29. CI 28. © A. S. Ferguson.

LETTERING: Gothic majuscules cut in V-section. The text is spaciously laid out with generous distance between letters and words, the latter additionally separated by mid-high interpuncts. It is justified on the left. The characterful lettering is 3 cm high and vigorously uncialesque. Prominent are the very long curving hairstrokes on <c>, <e> and <f>, the extended tapering upstroke on <l> that matches the stem length, the sinuous arms of <a>, <h> and <n>, and the extravagant and shapely leg of <r> in *decenbrio* (l. 1) which curves below the baseline to touch the letter beneath. Unusual among the Gothic inscriptions in the corpus is the straight-sided <u/v> in *questo* (l. 2) and *perchurador* (ll. 2–3) with a horizontal underbar as on a truncated capital upsilon. On this Byzantine Greek feature see CI 37. Two different forms of <m> are featured, the capital type on *miser* and the uncial elsewhere. There are no abbreviations, but ligatures are present on two of the three examples of <an>. The punctuation at the end of the text, with five dots in a diamond formation followed by an acanthus-leaf motif, is rare in the corpus. For a similar example see CI 41.

LANGUAGE: *Chanpanil* 'bell tower' (l. 2), from Early Venetian *c(h)anpana* 'bell', survived into Modern Venetian in the forms *campanil* or *campaniel*. The Early Venetian spelling characteristically suggests nasalisation at the end of the first syllable (also seen on the second syllable of *decenbrio*, l. 1) and employs the common <ch> digraph for /k/. On the ending of *decenbrio* (December) see CI 79. The passive *fo fato questo chanpanil* (ll. 1–2) shows complete agreement between noun and past participle as was inevitable with a masculine singular noun. *Siando* 'being' (l. 2) is from *eser* 'to be' and features the regular Venetian reduction of gerunds to the first (*-ar*) conjugation that we have already seen in CI 2, CI 3, CI 13. *Perchurador* 'procurator' (ll. 2–3) shows the metathesis of *pro-* to *per-* on reflexes of PRŌCŪRATŌREM that occurs regularly in the corpus. This time, however, the title referred to is not that of proctor, as in CI 17, but of the powerful and prestigious Procurator of St Mark — specifically the *Procurator de Ultra* whose jurisdiction encompassed the *sestieri* of Dorsoduro, S. Crose and S. Polo. *Felipo* (l. 3) is an example of Early Venetian lowering of pre-tonic /i/ to /e/ compared to Tuscan/Italian, while *nobele* (l. 3) shows the same phenomenon post-tonically. Interestingly, *miser* 'Sir, Mr' (l. 3) has resisted the wave of diphthongisation of tonic mid-high vowels which we have already noted.

RECENT STUDIES: FERGUSON (2013c: 106–07). First published by Flaminio Corner (CORNER 1749, II: 309–10) then by SORAVIA (1822–24, II: 175).

Corpus Inscription 29

· M⁰ · CCC⁰ · LXII · ADI X D(E) AVRIL SIA͡NDO ₁|
PLOVA͡N D(E) SE(N) M(AR)TIN MIS(R) P(RE) FRA͡NÇESCO ₂|
A͡LBAREGNO S(R) PIERO MASER FE FA͡R Q(V)ESTA O[VR]A ₃

[MCCCLXII, adì x de avril, siando plovan de Sen Martin mis. pre' Françesco Albaregno, sr Piero Maser fe' far questa ovra.]

TRANSLATION: On the 10th of April 1362, when the very reverend Françesco Albaregno was parish priest of St Martin's, Mr Piero Maser had this object made.

DATE: April 1362.

LOCATION: Campo S. Martin (*sestiere* of Castello). Affixed just above eye level to the left-side outside wall of the church of S. Martin.

TYPE AND DESCRIPTION: Dedicatory and documentary. The inscription documents the completion (or perhaps the commissioning, since the wording is ambiguous) of a *Madonna and Child* devotional object (*c.* 70 × *c.* 60 cm) made, presumably, to be displayed on or near the church of S. Martin (Italian, S. Martino). The church and its square are in what is nowadays a very quiet part of eastern Venice, little visited by tourists, around the corner from the Arsenal. The inscribed message records the name of the parish priest at the time (Françesco Albaregno) and of the work's commissioner (Piero Maser). Wedged between two chevroned coats of arms it occupies the extended bottom frame of the *ancona* in Istrian stone (*c.* 60 × *c.* 9 cm including the escutcheons). The other three sides of the artefact have a crenellated edge. The wooden frame at present round the whole plaque was added in the twentieth century. The low relief depicts a gentle-faced standing Virgin Mary, crowned and haloed head slightly inclined, holding a calm baby Jesus. It is an example of the *Hodegetria* Madonna genre inherited from Byzantium, and the relief in fact shows the influence of both Byzantine and Gothic styles. It was moved at some time in the twentieth century to its present position from the opposite side-wall of the church, facing the Rio del Arsenal, where an inscription plaque in Italian recorded by Cicogna once stated that it was restored by a group of pious parishioners in 1829 (PAZZI 2001, II: 1301). Earlier it may have been part of a shrine of which we have no surviving information. The writing is worn down but the epigraph, although in need of restoration, is in reasonable shape. There is unsightly atmospheric blackening along the middle of the sculpture while the inscription plaque is chipped along the central part of the bottom edge, affecting in particular the reading of the name *Maser* (l. 3).

The citizen family *Albaregno* (l. 3) or Alberegno, connected notably with the cloth trade, is well recorded in Venice in the Trecento. Cicogna transcribed details of the Latin inscriptions on a number of fourteenth-century Alberegno tombs in the church of S. Maria dei Servi in Cannaregio, the third largest church in Venice, which was demolished after the Napoleonic suppressions. Françesco Albaregno's rectorship of S. Martin was no small matter. His predecessor was, in fact, the

FIG. 3.30. CI 29 in context. © Ronnie Ferguson.

Andrea Dotto we have come across already (CI 20) who was to become Bishop of Chioggia then Patriarch of Grado. As was normal for priests in Venice, Albaregno also acted as a notary public (Venetian, *noder*). He is recorded as the lawyer in a transaction of 13 January 1364 involving the sale for 40 ducats of a female Tartar slave by Polo Antiollo, a resident of S. Martin, to Jacobello Negro (ASV, Cancelleria Inferiore, Notai, *busta* 5).

LETTERING: Gothic majuscules cut in V-section. The script, which has a rather compressed module, is not always perfectly aligned so that letter height varies a good deal around an average of 2.3 cm. The groove depth has been worn down but enough remains to show that the mason achieved good stroke contrast. Space between letters and words has been relatively well maintained but the craftsman, given the constraints of space he was working under, resorted to a higher than average proportion of abbreviations. A kinked bar was inserted over <e> in *sen* (l. 2). Tironian 7 cuts diagonally through <s> on *mis(r)* and also through the ascender, rather than the body, of <d> for *de* (ll. 1, 2). An odd canopy abbreviation mark over the <m> of *Martin* (l. 2) expresses the missing <ar>, and a vertical stroke inside the bowl of <q> in *questa* (l. 3) points to missing <u/v>. To indicate *pre* 'priest' (l. 2) a short bar has been inscribed above the <p> and the bowl of the letter has been deliberately opened out and curled. There is an unusually simplified cedilla on the <ç> of *Françesco* (l. 2). Elsewhere, the sides of <u/v> are gently bowed and quite strongly serifed. The <an> ligature is used three times and the <ar> ligature twice. The <al> on *Albaregno* (l. 3) is also ligatured, with a rather peculiar weak <l> employed. The sculptor, pushed for space, has ingeniously taken advantage of the chevrons of the escutcheon on the bottom right to suggest the letters <vr> in *ovra* (l. 3).

LANGUAGE: *Plovan* (Tuscan/Italian, *pievano*) is 'parish priest, rector' (l. 2) < PLEBANUS, with the variants *ploban* and *pleban* also present in Early Venetian. It shows normal fourteenth-century retention, in writing at least, of the PL nexus which would evolve over time into /pj/. For *siando* 'being' (l. 1) see CI 2, CI 13, CI 28. *Pre* or *pre'* (l. 2) is the vocative shortening of Early Venetian *preve* (also *prevedo* or *prevede*, the latter surviving into Modern Venetian as an archaism) meaning 'priest' or 'reverend'. *Ovra* 'work, piece of work, object' (l. 3) derives from the Latin plural OPERA 'works', with syncope of the post-tonic /e/ and regular Venetian lenition of -PR- > /vr/. The neologism *opera* appears in the vernacular of CI 105. The surname *Maser* (l. 3) or Masser (also Massaro on the mainland) had meanings ranging from 'administrator or treasurer' (as in CI 75) to 'tenant' or 'factor' (BOERIO 1865, *s.v. massèr*). It is probably, in fact, a proto-surname like the artisan names in CI 23.

RECENT STUDIES: RIZZI (1987: 182–83); FERGUSON (2013c: 107–08). Recorded, but not published, by Cicogna.

Corpus Inscription 30

:✝: URBAN UESCOVO . SERVO DELI SERVI DE DIO. A TVTI LI FEDELI ·₁ | DE
CRISTO. CHE LLE PREXENTE LETERE VEDERA SALVDEMO CO(N) ·₂ |
LA APOSTOLICHA BENEDICION · LO SPLANDOR DELA PATERNAL ₃ |
GLORIA. LOQVAL PER LA SOA INEFFABELE CLARITADE INLVMIN |
A EL MONDO. CVM ÇO SIA CHOSA CHE LI PIETOSI VODI DELI FED |
ELI. SPERANDO DELA CLEMENTISSIMA MAIESTADE DE QVELLO ₆ |
IN QVELA FIADA GRANDEMENTE CON BENIGNO OLTVRIO EL LI ₇ |
RECEVERA E PER LA DEVOTA HV(M)ILITADE D(E) QVELLI PER LI PRIE |
GI E MIERITI DELI SENTI QVELLI SERA AIDADI. DESIDERANDO ₉ |
ADONQVA CHE LLA CHAPELLA METVDA IN LO PALLAÇO DELO ₁₀ |
DOXE DE VENIESIA IN HONOR E NOME DE SEN NICHOLO I(N) LAQV |
AL SI COMO NV AVEMO INTENDVDO DE MESSE (E) D(E) OLTRI DEVINI ₁₂ |
OFFICII SOLEMNI CONTINVAMENTE SIA CELEBRADI E CON ₁₃ |
CONVEGNIVELLE HONORI CONTINVADA. E A ÇO CHE LI FEDELI ₁₄ |
DE CRISTO PLV VOLENTIERA PER CHASION DE DEVOCION AL |
O DITO LVOGO VADA. IN LOQVAL LVOGO PLV VBERTOSAMENT |
E DE CELLESTIAL DON DE GRACIA E(L)LI SE VEGA SATISFATI DE |
LA MISERICORDIA DELO OMNIPOTENTE DIO. E DELI BIADI APOS |
TOLI. SEN PIERO E SEN POLO. E PER LAOTORITADE DE QVELI A NV ₁₉ |
CONCEDVDA A TUTI VERAMENTE PENTIDI. E CONFESSI [LL]IQVAL ₂₀ |
ANDERA IN LA FESTA DELA NATIVITADE. E DELA CIRCONCISI |
ON. DELA EPIPHANIA. DELA RESVRECION. DEL CORPO D(E) CRI |
STO. ECIAMDIO. LE QVATRO PRINCIPAL FESTE DELA BIADA ₂₃ |
VERGENE MARIA. E DELO DITO SEN NICO⟨L⟩LO. E LA DITA CHA |
PELA VISITERA DEVOTAMENTE. E PER SOSTENTACION DE |
LI PVOVERI PRISONIERI DETEGNVDI. IN LE CHARCERE ₂₆ |
DELO DITO PALAÇO. DELI BENI CHE DIO LI A DADI PIETOXE ₂₇ |
HELEMVOSENE ELI DARA : VN ANNO. E QVARANTA. DI. DE |
LE INÇVNTE PENETENCIE PER ÇASCADVNA DE ⟨Q⟩ |
VESTE FESTE. LI DI LIQVALI. LA DITA CHAPE |
ELA. ELLI VISITERA. ET HELEMVOSENA ELI ₃₁ |
DARA SI CHOME DITO. MISERICHORDIEVOLE |
MENTE MO LASEMO : DADO IN VIGNON. VII. I |
DI DE MAÇO L·ANO PRIMO DELO NOSTRO PON |
TIFICHADO : AMEN :~

[+ Urban vescovo, servo deli servi de Dio, a tuti li fedeli de Cristo che lle prexente letere vederà, saludemo con la apostolicha benedicion. Lo splandor dela paternal gloria, loqual per la soa ineffabele claritade inlumina el mondo, cum ço sia chosa che li pietosi vodi deli fedeli, sperando dela clementissima maiestade de quello, in quela fiada grandemente con benigno olturio el li receverà, e per la devota humilitade de quelli per li priegi e mieriti deli

FIG. 3.31. CI 30. © A. S. Ferguson.

Fig. 3.32. CI 30 (lines 29–35). © A. S. Ferguson.

senti quelli serà aidadi. Desiderando, adonqua, che lla chapella metuda in lo pallaço delo Doxe de Veniesia in honor e nome de Sen Nicholò in laqual, sì como nu avemo intendudo, de messe e de oltri devini officii solemni continuamente sia celebradi e con convegnivelle honori continuada; e a ço che li fedeli de Cristo plu volentiera per chasion de devocion alo dito luogo vada, in loqual luogo plu ubertosamente de cellestial don de gracia elli se vega satisfati dela misericordia delo omnipotente Dio e deli biadi apostoli Sen Piero e Sen Polo e per l'aotoritade de queli a nu conceduda, a tuti veramente pentidi e confessi lliqual anderà in la festa dela nativitade e dela circoncision, dela epiphania, dela resurecion del corpo de Cristo, eciamdio le quatro principal feste dela biada Vergene Maria e delo dito Sen Nichollò, e la dita chapela visiterà devotamente, e per sostentacion deli puoveri prisonieri detegnudi in le charcere delo dito palaço — deli beni che Dio li a dadi — pietoxe helemuosene eli darà: un anno e quaranta dì dele inçunte penitencie per çascaduna de queste feste li dì liquali la dita chapeela elli visiterà et helemuosena eli darà sì chome dito, miserichordievolemente mo lasemo. Dado in Vignon VII idi de maço, l'anno primo delo nostro pontifichado. Amen.]

TRANSLATION: Bishop Urban, servant of the servants of God, to all the faithful in Christ who see the present letter, we salute (you) with the Apostolic blessing. The splendour of paternal glory which through its ineffable clarity illuminates the world, in consideration of the pious vows of the faithful hoping in its most clement majesty, will on this occasion greatly, with benign help, receive these (vows); and through the devout humility of those (vows) and the prayers and merits of the saints they will be supported. Desiring, therefore, that the chapel housed in the palace of the Doge of Venice to the honour of, and in the name of, St Nicholas — in which, as we have heard, masses and other divine and solemn services are continually celebrated — be supported worthily; and so that the faithful in Christ more willingly for the sake of worship attend that place; and so that when there they can profit more fruitfully from the celestial gift of grace and pity of almighty God and of the blessed apostles Saints Peter and Paul, on the basis of their authority handed down to us, we now mercifully give out — to all those who are genuinely repentant and have confessed and who attend on the feast days of the Nativity, Circumcision, Epiphany, and the Resurrection of Christ's body, as well as the four main feast days of the Blessed Virgin and (the feast of) St Nicholas; and who visit the said chapel reverently, and for the maintenance of the poor prisoners held in the prisons of the said palace give alms charitably from the goods that God has given them — : one year and forty days from imposed penances for each feast day, on the day that they visit the said chapel and give alms charitably as stipulated. Issued in Avignon on the seventh of (the) Ides of May in the first year of our pontificate. Amen.

DATE: 1362 or soon thereafter.

LOCATION: Embedded in situ, or in close proximity, on the wall of the first floor loggia of the eastern tract of the Doge's Palace (*sestiere* of S. Marco), to the right of the Scala d'Oro. In the context of the papal indulgence offered on the plaque the inscription makes extensive reference to two locations in the palace originally in the vicinity of the inscription but now gone: the chapel of St Nicholas and the ducal prisons known as the *Toresele*, literally 'turrets, little towers'. The chapel of St Nicholas, the patron saint of sailors and merchants — whose stolen body was brought back to Venice and interred in 1100 in S. Nicolò del Lido — was built under doge Piero Ziani (in office 1205–29) but was probably instigated by the preceding doge Endrigo (Italian, Enrico) Dandolo, in office 1192–1205, to commemorate the capture of Constantinople by the Venetians and other Crusader forces in 1204. The church, the doge's private chapel on the first floor of the eastern part of the courtyard, was located to the left of our inscription at the end of the loggia. It was demolished in 1525 so that the eastern wing of the palace could be enlarged. The prisons were housed, before the sixteenth century, on the ground floor of the palace and could be reached via a staircase on the other side of the wall where the inscription is located. On the church of St Nicholas, with the relevant documentation, see FORTINI BROWN (1988: 259–60).

TYPE AND DESCRIPTION: Proclamatory, with charitable appeal and concessionary indulgence. The text is the epigraphic transcription into the vernacular of a papal bull issued in Latin by Pope Urban V from Avignon in the first year of his pontificate, probably at the request of the Venetian government. The Latin original was copied into the Venetian state records at ASV, *Libri Commemoriali*, VII, fol. 34*v*. It is not without interest that the inscription which would have been read by the Venetian elite, most of whom had studied Latin, was felt by the authorities to have a greater impact if carved in the vernacular. The missive, obviously translated into Venetian prior to being sculpted in stone, offered 140 days remission of sins to those who visited the chapel of St Nicholas in the Doge's Palace in Venice on given feast days and donated alms for the maintenance of the 'poor prisoners' (*puoveri prisonieri*, l. 26) held in the contiguous ducal prison.

The inscription consists of 35 lines of densely packed text in raised lettering on a handsome, rather austere, marble tablet with crenellated frame. Standing some 170 cm off the loggia pavement, the imposing artefact with its frame measures 154 × 114 cm, while the epigraphic surface is 150 × 110 cm. Below the text itself a strip, roughly 20 cm high, runs along the bottom of the plaque and features a row of low-relief insignia. In the middle a Venetian lion *in moleca* (restored after being vandalised, like almost all Venetian lion symbols, by the post-1797 Republican goverment) is flanked on either side by sculpted ankle fetters, in reference to the nearby prisons, and by the ducal shield of the reigning doge Lorenço Celsi. The marble of the plaque has weathered well and there is no major structural damage.

Letters have occasionally suffered some chipping and in one case, the double <ll> on l. 20, have fallen out but overall the epigraph remains intact and impressive. Clearly recognised as a significant historical document, the inscription was transcribed (not always accurately) in the nineteenth century by Pietro BETTIO, the Marciana librarian, in his book on Francesco Sansovino's letter concerning the Doge's Palace (1829: 42), by Bartolomeo GAMBA in his collection of early Venetian texts (1832: 15–17), by Francesco ZANOTTO in his study of the palace (1842–58, I: 7–8), and by Giovanni FERRO in his article on early Venetian inscriptions (1889: 449–50). It was transcribed, but not published, by Cicogna.

It is not unique to Venice that a papal bull should be sculpted in stone, or even painted, for public display. One thinks of two conspicuous examples elsewhere in Italy: the record of a bull by Pope Innocent III frescoed *c.* 1200 by Magister Conxulus in the Benedictine monastery of the Sacro Speco in Subiaco; and the screeds of papal privileges inscribed in stone in the later Trecento on the façade of Ferrara cathedral, alongside the statue of Alberto d'Este. However, these are in Latin. What is unique in the Middle Ages, as far as I am aware, is that a papal letter should be translated into the vernacular and then transferred on to stone. On two different types of *charta lapidaria* in the present corpus see CI 8 and CI 49.

LETTERING: Gothic majuscules in raised lettering. The script is 3 cm tall and is elevated from the plaque by just under 0.5 cm. It was almost certainly gilded originally although no traces remain.

It is reasonable to suppose that the civil servant charged by the Signoria with translating Urban's letter would have provided the stonemason with a text written in a minuscule chancery hand, including the punctuation customary (but with a good deal of inconsistency from text to text) in careful handwritten documents. The mason then transferred the minuscule into the usual Gothic majuscules but maintained the original written punctuation, apart from capitals, probably on orders. Consequently, the sculpted marks on the epigraphic text differ fundamentally from those on all other inscriptions in our collection in being concerned less with word or syntagm separation than with breathing and declamatory pauses. The range of marks is interesting and basically follows the *positurae* recommended by Donatus's *Ars Grammatica*. We find the mid-high interpunct (*media distinctio*) representing a period after *benedicion* (l. 3). In the original bull it is followed by a full stop and a capital letter at the start of the next word. Also present on the inscription are a series of single *puncti* on the baseline representing commas (*subdistinctiones*). Finally, there is the declaratory conclusion featuring a sequence of three strong-pause colons between ll. 28 and 35, the last of these, the end-of-text *periodos*, accompanied by a wavy line. Only on *l·ano* 'the year' (l. 34) does one come across an interpunct apparently indicating word separation, and here it is about avoiding the awkwardness of a hanging article (as on CI 61). The epigraph begins with a cross studded with four dots as in CI 13, another solemn ecclesiastical text.

The spelling on the inscription is as expected apart from one recurring feature, the surprising and seemingly haphazard distribution of single and double <l> as in *la* ~

lla 'the', *quelli* ~ *queli* 'those', *Nicholo* ~ *Nichollo* 'Nicholas'. This can be explained by the mason's slavish copying of the translator's text. The use of double <l> appears to have had no phonetic rationale but it was common practice in longhand writing in Early Venetian and in other early Italo-Romance varieties, possibly because the long stem of a single handwritten <l> was easily confused with that of <f> or <s> (DOTTO 2008: 154–57). The practice is seen more rarely in *littera textualis* bookscript and is very rare in vernacular epigraphic script where majuscules and, later, Roman capitals reduced or removed visual ambiguity.

Pagination on the epigraph is exceptionally dense although the lining is quite regular. The stonecutter, probably on orders from the commissioner, seems to have striven for perfect justification on both sides, adding not only a mid-high interpunct when there was any kind of space at line-end (l. 1) but even, in one case (l. 10), filling the gap with a squiggle. The latter is a particularly interesting instance of the sculptor's preoccupations and *modus operandi*. Having originally decided to end l. 10 with *del* — in other words, the first three letters of *delo* 'of the' — the craftsman inserted an end-of-line interpunct. To his dismay he then realised that he had still left too much space and that his solution spoiled the aesthetic unity he was endeavouring to achieve. He went on to rectify his 'mistake' by inserting the final <o> of *delo* after all, sculpting it round the interpunct itself. Finally, he filled the gap that still remained with the squiggle.

Gaps between letters are, in general, quite generous but word spacing as such hardly exists except towards the bottom of the inscription where the sculptor was, again, preoccupied to fill the available space. This creates an overall effect of *scriptio continua* which makes the text difficult to absorb for the modern eye even though the letters themselves are sober in ductus. In this respect the script, while broadly similar to that of CI 9 and CI 14 — the other two raised stone epigraphs in the corpus — differs from both. In CI 9, whose ductus is rather more sinuous, words or syntagms are separated, while in CI 14 they are carefully demarcated by mid-high interpuncts. Overall, the Palace inscription is more functional than decorative compared to CI 9 and CI 14. Interesting and unexpected is the uncial <u> on *Urban* and *vescovo* (l. 1). This choice is certainly conditioned by the original papal text where, as in all his correspondence, Urban began with the formula *Urbanus ep(iscopu)s servus servorum dei*. The <u/v> is always represented at the outset of his papal missives by a striking uncial display capital <u> with horizontal hairstroke. In our inscription the uncial form replicating this quickly gives way to a bowed <v>, presumably because the latter provided greater distinctiveness in the raised format vis-à-vis other rounded letters such as <c> and <e>. The double <l> in both *chapella* and *pallaço* (l. 10) is run together in a quasi-ligature as is the <ff> in *ineffabele* (l. 4) but, otherwise, ligatures are absent. Mistakes as such are rare: in ll. 29–30 the <q> of *queste* has been sculpted as an <o>; on l. 24 the first <l> of *Nicollo* has been carved as an <i>, with the mason probably intending originally to link it up to the following <l> with a baseline stroke; and the double <e> in *chapeela* (ll. 30–31) is an error caused by the copyist splitting the word at line-end and reprising the last letter at the start of the new line. Abbreviations are few and far between.

LANGUAGE: Directly based on a high-register written text translated from Latin into Venetian by, one assumes, a senior functionary in the ducal chancery, the inscription is quite different from anything else in the corpus in terms of syntax, vocabulary and punctuation. As such, it is a critical piece of linguistic and sociolinguistic testimony. It shows what mid-fourteenth-century Venetian was capable of at the highest non-literary stylistic level. In addition, as an eminent piece of public writing exhibited in the most central and prestigious location imaginable in the Venetian state, it is a precious example of what must have been regarded — in terms of phonology, morphology, lexis and spelling — as the Venetian written 'standard' of the time.

In contrast with the paratactic structures that characterise most of our inscriptions, this epigraphic text is hypotactic, deploying long, complex, rhetorical sentences that contain a high level of abstract nouns and syntactic recurrence with relative pronouns. The Venetian translator of Urban's letter has done a decent job overall in conveying what is very difficult stylistic material, although occasionally his attempts to stay faithful to the convoluted syntax of the original Latin verge on the obscure. While the translator's rendering is genuinely Venetian it is inevitably affected by the Latin of the original, and not only in terms of the extreme dependent-clause syntax. The plural morphology of *lle prexente letere* 'the present letter' (l. 2), for instance, is directly conditioned by the *presentes litteras* of the original Latin. The officialese *cum ço sia chosa che* 'in consideration of the fact that' (l. 5) uses Latin *cum* 'with'. Terms such as *ineffabele* 'ineffable' (l. 4), *clementissima* 'most clement' (l. 6), *solemni* 'solemn' (l. 13), *omnipotente* 'omnipotent' (l. 18), *aotoritade* 'authority' (l. 19) and the mouthful of an adverb *miserichordievolemente* 'mercifully' (ll. 32–33) are semi-learned and calque the Latin original. Latinising spelling with <h> is used on *humilitade* 'humility' (l. 8) and *helemuosena* 'alms' (l. 31). One notes, however, that the pull of Latin onset AU on *aotoritade* < AUCTŌRĬTATEM is less than on the more usual form *autoritade*, and that the diphthong is fully resolved to /o/ in the popular *Polo* (l. 19) Paul < PAULUS, still used in Venice in the name of the square and church of S. Polo. *Ubertosamente* 'fruitfully' (ll. 16–17) is from the semi-learned and rare adjective *ubertoso* 'fertile', itself from ŪBERTAS 'fertility of the soil'.

The inscription provides interesting evidence of the status of important variants in the history of Venetian. One notes, first, that the wave of diphthongisation of stressed mid-high vowels which swept over Early Venetian from the mid-fourteenth century appears to have been socially unmarked, if the frequency with which it occurs here is anything to go by: *priegi* 'prayers' (ll. 8–9), *mieriti* 'merits' (l. 9), *Veniesia* Venice (l. 11), *luogo* 'place' (l. 16), *Piero*, Peter (l. 19), *helemuosena* 'alms' (l. 31). Also important is the strong suggestion given off by the inscription that vowel raising — of /al/ to /ol/ before a dental consonant and of /an/ to /en/ — was still perfectly acceptable at this juncture and level, although it would die out in both cases in the fifteenth century. So *olturio* (rather than *alturio*) 'help' (l. 7) < late Latin ADIUTORIUM; *oltri* 'others' (l. 12); *sen* 'saint' throughout and *senti* 'saints' (l. 9) rather than *santi*. *Lo* and *li* remain the dominant forms of the masculine definite article. The epigraph also confirms what was suggested by previous inscriptions, that the standard written form of regular past participles and of nouns from Latin -ĀTEM had crystallised around the maintenance of intervocalic /d/, rather than allowing the weakening or loss seen in some less formal Early Venetian texts and destined to prevail long-term in Venetian: *aidadi* 'helped' (l. 9), *metuda* 'put, placed' (l. 10), *intendudo* 'heard, understood' (l. 12), *celebradi* 'celebrated' (l. 13), *continuada* 'continued' (l. 14), *conceduda* 'conceded' (l. 20), *pentidi* 'repented' (l. 20), *detegnudi* 'held, detained' (l. 26); and *claritade* 'clarity' (l. 4), *maiestade* 'majesty' (l. 6), *humilitade* (l. 8), *nativitade* 'nativity' (l. 21). Also confirmed is the preference for the traditional -*er*- over the variant -*ar*- in the stem of the future tense: *vedera* 'will see' (l. 2), *recevera* 'will receive' (l. 8), *sera* 'will be' (l. 9). On the other hand, adverbial endings show a decisive preference for the formerly minority -*mente* morph, aligned with Tuscan and destined to prevail in Venetian, over the traditional -*mentre* seen in CI 14: *grandemente* 'greatly' (l. 7), *continuamente* 'continually' (l. 13), *ubertosamente* (ll. 16–17), *miserichordievolemente* (ll. 32–33). On the common adverb *mo* 'now' (l. 33) see CI 32. For the first time in the corpus we see the deployment of the typical Venetian 1st person plural of the present tense in -*emo*: *saludemo* 'we greet' (l. 2), *lasemo* 'we leave' (l. 33). There is also a display of present subjunctives: *sia* 'be' (l. 13), *vada* 'go' (l. 16), *se vega* 'see themselves' (l. 17). *Ineffabele* (l. 4), *recevera* (l. 8), *devini* 'divine' (l. 12), *vergene* 'virgin' (l. 24), and *penetencie* 'penances' (l. 29) show characteristic Venetian atonic vowel lowering compared to Tuscan/Italian. In *chosa* 'thing' (l. 5), *chapel(l)a* 'chapel' (l. 10 passim), *Nicholo* (l. 11 passim), *chasion* 'occasion' (l. 15), *charcere* 'prisons' (l. 26) and *pontifichado* 'pontificate' (ll. 34–35) the digram <ch>, as expected, represents velar /k/ before a back vowel. *Inlumina* 'illuminates' (ll. 4–5) has the typical Venetian verbal prefix in *in*-, as in *inpensar* (see CI 1, l. 2). *Splandor* 'splendour' (l. 3) coexisted in Early Venetian with *splendor* < SPLENDOREM. The aphaeresis of initial *a*- in *Vignon*, Avignon (l. 33), was common both in Early Venetian and Early Tuscan.

RECENT STUDIES: STUSSI (1995a), with the original Latin text at p. 487; STUSSI (1997a: 170–71); STUSSI 1997b: 918); FERGUSON (2013c: 108–11).

Corpus Inscription 31

M · CCC · L · XIII · I(N) ·[TE]NPO · D(E) · MISIER ·P(RE) ₁|
AGNOLO · D(E) CHA(N)DIA · E · D(E) · SIER · BORT|
OLAMIO D(E) · CE(C)HIN · FO FATO ₃

[MCCCLXIII, in tenpo de misier pre' Agnolo de Chandia e de sier Bortolamio
de Cechin, fo fato.]

TRANSLATION: Made in 1363, in the time of the very reverend Agnolo de Chandia and of Mr Bortolamio de Cechin.

DATE: 1363.

LOCATION: Displayed since 1960 on a stand in the stairway near the entrance to the picture gallery of the Museo Correr. Its original provenance is not known for certain. In the Correr's late nineteenth-century inventory it is simply down as an 'Acquisition' (*Acquisto*), without date or seller. This is undoubtedly, though, the object listed in the Museum's acquisitions register, *Registro doni e acquisti*, on 14 February 1878 as: 'Una vasca operata (epoca intorno al 1000) con iscrizione del 1363'. Again, no further details of its origins and of how it came to the Museum are provided. My personal conviction is that the carvings on the capital must indeed have been sculpted around the turn of the first millennium, and that the ultimate provenance of the inscribed artefact was the northern lagoon area of Venice with its many churches and religious foundations, most of which have disappeared — often systematically or casually pillaged in the later Middle Ages (CROUZET-PAVAN 2017: 436–38) — leaving little or no trace. The chief curator of the Museo Correr, Arch. Andrea Bellieni, is of the same opinion on both counts (personal written communication, 15 January 2018) and has pointed out that such objects were acquired by the Museum in the period in question from the local Venice area and not beyond.

TYPE AND DESCRIPTION: Commemorative. The inscription is on the front entablature of a marble Romanesque cushion capital modified for use as a baptismal font. The capital is decorated on three sides with sculptured reliefs. The lateral faces show gryphons rampant and vegetation while the front, beneath the inscription, depicts two archaic-looking lions with raised hind legs, tapered bodies and curled-back tails, on either side of a small palm which they appear to be grazing on. The lions look out towards the spectator. The style is commonly found on Romanesque capitals across Europe. The complex symbolism on our particular example seems to centre on the tree of life which the mythical beasts are feeding off. It is reminiscent of the gryphons with tree-of-life motif on another re-used northern lagoon object now housed in the Museo Provinciale on Torcello. This is the well head with reliefs, carved *c*. 1000, converted from the Roman funeral altar-front of the *dispensator* Chaerons (CIL, V, 2155). As noted, it is not improbable that our capital-cum-font itself originated in one of the churches or foundations in the northern Venetian lagoon, most of which (and there were many dozens) have now vanished (VECCHI

Fig. 3.33. CI 31 in context. © A. S. Ferguson.

1982). A similar holy-water font converted from a Romanesque cushion capital and probably from the Venice area — with analogous but not identical motifs to ours and with no inscription — is in the Metropolitan Museum of Art (CASTELNUOVO-TEDESCO and SOULTANIAN 2010: 87–89).

The language of the epigraph is unequivocally Venetian and the lettering style falls within Venetian practice of the time. It records the date of the conversion of the capital to a christening stoup as well as the names of the priest and one other in office at the time. Either or both of the named individuals may have sponsored the renovation of the font. The priest's surname *de Chandia* (in other words, from Crete) might possibly suggest a Venetian colonial provenance for the object, but that seems far-fetched. Another inscription in our corpus — CI 76 from the builders' guild, the *Scuola dei Mureri* — is entirely Venetian in provenance and execution yet carries the name of two guild officials with surnames evoking Venice's Levant interests: Antuonio da Modon and Andrea d'Acre.

The artefact is 43 cm high, 80 cm at its widest point and 55 cm deep. The inscription tablet itself is 78 × 11 cm. It has suffered some damage, with a large rectangular chip on the top rim impacting partially on the legibility of the first two letters of *tenpo* (l. 1). The chip becomes a crack which extends down the middle of the inscription and bisects the two lions. On the whole the epigraph is reasonably well preserved, although the letter grooving is notably worn down, rendering abbreviation marks and interpuncts almost invisible.

LETTERING: Gothic majuscules cut in V-section with measured stroke contrast.

The ductus is confidently uncialesque with sweeping hairstrokes on <c>, <e> and <f> that curve beyond top and bottom line, a parallel upstroke on <l> that is sometimes higher than the stem itself, and fine flared downstrokes on <t>. Sinuosity is very marked on the <m>, with left bow always closed, on <a> with wavy left stem, and on the curved legs of <h> and <n>. Most memorable in this regard is the beautiful <g> in *Agnolo* (l. 2) with its unusually elongated snail-shell spiral. It opens out into hornlike splay serifs, picked up by those on the uncial <d> which are themselves almost claw-like. Letter and word spacing is quite generous and there are no ligatures. Legibility, further aided by interpuncts and by letters averaging 2.6 cm in height, would have been reasonably good although there are more abbreviations than was strictly called for by space constraints. On three occasions an elegant Tironian 7 slash bisects <d> to indicate *de* 'of'. An overbar appears on <i> (l. 1) to express the missing <n> of *in*. A similar suspension bar, now almost obliterated, appears above the <p> to abbreviate the title *pre* or *pre'* 'priest, reverend' (l. 1; see CI 29, l. 2). As in CI 29 the bowl of <p> has been opened out and curled. There seems to be a line over the <a> of *Chandia* (l. 2) denoting the missing <n>, but the area above the letter is so worn that one cannot be certain. Most interesting of all is the diagonal hooked bar through the stem of <h> in *Cehin* (l. 3), indicating the missing <c> that precedes it on the common Veneto surname Cechin: a feature much easier to detect before the object was restored. Until now this abbreviation has been overlooked, with the <h> taken at face value and linked to the very occasional manuscript use of <h> in old texts to indicate velar <k> (DOTTO 2008: 134 n. 162). However, in Venetian inscriptions <ch> is occasionally represented by an <h>, kinked or hooked, as in CI 8 and CI 23. This key feature has been almost worn away in the present case. The presence of the <ch> in Chandia itself alerts us to the fact that the stonemason was perfectly aware of the strong convention of using <ch> for /k/. There does not appear to be the expected cedilla on the initial <c> of *Cechin* but the position of the word, sitting on the bottom rim of the entablature, would have made this awkward. The same name appears twice, with the normal cedilla, in CI 41. There are no ligatures.

LANGUAGE: Apart from the presence of the Venetian <ch> spelling convention in *Chandia* and *Cechin* and the end-of-syllable <n> suggesting nasalisation in *tenpo* 'time' (l. 1), the most interesting linguistic feature is the evidence of the widespread advance of mid-vowel diphthongisation in *misier* 'Sir, Mr' (l. 1) and *sier* 'Mr' (l. 2) and the implied social distinction, as in CI 29 and CI 38, between these juxtaposed terms. *Chandia* (l. 3) could refer both to the city of Heraklion or, by metonymy, to the island of Crete itself which was a Venetian colony from 1207 until 1669.

RECENT STUDIES: STUSSI (1997a: 165–66).

Corpus Inscription 32

[DE BAIA]M[ONTE FO] ₁| QVESTO · TERENO · E · MO ₂| P(ER) LO · SO INIQVO · TRADIME(N)TO ₃| SE · PO[S]TO · IN · CHOMV(N) · P(ER) · ALTRV[I] ₄| [SPAV]ENTO · E · P(ER) · MOSTRAR ₅| [A TVTI] · SENPRE · SENO ₆

[De Baiamonte fo questo tereno, e mo per lo so iniquo tradimento se posto in chomun, per altrui spavento e per mostrar a tuti senpre seno.]

TRANSLATION: This plot of land was Baiamonte's and now, because of his evil betrayal, it has been made common land to frighten others and forever show all people (the benefits of) good sense.

DATE: Around 1364, when the Venetian Senate decreed that a column of infamy be erected to remind people of Baiamonte's traitorous insurrection and its consequences for him (CICOGNA 1824–53, VI: 770).

LOCATION: Originally the column stood in what is now the Campiello del Remer, off Campo S. Agostin (*sestiere* of S. Polo), at the location of the house of the traitor patrician Baiamonte Tiepolo (died 1328). Subsequently it was moved into Campo S. Agostin itself and erected against the apse at the rear of the church of S. Agostin. The damaged object was given over in 1785 to the nobleman Angelo Maria Quirini who took it to his mainland villa. The church itself, disaffected after the Napoleonic suppressions, was demolished in 1873 to make way for low-cost housing. At some point in the eighteenth or nineteenth century the spot where the column once stood in Campo S. Agostin was marked by a stone plaque on the ground, now badly split, with the terse statement in capitals: *Loc. col. / bai. the. / MCCCX*. After passing through a number of hands the remains of the column ended up with the Melzi family, becoming a garden ornament in their grounds near Lake Como. Eventually, in the late 1800s, the duchess Joséphine Melzi d'Éril donated it to the Museo Correr where it spent the best part of a century in store. It is now kept by the Fondazione Musei Civici di Venezia in a storeroom of the Doge's Palace. The Venice in Peril Fund has lobbied to have the column restored and returned to its former location in Camps S. Agostin.

TYPE AND DESCRIPTION: Commemorative and didactic *damnatio memoriae*. The admonitory text, in four rhyming hendecasyllabic verses (rhyme scheme ABBA), is engraved over six lines on a severely damaged marble column. The object recalls those Roman milestones which during the later Empire increasingly had a political complexion, with declarations of allegiance on them to an emperor. SANSOVINO and STRINGA (1604: 153) gave a transcription of our column text which, apart from the first two lines, was very approximate. Stringa provided additional lines (which, if they ever existed, are no longer visible) to the effect that in 1310 Baiamonte crossed the bridge in the middle of the month of cherries and that this led to the founding of the Council of Ten.

Giving definitive dimensions is problematic owing to the erosion and splitting that have affected the artefact. What is left of the column is about 93 cm high.

Fig. 3.34. CI 32. © A. S. Ferguson.

The circumference at the top end where the inscription is located is roughly 190 cm. Towards the bottom it is much reduced in girth and the wasted object is in fact held together and upright by a metal rod embedded in a stone pedestal. The damage to the inscription itself is worst along the top line which has been altogether obliterated except for an isolated <m>. Further down it has suffered considerably from wear and tear, especially on l. 6. The missing parts of the script have had to be reconstructed from the rubbings and transcription made in the nineteenth century for Cicogna by his collaborator Giovanni Casoni when the column was in private hands, and from the history of the transcriptions of the epigraph critically evaluated by CICOGNA himself (1824–53, III: 28–40).

The unsuccessful 1310 conspiracy attached to Baiamonte Tiepolo's name is notorious for being one of the few attempts in the history of Venice to overthrow the established order. It was occasioned ostensibly by the so-called *Serrata del Maggior Consiglio*, the closure to all new members of the Great Council in 1297, with the consequence that thereafter a relatively large but exclusive hereditary caste would run the state. Tiepolo, who may have had a personal grudge against doge Pietro Gradenigo, was a ringleader of the plot which involved members of the Querini, Badoer, Doro and other patrician families as well as a section of the general population. The armed uprising on the night of 14–15 June failed as the doge was ready and waiting. The coup leaders were put to flight and Marco Querini, its most prominent leader with Tiepolo, was hanged. Baiamonte was exiled and his palace raised to the ground. The resulting wasteground, where the column of infamy was raised, can be seen to the north west of the church of S. Agostin in the meticulous plan of the parish in the mid fourteenth century reconstructed by DORIGO (2003, II: 892–93). On the conspiracy see GULLINO (2010).

LETTERING: Gothic majuscules carved in V-section. What remains of the inscription — with its grooving drastically worn down — reveals an accomplished and attractive uncialesque script, averaging 3 cm in height, with fine stroke contrast. Striking are the long curving hairstrokes on <c> and <e>, the sinuous arms of <m> and <n>, and the vigorous spike serifs on <s> throughout. Very characteristic is the almond-shaped <o>, with beautiful stroke modulation that is replicated in the bowl of <d>. Some abbreviations are used. *Per* (ll. 3, 4, 5) is rendered by a horizontal bar through the stem of <p>. The missing <n> in *tradimento* (l. 3) and *chomun* (l. 4) is indicated at word end by the symbol in the shape of a 3 that was commonly used in manuscripts in Latin for the accusative *-m* ending but is unique in Venetian vernacular stone inscriptions of the period. This is clearly the result of the stonecutter working from a manuscript layout of the text given to him by the government *scriptor* of the epigraph. Word spacing is emphasized by mid-high interpuncts. This — in addition to good interlineal gaps and an apparent absence of ligatures — would, as was intended, have made the admonitory message (probably picked out with black infilling) unmistakably clear to the passer-by.

LANGUAGE: *Tereno* 'plot, land' (l. 1) is a minority Early Venetian variant of *teren* (see CI 70). It was undoubtedly preferred because of the rhyme with *seno* (l. 6), the normal form for 'wisdom, good sense' (Italian, *senno*). *Mo* 'now' < MODO (see also CI 30, l. 33) was common in Venetian up until the modern period, when it became relegated to a filler in expressions like *vien mo* 'come on, now!' While *chomun* (l. 4) seems the likely spelling, it is not impossible that the 3 abbreviation on it represents an <m> (see CI 25). *Altrui* 'others, other people' (l. 4) is essentially a Tuscan and central Italian term familiar to the Venetian elite from Tuscan verse (and our epigraph is, of course, in verse). *Se* (l. 4) '(it) is' is the first example in the corpus of the characteristic — and unique within the Romance area — Venetian 3rd singular of the verb 'to be' (Early Venetian, *eser*). Better known nowadays with its iconic spelling *xe*, it developed as an alternative to the *ab initio* form *è* which remains typical of the Veneto mainland outside of some of the cities which have been historically influenced by Venetian. Abundant evidence from Early Venetian texts suggests that *se* ~ *xe* developed as a rapid speech variant of the emphatic construction *si è* '(it) is' (spelled *si e* or run together as *sie*: see CI 42) with which it long co-existed. A fuller history of the form is in FERGUSON (2007: 151–52). For other hypotheses about this vexed question see ROHLFS (1949–54, II: 314) and SATTIN (1986: 116 n. 152). The spelling *senpre* 'always' (l. 6), rather than *sempre*, conveys the characteristic Venetian nasal pronunciation at the end of a syllable.

RECENT STUDIES: STUSSI (1997a: 157); STUSSI (1997b: 916); FERGUSON (2013c: 111–12); GEYMONAT (2014: 69).

Corpus Inscriptions 33, 34

•ᵒ Mᵒcᵒcᵒcᵒ • L•X•VI • ADI • PRIMO • D(E) AVOSTO • ₁| • FO FATO • Qᵛ ESTO
• PENELO • D(E) • S(AN)C(T)A • FOSCA •

[MCCCLXVI, adì primo de avosto, fo fato questo penelo de Sancta Fosca.]

•ᵒ Mᵒcᵒcᵒcᵒ • L•X•VI • ADI • PRIMO • D(E) AVOSTO • FO FA̤TO̤ • ₁|
Q̤VE̤STO̤ • PE̤NE̤LO̤ • DE̤ • S̤(AN)C̤(T)A̤ • FO̤SCA • D(E) • TORÇE̤LO̤ •

[MCCCLXVI, adì primo de avosto, fo fato questo penelo de Sancta Fosca de Torçelo.]

TRANSLATIONS: CI 33: (In) 1366, on the first of August, this banner of Saint Fusca was made.

CI 34: (In) 1366, on the first of August, this banner of Saint Fusca of Torcello was made.

DATE: August 1366.

LOCATION: Embroidered on both sides of the so-called banner of S. Fosca. Originally the confraternity banner was housed in the church of S. Fosca on Torcello. By the nineteenth century, with the disbanding of all confraternities in Venice and the islands, one side of the banner was being used in the church as a rag. The other ended up with a Capuchin friar in the monastery of the Redentore on the Giudecca in Venice who donated it in 1861 to the Museo Correr. The two sides were reattached in 1870, and the banner was subsequently displayed in the Museo Provinciale on Torcello in a glass case (CALLEGARI 1930: 39). Between 2014 and 2019 the banner underwent full restoration at the Ca' d'Oro in Venice.

TYPE AND DESCRIPTION: Documentary and commemorative. The two-line inscriptions, one slightly different from the other, are embroidered on a processional banner (Venetian, *penelo*) belonging to the penitential confraternity of S. Fosca on Torcello. As with all confraternities the banner was the symbol of the brotherhood and was carried in processions. The vast majority of these once common and culturally important objects have disappeared so that, in the case of Venice, they are known to us mainly from incidental painted representations of them by artists such as Paolo Veneziano and Gentile Bellini. Occasionally they are depicted in sculptured relief as on CI 42 from the guild of German shoemakers. Details of pictorial recording and of surviving banners from Torcello and Venice are in FERGUSON (2015b).

The S. Fosca banner is unique in terms of its age, survival, quality and vernacular writing. Overall, including the tasselled fringes at top and bottom, it measures *c*. 136 × 68 cm. The embroidered part proper is 101 × 61cm. While these dimensions are average for a medieval or Renaissance processional banner, the nature of the written messages on ours marks it off from all other surviving Italian examples of the period, most of which are from central Italy (DEHMER 2004). These sometimes have writing stitched on them but invariably in Latin. On the rare occasions when

Fig. 3.35. CI 33 in context. © Città Metropolitana di Venezia — Museo di Torcello.

the vernacular is used the message is religious and never purely descriptive as here. This fact is not incidental. It typifies the culture and strong self-consciousness of the Venetian confraternities.

The *penelo* is superficially identical on both sides but on closer inspection the different positioning of S. Fosca's hands is evident, as is the location of the processional mace and the different wording and line division of the messages. The fabric of the banner is taffeta silk. It combines embroidery and tempera painting on a red and gold ground with silver thread appliqué and, as such, is a rare survivor of the *tela picta* genre which was a Venetian speciality of the period (DAVANZO POLI 2000). The edging frame, with the Evangelists in the corners, is richly decorated with flowers and stems in a rhythmic pattern. The upper two thirds of the banner show a sequence of three niches with pointed arches. The central one has in it a standing Virgin and Child. In the niche to her right is St Fusca, the patron saint of the confraternity, wearing a crown (POLACCO, NEPI SCIRÉ and ZATTERA 1978: 101–02). To her left is another female saint, almost certainly Maura. The face and hands of the figures are in tempera. In the bottom rectangle of each side, below the panel of script, is depicted a group of kneeling penitential brothers, in dark hooded habits, whose faces are also painted. The brothers in the middle hold aloft a gilded processional mace with a cross on top. In CI 33 this object intrudes into the writing above, bisecting the first two syllables of *penelo* (l. 2) which are, of necessity, spaced apart. Separating the scenes above and below on both sides of the banner is the panel of writing measuring *c.* 61 × 11 cm, with the letters embroidered cross-stitch in silver thread on a red ground. There was no silk production, as far as we know, on Torcello itself so the banner provides another connection to the Venetian silk manufacturing industry of the fourteenth century which has already figured in CI 8 and CI 26. As for the iconography of the banner, PALLUCCHINI (1964: 212) thought that the artist who provided the cartoon might be the same one who in this period illuminated the statute book of the *scuola* of S. Caterina in Venice. Illustrations from the *mariegola* of this confraternity, which is held at the Museo Correr (ms CI. IV, 118), are in HUMPHREY (2015: ill. VII a, b, c).

The legend of St Fusca explains the presence of the church in her name on Torcello and the confraternity devoted to her on the lagoon island. Fusca, a young virgin from Ravenna, converted to Christianity in the third century, along with her wet nurse Maura. After her conversion was discovered she was tried, found guilty and executed by being stabbed to death with a lance, with Maura asking to follow her mistress. The remains of the two martyred women were transported by Christian sailors to Libya where they lay buried for centuries. Sometime in the early eleventh century their bodies were rescued from pagan Libya by a Venetian and brought to Torcello. The delightful little martyrium church of S. Fosca — with its Byzantine and Islamic architectural echoes — was built (or perhaps rebuilt) in her honour, and her bones and those of Maura were placed under the main altar. In 1247 the Bishop of Torcello, Stefano Nadal, had the relics placed on top of the altar and in 1592 one of Fusca's shin bones was given to the church of S. Fosca in Venice (*sestiere* of Cannaregio), the other medieval church in the lagoon devoted to Fusca (PIEGADI 1847). The recovery and exposure of her bones in 1247 is recorded on an inscription carved around that date on a plaque embedded outside the Torcello church over the left-side door, transcribed in full in BATTAGLINI (1871: 107). The opening lines, carved in a mixed capital-uncial script, and essentially in *scriptio continua*, are still legible in situ: + *ann(o) ab i(n)carnatio(n)e d(omi)ni mill(esimo)* / CCXLUII *die non(o) intr(an)te apr/ili corpus s(ancte) Fusce uirginis q(u)o[...]*. The nearby Museo Provinciale houses a polychrome wooden statue (151 cm in length), depicting the dead Fusca, dateable to the early fourteenth century. It was the lid of a sarcophagus containing Fusca's remains that was kept on the altar in the church itself until well into the twentieth century.

Archival research by Maurizia VECCHI (1982: 57–62) suggests that a confraternity dedicated to the saint (whose name, like that of her wet nurse, alludes to darkness of complexion associated with north Africa) was already in existence in the eleventh century. The iconography of the great stone plaque of *c.* 1400 made for the confraternity and inscribed in the vernacular — displayed outdoors to the side of the church (CI 46) — very much suggests that it was a flagellant brotherhood. It strongly resembles two other relief plaques from *scuole grandi* in Venice (CI 17) and

Murano (CI 26) in our corpus. Our knowledge of the confraternity on Torcello is limited, but it appears from the few references to it in the *buste* of the ASV *Podestà di Torcello* that it was the larger and more influential of the two *scuole* on the island (the other dedicated to St Mary was connected with the cathedral); that it recruited members not only from Torcello but from the nearby islands of Burano and Mazzorbo; and that from 1351 and well into the fifteenth century it was responsible for the running of a small hospital on Torcello. What is also certain is that it was not linked in any way to a trade guild. These, as far as we know, did not exist on Torcello.

LETTERING: Gothic majuscules, beautifully sewn in imitation of their inscriptional or manuscript equivalents, with all the expected characteristics of serifing, hairstroking and abbreviating. CI 33, where the thread has sustained less wear and damage, is the more legible of the two sides. Particularly noticeable in the script are the tapering downstrokes on <t>, the uncial <d> and the uncial <m> with its left bow closed. The message on CI 33 is the shorter of the two and this leads to contrasting line divisions between the two captions. CI 33 would ideally have included the final words *de Torçelo* 'from Torcello' as on CI 34 (l. 2). However, the length of the caption was constrained by the intrusion into the inscriptional space on CI 33 of the mace held aloft by the supplicants on the panel below. This led, as we noted, to the word *penelo* 'banner' being split into two segments, *pe* and *nelo* (l. 2), widely separated on either side of the mace. The body of the <ç> in *Torçelo* (CI 34) is noticeably raised above the baseline border of the embroidered panel to allow space for the cedilla, of which only the stump is now visible. The threaded suspension bar, which must presumably have been stitched over *sca = sancta* 'saint' (l. 2) on both sides, is now invisible. The straight <u/v> of *questo* on CI 33 (l. 1) has been appliquéd in superscript. The usual superscript <o>s on the date of both inscriptions are actually placed above, rather than to the side of, the digits. Words are separated by large mid-high interpuncts on both sides, except for *de avosto* 'of August' and *fo fato* 'was made' which are clearly treated as unitary syntagms. The only mistake in the lettering is the missing <s> in *avosto* (CI 34, l. 1) which I have integrated in italics. There are no ligatures. Both epigraphs are preceded by an enlarged mid-high interpunct with a purely decorative superscript <o> over it.

LANGUAGE: Belonging to the first and earliest of only three inscriptional artefacts from Torcello in the corpus, the language of these brief messages is not without interest in the context of Early Venetian norms and tendencies. All the linguistic features of the banner's writing conform, as it happens, to what we would expect. There is the absence of consonant gemination in *fato* (CI 33, CI 34, l. 1), *penelo* and *Torçelo* (CI 34, l. 2), and the presence of the normal passive construction with *fo fato*. The affricate pronunciation in Torcello is confirmed by the cedilla, which was not always present on the name of the island in contemporary Venetian written documents. *Avosto* August (CI 33, l. 1; CI 34, l. 1) < A(U)GUSTUS — via **aosto*, with an epenthetic /v/ covering for the lenition of /g/ — was the dominant Early Venetian form (see CI 48). It was gradually replaced by the more Italianate variant *agosto* from the fifteenth century (see CI 55, CI 79). *Penelo* 'banner' (CI 33, l. 2;

CI 34, l. 2) was a traditional Venetian term, surviving through to the nineteenth century, related to English *pennon*. The medieval Italian terminology for banners and standards of confraternities was very varied. *Stendardo, gonfalone, vessillo, pen(n)-el(l)o, segno, pennone, pal(l)io, insegna, drappo* and *bandiera* were the terms employed, and there were subtle differences in usage from centre to centre. The terms found in Early Venetian are *penel(l)o, c(h)onfalon* and *stendardo*, all three of Germanic (Frankish) origin via Old French *penel ~ penon, gonfanon ~ gonfalon* and *estandart*. It is not always easy when reading the Early Venetian documentation to pin down the differences in emphasis between these designations. According to BOERIO (1865, s.vv.), *Penelo de le scole e compagnie* is defined as '*Pennone; Segno, Paliotto*, cioè l'Insegna delle Compagnie e Confraternite religiose'. *Confalòn*, confusingly, is said to refer to 'sacri stendardi che servono d'insegne alle Confraternite e compagnie religiose, detti pure *Pennoni, Segni, Vessilli* etc. V. *Penelo*'. *Stendardo*, as well, is 'Insegna o Bandiera principale'.

RECENT STUDIES: CONTON (1927: 84); POLACCO, NEPI SCIRÈ and ZATTERA (1978: 101); DEHMER (2004: 210); HUMPHREY (2015: 76–77, 125 n. 80); FERGUSON (2015b).

Corpus Inscription 35

M⁰· C·C·C·L·X·VIII DIE P·|RIMO · DE · NOVE(N)BRIO · FO FAT|O · QVESTO ·
LAVORIERO I(N) TENPO D(E)|LA EGREGIA E · NOBELE · E · RELIGILIO|
SA · MADONA · BETA · DOLPHIN · REVE|RENDA · BADESA · DE QVESTO · L|
OGO · SIANDO · PROCVRAT|OR · Ç(ANE) M(ICHIEL) 8

[MCCCLXVIII, *die* primo de novenbrio, fo fato questo lavoriero in tenpo dela egregia e nobele e religiliosa madona Beta Dolphin, reverenda badesa de questo logo, siando procurator Çane Michiel.]

TRANSLATION: 1368, on the first *day* of November, this piece of work was made in the time of the esteemed, noble and religious lady Beta Dolphin, reverend abbess of this place, when the procurator was Çane Michiel.

DATE: November 1368.

LOCATION: Carved in situ on the lunette above the entrance to the church of S. Caterina on the lagoon island of Mazzorbo. This is one of the very few inscriptions left on the island — all of them in this church — and the sole surviving vernacular one. This was not always the case. Around the turn of the first millennium the island was a flourishing commercial centre in the northern Venetian lagoon. In spite of the decline of prosperity there in the succeeding centuries, Mazzorbo went on to generate a remarkable concentration of religious activity for such a small place, with five parish churches at one point: S. Bartolomeo, SS. Cosma e Damiano, S. Michele Archangelo, S. Pietro and S. Stefano. It also boasted five religious houses: S. Caterina, S. Eufemia, S. Maffio, S. Maria in Valverde and S. Maria delle Grazie. These convents, which produced many inscriptions, were patronised by the Venetian nobility some of whom sent their children to be educated there. The church of S. Caterina di Mazzorbo (Early Venetian, S. C(h)atarina de Maçorbo) was in fact the convent church of a community of Benedictine nuns whose population fluctuated over the centuries up to a maximum of forty women. Its patrons were the patrician Michiel family of Venice, one of whose number is the procurator sculpted on the lunette and evoked in our inscription. He is probably the sponsor or co-sponsor of the sculpted artefact itself. The Michiel presence in the church is still evident in their coat of arms and in the few remaining inscriptions, although most of the formerly numerous artefacts connected with them have been destroyed or removed to other locations.

The churches and convents on Mazzorbo either withered away between the fourteenth and nineteenth centuries as the island and its population declined or else were swept away by the Napoleonic suppressions. S. Caterina was abolished in 1806 and the twenty-six nuns left there were moved the following year to the convent of S. Giovanni Evangelista on Torcello (Early Venetian, S. Çan de Torçelo) which was itself abolished in 1810. The numerous paintings and sculptures in their original institution were sold off or looted. Their former church with its bell tower of *c.* 1318, one of two remaining historic religious buildings on the island (the other is

FIG. 3.36. CI 35 in the 1970s. © A. Scarpa.

the derelict *campanile* of S. Michele Arcangelo), was subsequently converted into a parish church for the modest local population. Dating back possibly to the late eight century, the attractive little single-aisled building has maintained its fourteenth-century interior in spite of subsequent modifications and restorations. Its most striking features are the wooden ship's keel roof and the nun's gallery (Venetian, *barco*) at the back. The outside of the church on the quayside overlooking the canal, where the main door and lunette with the inscription are located, has clearly been radically altered in structure since the nineteenth century. One is in fact surprised, upon approaching the portal, to see that it appears to be embedded in a normal house front.

TYPE AND DESCRIPTION: Documentary and commemorative. The 8-line epigraph is inscribed across the right-side middle section of the arch above the doorway of the church on the Fondamenta S. Caterina facing the Mazzorbo canal. It records the completion date of the sculpted lunette (the *lavoriero* of l. 3), the name of the abbess of the convent at the time, and the initials of its procurator. The base length of the lunette is *c.* 210 cm and its maximum height is *c.* 144 cm. It stands *c.* 233 cm above the pavement of the *fondamenta*. The scene, sculpted in high relief within the Istrian stone Gothic archway flanked by pinnacles, depicts the mystic marriage of St Catherine of Alexandria with Christ. This is based on the story that after He had initially rejected her, Christ came to the newly baptised Catherine in a dream, put a ring on her finger and took her as His celestial spouse. The majestic figure of the enthroned Christ, His bearded face stately and benevolent, occupies the centre of the arch. To His right the kneeling St Catherine, a sweet smile on her face, receives the ring from Him. Above them the scene is framed by two flying angels. On either side of Christ kneel two donors on a smaller scale. On His right is the charming figure of the abbess, smiling radiantly beneath her wimple and proudly clutching a crosier. On Christ's left, in an attitude of prayer, kneels the serious figure of the procurator, the long flap of his headgear protruding stiffly over his right shoulder and the initials of his name carved on his left shoulder towards the spectator. The reliefs have been worn down by time and have suffered some abrasion and chipping but, apart from the severe damage to the head of one of the angels, they remain in reasonable shape. The whole artefact, while perhaps not of the very highest artistic quality, has an appealing, unprepossessing naivety.

The inscription itself occupies an area very roughly 50 × 25 cm between Christ's throne and the right-side edge of the arch. It is bounded at the top by one of the flying angels. At the bottom it is encroached upon by the head of the procurator. One is struck immediately by the presence of the epigraph within the sculpted space of the artefact itself. In Venice it was usual practice to confine inscriptions relating to a sculpture to an accompanying plaque rather than incorporating them into the surface area as here. In fact the lunette's surface has been treated in this respect as if it were a painting, where the presence of script was not unusual. The blank space for our inscription was selected more by necessity than design, and is hardly ideal. It has forced the mason into awkward cramping at line-end and is especially disruptive at the epigraph's conclusion, where the procurator's upper body intrudes. However, the stonecutter went on to exploit this necessity cleverly for his own purposes, almost in the manner of an in-joke. He devised the unorthodox but economical expedient of simply carving the procurator's initials on his protruding sleeve, in imitation of embroidery, rather than cutting his name, isolated and in full, on the far side of the relief figure. Michiel in any case would have been a familiar figure to those associated with the monastery, church and island, and his likeness (or so one presumes) was there for all to see. In the absence of archival evidence it is only possible to conjecture that he is the Çane Michiel who, according to chronicler Gian Giacomo Caroldo, was one of the forty-one patricians mandated to select a new doge (Andrea Dandolo) in 1343, and who in 1378 was a prison-ship

Fig. 3.37. CI 35 in 2019. © A. S. Ferguson.

commander (*Sopracomito prigioni*) during the war against Genoa (MARIN 2008-12, II: 6-7 and III: 69-70). The fifteenth-century chronicler Zorzi Dolfin lists him as one of the twelve Venetian patrician ship commanders taken prisoner that year by the Genoese (CARACCIOLO ARICÒ 2007-09, II: 63). He was resident in S. Samuel and his tax return was modest (MUTINELLI 1841: 217).

LETTERING: Gothic majuscules cut in V-section. The carving is vigorous, bold and effective, but only sporadically subtle. The aspect is chunky and stroke modulation, while present, is limited. This can best be appreciated on the thickish hairstroking on <c>, <e> and <f> and on the rather crude overarm of the uncial <d> on *die* (l. 1). Stems on <i>, <p> and <v> show moderate tapering although at times, as on the two sinuous <n>s of *novenbrio* (l. 2), the mason's skill shows through more fully. Two types of <d>, capital and uncial, are deployed in the inscription, but <u/v> is always straight-sided. The <m> is of the uncial type with the one on the date having its left bow closed, as was often the case. The abbreviation on the uncial <d> of *de* (l. 3) is unusual in being a hooked wavy line above (and not through) the arm of the <d>. Letter height, wavering between 2.5 and 3 cm, is greater towards the top of the inscription, perhaps deliberately, and letter spacing is slightly variable. There are no ligatures. The text is justified on both sides: straight on the left, curved on the right. The remains of black infilling in the letters are still clearly visible in the top lines, while older photographs show its presence throughout the epigraph. With wear and tear to the script and the progressive disappearance of the infilling the inscription is no longer easy to read on a casual basis. In particular, the finely carved large initials ÇM on Michiel's clothing — with a prominent cedilla on the <c> and elegant uncial <m> — have left only a faint trace. They were clearly visible, though, in the recent past (WOLTERS 1976, II: ill. 286) — as was the now-effaced insertion mark after *procurator* of the type seen on CI 95 and CI 108 — and it is surprising that they have been missed by all epigraphers from Cicogna onwards. These experienced observers were deceived into thinking that the inscription ended abruptly, with the procurator's name inexplicably omitted.

LANGUAGE: A unique surviving example from the Middle Ages of vernacular public writing executed on Mazzorbo. Although the text is brief it may, potentially at least, yield interesting clues about linguistic divergencies between the northern lagoon and Venice itself in this period, although it has to be borne in mind that the commissioning nuns and procurator were themselves Venetian and from the city's aristocracy. The crucial factors here are likely to be the mediating role of the sculptor himself, if he were a local craftsman — and this is not certain — and the degree of linguistic latitude within the Venetian diasystem that his employers were willing to tolerate. One is struck in this context by two words in particular. *Lavoriero* 'work, piece of work, artefact' (l. 3) was a minority variant in Venice in the early fourteenth century, but by 1368 it was very much an anachronism there. This is, in fact, its only occurrence in the corpus alongside the many instances of *lavorer* ~ *lavorier*. Slightly surprising, too, is *logo* 'place' (ll. 6-7). By the seventh decade of the Trecento one would have expected to see diphthongisation of the stressed /o/ to /wo/. *Luogo* is, in fact, already present twice in the very high-register CI 30 of

1362 from the heart of Venice. Evidence of tolerance of variation or deviance from the norm is suggested by the uncorrected malapropism *religiliosa* 'religious' (ll. 4–5) for *religiosa*, although it may already have been too late to rectify it by the time it was noticed. For another example of apparent linguistic latitude by an epigraphic commissioner see CI 25.

Our stonemason must certainly have been given a written text to work from. Elevated terms such as *egregia* 'esteemed, distinguished, eminent' (l. 4) and *reverenda* 'reverend' (ll. 5–6), as well as the Latin *die primo* 'on the first day' (l. 1) rather than the Venetian *adi primo* — which craftsmen would have been used to in vernacular inscriptions — strongly indicate this. Indeed the string of four epithets to describe the abbess will probably have come from the procurator of the convent, with the consent or collaboration of the abbess herself. That this is so seems confirmed by the charming familiarity of the abbess being called *Beta* (Betty, Liz), l. 5, rather than her formal Christian name Isabet(t)a. Paradoxically, the rarer classicising spelling of the patrician surname Dolphin, rather than the more usual Dolfin, may also point to the abbess's hand. The procurator's input might explain that the term *procurator* 'procurator, administrator' (ll. 7–8) itself is given in its 'correct' form rather than in one of the many metathetic variants seen elsewhere in our corpus. This assumption seems to be contradicted, though, by the form *percolatori* 'procurators' chosen by two Procurators of St Mark in CI 39. The short biblical text carved in majuscules on the book held by Jesus would, presumably, have been provided by Beta and her sisters: *Ego sum lux mundi* 'I am the light of the world' from John 8.12. The sculptor rendered this sacred text with a spelling strongly coloured by vernacular pronunciation: *Ego / svm / lvs // mon/di:~*. Was this on his own initiative? Were the nuns happy with it? At all events no attempt has been made to have it rectified. On the basis of *tenpo* 'time' (l. 3) with an <n> (l. 3) I prefer *novenbrio* (l. 2) to *novembrio*. On the peculiar Early Venetian ending of *novenbrio* see CI 79. *Siando* 'being' (l. 7) exemplifies the standard Venetian gerund metaplasm we have observed elsewhere. *Badesa* 'abbess' (l. 6), pronounced with the unvoiced sibilant /s/, represents the normal evolution of late Latin ABBATISSA and is found in Tuscan/Italian *badessa* too. The Latinising variant *ab(b)atis(s)a* was also found in Venice in our period and is present, hybridised with *badesa*, on CI 106.

RECENT STUDIES: WOLTERS (1976, I: 198); STUSSI (1997a: 164–65). Recorded, but not published, by Cicogna.

Corpus Inscription 36

+ QVESTO · E · EL · DENTE · D(E) · S͡AN · ÇV͡ANE · BATISTA

[+ Questo è el dente de San Çuane Batista.]

TRANSLATION: This is the tooth of St John the Baptist.

DATE: Undated but possibly later fourteenth century. The dating conjectures for the reliquary carrying the inscription range from the late fifteenth or early sixteenth century (PASINI 1887: 47) back to 1320–1330 (HAHNLOSER 1971: 160). The former is far too late for the epigraph's Gothic lettering. The latter is more plausible although the weight of evidence from script and language suggests the second half of the Trecento for the inscription itself.

LOCATION: On a reliquary, in situ, in the Treasury of St Mark (*Santuario* no. 107), St Mark's Basilica.

TYPE AND DESCRIPTION: Documentary. The brief message identifies the relic displayed within the vessel as the tooth of the precursor of Christ. The raised lettering appears to be in metal appliqué. It is soldered on to a metal band running around the top of the rock crystal chalice within which the relic is mounted. The reliquary is 23.2 cm tall and 9.1 cm in diameter, while the transparent chalice itself is only 4.7 cm in height and averages 4.8 cm in width. Structurally this small object, delightfully balanced and decorated, is one of the most attractive reliquaries in the Treasury. The sloping palmate base covered in filigree work is studded with large blue enamel roundels, each with a separate religious theme. On the base stands the gently flared stem, its middle section decorated with a delicate lattice-work cage projection. Within the crystal vessel the relic molar is held in a gold grip set on a gold base. The vessel is bounded at the bottom by a silver band with an engraved floral motif. At the top a band carries our inscription. The lid of the chalice is highly distinctive, covered all over with small embossed gilded balls and topped by the strongly end-curved cross of S. Marco. Given that its dimensions are out of proportion with the rest of the reliquary one suspects that the cross is a later addition. Puzzlingly, the artefact has traditionally been called the reliquary of the tooth of St Mark, although the inscription indicates that it has held the molar of St John the Baptist since the fourteenth century. The reliquary and its inscription can be viewed in detail at http://www.meravigliedivenezia.it/it/oggetti-virtuali/CAT_157.html [accessed 25 June 2020].

LETTERING: Gothic majuscules in raised lettering that is *c.* 0.5 cm in height. The Gothic employed is confident and expansive. The <e> has strong hairstrokes, the lateral arms of <t> are long and curving, the <s> shows spike serifs, and <i> has prominent, forked terminals. Ligatures appear twice on <an>, and the cedilla on <ç> is vigorous. The <a> is uncialesque, with the left arm curving back inwards. There is good contrast between thick and thin strokes, although this is not apparent in places because of occasional smudging and distortion of the solder, particularly on the section with the words <*e el dente*>.

Fig. 3.38. CI 36 (detail). © Ronnie Ferguson.

LANGUAGE: It is not at all impossible for the forms *el* 'the', *san* 'saint' and *Çuane* (John) to be present singly in a Venetian inscriptional text from the early fourteenth century. However, the presence of all three together in a period when their equivalents *lo*, *sen* and *Çane* were commoner is unlikely. This, in conjunction with the nature of the script, argues for a date in the later Trecento.

RECENT STUDIES: GALLO (1967: 317); HAHNLOSER (1971: 160–61).

Corpus Inscription 37

S(ANCTVS) MAFEV(S) [ ] S(ANCTVS) | MAFE | V(S) [ ] EFIENIA · FIA DE RE $_1$ | |
· S(ANCTVS) MAF[...]S $_2$ | | [ ] $_3$ | | IRTACHV(S) | RE $_4$ | |
LARCHA DE S(ANCTVS) MAFEV(S) [ ] · S(ANCTVS) | MAFEV(S) [ ] · LIDO ·
DE ANTIOPIA $_5$ | | · LARCHA · DE · S(ANCTVS) · MAFEVS $_6$

[*Sanctus Mafeus. Sanctus Mafeus.* Efienia, fia de re. *Sanctus Mafeus.* Irtachus re. L'archa de *Sanctus Mafeus. Sanctus Mafeus.* Lido de Antiopia. L'archa de *Sanctus Mafeus.*]

TRANSLATION: *St Matthew. St Matthew.* Ephigenia, daughter of the king. *St Matthew.* King Hirtacus. The tomb of *St Matthew. St Matthew.* Shore of Ethiopia. The tomb of *St Matthew.*

DATE: Undated, but attributable to the later fourteenth century.

LOCATION: Painted on an altarpiece screen now displayed in the Vittorio Cini collection in the gallery of Palazzo Cini at S. Vio (*sestiere* of Dorsoduro). The screen came to the Cini collection in 1941 via the antiquarian Antonio Carrer in Venice and the Achilito Chiesa collection in Milan (DELORENZI 2016). Its original provenance is not known. The Venetian of the captions as well as the Venetian-influenced Latin spelling *Mafeus* of the saint's name on the panels suggest a location in Venice. It would not be surprising if it had been originally commissioned for the Church of S. Mafio (or Mat(t)io) near the Rialto which figures in CI 41 and CI 108. It may have been sold or auctioned off when that church was destroyed in the early nineteenth century following the Napoleonic suppressions.

TYPE AND DESCRIPTION: Picture captions. The terse legends are painted (in black, but with one instance in white) on to five of the six panels of an altarpiece screen known as the *Storie di san Matteo*. The screen measures 71 × 64.5 cm and is coloured in tempera and gold. It is divided into six equal sized oblong compartments framed in wood. The scenes painted in the compartments read from top left to bottom right, with each depicting an episode from the mission of St Matthew in Ethiopia derived, for the most part, from the thirteenth-century *Legenda Aurea* compiled by Jacobus de Voragine. The scenes are illustrated in vivid colours and combine a static Byzantine quality — with characters only roughly to scale and scenes summarily conjured up — with an earthy cartoonish realism. In panel 1 the saint appears twice: once blessing princess Ephigenia, daughter of king Egippus, and her fellow virgins; then being stabbed to death before the altar by the killers sent by the new king Hirtacus who covets Ephigenia. In panel 2 the dead Matthew is being blessed by the priests and deacons who celebrate his martyrdom. Panel 3, which presumably speaks for itself and is therefore captionless, depicts angels intervening to turn King Hirtacus's arson, directed at Ephigenia and the virgins, against the royal palace itself. In panel 4 we witness the dramatic suicide of Hirtacus, stricken by leprosy, in the burning royal palace. As he drives a dagger into his own chest a naked female figure issues from his mouth and a black horned

FIG. 3.39. CI 37 (detail). © A. S. Ferguson.

devil stands on his shoulder. Simultaneously Hirtacus's son, possessed by the devil, confesses his father's sins in a torrent of words. In panel 5 the saint, in the guise of a boy, walks across a kind of golden gangway that represents the shore of Ethiopia. He points out to two sailors the site of his tomb. In panel 6 the two mariners kneel and pray before the sarcophagus of Matthew which is now safe within a church. In my transcription each 'line' — marked off by a double vertical — represents a panel. A single vertical indicates a caption split within the panel. Spaces between captions within an individual oblong are represented by empty square brackets.

The artefact, which is in excellent overall condition, appears to be the right-side wing of a reredos dedicated to Matthew the Apostle and Evangelist that presumably involved two screens flanking an image of the saint. Since the surviving board evokes scenes from the later phase of the life of St Matthew, the lost left side must have illustrated his earlier life. The unsigned panels are sometimes attributed to the Venetian painter known as Vielmo or Guglielmo Veneziano who was active between 1352 and 1386. On Vielmo, his work and its dating see GUARNIERI (2006: 34–35). I have examined the explanatory writing in Venetian and Vielmo's signature (*Gvielmvs pinxit*), both painted in Gothic majuscules across the foot of his panel with *Madonna, Child and Saints* (1382) now in the Museo Diocesano in Recanati. Neither can be convincingly matched to the captions on the Cini altarpiece.

LETTERING: Painted Gothic majuscules with archaic features. The writing is somewhat uneven and therefore not perfectly aligned. It varies in height from scene to scene — between *c.* 0.3 cm and *c.* 0.55 cm — and word spacing is similarly irregular. The script has none of the calligraphic finesse we saw in the painted lettering of Lorenzo Veneziano's authorial statement (CI 24), with its careful stroke contrast and decorative flourishes. Although clumsier in execution it has more in common with the archaic flavour of the epigraph on the great 1310 *ancona* of St Donatus from Murano (CI 2). As on that devotional image, the <t> has short end-stop serifs rather than the usual fine Gothic downstrokes, while the expected upstroke on <l> is cursory. This restraint is reminiscent of twelfth- and thirteeenth-century Byzantine Romanesque lettering in St Mark's. Most striking on the Cini captions is the initial <m> used on the saint's name, *Mafeus*, throughout. It is in the unmistakable form of the Greek mu that we commented on in CI 2. Also present on the St Matthew screen is another highly distinctive Byzantine Greek feature: the <u/v> on *Mafeus* and *Irtachus* (l. 4) is painted with a short understroke, in effect an upsilon (see CI 28 for another example). This combination of mu and upsilon appears to have been impressed on the mind of artists working with sacred subjects in Venice by its prominent presence on the great mosaics of Murano, Torcello and St Mark's, where it invariably accompanies representations of the Virgin Mary. These often feature the capital initials mu-rho-theta-upsilon (MP ΘY), standing for Μήτηρ (του) Θεού 'Mother of God', that are also highly visible in Sancta Sophia in Constantinople. In the sacred context in Venice the two iconic Greek letters even survived the onset of the Gothic fashion in the Trecento, becoming sometimes integrated into uncial script. They feature conspicuously on two of the most prestigious examples of Latin inscriptional writing in the city from the mid-thirteen hundreds, both in St Mark's and both strongly Gothic: the Baptistery mosaics and the large painted epitaph in the chapel of St Isodore. The understroked upsilon can also be admired in the elegantly ornate gold lettering in Latin, from the same period, along the bottom of the so-called *pala feriale* altar screen in S. Marco — painted by Paolo Veneziano and sons — on the panel depicting the transportation of Mark's body. It is no coincidence that these very letters re-appear in the vernacular inscription at the foot of the *Coronation of the Virgin* panel by Catarino that we consider in CI 40. The archaic feel of the Cini captions is accentuated by the constant use of the saint's name in its Venetian-influenced Latin form *sanctus Mafeus* (ll. 1, 2, 5, 6). *Sanctus* is abbreviated with a wavy overbar, while the <s> of *Mafeus* is sometimes represented by the curled symbol for <s> or <us> at word-end which is common on Latin epigraphs. Surprisingly, there is no hairstroking on <c> or <e>, while on <f> it is strongly present.

LANGUAGE: Two spelling features stand out. The first is the typical Venetian <ch> digraph for /k/, present in *Irtachus* and *archa* = /arka/. The second is the <f> in *Mafeus* (Matthew), where Tuscan/Italian has *Matteo*. It stems from a Venetian rendering of the Greek theta in Ματθαῖος which gave native *Maf(f)io* or *Maf(f)eo* (see CI 41) alongside *Mat(h)io*. Unusually this vernacular pronunciation has been transferred back to the Latin spelling, whereas in Latin documents and mosaics in Venice the forms *Matheus* or *Mateus* remained normal. *Fia* 'daughter' (l. 1) < FĪLIAM has been present throughout the history of Venetian. *Re* 'king' (l. 4) < RĒX, identical with Tuscan/Italian, makes its first appearance in the corpus, as does the quintessentially Venetian *lido* 'shore' (l. 5) < LĪTUS which would eventually spread to English and to other languages. *Efienia* Ephigenia (l. 1) manifests the tendential Early Venetian loss of original Latin intervocalic G, as in *vinti* 'twenty' < VĪGINTI. The odd form *Antiopia* (l. 5) is probably a cross-contamination between *Etiopia* (Ethiopia) and the city of *Antiochia* (Antioch) familar from the Bible, from the

Golden Legend itself and from Venice's Levant trade. *Archa* 'sarcophagus, tomb' is from ărcam 'chest, box, ark', while the syntagm *larcha* (ll. 5, 6) represents it preceded by the definite article, with no apostrophe or space between the two. For the juxtaposition, as here, of Latin and vernacular elements in Italian medieval artwork captions see Formentin (2015).

RECENT STUDIES: Delorenzi (2016).

Corpus Inscription 38

· M⁰CCC·LXXIIII · DI XXX · OTVBRI⁰ · ₁| SOTO · EL NOBEL · E SAVIO ·
MIS(IER) · ₂| ÇACHARIA · GABRIEL · PODESTA · ₃| DE MVRAN · FO
FRA(N)CHADO · (QVE)S | TO · ALBERGO · SIA(N)DO · VARDIAN · ₅|
S(IER) ÇAN · BVXELO · E I SVO (CON)PAGNI ₆| OFICIALI · D(E)LA SCVOLA ·
DI BAT | VDI · D(E) MISIER · S(-N) ÇANE · BATIS | TA · DE MVRAN · S(IER) ·
IACHOMELO · D | A MOLI(N) · S(IER) · OLIVIER · DARPO · S(IER) · M | AFIO ·
ROSO · S(IER) · NICHOLETO · D(E) ₁₁| GREGVOL · S(IER) · IOANE · CHAVO ·
D | VRO · S(IER) · PARIS · SARTOR · S(IER) · NI | CHOLO · DAL SOLER · S(IER) ·
ALVIS | E · MA(R)ÇANTE · S(IER) · MENEGELO · D | ASTRA · S(IER) · ANTHONIO ·
ÇIO · S(IER) · ₁₆| BE(N)VEGNV · PISTOR · S(IER) · MAR | CHO · SANTO ∶~

[MCCCLXXIIII, dì xxx otubrio, soto el nobel e savio misier Çacharia Gabriel, podestà de Muran, fo franchado questo albergo, siando vardian sier Çan Buxelo e i suò conpagni oficiali dela Scuola di Batudi de misier S. Çane Batista de Muran: sier Iachomelo da Molin, sier Olivier d'Arpo, sier Mafio Roso, sier Nicholeto de Greguol, sier Ioane Cavoduro, sier Paris Sartor, sier Nicholò dal Soler, sier Alvise Marcante, sier Menegelo d'Astra, sier Antonio Çio, sier Benvegnù Pistor, sier Marcho Santo.]

TRANSLATION: 1374. On the 30th of October, under the noble and wise Sir Çacharia Gabriel, mayor of Murano, this meeting hall was (completed and) released for use. The warden was Mr Çan Buxelo, and his fellow officials of the Flagellant Brotherhood of St John the Baptist of Murano (were): Mr Iachomelo da Molin, Mr Olivier d'Arpo, Mr Mafio Roso, Mr Nicholeto de Greguol, Mr Ioane Cavoduro, Mr Paris Sartor, Mr Nicholò dal Soler, Mr Alvise Marcante, Mr Menegelo d'Astra, Mr Anthonio Çio, Mr Benvegnù Pistor, Mr Marcho Santo.

DATE: October 1374.

LOCATION: At present the inscription plaque is displayed in Germany, embedded in the outer south-west wall of the so-called *Klosterhof* in Glienicke Park in Potsdam (*Land* Berlin-Brandenburg). It forms part of the collection of medieval *objets d'art*, some from Venice and Murano, put together by Prince Carl (or Karl) of Prussia and housed there since the late 1850s when the *Klosterhof* was purpose-built. On this collection and its history see ZUCHOLD (1993). However, the original location of the plaque was on Murano, in or on the meeting house of the *Scuola* of S. Giovanni Battista (Early Venetian, S. Ç(u)ane Batista) in the S. Stefano parish of the lagoon island. By the early nineteenth century it was mounted on a wall inside the main *scuola* building at the top of the stairs (CICOGNA 1824–53, VI: 375). It was obscured, though, by the beautifully sculpted seventeenth-century walnut wainscotting that adorned part of the meeting hall and some of which still survives, along with religious objects salvaged from the *scuola*, in the *Museo parrocchiale* of the church of S. Pietro Martire on the island. All the confraternity's premises, including its hospital for the poor, were demolished in 1837 in the wake of the Napoleonic suppressions. It is only thanks to several eighteenth-century artworks, notably Canaletto's oil

Fig. 3.40. CI 38. © Ronnie Ferguson.

FIG. 3.41. CI 38 (lines 1–5). © Ronnie Ferguson.

painting *View of S. Giovanni dei Battuti at Murano* (*c.* 1727) in the Hermitage, and his slightly later pen-and-ink drawing of the same subject in the Royal Collection, that we know what this important cultural and charitable complex looked like. On the wainscotting and other works of art which once adorned the confraternity, and most of which were sold off or looted, see Toso Borella (2009).

Our inscription plaque found its way to Venice and was seen twice there by Cicogna, the last time in May 1856 when it was in the workshop of a stonemason called Seguso in the area of the Eremite, near S. Trovaso, in the *sestiere* of Dorsoduro. Sadly but unsurprisingly the handsome artefact, with its large size, strikingly vivid Gothic lettering and frieze featuring the lion emblem of Venice — a Venetian medieval statement-artefact *par excellence* — was an object of desire for unscrupulous sellers and buyers in the nineteenth century free-for-all despoliation of the city. Like so much of Venice's material heritage, including devotional objects, reliefs, wall plaques, well heads, paintings and illuminated guild and confraternity statute books, it ended up abroad in private and public collections. For another important inscribed object which suffered the same fate see CI 47.

TYPE AND DESCRIPTION: Commemorative and declarative. The inscription celebrates the completion and handing over in late October 1374 of a new executive meeting room or hall (*albergo*, l. 5) to the flagellant confraternity of St John the Baptist on Murano (*Scuola di batudi de misier S. Çane Batista de Muran*, ll. 7–9), recording at the same time the name of the then mayor of Murano, that of the warden (*vardian*, l. 5) of the brotherhood, and the composition of his executive (*conpagni oficiali*, ll. 6–7). The elongated rectangular marble tablet itself measures 109 × 55 cm and its castellated frame is *c.* 7 cm wide. It is topped by an attractive frieze around 30 cm high. This features, in the centre, an intact Venetian winged lion, in the *a moleca* posture, holding open the Gospel of St Mark. On its right stands the figure of John the Baptist, scroll in hand; on its left is a bearded and mitred bishop, probably St Donatus, with a crosier (see CI 2). The three symbolise respectively Venice, the confraternity itself, and the island of Murano.

The plaque was until recently in an exceptionally good state, having spent most of its existence indoors. However, its outdoor positioning very close to the ground in the *Klosterhof* — probably chosen so that spectators could admire at eye-level the sculpted frieze on the top section — has in recent decades had negative consequences for the long-term condition of the object. The right-hand side of the plaque has suffered greater weathering, because of its direction of exposure, and this has gradually bleached the lettering there. More seriously still, rising damp has seeped up into the lower part of the tablet, darkening it and making the bottom lines of the inscription increasingly hard to decipher. Otherwise the plaque is still largely undamaged, apart from a pattern of superficial cracks and one deeper fissure, which may be old, running down part of the right-hand side. The crenellation on the frieze directly above the lion is deeply chipped.

The confraternity of St John the Baptist was a flagellant brotherhood, just like the great *scuole grandi* in Venice itself, and attracted hundreds of members. It was in fact elevated to the rank of a *scuola grande*, with its attendant privileges, in 1466 by the Council of Ten. Its special vocation, *ab initio*, was the care of the poor. In fact its history and physical presence were intimately entwined with that of a hospital for the poor founded in 1337. The latter originated in a legacy from a Florentine merchant resident in Venice — Corsolino (or Chersolino) degli Ubbriachi (or Ubriati) — of 10,000 Venetian *lire de piçoli* for the construction of a hospital for the poor in Murano in the parish of S. Stefano. The already existing devotional brotherhood on the island joined forces with the hospital and was granted use of its premises around 1348, which is when its *mariegola* may date from. The membership having quickly grown to the point where the brotherhood required more space, an exchange of properties between the two entities allowed the new flagellant confraternity dedicated to St John the Baptist to build a proper meeting room or hall next to the hospital. This could well be the *albergo* referred to in our inscription. In fact the unexpected legal term *franchado* 'released for use' may have been triggered by the fact that the granting of the nearby land to the confraternity by the hospital authorities was conditional on the completion of the *albergo* (CICOGNA 1824–53, I: 371). This fusion of devotion and charity explains the nature of the complex of buildings which gradually arose on the quayside still bearing the *scuola*'s name. As Canaletto's illustrations show, this involved an oratory, a meeting hall and a hospital clustering around a church. On the *mariegola* of the confraternity, held in the British Library, see HUMPHREY (2015: 221–25 and ill. XIVa-XIVb). Another inscription in our corpus originating in this *scuola* is examined at CI 26.

LETTERING: Gothic majuscules carved in V-section. The lettering is tall, with a semi-condensed module, as can probably best be appreciated in the compression of <o> and on the succession of <x>s on the top line. The ductus is strong, with well-balanced stroke contrast. The decorativeness of the writing remains sober and functionally very effective in creating a script that is both pleasing to the eye and eminently legible. Clarity is further enhanced by regularity of alignment and pagination, comfortable word and line spacing, exceptional letter height (at around 5 cm), black infilling in the letters, some of which still survives, and by the prominent interpuncts clearly separating words or, sometimes, syntagms. It is interesting to note, in this context, how the mason has made an obvious effort to differentiate between <c> and <e> which are notoriously similar in Gothic majuscular writing. Instead of hairstroking both he has chosen to leave <c> open, highlighting and decorating it instead with crescent serifs which are picked up by other letters, including the <g> and, in counterpoint, the upswept topstroke of <a>. The unusually high number of ligatures deployed, 18 in all — involving <a> and a following consonant –, lends elegance while in no way impairing legibility. These involve <al>, <an>, <ar> but also, for only the second time in the corpus, <ab>. Straight-sided <u/v> is employed throughout. Two errors of omission have been corrected, either directly by the mason or at the behest of his patrons. Firstly, a superscipt <o> has been inserted at the end of *otubrio* October (l. 1). Secondly, on the name *Marcante* (l. 15) a hyphen with a trailing wavy line that extends below the following two letters has been inserted between <a> and <c> to indicate the missing <r>. Nowadays this correction is largely obscured but it is perfectly visible in earlier photographs: see ZUCHOLD (1993, I: ill. 8). The abbreviations employed are clean-lined. They are the Tironian 9 on *conpagni*; the kinked and serifed slashes through <s> on *s(ier)*, with the slash on *misier* (l. 2) actually elongated and inverted and made to represent both <s> and the abbreviated syllable; *sier* abbreviated once (l. 6) by means of the the Latin *pro* symbol, looking like a P with the lower part of the bowl snaking down through, then behind, the stem (as on CI 15, CI 16); the keyhole suspension bars representing <n> and also <san> (or perhaps <sen>); and, most unusually in a vernacular epigraph, the <que> on *questo* (ll. 4–5) represented by what looks superficially like a wide, swashed <s> shape. It seems to be a stylised version of an abbreviation sometimes seen in Latin inscriptions from the twelfth and thirteenth centuries: <q> with an elongated tail bisected by a diagonal stroke.

LANGUAGE: The language of this inscription from Murano displays no perceptible divergence from the Early Venetian of Venice proper, and clearly participates in contemporary trends such as the onset of diphthongisation on mid-high vowels, as can be seen on *scuola*, *sier* and *misier*. We have already noted the interesting presence in the epigraph of terms related to confraternity governance, including *oficiali* 'board officials, officers' (for which see CI 3) and *albergo* (see CI 18). *Podesta* (in other words, *podestà*) 'mayor', which was present on an early inscription from Murano, appears again here in the perhaps unexpectedly apocopated form instead of the majority variant *podestade* (see CI 2 and CI 51). As mentioned above, the likely reason for the recourse to the legal term *franchado*, literally 'freed', from *franc(h)ar* 'to liberate, free, remove an obligation', is the fulfilment of a legal commitment on the *scuola*'s part to complete the building of their hall on the land granted to it. *Di* in *scuola di batudi* (ll. 7–8) is the first chronological appearance in the corpus of the contracted Early Venetian masculine plural partitive article, originating in speech, which became generalised in writing in the fifteenth century, ousting the traditional *deli* and competing with *dei* (see CI 18, CI 41, CI 60, CI 77). When freestanding, *nobel* 'noble' (l. 2) would normally be *nobele* in Early Venetian. The apocope here is provoked by its position in the syntagm *nobel e savio* 'noble and wise'. Based on the full form of *misier* (l. 7) I have opened out the slashed <s> throughout as *sier* and not *ser*. The digraph <ch> is used constantly for the velar /k/, and the traditional <ç> is employed for the palatal affricates /ts/ and /dz/. *Çacharia Gabriel* (l. 3), the mayor of Murano in 1374–75, was of course a Venetian patrician. *Çan Buxelo* (l. 4), however, was a citizen from Murano, the position of confraternity *vardian (grando)*, l. 5, being the preserve of the citizen class. *D'Arpo* (l. 10) was the surname of a well-known Muranese family of glass manufacturers (FORMENTIN 2017: 127). *Cavoduro* (ll. 12–13) is actually spelled as two words on the inscription itself. It was originally a nickname meaning 'hard head'. *Sartor* 'tailor' (l. 13) and *pistor* 'baker' (l. 17) are occupational surnames, hovering between trade designations and settled family names, like those we examined in CI 23. The two terms are considered in CI 100 and CI 95 respectively. Another occupational surname is *Marcante* 'merchant' (l. 15), with the typical Veneto raising of /er/ to /ar/ which is matched by the alternation in English of the surnames *Merchant* and *Marchant* (see CI 107). The two Christian names *Alvise* (Italian, Luigi) and *Mafio* (Italian, Matteo) are characteristically Venetian in form. On *otubrio* (l. 1) for October see CI 8 and CI 79.

RECENT STUDIES: TOMASIN (2012b); FERGUSON (2015c: 63–64). First published and commented on in CICOGNA (1824–53, VI: 375).

Corpus Inscription 39

MCCCLXXV · QVES|TA · PIERA · E · PROP|IA · DELA · CHOLONA ₃|
CHE · CHR(IST)O · FO BATVD|O · MIS(R) · MICHIEL ₅| MORESINI · MIS(R) ·
PI|ERO · CHORNER · P(ER)C|OLATORI · FE FAR :

[MCCCLXXV. Questa piera è propia dela cholona che Christo fo batudo. Mis. Michiel Moresini, mis. Piero Chorner, percolatori, fe' far.]

TRANSLATION: 1375. This stone is from the very column where Christ was scourged. The procurators Sir Michiel Morosini (and) Sir Piero Chorner had it made.

DATE: 1375.

LOCATION: On a reliquary, in situ, in the Treasury of St Mark (*Santuario* no. 59), St Mark's Basilica.

TYPE AND DESCRIPTION: Documentary and commemorative. The inscription is engraved on eight oblong plaquettes running round the column capital of the fourteenth-century reliquary of the *Column of the Flagellation of Christ*. It confirms that the relic displayed is a true fragment of the column against which Christ was scourged. It also records the year when the artefact was made and the names of its two commissioners. The reliquary is displayed in a glass case in the Sanctuary part of the Treasury. On feast days it is occasionally brought out on to the main altar of the Basilica, a tradition dating back to the Middle Ages.

The relic itself is a fist-sized piece of red granite mounted on a collar on top of the column, just above our inscription. The date and circumstances of its arrival in Venice are not known. The reliquary strikes the viewer immediately as an impressive piece of work. Standing 67 cm high and 19.2 cm in diameter at its widest point, it is the largest among the priceless objects in the Treasury and weighs close to 4 kg. In remarkably good condition it is an exquisite example of medieval Venetian goldsmithery. The artefact is crafted and engraved in partly-gilded solid silver. It depicts with elegance and dramatic economy the scene of the scourging of Christ evoked in the Gospels. The fulcrum of the reliquary is the composed figure of Jesus bound to the column and about to be flogged by the two guards or soldiers standing on either side of Him, each with one arm raised. The whips which they originally carried are now lost. The composure of Christ contrasts with the angry sneers of His torturers and their dynamic twisted posture. The decorative detail of the hair, beards and costumes of the two guards is beautiful but does not detract from the frozen violence and pathos of the scene. The presence of the stringent inscriptional message, at just under 1 cm high, is suitably discreet. The object and its inscription can be examined in detail at http://www.meravigliedivenezia.it/it/oggetti-virtuali/CAT_164.html [accessed 26 June 2020].

It seems likely that the iconography of this prestigious reliquary influenced subsequent representations of the flagellation. HAHNLOSER (1971: 167) even thought that the figures of the so-called *Mori* on the clock-tower in St Mark's square might

Fig. 3.42. CI 39 (detail). © A. S. Ferguson.

be attributable to its visual impact (see CI 80). What it does appear to have links with, although the influence must be in the other direction, are the illuminated scenes of scourging sometimes found in the fourteenth-century membership-and-rule books of the *scuole grandi* of Venice that were founded, of course, as flagellant confraternities. Particularly striking is its resemblance to the illustration of the flogging scene in the *mariegola* of the Scuola Grande di S. Giovanni Evangelista — from the first third of the Trecento — now in Paris in the Musée Marmottan Monet (Wildenstein Collection M 6098), of which a good reproduction is in HUMPHREY (2015: ill. IIIb).

LETTERING: Gothic majuscules in gilded silver inscribed in V-section on a dark blue niello ground. The goldsmith's work on the letters is of the highest order. He achieves an exceptional balance between roundedness and verticality, delicacy and forcefulness. The result is an inscription which is aesthetically pleasing while remaining eminently legible. Particularly revealing of the smith's finesse are the fine hairstrokes on <c>, <e> and <f>, the tapering parallel upstroke on <l>, the serifing on <s> and the diagonal Tironian abbreviation stroke through the <s> of *mis(r)*. The <h> has an attractively curved tucked-in leg, and the <m> throughout has delicately incurved arms. The <q>, unusually, has its tail left-aligned: a feature that occurs on only two other occasions in the corpus (CI 2, CI 48). Christ's name (l. 4) is represented by the Chi-Rho in the forms of <xpo> with a horizontal overbar. There are no ligatures. Words or syntagms are nearly always separated by a prominent mid-high interpunct, and the epigraph ends with a conspicuous triple row of vertical dots.

The order of the plaquettes was unfortunately altered during one of the restorations of the reliquary, probably either in 1489 or, as appears more likely, in 1721 (GALLO 1967: 100). With oblongs 3 and 7 switched round, the syntax of the message has become jumbled, a fact that was already apparent to nineteenth-century observers. I have restored the plaquettes to their correct order in my transcription, as did FERRO (1889: 451). The authorities and organisations dedicated to the preservation of Venetian works of art should make it a priority to restore the original word order on this outstanding artefact.

LANGUAGE: Although short, the language of the inscription takes on particular significance in the light of the status of its two commissioners who stood at the heart of the Venetian patriciate and state. Piero C(h)orner from S. Samuel had a distinguished diplomatic career. He was the Venetian ambassador who accompanied Pope Urban V on his return to the Holy See in Rome from Avignon in 1367, and he was in charge of the Republic's supplies in the wars with the Carrara dynasty, Austria and Hungary. He was made a Procurator of St Mark the year before the commissioning of the column inscription. He died in 1407 and his fine wall tomb, with Latin inscription underneath, is in the chapel of the Magdalene in San Zanipolo. Michiel Morosini *quondam* Marin had a glittering career as Venice's ambassador to the Carrara, to Genoa and to Hungary. He used his immense wealth from trade to support the city during the wars with Genoa. Like Corner he was made a Procurator in 1374. He went on to be elected doge in 1382, dying four months and five days after his accession as the Morosini codex confirms (NANETTI 2010, I: 167). His tomb in S. Zanipolo, on the south wall of the presbytery, is a remarkable multi-media creation with its great Gothic tabernacle adorned by sculpted figures, its brightly coloured mosaic canopy with Morosini and his wife presented to the crucified Christ, and its huge (and now ruined) background wall painting. The concise message that the goldsmith engraved on the plaquettes of the *Column of the Flagellation* — a commission of outstanding religious and political significance and a gesture of exceptional patronage — was given to him by one or both of these two politicians. It is reasonable to suppose that their sponsorship of the *Column* was an act of celebration and/or thanks for their elevation to the Procuratorship of St Mark. The written vernacular they employed is guaranteed to have been the Venetian of the city's elite.

One immediately notes the characteristic absence of consonant doubling in *cholona* 'column' (l. 3) and *batudo* 'beaten' (ll. 4–5) compared with Tuscan/Italian *colonna* and *battuto*. Also expected is the voicing of T > /d/ in *batudo*, with the lenition going no further than /d/ in prestige writing such as this. By 1375 diphthongisation of stressed /e/ was widespread, affecting a noun like *piera* 'stone' (l. 2) and the Christian names *Piero* (Peter; ll. 6–7) and *Michiel* (Michael; l. 5), where early in the century the predominant forms were *pera*, *Pero* and *Michel*. This suggests that the abbreviated title *mis.* (ll. 5, 6) should be expanded to *misier* and not *miser*, but out of prudence I have preferred *mis(r)* in both cases. In the construction *fe far* '(they) had (it) made' *fe* or *fe'* is the usual 3rd plural past historic of *far* 'to make'. It shows one of the most constant features of Venetian verb morphology: that 3rd singular and plural verb forms are identical. The Tuscan/Italian equivalents are *fece fare* (3rd singular) and *fecero fare* (3rd plural). In Early Venetian and Early Tuscan the spoken adjectival form *propio*, *propia* 'the very, (the thing) itself, the one, proper' (ll. 2–3) < PRŌPRĬUS — agreeing here with *piera* — coexisted with the more strictly 'correct' form *proprio/a* (see CI 45). The adverb *propio* 'really, genuinely', with deletion of the second /r/ by dissimilation, was still common in Modern/Contemporary Venetian. It is amusing to note that the two *Procuratores Sancti Marci* themselves considered the written vernacular form of their conjoined title to be *percolatori* (ll. 7–8), with initial metathesis and dissimilation of the second /r/. The use of the catch-all relative *che* 'that, which' (l. 4) strikes the modern reader as ungrammatical, but it was perfectly acceptable in Early Venetian. *Moresini* (l. 6), also spelled Morexini (see CI 13), vied in Early Venetian with the variant Morosini which eventually predominated. The presence of the digraph <ch> for /k/ remains prevalent, except in the case of *percolatori*, although the arrangement of letters at the end of the plaquette (stem-barred <p> for *per-* followed by a <c> hard against the metal frame) left some room for doubt. I have now been able to examine the inscription close up and am convinced that the <h> is absent.

RECENT STUDIES: GALLO (1967: 99–100); HAHNLOSER (1971: 166–68); WIXOM (1984: 306); FERGUSON (2015a); HUMPHREY (2015: 95); MENEGUOLO (2019: 51–53). First transcribed in MOSCHINI (1815, I: 381). First transcribed with the correct word order in FERRO (1889: 451).

Corpus Inscription 40

M CCC LXXV · D(EL) MEXE · D(E) ₁| MARÇO · CHATARINV(S) · ₂| · PINXIT ₃
[MCCCLXXV, del mexe de março. *Chatarinus pinxit*.]

TRANSLATION: 1375, in the month of March. *Chatarinus painted (it)*.

DATE: March 1375.

LOCATION: At present, and since the nineteenth century, in the Accademia galleries (*sestiere* of Dorsoduro), inventory 545, catalogue 16. Its original provenance is unknown but both its subject and use of the vernacular suggest a commission by a confraternity, or possibly a church, in Venice.

TYPE AND DESCRIPTION: Statement of authorship of a painting, with date. The epigraph is painted in black on three lines at the bottom of a tempera panel (89 × 58 cm) depicting the *Coronation of the Virgin* by the Venetian painter usually known in Italian and English as Catarino or Caterino (di Marco Veneziano) and in Venetian as Catarin. He signed himself on his work as *C(h)atarinus*. Catarino, resident at different periods in the parishes of S. Luca and S. Anzolo, was active between 1367 and 1390, first in partnership with an older painter who signed himself *Donatus*, then alone. He is documented as executing various commissions in Venice, including for the church of S. Agnese (*sestiere* of Dorsoduro) and for the monastery of S. Giorgio (Venetian, S. Zorzi), as well as on the mainland.

The present panel depicts Christ symbolically crowning the Virgin Mary, His right hand on her halo, while in the background, behind a blue panel with gold stars, eight angel-musicians play music to accompany the ceremony. The solemn figures of Jesus and the Madonna are unified by the interplay of grave hand gestures, by the golden discs of their haloes and by their identical garments: a pink gold-fringed undershirt overlain with a gorgeous dark blue mantle picked out in a golden brocaded flower pattern which flattens the picture surface. These motifs and colours are picked up by the fabrics on the divan on which the two figures are seated and by the panel at the back. Foreground and background are linked by the two outer angels reaching over to hold in place the golden divan cover. The solemnity of the scene and the involvement of the spectator are evoked by Catarino through the sad expression of Christ, looking away from us into the middle distance, while Mary, her hand indicating her son, glances pointedly towards us. While the faces of the two main figures have a static, almost Byzantine quality, the eight figures in the background are more animated and individualised. The angel in red at the centre runs her fingers over the keyboard of a portative organ. She is flanked by a viol player and a lute player. Our panel repeats on a simpler, more human and less grandiose scale, the identical themes and motifs explored in the slightly earlier *Coronation of the Virgin* painted together by Catarino and Donato. It is displayed in the Querini Stampalia gallery in Venice and bears a Latin inscription inflected by Venetianisms in spelling and syntax: *MCCCLXXII / m(en)xe agvsti // Donatv(s) (et) Cat/arinv(s) picxit*.

FIG. 3.43. CI 40. © A. S. Ferguson.

LETTERING: Gothic majuscules. Thin, dark, slightly spidery writing that looks almost as if it has been traced with a pen. The letters, averaging *c.* 0.7 cm in height, increase slightly in size line by line. Their Gothic roundedness is balanced by a certain spikiness that makes the script rather distinctive. As on CI 37 the <t> is modelled with sober end-stop serifs, but overall Caterino's script has greater sophistication. This is apparent in the very fine hairstroking on <c> and <e> and on the bowed, exaggeratedly elongated, legs of <h> and <n>, on the uncialesque <m> of the date, whose left stem is a bowl, and on the curled, raised Latin abbreviation mark for the <s> of *Chatarinus* (l. 2). As on CI 37 the Greek influenced mu-type <m>, very attractively drawn, appears on *mexe* (l. 1) and *março* (l. 2). Alongside it, too, is the <u/v> on *Chatarinus* in the form of an upsilon with short understroke. Surprisingly, the painter has also employed this letter form for the Roman numeral V on the date. The <ç> on *março* is unusually bold. The two Tironian 7 slashes through <d> (l. 1) are crisply drawn. The second clearly indicates *de* 'of'. I assume that the first one stands, instead, for the <el> of *del* 'of the', although such an abbreviation is unusual.

LANGUAGE: Caterino's statement juxtaposes the date of execution of the panel in Venetian with his trademark signature in Latin, in a formula that was not uncommon in Venice in the later Trecento. Three of the iconic traits of Early Venetian spelling are present: the <x> for the voiced sibilant /z/ in *mexe* 'month' (l. 1), the <ç> for the unvoiced affricate in *março* March (l. 2), and the digraph <ch> for /k/, even on the Latin spelling of the painter's name *Chatarinus*. On *março* see CI 18, CI 58.

RECENT STUDIES: TESTI (1909, I: 239–42).

Corpus Inscription 41

A̅NOME · DE · DIO · E DE · MADONA · S(-NTA) · MA̅RIA E ·S(-N) · GOTA̅R|DO
· FO · CONCESSO · GRACIA · P(ER) · LA · DOGAL · SIGNORIA · E ₂|
IN · TEMPO · DE · MIS(R) · A̅NTHONIO · UENIER · DOXE · DE · UE|NIEXIA ·
E · P(ER) · LO · CONSEIO · DI · D^{I}EXE · A · S(R) · ÇECHIN · DAL · ₄| MELON ·
(CON)DAM · S(R) · BERTUÇI · IN · M^O·CCC·LXXXIII · DI · IIII · ₅| FEURER ·
CHE LO · DITO · S(R) · ÇECHIN · POSSA · FAR · UNA · ₆| SCUOLA · (E) UNO ·
ALTA̅RO · DE · S(-N) · GOTARDO · A̅LA · GLEXIA ₇| DE · S(-N) · MAFIO · DE
RIALTO · E · QUESTO · LAUORIER · FO · ₈| FATO · TUTO · P(ER) · LO · S^{O}URA ·
SCRITO · S(R) · ÇECHIN · E · DELI · S|UO · BENI · AL ONOR · DE · DIO · E DE
· S(-N) · GOT|A̅RDO · AMEN :::≫

[A nome de Dio e de madona S. Maria e S. Gotardo fo concesso gracia per la Dogal Signoria — e in tempo de mis. Anthonio Venier, Doxe de Veniexia, e per lo Conseio di Diexe — a sr Çechin dal Melon, *condam* sr Bertuçi, in MCCCLXXXIII, dì IIII fevrer: che lo dito sr Çechin possa far una scuola e uno altaro de S. Gotardo ala glexia de S. Mafio de Rialto. E questo lavorier fo fato tuto per lo sovrascrito sr Çechin, e deli suò beni, al onor de Dio e de S. Gotardo. Amen.]

TRANSLATION: In the name of God and of Our Lady St Mary and of St Gotthard a grace was granted by Ducal Authority — and (this was) in the time of Sir Anthonio Venier, Doge of Venice, and by the Council of Ten — to Mr Çechin dal Melon, *son of the late* Mr Bertuçi (dal Melon), on February the 4th 1383. Whereby the said Mr Çechin can set up a confraternity and an altar to St Gotthard in the church of St Matthew at the Rialto. And this present piece of work was made in its entirety thanks to the above-mentioned Mr Çechin, from his own funds, to the honour of God and of St Gotthard. Amen.

DATE: February 1383 (1384 by modern reckoning).

LOCATION: The inscription plaque is now on display among the collection of epigraphs and other classical artefacts at the grand Villa Contarini-Camerini at Piazzola sul Brenta, north west of Padua. It is affixed, roughly 2 m off the ground, on the sheltered side of one of the pillars in the open arcade in the eastern wing at the front of the Villa where the archaeological collection is housed. How and when it came to the Villa is not clear. The collection was originally put together at Piazzola by the Nani family in the eighteenth century, when Antonio Nani and his two sons acquired Graeco-Roman pieces during their periods in office in Venice's eastern Mediterranean possessions. The original collection was sold off in 1822 and scattered to museums across Europe and America but a nucleus was acquired by the new owners of the Villa, the Camerini, and housed at Piazzola. It is possible that our inscription came to the collection before 1822.

The original location of the plaque was in the church of S. Mafio (or S. Mat(t)io: see CI 108) near the Rialto, beside the new altar, commissioned by the grocer Çechin dal Melon and dedicated to St Matthew, that is mentioned in the epigraph.

FIG. 3.44. CI 41. © Ronnie Ferguson.

FIG. 3.45. CI 41 (lines 10–11). © Ronnie Ferguson.

The small church was located near the extremely busy commercial centre off the Ruga Rialto (*sestiere* of S. Polo) on the approaches to the bridge. The church was demolished in 1810 following the Napoleonic suppressions (BASSI 1997: 98–102).

TYPE AND DESCRIPTION: Documentary and commemorative. The marble plaque with the inscription measures 73 × 55 cm and is surrounded by a crenellated frame some 5 cm wide. The object is in excellent condition, probably on account of its being inside a church for most of its existence and because of the relative absence of airborne pollution in its present rural location. The tablet features low-relief coats of arms on both sides towards the bottom. These belonged presumably to the dal Melon family, although confirmation of this has yet to be found. The inscription is the proud announcement by an obviously wealthy grocer, Çechin dal Melon (of whom we have no further information), that the Venetian authorities had given him permission to found a confraternity dedicated to St Gotthard and to have an altar built in the church of S. Mafio, dedicated to that saint, where the brotherhood would worship. The epigraph in effect records the birth of the *scuola* of S. Gotardo belonging to the guild of the wholesale grocers or duggists (Early Venetian, *speçieri* — or *spiçieri* — *da grosso*) who dealt in spices, dried fruit, sugar and confectionery. As such, it is exceptional documentary evidence of the founding of a confraternity through individual initiative and patronage. It is highly likely that the stonemason charged with executing this commission was provided with a written text by dal Melon himself.

It is interesting to note that the *speçieri* were in fact not happy to worship for long in their original location. A decade later, on 9 September 1394, they obtained permission from the Council of Ten to transfer to the nearby church of S. Aponal (Italian, S. Apollinare) on account of the alleged proliferation of prostitutes and lowlifes in the vicinity of S. Mafio (SBRIZIOLO 1967–68: 421; TASSINI 1863, *s.v. Speziali*). In Calle del Campaniel, immediately to the left of S. Aponal, they acquired a meeting house on the first floor, above what would soon be a meeting room of the German bakers and beneath what was to be the headquarters of the stonemasons' guild (see CI 95).

LETTERING: Gothic majuscules cut in V-section. The script is unusually elegant and stylised, while remaining balanced and rigorously aligned. Although exceptionally fine-lined in ductus it displays subtle stroke contrast. It is obvious that the stonemason was aesthetically aware by the way he meticulously pursued individual curviness and overall roundedness. This is particularly evident on the sinuous legs of <h>, <m>, <n> and <r> and on the left leg of <a>, all descending below the baseline. It is also present in the strongly curved serifs on <s> and <g>, on the highly elongated and curved hairstrokes on the <c>, <e> and <f>, on the unusually upswept topstroke of <a>, and on the abbreviation signs: particularly the snaking line through <s> for *ser* or *sier* and the Tironian 9 on *condam* (l. 5). The search for decorativeness is evident in the sensitive rendering of <ç> and in the delicately balled serifs on <u>, <d> and <t>. Unsurprisingly, the stonecutter has gone throughout for a flowing left-curved <u> for <u/v>. He makes regular use of ligatured letters, including the usual <al>, <an> and <ar> but also, uniquely in the corpus, <eu> and <ur>. Unexpected are the insertion twice of superscript letters — on *diexe* (l. 4) and *sovra* (l. 9) — and the hooked abbreviation sign on the first <e> of *fevrer* (l. 6) to indicate the insertion of a missing <u/v>. This suggests that the finished work was revised with care, either by the mason on his own initiative or at the instigation of the sponsor. The text is perfectly paginated, with justification on both sides: no mean feat given the awkwardness of layout. The epigraph tapers at the bottom of the tablet because of the presence of the two escutcheons, but the mason has negotiated these obstacles expertly. The inscription concludes with a cluster of dots followed by a low-relief acanthus leaf, a decorative motif that we already noted on CI 28.

LANGUAGE: One is struck immediately by the exceptional string of references to the Venetian authorities, expressing the commissioner's pride in his achievement and the prestige attached to his initiative. In quick succession we have *dogal signoria* 'government, Ducal authority' (l. 2); *Anthonio Venier* (l. 3), the name of the reigning doge; *doxe de Veniexia* 'doge of Venice' (ll. 3–4); and *conseio di diexe* 'Council of Ten' (l. 4). One notes here the hyper-Graecism of *Anthonio* with an <h>, and the regular use of <x> for the voiced sibilant /z/ in *doxe*, *diexe* and also *glexia* 'church' (l. 7). This contrasts with the unusually consistent use of <ss> for the unvoiced sibilant /s/ on *concesso* 'conceded' (l. 2) and *possa* 'can, may' (l. 6). For a discussion of the complex problem of how the <x> in *Ven(i)exia* (ll. 3–4) may originally have been pronounced, see FERGUSON (2007: 76 n. 11). *Fo concesso gracia* 'grace was granted' (l. 2) is an example of lack of agreement in the passive construction, frequent in Early Venetian but rare in the corpus. On the contracted partitive form *di* (l. 4) for *de(l)i*, see CI 18, CI 38, CI 60, CI 77. Expected at this point in time is the diphthongisation of the stressed mid vowel in *Veniexia*, *diexe*, *scuola* 'confraternity' (l. 7) and *lavorier* 'work, piece of work, artefact' (l. 8). It suggests strongly that the forms *sier* 'Mr' and *misier* 'Sir, Mr' underlie their respective abbreviations, although I have remained neutral in my transcription. The ending *-eio* of *conseio* < CONSĬLIUM displays the dominant Early Venetian reflex of Latin L + yod. In Modern/Contemporary Venetian this outcome would be superseded by the palatalised variant in *-egio* already present in Middle Venetian.

The *lavorier* referred to here (l. 8) is probably the confraternity altar itself rather than the inscription plaque. The use of the metaplasmic *altaro* 'altar' (l. 7) is somewhat surprising. *Altaro* was a common Trecento form on the Veneto mainland and may have been a minority variant present in Venice where *altar* was usual (see CI 47). *Glexia* 'church' retains the traditional Early Venetian consonant + L cluster and the masculine singular definite article is always *lo*. However, other features appear more 'modern', such as the <m>, rather than <n>, in *tempo* (l. 3) and the preference for /al/ rather than /ol/ in *Rialto* (l. 8). One suspects that *san* rather than *sen* underlies the abbreviations for 'saint', but again I have settled for a neutral transcription. *Fevrer* (l. 6) is the commonest form for February in Early Venetian, contrasting with the variant *fevraro* which appeared in CI 24. It shows the characteristic Venetian outcome in *-er* of -ĀRIUS. *Condam* '(son of) the late' (l. 5) is a vernacular pronunciation form of Latin QUONDAM 'formerly', much used in early Italo-Romance vernaculars to express the relationship to a deceased parent, in this case 'son of' (see CI 49). *Mafio* Matthew (l. 8) is the result of a native Venetian rendering in /f/ of the theta in Greek Ματθαῖος (see CI 37). The Christian name *Çechin*, which we came across in CI 31, possibly without the cedilla, is a diminutive of *Çeco*, itself a shortened form of Françesco (Francis). *Bertuçi* (l. 5), derived from *Berto* (Robert), is undoubtedly of Germanic origin. It corresponds to Early Tuscan *Bertuccio*.

RECENT STUDIES: TOMASIN (2001a); FERGUSON (2015c: 65–66).

Corpus Inscription 42

QVESTA · FRADELITADE · SIE · DEI · LAVORENTI · TODESCI · CALEGERI ·

[Questa fradelitade si è dei lavorenti todesci calegeri.]

TRANSLATION: This is the brotherhood of the German shoemaking workers.

DATE: 1383 or shortly thereafter.

LOCATION: In situ on a strip running along the bottom of a plaque which depicts the Annunciation in high relief. The plaque is embedded *c.* 220 cm off the ground on an outside house wall in Calle de le Boteghe (*sestiere* of S. Marco no. 3128), the main artery connecting S. Stefano and S. Samuel.

TYPE AND DESCRIPTION: Declaration of ownership and presence. The inscription with its accompanying sculpture documents and advertises the new presence of the confraternity of the German shoemakers — the *Sc(u)ola dei caleg(h)eri todesc(h)i* or *Scola sancte Marie Theotonicorum calegariorum* (or *cerdonum*) in the contemporaneous Latin documentation — under the protection of the Virgin of the Annunciation. However, a legal agreement of February 1380 between the brotherhood and the nearby Augustinian friars of S. Stefano confirms the *de facto* existence of the confraternity at least three years before our inscription (BRAUNSTEIN 2016: 856). The inscription itself and the *scuola*'s bilingual Latin-German statute of 1383 make explicit that membership was originally restricted to journeymen ('geselschaft der deuczen schuster knechten in venedien'), with masters only being admitted from 1474 (BÖNINGER 2002: X).

The whole inscriptional artefact is in Istrian stone. From base to apex it measures around 60 cm. The inscription strip itself which forms the base of the plaque is *c.* 80 × *c.* 3 cm. The scene sculpted in relief above the epigraph is a vivid depiction of the Annunciation. With God the father at the apex, on the point of releasing the dove of the Holy Spirit, the kneeling angel Gabriel on the left raises one hand in benediction while in the other he holds a lily. He blesses Mary who kneels, arms folded across her chest, in front of a handsomely-sculpted lectern. By the lectern, on a smaller scale, kneel five confraternity brothers, all highly individualised facially. Some are bearded, others not; some wear headgear, others are bareheaded. They hold aloft their confraternity banner with its tasselled end flared out. The heavy folded draperies of angel, Virgin and supplicants are rendered with detailed vigour as are the paving stones beneath the figures.

The brotherhood of the German cobblers was officially licensed by the Council of Ten in July 1383. Throughout almost all of its 425-year existence its devotional activities were carried out at the altar of the Annunciation in the nearby church of S. Stefano. However, it owned a group of contiguous properties in Calle de le Boteghe corresponding to *sestiere* of S. Marco house numbers 3127–33. Here it established the charitable hospice-cum-hospital for sick and indigent members of the brotherhood, eventually also offering temporary accomodation to Germans passing through Venice. See SEMI (1983: 160); G. VIO (2004: 317–19). The origins

Fig. 3.46. CI 42 in context. © A. S. Ferguson.

Fig. 3.47. CI 42. © A. S. Ferguson.

of the hospital can be traced back to the donation of a house to the confraternity for the succour of the poor in 1411 by a German shoemaker, resident in Venice, called Heinrich son of Konrad (*Henricus quondam Conradi*). The legal document is reproduced in BRAUNSTEIN (2016: 855). The end stretch of Calle de le Boteghe up to the junction with Salizzada S. Samuel is still rich in echoes of the shoemaker's hospice whose original locale was sold off and turned into shops and flats in the nineteenth century after the Napoleonic suppression of the great network of confraternities and guilds in the city. The entrance to the main building, now a shop, retains sculpted Annunciation figures on its Istrian stone door jambs, while handsome outlines of fashionable Renaissance shoes mark the pillars at either end of the brotherhood's row of properties. Underneath our present relief and epigraph is embedded an inscription of 1659 in Roman capitals. Along the bottom of this plaque is sculpted a splendid fashion shoe in high relief flanked by two shoe outlines: *D.O.M. / fu restaurato il presente hospitale / de calegheri todeschi sotto / il governo di mistro Zuane Mestich / gastaldo et sopraintendente della / fabricha con / lassistenza di mistro Christoffollo Mensori soprastante / alla medesima / con consentimento del capitolo gieneral / adi primo ottobre* MDCLVIIII. From the *scuola* complex there survives a fine well head (63 × 98 × 88 cm) now in the Museo Correr (Cl XXV n. 0794a). On one side it carries an elongated shield motif with symbols of the confraternity (leather shoe strips arranged into a pattern and surmounted by an uncialesque majuscule M for Maria and by a crown) and the date 1486 in Roman numerals.

The presence in our period of the prosperous south German merchants housed in the Fontego dei Todeschi, who worshipped in the church of S. Bortolamio (Modern Venetian, S. Bortolomio) at the Rialto — where, according to Marin Sanudo, services were even conducted in German (CARACCIOLO ARICÒ 2011: 49) and for whom Dürer executed the sumptuous *Feast of the Rose Garlands* in 1506 — has been intensely studied. Less well known are the long-term nuclei of Germans resident elsewhere in Venice, especially those in the S. Stefano and S. Samuel parishes who were essentially involved either in the shoemaking or bakery trades (see CI 95 for the association of German bakers), and those in the area around the Rialto who worked as warehouse packers in the Fontego itself (see CI 73, CI 74).

LETTERING: Gothic majuscules cut in V-section. Both letters and words are well-spaced, with the latter separated by mid-high interpuncts, and there is a complete absence of ligatures and abbreviations. The module of the script is squarer than usual, as can be appreciated in particular by the width of <a>, <e>, <l> and <v>. The lettering, neatly contained within the strip, exhibits vigorous stroke modulation, serifing and hairstroking. These features are particularly noticeable on the strongly uncial <d>, its ascender spreading horizontally left then dipping to the baseline; on the sinuous <s> with its wide then narrow curves ending in bowed serifs; on the extravagant bowed hairstroke on <e>; on the long splayed downstrokes of <t>; and on the unusually outcurved parallel upstroke of <l> on *lavorenti*. Stems themselves show powerful wedge serifing. A striking consequence of the tendency of the sculptor to indulge in flourishing, allied to the rather square module he has given his script, is the almost inevitable letter conjoining that sometimes occurs, with, for example, the hairstroke of <e> on *dei* linking at both ends with the following <i>, and the four final letters of *todesci* almost run together. While this inscription is very much in the later Gothic manner exemplified by CI 38, CI 41 and CI 45 its combination of strong ductus, decorativeness and letter joining marks it off. Until very recently the legibility of the inscription and of the relief itself was impaired by a sooty incrustation over the object. This has been removed so that the vigour of the relief as well as the clarity of its accompanying epigraph are now fully revealed.

LANGUAGE: A brief but interesting example of later fourteenth-century Venetian. Regular, but unusual looking to the modern eye, are the <c> on *todesci* 'Germans' and the <g> in *calegeri* 'shoemakers, cobblers', where Modern/Contemporary Venetian would require a following <h> to mark the velar /k/ and /g/ respectively. *Todesco* is Venetian for 'German', noun or adjective, as in the great residence and trading warehouse of the Germans at the Rialto, the Fontego dei Todeschi (Italian, Fondaco dei Tedeschi). *Todesco/tedesco* are derived from the ancient Germanic ethnic name, represented by Old High German *diutisc*, meaning 'national, popular, vulgar', which eventually gave the modern outcome *deutsch*. *Caleg(h)er* 'shoemaker, cobbler' < CĂLĬGĀRĬUS (Mussafia 1873, s.v. *calig(h)er*) is familiar to all Venetianists. It is currently pronounced [kaeˈgɛr]. We encountered it in CI 23 and come across it again on the inscription from the shoemakers' guild at S. Tomà (CI 60). *Fradelitade* 'brotherhood' is unique in the corpus and contrasts with *fratirnitade* in CI 11, itself a one-off in our collection. By far the commonest Early Venetian form employed by the guilds and devotional confraternities themselves was *fraternitade*, with *fratirnitade* very much a minority variant. As for the *fradelitade* of the present inscription it is clearly a collective construction taking as its starting point not Latin but the Venetian plural noun *fradeli* 'brothers'. As such, it may be a lower register Venetian variant or, just possibly, a coinage influenced by the German of the shoemakers themselves. *Lavorente*, the common Early Venetian term for worker or journeyman, was shared in part by Tuscan. Despite appearances it does not seem to have originated as a metaphonic plural variant of *lavorante* which then spread back to the singular. On the originally emphatic form *si e* (in other words, *si è*) meaning 'is' which fused to *sie* and eventually settled down long term as the characteristic and unmarked Venetian 3rd singular present tense of the verb 'to be' — *se* or *xe* — see CI 32.

RECENT STUDIES: Böninger (2002: VII); Ferguson (2015c: 67). First recorded, but not published, by Cicogna.

Corpus Inscription 43

ÇVANE · DA BOLOGNA · PENSE ·

[Çuane da Bologna pense.]

TRANSLATION: John of Bologna painted (it).

DATE: Undated, but probably executed in the 1380s.

LOCATION: Now in the Accademia galleries, inventory 230, catalogue 17. Its original location, from the Trecento until the early nineteenth century, was inside the Scuola Grande di S. Giovanni Evangelista near the Frari. It was acquired by the Accademia in 1812 following the Napoleonic suppression of confraternities. It would be joined in 1820 in the Accademia by arguably the greatest cycle of narrative paintings in Venice, also originally housed in the *albergo* of the *scuola*: the priceless *teleri* from the late Quattrocento, illustrating the *Miracles of the True Cross*, by Carpaccio, Gentile Bellini, Lazzaro Bastiani and Giovanni Mansueti.

TYPE AND DESCRIPTION: Statement of authorship, without date, traced in black along the bottom of a tempera and gold panel (110 × 97 cm) painted by Çuane da Bologna (Italian, Giovanni da Bologna). The panel depicts *Our Lady of Humility*, with Saints John the Evangelist, John the Baptist, Peter and Paul, and with brothers from the Scuola Grande di S. Giovanni Evangelista. The image is very visually striking with its dominant bright red background. As befits what is, in effect, a kind of devotional icon there is no depth of field or attempt at realism, except to a limited extent at the bottom where the cluster of confraternity brothers — the only figures in the painting in the 'here and now' — is depicted. Appropriately, Çuane's statement of authorship appears just below this group. The central scene on the panel shows the Virgin Mary under a trilobe Gothic archway suckling the baby Jesus. Her blue robe and the stylised flower ground stand out powerfully against the intense red background irradiated by the aureole emanating from the two figures. The central panel is flanked by four narrow oblongs each featuring a haloed saint with his traditional attributes and his Latin name picked out in gold Gothic lettering. At the bottom kneel the group of fourteen confraternity supplicants in white hooded robes. Two bear candles while the *vardian grando* holds aloft a banner with the crosier symbol of the *scuola* which is also embroidered in red on each brother's garment.

Çuane da Bologna is recorded in Venice (where he resided in the parish of S. Luca) and in Treviso between 1377 and 1389, the year when he drew up his will. The four signed works left by the painter are all undated, but our panel and the *St Christopher* now in the Musei Civici in Padua, but which he painted for the Scuola dei Mercanti at the Madonna dell'Orto (*sestiere* of Cannaregio), suggest that he was in demand among Venetian confraternities.

LETTERING: Gothic majuscules. The strongly uncial script is rather clumsily laid out. The letters are emphatic and syntagms are demarcated by mid-high interpuncts, but overall clarity is impaired by the inconsistency in letter module,

FIG. 3.48. CI 43. © A. S. Ferguson.

height (averaging 0.75 cm) and spacing. This is best exemplified by the five letters of the painter's Christian name, *Çuane*. The space between <ç> and <v> is excessive and the width of the <v> is out of proportion. The excessive spread of the first two letters is then followed by the unnecessary compression of the <an> ligature and the over-small <e>. Individually, though, the letter tracing can be quite impressive. Hairstroking on <c> and <e> is marked, as is the serifing on the <s> and the strongly down-sloping ascender of <d>. Interesting is the <g> in *Bologna*, with good stroke modulation and the unusual rapprochement of the high swirl and the echoing bowed serif.

LANGUAGE: Noteworthy is the earliest appearance in the corpus of the form *Çuane* (rather than *Çane*) for John which would become predominant in the fifteenth century. *Pense* (or sometimes *inpense*) '(he) painted' is the normal Venetian rendering of the Latin *pinxit* which we saw in CI 40. Its noun equivalent, *pentor* 'painter', appeared in CI 24.

RECENT STUDIES: TESTI (1909: 299–301).

Corpus Inscription 44

· Q(UE)STOPERA DINTALGLIO E FATTO IN PIERA · ₁| · UN UENICIAN LA FE
CHA NOME POLO · ₂| · NATO DI IACHOMEL CHATAIAPIERA ·<~

[Quest'opera d'intalglio, e fatto in piera, un Venician la fe' ch'à nome Polo, nato di Iachomel Chataiapiera.]

TRANSLATION: This sculpted work, done in stone, was made by a Venetian called Polo, born of Iachomel Chataiapiera.

DATE: c. 1385. There are two inscriptions embedded in the wall beneath the tomb of Iacopo Cavalli in S. Zanipolo: the first in Latin, the second in the vernacular. The Latin plaque eulogises Cavalli, the Veronese warrior who gave distinguished service to Venice in the Chioggia conflict of the war against Genoa, as Captain General of the Republic's land forces, and who was ennobled for it in 1381. In his *Cronicha della Nobil Città de Venetia* Zorzi Dolfin records, in fact, that in 1380 'fo fatto Capitanio missier Jacomo deli Cavali, homo nobilissimo et notabile in fati d'arme, citadin de Verona' (CARACCIOLO ARICÒ 2007–09, II: 85). The plaque informs us that he died on 24 January 1384 (*more veneto*). Recently uncovered documentary evidence appears to confirm that work on the tomb began shortly after Cavalli's recorded death (D'AMBROSIO 2012a: 106). Our vernacular inscription is undated. We can surmise, however, that the sculptor Polo's signature tablet would have been prepared in advance — cut to size and inscribed with his trademark statement of authorship — possibly soon after the monument was commissioned and its measurements and layout established. It would thus have been ready to slot into place as the building project drew to a close.

LOCATION: In situ in the Basilica of S. Zanipolo, *sestiere* of Castello, in the left-side apse chapel dedicated to St Pius V (formerly to St Michael). Both inscriptions sit under a sumptuous polychromatic sarcophagus in Istrian stone (c. 260 × c. 160 cm) sculpted by Polo himself. The Cavalli tomb is topped by the formidable armoured *gisant* figure of the dead *condottiere*, his head cradled on two lions, his feet on a dog. Under the chain mail his face can be glimpsed, its lips and eyelids slightly parted. The burial chest is elaborately carved and coloured, with a deeply coffered front featuring relief figures and Evangelist symbols in its six *tondi*. The wall behind the tomb possibly bore an accompanying fourteenth-century fresco. It was re-frescoed in the sixteenth century by Lorenzino di Tiziano and features a vast battle scene with horses seen dramatically through pulled back curtains. The two inscriptions themselves are surmounted by the high-relief figure of an angel, coloured and glazed.

TYPE AND DESCRIPTION: Statement of authorship and advertising platform. The first example in the corpus in which a stonemason identifies himself. The rectangular inscription tablet in white marble measures 13 × 83 cm and has a crenellated frame 5 cm wide. It is in remarkably good condition, with no damage visible. Together with the Latin epitaph to Cavalli the two plaques form an inscriptional whole measuring in all 54 × 88 cm. Distinguished from each other by language and layout,

Fig. 3.49. CI 44. © A. S. Ferguson.

the plaques also feature different lettering techniques: the Latin epigraph employs the more expensive, and hence prestigious, raised characters; the vernacular one is inscribed. Additionally, the tablets are demarcated by the dividing length of their shared frame and by pigmentation. The epitaph plaque above is stained with what now looks like a dark brown colour but was possibly gold. This pigment is also used to highlight alternate segments of the outer crenellated frame surrounding both epigraphs, thus creating a chequered pattern. The vernacular tablet itself has been left uncoloured, as would have seemed appropriate, although infilling was applied by Polo to pick out the lettering. Our sculptor must have been aware that the eye of the onlooker was being subtly manipulated by his choices. Although attention was theoretically directed at the praise of the national hero, whoever examined the Latin inscription was bound to read Polo's self-advertisement below, their eye drawn down to its clear, spacious layout and more easily deciphered message. Such was the impact of the Cavalli tomb that its vernacular inscription was among the first to be recorded in print (SANSOVINO and STRINGA 1604: 122). It has consistently been transcribed and described by scholars and art historians, including Ruskin in the *Stones of Venice* (RUSKIN 1886, III: 82).

Some of the above remarks about the sculptor's intentions would be speculation but for the survival in Mirandola (Emilia-Romagna) of a later commission featuring another of Polo's authorship-advertising inscriptions. This confirms that he had indeed devised a fixed calling-card message, almost a jingle, which he in fact appears to have adapted to the local language variety of the audience likely to read it. It consisted of a three-line hendecasyllable, rhyming ABA, in a passe-partout form of Tuscan: the written variety familiarised throughout Italy by Dante, Petrarch and Boccaccio which was gradually becoming the written vernacular lingua franca up and down the peninsula. In Venice he tinged it with Venetian. In the church of St Francis in Mirandola, in a vernacular inscription (c. 1394) placed under the sarcophagus of another warrior, Prendiparte Pico, he instead inserted elements from the local Emilian dialect: *Questa opera de(n)tallio fata i(n) preda / un venician la fe cha nome Polo / nato di Iachomel Chataiapreda*. Most noticeable here is the substitution of the Venetian *piera* (< PĚTRAM) 'stone' and the occupational surname *Chataiapiera* with the metathetical equivalents *preda* (< *PRETAM) and *Chataiapreda*.

Our sculptor, who signs himself *Polo nato di Iachomel Chataiapiera* and now tends to be called Paolo di Jacobello by art historians, has traditionally been identified with Paolo delle (or *dalle*) Masegne, of the famous Venetian stonecutting family workshop operating in the late Trecento and early Quattrocento. In Venetian *masegne* are a type of stone slab, so both surnames are transparent references to the stonecutting trade. On the identification problem see WOLTERS (1976, I: 213–14).

LETTERING: Gothic majuscules cut in V-section. Smart, clear, well-aligned script, 3 cm high, that is elegant but unmannered. The stroke modulation is admirably controlled and effective. Polo's skill as a stonecutter can immediately be appreciated by the sheer balanced consistency of the repeated letters <c>, <e>, <f>, <h>, <l>, <n>, <o>, <t>, as well as by the <u/v> which in both instances takes the form of a left-curved <u>. If one were to pick out two letters for particular admiration it would be the <m>, which displays a subtle tension between its square module and the controlled sinuosity of its arms, and the <g> where the downward curl of the central swirl is in pleasing counterpoint with the upcurved serif on the arm. Legibility is further enhanced by ample letter height and spacing, by the absence of ligatures, by the single interpunct framing at the beginning and end of each line, and by the black infilling which is now much faded. The only abbreviation is the wavy bar over <q> and <s>. The three lines of writing are justified on the left.

LANGUAGE: The language of the inscriptional statement is Tuscan with a Venetian patina. *Questopera dintalglio* (l. 1) (= *quest'opera d'intalglio*) is perfect Tuscan, although Polo has hypercorrected the spelling of *intaglio* to render the palatal lateral sound /λ/. This phoneme did not exist in his native Early Venetian where the phrase would have been rendered by *questa ovra de intaio* (or *entaio*). The apocopated Tuscan forms in the phrase are unusual in our corpus (see CI 23), with the absence of apostrophes — never present in majuscule inscriptions — leading to rather awkward syntagmic amalgamations. *Nato di* 'born of' is clearly Tuscan too (Early Venetian, *nassudo de*), while *fatto* 'made' (l. 1) has the Tuscan double <tt> but fails to agree in gender with *opera*. *Cha nome* = *ch' a nome* 'who is called' (l. 2) and *la fe* or *fe'* 'made it' (l. 2) span both varieties. The Venetian overlay is clear in *piera* 'stone' (l. 1; Tuscan/Italian, *pietra*), in *un venician* 'a Venetian' (l. 2) and probably in the consistent use of the digraph <ch> for /k/. All proper names invoked are purely Venetian as well. The Christian name *Polo* (Paul; l. 2) — as in the *sestiere* of Venice called S. Polo and in Marco Polo — is the regular Venetian outcome of PAULUS. *Iac(h)omel* (l. 3) or *Iac(h)omelo* is a Venetian diminutive derivative of Jacobus (Jacob or James), the Early Tuscan cognate being Jacobello. *Chataiapiera* (= *c(h)a taia piera* 'who cuts stone') features Early Venetian *cha* 'who, which, that'. It appears, here, to be a proto-surname hovering between professional designation and established family name, like those we came across in CI 23 and CI 38. It is interesting to note that C(h)ataiapiera survived as a surname in Venice into the modern period, with MUTINELLI recording the sculptor Carlo Cataiapiera as a member of the city's Accademia di Pittura in the eighteenth century (1841: 19). Stoneman or Staneman is the exact occupational surname equivalent in English. It is not clear if Piero's surname is ultimately connected to the notable Venetian family name *de ca' Taiapiera* regularly recorded in the Early Modern period.

RECENT STUDIES: WOLTERS (1976, I: 212); CIOCIOLA (1995: 544–45); STUSSI (1997a: 160–61); D'AMBROSIO (2012a). First published in SANSOVINO and STRINGA (1604: 122).

Corpus Inscription 45

M°·CCC°·L·XXXX·III · D(E) · MAÇO · ₁| · FO FATO · FA͡R · QVESTO ·
OR|GA͡NO · E PERGOLO · DI BENI · ₃| · PROPRII · DE MIS(R) · LO VA͡RDI|A͡N ·
E (CON)PAGNI · CHE · IERA · IN · ₅| · QVEL · TENPO ·

[MCCCLXXXXIII, de maço, fo fato far questo organo e pergolo di beni proprii de mis. lo vardian e conpagni che iera in quel tenpo.]

TRANSLATION: In May 1393 this organ and pulpit were commissioned from the personal funds of the Warden and his executives in office at that time.

DATE: May 1393.

LOCATION: Now on display in the ground floor main hall, the *Sala delle Colonne*, of the Scuola Grande di S. Giovanni Evangelista (*sestiere* of S. Polo). The plaque is currently affixed to the wall immediately to the left as one enters the hall. Its original location was unquestionably in the nearby church of S. Giovanni Evangelista, directly facing the *scuola* building, in the vicinity of the pulpit and organ mentioned in the inscription. The considerable thickness of the plaque at the rear makes it certain that it was originally embedded in a wall. Given the radical restructuring of that church in the seventeenth and eighteenth centuries, which destroyed the original Trecento organ and pulpit, the inscription tablet is likely to have been removed to the confraternity premises at some point during those building works. It was certainly no longer in the church in the early nineteenth century when Giambattista SORAVIA carried out a careful survey of its contents, transcribing all the inscriptions he came across (1822–24, II: 195–214). CICOGNA (1855: 14) recorded it in its present location.

TYPE AND DESCRIPTION: Commemorative and documentary. The inscription tablet is a hefty rectangle of white marble measuring 44 × 29 cm with a castellated frame *c*. 4 cm wide around it. In places the angled crenellation of the frame retains faint traces of alternate dark green and pink pigmentation. The epigraph itself documents the commissioning of a new organ and pulpit in the church of S. Giovanni Evangelista and the fact that they were ordered to be made, and were paid for, by the confraternity warden (*mis(r) lo vardian*. ll. 4–5) and by his fellow elected officers (*conpagni*, l. 5) on the *scuola*'s executive board, the *banca*. The inscription plaque is exceptionally well preserved, with no appreciable damage either to support or lettering. This may well be the result of the object spending its entire existence indoors, protected from the effects of weather and pollution. The inscription surface is generous in relation to the five and a half lines of writing and there is a section of unused space at the bottom. On the confraternity of S. Giovanni Evangelista, one of the great *scuole grandi* devotional brotherhoods of Venice, see CI 3, CI 17, CI 18, CI 43, CI 48.

LETTERING: Gothic majuscules carved in V-section. This is an impressive piece of inscriptional work: striking in the controlled vigour and panache of its cut and in the clean regularity of letter- and word-spacing. The letters themselves, averaging

FIG. 3.50. CI 45. © A. S. Ferguson.

2.8 cm in height, are perfectly aligned in spite of the absence of explicit lining. The stonecutter is operating within the manner of the later Gothic period, with confident stroke modulation, marked serifing and fine, long hairstroking on <c>, <e> and <f>. Particularly characteristic are the prominent curved and tapered downstrokes on <t>, where the crossbar link with the central stem is tenuous, and the strong parallel upstroke of <l> which reaches the notional top line. The join between the strokes of the <l> is so slight as to give the initial impression of a pair of majuscule <i>s side by side. Two different uncialesque forms of rounded <m> are featured, with that on the date having its left bow closed, while <u/v> is always straight-sided. The <g>, employed twice, is distinctive in its narrow module, shallow swirl and very marked downward-pointing serif. The latter is a feature picked up by the overarm on the three instances of <d>. The wavy and serifed abbreviation line through the <d> of *de* (l. 1) is quite different from the inverted Tironian 7 on the <s> of *mis* (l. 4). It is very likely that the full form expressed by the latter abbreviation is the diphthongised *misier*, rather than *miser*, but I have preferred to play it safe. The Tironian 9 on *conpagni* (l. 5) is handsome in its measured swirl and tapered tail. I have opened it out with *con-* rather than *com-* on the basis of *tenpo* (l. 6). Ligatures are employed throughout on <an> and <ar>.

LANGUAGE: On *maço* May (l. 1) see CI 23, CI 56. *Fo fato far* 'were ordered to be made' (l. 2) is an interesting and unusually explicit reference to the commissioning process of an inscription in our collection. *Di* 'of the' (l. 3) is only the third appearance in the corpus, after CI 38 and CI 41, of the contracted spoken form of the masculine plural partitive article which would become generalised in the fifteenth century (see also CI 18 of 1453). The plural adjective *proprii* (l. 4), from *proprio* 'own, personal', contrasts with *propia* showing deletion of the second /r/ through dissimilation in CI 39. On the diphthongised imperfect *iera* 'was' (l. 5), see CI 14. Two nouns unique in the corpus are *organo* 'organ' (ll. 2–3) and *pergolo* 'pulpit' (l. 3). The former is from ORGANUM 'instrument', with the organ itself reaching Venice and the West generally from Byzantium after the first millennium and becoming common in parish churches. *Pergolo* appears to be a cross between PERGĂMUM (the citadel of Troy) and PERGŬLAM 'raised platform, awning, pergola': see SALLACH (1993, *s.v. pergolo*).

RECENT STUDIES: FERGUSON (2013C: 115–16); FERGUSON (2015C: 69). First published in CICOGNA (1855: 14).

Corpus Inscription 46

M⁰ · CCCC · VII · SETE(N)BRIO · FO FATO · STO LAUORIER · I(N) TE(N)PO ·
D(E) · S(R) · ÇU[L]IA(N) · D(E) · BONOMO · GASTOLDO · E (CON)PAGNI

[Mcccc, vii setenbrio, fo fato sto lavorier in tenpo de sr Çulian de Bonomo, gastoldo, e conpagni.]

TRANSLATION: (On) September 7th 1400 this piece of work was done, in the time (of office) of Mr Çulian de Bonomo, alderman, and his colleagues.

DATE: September 1400. However, the wording of the date is ambiguous since the expected *(a)di* 'on the day of' between *VII* and *setenbrio* was omitted, probably because of space limitation. The alternative interpretation, September 1407, although syntactically very awkward, is just possible. There is no independent documentation available to confirm either reading.

LOCATION: At present it is on display, mounted on three carved Istrian stone wall brackets, on the outer south-side wall of the church of S. Fosca on Torcello. It is partly sheltered from above by a small tiled wooden awning. It was also in this position when seen by Giulio Lorenzetti in the mid-1920s (LORENZETTI 2010: 828). However, it appears to have spent much of the twentieth century in the medieval collection of the Museo Provinciale on Torcello before being returned to its position on the outer wall of S. Fosca. Very few fourteenth-century references to artistic commissions by the confraternity of S. Fosca on the island, for which the relief and inscription were sculpted, are to be found in the *buste* of the ASV *Podestà di Torcello*, and nothing has come to light about our relief. This makes pinpointing its original location necessarily speculative. Like the banner of S. Fosca from the same brotherhood, which we examined in CI 33 and CI 34, the artefact is likely to have been kept in or on the church of S. Fosca itself, where the *scuola* worshipped and which it apparently financed (VECCHI 1982: 61–62). The confraternity was abolished by Napoleonic decree in 1806.

TYPE AND DESCRIPTION: Documentary and commemorative. The inscription is carved on to the inclined lower lip (173.5 × 6 cm) of an Istrian stone plaque which depicts in high relief a group of confraternity brothers kneeling before St Fusca. The impressive plaque, with its crenallated frame, measures 173.5 × 107 cm in all, while the sculpted surface itself is 165 × 100 cm. Overall the object is in good condition, with both relief and inscription perfectly legible. The only major damage is a crack extending through the whole tablet, increasing in depth and width as it proceeds from the right side of the top frame through to the bottom frame where it splits and chips the inscription lip itself, partly obliterating the <l> in *Çulian*. The fissure is bisected near the top-right corner of the tablet by a shorter and more superficial crack. Both cracks were sealed during the recent cleaning and restoration of the artefact.

The scene depicted on the relief is a variation on the iconography we observed on plaques from two other flagellant confraternities: CI 17 of 1349, from the Scuola

Fig. 3.51. CI 46 in context. © A. S. Ferguson.

Fig. 3.52. CI 46 (detail). © A. S. Ferguson.

Grande di S. Giovanni Evangelista in the heart of Venice, and CI 26 of 1361, from the Scuola di S. Giovanni Battista on Murano. All three feature, on the far left of their respective tablet, the patron saint of the confraternity clutching the staff of the *scuola*'s ceremonial banner. The banner is held out by the saint to the confraternity warden who grasps it. The warden, with a group of robed and hooded brothers behind him in pairs, kneels before the saint in order to be blessed. The 1349 relief includes twelve kneeling brothers in all and its inscription sits immediately underneath on a separate plaque. The two later reliefs feature nine brothers each and their written message is inscribed on an integrated angled ledge, on Torcello with one rim, on Murano with two. The iconography of all three reliefs clearly derives from the familiar image on Venetian coinage of the doge kneeling before St Mark who hands him the ducal banner. This can be seen on the ducat issued during the period of the Torcello inscription by doge Michiel Sten. The Torcello sculpture is arguably the most impressive of the three surviving examples of the genre. There is a strength and unfussiness to it which is both powerful and affecting. The serene, smiling St Fusca, crown on head and two fingers raised in blessing, looks down benevolently on the hooded brothers. The pair behind the alderman hold massive candles; the one at the back looks down towards the spectator. All nine are strongly characterised, with forceful outsized heads and individual expressions of fervour. Their collective intensity contrasts with the calm radiating from Fusca. The folds of her dress and of the brothers' habits are carved simply but sensually and serve to cement physically the spiritual union that is evoked. It is likely that the relief was sculpted by a Venetian workshop.

LETTERING: Gothic majuscules carved in V-section. A very accomplished piece of inscription work, with elegant and highly legible lettering. The tall, compressed script, averaging 3.4 cm in height, is admirably consistent, spaced and aligned, with words or syntagms separated by clear mid-high interpuncts and with no ligatures. In addition, the inscriptional lip is angled so that the epigraph is easily read from below. The letters are skilfully cut for stroke contrast, with the subtly modulated grooves still perfectly visible. The play of light and shade produced in this way is pleasing to the eye and can be best appreciated by the grooving on <o>, <b>, <r>, and especially on the curves of the <g>, <s> and <u/v>, the latter always in the form of a right-curved <u> contrasting with the straight-sided V of the Roman numeral in the date. The hairstroking is long and fine on <c>, <e> and especially <f> where the bottom of the stroke is upturned and matches in length and finesse the long, slightly curled-back downstrokes on the <t> and the delicately upcurved laterals on <m> and <n>. The scroll-curve at the top of the parallel upstroke on <l> and the serifs on <c>, <e>, <g> and <s> complete this sophisticated, unobtrusive decorativeness on both header and footer. The wavy overbar abbreviating <n> or <m>, the Tironian 7 on the <d> of *de* and the long sinuous Tironian 9 are in keeping with the stylistic unity of the script.

LANGUAGE: The language of this brief inscription from Torcello is entirely what one would expect from an epigraph cut in Venice itself or at least by a Venetian mason. On the basis of the definite nasal abbreviations in <n> on *i(n)* and *Çulia(n)* I opt tentatively for <n> rather than <m> on *sete(n)brio*, *te(n)po* and *(con)pagni*. On the ending in *-brio* of *setenbrio* see CI 79. The *gastoldo*, as we have noted elsewhere, was the head of a guild or devotional *scuola piccola*. The status of the devotional and probably flagellant confraternity of S. Fosca is unclear (see CI 33, CI 34 for our limited knowledge of the brotherhood) but the iconography of its plaque unequivocally recalls that of the *scuole grandi*. On the other hand, the use of *gastoldo* rather than *vardian* appears to contradict this assumption. The *conpagni* referred to are, as ever, the executive officials of the *scuola*. I have been unable to find information on Çulian de Bonomo.

RECENT STUDIES: FERGUSON (2015c: 71); MOCELLIN (2016: 9–11).

Corpus Inscription 47

MCCC | C · VIII · ₂ | ADI · X · ₃ | DOTV | BRIO · ₅ | S(IER) · GIRAR͡ | DO · TA | IAPIER͡ | A · FEX | E · QV | ESTO · ₁₁ | ALTAR͡ ₁₂ | · D(E) · MISI | ER · S(-N) · P | IERO · AR͡ | EVER | ENTIA · ₁₇ | D(E) · MIS(IER) ₁₈ | · DOME | NEDIO ₂₀ | · E · D(E) MA | DONA · ₂₂ | · S(-)NTA · ₂₃ | · MARIA͡ · ₂₄ | E DE T | VTALA͡ · | · CORTE · ₂₇ | · CELES̩ | TIAL · ₂₉ | AMEN ·

[Mcccviii, adì x d'otubrio, sier Girardo Taiapiera fexe questo altar de misier S. Piero a reverentia de misier Domenedio e de madona S. Maria e de tuta la corte celestial. Amen.]

TRANSLATION: On the 10th of October 1408 Mr Girardo Taiapiera made this altar of St Peter in veneration of the Lord God and of Our Lady St Mary and of all the heavenly court. Amen.

DATE: October 1408.

LOCATION: At present the inscribed altarpiece is in the Metropolitan Museum of Art, New York, accession no. 11.104. It was purchased by the museum's Frederick C. Hewitt fund in 1911. The original location of the piece was without doubt an altar dedicated to St Peter in the church of S. Beneto (Italian, S. Benedetto; English, St Benedict) now in the parish of S. Luca (*sestiere* of S. Marco) in Venice. On S. Beneto, founded in the tenth century and rebuilt in 1619, see CORNER (1758: 212–14). The church was not demolished after the Napoleonic suppressions but has instead lived on with a reduced status as an adjunct to the larger nearby church of S. Luca. It can still be seen with its classical frontage in the secluded Campo S. Beneto, while its original, quite different, configuration can be examined on de' Barbari's cityscape of 1500.

The Metropolitan's records state that our altarpiece was purchased in 1911 from Cooper and Griffith Co., London, so it is fair to surmise that it had appeared in the nineteenth century on the antiquarian market like so many objects sold off from Venetian churches and monasteries in that period. However, it is not clear how and when the artefact was removed from its original site in the church and by whom. Significantly, Cicogna recorded all the numerous inscriptions inside S. Beneto, but did not see *sier* Girardo's epigraph. What is more, all those he did find date from the seventeenth century or later. Both facts strongly suggest that the altarpiece was removed from the church at the time of the complete seventeenth-century rebuilding programme, when medieval tombs and objects in the church must have been discarded.

TYPE AND DESCRIPTION: Commemorative and dedicatory, with statement of authorship and date. The inscription records the making of an altar to St Peter by the Venetian stonemason Girardo Taiapiera. Uniquely, it is cut into the side of a coloured and gilded bas-relief altarpiece in Istrian stone made by Girardo himself. The object, which is in remarkably fine condition and retains a good deal of its original polychromy, measures 169.9 × 102 × 11.4 cm. The inscription runs down

Fig. 3.53. CI 47 (relief carving on front of inscription stone). © A. S. Ferguson.

Fig. 3.54. CI 47 (lines 1–20). © Scala Group S.p.A.

the length and width of the object's thickness on its right-hand side, and is still clear and perfectly legible. It was evidently meant to be visible to worshippers as they approached the altar from the right. The epigraph is doubly special in being only one of two in the corpus in which the stonecutter identifies himself (the other is CI 44). It is additionally unique in that the commissioner of the altar and altarpiece was unquestionably the stonemason himself, acting simultaneously as sponsor, *scriptor*, *ordinator* and *sculptor* of his own text. Omnipresent, he is depicted in miniature, kneeling in worship with his wife Ricadona, at the foot of the relief.

The inscribed altarpiece is in the form of a gabled dossal surmounted by a smaller medallion with a Madonna and Child. The whole is surrounded by a crenallated frame. In the middle of the relief tablet stands the calmly imposing haloed figure of St Peter, clasped book and keys in hand, in the act of blessing. He is flanked by two slightly smaller figures of saints, both haloed. On his right stands John the Baptist pointing to the scroll on which he announces the coming of Jesus. On his left, holding a clasped book and the sword with which he would be beheaded, is St Paul. At the feet of the Baptist kneels the diminutive figure of Girardo himself. The stonemason's wife prays at Paul's feet. The figures are all cut with vigorous realism. Peter's hair and beard are intensely curled, while those of John are wavy. Paul is depicted, in the traditional manner, as balding. Peter's outsized raised hand is prominent as are the bony forearm and index of the Baptist. The miniature figures of donor and wife are charmingly naive. The whole object still bears traces of the gilding and colouring which to modern tastes must have been very bright.

Girardo Taiapiera was a prosperous entrepreneur stonemason with house and premises in the parish of S. Beneto. He was a prominent and active citizen in both the stonemasons' confraternity-guild (Early Venetian, *Sc(u)ola del arte d(el)i taiapiera*) and in one of the most prestigious devotional confraternities of Venice, the Scuola Grande di S. Giovanni Evangelista. His three wills of 1405, 1411 and 1422 (the first two in Latin, the last in Venetian) reveal a successful businessman, well-connected across the city. He left considerable sums to individuals, including his wife, and to organisations, and he even possessed a slave called Martin whom he freed in his final testament. His full name, in his own words, was *Girardo Taiapiera [...] condam Mainardi* and he described himself as 'de la contra de San Benedeto de Venexia'. He asked to be buried in the family tomb in the church of S. Lorenzo 'in larcha che fo di antecessori mij' ('in the tomb that belonged to my ancestors'), and paid for masses to be said for him every Friday at the very altar of St Peter and before the very relief ('ad altare sancti Petri') that he had made for the church of S. Beneto. The three wills are reproduced in PAOLETTI (1893–97, I: 94).

LETTERING: Gothic majuscules cut in V-section. The inscription is highly unusual within the corpus in terms of its location and narrow format. It runs down the outer edge on the right hand side of the altarpiece, meaning that only a few words are able to fit in their entirety on to one line. Because of this space restriction the stonecutter has had recourse to abbreviations on seven occasions and to ligaturing on <al>, <ap> and <ar>. The epigraph is laid out in 30 tightly packed lines, justified on both sides, filling the available surface from the top to about 7 cm from the bottom. The script is expertly and sharply cut in mature Gothic on a surface 11.4 cm wide and the lettering, which averages 2.8 cm in height, was and is eminently legible because of the crispness of the chiselling, the regularity of spacing and the consistent use of mid-high interpuncts. The letters show an attractive balance between round, horizontal and vertical dynamics. Compression is most visible on the bowls of <d>, <o> and <q> which are markedly almond shaped. Sinuosity is striking on the <n> and on the leg of <r> which curves below the baseline. In this context the <g> is a surprise in that it is always squared off as in G. A compromise is represented by <u/v> which is cut with its sides subtly bowed. The serifs on <s> are strongly spiked, while the uncial <d> contradicts the curved nature of its bowl with an ascender which first extends out horizontally before dipping down vertically to the baseline. Long, curved hairstrokes ornament <c>, <e> and <f> and, as would be expected, the downstrokes on <t> are extended and tapered. The <m> appears in two uncialesque guises, the one on the date having its left loop closed. The notched overbar abbreviation is used once for what is probably *santa* (l. 23); otherwise the Tironian 7 is employed on *sier* and *misier*.

LANGUAGE: The text illustrates the drift towards diphthongisation of stressed mid-high Ě at this stage in Early Venetian, with *Taiapiera*, *Piero*, *misier* and *sier*. I have hesitated to open out the 'saint' abbreviations, but it is highly likely that they represent *san* and *santa*, the increasingly dominant forms which actually appear in Girardo's Venetian will. *Fexe* '(he) made' (ll. 9–10) and *fese*, both possibly pronounced /fese/, coexisted in Early Venetian although the <x>, as we have noted throughout, was mainly used for the voiced sibilant /z/. *Domenedio* 'the Lord God' as a single syntagm coexisted with *Dio* in both Early Venetian and Early Tuscan. *Girardo* (Gerard, Gerald), ll. 6–7, shows raising of pre-tonic /e/ to /i/. In his Latin wills Girardo is called *Gerardus*. It is interesting but not surprising that *reverentia* 'reverence' (ll. 15–17) and *celestial* 'celestial' (ll. 28–29), as high-register terms, have retained their Latinising spellings for what is presumably still the palatal affricate normally rendered as <ç>. On *otubrio* October (ll. 4–5) see CI 8, CI 79.

RECENT STUDIES: BRECK (1912); CASTELNUOVO-TEDESCO and SOULTANIAN (2010: 226–34).

Corpus Inscription 48

ṣç M cccc xiiii in tempo del egregio et nobel homo mis(r)
nicolo badoer prior ₁| d(e) questo luo‹g›o del mexe de auosto
fo principiada questa fabrica . e com|plida di beni dela scuola di
batudi de mis(r) s(-n) çuane euangelista per ₃| la concession fata
ala dita scuola per lo dito mis(r) lo prior del hospedal ₄|
et dela riua che iera soto la caxa dela dita scuola ₅

[ṢÇ MCCCCXIIII, in tempo del egregio et nobel homo mis. Nicolò Badoer, prior de questo luogo, del mexe de avosto fo principiada questa fabrica . e complida di beni dela Scuola di Batudi de mis. S. Çuane Evangelista per la concession fata ala dita Scuola, per lo dito mis. lo prior, del hospedal et dela riva che iera soto la caxa dela dita Scuola.]

TRANSLATION: ṢÇ. In the month of August 1414, in the time of the distinguished nobleman Sir Nicolò Badoer, prior of this place, this building was commenced. And (it) was completed from the funds of the Flagellant Confraternity of St John the Evangelist in return for the concession to the said Confraternity — by the aforementioned prior — of the hospital and of the embankment that was under the meeting house of the said Confraternity.

DATE: Post 1414. Although the inscription records the start date of the building project in question as August 1414, this is clearly not when the works were finished and the new Badoer hospice handed over to the prior of that institution. Nor can it be the date of the inscription itself. The epigraph in fact remains curiously silent on the completion date, confining itself in rather legalistic language to exposing two points. The first that the project was completed and paid for by the *scuola* of S. Giovanni Evangelista out of its own funds. The second that what enabled the project was the ceding to the *scuola* of the original Badoer hospice (the *hospedal* of l. 4) and of an embankment at the rear of the *scuola* (*la riva che iera soto la caxa dela dita scuola*, l. 5). At first sight the wording of the epigraph is ambiguous on the date, seeming to associate both *principiada* 'begun' (l. 2) and *complida* 'completed' (ll. 2–3) with August 1414 in an impossibly tight timeframe. However, closer inspection reveals a clear full-stop punctuation mark after *fabrica*. The puzzling dissociation of the two parts of the inscription and the absence of the completion date is explained by a complex background story. In essence, the confraternity — wishing to expand its premises and clear out of them, on the pretext of safety, the original Badoer hospice — did a deal with the Badoer. In return for the removal of the hospital from the ground floor of the *scuola* and the right to extend on to the embankment at the back of the *scuola* building (both concessions mentioned in the inscription) the brotherhood undertook to rebuild the Badoer hospice on a separate site. The initial accord was drawn up in June 1414 (ASV, *Scuola Grande di S. Giovanni Evangelista*, reg. 2, fols 14–16 and reg. 140, fols 251–52) and, according to our epigraph, the agreed rebuilding was started in August of that year. However, the situation between the *scuola* and the Badoer deteriorated, probably due to the

Fig. 3.55. CI 48 in context. © A. S. Ferguson.

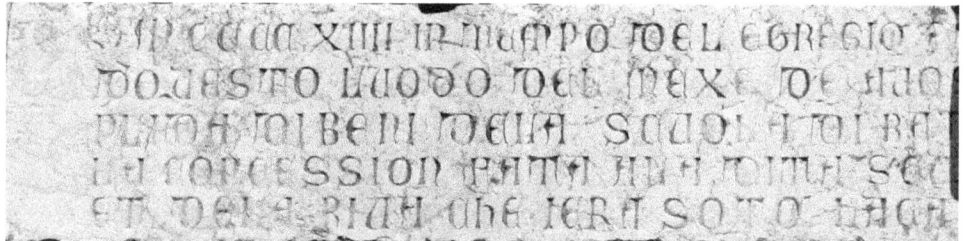

Fig. 3.56. CI 48 (detail). © A. S. Ferguson.

scuola's being financially stretched at that point by its own ambitious rebuilding and redecorating plans. The upshot appears to be that work on the new hospice dragged on so that an updated agreement had to be drawn up between the parties in 1424 (ASV, *Scuola Grande di S. Giovanni Evangelista*, reg. 38, fols 21–23, 51–52). This all suggests that our inscription was probably not carved until at least a decade after the 1414 start date. Understandably, nobody — least of all the *scuola* — had an interest in advertising a belated, potentially embarrassing, completion date.

There had been a hospice for women funded and run by the Badoer — the distinguished local landowning patrician family who supported, as we have already noted, the confraternity of S. Giovanni Evangelista — since the early thirteenth century. The hospice was originally situated a few hundred yards further back from its present location in Campiello S. Zuane, in the ground floor area of what was to become the meeting house and courtyard of the *scuola*. Its eventual removal from this original site was clearly the long-term aim of a confraternity which had grand ambitions to expand and embellish its headquarters. Although the *scuola* was, of course, abolished by Napoleonic decree in 1806 the Ospizio Badoer was left untouched. Funding for it was maintained by the remaining members of the Badoer family then, towards the end of the nineteenth century when the family line died out, it was taken over by the state-run charitable foundation, the Congregazione di Carità. Now known as the Residenza Badoer it is run by its successor, the Istituzioni di Ricovero e di Educazione. The building (accessible from a door under the Sotoportego de la Laca at S. Polo no. 2467) has recently been refurbished. It consists of a ground floor with entrance hall and storerooms and a first floor with a central communal hall and twelve individual rooms. Continuing its original mission, it offers sheltered accomodation to twelve Venetian widows of modest means who are over fifty years of age. The communal room has a small oratory near the window where our inscription is located. On the hospice, with plans of the building and of the whole Badoer-Scuola di S. Giovanni Evangelista complex, see SEMI (1983: 228–34).

LOCATION: Carved in situ on the windowsill of the Badoer almshouse. The inscribed ledge is situated over the Sotoportego de la Laca, the underpassage that leads away from the complex of buildings connected with the Scuola Grande di San Giovanni Evangelista as one heads along Calle Vitalba then Calle de la Laca in the direction of S. Rocco.

TYPE AND DESCRIPTION: Commemorative and documentary. The inscription commemorates the (dated) start and the (undated) finish of the building that would become the new Badoer hospice for women. The epigraph, covering an area roughly 180 × 20 cm, is inscribed on a rectangular block of Istrian stone that forms the sill of the two square-shaped windows, connected by a mullion, above. The inscription has undergone some wear and tear, with superficial pitting, but is in relatively good condition. There are now two largish chips on the top edge of the lintel and a diagonal crack runs through the middle of the stone, but the epigraph is largely unaffected by these imperfections. In fact, although situated roughly 450 cm above pavement level it remains legible from below. The windows in turn are surmounted by an early fifteenth-century crenellated Istrian stone shield measuring c. 60 × c. 40 cm. This bears the coat of arms of the Badoer family, with a lion rampant on a blue and gold striped ground flanked by crosiers and, above, a low-relief bust of St John the Evangelist. The shield is held aloft by two relief-sculpted brothers of the *scuola* in their hooded robes. The artefact — with blue and gold pigmentation, possibly original, still visible on the shield itself — is clearly symbolic of the collaboration between the *scuola* and the Badoer. The ensemble, with framing balcony, coat of arms and the inscription picked out in black against a gleaming white ground, was and is modestly impressive.

LETTERING: Gothic majuscules cut in V-section. A stylish example of mature Gothic epigraphy. The five-line inscription, laid out along the length of the windowsill and justified on the left, has generous, regular spacing between letters, words and lines. The letter height at 3.5 cm is deliberately large to ensure visibility from the street below, so that even after 600 years the message catches the eye of the passer-by. The airiness of the layout is matched by that of the script itself which, not surprisingly, has a minimum of abbreviations, no ligatures and no interpuncts. The writing is aesthetically pleasing, with attractive stroke contrast within individual letters. Its relatively open module achieves a delicate balance between decorative sinuosity and basic structure. This subtlety can be appreciated on the hairstroked <c> and <e>, on the downstroke and upstroke on <t> and <l>

respectively (the latter actually peaking above the headline), on the leg of <n>, and on the contrasting cross-strokes of <x>. The internal curves of the <s> are matched externally by its arched serifs. A number of distinctive features catch the eye. The ascender on <d> juts vigorously to the left before plunging with a confident curve right down to the baseline. The <u/v> is always sweepingly curved inwards on the left side, with the leg straightening out to the left at the top, but is vertically straight-sided on the right. The rather compressed bowl of <p> reaches unusually far down the stem. The long, undulating tail of the <q> on *questo* (l. 2) bears right, but on the following *questa* (l. 2) it snakes to the left as in CI 2, CI 39. There is one obvious mistake: the mason has inverted the <g> in luogo, treating it almost as a <d>. I have rectified this in my transcription with angled quotation marks. This is the first inscription in the corpus to mark off the first letter of its statement — the <m> of the date — as an actual capital. The beginning of the text itself is indented to make way for the swashed abbreviation SÇ (= S. Çuane) of the confraternity's name. The <ç> appears to be in inverted form although wear and tear on the letter makes it hard to be sure. The epigraph may have ended with a mid-high dot but, again, the large crack running through the area in question makes it impossible to be certain.

LANGUAGE: The legalistic tone of the second half of the inscription is evident in the fussy repetition of *dito*, *dita* (l. 4), *dita* (l. 5) 'the said, aforementioned' — also, interestingly, present in C17 and C 18 from the same *scuola* — and in the terms *beni* 'goods' (l. 3) and *concession* 'concession' (l. 4). The Latinism *egregio* 'esteemed, distinguished, eminent' (l. 1) < ĒGRĔGĬUS was common to both Early Venetian and Early Tuscan. *Prior* 'prior' (ll. 1, 4) derives from PRĬOR 'first, top, superior'. The Badoer family had the right to nominate the *prior* of the Badoer hospice who had himself to be a Badoer and who served for life. His duty was to run the institution and manage its property incomes. On the Latinising <h> on *hospedal* 'almshouse, hospital, hospice' see CI 4. One notes the conservative spelling *complida* 'completed' (ll. 2–3), with retention of the <pl> cluster, compared with *conpido* in C18 (from 1453 and from the same confraternity). *Çuane evangelista* stands out as conservative, too, compared to the equivalents *vangelista* of C17 and *evançelista* of CI 18. *Luogo* 'place' (l. 2), *scuola* 'confraternity' (ll. 3, 4, 5) and *iera* 'was' (l. 5), already present on CI 45 from the same brotherhood, show the expected advance of the diphthongisation trend in Early Venetian, but *homo* 'man' (l. 1) resists. *Principiada* 'begun, commenced' (l. 2), where there appears to be no cedilla under the <c>, and *complida* have halted the /t/ voicing at /d/ on the past participle, as in Modern/Contemporary Venetian. As is frequently the case in the corpus *fo principiada questa fabrica* 'this building was commenced' (l. 2) displays agreement in gender and number in the passive construction. Not unexpected is the contracted plural partitive *di* 'of the, from the' (l. 3) which became a strong competitor of *deli* and even *dei* in the fifteenth century, and which first appeared in our corpus in CI 38 of 1374.

RECENT STUDIES: FERGUSON (2015c: 73); MOCELLIN (2016: 12–15). First published by SORAVIA (1822–24, II: 220–21).

Corpus Inscription 49

+ MCCCCXXI : ADI : XXIIII : ZVGNO : NEL TE(M)PO : DE : S(ER) :
FRA‹N›CISCO : POSCA : (CON)DA(M) ₁| S(ER) : (CHRIST)OFALO : POSCE :
MERCADA(N)TE : D(E) : MILANO : E : S(ER) : ZORÇI : DA : MOLTEN : DA :
₂| MILANO AL : P(RE)SENTE : P(RI)ORI : E : GVBERNADORI : D(E) : QVESTA
: BENEDICTA : SCVO|LA D(E) MISER : S(AN)C(T)O : IOHAN(N)I : BATISTA : E
: DI : MISER : S(AN)C(T)O AMBROSIO CON|FESSOR : E : DOCTOR : DE : LA
S(ANC)T(A) : GLEXIA : POSTA : NELA : GLEXIA D(E) : MA|DON(N)A :
S(AN)C(T)A : MARIA : D(E) : LI : FRA : MENORI : D(E) : VENEXIA : E : ANCHE
: IN : PRE|SENTIA : D(E) : TVTI : OFFICIALI : E : FRADELI : D(E) : ‹L›A : DICTA
SCHVOLA : TVTI ₇| NOTI : A : QUESTO : INSTRVMENTO : D(E) : CARTA :
R(O)GATA : P(ER) : MIS(ER) : P(RE) : FRA(N)CISCHO : DE ₈| FRA(N)CISCHI :
AVCTO(R)ITAD(E) : IMP(ER)IALE : PVBLICO : NODER : D(E) : VENEXIA : COMO
: ÇIO : SIA ₉| CHE AL P(RE)SENTE DI : E : ANNO : FO : (CON)SECRATO :
QVESTO : BENEDETO : ALTARE : P(ER) : REV(ER)END(O) : ₁₀| IN CHRI(ST)O :
PATER : ET : D(OMI)N(V)S : D(OMI)N(V)S : FRATER : ANTONIVS : DEI : ET :
AP(OSTO)LICE : SEDIS : GRATIA : EP(I)S(COPVS) : ₁₁| CVMANVS : ET : AD :
P(RE)SENS (CON)STITVT(VS) : IN : ECCL(ES)IA : D(OMI)NE : S(AN)C(T)E :
MA(R)IE : ORDINIS : FRATRVM ₁₂| MINORV(M) : D(E) : VEN(ETIIS) : SVB
: TIT(V)LO : (ET) : NO(M)INE : SCOLL(E) : IOH(AN)IS : BAPTISTE : (ET) :
AMBROSI(I) : (CON)FESS(ORIS) :

[+ MCCCCXXI, adì XXIIII zugno, nel tempo de ser Francisco Posca, *condam*
ser Christofalo Posce, mercadante de Milano e ser Zorçi da Molten da
Milano — al presente priori e gubernadori de questa *benedicta* Scuola de miser
Sancto Iohanni Batista e di miser Sancto Ambrosio, confessor e doctor de la
Sancta Glexia, posta nela glexia de madonna Sancta Maria de li fra menori de
Venexia — e anche in presentia de tuti officiali e fradeli de la dicta Schuola,
tuti noti a questo instrumento de carta rogata per miser pre' Francischo de
Francischi *auctoritatis imperiale* publico noder de Venexia: como çiò sia che
al presente dì e anno fo consecrato questo benedeto altare per reverendo
in Christo *pater et dominus dominus frater Antonius dei et apostolice sedis gratia
episcopus cumanus et ad presens constitutus in ecclesia domine Sancte Marie ordinis
fratrum minorum de Venetiis sub titulo et nomine scolle Iohanis Baptiste et Ambrosii
confessoris.*]

TRANSLATION: 1421, on the 24th of June, in the time (of office) of Mr Francisco Posca, *son of the late* Christofalo Posca, merchant of Milan, and of Mr Zorçi da Molten from Milan — at the present time priors and governors of this *blessed* Confraternity of St John the Baptist and of St Ambrose, confessor and doctor of Holy Mother Church, situated in the church of Our Lady St Mary of the friars minor in Venice — and also in the presence of all the officials and brothers of the said Confraternity, all known to this legal charter drawn up by the reverend Mr Francischo de Francischi notary public of Venice *by imperial authority*, to the following effect: that on this day and year this blessed altar was consecrated by the

FIG. 3.57. CI 49 (detail, ll. 5–12). © A. S. Ferguson.

reverend in Christ *father and lord brother Antonius, by the grace of God and of the Holy See Bishop of Como, and at present established in the church of our Lady St Mary of the order of the friars minor of Venice under the title and name of the Confraternity of John the Baptist and Ambrose the Confessor.*

DATE: June 1421.

LOCATION: Cappella dei Milanesi, Basilica dei Frari (*sestiere* of S. Polo). The inscription plaque is embedded in situ 184 cm off the ground in the great pillar on the right-hand side of the altar — which is the subject of the inscription itself — as one enters the *cappella*. This is the third chapel on the left in relation to the main altar in the Frari displaying Titian's *Assumption of the Virgin*. Situated prominently in the Basilica, in the jewel-like place of worship of the Lombard confraternity, with its finely sculpted altar and the splendid altarpiece painting of *St Ambrose with Saints* (500 × 250 cm) of *c.* 1500 by Alvise Vivarini and Marco Basaiti, our inscription is in a setting of exceptional religious and cultural significance.

TYPE AND DESCRIPTION: Commemorative and celebratory. The inscription plaque in Istrian stone measures 86 × 48 cm and is largely undamaged. There is some surface abrasion, especially towards the bottom left-hand side, but this does not affect legibility. The tablet looks as if it has a dingy yellowish-brown stain on it, but this is in fact what remains of its original gold background. The inscription commemorates the official dedication by the Bishop of Como, Antonio Rusconi, of an altar of the *scuola* of St John the Baptist and St Ambrose — known commonly as the *Scuola d(e)i Milanesi* or *d(e)i Lombardi* — in the chapel belonging to the confraternity. It records the date, the names of the two priors of the brotherhood at the time, and the presence of all its executive and membership at the ceremony. The fact that it also states the name of the notary public who drew up the act, alongside the phrase *tuti noti a questo instrumento de carta* 'all known to this legal charter' (ll. 7–8), confirms that the inscription is a legal document. In other words it is a form of *charta lapidaria* like CI 8 and CI 30. The dedication of the altar, with all the details listed in the inscription, is described in the confraternity's *mariegola* in the ASV, Sta Maria Gloriosa dei Frari, *busta* 100, fol. 40v. It is reproduced in SARTORI (1983–89, II: col. 1877).

The wealthy Scuola dei Milanesi, set up by and for Lombard merchants resident in Venice, particularly those from Milan and Monza originally, was licensed by the Council of Ten in 1361 with a maximum membership of 300. In the Latin documentation it is called the *Scola sanctorum Johannis Baptiste et Ambrosii confessoris*. Among its notable features was the fact that it combined, unusually, three categories of *scuola piccola* in one, in that it was simultaneously a professional guild, a devotional confraternity, and a 'national' brotherhood. On its *mariegola* of 1427–28 see HUMPHREY (2015: 336–47, ill. XXXIVa, b, c); CANTÙ (1856: 176–94); SARTORI (1983–89, II: coll. 1871–83).

LETTERING: Gothic majuscules cut in V-section. The inscription is unusual for late Gothic in that the script, while exhibiting sinuosity (notably on the leg of <r>, on the left stem of <a> and on the hairstroke of <e>), is more powerful than decorative. With its strong deep cut, prominent wedges on head and base of uprights, modestly developed upstroke on <l> and absence of downstrokes on <t>, it is effective rather than pleasing on the eye. Perfectly justified on both sides, with great regularity of letter spacing and letter height (averaging 2.5 cm) and with rigorous interlinear distance, the text conveys its message powerfully. It must have been impressive, with its black lettering on a gold ground, within the sumptuously decorated chapel. Word spacing on the epigraph is further emphasized by an unusual and highly consistent punctuation-separation pattern which I have rendered in my transcription by colons. In the original this actually consists, within each word space, of a mid-high interpunct with a wedge mark punched beneath it on the baseline. While there are no ligatures to distract the eye there are a surprising number of abbreviations of different kinds. Three types of suspension bar are featured: straight, wavy and eyehole. These abbreviate a variety of letters, single and double, ranging from nasals to the more complex groups in *dns* (= *dominus*) and *sca* (= *sancta*), via the XPO *Chi-Rho*, to the final <e> of *scolle* (l. 13) and the <re> on *presente* 'present' (l. 3). Interesting is the presence, in proximity, of the <p> barred on its stem for *per* 'by' (l. 8) and the overbarred <p> for *pre* or *pre'* 'priest, reverend' (l. 8). The usual Tironian 7 and Tironian 9 (for *con-*) are employed, the latter striking for its small bowl, sweeping extended tail and its frequency. The smaller 9 abbreviation, curling from the end of several Latin words, expresses final *-us* or final *-i*, and the hook-and-wedge arm symbol we have noted before may replace a number of letters such as the <u> on *titulo* (l. 13), the <ann> on *Iohannis* (l. 13) or the *-oris* of *confessoris* (l. 13). The inscription is also notable for the first appearance of <z> in the corpus (for what we may presume was the voiced affricate /dz/), in its capital form, on both *zugno* June (l. 1) and in conjunction with the usual, up until now, <ç> in *Zorçi* George (l. 2). In both occurrences this Z exhibits an unusual vertical upstroke on its base.

The inscription beneath, in Latin, is undated but was undoubtedly carved by the same stonecutter not much later. It also features black lettering against a gold ground. It begins: *Et : in : dicto : isti : altari : posite : fverint : quamplvres : re/liq(vi)e : s(an)ct(orvm) : vsque : ad : nvmerv(m) : triginta* ('And in this aforementioned altar were placed numerous relics of saints, up to the number of thirty'). It goes on to detail the forty days of indulgence to be accorded to those who visit the altar reverently. In this it recalls a similar concession on CI 30. The epigraph is palaeographically interesting for a number of reasons, including the panoply of Latin abbreviations on display. Most of all, though, it is significant for the way the same sculptor (who had already reined in Gothic decorativeness on the vernacular inscription) can be seen edging his script on the Latin epigraph towards the new revival Roman quadrate lettering that would shortly become the norm. This is especially evident on <d>, <e>, <m> and <n>. A third inscription, from 1547, is embedded beneath the second one. Here the letters are, of course, monumental capitals.

LANGUAGE: Although emanating from a Lombard confraternity, the default language of the inscription in terms of phonology, morphology, syntax, lexis and spelling remains Early Venetian. This is lightly veined by a few supra-regional 'Italian' features (that are also present in the substantially Venetian *mariegola* of the brotherhood), such as *altare* 'altar' (l. 10), rather than the expected *altar*, *Milano* Milan (ll. 2, 3) rather than *Milan*, and *di* 'of' (l. 3) for the otherwise predominant *de*. More conspicuous are the Latinisms and fully Latin intrusions which one may ascribe to the notary who, in collaboration with the confraternity heads, drew up the inscriptional document: the priest-lawyer Francischo de' Francischi. He is listed in the ASV, *Archivi Notarili* (*Notai di Venezia*) as a practicing notary in Venice between 1402–33. This means, one assumes, that he was *veneta auctoritate notarius*, while also practising by imperial authority, *auctoritade* (in other words, *auctoritate*) *imperiale*, l. 9 (see ZABBIA 2009). The Latin presence is unsurprising in a document that is an *instrumentum* or *instrumento* 'legal act' (l. 8), in the semi-learned Venetian form of the term adopted by the inscription. I have indicated the Latin intrusions in italics in my transcription. Latinisms include *benedicta* 'blessed', l. 3 (but note the normal *benedeto* in l. 10); possibly the lawyer's name *Francisc(h)o* (l. 8) for *Francesco* or *Françesco*; the forms *sancto* and *sancta* 'saint' throughout; the probably genitive *Posce* (= *Poscae*), l. 2, for the name *Posca* (l. 1), apparently determined by the preceding *condam* (= *quondam*); *doctor* (l. 5), where the *mariegola* employs the usual Venetian *dotor*; *presentia* 'presence' (ll. 6–7); *gubernadori* 'governors' (l. 3) for Early Venetian *governadori*; and the past participles *rogata* 'drawn up' (l. 8) and *consecrato* 'consecrated' (l. 10) for Early Venetian *consegrado*. This Latinising patina lends a deliberate formality and solemnity to the document. It is reinforced by the *signum crucis* at the outset, by the officialese of *como çio sia* 'to this effect' (l. 9), by the evoking of the officials and members of the confraternity, and by the exceptional presence of the bishop.

We have not met *priori* 'priors' before in the sense of 'heads of confraternity'. Whereas other *scuole piccole* usually elected a *gastaldo ~ gastoldo* annually, the Milanese elected two *priori* every six months. St Ambrose (l. 4) was, of course, the Milanese patron saint. *Glexia* 'church' (l. 5) interestingly maintains the <gl> combination, in writing if not in pronunciation. Also of interest is the contrast between the diphthongisation of stressed mid-high vowels affecting /o/ but not /e/, with *sc(h)uola* throughout versus *ser* and *miser*. *Noder* 'notary, lawyer' (l. 9) < NŎTĀRIUS 'clerk, secretary, amanuensis' survived into Modern/Contemporary Venetian. The *fra menori* (l. 6) are the Franciscans of the Frari church. They were known in Early Venetian as the *frari* ('brothers', ultimately from FRATRES), *frar* or *fra menori* — in other words, the friars minor founded in 1209 by Francis of Assisi. *Zugno* June (l. 1) is the first example in the corpus of the replacement of the traditional *çugno* with the innovative spelling in <z>.

RECENT STUDIES: FERGUSON (2015c: 75–77); MOCELLIN (2016: 19–24). The inscription was published three times in the nineteenth century: by CICOGNA (1824–53, II: 984) with some inaccuracies; by CANTÙ (1856: 153–54), with interesting details about the *scuola* and its chapel; and by SORAVIA (1822–24, II: 112) who transcribed it diplomatically but with <c> for <ç>.

Corpus Inscription 50

[MCCCC]XX · IIII ·ADI · P[(RIMO) · DE LVI]O ·₁| [FO LEVADA] ST[A SCVOLA] IN ₂| [SOLER] · I(N) · [TEMPO DEL SERENISIM]O · ₃| [P]RINCIPO MIS[IER FRANCESCO FO]SC|ARI [SIANDO] GAS[T]OLDO SIER BORTO[LA]MIO ₅| [LO]TO · A[VI]C[A]RIO · SIER · PIERO · POLO [SCR|IV]AN · SIER · [LVN]ARDO · TRIVIXAN · E DE · ₇| TVTI · I SUO · CHONPAGNI · ₈

[Mccccxxiiii, adì primo de luio, fo levada sta scuola in soler in tempo del serenisimo principo misier Francesco Foscari, siando gastoldo sier Bortolamio Loto, avicario sier Piero Polo, scrivan sier Lunardo Trivixan, e de tuti i suò chonpagni.]

TRANSLATION: In 1424, on the first of July, this *scuola* was given an upper floor. This was in the time (of office) of the most serene prince Sir Francesco Foscari, (with) the alderman Mr Bortolamio Loto, the deputy Mr Piero Polo, the clerk Mr Lunardo Trivixan and all their colleagues.

DATE: July 1424.

LOCATION: The inscription plaque is embedded, probably in situ, on the outside wall of the former meeting house of the devotional confraternity of S. Maria delle Grazie. Now converted to private properties, the former brotherhood headquarters stand at house number 2491 (*sestiere* of Cannaregio), beside the church of S. Marziale (Early/Middle Venetian, S. Marcilian or S. Marzilian) in the *campo* of the same name.

TYPE AND DESCRIPTION: Commemorative. The inscription announces the brotherhood's move in July 1424 to more spacious and presumably prestigious premises than formerly. It lists the doge of Venice at the time and the principal office holders of the confraternity. The unframed plaque, in Istrian stone, measures 90 × 40 cm and is embedded to the right of the ground floor door, under the jutting *barbacani* of the building, at around 2 m above pavement level. The badly worn symbol of the confraternity is sculpted in low relief within a roundel 15 cm in diameter in the centre of the top part of the tablet. The large uncialesque M for Maria in the middle of the roundel can still just be made out.

The devotional *scuola piccola* of S. Maria delle Grazie had been at S. Marcilian, worshipping in the nearby church and meeting in rooms of its own, probably since 1296. It is recorded as being re-dedicated in 1409 and as already possessing at that time a locale of its own. It was devoted to the miracle-working statue of the Virgin said to have reached the parish in a boat by itself from Rimini in the thirteenth century. As Marin Sanudo noted: 'A San Marcilian: è una nostra Donna in la chiesia, portata da Rimano per miracolo' (CARACCIOLO ARICÒ 2011: 49). A medieval wooden statue of the Virgin is still venerated in the church. It seems reasonable to surmise that the *scuola*'s move in 1424 was prompted by practicalities. It had recently been joined at S. Marcilian by a breakaway faction of the Scuola dei Mercanti in the adjoining parish of the Madonna dell'Orto. This latter brotherhood, also dedicated

Fig. 3.58. CI 50. © A. S. Ferguson.

to the Virgin and known as S. Maria Odorifera, was given permission by the Council of Ten to move to S. Marcilian and to join the older Marian confraternity on 29 March 1424, three months before the move recorded in our epigraph. See SBRIZIOLO (1967–68: 426, 428–29) and G. VIO (2004: 522).

LETTERING: Gothic majuscules, around 2.5 cm high, cut in V-section. The inscription is in very poor condition. Rapidly advancing corrosion and exfoliation have attacked the whole tablet, so that grooving is drastically reduced and legibility is severely affected by letter distortion. The bottom half of the inscription can just about be deciphered with great care. In transcribing the top half I have recovered what I can from high-resolution computer enhanced photographs, completing the obliterated sections with the help of the independent early nineteenth-century readings of B. GAMBA (1832: 18) and Cicogna (BMC, mss Cicogna, *Inedite* 2008, *busta* 499, no. 305) whose transcriptions of these lines coincide closely apart from the date which can, fortunately, still just be made out.

Primo 'first' (l. 1) seems to consist solely of a <p>, with what may be a back-curved abbreviation sign indicating <pri>. The mason, however, appears to have cleverly employed the nearby roundel, with its large uncial <m> for *Maria* in the middle and the <o> of the roundel itself, to suggest the missing <mo> of the word. One is reminded of a similar expedient resorted to for lack of space by the stonecutter of CI 29. The <u/v> has noticeably bowed arms. Interpuncts appear to have been employed systematically for word or syntagm division, although some can no longer be detected in the obliterated sections. The inscription ends with an interpunct followed by what looks like a rather elaborate stonemason's mark. Traces of what may be the original black infilling are still visible in the later lines.

LANGUAGE: The most intriguing lexical and semantic item in the inscription is the phrase *fo levada sta scuola in soler* (ll. 2–3). *Soler* in Venetian is a floor, storey or platform, and a *casa in soler* is a house on several storeys. The sense here is likely to be that the confraternity moved into the upper floor of the building whose ground floor they already occupied, or else that they actually added a second storey to it. The Latin equivalent of *in soler* in the fifteenth- and early sixteenth-century Venetian documentation is *in solario*, from SŌLĀRIUM 'terrace': see SALLACH (1993, *s.v. soler, solaro*). The construction itself is fully regular in its agreement as are the majority of passives in our collection. The terminology of the officialdom of the *scuole piccole* is present with *gastoldo* 'alderman' (l. 5), *avicario* 'deputy' (l. 6) — appearing here for the first time with a prosthetic <a> that was to become increasingly common — and *scrivan* 'clerk, secretary, scrivener' (ll. 6–7), terms and their forms that are discussed at CI 23. Interesting linguistically, and perhaps ideologically, is the use of *principo* 'prince' for the doge of Venice: its first occurrence in the corpus where until now the Venetian head of state has always been referred to as *doxe*. As is well known, the elitist turn in the figure of the doge would culminate in the early to mid-sixteenth century with the self exaltation of the notoriously authoritarian Andrea Gritti. It is no coincidence that the word *principe* is prominent in the inscription to him from 1525 — appropriately in imperial-style Roman capitals — in the heart of the Rialto on the wall of the Palazzo dei Camerlenghi: *Andrea Gritto / Venetiarum Principe / MDXXV*. The metaplasmic form of the word in *-o* in our inscription, rather than the regular *-e* < PRINCĬPEM, was not uncommon in early Italo-Romance varieties and was particularly favoured in Venice and the Veneto. We have already noted in CI 14 (l. 12) the surname *Trivisan* ~ *Trivixan* (l. 7), literally meaning 'from Treviso', with raising of pre-tonic /e/ to /i/, as well as the typical Venetian form of the Christian name Leonard in *Lunardo* (l. 7). Diphthongisation is consistently present here on words derived from stressed /o/ and /e/, so *scuola* (l. 2) and *sier* ~ *misier* throughout. The wavering Early Venetian rendering of nasals is exemplified by the presence of the <m> in *tempo* 'time' (l. 3) alongside the <n> in *chonpagni* 'colleagues, fellow executives' (l. 8).

RECENT STUDIES: RIZZI (1987: 257); FERGUSON (2015c: 79–80); MOCELLIN (2016: 25–28). First published in B. GAMBA (1832: 18). Recorded, but not published, by Cicogna.

Corpus Inscription 51

M · CCCC [·] XX · VIII · A[DI XXII NOVEMBRI]O · AL TEMPO [·] ₁|
DEL NOBELE · HOMO · MISIER · IACHOMO · DONADO · ₂|
HONOREVELE · PODESTADE · DE MVRAN · ~ ·

[Mccccxxviii, adì xxii novembrio, al tempo del nobele homo misier
Iachomo Donado, honorevele podestade de Muran.]

TRANSLATION: 1428, on the 22nd of November, in the time (of office) of the nobleman Sir Iachomo Donado, right honourable mayor of Murano.

DATE: November 1428.

LOCATION: In situ on a well head in Campo S. Stefano on the island of Murano.

TYPE AND DESCRIPTION: Commemorative. The inscription, carved in three lines along the widest point on the eastern face of the well head, celebrates the completion and unveiling of a well in Campo S. Stefano on Murano, recording the date and the name of the incumbent mayor of the island. The *vera da pozzo*, in Istrian stone, is 89 cm high and 116 cm wide at its maximum width where the inscription is carved. The inscription area is approximately 104 × 10 cm and has suffered a good deal of abrasion and superficial cracking. The epigraph itself is now very worn down, with the grooving so shallow that the message has become hard to read. In addition, the upper lip on the inscription side of the well has suffered substantial damage, already partly present in the early nineteenth century when Cicogna transcribed the message. The damage was probably caused originally by a metal lid being installed. The chipping along this curb of the well has now obliterated the central part of the top line, which has been infilled at some point in recent times with a layer of cement. I have reconstituted some of the missing words on the top line with the help of CICOGNA (1824–53, VI: 498). It seems reasonable to assume that *nove[...]o* in Cicogna's reading was *novembrio* with an <m>, given the spelling *tempo* (l. 1) rather than *tenpo* although, as CI 50 shows, there is no certainty in such matters.

This is the second of only two surviving well heads in Venice and the islands from our period with vernacular writing on them. For the first, at S. Rafael in Venice, see CI 15, CI 16. According to Elisabeth CROUZET-PAVAN (2015: 347; 921 n. 140) the decision by the *podestà* of Murano (recorded on 6 March 1424) to dedicate communal funds to the building of the S. Stefano well was a sign of the new interest shown by prosperous Venetian and Muranese residents in beautifying the island. This campaign of embellishment would lead to Murano, with its palaces and gardens, being the *locus amœnus* of Venice's elite in the sixteenth century.

LETTERING: Gothic majuscules carved in V-section. The absence of ligatures and abbreviations and the ample spacing between words and lines, with mid-high interpuncts, must have made the inscription perfectly legible in the past, even from a distance. In addition, letter size was generous at 3.5 cm high on average, and older photographs show black infilling in the grooves (RIZZI 1981: 276–77). However,

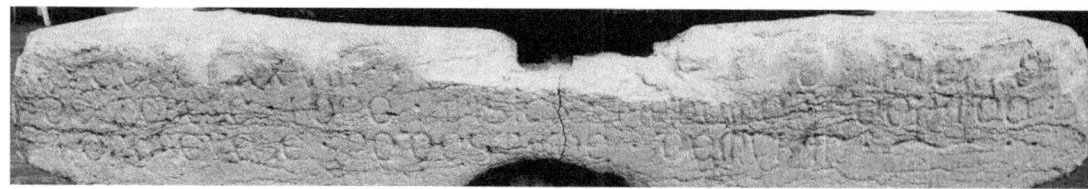

FIG. 3.59. CI 51. © A. S. Ferguson.

even taking into account the present deterioration of the script, the overall layout is less that perfect in terms of positioning, with particular cramping on *de Muran* (l. 3), while letter height is undoubtedly shaky at times. The Gothic nature of the script seems very reduced: essentially monoline with little hairstroking. It led Cicogna to see the lettering as transitional between Gothic majuscules and Renaissance Roman capitals. However, this is only an optical illusion, the result of the drastically worn down state of the writing. On closer inspection, and with the aid of high-resolution photographs, one can detect the expected curved hairstrokes on <e>, the sinuosity of <h>, <m> and <n>, and the long curving upstroke on <l> which even starts below the baseline.

LANGUAGE: The brief message, although carved on Murano, is entirely consistent with Early Venetian norms. As on two of the previous three inscriptions from the island in the corpus the term for 'mayor' crops up here. Surprisingly, though, *podestade* (l. 3) < PŎTESTĀTEM is the first occurrence of this conservative form of the word, with the *-ade* ending, instead of the more 'modern' *podesta* (= *podestà*) present on the other two. See CI 2 (l. 8) from 1310 and CI 38 (l. 3) from 1373. It is unlikely to be a coincidence that the patrician surname of the mayor is in the conservative form *Donado* (l. 2) rather than the innovative *Donà* which would predominate in the Renaissance, and that *honorevele* (l. 3), like *homo* (l. 2), retains the Latinising <h>. *Nobele* 'noble' (l. 2) shows characteristic Venetian post-tonic vowel lowering compared to Tuscan/Italian. On the ending in *-brio* of *novembrio* (November; l. 1), see CI 79.

RECENT STUDIES: RIZZI (1981: 276–77); TOMASIN (2012b: 2); MOCELLIN (2016: 29–31). First published by CICOGNA (1824–53, VI: 498).

Corpus Inscription 52

DELA LATE DELA VERGENE MARIA

[Dela late dela Vergene Maria.]

TRANSLATION: Milk of the Virgin Mary's.

DATE: Undated but assignable to *c.* 1420–30 on stylistic grounds (HAHNLOSER, 1971, II: 181–82). Nothing in the lettering or language of the inscription contradicts this dating.

LOCATION: In situ on a reliquary in the Treasury of St Mark (*Santuario* no. 106), St Mark's Basilica.

TYPE AND DESCRIPTION: Descriptive. The inscription is in raised gilded lettering running around the narrow collar of the lid of the reliquary. It informs the viewer that the golden ampulla within contains breast milk from the Virgin Mary. This statement contrasts with the surprising fact that the reliquary actually holds the relic of the thumb of the Evangelist St Mark. PASINI (1887: 40) believed that the thumb had been removed from the body of the saint when it was recovered in the Basilica in 1094, and he noted that it was first registered as present in the Treasury in the inventory of 1463. He considered that the thumb might have been switched — from its original delapidated reliquary to that previously containing the Madonna's breast milk — sometime in the nineteenth century.

The highly ornate Gothic reliquary in gilded silver is 35.8 cm high and 13 cm in diameter around the base. This hexagonal lobed base has miniature lions at the lobes and complex foliage decoration on the surface. The tall stem, with an intricate wrought ogival projection in the middle, holds the transparent chalice. The latter displays the relic of the thumb of the patron saint of Venice held within a gold clasp which resembles a small Gothic chapel. The domed lid of the vessel features attractive large enamel scales and is topped by a little cupola that can be raised. This itself is surmounted by a tuft of metallic leaves. The inscription is fashioned on the collar ring of the cupola.

LETTERING: Gothic majuscules. The script is regular in height and spacing, following the top and bottom of the collar as if between guidelines. While it is relatively easy to read at around 0.3 cm in height, the uncialesque lettering appears to lack subtlety, with the contrastive strokes tending to the same thickness as the main ones. This chunkiness can be seen on the hairstroking of <e>, the upstroking of <l> and on the thick vertical downstroke on the ascender of <d>. The extreme extent of this downstroke is typical of later Gothic practice in Venice, as are the strong parallel upstroke on <l> and the long downstrokes on <t>.

LANGUAGE: The brief inscription is most notable for containing rare public written evidence of the feminine gender of *late* 'milk' in Early Venetian. The third declension LAC, LACTIS was neuter in Latin, and like similar nouns in this declension was re-assigned to masculine or feminine in the Romance languages, but not

246 CORPUS OF INSCRIPTIONS

FIG. 3.60. CI 52 (detail). © A. S. Ferguson.

always consistently across them. Hence French *le lait* and Italian *il latte* contrast with Spanish *la leche*. Venetian, undoubtedly influenced by Tuscan/Italian, has gradually drifted towards the masculine option but originally preferred the feminine, as can still be seen on the street sign for the *Ponte de la Late* bridge over the Rio S. Zuane (*sestiere* of S. Crose).

RECENT STUDIES: GALLO (1967: 118–19); HAHNLOSER (1971: 181–82).

Corpus Inscription 53

· ÇEREXIS · | · PIRI · | · CH[U]CUM͡ERIS · | · PERSICI · | · ÇUCHE · |
· MOLONI · | · FICI · | · HUUA ·

[Çerexis, piri, chucumeris, persici, çuche, moloni, fici, huva.]

TRANSLATION: Cherries, pears, cucumbers, peaches, gourds, melons, figs, grapes.

DATE: Between *c.* 1422 and *c.* 1442. See CI 54.

LOCATION: Carved on capital no. 10 (Piazzetta side — counting from the Porta della Carta) on the ground-floor arcade of the Doge's Palace. The capital was badly damaged by frost in the winter of 1857 and was replaced by a copy made between 1879 and 1884. The original is now on display, along with twelve others of the *ab initio* 36, in the *Museo dell'opera* rooms on the ground floor of the Doge's Palace. Ours is the only fourteenth-century capital to have been replaced.

TYPE AND DESCRIPTION: Captions over sculpted depictions of a series of fruit and vegetables in baskets. The anonymous capital itself, in Istrian stone, sits atop its *pietra d'Istria* column *c.* 275 cm above ground level. Its sculpted decoration consists of a series of eight evenly spaced acanthus leaves rising from the base of the capital bell. Each leaf bears upon it a similar plaited wicker basket heaped with one type of fruit or vegetable. The baskets are separated by overlapping pairs of acanthus leaves. Wedged between the top of each basket of fruit and the abacus there emerges a smooth necking of convex stone, with the repeated moulding seeming to form a linked ring round the whole bell. The inscriptions are carved on the middle part of each bulge, so that they project forward prominently. The baskets convey their contrasting weaves simply but effectively, while the succulent and highly individualised fruit and vegetables are heaped on top with realistic freshness. RUSKIN (1851–53, II: 361) described the carving on this capital as 'well designed, though a little coarse [...] the characters [*scilicet* of the fruit and vegetables] well given, and groups well arranged, but without much care or finish'.

Parts of the original capital have sustained damage, most apparent around the abacus and on the area of the basket of figs, which is affected by abrasion, and at the top of the melon basket which is badly chipped. The only caption to be substantially damaged is that of the cucumbers where the first <u/v> of *chucumeris* has been swallowed up by a deep split running down from the abacus. The originals are grey with age and atmospheric pollution compared to the gleaming white copies in the Piazzetta which have been recently restored.

LETTERING: Gothic majuscules cut in V-section. Splendid examples of late Gothic letter carving. The script is delightfully sinuous, elegant and flourished, while remaining perfectly legible thanks to its generous size (*c.* 4 cm high on average) and spacing, as well as to the volumetric balance between thick and thin strokes throughout. The notional headlines and baselines are maintained firmly by the body of the letters with their sturdy wedged stems, giving the mason the

248 CORPUS OF INSCRIPTIONS

FIG. 3.61. CI 53 (detail). © A. S. Ferguson.

FIG. 3.62. CI 53 (detail). © A. S. Ferguson.

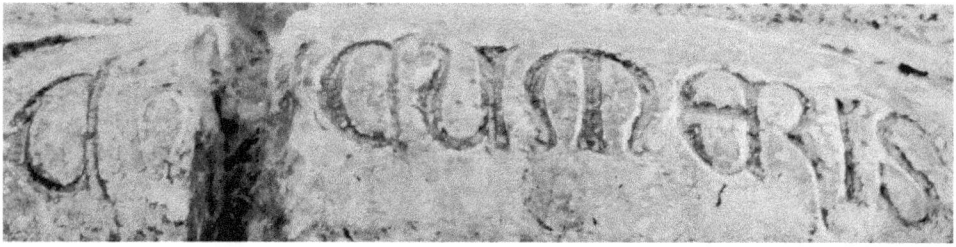

FIG. 3.63. CI 53 (detail). © A. S. Ferguson.

freedom to elaborate above and, especially, below them. This he did with delicate elongated serifs on the <s>, with fine long hairstroking on <c>, <d> and <f>, and with elongated threads, tapered and curved, on the left stem of <a> and on the leg of <h>. Remarkable in this respect are the virtuoso <r> on *persici* and *piri* and the audacious <ç> on *çuche* and, particularly, on *çerexis*. Here the elaborate tail on the cedilla takes up more than half the letter length and extends confidently and attractively below the baseline. Sinuosity is marked on the uncial <x>, on the almond <o> of *moloni*, on the parallel upstroke of <l> and, especially, on the left curved <u/v>. The sequential presence of curved <u/v> on *huva* is unusual and slightly awkward visually. Each individual caption is framed at start and finish by a mid-high interpunct. Traces of black infilling are still present in the grooving of some of the letters and middle dots.

LANGUAGE: Apart from CI 54 this is the only inscribed capital on the Doge's Palace where the vernacular is featured. In the case of our captions two of the designations are unequivocally in a Venetian (or at least Veneto) vernacular form: *çuche* 'gourds' and *moloni* 'melons'. The others appear to hover between the vernacular and Latin — in the case of *huva* 'grapes' and *piri* 'pears' — or else to be vernacular terms Latinised or overlaid to a greater or lesser extent with Latin: *çerexis* 'cherries', *chucumeris* 'cucumbers', *persici* 'peaches' and *fici* 'figs'. In the absence of documentation one can only conjecture as to what was behind these linguistic choices. From the evidence of the captions themselves it would appear that the *scriptor* and sculptor, faced with concrete and well-known natural objects, some of which did not have immediately familiar Latin plurals, came to a compromise. They simultaneously made the inscriptions as transparent as they could to onlookers while retaining as much of a Latin patina as possible. That this was their aim is suggested immediately by the spelling of *huva*. Latin ŪVA '(bunch of) grapes' coincided with the Early Venetian equivalent *uva* (Modern Venetian, *ua*), but the need seems to have been felt to emphasise its Latinity by adding an etymologically unjustified <h>. *Piri* 'pears' coincided with the lowland rural Veneto metaphonic plural *piri* 'pears' (singular *pero*). It was also a Latin plural meaning 'pear trees'. The plural PĬRA 'pears' (from neuter PĬRUM) was rejected, probably because it would have felt like a singular to viewers. It is possible, on the other hand, that Latin CŬCURBĬTAE 'gourds' was considered to be both too unfamiliar and too unrelated to the vernacular equivalent to be of use, so the purely Venetian *çuche* was opted for. When it came to designating the basket of melons the rare classical MELŎPOPON must have been out of the question. The Veneto forms *meloni* or *moloni* could have been seen as appropriate in that they were close to the later Latin MELONES of medical treatises. It was perhaps natural that the variant *moloni* was selected as it was the favoured term in the mainland areas round the lagoon where melons were grown (PACCAGNELLA 2012, *s.v. molon*). *Çerexis* 'cherries' strongly evokes, even in its spelling with <ç> and <x>, the Early Venetian *çerexe* or *çerese* (and not at all the classical CĒRASA) while *chucumeris* 'cucumbers', with the typical Venetian spelling <ch> for /k/, recalls both Latin CUCŬMERES and Early Venetian *c(h)uc(h)umeri, c(h)ugumeri* or *c(h)ugumari* (see SALLACH 1993, *s.vv. cogumaro, cogumero, cugumaro*). The late Latin *-is* plural endings on both *çerexis* and *chucumeris* are reminiscent of *-is* for *-es* accusative plural third declension endings in older Latin. One suspects the influence here of medieval treatises on medicinal plants like the *Antidotarium Nicolai* (FONTANELLA 2000) where plural spellings such as *semis* or *seminis* 'seeds' are found whenever the classical Latin plural (in this case the neuter SĒMINA) is perceived as obscure or awkward. Our hypothesis appears to be supported by the presence of *çeresis* 'cherries' on another capital on the Piazzetta-side arcade of the Doge's Palace. This is the nearby capital no. 12 from the mid-fourteenth century, dedicated to the months of the year, where the eight inscriptions are all in Latin. June is described here as *Iunius cum çeresis* 'June with cherries' using the same vernacular-based designation for cherries as on our caption, but this time dressed up as a pseudo-ablative. The fact that the Latin neuter plural PĔRSICA 'peaches' looked like a singular may have driven the choice of *persici*, a Latin second declension plural which recalled Early Venetian *perseg(h)i*. Similarly, the Latin neuter plural FĪCA 'figs' may have looked inappropriately singular — and evocative of the obscene connotations of *figa* 'fig' — thereby encouraging an alternative nominative plural *fici*. Although close enough to the vernacular *fig(h)i* to be understood as 'figs', *fici* actually meant 'fig trees' in Latin.

That the type of linguistic adaptation discussed above was not unusual is confirmed by the impeccable Latin of Venetian decrees and other official documents of our period where scribes were uninhibited in inserting superficially (if at all) Latinised vernacular forms for local terminology — including designations of fruit and vegetables — when the employment of strictly Latin equivalents would have led to ambiguity or obscurity.

RECENT STUDIES: MANNO (1992: 47–48); MANNO (1999: 88–89). Transcribed in WOLTERS (1976, I: 250). First recorded in B. GAMBA (1832: 14).

Corpus Inscription 54

· IVSTITIA · $_1$| · ARISTOTILE · CHE · DIE · LEÇE ∶ $_2$|
[---] P^{O}VOLO · P(ER) L^E · SVO ·
ISEL^E RITA · $_3$| · SAL^O(N) · VNO · DEI SE(T)T$_E$ · SAVI · DI GREÇ^{I}A · CHE · DIE
· LE(Ç)ÇE · $_4$| · ISIPIONE · A CHASTITA CH[-------------] FIA · A(L) RE $_5$| ·
NVMA · PONPIL^{I}O · I(N)PERADOR · EDIFICHADOR · DI TE(N)PI · E CHIESE $_6$| ·
QVA(N)DO · MOISE · RICEVE · LA LEÇE · I(N) · SVL MONTE ∶ $_7$| · TRAIANO ·
I(N)PERADORE · CHE · FE · IVSTITIA · AL(L)A · VEDOVA ∶·

[1. Iustitia. 2. Aristotile che dié leçe. 3. [----------------] povolo per le suo iselerita. 4. Salon, uno dei sette savi di Greçia che dié leççe. 5. Isipione à chastità ch[---------] fia al re. 6. Numa Ponpilio inperador, edifichador di tenpi e chiese. 7. Quando Moisè ricevé la leçe in sul monte. 8. Traiano inperadore che fe' iustitia alla vedova.]

TRANSLATION: 1. Justice. 2. Aristotle who gave laws. 3. [--------------] for his Israelite people. 4. Solon, one of the seven sages of Greece who gave laws. 5. Scipio is chaste in that [----------] daughter to the king. 6. Numa Pompilius, emperor and builder of temples and churches. 7. When Moses received the law on the mount. 8. Emperor Trajan who rendered justice unto the widow.

DATE: *c.* 1422–*c.* 1442. In his fifteenth-century *Cronicha dela Nobil Città de Venetia* (CARACCIOLO ARICÒ 2009, II: 218) Zorzi Dolfin recorded that:

> El pallazo nuovo de Venezia, zoè quella parte che è sopra la piaza verso la giesia de missier San Marcho — del 1422 de settembrio — fo prencipiado, el qual fu fatto e finito molto bello come al presente se vede nobilissimo; et a la fabricha fu deputado missier Nicolò Barbarigo soprastante con duchati x d'oro al mexe e fusse fatta la spexa dela ditta fabricha per quelli da l'Offitio del Sal.

Work on the Porta della Carta, adjacent to the Justice capital, brought renovation on the Piazzetta side of the palace to an end. It appears to have been completed by the Bon brothers around 1442 (ZANOTTO 1842–58, I: 356–57).

LOCATION: The inscription sequence is in situ on the abacus of capital no. 1 on the ground-floor arcade of the Doge's Palace. The so-called Justice capital sits just beneath the magnificent sculpted ensemble of the *Judgement of Solomon* on the south-west Porta della Carta corner of the palace facing the Piazzetta. The Solomon group has been attributed to Bartolomeo Bon or to Jacopo della Quercia, while the Justice capital itself has often been attributed to the hand of Florentine sculptors (WOLTERS 1976, I: 249–50; TIGLER 1999). More recently, Anne MARKHAM SCHULZ (2011: 41–42) has demonstrated the important presence of Tuscan stonemasons in Venice in our period, and has underlined the likelihood that our capital and its captions were the work of Florentines. The palaeographic and linguistic evidence set out below confirms this conclusion.

TYPE AND DESCRIPTION: A related series of inscribed captions running along the sides of the abacus on the Justice capital which sits atop its shaft some 225 cm

FIG. 3.64. CI 54 (line 7) in context. © A. S. Ferguson.

above pavement level. The abacus location of the inscriptions is unusual on the Palazzo Ducale capitals where legends were invariably cut along the necking of the bell below. Our captions summarise the content of the accompanying sculptures beneath them on the eight facets of the Istrian stone capital. This succession of carved scenes brings to life the theme of Justice through the actions of exemplary lawgivers and righteous men. The popularity of the Justice theme during our period is suggested by two surviving fresco fragments, now in the Castelvecchio in Verona, depicting the restraint of Scipio and the justice of Trajan. They originally decorated the interior walls of a private house in Verona and are very much along the lines of the figurations on the Justice capital. They were painted in the early sixteenth century by the Venetian artist Girolamo Mocetto who had himself worked in the Doge's Palace.

MANNO (1999: 69) pointed out the inscriptional anomalies on the Justice capital. These are: the missing sections on ll. 3 and 5; the apparently jumbled wording of what remains of l. 3; and the sometimes imperfectly spaced overall layout, with blank stretches of abacus. He suggested tentatively that these puzzling features might be the result of restoration, displacement or replacement of the original epigraphs during renewal work in the late 1850s. What does seem likely is that the now blank stretches of the abacus on sides 3 and 5 result from new stone being inserted there to replace badly deteriorated parts. The original damaged sections undoubtedly carried those segments of the inscriptions now missing, or what was left of them. In fact the wedge of stone inserted into side 5, covering what was the middle part of the inscription on that side, is still perfectly visible today. Be that as it may, Ruskin's transcriptions, carried out before the restoration, show that on at least seven of the eight epigraphs the wording was as it is now (RUSKIN, 1851–53, II: 362–64). He thus confirmed what had already been suggested by MOSCHINI (1815, I: 476–77). Ruskin's accompanying sketch of the capital, showing the inscriptions on sides 1 and 2, proves that on those epigraphs at least the wording was not tampered with by the restorers. That said, Ruskin's insertion of several asterisks after the second <t> of *Aristotile* (l. 2) — where that segment, at present bisected by a clean cut in the stone, is now clearly legible — suggests restoration of the following <il>. One other lettering detail on the inscriptions as they are today could be considered suspicious: the threaded serifs on the <s> of *iustitia* on side 8. However, as letter uniformity on the captions is far from absolute this is not conclusive. Unfortunately, Ruskin did not sketch side 8. In addition, and more seriously, he mislaid his notes relating to side 3 where damage is currently greatest and where the wording of what remains seems confused. Fortunately, Moschini's transcription appears to confirm that the wording there was already the same in the nineteenth century as it is now.

The sculpted carrousel of scenes around the capital stands on the summit of a crown of beautiful dense and swirling foliage from which it appears to emerge organically. Vivid and intricate, the scenes bring to life the actions of the men of justice mentioned in the captions. Side 1 depicts the crowned and winged figure of Justice herself, sitting on two lions and bearing the symbols of justice. She held scales in her left hand and a sword in her right (both symbols are now missing, although they were present in mid-nineteenth century images). She mirrors the large figure of Justice sitting prominently at the top of the Porta della Carta itself. On side 2 Aristotle, with cap and beard, stands holding a tablet of the law in each hand while two bearded kneeling men look at him. On side 3 a dignified, bearded Moses points to a book lying open on his lap while two adoring Israelites look on and prepare to swear on the book. Side 4 shows a bearded Solon reading from a book of laws to two Athenians at his feet. On side 5 the notorious womaniser Scipio Africanus demonstrates the just restraint of his passions during the Second Punic War, according to the version of events handed down by Polybius rather than by Livy. Scipio is depicted here turning away thoughtfully from the kneeling young female prisoner presented to him by a soldier in a plumed bonnet. He then returns the maiden to her father, the king mentioned in the caption. Polybius does not actually call her father a king, though, so it may be that the *scriptor* was influenced by Livy's version of the story where the girl is handed back to her betrothed, the Celtiberian chieftain Allucius. Side 6 celebrates the legendary second king of Rome, Numa Pompilius, religious reformer and builder of temples. Wearing a tall hat, Numa is depicted discussing the building project of a three-storey church bell tower — reminiscent in its shape of Giotto's *campanile* of the Duomo in Florence — with a helmeted Roman. On side 7 God emerges from the sky, represented by the necking of the capital, and presents the tablets of the law to Moses. The latter kneels before a beautifully sculpted tree which, presumably, represents mount Sinai. On side 8 Trajan on horseback, cape flowing behind him, rides up vigorously to do justice to the kneeling and imploring widow whose son has been murdered. In the *Stones of Venice* Ruskin described the capital as follows:

> This is the last of the Piazzetta façade, the elaborate one under the Judgment angle. Its foliage is copied from the eighteenth at the opposite side, with an endeavour on the part of the Renaissance sculptor to refine upon it, by which he has merely lost some of its truth and force. This capital will, however, be always thought, at first, the most beautiful of the whole series: and indeed it is very noble; its groups of figures most carefully studied, very graceful, and much more pleasing than those of the earlier work, though with less real power in them; and its foliage is only inferior to that of the Fig-tree angle. It represents, on its front or first side, Justice enthroned, seated on two lions; and on the seven other sides examples of acts of justice or good government, or figures of lawgivers. (RUSKIN 1851–53, II: 362)

It is worth considering the central ideological location occupied by this whole sculptural ensemble, including the inscriptioned capital, placed as it is at the passageway into the Doge's Palace. Venice's self-image as the home of justice and good government is here given elaborate figuration at the entrance to the centre of the Republic's political and judicial power. Indeed the *Procession in St Mark's Square* from c. 1496 by Gentile Bellini (Early/Middle Venetian, Zentil Belin) shows clearly that our capital was important enough to be gilded, like the decoration of the Porta della Carta itself.

In my view, likely candidates for the authorship of the Justice capital and their inscriptions are the Florentine sculptors Piero di Niccolò Lamberti and Giovanni di Martino da Fiesole. Their presence in Venice in our period makes this attribution a possibility. The following palaeographic considerations strengthen the case. In 1423 Piero and his workshop, with Giovanni, completed a huge commission in Venice: the sculpting of the elaborate wall tomb of Doge Tom(m)aso Mocenigo in S. Zanipolo (MARKHAM SCHULZ 2012). No strangers, therefore, to prestigious commissions in the city they were then available to work on the Doge's Palace. Like the sarcophagus of Iacopo Cavalli by Polo Chataiapiera in S. Zanipolo which we have examined previously (CI 44), the Mocenigo tomb features two inscriptions of contrasting types beneath it, one below the other. On the Cavalli monument the two separately framed inscriptions are distinguished by language and function: Latin for the eulogy, the vernacular for the authorship proclamation. Under the Mocenigo monument the epigraphs are both in Latin. However, they are equally sharply separated by function, a fact emphasized by the contrast between the elaborate plaque of the doge's epitaph and the simple frame of Istrian stone along the bottom carrying the masons' single-line statement of authorship: *Petrvs magistri Nicholai de Florencia et Iovannes Martini de Fesvlis inciservnt hoc opvs 1423*. The two Mocenigo epigraphs could not differ more radically in the scripts they deploy. The alphabet of the eulogy is unusual for this late date in its curious amalgam of uncial and antiquarian capital forms in thick black lettering. In spite of the presence of uncials it has little of the Gothic spirit about it. It is an impressive and elaborate piece of inscriptional work which retains the careful hallmark of a written model provided by a learned *scriptor*. The overall impression is of a deliberate attempt to appear old-fashioned. The author's statement underneath is starkly different in appearance. Its alphabet has minimal uncial intrusions (the occasional <e>). Otherwise we are in the presence of unfussy revival Roman lettering characteristic of the early fifteenth century in Florence. The line is thin, the module condensed, the serifing hardly present. At first glance this script reminds one of the captions of the Justice capital, but shorn of their deliberate archaisms. Strikingly similar on both are the <e>, <s> and <t> as well as the almost square <c> and the inclined <v>. One can see how the <a> with looped overarm here might have become the /λ/-type discussed below. The suggested link between Piero Lamberti's workshop, the Mocenigo tomb and the Justice capital appears to be reinforced by the palaeographic evidence provided by the two inscriptions on the tomb of the jurist Raffaello Fulgosio executed by Lamberti, possibly with Giovanni di Martino (LAZZERINI 1923), in the Basilica del Santo in Padua in the late 1420s (FOLADORE 2010: ill. 20; MARKHAM SCHULZ 2017, II: ill. 26). We find ourselves again in the presence of sans-serif early Florentine revival capitals with similar script line and compression as before. Comparison of individual letters — including, most compellingly, Lamberti's unique signature <a> tending to the shape of a lambda — supports our suggested rapprochement.

LETTERING: Antiquarian majuscules cut in V-section. At first sight the script looks essentially capital. It recalls, in fact, the early Quattrocento Florentine revivalist experiments with condensed sans-serif republican Roman capitals seen, notably, on the epitaph at the foot of Masaccio's fresco of the *Trinity* (*c.* 1425–27) in S. Maria Novella. Closer inspection reveals a more complex and intriguing picture. One becomes gradually aware that there are a considerable number of uncial forms. These are as follows: <d> 9 times out of 9; <h> all 4 times; <m> 2 out of 2; <n> 6 times out of 6; and 21 examples of uncial <e> as against 12 capital ones. Of these uncial letters only <h> (featuring a noticeably high starting point for its leg), <m> and <n> show anything like the kind of sinuosity on the leg associated with Gothic. On the contrary, the ascender on uncial <d> is horizontal, short and briefly serifed while <e> is not hairstroked and is only very lightly serifed. Highly unusual is the <a> used in all 18 cases: an archaic type shaped like an enlarged lower-case lambda. It is derived ultimately from a Roman rustic capital form re-employed in Carolingian literary works.

The 42 uncial letters in the inscription and the 18 cases of the /λ/-type <a> stand alongside some 150 capital characters. These are not derived directly from classical Roman capitals but from twelfth- to thirteenth-century Romanesque script and show in almost all cases the unserifed, condensed, tendentially monoline ductus of that period and style. Some are particularly striking. The condensed <r> features a bowl which curves in and up at the end without touching the stem. From the tapered end of the bowl the leg projects down to the baseline at an acute angle. The bowl of <p> sometimes fails to touch the stem as it curves back, snaking instead inside and up or, in one instance (*per*, l. 3), down. At other times, as in the first <p> of *Ponpilio* (Pompilius) on l. 6 and on that of *Isipione* (Scipio) on l. 5, it does curve back to touch the stem, albeit very low down. The <e>, <l> and <t> are characteristically Romanesque, with thin lines and short unserifed projections. The <c> and <ç> are also condensed, monoline and sans-serif, curving only briefly at the ends. The straight form of <u/v> is always employed. Occasionally, as in *riceve* 'received' (l. 7), one side of the <v> is strongly tilted after the fashion sometimes seen on Romanesque epigraphs. The <g> is reduced to its essentials: condensed and elbow-curved on the bottom stroke, with no swirl and no serifs. The use of the cedilla is, of course, anachronistic in that it was not found in Romanesque inscriptions. Immediately recognisable as Romanesque-inspired is the letter-nesting on ll. 3 and 4, with subscript and superscript capital insertions.

All in all, the presence of such Romanesque revival characters, hybridised with uncial residues, is unlike anything on the capitals of the Doge's Palace where only full-blooded Gothic majuscules appear. There is probably no single source for this eclectic historicising alphabet. If commissioner and stonemason(s) were seeking an archaic-looking script, mingling capitals and uncials, for this prestigious commission — one that suggested solemnity and age — they needed look no further than the older mosaics in St Mark's. However, the mason(s) are also likely to have had prominent in their mind late twelfth-century Tuscan models such as those in Pisa (BANTI 2000: 98, fig. 2), where the compressed elbow-curve on <g>, <a> with protruding right stem, and the alternation of two sorts of <e> — alongside uncial <h>, <m> and <n> — are present in a sans-serif monoline script.

Among the many oddities of our captions is their unique abbreviation system. The only 'normal' abbreviation mark present is the barred stem of <p> for *per* (l. 3). Otherwise the mason(s) puzzlingly opted to indicate missing letters with a strong overdot. This can refer back to the usual dropped <n>, as in *Salo(n)* (l. 4), *i(n)perador* and *te(n)pi* (l. 6), *qua(n)do* and *i(n)* (l. 7), and *i(n)peradore* (l. 8) but also, much more surprisingly — and uniquely in the corpus —, to one letter missing from a double consonant combination. This applies to the suspended <l> in *al(l)a* (l. 8), to the <t> in *set(t)e* (l. 4), but also, apparently, to the <ç> in *leçe* 'laws' (l. 4). The latter, very rarely seen in Early Venetian documents, can only be explained by the sculptor(s) having the underlying Tuscan form *legge* or *leggi* in mind. There is even an overdot above the first <o> of *povolo* 'people' — raised as it is above the notional headline — to indicate that it should be inserted below. Ligatures, perhaps also felt to be particularly associated with more recent Gothic inscriptions, are not present on the captions.

It has been alleged by various scholars since the nineteenth century that an irregular sequence of small letters cut at the bottom of the capital foliage just before it meets the shaft — and reading, in a Latin of sorts, *duo sotii florentini incise* 'two Florentine partners cut (this)' — is *ab initio*. Others think they are more likely to be a hoax perpetrated during the restoration process on the capital. It is undoubtedly true that the apocryphal message would be in line with the conclusions we have reached regarding the authorship of the Justice capital inscriptions. However, while it is the case that the miniature lettering (some of it, at least) is indeed visible upon careful scrutiny, it is genuinely problematic to interpret this meagre palaeographic evidence with any degree of certainty. The authenticity question therefore remains open.

LANGUAGE: As with its lettering, the language of the inscription surprises by its hybridity, combining underlying Early Tuscan with Early Venetian forms. It is not without interest, and cannot be without significance, that this is the only capital on the Palace arcades to be entirely in the vernacular. It reminds us that CI 1 which faces it on the great corridor leading into the Doge's Palace and CI 30, the translated papal bull inscription in the Loggia above, are carved in Venetian. It would seem that whenever a lapidary message was considered essential reading the authorities privileged the use of the vernacular. We have already noted a spectacular instance of linguistic code switching and code mixing in CI 8, involving a Tuscan settled in Venice, and a hint of *Sprachmischung* in the short CI 26, again involving someone with a Tuscan background. In the case of the the Justice capital captions it appears that the native Tuscan of the mason(s) has been infiltrated consciously or unconsciously by the Venetian of their patrons, fellow craftsmen and urban surroundings. Lamberti, at least, may actually have been living in Venice for some time. This type of linguistic fluidity is unsurprising in a cultural and linguistic context where mutual understanding between these two prestigious Italo-Romance varieties was probably relatively high and where there were, as yet, no formal boundaries laid down by prescriptive standardisation.

Aristotile (l. 2) is Early Tuscan, the Early Venetian form being *Aristotele*. The Latinising *iustitia* (ll. 1 and 8) is common to both varieties. The past historic verb forms *die* (= *diè*) '(he) gave' (ll. 1 and 4) and *riceve* (= *ricevé*) '(he) received' on l. 7 are both Venetian and Tuscan, but *fe* (= *fe'*) '(he) made, gave' (l. 8) is likely to be Venetian. *Leçe* 'law, laws' (ll. 1 and 7) can only be Venetian; on the other hand, as noted above, the doubling on *leççe* (l. 4) is certainly prompted by underlying Tuscan, as is the <tt> in *sette* 'seven' (l. 4). *Edifichador* 'builder' (l. 6) and *inperador* 'emperor' (l. 6) are utterly Venetian in form and spelling whereas *inperadore* (l. 8) is Tuscan. *Moise* or *Moisè* (Moses), on l. 7, and *Numa Ponpilio* (l. 6) could be from either variety. *Traiano* Trajan (l. 8) is definitely Tuscan. The hapax *Isipione* Scipio (l. 5) with its prosthetic <i> before initial <s> appears to reflect a popular pronunciation, partly influenced by Venetian, of the usual Early Tuscan *Scipion(e)*. The Venetian form would likely have been *S(c)ipion*. Similarly, *tenpi* (or just possibly *tempi*) 'temples' (l. 6) could be either Venetian or Tuscan but *chiese* 'churches' can only be the latter. The normal Tuscan form *vedova* 'widow' (l. 8) was possible in Early Venetian but *vedoa* was commoner. The preceding *alla* 'to the' confirms its Tuscan-ness. Similar considerations apply to *chastita* (= *chastità*) on l. 5, where in fifteenth-century high register Venetian one might have anticipated *c(h)astitade*. Ambiguity hangs over *Greçia* (Greece) on l. 4, although the cedilla gives it a Venetian appearance. Unquestionably Venetian are *povolo* 'people' (Tuscan, *popolo*) on l. 2 and *fia* 'daughter' (Tuscan, *figlia*, *figliola*) on l. 5. Finally, the ending of the very incomplete third caption remains a puzzle. The meaning would appear to be 'for his Israelite people', referring back to Moses. However, the syntax looks incoherent and the two elements of 'Israelite people' seem bizarrely separated.

In addition, *iselerita* is a clumsy and unattested metathesis of *israelita*. Nevertheless, it would be unwise to rush to judgement given our ignorance of the first part of the inscription.

The remarkably eccentric lettering selected for this inscription and its fluid linguistic hybridity, with the awkward elements noted above, again bring into sharp relief the question of the autonomy exercised by masons over their inscriptional commission. The sculptor(s) of the capital obviously learned in detail from the commissioner's agent or *scriptor,* as well as from their contract, the precise subject of the scenes to be carved. Were they then given fairly general instructions about the captions for each one and allowed to express them in their own words, with the proviso that a Venetian public should have no problem with understanding them and that the lettering should look somewhat archaic? What is on the abacus makes it hard not to draw such a conclusion.

RECENT STUDIES: ROSSI and SALERNI (1952: 120–25); MANNO (1992: 35–39); MANNO 1999 (69–77). Transcribed in WOLTERS (1976, I: 250). First recorded in MOSCHINI (1815, I: 476–77) and in B. GAMBA (1832: 13).

Corpus Inscription 55

☩ M(AISTRO) LORE(N)ÇO ☩ E IACHOMO ☩ DA UENEXIA ☩ A FATO ☩ QUESTO ☩
LAUORO ☩ 1429 $_1$ | ADI 8 AGOSTO $_2$

[Maistro Lorenço, e Iachomo, da Venexia a fato questo lavoro. 1429,
adì 8 agosto.]

TRANSLATION: Master Lorenço, and Iachomo, from Venice did this work. 1429, on the 8th of August.

DATE: August 1429.

LOCATION: On a banderole running along the bottom of the painting of the *Coronation of the Virgin* by Lorenzo da Venezia (Early Venetian, Lorenço da Venexia) and an assistant called Iachomo, also from Venice. The painting is now held in the collection of the Fondazione Cini in Venice. Previously it belonged to count Vittorio Cini and was hung in the Cini castle at Monselice, in the Paduan countryside, in the count's remarkable medieval and Renaissance collection. Vittorio Cini donated it to the Fondazione Cini in 1972. Before him the painting had passed through the hands of a series of collectors. Its ultimate provenance is uncertain.

TYPE AND DESCRIPTION: Painted statement of authorship with date of completion that mimics ink writing on a parchment banderole. The epigraph appears on the panel of the *Coronation of the Virgin* (105 × 53 cm) painted in tempera and gold on what was probably the central compartment of a polyptych whose lateral panels are now lost. At present it is mounted in an elaborate gilded frame and is flanked by a series of medieval-style framed panels of saints, and one of the Virgin Mary: all actually painted in the nineteenth century. The figure of the artist Lorenço da Venexia, also sometimes identified with the so-called Master of Ceneda (from an altarpiece now in the Accademia but originally in Ceneda, in other words, Vittorio Veneto, in the northern Veneto), has only recently come to be associated with a body of work and to be given a still tentative identity (DE MARCHI 2003). His *Coronation* panel depicts, against a gleaming gold ground, a bearded God the Father, in royal blue and crimson tunic, placing His hands on the shoulders of Jesus and the Virgin Mary who sit below Him. Christ, holding a fine golden rod topped with the gold lillies of purity, in turn places a crown on the bowed head of His mother who has her arms crossed in modest devotion. The Madonna and Jesus are sumptuously dressed in pink and brocaded blue fabrics. They sit on a pale pink raised stone platform with sculpted edges under which is a dark green marble floor. The white banderole with our inscription unfurls across the pink floor space at the foot of the Gothic artwork, its elegant message picked out in black.

LETTERING: Painted Gothic minuscules. This highly stylised lowercase hand — in effect, a form of Gothic minuscule display script — makes its first appearance in the corpus. It reappears, inscribed on a stone banderole, in CI 61. The script is an artificial, de luxe offshoot of *littera textualis* not classifiable as either *rotunda*, *quadrata* or *praescissa*. As an outlier it is sometimes categorised rather vaguely as *fere textura*. It is northern European in its compression, angularity and decorativeness and

Fig. 3.65. CI 55. © Ronnie Ferguson.

appears commonly, in forms similar but not identical to ours, on the banderoles and captions of fifteenth-century tapestries and stained glass from France, Burgundy and Germany. Fine examples are on view in the Musée de Cluny in Paris and the Burrell Collection in Glasgow.

With its thin strokes, elongated module, delicate ductus, angular shafts and decorative filigree hairstroking, the effect of Maistro Lorenço's banderole alphabet — standing *c.* 1.6 cm high — is markedly calligraphic. The <a> which appears seven times over the two 'lines' is exemplary in this respect. Its ascender has a short tail stroke parallel to the baseline. It rises to the headline via a sequence of two kinks before releasing a descending curlicue hairstroke at its end. Its bow, meantime, is a narrow rectangle intersecting with the ascender just above mid point, passing through and just beyond the stem, before descending in a curved hairstroke parallel to the stem. Interesting is the <e> which appears four times. It is tall, almost rectangular, and its two short end-curves are peaked. The top one finishes in a diagonal bowed hairstroke serif, touching the main stem at one end and curling down at the other. The eight examples of <o> are all strongly lozenged, while the two occurrences of <r> have kinked flares at top and bottom of their perpendicular, and a flared horizontal topstroke which ends in a long, descending-then-upcurved, hairstroke. The <st> in *questo* (l. 1) is ligatured, the <ch> in *Iachomo* (l. 1) is conjoined, while the <q> of *questo* forms an underloop join with the following <u>: a type only seen in CI 2 (in paint) and CI 57 (on stone). *Agosto* (l. 2) has an unusual <g>, also present on CI 61, joined both to preceding <a> and following <o>.

Although this is a minuscule script and the <h> in *Iachomo* clearly reaches a little beyond the headline, there is undoubtedly an attempt to regularise it into bilinearity. The tendency — which has <f> and <s> fitting between headline and baseline, the <g> in *agosto* adapted from a capital form, and the tailed <q> of *questo* (l. 1) standing on the baseline — is in keeping with a display script. This propensity of our inscription is taken to its logical conclusion of full bilinearity in CI 61. The decorative effect of the present script is rounded off by the elegant spiral interpuncts between syntagms, also adapted for the <n> abbreviation bar in *Lorenço* (l. 1), and by the modulated and flourished 9 in the date. Arabic numerals for dating purposes — common in Venetian chancery documents since the fourteenth century — appear here for the first time in the corpus.

LANGUAGE: A number of linguistic features also make their first appearance in our collection. The designation *maistro* was a common term of address and respect for a master tradesman (see CI 56). The perfect *a fato* '(they) did, made' (Italian, *hanno fatto*) exemplifies the fact that 3rd singular and 3rd plural verb endings on all tenses were and are identical in Venetian. This is also the earliest appearance in the corpus of the innovative Italianate spelling *agosto* (see CI 79) for the traditional *avosto* (see CI 33, CI 34, CI 48). One notes, though, the continued use of two key Venetian spelling conventions: the <ç> for the unvoiced affricate and <ch> for the velar /k/.

RECENT STUDIES: LUCCO (1989: 33); DE MARCHI (2003: 72).

Corpus Inscription 56

·M⁰ CCCC⁰ XXXVI ADI · XX · MAÇO · ₁| · SEPVLTVRA · DE · M(AISTRO) ·
IACOMELO · ₂| · DA GAIO · CIROICO · IN · TORCELO E · DE[I] · ₃|
SOI · ERIEDI ·₄

[Mccccxxxvi, adì xx maço. Sepultura de maistro Iacomelo da Gaio, ciroico in Torcelo, e dei soi eriedi.]

TRANSLATION: 1436, on the 20th of May. Burial place of master Iacomelo da Gaio, surgeon on Torcello, and of his heirs.

DATE: May 1436.

LOCATION: Torcello. On a sarcophagus, presumably in situ, under the portico that runs along the left-side outside wall of the church of S. Fosca. The burial chest is set directly against the outer wall of the church.

TYPE AND DESCRIPTION: Announcement of tomb ownership. The inscription records that the tomb belongs to the surgeon Iacomelo da Gaio and his heirs. The date on it appears to refer to when the tomb was completed rather than to the time of Iacomelo's burial. This is confirmed by documentation showing that the surgeon was alive and well around 1440 (CROUZET-PAVAN 2017: 203). We can therefore be sure that he commissioned the inscribed text himself.

The epigraph is carved in four lines in the centre of the front surface of a large Istrian stone sarcophagus and is flanked, as was common practice in Venice, by two large trilobe crosses. The full front surface measures 230 × 74 cm while the inscription area on it is 65 × 17.5 cm. The surface of the chest where the inscription is located is in a run-down state, with a criss-cross pattern of cracks running through the script. If anything, though, legibility is impeded more severely by the faded state of the lettering itself which can just be made out overall but is becoming almost invisible in some parts. The sloping top of the sarcophagus, 108 cm long, is decorated with an ogival-shaped relief, now severely damaged but still showing interesting features such as a low-relief crow surrounded by a moon-and-stars motif. The whole artefact is in urgent need of intervention. Without it the epigraph risks obliteration in the near future.

As a licensed surgeon in the Republic, Iacomelo could theoretically have occupied either the second or third rung on the Venetian tripartite hierarchy of medical practitioners. At the top were the university-qualified physicians — often trained in nearby Padua, one of Europe's leading medical schools — who as a rule confined themselves, although in Venice not exclusively, to internal medicine. The practice of the physician, the *m(i)edego de fisic(h)a* or *de fixic(h)a*, was more preventative than interventionist, with the aim of re-establishing the sick body's humoral balance by correct regimen. He was enrolled in a prestigious college of physicians. The practical treatment of the outer body, from blood-letting to the mending of fractures and even to surgical operations, was as elsewhere in late medieval Europe the province of the barber-surgeon, Early Venetian *m(i)edego ciroico, ceroico* or *ciroigo*,

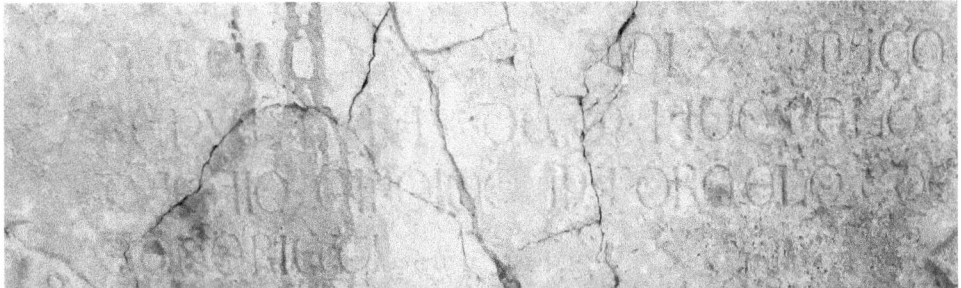

Fig. 3.66. CI 56. © A. S. Ferguson.

who belonged to his own guild. However, in Venice there was an intermediate category of surgeons proper. This was the *m(i)edego de plag(h)e*, enrolled in a separate college of surgeons. Some of these were actually university-trained, while others acquired a licence from the college of surgeons in Venice via an examination in Latin or the vernacular. They enjoyed higher prestige than their barber colleagues whose training was apprenticeship-based (EAMON 2013; BARTOLINI 2015). The Venetian Senate records suggest that the salary of a physician was around five times higher than that of a surgeon. The practice on Torcello in our period, when the island's population was already in decline and its prosperity modest, appears to have been to hire a barber-surgeon on renewable two-year contracts which also involved him acting as town crier. Master Iacomelo da Gaio, who is recorded as having resigned his position in 1430, but being back in office at least by 1440 (CROUZET-PAVAN 2017: 203), was obviously a well-known local personality whose social status and earnings allowed him to have a respectable family sarcophagus in a prominent position on the island. The need later in the century to stabilise the post is suggested by the 1487 record of Torcello council hiring a barber-surgeon for a five-year term (CONTON 1927: 85).

The surname of our surgeon means 'from Gaio', indicating that he was probably a local man. Gaio was a village on the mainland, set back from the edge of the lagoon opposite Torcello. The name evolved normally in Middle and Modern Venetian into the form Gagio, which was later Italianised as Gaggio. The locality of Gaggio is now, administratively, in the district of Marcon.

LETTERING: Gothic majuscules cut in V-section. The wearing down of the grooving of the letters, which average 2.5 cm in height, makes it difficult to make definitive judgements on the quality of the carving. This is especially the case as regards stroke contrast which, on the face of it, looks limited. The impression is of a rather subdued script, with little stylistic distinction, far less panache. The expected hairstroking is detectable on <c> and <e> and on the ascender on <d> pointing towards the baseline. A long, but not excessive, parallel upstroke ornaments the <l> while the usual downstroke threading on <t> can just be detected. There is simple, contained sinuosity on the arms of <n> and <r> and on the closed left bow of the initial <m> on the date. The cedilla on *maço* (May) on l. 1 is still clearly visible. There may well have been another cedilla under the <c> of *Torcelo* (l. 3), but it is impossible to be certain of its presence given the extent of roughing on the stone at the foot of the letter. Very faint traces of black infilling can be detected in some letters. There are no ligatures and abbreviations are restricted to the superscript <o> over the <m> on *m(aistro)* 'master' (l. 2). Interpuncts are regularly used to separate words and, in one case, the surname syntagm *da Gaio* (l. 3). The epigraph is justified on the left, and the fourth line is considerably shorter than the other three.

LANGUAGE: *Ciroico* 'surgeon' (l. 3) was *ceroico* in Modern Venetian. Like Italian *cerusico* and the Middle English equivalent *chirurgeon* it is probably from *CIRUGICUM, a dissimilated derivative of late Latin CHIRURGICUM 'surgeon'. On the other hand, the standard Italian *chirurgo* is from CHĪRURGUM. All derive ultimately from Greek χειρουργός 'someone who works with their own hands'. *Eriedi* 'heirs' (l. 4), rather than *eredi*, looks superficially unusual. In the later part of the fourteenth century and in the first half of the fifteenth *(h)erede* 'heir' < HĒRĒDEM was — in spite of its stressed Ē rather than Ĕ (see CI 1) — influenced by the prevailing wave of diphthongising affecting mid-high vowels in Early Venetian to become *(h)eriede* (see CI 78). The craft-trade title *maistro* 'master', which also figures in CI 55, CI 76 and CI 78, is one of the two outcomes in the corpus from MĂGISTRUM. *Maistro* was used figuratively as an adjective in fifteenth- and sixteenth-century Venetian, as in *porta maistra* 'master door' and *strada maistra* 'main road'. The other outcome is *mistro* which appears in CI 70 from the carpenters' guild. On the Christian name *Iacomelo* (l. 2) see CI 44.

RECENT STUDIES: MOCELLIN (2016: 32–34). Transcribed in CONTON (1927: 85). First recorded, but not published, by Cicogna. First published in BATTAGLINI (1871: 111).

Corpus Inscription 57

Sia ✲ al nome ✲ de ✲ lonipote(n)te ✲ dio ✲ e dela biada ✲ ₁|
verzene ✲ maria ✲ e del precioxo ✲ misier ✲ san pie(r)o ✲ ₂|
martore [✲] fo fato ✲ qvesto [✲] lavorom°ccccx[x]xxiiii ✲ adi
p(ri)m[o ✲] mar | co ₄

[Sia al nome de l'onipotente Dio e dela biada Verzene Maria e del precioxo misier San Piero martore. Fo fato questo lavoro MCCCCXXXXIIII adì primo marco.]

TRANSLATION: Let it be in the name of Almighty God and of the Virgin Mary and of the precious St Peter Martyr. This work was done on the first of March 1444.

DATE: March 1444.

LOCATION: At present on the architrave of a door jamb on the outside of the church of S. Zanipolo (*sestiere* of Castello). The jamb surrounds a bricked-up door on the side of the meeting hall, attached to the basilica, of the former Santissimo Nome di Dio devotional confraternity. This one-storey oblong building, set just back from the Colleoni monument, is now the hall of the Conferenza di S. Tommaso d'Aquino. It is depicted in Canaletto's oil painting of *Campo S. Zanipolo* in the Royal Collection. However, this is neither the building nor the *scuola* where the inscription was once located. Jamb and inscription originally framed the front door of the nearby confraternity of S. Pietro Martire (Early Venetian, S. Piero Martore). This *scuola* was housed in the two-storey building, jutting out from the apse of the church, which used to delimit the *campo* from the Dominican monastery precincts. It too is visible in the Canaletto oil and on de' Barbari's cityscape, although it is unclear if it had two floors in 1500. This is the construction which also accomodated the Scuola di S. Vincenzo, the confraternity which fused with that of S. Piero Martore in 1565. It was demolished following the Napoleonic suppressions (D'Ambrosio 2012b), but our inscribed doorway was saved along with another jamb featuring reliefs of St Peter Martyr and St Vincent. Both were transferred to the outside of the former Santissimo Nome di Dio meeting house. The latter frames the entrance door of the building.

TYPE AND DESCRIPTION: Dedicatory and commemorative. The inscription celebrates the completion in 1444 of the first meeting house (*questo lavoro*, l. 3) of the confraternity of *san Piero martore* (ll. 2–3). It records its invocatory dedication to God, to the Blessed Virgin and to St Peter Martyr, the new Dominican saint whose cult the order was encouraging. The door jambs are 245 cm high. The Istrian stone architrave on which the inscription is carved is 182 × 17 cm while the inscription area itself is approximately 160 × 14 cm. Three-quarters of the way up both jambs low-relief sculptures of S. Peter Martyr can still be seen quite clearly. These are probably contemporaneous with the inscription. The thirteenth-century Veronese saint, who was a Dominican preacher, was ambushed and murdered in a wood according to legend. The scene was notably painted in an oil and tempera panel of *c.* 1507, the *Assassination of St Peter Martyr* by Giovanni Bellini (Early/Middle

Fig. 3.67. CI 57 in context. © A. S. Ferguson.

Fig. 3.68. CI 57 (detail). © A. S. Ferguson.

Venetian, Zuan(e) Belin), now in the National Gallery in London. On our Istrian stone doorposts the saint is depicted in the traditional way, with a hatchet lodged in his head, a knife stuck in his back, a book in one hand and a palm frond in the other. A number of holes have been deliberately pierced in the architrave at some point, two of which have almost obliterated sections of the date. Apart from this the inscription is in good condition, with grooving and detail still largely intact.

The earliest date when the Scuola di S. Pietro Martire is mentioned is 1433. According to its *mariegola* the brotherhood, which probably worshipped originally at an altar in S. Zanipolo, had already obtained permission from the Dominicans by 1443 to build an independent hall of its own on land beside the church ceded to them by the friars. In return the brothers committed themselves to animating at their own expense the processions in honour of St Dominic and St Thomas Aquinas (G. VIO 2004: 180). The confraternity joined forces with that of St Vincent Ferrer in 1565 before eventually becoming one with the *scuola* of St Catherine of Siena in 1618.

LETTERING: Gothic majuscules cut in V-section. An outstanding example of late Venetian Gothic script carving that achieves a delightful blend of strength with subtlety and legibility with decorativeness. The lettering, which is a generous 3.5 cm in height, is beautifully balanced, spaced and stroke-modulated, and the embellishments added by the mason to characters and interpuncts are both highly sophisticated and consistent. In finesse of ductus and execution, as well as in its layout, the epigraph is strikingly reminiscent of the epitaph (dated 1421) of the priest Dominico which was formerly in the monastery of SS. Agata e Cecilia in Padua and is now in storage at the Museo Eremitani in that city (BENUCCI 2015: 219–20).

The brief inscription incorporates three important script innovations not seen before in our corpus. It is the first example of an epigraph (if one discounts CI 48 where the initial <m> of the date is enlarged) beginning with a capital letter proper — the <s> on *Sia* (l. 1) — that is deliberately bigger than the majuscules which follow. In addition, it incorporates an example of letter-joining entirely different in kind from the ligatures we have previously witnessed and which are also present here. The thread looping under, and purposely linking, *e* and *dela* (l. 1) is formed by joining the hairstroke on the <e> with the threaded extension to the serifed ascender on <d>. We are in the presence here of a calligraphic awareness on the sculptor's (or commissioner's) part which strongly suggests familiarity with manuscript titling capitals. The only other examples in the corpus of similar letter joining are in CI 2 and CI 55, both painted epigraphs. The /z/ of *verzene* (l. 2) is the first example in the corpus of the minuscule form of this letter adjusted to a bilinear script. Previously it had only appeared in CI 49 in its capital form.

It is worth paying some attention to the detail of decoration on the characters. The fine wavy serifs on the heads and feet of perpendiculars stand out as new in the corpus. They are echoed by the consistent presence of slender decorative filament volutes. These appear on the terminals of the hairstrokes on <c>, <e> and <f>; on the threaded downstroke of the <d> ascender reaching well below the baseline; on the parallel upstroke of <l> at headline level; at the end of the long, sweeping left stem of <a>; on the curved tapering leg of <n> and <r> where, uniquely, the volute plunges below the baseline; on the outer limbs of <m>; on one of the cross strokes of <x>, again descending below the baseline; on the bottom end of the enlarged minuscule <z> of *verzene* (l. 2) which curves below the baseline, almost touching the <t> on the line below it; and on the flourish on the line-end final <a> of *biada* (l. 1). The capital <q> on *questo* (l. 3) is exquisite, with its right-side tail arched up and ending in a volute. This calligraphic elegance is repeated by the smartly executed ligatures on <an> and <ar>, by the keyhole abbreviation bars for <n> in *lonipote(n)te* (l. 1) and <r> on *Pie(r)o* (l. 2), and especially by the careful spiral interpuncts throughout, separating words or syntagms. The original layout plan had obviously been to justify the epigraph on both sides but it was spoiled by miscalculated *ordinatio*. In order to rectify things the mason saved space by cleverly co-opting the final <o> of *lavoro* (l. 3) as the billowing left side loop of the following <m> of the date. In spite of this, he was forced to spill on to the doorpost on the right side at the end of l. 3 and to leave the last two letters of *marco* (l. 4) hanging awkwardly at the close: a messiness that detracts from the overall effect of the beautiful script.

LANGUAGE: A short but linguistically interesting piece of mid-fifteenth century Venetian writing. *Lonipotente* 'the omnipotent' (l. 1) is carved as an amalgamated syntagm with no punctuation mark between article and noun as we find instead, and for the first time, in CI 61. *Precioxo* (l. 2) is the sole instance in the corpus of the word 'precious' in its original sense of 'beloved, held in high esteem, morally or spiritually valuable'. It was often applied in the Middle Ages to Christ, to His blood or to the saints. In Early Venetian the spelling with <c>, as here, alternated with the pronunciation orthography in <ç>. It may say something about the status of <ç> spellings at this point that they are avoided in the inscription, even on a common and expected case like *marco* 'March' (ll. 3–4), instead of the normal *março* as in CI 58. The up-and-coming written equivalent <z> for the voiced affricate appears in *verzene* 'Virgin' (l. 2), in place of the semi-learned *vergene* used until now in the corpus. Another *unicum* in our collection is the term *lavoro* 'work, piece of work, artefact' employed instead of the dominant *lavor(i)er*. Similarly, *martore* 'martyr' (l. 3) is found only here. From post-Classical Latin MARTYR 'witness, martyr', adapted from an equivalent Greek form, it shows the regular outcome of Latin Y treated as a Ŭ. The form *martore* was common in Early Venetian and Early Tuscan but very unusual among the continuers of MARTYR in the Romance languages generally. On the other hand, *biada* 'blessed' (l. 1) < BEĀTA 'fulfilled' shows the raising of pretonic /e/ to /i/ on this word that we have already noted several times (CI 9, CI 14, CI 30). *Piero* Peter (l. 2) is from ecclesiastical late Latin PETRUS, with the Venetian *muta cum liquida* reduction of -TR- > /r/. It also displays the diphthongisation that affected the thirteenth- and early fourteenth-century equivalent *Pero*. The full form *misier* (l. 2), rather than *miser*, confirms the now dominant diphthongised variant of the word, while *san* 'saint' suggests that *sen* was by now archaic, in writing at least.

RECENT STUDIES: FERGUSON (2015c: 81–82); MOCELLIN (2016: 35–38). It is transcribed in TOMASIN (2012b: 7 n. 11) and D'AMBROSIO (2012b). The inscription was first recorded, but not published, by Cicogna.

Corpus Inscription 58

M°CCCC°XLIIII ⸱ DI ⸱ P(RIMO) ⸱ 1 |
MARÇO [⸱ F]O ⸱ PREN |
CIPIADA ⸱ QVESTA ⸱ 3 |
CASA 4

[Mccccxliiii, dì primo março, fo prencipiada questa casa.]

TRANSLATION: In 1444, on the first of March, this house was begun.

DATE: March 1444.

LOCATION: Carved on the pedestal of a column. The column, standing against a brick wall, is the first one supporting the elegant little portico in the open courtyard of the Archivio di Stato at the Frari (*sestiere* of S. Polo) that leads to the cloister of the Trinity.

To judge by the wording of the inscription and by its accompanying symbol, the inscribed stone was commissioned for the confraternity of the Twelve Apostles and may originally have been intended for the outside of a house in the parish of the Santi Apostoli in the *sestiere* of Cannaregio — at the confluence of what is now the Strada Nova and the direct artery from the Rialto — where the prosperous *Scuola de(l)i Dodexe Apostoli* had its meeting house and where it owned properties. On this *scuola piccola* and another of its inscriptions see CI 19. How long, if ever, the present inscription fulfilled its original purpose is an open question. The so-called *chiostro dei Fiorentini* in the Frari, where it is at present located, is undoubtedly a Quattrocento structure. The confraternity of the Florentines resident in Venice had the cloister built in the first space ceded to it by the Franciscans when it moved to the Frari from S. Zanipolo after 1435 (CECCHINI 2015: 130–31). Rather than being *spolia* it is more likely that the recycled stone, perhaps judged to be faulty in some way, was sold by the Dodexe Apostoli or by its stonemason to the Florentines who do not seem to have minded that the writing on the column pedestal remained visible on their new structure.

The Scuola dei Fiorentini, whose members were drawn from the Florentine artisans, merchants and bankers living in Venice, was dedicated to St John the Baptist. It had its altar in the Frari from the mid-fifteenth century and eventually built premises in the adjacent *campo*. Its Renaissance colonnade in the Archivio courtyard, with its tiled wooden roof and recessed timber supports known as *barbacani* (see CI 101, CI 102), is of the type depicted by Carpaccio on the Riva del Vin at the Rialto in his *Miracle of the Relic of the Holy Cross* canvas (*c.* 1494) painted originally for the Scuola Grande di S. Giovanni Evangelista and now in the Accademia. On the Scuola dei Fiorentini see G. VIO (2004: 638–39).

TYPE AND DESCRIPTION: Declarative and commemorative. The message and the confraternity symbol above it simultaneously record the start of building works on a property (*questa casa*, ll. 3–4) and its ownership by the devotional confraternity

Fig. 3.69. CI 58 (detail). © A. S. Ferguson.

of the Twelve Apostles. The epigraph is cut at the base of the Istrian stone pedestal that supports a slender marble column. Above the inscription, on the same block face, is carved in low relief the symbol of the confraternity: the enlarged initials AP (= *Apostoli*) within a roundel, with the letters centrally ligatured by a tall Latin cross which rises out of the circle. The total surface area of the block face is 37 × 35 cm. The area of writing on it is roughly 31 × 16 cm, while the diameter of the carved roundel above is *c*. 16 cm. The script itself is largely undamaged except for a patch in the middle which obscures the <f> in *fo* 'was' (l. 2). Otherwise it seems to have benefited from its relatively sheltered location. The principal problem at present is the sedimentation at the foot of the column, with the inscribed base slowly sinking into the softish ground in the entrance area of the Archivio. The writing, which until a few years ago could be seen in its entirety if one scraped away the surrounding dirt, is now obscured except for the first two lines. When I visited the inscription to take photographs in July 2017 and 2018 I had to remove a good deal of soil even to view those lines adequately.

LETTERING: Gothic majuscules cut in V-section. This is a brief but interesting example of late Gothic carving, with vigorously uncialesque lettering (averaging 2.5 cm in height), good contrastive stroking and a balanced, rather open, module. It embodies a number of distinctive features found in some later Gothic inscriptions in the city. Most notable are the very contrastive curved limbs on <m> which are almost detached from the central stem; the exaggeratedly elongated curved upstroke on <l> reaching slightly above the headline; and the long undulating ascender on the uncial <d>, with splay serif from which a bottom stroke descends in a curve to the baseline. Also typical of late-phase Venetian Gothic is the method of closing the <c> and <e> with hairstrokes whose protruding extremities, curved in earlier epigraphs, have morphed into spikes. Decorative emphasis is also present on the excessively long serifs on <s> and on the in-and-out curved and tapered leg of <r>. There are no ligatures on the epigraph and the only abbreviation is the short suspension bar over the <p> of *p(rimo)* on l. 1.

LANGUAGE: The perfect agreement between past participle and noun in the passive construction *fo prencipiada questa casa* 'this house was begun' (ll. 2–4) is usually but not exclusively the rule in the corpus, as can be seen in the similar construction *fu comprado questa scolla* 'this *scuola* was bought' in CI 60. *Prencipiada* 'initiated, commenced' is itself the regular Venetian outcome from the late Latin learned verb PRĬNCIPIARE (compare Italian *principiare*). The more Latinising variant *principiada* is found in CI 70. The ellipsis *di* (= *dì*) for *adi* (= *adì*) 'on the (day)' is uncommon. The more 'modern' spelling *casa* 'house' (l. 4) here replaces the traditional *caxa* with its <x> for the voiced sibilant /z/. Unlike on CI 57 the cedilla is present on <c> for the unvoiced affricate on *março* March (l. 2).

RECENT STUDIES: MOCELLIN (2016: 16–18). The inscription was not recorded by Cicogna.

Corpus Inscription 59

CHRISTOFOL · [D]A FERARA I(N)TAIA · ZU(H)ANE E ₁|
ANTONIO DE MURAN P(E)NSE · 1444 ·

[Christofol da Ferara intaià. Zuhane e Antonio de Muran pense. 1444.]

TRANSLATION: Christopher from Ferrara carved (it). John and Anthony of Murano painted (it). 1444.

DATE: 1444.

LOCATION: The painting bearing the inscription is at present displayed in the chapel of the Holy Nail (cappella del Santo Chiodo) in the church of S. Pantalon (*sestiere* of Dorsoduro). It was commissioned for the chapel of the Ognissanti in the same church (SALSI 1837: 64) where it was seen by SANSOVINO (1581: 248). It was removed from its *ab origine* location shortly before the restoration of the church in 1668–86 during which the Ognissanti chapel was destroyed.

TYPE AND DESCRIPTION: Declaration of artistic authorship with date of execution. The inscription is painted in black along the unfurled grey illusionistic banderole (24 × 5 cm) at the foot of the tempera panel of the *Coronation of the Virgin*. The huge painting, measuring 220 × 170 cm, is by Giovanni d'Alemagna (Early Venetian, Zu(h)ane de Muran or Zohane Alaman) and his younger brother-in-law Antonio Vivarini (Early Venetian, Antonio Vivarin). The original frame of the painting, now lost, was carved by the ebonist C(h)ristofol da Ferara (Italian, Cristoforo da Ferrara).

The second part of our vernacular inscription mirrors its Latin equivalent carved on wood by Ludovico da Forlì — in *littera textualis* script like ours — at the bottom of the devotional image (*ancona*) of the *Redeemer* painted by Zuane and Antonio the previous year in the chapel of St Tarasius in the church of S. Zaccaria. It reads: *Iohanes et Antuonius d(e) Muranio pi(n)xeru(n)t*. This wording is repeated almost verbatim in the same chapel under the polyptych of St Sabina: *Iohanes et Antonius de Muranio pinxerunt*. Cristoforo da Ferrara's name appears as *Cristoph*, again preceding those of Antonio and Zuane, in another vernacular authorship epigraph: it is inscribed and gilded against a dark ground on the frame at the foot of the central panel (*Virgin and Child*) of the polyptych which they collaborated on for the Lion chapel in the church of S. Francesco Grande in Padua. The panel is now in the National Gallery in Prague. Its inscription reads: MCCCCXLVII *Cristoph d(e) Ferara intaia Antonio d(e) M(u)ra(n) e Zoha(ne) Alaman p(ense)*.

Antonio Vivarini (*c*. 1415-*c*. 1480) and Giovanni d'Alemagna (documented *c*. 1440–1450 and whose name indicates German ancestry), were in mid-century key members of the Vivarini workshop which dominated the market for altarpieces in Quattrocento Venice. Originating in, and working out of, Murano — as the consistent use of the island name in their signatures shows — they also opened a workshop in Venice in the 1440s. Zuane and Antonio are recorded as collaborating on a dozen or so major commissions in Venice and Padua in this period but their

FIG. 3.70. CI 59. © A. S. Ferguson.

works were also in demand elsewhere in Italy and in Venice's overseas empire. After the death of Zuane, Antonio would be joined by his younger brother Bartolomio (Italian, Bartolomeo).

The S. Pantalon *Coronation* by Zuane and Antonio, painted on a poplar panel, is an extraordinary composition packed with figures and rich in detail and religious iconography. It was executed in an eclectic style dominated by the international Gothic aesthetic. The scene is structured by a tall, elaborately decorated, multi-tiered marble throne. At the top stands the majestic bearded figure of God the Father whose arms enfold the sitting Jesus and His mother, with the hovering dove of the Holy Ghost between them. Jesus is in the act of crowning the sweetly smiling Virgin. Beneath them a group of naked Innocents carries the instruments of Christ's passion. Most remarkable of all are the soaring tiers of stalls rising heavenward as if in a towering church apse, each row packed with male and female saints, the whole structure topped by an angelic host in steep relief. At the foot of the throne stands a richly clad group of bearded and formidably dignified fathers of the church and Evangelists. The restoration of the altarpiece in 1996 revealed the intense colouring of the original, dominated by red and dark blue tones and by gleaming gold pastiglia work on crowns, mitres and haloes. The artefact was commissioned and paid for by the wealthy parish priest of the church, Francesco Gritti (*plebanus* 1427–58), who also had the new altar in the Ognissanti chapel built to house a number of saints' relics. Gritti, who became Bishop of Corfù but retained the living of S. Pantalon, is buried in the church.

LETTERING: Gothic minuscules painted in black. The lettering, *c.* 1.2 cm high on average, is in the rounded (*rotunda*) form of the *littera textualis*, the standard Gothic minuscule book hand of the period in Venice where it was variously known in the vernacular as *li(t)era/le(t)era formada* or *li(t)era/le(t)era de forma* — in other words, formal or well-formed letter. The unadorned black letters stand out strongly against the lighter ground of the illusionistic banderole, their size adapted to follow the receding folds of what is meant to be an unfurled roll of parchment. The paint effectively mimics the characteristics of 'inked' script, with the heavy minims giving a compressed feel to the writing, although much less so than on the more tightly vertical and angular French, and generally northern European, *textura* scripts. The typically lighter contrastive lines and flicks at top and bottom of letters such as <a> and <e> have largely been worn away on the *Coronation* epigraph but can just be detected on *Zuhane* (l. 1) and *Antonio* (l. 2). One of the characteristics of this writing style was the requirement that if two adjacent letters had facing bows, these had to be fused: a feature best appreciated on the conjoined *de* (l. 2). The quadrilinear nature of the minuscule is apparent on the <p> with tail below the baseline and, especially, on the <f> of *Christofol* (l. 1) — the ebonist's Christian name abbreviated on the first syllable by means of the Chi-Rho — which more or less spans the notional four-line stave. Interestingly, the lowercase <z> on Zuane's name on l. 1 has been squeezed between two lines, as in CI 57 which was inscribed on stone. A number of abbreviations are used. A short line over the <i> of *intaia* (l. 1) indicates the missing <n>, and another formerly visible over the <a> in *Zuane* suggests a Latinising <h>, as on the spelling used in full by the artist on the Prague polyptych. A stroke through the <p> linking to the <n> of *pense* (l. 2) confirms that the following <e> has been abbreviated. Wear and tear and, possibly, touching up associated with a previous early nineteenth-century restoration have taken their toll. The <d> on *da* (l. 1) has been obliterated while the initial section of *Muran* (l. 2) is badly faded. Mid-high interpuncts can still be detected sporadically. This is only the second epigraph in the corpus to express the date in Arabic numerals. However, the three 4s in the 1444 date (l. 2) are not in our normalised straight-line Western form but in the shape of a looped Arabic-derived glyph.

This blackletter *textualis* — familiar to all who were literate as the script of the *mariegola* statute books of confraternities and guilds in the city — had made one of its earliest painted appearances in Venice in the elegant explanatory and signatory gold lettering at the foot of the *Madonna and Child with the Patron Belgarçone* (1394) panel, by Nicolò di Pietro, now in the Accademia. Many long descriptive captions employing the script, painted again by Zuane and Antonio this time under the images of saints, can be read on the *Redeemer* polyptych (1443) in S. Zaccaria. One of its most flamboyant and influential exemplars in the city was the series of biblical texts on the three prominent banderoles of the *Justice* triptych of 1421 painted by Iacobello del Fiore for the office of the property court in the Doge's Palace, and also now at the Accademia. A late but highly prestigious consecration for this hand within the painted inscriptional context was the canvas of the *Lion of St Mark with Saints* by Donato Bragadin in the Palazzo Ducale, where it appears on two banderoles held by saints. The spectator is reminded of its origins by the legible text in the book held by the lion's paw.

LANGUAGE: *Intaia* (in other words, *intaià*) '(he) engraved', l. 1, shows the regular 3rd singular past historic ending of the 1st conjugation in Early Venetian. It would shift in Middle Venetian from -*à* to -*ò*, in line with Tuscan/Italian (see CI 107). *Pense* (or *inpense*) '(they) painted', l. 2, is the 3rd singular and 3rd plural past historic of Early Venetian *pençer* or *penzer* 'to paint'. Some art historians have been puzzled that the plural subjects *Zuhane* (l. 1) and *Antonio* (l. 2) could take a singular ending, but of course 3rd singular and plural verb endings are identical in Venetian across all tenses. *Ferara* (Ferrara) with one <r> is normal in Venetian, as it is in the Gallo-Italian dialects of northern Italy. *C(h)ristofol* (l. 1) or C(h)ristofolo, with an <l>, were common forms of Christopher in Venice and northern Italy in this period (see CI 83, l. 8 and CI 96).

RECENT STUDIES: DE MARCHI (2003: 71–100); MERKEL (1989: 72–73).

Corpus Inscription 60

1446 ADI 14 (DECEM)B(RI)° ₁ | FV COMPRADO ₂ |
QVESTA SCOLLA ₃ | DEL ARTE ₄ | DI CALEGERI ▲

[1446, adì 14 decembrio, fu comprado questa scolla del arte di calegeri.]

TRANSLATION: 1446, on the 14th of December, this *scuola* of the shoemakers' guild was bought.

DATE: December 1446.

LOCATION: Carved, in situ, on the left-side pilaster of the former meeting house of the shoemakers' confraternity-guild in Campo S. Tomà (*sestiere* of S. Polo), at the corner where the *campo* leads into the narrow Calle del Mandoler.

TYPE AND DESCRIPTION: Commemorative. The inscription proclaims the ownership and presence — with the date of purchase — of the shoemakers' meeting house. The epigraph is cut on to the Istrian stone pilaster (192 cm high) at a height of between 107 cm and 131 cm above pavement level. The inscribed writing occupies an unframed rectangular space of *c.* 36 × *c.* 23 cm. The inscription is still fully legible with care, although some letters are badly worn. The most severe letter deterioration has understandably occurred down the left hand side of the inscription where the writing is almost flush with the stone edge. For centuries passers-by and objects, carried or pulled, have rubbed or bumped against the side of the building at the corner of the cramped thoroughfare leading to the Frari and S. Rocco and, in the modern period, to Piazzale Roma and the railway station.

LETTERING: Roman square capitals, shakily realised. This modest inscription, cut in V-section, is the first surviving vernacular inscription in Venice to revive monumental capitals. As such it marks a watershed in the city's fifteenth-century epigraphy. Its groundbreaking selection of revival Roman monumental script is a choice that must have been down to the alderman and board of the guild-cum-confraternity who were, one assumes, alive to the brand new elite lettering fashion and its prestige. The precise model here was undoubtedly imperial inscriptional lettering of the type found on the base of Trajan's column in Rome and destined to become canonical: balanced, well-spaced quadrate characters, serifed throughout, with subtle nuances of thick and thin in the cut. As it is, the mason, who must have been given a written text in minuscule to work with, appears to be finding his way with a style unfamiliar to him. His letter- and word-spacing and, in general, his layout are hesitant. The module of the letters, which average 2.5 cm in height, is more or less 'square' (see the nicely realised <d> on ll. 1, 2, 4), but his attempt to calibrate the script is imperfect, with occasional variation between examples of the same letter. This can be seen on the <o> and especially <a>, with the <a> of *scolla* (l. 3) noticeably bigger than that of *questa* on the same line. There are also unbalanced outcomes, as in the contrasting length of the strokes in the X on l. 1 and the slightly off-centre cross stroke on the <a> of *comprado* (l. 2). The unorthodox use of the Roman numeral X to abbreviate <decem> in *decembrio* (December) on

Fig. 3.71. CI 60. © A. S. Ferguson.

l. 1 is a unique space-saving expedient in the corpus but was not uncommon as shorthand in account books. It is followed here, rather awkwardly, by a superscript <o> that looks like an afterthought. In spite of wear and tear and the overall fading that affects the inscription and makes it hard to judge the original groove depth, close inspection confirms that the mason has striven for modest stroke contrast. Wedge serifing too is well developed on all perpendiculars, and strong contrasting bracket serifs are present on the topstroke of <t>. The text is justified on the left and the only punctuation mark is the full stop in the form of a mid-high triangular mark at the end. This is the first inscription in stone in the corpus to carry the date in Arabic numerals, following the two painted examples which precede it closely (CI 55, CI 59).

The shoemakers' inscription appears to be only the second example of monumental epigraphic lettering in stone of this type in Venice. The earliest that I have come across, from 1432, is on the Istrian stone plaque, surmounted by a scaled-down fortified tower in high relief, on the wall of house no. 587 on Fondamenta Bragadin (*sestiere* of Dorsoduro) at the site of the former Ospizio delle Pizzocchere di S. Agnese: *Iesus // Mulieribvs / piae legata / anno / MCCCCXXXII*. On that epigraph, by contrast, the script is fully regular in its geometry and features impeccable spacing, layout and contrastive stroking.

LANGUAGE: On *calegeri* 'shoemakers, cobblers' (l. 5), with its regular Early Venetian velar <g> spelling, see CI 23, CI 42. *Comprado* 'bought' (l. 2) shows the dominant written Early Venetian masculine singular past participle in *-ado* from -ātum (Modern/Contemporary Venetian, *comprà*). *Fu comprado questa scolla* 'this *scuola* was bought' (ll. 2–3) is one of the minority cases in the corpus of lack of agreement in the passive between past participle and noun. One notices that for the 3rd singular past historic of 'to be' *fu* — coinciding with the equivalent Tuscan outcome — is employed rather than the overwhelmingly more frequent *fo*. I have tentatively recomposed *decembrio* (December), l. 1, with an <m> on the basis of *comprado* being used rather than *conprado* and the hint of awareness on the part of the *scriptor* of Tuscan outcomes, exemplified by the presence of *fu* and perhaps by a hypercorrect doubling of the <l> in *scolla* (l. 3). The geminated <ll>, though, may just possibly be the result of the the sculptor following the *scriptor*'s minuscule hand where /l/ was frequently doubled for reasons of clarity (see CI 30). For the ending in *-brio* of the months from September to December in Early Venetian see CI 79. On the contracted Early Venetian partitive *di* 'of the' (= *dei* or *deli*), present in the corpus from the end of the fourteenth century onwards, see CI 38, CI 41, CI 48. The contiguous presence of the terms *arte* (l. 4) and *scolla* (l. 3) is interesting and unique in the corpus. It lays bare the composite nature of the Venetian craft guild-cum-*scuola piccola* which was simultaneously a trade union and a spiritual brotherhood. In addition, the designation *sc(u)ola* itself hovered between its senses of devotional congregation and of the actual building, as here, where the confraternity-guild was housed and gathered. On the shoemakers' meeting house at S. Tomà and its other vernacular inscriptions, see CI 75.

RECENT STUDIES: Ferguson (2015c: 83); Mocellin (2016: 39–41). First recorded, but not published, by Cicogna.

Corpus Inscription 61

CHOGNOSIE L * HOMO

[Chognosié l'homo.]

TRANSLATION: Know the man.

DATE: Undated. Lettering, language and style suggest the mid-fifteenth century.

LOCATION: On the façade of the Ca' Da Lezze palace on the Rio Terà Lista de Spagna thoroughfare in the parish of S. Geremia (*sestiere* of Cannaregio no. 132). The coat of arms is embedded in the middle of the palace façade on the second floor and appears to be in situ, although there is no evidence available to confirm this.

TYPE AND DESCRIPTION: Motto on a coat of arms sculpted in Istrian stone. The words are carved on a stone banderole held by a raised fist atop a helmet, itself over a striped shield with lion rampant. The large, impressive crenellated coat of arms (*c*. 100 × *c*. 100 cm) is in the shape of a square with ogival niches protruding on all four sides. The inscribed banderole curls around inside the top niche, its folds falling back on to the central ground. The decoration of the escutcheon is completed by swashed foliage radiating from the central trophy area into the lateral and bottom niches. Although the artefact is probably in situ it appears to feature an exuberant variant of the Pisani, rather than Da Lezze, coats of arms. The great Pisani clan had properties in this neighbourhood of Cannaregio, so the palace may originally have been theirs. Our Delphic maxim is not attested on any other surviving coat of arms in Venice.

LETTERING: Gothic minuscule carved in V-section. This highly-stylised Gothic minuscule display script — a luxury derivative of the *littera textualis* book hand that is sometimes categorised as *fere textura* — makes its second and final appearance in the corpus after its occurrence in painted form on a banderole in CI 55. Unlike CI 55, though, its origins can be located more clearly in *textualis quadratus*. It is undoubtedly northern European in its compressed, angular and decorative look and, as such, was appropriate for use as a Gothic show script on the scrolls and captions of fifteenth-century tapestries and stained glass. An essentially aristocratic alphabet it was also ideally suited to, and therefore much employed for, mottoes on escutcheons. It is most familiar from the compressed, beautifully flourished incised tomb inscriptions on brass in English churches.

Angularity is a hallmark of our scroll motto, with the <c> on *chognosie* employing four strokes, the <e> five, the <n> seven, the <s> eight and the <g> a remarkable nine. Stylistic unity is achieved, paradoxically, by the staccato, broken feel of the letters, with curves and smooth joins studiously avoided. This is very obvious on the <m> of *homo* where the three jaggedly serifed minims stand side by side without touching. Compression is also a key feature, most apparent on the four examples of <o> which are strongly lozenge shaped. The whole script tends to a kind of self-conscious aesthetic abstraction typical of *fere textura*, to the extent that some realisations such the <i>, <e> and <g> might have been hard to recognise

Fig. 3.72. CI 61. © A. S. Ferguson.

in isolation. Although it is derived from Gothic minuscule, our script strives, even more than CI 55 did, to be bilinear. This is clear from the shortening of the perpendicular on the first <h> and the kinking back to the headline of the stem on the second <h>. A modified capital <g> form (as on CI 55) has been employed to avoid a minuscule <g> whose tail would have dipped below the baseline. The script is cut deeply and cleanly, producing stong contrasts of light and shade, and averages a generous 4 cm in height. It is in surprisingly good shape, with only superficial abrasion affecting the middle letters of *chognosie*.

It may not be a coincidence that the only other example in stone of a *fere textura* vernacular inscription in Venice is the Lusignan motto in Old French on the banderole of a coat of arms from the mid-1360s. It is on the scroll, wound across an upright sword on an Istrian stone shield, on the façade over the *piano nobile* balcony of Ca' Loredan. The palace, formerly Ca' Corner-Piscopia, stands on the Riva del Carbon (*sestiere* of S. Marco no. 4137) just south of the Rialto bridge. The motto is cut in raised *textualis quadrata* sculpted in highly stylised, densely packed and steeply horizontal staves. It reads: *Pour leaute maintenir* ('To safeguard loyalty'). The shield with its sword emblem and motto represents the Lusignan order of chivalry, the Order of the Sword. To its left on the building is another shield with the Lusignan colours. Together they commemorate the seven-month stay in the Corner palace in 1365 of Pierre I de Lusignan, King of Cyprus, returning from his fundraising tour for a new crusade in the Holy Land.

LANGUAGE: *Chognosie* (in other words, *chognosié*) is the 2nd person plural imperative of Early Venetian *c(h)ognoser* 'to know' < COGNOSCERE. The form of the verb with <gn> survived intact from Early to Modern Venetian (compare Tuscan/Italian *conoscere*). This is the only example in the corpus of a verb in the plural imperative mode. *Homo* 'man' has the Latinising initial <h> (see CI 4). The triskelion interpunct used as an apostrophe between the elided definite article and *homo* betrays the textual origin of the motto which the sculptor has endeavoured to replicate.

RECENT STUDIES: RIZZI (1987: 239).

Corpus Inscriptions 62–66
[Fra Mauro's *mappa mundi*]

CI 62 [★2240]

Questa nobilissima cita dita chansay e i(n) uno lago ₁| come ueniexia e uolta mia 100 et e molto apopula|ta . et ha borgi gra(n)dissimi e 12 porte principal e ₃| lu[n]ta(n) da quele p(er) 8 mia sono citade maçor de ueni|exia . et ha 12000 ponti e 14000 stue . et i(n) meço de ₅| questa e uno lago che uolta 30 mia . nel qual so|no palaçi grandissimi . doue queli de li fano ₇| le suo feste . (et) e i(n) questa tal casa . che ha 12 fa|meie . e pur sono co(n)putade p(er) uno fuogo . e tu|ti q(ues)ti fuogi sono 90 tuni . e uno tuno fa ₁₀| 10000 fuogi . che seria 900000 fuogi . e q(ui) ₁₁| e studio de ogni scientia . e gra(n) magnifi|ce(n)tie . et ordine . et copia de ogni mesti|er (et) altre cosse le q(ua)l q(ui) no(n) dico ₁₄

[Questa nobilissima città, dita Chansay, è in uno lago come Veniexia, e volta mia 100 et è molto apopulata et ha borgi grandissimi e 12 porte principal. E luntan da quele per 8 mia sono citade maçor de Veniexia, et ha 12.000 ponti e 14.000 stue. Et in meço de questa è uno lago che volta 30 mia, nel qual sono palaçi grandissimi dove queli de lì fano le suò feste. Et in questa tal casa che ha 12 fameie e pur sono conputade per uno fuogo. E tuti questi fuogi sono 90 tuni, e uno tuno fa 10.000 fuogi: che seria 900.000 fuogi. E qui è studio de ogni scientia, e gran magnificentie et ordine, et copia de ogni mestier, et altre cosse le qual qui non dico.]

CI 63 [★2314], [★2299]

Chathaio || Questo excelle(n)tissimo e ₁| pote(n)tissimo i(n)perador el qual ₂| ha . lx^A . re de corona soto el suo ₃| dominio qua(n)do el ua a spaso ₄| el senta i(n) un caro doro e dauo|lio ornado de çoie el priesio de|le qual e i(n)extimabile . e questo ₇| caro uie(n) menado da uno elefan|te bia(n)cho . e ha IIII° . re di piu nobili ₉| del suo regno uno per canton ₁₀| che regeno questo caro . e . l^A . al|tri li uano auanti . con assai ₁₂| numero de homeni darme dauanti e dadriedo e qui sono tuti i piaceri çentileçe e costu|mi del mo(n)do · ₁₄

[Cathaio. Questo excellentissimo e potentissimo inperador, el qual ha lx re de corona soto el suo dominio, quando el va a spaso el senta in un caro d'oro e d'avolio ornado de çoie, el priesio dele qual è inextimabile. E questo caro vien menado da uno elefante biancho. E ha IIII re di più nobili del suo regno, uno per canton, che regeno questo caro. E l altri li vano avanti, con assai numero de homeni d'arme davanti e dadriedo. E qui sono tuti i piaceri, çentileçe e costumi del mondo.]

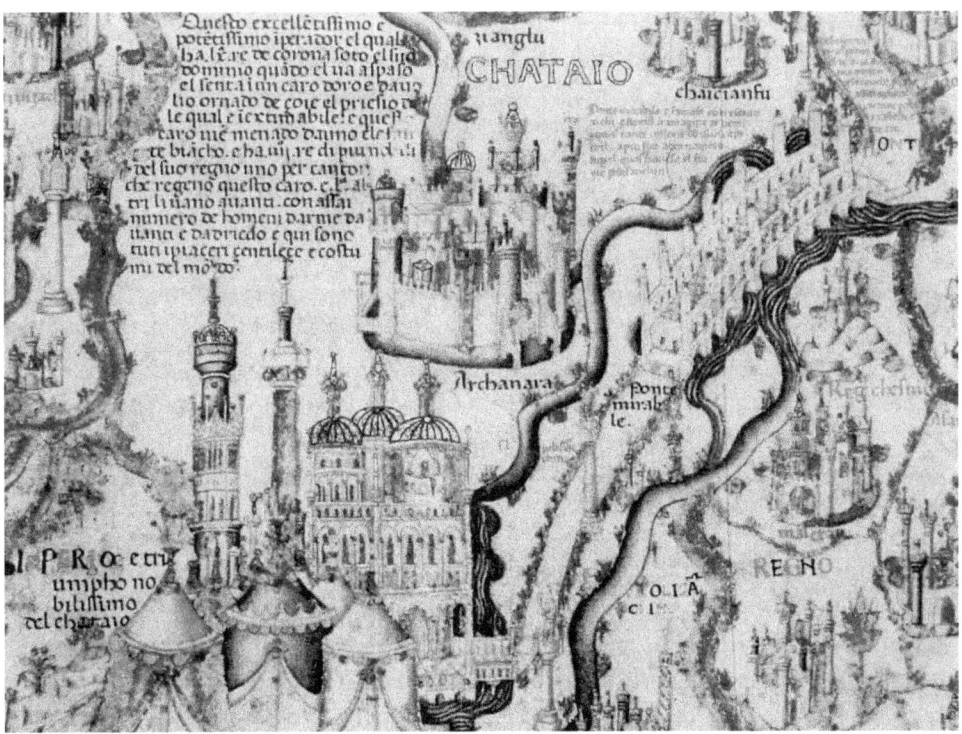

Fig. 3.73. CI 62, CI 64, CI 65. © A. S. Ferguson.

CI 64 [★2315]

Ponte mirabile e famoso con tresento $_1$ | archi e siemil[i]a imagine de lioni $_2$ | i qual <reze> tante collone co(n) i suo capi | telli a piu suo adornamento $_4$ | su p(er) el qual <se> traue(r)sa el fiu | me polisanchin

[Ponte mirabile e famoso con tresento archi e siemilia imagine de lioni — i qual reze tante collone con i suò capitelli a più suo adornamento — su per el qual se traversa el fiume Polisanchin.]

CI 65 [★2330]

imperio e tri | umpho no | bilissimo $_3$ | del chataio $_4$

[Imperio e triumpho nobilissimo del Cathaio.]

CI 66 [★2734], [★2729]

sepvltvra imperial | | Questa pretiosa e mirabile sepultu | ra che e posta sul nobel monte dito $_2$ | alchai e deputada solo a hi impera | dori del chataio e a lalta sua gene | ration $_5$

[Sepultura imperial. Questa pretiosa e mirabile sepultura, che è posta sul nobel monte dito Alchai, è deputada solo a hi imperadori del Chataio e a l'alta sua generation.]

TRANSLATIONS: CI 62: This most noble city called Chansay is in a lagoon like Venice. And it is 100 miles all round and heavily populated, and has great suburbs and 12 main gates. And 8 miles distant from them are cities bigger than Venice. And it has 12,000 bridges and 14,000 hot baths. And in the middle of it is a lake 30 miles round on which there are great palaces where the people there have their parties. And there is a house there with 12 families and yet it is counted as one household. And all these households come to 90 *toman* and one *toman* comes to 10,000 households, which would amount to 900,000 households. And here the study of every branch of knowledge is found, and there is great luxury and order and abundance of every trade, and many other things which I do not mention here.

CI 63: Cathay. This most excellent and powerful emperor, who has 60 crowned heads under his dominion, when he goes out and about sits in a carriage of gold and ivory decorated with gemstones of inestimable price. And this carriage is pulled by a white elephant. And he has 4 of the most noble kings of his kingdom, one per corner, who escort this carriage and 50 others go on ahead of him, with a very great number of men-at-arms at front and rear. And here are all the pleasures, delights and manners in the world.

CI 64: Marvellous and famous bridge with three hundred arches and six thousand images of lions — which support as many columns with their capitals for its adornment — over which one crosses the river Polisanchin.

CI 65: Most noble empire and splendour of Cathay.

CI 66: Imperial burial site. This precious and marvellous mausoleum, which is sited on the noble mountain called Alchai, is reserved only for the emperors of Cathay and their high lineage.

DATE: *c.* 1448-*c.* 1460. On the dating of Fra Mauro's *mappa mundi* see FALCHETTA (2006: 143–46); FALCHETTA (2013: 16–29). On the back of the wooden frame of the map is the following written inscription in a hybrid minuscule: MCCCCLX adi XXVI / avosto. Fo chonplido / questo lauor ('1460, on the 26th of August. This work was completed').

LOCATION: On the southwestern corner of Fra Mauro's *mappa mundi* in the Marciana library. The great map of the world was on display until May 1811 in its original location: the Camaldolese monastery of S. Michele di Murano (Early Venetian, S. Michiel de Muran), not on Murano itself but on the small lagoon island of S. Michele — now the Venetian cemetery site — between Murano and Venice. It was first in the church on the island, then after work on the church in the 1470s it was transferred to a nearby room known as the *mappamondo* room. From 1655 it was shown in the library area of the monastery. After the Napoleonic abolition of religious orders in the nineteenth century, the 600-year settlement of the Camaldolese order on S. Michele was brought to an end on 25 April 1810, and the large library of the monastery, full of *incunabulae*, precious editions and artefacts, was dispersed to many institutions. Some fortunately ended up in the Correr and Marciana libraries, while Fra Mauro's priceless *mappa mundi* eventually went to the

Biblioteca Nazionale Marciana in St Mark's Square where it is now prominently displayed.

This remarkable object is a vivid graphic summum of geographical knowledge at the end of the Middle Ages. It combines traditional Ptolomaic cosmography with the narratives of medieval voyagers, notably Marco Polo, Odorico da Pordenone and Nicolò de' Conti and, most interestingly, accounts communicated to Fra Mauro by travellers and merchants with first-hand experience of Africa, Asia Minor, Russia and central and eastern Asia. Above all, the whole enterprise and its declared limits and sources are constantly laid bare in the inscriptions by Fra Mauro's stream of reasonable, although occasionally polemical, first-person commentary. He has no truck with alleged fabulous monsters in Africa, treats Ptolemy critically, and is receptive to the practical experience of navigators and merchants: *i(n)vestigando p(er) molti a(n)nni / e pratica(n)do p(er)sone degne de fede le qual hano ueduto ad ochio q(ue)lo che / qui suso fedelme(n)te demostro* [★2834] ('researching for many years and frequenting trustworthy people who have seen with their own eyes what I lay out faithfully above').

Fra Mauro (Early Venetian, Frar Mauro or Frar Moro) appears to have spent most of his life in Venice and on S. Michele, possibly as a *conversus* or *commissus* in the monastery. He worked in the famous manuscript workshop of the Camaldolese within the monastery where there were records of his purchases of pigments and gold for illlustrations and where he was the centre of a notable and well-known map-making enterprise which was patronised, at one time or another, by Venice itself and by the king of Portugal. Fra Mauro explicitly dedicated the *mappa mundi* (he calls it *cosmographia over ma/pamu(n)di*) to Venice itself: *Qvesta opera fata a conte(m)platio(n) de qvesta illustrissima Signoria* ('This work made for the scrutiny of this most illustrious Signoria' ★2834). Fra Mauro's status even in his own day is attested by a fifteenth-century medal with his effigy, struck in his honour by the monastery and describing him as a peerless cartographer (ZURLA 1806: 80). The full legend, inscribed in Roman capitals on the medal which was once kept on S. Michele and is now in the Museo Correr numismatics collection, reads: *Frater Mavrvs S Michaelis mvranensis de Venetiis ordinis camaldvlensis chosmographvs incomparabilis*. On Fra Mauro and all aspects of the atlas see ZURLA (1806); GASPARRINI LEPORACE (1956); FALCHETTA (2006); CATTANEO (2011); FALCHETTA (2013); BOELHOWER (2018).

TYPE AND DESCRIPTION: Explanatory and descriptive captions on a planisphere map of the known world. The map is drawn, painted and inscribed on parchment stretched out on a square wooden support with a gilded frame (223 × 223 cm). Within this is a second, circular, gilded frame containing the slightly elliptical map proper, laid out with south at the top. The map has a diameter of 195 × 193 cm. The cosmographical notes, as well as a painted representation of the earthly Paradise, are contained in the corners, in the space between the two frames, while the actual captions, long or short, are spread densely across the surface of the map itself. Even on a superficial viewing the planisphere is breathtakingly impressive. Against a plain ground picked out in a range of hues the map teems with details of cities, monuments, bridges, mountains, rivers and ships. The dominant colours are dark blue for the seas and inland waters, with white waving; green for natural features on land; and blue, red and gold for the captions. These legends, freestanding or within cartouches over the sea and ocean sections, are everywhere, drawing the eye in and expanding the viewers' understanding of what has piqued their curiosity. The strong bright colours of the inscriptions and their careful layout and spacing ensure ease of consultation.

Widely known and admired in fifteenth- and sixteenth-century Venice and beyond, this map by the foremost cartographer of his day was permanently exhibited and was the pride of S. Michele. Given the *mappa mundi*'s geographical, historical and cultural significance, as well as its craftsmanship and beauty, this artefact undoubtedly constitutes an outstanding example of vernacular writing for public display produced in Europe's greatest international emporium on the cusp between Middle Ages and Renaissance. The particular captions chosen, from the map portion devoted to northern China, are a related group of five out of some 200 extended legends displayed on the atlas. The asterisked numbers added alongside them and other quotations taken from the map are from the complete classification of the captions elaborated in FALCHETTA (2006). When added to the hundreds of toponyms on show the captions on the planisphere (around 3,000 altogether) total more than 115,000 characters. The captions in and around Venice itself have unfortunately been completely worn away by human touch over the centuries.

CI 63, CI 64 and CI 65 cluster round dazzling illuminated illustrations of the great city Fra Mauro calls *Cha(n)balec* (in other words, Peking) which also show, at the bottom, the exotic tents of Kublai Khan's hunting lodge as related by Marco Polo. The bridge described in CI 64, and fascinatingly painted in detail, is the Lu-Kon bridge over the Yongding river (called *Polisanchin* by Mauro). To the south, across the river, is the huge imperial mausoleum described in CI 66, accompanied by an illumination showing its pinnacled, multi-tiered structure. To the north-west of Chanbalec stands the important coastal city called *Chansay* (in other words, Hangzhou) described in CI 62, the red inscription filling a large scroll-cartouche just off the coast.

LETTERING: The main text of all five inscriptions is in Gothic minuscule, with headings and rubrics in *capitalis*. Like all Fra Mauro's legends the present group are handwritten in *littera textualis* of the *rotunda* type — the standard Gothic book hand in Venice. Blocks of text vary in the letter size employed (CI 62 and CI 65 are much larger than CI 64) and in colouring: some all blue (CI 62) or all red (CI 61 and CI 64), others with display letters alternating the two colours (CI 65 and CI 66). In the body of the text capitals are restricted to the initial letter of the first word. Major pauses are marked by a period. Full stops are also used, as was normal in manuscripts, to mark off numbers. The only abbreviations utilised are the short overbar or tilde on vowels to indicate a missing nasal consonant or, occasionally, <r>; the horizontal bar through the tail of <p> = *per(-)* and through or under the tail of <q> (= *qui*) or else above <q> = *q(ues)ti* or *q(ua)l*; and the occasional Tironian

7 for *et* 'and'. No apostrophe is inserted between article or preposition and noun or adjective, so *doro* 'of gold' (CI 63, l. 5), *davolio* 'of ivory' (CI 63, ll. 5–6) and *lalta* 'the high' (CI 66, l. 4) are run together as single syntagms.

The hand deployed by Fra Mauro and his collaborators (and we know from the records that he paid at least one other person to work under his supervision) comes across at first as familiar and unexceptional. On closer inspection it is seen to be out of the ordinary. In a sense it mirrors the practical nature of the *mappa mundi* in being a clear, unfussy *textualis* that concedes nothing to aesthetics. It is eminently readable, with ample space between both words and most letters (the exception being the usual fusion of adjoining bows), as well as between lines. It has few of the difficulties in legibility that Gothic minuscule sometimes presents, with its tendential compression, contrasted stroking and consequent profusion of thick blackletter minims with thin hairstrokes. Here we find no emphasis on stroke contrast of this type and no decorativeness, and the letters have a lower, squarer module than is usual even with *rotunda*. The script is tendentially uniform throughout the map, but differences in execution are visible on close inspection. In our group of captions the writing in red on CI 64 appears to be more hasty: a feeling confirmed by the two corrected omissions indicated on my transcription. In addition, not only is the verb *reze* re-inserted here in its Venetian singular form, where Fra Mauro's practice was always to use a disambiguating plural, but a minuscule <z> has been employed for the voiced affricate, whereas Fra Mauro preferred the <ç>. While still quite clearly Gothic — as one would expect from the pen of someone trained in an early fifteenth-century monastery with a *scriptorium* — this plain writing is moving, overall, towards the clarity of the new Humanist bookscript.

On this basis one might have expected Fra Mauro's display lettering to be in the Gothic majuscule, of manuscript or inscriptional derivation, that dominates our corpus. Instead the script employed for larger introductory words or bold headings on the *mappa mundi* is, in fact, square capitals. However, as with Fra Mauro's minuscule the bald description of his lettering as Roman and quadrate comes with a proviso. There is little or no interest in emphasising stroke contrast, and serifing is minimal or variable. In addition, the script is not always strictly majuscular, with <p>, notably, having its tail well below the baseline, and there are occasional uncial-type intrusions, particularly the round <e>. What Fra Mauro is interested in, with the spectator in mind as always, is prominence and clarity. To this end his rubrics use alternate blue and red characters, as in *Imperio* 'Empire' (CI 65) and *Sepultura imperial* 'Imperial burial ground' (CI 66), while his block-capital section headings, such as *Cathaio* 'Cathay' (CI 63), are in gold edged with black.

LANGUAGE: Early Venetian veined with some Tuscanisms. Fra Mauro would have been perfectly aware that he was breaking new ground by abandoning Latin for his great work. Although less estimable than Latin the vernacular was the only choice if accessibility was a prime consideration. In fact he explicitly noted: *In questa opera p(er) necessita ho conuenuto usar no/mi moderni e uulgar . p(er)che al vero se io hauesse fa/to altrame(n)te . pochi me haueria inteso saluo q(u)alche literato* ('In this work I decided out of necessity to use modern, vernacular names, because if I had done otherwise few would have understood me apart from the occasional man of letters' ★2202). As in his alphabets which stood between tradition and innovation, with practicality and transparency paramount, so it is with Fra Mauro's language. A Venetian working in and for Venice he used his own *venexian* vernacular — ubiquitous in every spoken domain in the city and its empire and still prestigious in writing — as the dominant basis of his textual communication. However, with the undoubted aim of reaching the widest possible audience outside of Venice he occasionally compromised, lightly modifying some phonological and morphological features of his Venetian in the direction of literary Tuscan which was increasingly well known to the educated in Italy and even beyond.

That he did so in the main to avoid any syntactic ambiguity is obvious from his most consistent application of the tendency: making plural verb forms explicit because in Venetian singular and plural verb endings are identical. This was a practice also common at the time in vernacular wills and contracts where any ambiguity was unacceptable. It can be seen in *sono* 'are' (CI 62, ll. 4, 6–7, 9, 10; CI 63, l. 13), *fano* '(they) make' (CI 62, l. 7), although without consonantal doubling as in Tuscan 'fanno', *regeno* '(they) support, escort' (CI 63, l. 11), and *vano* '(they) go' (CI 63, l. 12), again with no doubling. One exception here in *reze* '(they) support' (CI 64, l. 3) which, although plural in sense, is given its Venetian singular form. This was perhaps due to the oversight mentioned above: the verb was left out in error then added subsequently in the left margin with a diagonal insertion mark. Other possible Tuscanising tendencies are more sporadic. The high-register past participle *apopulata* 'peopled, populated' (CI 62, ll. 2–3) appears to be Tuscan, although a Latinism cannot be ruled out. It stands in contrast with the other 1st conjugation past participles in the extracts which are all fully Venetian: *conputade* 'counted, computed' (CI 62, l. 9), *ornado* 'adorned, decorated' (CI 63, l. 6), *menado* 'pulled, drawn' (CI 63, l. 8), *deputada* 'reserved, allocated' (CI 66, l. 3). The present tense *dico* 'I say' (CI 62, l. 4), rather than Venetian *digo*, happens to coincide with both Tuscan and Latin. *Imagine* 'images' (CI 64, l. 2) is pan-Italian in this period, although the invariant plural is Venetian. *Triumpho* 'triumph' (CI 65, ll. 1–2), *inextimabile* 'inestimable' (CI 63, l. 7), *scientia* 'science' (CI 62, l. 12), *studio* 'study, diligence' (CI 62, l. 12), *pretiosa* 'precious' (CI 66, l. 1), *magnificentie* 'luxury, luxuries' (CI 62, ll. 12–13), *mirabile* 'marvellous' (CI 66, l. 1), *copia* 'abundance' (CI 62, l. 13) and *capitelli* 'capitals' (CI 64, ll. 3–4) < CĂPĬTELLI, as well as the initial <h> of *homeni* 'men' (CI 63, l. 13), are Latinisms found in Early Venetian and other early Italo-Romance writing. They are clearly intended to dignify the text. The spelling of *collone* 'columns' (CI 64, l. 3), with a double <l> alongside the expected single <n>, is usual in Early/Middle Venetian (see CI 30).

Many fundamental long-term trends of Venetian phonology and spelling are present in the captions. *Inperador* 'emperor' (CI 63, l. 2) < IMPĚRATOREM shows final /e/ dropping after /r/ on an original paroxytone, intervocalic T voiced to <d> and the syllable final nasal rendered as <n>. In *generation* 'offspring' (CI 66, ll. 4–5) < GĚNĚRĂTĬONEM and *canton* 'corner' (CI 63, l. 10), from an augmentative of

CANTO 'corner, edge', the /e/ drops after word-final /n/. Double consonants are, and were, absent from Venetian speech and this is reflected in our captions, with *soto* 'under' (CI 63, l. 3), *caro* 'carriage' (CI 63, l. 5), *fano* '(they) make', *vano* '(they) go', *cita* 'city' (CI 62, l. 1), *queli* 'those (people)' (CI 62, l. 7), and *dito* 'called, known as' (CI 66, l. 2). Venetian pre-tonic vowel raising is striking in *luntan* 'far' (CI 62, l. 4; Italian, *lontano*), and *lioni* 'lions' (CI 64, l. 2) compared to Italian *leoni*. Notable is the continuing strong presence of diphthongisation on stressed mid vowels, with *Veniexia* (CI 62, ll. 2, 4–5), *priesio* 'price' (CI 63, l. 6) < PRĔTĬUM and *fuogo* 'fire, hearth' (CI 62, l. 9) < FŎCUS 'hearth'. Where Modern Venetian prefers /ʤ/, the normal Early Venetian outcome of L + yod in /j/ is present in *fameie* 'families' (CI 62, ll. 8–9) and *mia* 'miles' (CI 62, l. 2) < MĪLIA. The Latinism *milia* 'miles' (CI 64, l. 2) predominated, however, in fourteenth-century written Venetian. The stressed /e/ in *fameie* is the phonologically regular outcome of Latin tonic Ĭ which Tuscan/Italian raised to /i/ in *famiglie* because of the following /ʎ/. A noteworthy feature of spelling is the constant and conservative use of <ç> for affricates, voiced and unvoiced, rather than <z> which would predominate within a few decades: so *çentileçe* 'delights' (CI 63, l. 13), *maçor* 'greater, bigger' (CI 62, l. 4); *meço* 'middle' (CI 62, l. 5), *palaçi* 'palaces' (CI 62, l. 7), and *çoie* 'jewels' (CI 63, l. 5). The singular *çoia* of Early Venetian *çoie*, meaning both 'jewel' and 'joy', was probably a derivative of GAUDIA, the plural of GAUDIUM 'joy', via Old French *joie*/Old Provençal *joia*. Traditional, too, is the single <s> spelling of the unvoiced sibilant /s/ in *a spaso* 'out and about' in CI 63. In line with the above conservatism is the persistence of the <g> for the velar /g/ in *borgi* 'suburbs' (CI 62, l. 3) and *fuogi* 'fires, hearths' (CI 62, ll. 10, 11).

The masculine definite articles appear to have assumed their modern pattern with singular *el* and plural *i* now exclusive, whereas our fourteenth-century inscriptions have *lo* dominating *el*, especially in the first half of the century, and *li* commoner than *i*. Evidence of a fascinating morphonological complication of this system is found in CI 66 (ll. 3–4) and elsewhere in the *mappa mundi* legends. It involves the unexpected spelling of the plural article as <hi> in the partitive construction *a hi* 'to the' or else when the prepositions *de* is followed by the masculine plural article (*de hi*). This peculiarity, found on only one other inscription in the corpus (CI 94, on stone, from 1507), appears to be an attempt to render graphically the voiced palatal approximant yod sound /j/ generated by such phonetic contexts. The fully palatalised variant [ʤ] is recorded in the contemporaneous central-southern Veneto dialects, and is found as such in Ruzante's early sixteenth-century rural Paduan texts written <gi>, although it is preceded in some earlier Veneto and northern texts by the <hi> spelling (OVI, s.v. *hi*). *Di più nobili* 'of the most noble' (CI 63, l. 9) features the contracted partitive *di* 'of the', whose increasing presence from the later fourteenth century onwards we have noted regularly.

The first and only use in the corpus of the 3rd singular impersonal construction is found with *se traversa* 'one crosses' (CI 64, l. 5), and the only uses of the obligatory 3rd person subject pronouns in Venetian occur in *el va a spaso* 'he goes out and about' (CI 63, l. 4; Italian, *va a spasso*) and *el senta* 'he sits' (CI 63, l. 5). Also unique in our collection is the use of the auxiliary *vegnir* 'to come' in the ongoing passive construction *vien menado* 'it is led/it gets led' (CI 63, l. 8). Syntactic recurrence with relative pronouns appears for the fourth time in the corpus with *el qual* 'who' (CI 63, l. 2) and *i qual* 'which' (CI 64, l. 3). See CI 13, CI 23, CI 30. Lexically interesting is *avolio* 'ivory' (CI 63, ll. 5–6), with /l/ instead of /r/ (compare Italian *avorio*), from EBUREUS 'made of ivory', a derivative of ĔBUR 'ivory'. It is the dominant form in Early Venetian but is also present in northern dialects generally in the period and occurs occasionally in Early Tuscan. On *dadriedo* 'behind' (CI 63, l. 13; Modern/Contemporary Venetian, *dadrio*), see CI 8, CI 14. *Stue* 'stoves' (CI 62, l. 5) is the plural of *stua* (Italian, *stufa*) present from Early to Contemporary Venetian. In *tresento* 'three hundred' (CI 64, l. 1), one is initially surprised by the presence of <s> where <ç> might have been expected from the palatalisation of Latin C + front vowel. However, as in the traditional Venetian *dusento* 'two hundred', the <ç> appears to have been treated as an intervocalic /s/ and to have undergone voicing.

RECENT STUDIES: GASPARRINI LEPORACE (1956); FALCHETTA (2006).

Corpus Inscriptions 67, 68

1456 ADI 20 ₁| ZENER FUI ₂| FATO MI PI|LASTRO AVA|NTI DEI MIE ₅|
COMPAGNI ₆

[1456, adì 20 zener, fui fato mi, pilastro, avanti dei mie compagni.]

1456 FO ₁| FATO QUESTO ₂| PILASTRO ₃

[1456 fo fato questo pilastro.]

TRANSLATIONS: CI 67: 1456, on the 20th of January, I pillar was made ahead of my companions. CI 68: 1456 this pillar was made.

DATE: 1456

LOCATION: In situ on two of the great brick piers supporting the row of sheds in the oldest part of the Arsenal, the so-called western boatyards or sheds (Venetian, *tezoni a ponente*). CI 67 is embedded on western shed no. 7 and CI 68 on western shed no. 8. Both are roughly 4 m off the ground.

TYPE AND DESCRIPTION: Commemorative. The writing is carved on plaques of Istrian stone embedded in the brickwork, with CI 67 measuring *c*. 50 × *c*. 46 cm while CI 66 is *c*. 44 × *c*. 28 cm. The lettering on CI 68 is extremely variable, but is very roughly 7 cm high on average, while CI 67 is somewhat less variable, with the letters averaging around 6.5 cm. The plaques have been cleaned and restored in recent times and are in excellent condition, the *pietra d'Istria* gleaming white. Occasional chipping round the edges of the plaques does not affect the lettering which is still clearly legible. DE LUCIA's photograph taken in the early twentieth century (1908: 185–86) shows the inscription plaques as greyer and more scuffed, with a small dark tag around the <ei> of *dei* (CI 67, l. 5). For comparison the restorers have intelligently left this patch which also reveals that the letters of the inscription(s) had originally been picked out with black infilling. In 1885 the Italian Royal Navy, the *Regia Marina*, added a small Istrian stone memorial plaque to the bottom of CI 67 with the following inscription in capitals: RMDCCCLXXXV.

LETTERING: A rudimentary assortment of Gothic-type majuscules and minuscules, with some cursive insertions, cut in shallow V-section. The two epigraphs together form a unique example in the corpus of 'popular' or semi-educated inscriptional writing on stone. Indeed, this precious testimony of basic, shaky literacy on writing for public display is without parallel in Venetian epigraphy of the period. Both commission and execution appear to be at the initiative of the *Arsenalot(t)i*, the workmen of the shipyards, themselves. This is strongly suggested by the fact that there has been no expert intervention on either the language, lettering or carving of the inscriptions, and by the simple, unframed plaques. They contrast strongly in these respects with the nearby and highly official CI 69 on another Arsenal shed.

CI 67 and CI 68 may or may not have been carved by the same hand. Their overall appearance is similar and some particular traits are identical, notably the cursive <st> conjoined on *pilastro* (CI 67, l ll. 3–4) and *questo* (CI 68 l. 2). However, other

FIG. 3.74. CI 67. © A. S. Ferguson.

FIG. 3.75. CI 68. © A. S. Ferguson.

features are unexpectedly different, such as the cursive minuscule <e> of *questo* (CI 68) compared to the four uncial-type <e>s of CI 67. The <f> on *fui fato* (CI 67, ll. 2–3) seems to be a minuscule, whereas that on *fo fato* (CI 68, ll. 1–2) appears to be a majuscule. The <r> of *pilastro* (CI 68, l. 3) is a clumsy minuscule whereas the <r> of *zener* and *pilastro* (CI 67, ll. 2, 3–4) is clearly a capital. The capital <a> used in both inscriptions is similar but not the same: both have a long topstroke, straight on CI 68, kinked on both sides on CI 67 where the crosspiece is also forked in the Byzantine style. The Arabic date on both plaques is very similar.

The mixed bag of letters on these tablets reveals basic familiarity with Gothic alphabets, majuscule and minuscule. The two <e>s of *zener* (CI 67, l. 2) and the <c> of *conpagni* (CI 67, l. 6) show closure with 'hairstrokes' in a rigid, mechanical way that is anything but hairstroking. Gothic majuscule <n>, though, is followed throughout and is generally well formed. The <i> is mostly deployed in its straight-line form: sometimes clearly majuscule, at other times minuscule. However, on three occasions — with *fui*, *dei* and *compagni* (CI 67, ll. 2, 5, 6) — it appears in a capital J form. On CI 68 the <t> is used three times: twice as a cursive minuscule on *fato questo* (CI 68, l. 2), once as a fully realised Gothic majuscule with long downstrokes on *pilastro* (CI 68, l. 3). It is not clear if the classic uncial <d> employed twice on CI 67 is uppercase or lowercase. The <u/v> of *fui* and *avanti* (CI 67, ll. 2, 4–5) is almost extravagantly cursive, the <q> of *questo*, the <m> of *mie* and *compagni* (CI 67, ll. 5, 6) and the <g> of *compagni* are genuine freaks, while the <f> of *fo* (CI 68, l. 1) actually spans the four lines of an imaginary stave. In these conditions letter height and linear regularity obviously leave something to be desired. Stroke contrast is only marginally present.

LANGUAGE: Early Venetian with some spoken inflections. *Zener* (CI 67, l. 2) — formerly spelled *çener* — is the overwhelmingly common designation for January in Early Venetian (see CI 79). *Fui* '(I) was' (CI 67, l. 2) and *fo* ('it) was' (CI 68, l. 1) are the regular 1st singular and 3rd singular forms of the past historic of *eser* 'to be' in Early Venetian, with the appearance of *fui* unique in the corpus. Also unique is the presence of *mi* 'me' (CI 67, l. 3), an extremely rare attestation at this early date of the emphatic 1st singular personal pronoun used as the subject pronoun instead of the 'regular' *io* 'I'. It is a development which started in informal speech in Early and Middle Venetian, gaining traction to such an extent that in Modern/Contemporary Venetian it was the norm. The unusual context of lower-class epigraphic commissioning and the idea of having the pillar speak for itself explain its appearance here. *Mie* 'my' (CI 67, l. 5) is the normal masculine plural possessive adjective in Early Venetian. It survived into Modern Venetian where it was gradually supplanted by *me* which is the norm in Contemporary Venetian. *Avanti dei* 'before, ahead of' (CI 67, ll. 4–5) is the only example in the corpus of this prepositional construction, as is the presence of the building feature *pilastro* 'pillar, pier' (CI 67, ll. 3–4; CI 68, l. 3), a form common to Early Venetian and Early Tuscan.

RECENT STUDIES: DE LUCIA (1908: 185–86); MOCELLIN (2016: 42–44). Both inscriptions were first drawn and transcribed by CASONI (1829: 34). Cicogna recorded (with the date misread), but did not publish, these inscriptions.

Corpus Inscription 69

M⁰ ‡ CCCC ‡ L ‡ VII | ADI ‡ PR(IMO) ‡ S(E)TE(NBRIO) ₂
[MCCCCLVII, adì primo setenbrio.]

TRANSLATION: 1457, on the first of September.

DATE: September 1457.

LOCATION: Embedded in situ, about 3 m off the ground, on the wall under the awning of the first shed of the Via Stradal Campagna thoroughfare on the south side of the Arsenal complex.

TYPE AND DESCRIPTION: Commemorative. The inscription records the completion of the two boatyards at the starting point of the Stradal Campagna artery running through the southern section of the Arsenal in a west-to-east direction. The epigraph is cut on a crenellated Istrian stone plaque whose inscriptional surface measures *c.* 55 × *c.* 27.5 cm. The bottom edge of the plaque dips down in a curved, squared-off triangle shape roughly 25 cm long which contains a tall acanthus leaf carved in high relief. The inscription plaque is embedded beneath a larger plain-framed tablet, measuring *c.* 150 × *c.* 75 cm, containing three coats of arms in relief. These are the shields of the patrician Barbaro, Contarini and Barbarigo families, whose members held high office as *Patroni* in the Arsenal at the time of the commemorated construction work. The important and privileged role of the *Patroni all'Arsenal* was summarised by Marin Sanudo:

> Patroni all'Arsenal [...] sono tre — et si chiama rezimento — stanno 32 mesi ivi, è da Pregandi in suso; si ellezze per scrutinio del Conseio d'i Pregadi et 2 man d'elettione. Hanno case tutti tre all'Arsenal dove convien habitar per esser lì vicino a custodia dell'Arsenal, et ivi sentano, fanno cassa, et attendono a scuoder li denari dalli officii diputati per pagar l'Arsenal, el qual [...] vuol di spesa all'anno ducati cento millia et ogni sabado pagano tutti quelli hanno lavorato in l'Arsenal che sono cottidiane 1000 operarii. Questi governano le salle di munitione, fanno far galie grosse per li viazi et galie sottil per l'armada, et tenghono conto diligentemente del tutto et, volendo per mal muodo tuor, si puol farsi ricchi. Vanno in Pregadi mettendo ballotta et a Conseio [...] che niun altro rezimento ritrovandosi in questa Terra ha questa auttorità — et *ut plurimum* a tal dignità si fa homeni esercitati in cose maritime. (CARACCIOLO ARICÒ 2011: 101–02)

I was unable, for safety reasons, to visit the inside of the nearby *Forza e Luce* shed where a similar commemorative inscription in Venetian is embedded on the wall. It too carries the Barbaro, Contarini and Barbarigo escutcheons, but this time with the shields below rather than above the epigraph. I transcribe it from photographs: + *1457 · adi ∵ / · hvltimo · dece(n)/ · brio ∵* '1457, on the last day (of) December'. The Gothic majuscule script employed is strongly uncialesque but not so decoratively fussy as on CI 69. The unusual enlarged minuscule <b> on *decenbrio* stands out, as does the hypercorrect insertion of an initial <h> on *hultimo*.

Fig. 3.76. CI 69. © A. S. Ferguson.

The presence of these inscriptions, as well as CI 67 and CI 68, bears concrete witness to the exceptional renewal and extension of the Arsenal dockyards from the mid-fifteenth century, after the fall of Constantinople to the Ottomans (CROUZET-PAVAN 2015: 138–39). The importance of the Arsenal to Venice's trading and military power in this period was underlined by the contemporaneous construction of the great triumphal arch — with prominent and interesting inscriptions in Latin — over its entrance: possibly the earliest piece of Renaissance architecture in the city. This and the key role of the *Patroni* is a reminder that the vast shipyard at the eastern end of Venice, with its arms production and strategic storage facilities, remained what it had been when Dante described it in *Inferno* XXI, 7–18: the greatest military-industrial complex in Europe. Originally *arsenà* ~ *arsanà* then *arsenal* in Early Venetian, the term derives from Arabic *dār aṣ-ṣinā* 'house of work/skills, factory'. Borrowed from Venetian, *arsenal* is attested in English from the early sixteenth century.

LETTERING: Gothic majuscules cut in V-section. The very large letters (*c.* 7.5 cm high) are highly decorative, to the point of being mannered. The bowed and tapered billowing outer arms of the numeral M (l. 1) are delicately and uniquely crossed at their ends. Each numeral C (= 100) has horn-shaped serifs, top and bottom, which are again unheard of in the corpus, while those of the <e> on *setenbrio* (l. 2) are actually hooked. The numeral I (l. 1) unexpectedly stands over the bottom stroke of the L = 50, while the top stroke of the <t> on *setenbrio* is strongly downtilted, once more like nothing else in our collection. The florid decorativeness is rounded off by notches in the middle of the perpendiculars throughout and by the elaborate knotted-string interpuncts. *Primo* (l. 2) and *setenbrio* are drastically abbreviated by means of keyhole overbars.

LANGUAGE: I make the assumption that the drastically abbreviated form of the month of September — <ste> with a suspension bar above it — has the majority Early Venetian spelling in <n>. On the *-brio* ending on the months from September to December in Early Venetian, see CI 79.

RECENT STUDIES: DE LUCIA (1908: 186–87). Recorded, but not published, by Cicogna.

Corpus Inscription 70

+ IN ⁕CHR(IST)I ⁕NO(M)I(N)E ⁕AMEN ⁕ M°CCCC°LXIII ⁕IN TENPO ⁕DE ⁕
M(ISTR)° ⁕ÇORÇI ⁕BIA(N)CO ⁕GASTOLDO ⁕E ⁕(CON)PAGNI ⁕M(ISTR)°
⁕NIC[...] ₁| ⁕SCRIVAN ⁕M(ISTR)° ⁕ NICOLO ⁕DE ⁕SIMON ⁕ M(ISTR)°
⁕VALENTIN ⁕ DE ⁕MICHIEL ⁕M(ISTR)° ⁕PIERO ⁕BRVTO ⁕M(ISTR)° ⁕
ALEG[...] ₂| MATIO ⁕DE ⁕CHIMENTO ⁕FO COMPRADO ⁕QVESTO ⁕TEREN ⁕
E PRINCIPIADA ⁕ QVESTA ⁕FAB[RICA] ₃

[*In Christi nomine* amen. MCCCCLXIII, in tenpo de mistro Çorçi Bianco, gastoldo, e conpagni — mistro Nic[...], scrivan; mistro Nicolò de Simon, mistro Valentin de Michiel, mistro Piero Bruto, mistro Aleg[...] Matio de Chimento — fo comprado questo teren e principiada questa fabrica.]

TRANSLATION: *In Christ's name*, amen. 1463, in the time (of office) of master Çorçi Bianco, alderman, and his colleagues — master Nic[...], secretary; master Nicolò de Simon, master Valentin de Michiel, master Piero Bruto, master Aleg[...] Matio de Chimento — this plot of land was bought and this building commenced.

DATE: 1463.

LOCATION: At present the inscription plaque is affixed to a wall at the back of the garden of Ca' Rezzonico (*sestiere* of Dorsoduro), along with a selection of sculpted artefacts of various periods. Although the inscribed object is actually listed in the online catalogue of the Museo Correr its whereabouts were unknown to modern epigraphers until I uncovered it in its present location in 2014 and published an edition (FERGUSON 2015c: 85–86). According to Cicogna, who viewed it in situ in the first half of the nineteenth century, it was originally to be seen in 'Calle fianco San Samuel — sopra porta n. 2744' (PAZZI 2001, III: 1899). In other words it was embedded above a door of the meeting house of the carpentry and joinery workers' confraternity-guild, the *Sc(u)ola d(e)i Marangoni*, located at the junction of Calle de le Carozze and Calle Lezze at S. Samuel (*sestiere* of S. Marco). It was probably stripped from that location in the nineteenth century and handed over to the Museo Correr. A similar fate, in fact, befell the sculpture dated 1558 which was removed from the façade of the *scuola* in order to be sold off but fortunately ended up with the Correr in 1883 (TASSINI 1863, *s.v. Marangon, Calle del*). That splendid oblong marble bas relief of *St Joseph in his Workshop and the Birth of Christ*, measuring *c.* 140 × *c.* 65 cm, is now stored in the Doge's Palace (Cl. XXV n. 0721a). It displays for the spectator all the tools of the carpenter's trade, and carries in Roman capitals the inscription: *MDLVIII in tenpo de m(aistr)o Andrea de Matio gastaldo et co(n)pagni*.

TYPE AND DESCRIPTION: Commemorative. The inscription records for posterity the guild's purchase of a plot of land for its headquarters in 1463 and the beginning of building work on it. It also lists the names of its elected officials at the time. The epigraph is lined off top and bottom by parallel furrows which focus the spectator's gaze on the writing. The plaque itself is unique in the corpus in terms of size and shape. It is a massive Istrian stone beam measuring in its present state

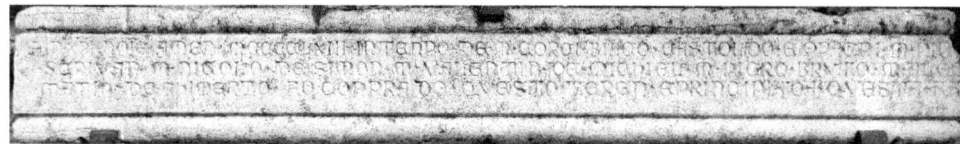

FIG. 3.77. CI 70. © A. S. Ferguson.

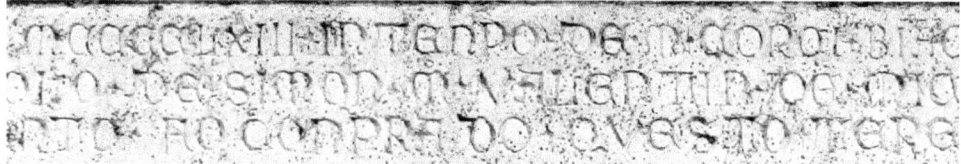

FIG. 3.78. CI 70 (detail). © A. S. Ferguson.

c. 150 × 21 cm, with the actual inscription area covering *c.* 150 × 12 cm. It would originally have been slightly longer in as much as the end of the right hand side of the artefact has been broken off diagonally to a width of between three and four letters. Judging by Cicogna's transcription it was already damaged on that side, although not quite so extensively, when he examined it. Otherwise the object is in reasonable shape in spite of being pockmarked by contact with the surrounding ivy vegetation. The letter grooving has been worn down by weathering but what remains of the epigraph is legible with care.

The confraternity of *S. Isepo* (Italian, S. Giuseppe) *del Arte dei Marangoni* was founded in 1335, worshipping at the ancient church of S. Maria in Broglio just behind Piazza S. Marco in what is now Calle Larga de l'Ascension. Our inscription confirms that it moved in 1463 to S. Samuel, where it occupied house numbers 3267–72 (*sestiere* of S. Marco). The documents relating to the purchase of the building plot and to the construction of the *scuola*'s headquarters are in CANIATO and DAL BORGO (1990: 226–30). Over the door of house no. 3272 in Calle Lezze one of the guild's vernacular inscriptions, from 1573 but still entirely in Venetian, survives in situ. The plaque is in Istrian stone and the letters are in Roman capitals: MDLXXIII *in tenpo de mistro Paulo chastaldo e chonpagini* [sic] / *proprieta dela Scola d(i) Marang(oni)* '1573, in the time (in office) of master Paulo, alderman, and his colleagues. Property of the carpenters' confraternity'. It is followed by the plumb-line symbol.

This great craft guild, with its hundreds of masters, apprentices and labourers, was divided into a number of branches, of which the main ones were: the *marangoni da case* (or *c(h)axe*), building carpenters and joiners; the *marangoni da noghera* specialising in furniture (Early/Middle/Modern Venetian, *noghera* 'walnut wood'); and the *marangoni da soaze*, the picture-frame makers (Early/Middle/Modern Venetian, *soaza* 'picture frame' from Old French *souage* 'border or edging on a porcelain dish or pewter plate': GODEFROY 1881–1902, *s.v. souage*). The term *marangon* 'carpenter, joiner' originated in Venice but has spread out widely into northern Italian dialects. On its much debated etymology see SALLACH (1993, *s.v. marangone*) and CORTELAZZO and MARCATO (1998: 269). A separate, numerous and strategically important category of carpenters, the *marangoni da nave*, ship's carpenters, worked in the yards of the Arsenal.

LETTERING: Gothic majuscules cut in V-section. This is a watershed inscription, the last in the corpus to employ the traditional Gothic lettering which had dominated the previous 150 years of epigraphy in Venice. Unsurprisingly, it was a script choice made by a confraternity-guild, one of the inherently conservative *scuole piccole* which — while adapting over a period of decades to the new Roman monumental lettering — would, in the main, remain loyal for many more years to the Venetian vernacular in their writing for public display. As we saw above, the *marangoni* were still using Venetian for their inscriptions more than a century later.

The vigorous epigraph is very much late Gothic in ductus without tipping over into the excessive decorativeness of CI 69. The stonemason has consistently striven, though, for roundedness — as can be seen on the bowed <m> and the closed-off <c>, <e> and <f> throughout — and for curviness. The latter is very visible on the legs of <m> and <n>, and is particularly marked on the <h> of *Chimento* (l. 3) which snakes extravagantly below the baseline, as well as on the wavy tail of the <q> on *questo* (l. 3). It is also striking on the left leg and crossbar of the <a> and on the swept-out downstrokes of <t>. The drive for curvature of line has even led him to shape the two keyhole suspension bars over *Christi* and *nomine* (l. 1) like cow horns, and to contrive two extraordinary letter joins: the <le> of *Valentin* (l. 2) and the calligraphic <at> of *Matio* (l. 3). The striving for the uncialesque sometimes works to the detriment of balance, as on the <r> of *scrivan* (l. 2) where the emphasis on the roundedness of the bowl detracts from the overall shape of the letter. In general, it somewhat disturbs the alignment of the letters which stand 2.5 cm tall on average but show considerable height variation. Any tendency to busyness in the ductus of the epigraph is counteracted by a certain strength of line, particularly apparent in the deep cut of the lettering and in the vigorous wedge-serifed stems. The epigraph is justified on the left (and perhaps on the right, although it is now impossible to tell) and words or syntagms are divided by interpuncts. The repeated title *mistro* 'master' is abbreviated by a hooked symbol protruding from high on the right leg of the <m> and by a superscript <o> over the <m>.

LANGUAGE: In line with the choice of the, by then, unfashionable Gothic script are traditional spellings like *gastoldo* 'alderman' (l. 1) instead of *gastaldo*; *tenpo* 'time (of office)' (l. 1) rather than *tempo*; and *Çorçi* George (l. 1) in preference to *Zorzi*. *Mistro* 'master' (l. 1 passim), rather than *maistro*, was the term sometimes preferred in the building trades, and was also associated with teachers, dancing masters and fencing masters (CORTELAZZO 2007, s.v. *mistro*; BOERIO 1865, s.v. *mistro*). On *maistro* see CI 56, CI 76, CI 78. *Teren* '(plot of) land' shows the usual Venetian absence of doubling on the <r> and the apocope of final /o/ following /n/ (in contrast to *tereno* on CI 32). Striking, and consonant with the majority tendency in our collection, is the perfect agreement running through the double passive construction: *fo comprado questo teren e principiada questa fabrica* 'this plot of land was bought and this building commenced' (l. 3).

RECENT STUDIES: FERGUSON (2015c: 85–86); MOCELLIN (2016: 47–50). Recorded, but not published, by Cicogna. His transcription was published by SAGREDO (1856: 104).

Corpus Inscriptions 71, 72

CAXE ▲ DEL^I $_I$| CO(N)VEXINI ▲ D{E $_2$| S(AN) ▲ MARZIL^{I}A^N $_3$

[Caxe deli convexini de San Marzilian.]

CAXE DELI $_I$| C(O)NVECINI $_2$| DE ✣S ✣MAR^{ÇILIAN} ✣

[Caxe deli convecini de S. Marçilian.]

TRANSLATIONS:

CI 71: Houses of the St Martial neighbourhood association.

CI 72: Houses of the St Martial neighbourhood association.

DATE: Undated, but lettering and language suggest the second half of the fifteenth century.

LOCATION: CI 71 is embedded on a house front in campo S. Marcilian (Italian, S. Marziale) at no. 2498, by the side of the church of S. Marcilian and just before the bridge leading to the Fondamenta de la Misericordia. The plaque is located between two first floor windows, about 5 m above pavement level, and is perfectly legible from the street below. CI 72 is on a nearby building that forms the corner of Calle Zancani and Fondamenta Moro just by the Ponte Zancani, the bridge leading into Campo S. Marcilian. The cartouche is situated between the second and third floors and is again perfectly legible from the bridge and the *fondamenta*. Both plaques appear to be in situ, and their existence was recorded in the nineteenth century — CI 71 by Cicogna, CI 72 by Tasssini.

TYPE AND DESCRIPTION: Declaration of ownership. The two oval Istrian stone cartouches, which may be contemporaneous or roughly so, proclaim the ownership of the properties in question by the local S. Marcilian neighbourhood residents' association. It is difficult to measure the two plaques accurately but I estimate them to be roughly 60 × 40 cm at their highest and widest points. Although CI 71 is perfectly legible the inscription surface has suffered considerable abrasion. CI 72, located in a more sheltered spot, has suffered some roughening along the edges and a hairline crack through the middle but otherwise is in excellent condition, with the writing perfectly clear. According to TASSINI (1863, *s.v. Zancana*) the S. Marcilian residents' association was active for at least four centuries and was still recorded as collecting rents from a neighbourhood grocer in the eighteenth century. Consisting of a grouping of local property owners, its funds are said to have come originally from profits made on raising money to build a bridge in the parish. It invested its funds in properties nearby, and with the rental income from these it financed good works and improvements to the church of S. Marcilian. It is relevant to our understanding of the organisation which commissioned the two inscriptions that BOERIO (1865, *s.v.*) defined *convicinato* as: 'Termine che usavasi sotto il Governo Veneto, anche nelle pubbliche carte, nel sign. di *Parrocchiani* o popolo della parrocchia; ma intendevasi una specie di Corporazione di parrocchiani rappresentata da' Capi, per l'esercizio di qualche diritto o amministrazione'.

CORPUS OF INSCRIPTIONS 301

FIG. 3.79. CI 71. © A. S. Ferguson.

FIG. 3.80. CI 72. © A. S. Ferguson.

LETTERING: Stiff, thin-cut square capitals in V-section featuring the type of ligatures, miniature letters and nesting associated with the Romanesque aesthetic. It is also reminiscent of Romanesque in being essentially monoline with minimal serifing. Only in its square module does it conform to Roman monumental capitals. The effort to make the letters quadrate is particularly clear on <a>, <d> , <n>, <s> and <x>, although the latter is more condensed on CI 72. On both inscriptions the ligatures, miniaturising and nesting appear to be motivated by the need to keep the message large and clear within the space constraints of the oval cartouches with their inset line framing. CI 72 opts to keep the first two lines of script full size, allowing only for the (redundant) keyhole-bar abbreviation of <n> on *convecini* (l. 2). CI 71, on the other hand, begins the space saving on ll. 1 and 2 by insetting the reduced <i> on *deli* (l. 1) and by dwarfing, then nesting, the <e> of *de* (l. 2). The inevitable consequence is that CI 72 is obliged to drastically reduce the linearity of *Marçilian* (l. 3) by a daring triple ligature of the first syllable <mar>. This is then topped by a reduced <an>, the right leg of whose <a> has been given a deliberately extended serif. From the serif emerges a tiny composite letter form, based on square <c> with end-hook cedilla, that simultaneously suggests and encompasses the missing <cili>. CI 71, with the space already saved on the first two lines, is allowed greater latitude on the third line, so that although *Marzilian* is also contracted with a triple ligature on <mar> the linearity of the remaining two syllables is kept intact, albeit at the price of reducing and raising <i> and <n>. It is tempting to see the same stonemason at work here, experimenting with different solutions and appearing to relish the challenge. Arguing against this are the short straight 'dots' over the <i>s in CI 71, absent in CI 72; the contrasting punched interpuncts, triangular on CI 71, spiral on CI 72 (and restricted to l. 3); and the different suspension bars. Aided by the size of their lettering and a certain elegant simplicity of line both epigraphs remain, despite their contraction trickery, eminently legible.

LANGUAGE: The twin inscriptions show a series of Early Venetian spelling conventions with variants. The traditional orthography with <x> for the voiced sibilant /z/ is still maintained in both inscriptions on *caxa* 'house' (CI 71, l. 1; CI 72, l. 1). However, on *Marzilian* (CI 71, l. 3) and *Marçilian* (CI 72, l. 3) we find the alternation of the innovative <z> with the traditional <ç> for what we presume to be the unvoiced affricate of the /ts/ type. *Convexini* (CI 71, l. 2) versus *convecini* (CI 72, l. 2) may reflect Early Venetian pronunciation variation or uncertainty over the reflex of Latin C followed by the front vowels /e/ or /i/, in this case on VICĪNUS 'neighbour'. The latter is believed to have evolved into the unvoiced affricate before simplifying out by Modern Venetian into the unvoiced sibilant /s/. The intervocalic /x/ in Early Venetian is always a sibilant, although more often than not, as in *caxa*, it represents the voiced /z/ rather than the voiceless /s/. The uncertainty over the spelling of the word for 'neighbour' continued into Modern Venetian where BOERIO (1865, *s.v. vicìn*) recorded *vicin* alongside *visin*. The modern forms with the first syllable in <i> have been influenced by Italian *vicino*. Interestingly, the more traditional partitive *deli* 'of the' is used in both inscriptions in preference to *dei* or to the innovative contraction *di* of spoken origin.

RECENT STUDIES: None. The present published editions are the first.

Corpus Inscriptions 73, 74

SEPVLTVRA DE I LIGADO | RI DE FONTIGO ₂ | | M · CCCC · LXXII ·

[Sepultura de i ligadori de fontigo. MCCCCLXXII.]

SEPVLTVRA ▲ DI ▲ LIGADOR ₁ | DE ▲ FONTEGO ▲ DI ▲ TODESHI ₂ |
ADI ▲ PRIMO ▲ MARZ[O] ▲ 14‹7›8

[Sepultura di ligador de fontego di Todeshi. Adì primo marzo 1478.]

TRANSLATIONS: CI 73: Burial place of the warehouse packers. 1472.

CI 74: Burial place of the German warehouse packers. On the first of March 1478.

DATE: CI 73: 1472. CI 74: March 1478.

LOCATION: CI 73 is carved on an in situ floor tomb in the Basilica of SS. Giovanni e Paolo (Venetian, S. Zanipolo). The tomb lies directly in front of the chapel of the Santissimo Nome di Dio, formerly dedicated to St Louis (Venetian, S. Alvise). This is the first apse chapel on the right (southern) side of the church. CI 74 is also carved on an in situ floor tomb in the same church but this time in front of the altar to the Holy Trinity in the Cappella della Santissima Trinità, the chapel to the left of the high altar.

A legal agreement of 31 August 1472 between the Dominican authorities of S. Zanipolo and the *scuola* of the German-warehouse packers accorded the packers, on condition of donating 30 ducats and carrying out the work at their own expense, 'certo terren over luogo posto nela giesia de sen Çuane e Paulo davanti laltar over capella de la santissima Trinita per farsi una archa over sepoltura per sepelir e far sepelir i corpi [...] de tutti i ligadori de la predetta schola'. The full agreement is reproduced in SIMONSFELD (1887, I: 287–89). A location in front of the chapel of the Holy Trinity, as stipulated in the agreement, was a logical choice for the *ligadori*. This was where they worshipped and gathered as a brotherhood and where they had built their chapel some fifty years before. However, the plot was not excavated in this location in 1472. We do not know what occasioned the change of plot location that year but two, perhaps not coincidental, facts are worth noting. The first is the erasure, discussed below, of a preceding inscription on the 1478 tomb slab. The second is the likely convenience and availability of ample room for a first burial plot beside the chapel of S. Alvise, a space that was in the process of being entirely redeveloped by a building campaign between 1458 and 1499 (MORETTI and TODESCO 2008). The space in the original location agreed with the church authorities was only excavated and made ready for use some six years later in 1478, as confirmed by CI 74.

TYPE AND DESCRIPTION: Announcements of tomb ownership. The inscription on CI 73 is carved on a marble tomb slab measuring 230 × 143 cm. The statement of ownership is laid out on one and a half lines about a quarter of the way down the large rectangular yellowish-pink ledgerstone. The date in Roman numerals

Fig. 3.81. CI 73. © A. S. Ferguson.

Fig. 3.82. CI 74. © A. S. Ferguson.

is displayed across the foot of the stone. The centre of the slab is dominated by large-scale relief depictions of what would have been to the spectator of the time the unmistakable objects associated with the packers' trade. A trussed bail of merchandise within a network of thick ropes is flanked on both sides by the bailers' special sticks. The one on the right, thinner and with curved pointed ends, served to tighten the ropes. The other thicker one, flattened at one end, was possibly for sealing or marking. At the top of the slab, separated by a gap from our inscription, are sporadic traces of a cancelled three-line epigraph which Cicogna (BMC, mss Cicogna, *busta* 502, *fasc.* 1) believed, on the basis of an unnamed manuscript seen by him, might have read: *Ligatores de fontico Theotonicorum posuerunt pro se* MCCCCLXXII. If this is the case then the packers must have decided to erase their original Latin statement and have it replaced by an exact vernacular equivalent comprehensible to all.

CI 74 is carved on the tomb lid of an identical marble slab to the first. The gravestone lies before the chapel and altar of the *ligadori*, dedicated to the Holy Trinity, at the far end of the church near the main altar. The inscription is carved in three lines towards the top of the slab, with the date (this time in Roman numerals) at the end of the third line. Traces of an underlying, effaced, inscription can be seen on the top line, particularly between *di* and *ligador*. The identical bale and stick motif is carved in the middle of the plaque. The ledgerstone, although generally in good shape, has been affected by two cracks. The substantial one at the top, starting top left and running through the middle of the inscription, troubles the legibility of the <o> at the end of *fontego* (l. 2) and *marzo* (l. 3). The crack itself has been infilled. It is not clear why the 7 on the date (l. 3) has been altered, possibly at the same time as the crack was filled in, with a <z> shape clearly overlaid. This looks rather like a 2, giving the mistaken impression to the onlooker that the date might be 1428 rather than 1478. This is, in fact, how it was read by Cicogna, even though 1428 would have been an improbably early date for combined Roman script and Arabic numerals in a Venetian vernacular inscription. However, the underlying 7 can just be made out on high-resolution photographs. The lighter fissure near the bottom of the slab does not affect the inscription.

The German-warehouse packers set up their trade association in 1418 and were given permission by the Council of Ten in 1423 to form a brotherhood dedicated to the Holy Trinity known as the *Schola di ligadori del Fontego di Todeschi*. Their confraternity-guild was a very particular one. It was small, with membership varying from a minimum of eighteen to a maximum of about forty, and it was essentially a closed shop. Potential members were recommended by the guild itself and had to meet the approval of the German merchants in the Fontego. They had themselves to be German. The packers thus formed a kind of caste which tended to perpetuate itself from father to son, although it was regularly renewed by new blood from the German territories. The provenance of the membership was German in the widest sense but the records confirm that the majority of packers came from the great Alpine arc of the southern German lands, from Lake Constance, through Bavaria and the Tyrol, to Bohemia and beyond. Their job made them an essential component of the transitting of goods, perishable or otherwise, from the Mediterranean to beyond the Alps via Venice. They had responsibility for the wrapping — at a fee set by them in agreement with the German merchants and the Venetian warehouse officials — of goods which had to travel overland in hazardous conditions, and for ensuring that there was no evasion of tax duties owed to the Venetian authorities. Their packing had to be done within the Fontego itself in the courtyard spaces, and not in rooms or corridors. The materials of their trade were canvas, leather and rope and their tools were the rods depicted on the floor tombs. Unlike the German merchants themselves who had to reside in the Fontego, the packers lived outside, mainly in the nearby parishes of S. Maria Nova, S. Lio, S. Cancian, SS. Apostoli and S. Salvador, and through marriage and everyday contact they became absorbed over time into the fabric of Venetian society.

On the *ligadori de fontego* see BRAUNSTEIN (2016: 110–20) who reproduces a detailed fifteenth-century price list for their services, by weight and type of goods, as well as a record of the names, provenance and Venetian residence of all the *ligadori* registered for 1419. On the confraternity's *mariegola* see PICHI (2013). In 1472 the Fontego, operational from 1268 as the official residence and warehouse of German merchants in Venice, was still the structure to be seen prominently, with the legend *Fontico · dalamani*, on de' Barbari's woodcut view of Venice of 1500 (see CI 85, l. 2). Soon after this date it was destroyed by fire and was rebuilt between 1505 and 1508 in the form still surviving today. It carries on its canalside frontage a scroll, on a shield featuring the German imperial eagle, that bears a terse large-scale Latin inscription carved in Roman capitals: *Ger/manicis/ ⁂ D ⁂* ('For the Germans. 1500'). The façade was frescoed in the Cinquecento by, among others, Giorgione and Titian. The magnificent structure of the Fontego, with its unique four arcaded floors, served for most of the modern period as Venice's central post office. Since 2000 it has passed through several business owners and is now (in 2020) a luxury emporium in Chinese hands.

LETTERING: Both CI 73 and CI 74 are in Roman square capitals cut in V-section. The brief statements of ownership commissioned by the *ligadori* are carved in two lines on CI 73, towards the head of the slab, with the date centred at the bottom, and on three lines at the top on CI 74. Letter height on both inscriptions is conspicuous at *c.* 6 cm on the wording and at 8.3 cm, on average, on the date of CI 73. The large-scale lettering, although eroded by half a millennium of being trodden on, remains legible, particularly on CI 74. The writing would have stood out much more clearly in the past, especially as the grooving was infilled in black as can still be seen in places. The script on both epigraphs is similar. It is competently cut and unpretentious, with little obvious attempt to accentuate stroke contrast or serifing, although wear and tear on the writing makes value judgements hazardous. On CI 73 the announcement of ownership is justified on the left, with the first line occupying most of the width of the tomb lid. The alignment of the inscription appears rather shaky, and this uncertainty is confirmed by some variable heights on the date, with the final four digits noticeably taller than the rest and uneven in size among themselves. Interpuncts between the main elements of the date can just be made out. CI 74 tapers inwards on both sides and shows better aesthetic balance and regularity. The words are separated, here, by triangular interpuncts.

LANGUAGE: *Ligadori* (CI 73, ll. 1–2) is the plural of *ligador* 'packer, bailer', from the Early/Middle/Modern Venetian verb *ligar* 'to tie (up)' pronounced [iˈgar] in Contemporary Venetian. The singular form *ligador* used as a plural on CI 74 (l. 1) may be a slip on the stonemason's part or may be down to the uncertain Venetian of the Germanic commissioning *scriptor*. This latter supposition would appear to be confirmed by the incorrect construction *de* (rather than *del*) *fontego* (CI 74, l. 2) and by the misspelling of *todeschi* 'Germans' as *todeshi* (CI 74, l. 2). On CI 73 (l. 2) *fontigo* is a curious mixture of Venetian and Latin. The vernacular name of the great German warehouse at the Rialto was, from Early to Modern Venetian, *Fontego d(e)i Todeschi* (Tuscan/Italian, *Fondaco dei Tedeschi*). *Fontego* — which appears correctly on CI 74 (l. 2) — seems to have been contaminated here by the influence of the Latin form used in legal documentation, where the German warehouse packers were referred to as *ligatores in fontico theutonicorum*. In the Latin statutes (Early Venetian, *capitolar*) of the Visdomini, the Venetian officials responsible for the warehouse, the building is in effect always called the *Fonticus Theutonicorum* (THOMAS 1874), and de' Barbari even employed *fontico* on his vernacular caption on the building. If CI 73 was, as suggested above, originally carved out in Latin on the slab, then it would hardly be surprising if some crossover occurred. *Fontego* and *fondaco* derive from Arabic *funduq* 'warehouse, merchant quarters, inn, hotel', itself from Greek πάνδοκος 'lodging, hostel, inn'. On the Venetian form *todesco* 'German' see CI 42. The partitive *de i* 'of the' (CI 73, l. 1) is, unusually for our corpus, separated clearly into two words. On CI 74 (l. 2) its equivalent is in the contracted *di* form.

RECENT STUDIES: None. The present editions are the first. Cicogna recorded both inscriptions but did not publish them.

Corpus Inscription 75

M°CCCCLXXVIIII *| ADI XIIIIII SE}EN^T{BRIO NE^L ₂| TE(N)PO{DE
M(ISTRO) POLO DE ₃| GRIGVOL *₄| MAS(ER) LVCHA DE ₅| ZVANE *₆

[MCCCCLXXVIIII, adì XIIIIII setenbrio, nel tenpo de mistro Polo de Griguol.
Maser: Lucha de Zuane.]

TRANSLATION: 1479, on the 16th of September, in the time (in office) of master Polo de Griguol. (The) treasurer (was) Lucha de Zuane.

DATE: September 1479.

LOCATION: Sculpted, in situ, on the architrave over the entrance to the former shoemakers' confraternity-guild meeting house in the picturesque and busy Campo S. Tomà (*sestiere* of S. Polo).

TYPE AND DESCRIPTION: Commemorative. Although it does not say so explicitly, the precisely dated inscription — standing out on its white Istrian stone architrave against the brickwork of the building — appears to commemorate the completion of the meeting house of the *Scuola de S. Aniano de l'Arte d(e)i Caleg(h)eri*, including the relief sculpture in the lunette above the epigraph. Recorded on the inscription are the names of the alderman in office at the time and his treasurer. The text is laid out between two bas-relief shoes in profile and is divided in the middle by the outline of a patten in low relief. The architrave is *c*. 200 × *c*. 22 cm, while the inscribed area itself, excluding the flanking shoe outlines, measures some 132 × 18 cm. The whole plaque, *c*. 272 cm above pavement level, is exceptionally well preserved, with the inscription remaining legible even from a distance.

In the ogival *pietra d'Istria* lunette above the architrave is an outstanding relief of *St Mark healing the cobbler Anianus*. This relief is generally, but not exclusively, attributed to Pietro Lombardo and his workshop, with some scholars, MARKHAM SCHULZ (2017, I: 168) in particular, ascribing it to Antonio Rizzo and his *bottega*. It is presumably contemporaneous with our inscription. It depicts St Mark in Alexandria healing the hand of Anianus, the cobbler-saint and patron of this confraternity-guild, with his blessing. The bearded and turbaned cobbler had hurt his hand mending the saint's shoe and is shown at the moment of his conversion as he witnesses Mark's miraculous intervention on his wound. Anianus's left hand is held by the saint; in his right hand the cobbler holds a shoe and a shoemaker's awl. On the ground behind him are a row of shoes and a tray with other tools of the cobbler's trade. A wall of buildings is visible in the background, to the rear of a grassy rise, while two exotic trees appear behind the saint. Traces of the original colouring of the relief are still present: notably the saffron robe of St Mark and his blue-green tunic; the brown hair and beard of St Mark and the beard of St Anianus; the patch of clear blue sky in the upper background above Mark's head; and the dark foliage and yellow and orange fruit on the two trees in the right foreground. The inscription and accompanying relief are a perfect example of the fusion of guild and devotional elements in the Venetian *scuole piccole*. The importance of

Fig. 3.83. CI 75 in context. © A. S. Ferguson.

the iconography of St Mark and Anianus to the shoemakers is underlined by the *scuola*'s commissioning of the anonymous mid-sixteenth century oil painting of the *Reception of the Scuola dei Calegheri by the Doge* now in the Accademia.

The *Scuola del Arte dei Calegheri*, dedicated to St Anianus, bringing together shoemakers, makers of pattens and clogs, and cobblers, appears to have been founded in the thirteenth century (MONTICOLO, II: 137–68) and to have been originally based, like the carpenters' and builders' trade associations, in the vicinity of S. Samuel. It moved to its S. Tomà location in the fifteenth century where it is recorded as buying a plot of land for its headquarters from the parish priest of S. Tomà in 1439 (G. VIO 2004: 617). However, the earliest recorded vernacular inscription from the *scuola*, dated 14 December 1446 and carved on the left-side pilaster of their meeting house, proclaims that the building was bought (*comprado*) on that date (see CI 60).

The charming shoemakers' meeting house, largely intact on the outside and preserving part of the structure and some original vestiges on the inside, including traces of wall fresco on the upper floor, is now a district library and community centre. It is a modest but important locus of vernacular inscriptions. We noted that CI 60 was the first vernacular epigraph in the city in revival Roman lettering. Our present inscription, beneath its outstanding relief lunette, is striking and relatively well known. In addition, the right-side Istrian stone pilaster on the front of the guildhouse bears a vernacular inscription from 1580 commemorating a restoration of the building. It remains mostly Venetian in language and reproduces the nomenclature of officials as cited in 1479: MDLXXX / in tempo de mis(tro) / Marcho Capo/grosso dal Chanpaniel / gastaldo et / mistro Zuane / dal Frate mas(er) / et mistro Giul[io] / dala Noviza / schrivan et chonpagni / fu restaurata. '(In) 1580, in the time (in office) of Marcho Capogrosso dal Chanpaniel, alderman, and of master Zuane dal Frate, treasurer, and master Giulio dala Noviza, secretary, and (their) colleagues (this building) was restored'. Two further vernacular inscriptions are to be found on the inside of the building, immediately to the right as one enters, on the staircase leading up to the former *albergo*. The earlier of the two, dated 1595, is still strongly Venetian in language. The second, from the late eighteenth century, is in Italian but with Venetian residues, especially in the designations of the confraternity officers. On the etymology and spelling of *caleg(h)eri* 'shoemakers, cobblers' see CI 42.

LETTERING: Eccentric Roman square capitals cut in V-section, featuring unorthodox sorts and Romanesque-style nesting. This is an attractive, sharply cut inscription that is legible in spite of a quirky series of rebuses — involving abbreviations, letter dwarfing and letter insertions — and despite its confusingly inconsistent layout.

The six lines of the epigraph are bounded by the two inward pointing shoe outlines. This intrusion into the writing space on either side precludes the text being justified either left or right. More serious for the legibility of the text is the presence in the middle of the inscription tablet of the shapely patten relief. This understandable desideratum of the guild commissioners has clearly presented the stonecutter with a logistical conundrum: how to combine textual equilibrium on the tablet with lines ideally laid out left to right along its full length. In the end he had to compromise. The first line is indeed spread across the full length of the inscription surface, albeit with a large gap in the middle of the date occasioned by the outline sole and marked by an outsized triangular interpunct. The remaining two lines force the reader to adjust to a different format involving two discrete blocks of text on either side of the patten: on the left is *tenpo de mis. Polo de / Griguol*; on the right is *mas. Lucha de / Zuane*. The result is aesthetically pleasing but awkward to read. It is clear that space constraints and the need for visual balance are also behind the lettering acrobatics on display, although one has to admire the ingenuity and almost playful solutions that the mason has come up with. He may have been influenced directly by Romanesque inscriptions in the city or even by the example of the remarkable Romanesque-inspired letter contractions and ligatures on the newly sculpted script over the portal entrance to the Arsenal (1460). Be that as it may, he has given his creativity free rein. Most bold are his nesting of miniature <e> and <t> either side of the diagonal of the much larger <n> in order to abbreviate *setenbrio* (l. 2); and the astonishing contraction of *tenpo de* (l. 3) into a single word by means of an overbar for <n> followed by Russian-doll nesting of <d> within <o> and of <e> within the already nested <d>.

The aspectually spare capital lettering of the inscription, with very marked wedge serifs on perpendiculars, is unorthodox and distinctive. The letters are large at around 4.5 cm, although the miniaturised and nested ones are considerably smaller. A number of idiosyncracies stand out. The three examples of spreading <m>, with the left arm of the fork descending to the baseline, are unique in the corpus and remind one of early manuscript display titling (most notably employed by the scribes of the so-called *Missale Gothicum* of the seventh or eighth century: Vatican, MS Regin. Lat. 317). Also archaic looking and without parallel in the collection are the two examples of <g> on *Griguol* (l. 4), with a perpendicular descending at right angles from the cross stroke. Quite extraordinary is *nel* 'in the' at the end of l. 2, where <l>, in superscript for lack of space, seems to be deliberately compensated by the elongation of the preceding <e>. The eclecticism of the inscription is reinforced by its reversion to Gothic abbreviation habits, involving the superscript <o> over <m> in the date; the suspension bar for <n> over *tenpo* (l. 3) and, very unusually, for <istro> over the <m> of *mistro* (l. 3); and the Tironian diagonal through the <s> on *maser* (l. 5). One is surprised by the sculptor's apparently clumsy rendering of the Roman numeral sixteen on l. 2, where the choice of XVI would have saved precious space. His alignments are also apparently wobbly at times. This can be appreciated on the contiguous <an> on *Zuane* (l. 6) where the left stem of <a> dips noticeably below the baseline and appears to be balanced by the right side of the <n> dipping down likewise.

There is more than a passing resemblance between the script employed here and that carved, albeit more elegantly, along the bottom stone frame of the Brenzoni mausoleum in S. Fermo in Verona by the Florentine sculptor Nanni di Bartolo in 1426. The rare archaic <g> on both is found notably, as it happens, in Verona on the epitaph (*c.* 978) of the Abbot Hubertus that is now on display in the Castelvecchio. Overall, one has the distinct impression that the inscription was not the product of a workshop with settled roots in the Venice's epigraphic traditions. It is perhaps worth remembering that a *mistro Piero Lombardo*, originally a foreigner, would rise to become by 1514 *gastaldo* of the stonemason's guild, the *Arte d(e)i Taiapiera*, in Venice (Sagredo 1856: 309). On the other hand, it is interesting to recall that Antonio Rizzo was originally from Verona.

LANGUAGE: On the Early Venetian *-brio* ending in *setenbrio* (l. 2) and on the months from September to December see CI 79. *Polo de Griguol* (ll. 3–4; Tuscan/Italian, Paolo di Gregorio) is the alderman of the *scuola*, although this is left implicit in the inscription. The overbar abbreviation on the <m> before his name certainly indicates *mistro* 'master', as on the later inscription on the right-side pilaster of the guildhouse where it is twice spelled out in full. The typically Venetian *Griguol* < Gregorius shows the raising of pre-tonic /e/ to /i/, the diphthongisation of stressed /o/, and the dissimilation of the second <r> to <l>. The other official named (l. 5) is the *maser* — in other words, treasurer — *Lucha de Zuane* (Tuscan/Italian, Luca di Giovanni), which shows the characteristic Early Venetian digraph spelling of <ch> for velar /k/. On *maser, masser* or *massaro* 'pubblico custode di masserizie' see Boerio (1865, s.v. *massèr*). The term, pronounced with an unvoiced /s/ and stressed on the second syllable, is also present on the inscription on the right-side pilaster. I resolve the nasal suspension as <n> in *tenpo* 'time' (l. 3) on the basis of *setenbrio* (l. 2).

RECENT STUDIES: Monticolo (1896–1914, II: lxxxix); Gramigna and Perissa (2008: 51); Ferguson (2015c: 87–88); Mocellin (2016: 51–54). Recorded, but not published, by Cicogna.

Corpus Inscriptions 76, 77

M°CCCC° · LXXXII · ADI · XXV · M | ARZO · IN TE(N)PO · DE · MA(ISTRO) · ANT | VONIO · DA · MODON · E · SOI · CON | [P]AGNI · [MA(ISTRO)] · ANTONIO · NEGRO ₄ | E [·] MA(ISTRO) · BONAZA · E · MA(ISTRO) [·] ANDR[EA] ₅ | DACRE · SCRIV[A]N · [M]A(ISTRO) · D[O]L[ZE] ₆

[MCCCCLXXXII, adì xxv marzo, in tenpo de maistro Antuonio da Modon e soi conpagni: maistro Antonio Negro, e maistro Bonaza, e maistro Andrea d'Acre. Scrivan maistro Dolze.]

LA SCOLA DI M[URERI]

[La scola di Mureri.]

TRANSLATIONS: CI 76: 1482, on the 25th of March, in the time (in office) of master Antuonio da Modon and his colleagues: master Antonio Negro, and master Bonaza, and master Andrea d'Acre. (The) secretary (was) master Dolze.

CI 77: The builders' meeting house.

DATE: CI 76: March 1482. CI 77: 1482?

LOCATION: The inscription plaque carrying CI 76 is at present embedded near the top of the façade of the former builders' confraternity-guildhouse, the *Scola d(e)i Mureri*, at S. Samuel (*sestiere* of S. Marco) house no. 3216. As the plaque is around 10 m above pavement level and the letter height is modest the inscription cannot be read by the passer-by. In all likelihood it has always been embedded on the front of the meeting house, but originally much closer to ground and eye level. This supposition is confirmed by testimony from the mid-nineteenth century. According to Agostino Sagredo CI 76 was located above the entrance to the building. It stood under a bas-relief which was sold off and taken abroad following the suppression of the confraternity and the selling off of the meeting house earlier in the century (SAGREDO 1856: 84). Presumably our inscription plaque was moved at that point to its present inaccessible location. The Renaissance bas-relief of the *Deposition of Christ*, now lost, was reproduced in line drawing by CICOGNARA (1813–18, I: ill. XIX). CI 77, on the other hand, is in situ on the main-door lintel of the building.

TYPE AND DESCRIPTION: CI 76 is commemorative while CI 77 is documentary. The former commemorates the inauguration of the confraternity-guild's headquarters. The latter advertises the *scuola*'s presence and ownership of the building. The entire artefact containing CI 76 is *c*. 85 × *c*. 55 cm, while the inscription surface itself, on the bottom section of the plaque, is *c*. 51 × *c*. 22 cm. It is in gleaming white Istrian stone embedded between two windows on the second floor of the building. In the upper compartment, taking up two thirds of the plaque and elegantly sculpted in relief within a quadrilobe shape, can be seen the tools of the builders' trade: set square with plumb line, trowel underneath on the left, hammer-pick on the right. In the four spaces between the quadrilobes and the frame are carved sprigs of foliage. CI 77 is carved on a rectangular slab of duller,

Fig. 3.84. CI 76 in context. © Ronnie Ferguson.

unrestored Istrian stone measuring 181 × 22 cm, with the writing placed exactly in the middle of the oblong architrave. The lintel is *c.* 259 cm above pavement level. CI 76 is largely undamaged, although the letters have been worn down and there is roughening of the stone at the bottom of the plaque. The lettering on CI 77 is more severely eroded. In addition, the final five letters of the word *mureri* have been obliterated by a metal support truss inserted into the plaque in modern times. The guild's plumb-line symbol is sculpted in low relief in the centre of the inscription, separating the words *scola* and *di*.

The *mariegola* of the *Arte dei Mureri* (Tuscan/Italian, *muratori*) was initiated in 1244. Dedicated to the apostle Thomas and to St Magnus bishop of Oderzo, the *arte*, perhaps the largest and most fundamental of the craft guilds in Venice, acquired a group of buildings for the site of its headquarters in S. Samuel — at the junction where Salizzada S. Samuel splits into Salizzada Malipiero and Calle de le Carozze — on 1 February 1482. Since CI 76 records the moving-in date as March 1482, it is reasonable to assume that the main building was already largely usable by then. The cultural damage occasioned by the nineteenth-century despoliation of confraternity buildings in Venice can be gauged by the loss from the meeting house of the *mureri* of the above-mentioned relief on the façade and also of numerous paintings housed in its rooms. These included the splendid oil of *Doubting Thomas with St Magnus* (*c.* 1505) by Cima da Conegliano which is now, by good fortune, in the Accademia.

LETTERING: Roman square capitals cut in V-section. As one would expect from a commissioning guild whose stock-in-trade was Istrian stone and a range of stone-cutting tools, the standard of lettering and of sculpting generally on CI 76 is high. The inscription itself is handsome, with the classic *capitalis* script fully and expertly regularised, justified on both sides and displaying measured stroke contrast. The latter can be appreciated most clearly on <a>, <d> , <m>, <n> and <o>. Serifing appears to be restrained, although letter fading makes it hard to judge. *Tenpo* (l. 2) is written as *tepo* and the five examples of *maistro* 'master' appear as <ma>, with abbreviating signs not (or no longer) discernable, even with the aid of enlarged high-resolution photographs. I expand *tenpo* with <n> rather than <m> on the basis of *conpagni* (ll. 3–4). Average letter height on CI 76 is 2.5 cm and with its balanced script, clear layout, and ample spacing reinforced by regular interpuncts, the epigraph must have been eminently legible. Average letter height on CI 77 is *c.* 5 cm and the now faded capitals would once have stood out prominently.

LANGUAGE: *Maistro* 'master' (CI 76, ll. 2, 4, 5, 6) is from MAGISTRUM which had two reflexes in the craft-guild context in Venice: *maistro* but also *mistro* (see CI 70, CI 75). The surname *Negro* (Black), CI 76, l. 4, is still fairly common in the Veneto. It derives regularly from NĬGRUM 'black'. Particularly interesting are two of the other guild officials' surnames — *da Modon* (l. 3) and *dAcre* (in other words, *d'Acre*; l. 6) — suggesting origins in Venice's overseas possessions, *de là da mar*, in the Peloponnese and the Levant. We already noted the presence on a fourteenth-century well head (CI 15, CI 16) of extreme diphthongisation on the Christian name *Antuonio* (CI 76, ll. 2–3). Here, however, it is counterbalanced by the undiphthongised *Antonio* (CI 76, l. 4). That the complex to-and-fro in Early Venetian between diphthongised and undiphthongised outcomes of original stressed Ŏ was moving at the end of the fifteenth century towards the latter again is suggested by *scola* (CI 77). Strongly present in CI 76 is the by now established use of <z> rather than <ç> for the unvoiced affricate: *marzo* (March; ll. 1–2); *Bonaza* (l. 5); *Dolze* (l. 6). *Mureri* 'builders' (CI 77), singular *murer* ('bricklayer' in Modern/Contemporary Venetian), is from Latin MURARIUS 'bricklayer, mason'. For the vernacular tomb inscription of a master *murer* see CI 78. *Di* 'of the' (CI 77) is a further example of the contracted partitive (of *deli* or *dei*) which had been on the rise since the late Trecento.

RECENT STUDIES: RIZZI (1987: 129); FERGUSON (2015c: 89–90); MOCELLIN (2016: 55–59). First recorded, but not published, by Cicogna. His transcription was published by SAGREDO (1856: 84).

Corpus Inscription 78

SEPOLTVRA ▲ DE MAISTRO ▲ MA | RCHO [▲] DE FIORIO ▲ MVRER ▲ E SVO ₂|
ᴇRIEDI [▲] M°CCCC°LXXXVIIII ▲ ADI XVII ▲ LVIO ₃

[Sepoltura de maistro Marcho de Fiorio, murer, e suò eriedi.
Mccccᴌxxxviiii, adì xvii luio.]

TRANSLATION: Burial place of master Marcho de Fiorio, builder, and (of) his descendants. 1489, on the 17th of July.

DATE: July 1489.

LOCATION: On a floor tomb in situ in the left-side cloister of the former Franciscan monastery attached to the church of S. Francesco della Vigna (*sestiere* of Castello).

TYPE AND DESCRIPTION: Announcement of tomb ownership. The inscription is carved towards the top end of the Istrian stone lid of a floor tomb measuring 197 × 102 cm, with the inscriptional area itself *c*. 100 × *c*. 12 cm. The epigraph records that this is the family burial site of a master builder, Marc(h)o de Fiorio, and his descendents. Presumably the date marks when the grave was completed and not when de Fiorio himself died. A master builder Marcho de Fiorio is in fact recorded as being alive in July 1490 in the payment records of the church of S. Giovanni in Bragora in the same *sestiere* (Castello) as S. Francesco della Vigna. He was employed with his team on the building of the choir screen designed by Sebastiano Mariani for that church. See *Archivio Parrocchiale di S. Giovanni in Bragora*, I, fol. 19r, cited by Humfrey (1980: 353 n. 15). On the confraternity-guild of the *mureri* see CI 76, CI 77.

De Fiorio's is one of only two early vernacular inscriptions still legible on what remains of the original pavements in the picturesque medieval cloisters of S. Francesco della Vigna which were formerly carpeted with burial plots of Venetian patricians, of substantial individuals like our master builder, and of confraternities and guilds. The other vernacular survival, positioned near that of our builder, is the splendid communal grave of the Arsenal caulkers' guild, undated but probably mid-sixteenth century and measuring 135 × 120 cm. In the centre of its slab is featured a fascinating depiction of a galleon in dry dock ready for the attention of the caulkers. The epigraph in Roman capital script reads: *Al nome* ▲ *de dio* ▲ / *in tempo* ▲ *de* ▲ *s(r)* ▲ *Domenego* / *de* ▲ *Antonio* [Cester] ▲ *gastaldo* ▲ *et* ▲ / *conpagni* ▲ *de* ▲ *larte* ▲ *deli* / *calafai* 'In God's name. In the time of office of Mr Domenego de Antonio [Cester], alderman, and his colleagues of the guild of caulkers'. The profession-cum-surname *Cester*, added in superscript, means 'basket maker'.

LETTERING: Roman square capitals cut in V-section. The unassuming text commissioned by de Fiorio is laid out neatly and rather elegantly in three lines that are justified on both sides. Stroke contrast and serifing are modest. However, with its accurate alignments and well-spaced words or syntagms, marked off clearly by large triangular interpuncts, the aspectually sober script, *c*. 3 sm high, remains

Fig. 3.85. CI 78, © A. S. Ferguson.

easily legible. It would have been even more so in the past since the letters were highlighted by black infilling which, even after five centuries of erosion, can still be detected. Although it is partly worn away the inscription is in surprisingly good shape. This is in spite of some serious damage to the ledgerstone itself which has sustained two parallel splits starting at the top and running diagonally through the epigraph to the left-hand edge of the lid. The cracks cut through the lettering and have caused a little line slippage, but the effect on legibility is negligeable.

LANGUAGE: This is the only one of the six tomb inscriptions in the corpus to prefer the fully vernacular form *sepoltura* (l. 1) to the more Latinising *sepultura* (both from SEPŬLTURA). See CI 3, CI 25, CI 56, CI 73, CI 74, although CI 25 may possibly be meant as Latin. The two variants contended for supremacy not only in Early Venetian but across the early Italo-Romance vernaculars generally. On *murer* 'builder', and on the builders' confraternity-guild, see CI 76 and CI 77 where *maistro* 'master' (l. 1) is also considered. It is interesting that the spoken Venetian variant *riedi* 'heirs, descendents' (see BOERIO 1865, *s.v. rede*) was corrected to the more formal *eriedi* (l. 3) by the insertion of a subscript <e> (see CI 56). On *luio* July (l. 3) see CI 79.

RECENT STUDIES: None. The present edition is the first. Cicogna recorded the inscription but did not publish it.

Corpus Inscription 79

[IANVARIVS] → ẒẸ[N]|ARO || [FEBRVARIVS] → [...] ||
[MARÇIVS] → MA[RZO] || APRILI^S] → APRIL || MAÇIVS → MAZO ||
[IVNIVS] → [Z]VGNO || IVLIVS → LVIO || AV[G]VSTVS → AGOSTO ||
SEP[TEMBER] → SETEMBR[IO]] || OC[TOBER] → OTOB|RIO ||
[NOVEMBER] → NOVEMBRIO || [DECEMBER] → DECEMBRIO

[*Ianuarius* → Zenaro. *Februarius* → [...]. *Marçius* → Marzo. *Aprilis* → April.
Maçius → Mazo. *Iunius* → Zugno. *Iulius* → Luio. *Augustus* → Agosto.
September → Setembrio. *October* → Otobrio. *November* → Novembrio.
December → Decembrio.]

DATE: *c.* 1493. The second arch of St Mark's main portal — whose underside features the captioned sculptures of the twelve months of the year — is ascribable stylistically to the early to mid-thirteenth century, with a likely date in the 1240s. The dating question and its bibliography are examined in TIGLER (1995b: 134). There is nothing palaeographically to contradict this conclusion in the few faint traces remaining of the original Latin epigraphic writing on the scrolls of the months. The *ab initio* Latin names of the months were replaced by the equivalent vernacular ones when the portal was refurbished, re-gilded and repainted in an upgrade that was completed in 1493. The restoration date is recorded in black paint at the bottom of the inscription plaque of the virtue of Charity on the archivolt of the second arch (a photograph of it is in PIANA (1995: 239)).

LOCATION: In situ. Painted on illusionistic sculpted banderoles. The legends, placed at the top of each figuration, accompany and make explicit the allegorical sculpures of the twelve months, with their respective zodiac signs, that decorate the underside of the second arch over the magnificent front entrance to St Mark's Basilica. The upper side of the arch is decorated with female personifications of the Virtues and Beatitudes holding large scrolls with biblical inscriptions.

TYPE AND DESCRIPTION: Explicative legends painted on twelve marble banderoles. These vernacular captions on carved, illusionistic scrolls explicate(d) the great thirteenth-century figurative cycle of the months, sculpted in marble and originally gilded and painted, spanning the entrance to St Mark's. For obvious reasons I leave them untranslated.

Heavily encrusted with salts, sulphides and soot — deterioration that was aggravated in the twentieth century by the generalisation of coal- and oil-fired heating in Venice and by exposure to atmospheric pollution from Mestre-Marghera — the inscriptions on both sides of the second arch had become virtually illegible before the restoration and stabilisation work carried out in the 1980s. The restoration also revealed clear traces of the original gold and paintwork.

The sculpted cycle of the months, personified mainly by their characteristic agricultural labours, was a familiar medieval theme on church portals. However, the months on St Mark's stand out not only for their earthy, almost expressionistic,

Fig. 3.86. CI 79 (detail with October and November). © A. S. Ferguson.

gusto but also for the eclectic originality of their figurations in which Venetian, northern Italian, French and Byzantine influences are detectable. They reflect in their own way the eclecticism that characterises the architecture, decoration and mosaic inscriptions of San Marco. On the sculpture and iconography of the St Mark's cycle see TIGLER (1993: 159–62); TIGLER (1995b: 153–218); TIGLER (1999); DORIGO (2003, I: 222–24).

LETTERING: Painted majuscules, mainly in *capitalis* but with the occasional unorthodox intrusion of enlarged minuscule <z>, most noticeably on *mazo* (May). The original Latin names of the months from the early to mid-thirteenth century were done in monoline Romanesque majuscules with uncial intrusions, as far as one can judge, on the <e> and <c> at least. This *ab initio* lettering appears in some cases (February and April for example) to have been first inscribed in shallow grooves on the stone before being painted or infilled. The restoration carried out between 1982 and 1987 not only made the vernacular overwriting clearer in cases where it had not been entirely effaced. It also revealed, on some of the scrolls, faint traces of the underwriting (PIANA 1995). This discovery allows us to reconstruct with some degree of certainty the nature and layout of the original lettering as well as the kind of modifications introduced by the late Quattrocento upgrade. The unearthing of these fascinating palimpsests is epigraphically significant. They provide a unique side-by-side case study of what letter forms were perceived by this date to be archaic and in need of modernisation. They confirm the fundamental transition in script norms in Venice, from Gothic majuscules to Roman capitals, after the mid-fifteenth century which has already emerged from our corpus. It is not insignificant that this highly visible recalibration was enacted on the prestigious great portal of St Mark's.

LANGUAGE: A review of the literature on the possible origins of the *-brio* (as opposed to *-bre*) endings of the ninth, tenth, eleven and twelfth months of the year, which are specific to Early and Middle Venetian, is in CRIFÒ (2016: 415–16). One theory is that analogy is at least partly involved in the emergence of these endings, given that six months of the year in Latin finished in *-ius*. However, this would not explain why the outcome was limited to the Veneto, even though MERLO (1904) implicated the Venetian bureaucracy in what he saw as analogical hypercorrection. Byzantine Greek had arguably the profoundest lexical impact on Early Venetian of any contact language, and the idea of a derivation from the Greek forms of September to December in -βριος is most persuasive. For the evolution of these designations over time in Venetian see FERGUSON (2007: 294–95). The vernacular preferences shown by the 1493 upgrade for January (*zenaro*), April (*april*), August (*agosto*) and October (*otobrio*) are of some interest. All four months had variant forms in Early Venetian and in each case the originally minority one, which happened to be closer to Tuscan and Latin, has prevailed here. So *zenaro* is preferred to *zener*; *april* to *avril*; *agosto* to *avosto*; and *otobrio* to *otubrio*. On this basis the obliterated inscription on the banderole for February may well have read *fevraro* rather than the commoner *fevrer*. March, May, June and July are represented by their usual Early Venetian forms: *marzo*, *mazo*, *zugno* (all three now with /z/ rather than the /ç/

which predominated in most of the Early Venetian period) and by *luio* via *LULIUS rather than the parallel variant *çulio* < IŪLIUS. The scraps of Latin underwriting show the fascinating influence of vernacular pronunciation and spelling habits on *maçius* (May) for *maius*, leading me to suggest *marçius* rather than *martius* for March. These outcomes are also reflected in Venetian chancery Latin for both months, where *madius* (alongside *maius*) and *marcius* were usual.

The zodiac signs on the clock-face of the nearby and almost contemporaneous Torre dell'Orologio in St Mark's square (see CI 80) carry raised and gilded metal capital inscriptions of the names of the months. The clock was made by the Emilian clocksmiths Zuan Paolo and Zuan Carlo Rainieri, and its month designations are curious for the mixture of Latin and vernacular terms, sometimes intermingled, which they display: *jannvario / febrario / marcio / aprille / maio / givnio / lvio / avgvsto / septembre / octobre / novembre / decembre.*

RECENT STUDIES: HEMPEL and JULIER (1979: 42–45).

Corpus Inscription 80

O ★ P ★ V ★ S ★ S ★ I ★ M ★ E ★ O ★ N ★ V ★ S ★ F ★ E ★ C ★ I ★ T ★ I ★ H
★ S ★ M ★ C ★ C ★ C ★ C ★ L ★ X ★ X ★ X ★ X ★ V ★ I ★ A ★ D ★ I ★ P ★ R
★ I ★ M ★ O ★ D ★ E ★ C ★ E ★ M ★ B ★ R ★ I ★ O ★

[*Opus Simeonus fecit*. IHS. MCCCCLXXXXVI, adì primo decembrio.]

TRANSLATION: *(This) work was done by Simion* in the year of Our Lord 1496, on the first of December.

DATE: December 1496. The literature, with very few exceptions (PUPPI and OLIVATO PUPPI 1977: 210), gives summer-autumn of 1497 as the date for the completion of the bell on the Torre dell'Orologio. This is largely on the basis that the cost of the bell materials was entered into the state debit account in June 1497 (ERIZZO 1866: 52). However, our inscription is unequivocal.

LOCATION: In situ on the great bell of the clock tower in Piazza S. Marco.

TYPE AND DESCRIPTION: Statement of authorship in raised metal lettering on the bronze bell of the Torre dell'Orologio in St Mark's Square. The bell is 156 cm high and has a maximum diameter on the lip of 127 cm. The inscription runs in a band round the roughly 4 m circumference of the bell at the point where the waist and soundbow meet, with the moulding wires acting as letter guidelines. The amply spaced letters are separated by raised rosettes so that there are no gaps in the epigraph except between *decembrio* and *opus*, the end and beginning words, bridged by a plaited relief. The bell is adorned by a band running just beneath the shoulder and featuring raised foliage and bird motifs. Four equidistant shields decorate the waist. Two of these feature the Barbarigo coat of arms in honour of the reigning doge Agostin Barbarigo, while the other two are wreath-framed lions *in moleca* symbolising Venice. As far as I know this is the only surviving bell inscription in Venice from our period which preserves vernacular elements. The metal for the bell was commissioned by the state from the Arsenal whose chief founder, (Si)gismondo Alberghetto, himself from a notable family of bell makers, provided 7,670 pounds of copper and 2,948 pounds of tin for the bronze at a total price of 682 ducats. The founder of the Torre bell Simion or Simon (Italian, Simone) Campanato, came from a famous Venetian dynasty of bell makers operating out of the *contrada* of S. Luca in the *sestiere* of S. Marco. Their lineage as *campanari* is recorded from *c*. 1300 until well into the sixteenth century (BOTTAZZI 2008: 368–75). The surname Campanato 'bell maker' must be of Paduan origin given the augmentative suffix *-ato* typical of that area and found in many common surnames such as Marcato and Cecchinato. The Campanato surname is still extant in the Veneto. On bells, bell making and bell inscriptions in Venice in the late medieval and Renaissance period, see BOTTAZZI (2008) and WOLTERS (2008). The *Mori* themselves, dating from the same period approximately as the bell, were cast by the Arsenal founder Ambruoxo (Italian, Ambrogio) dale Anchore.

The bell with the striking figures of the *Mori* ('Moors'), originally called the

Fig. 3.87. CI 80 (detail). © A. S. Ferguson.

Ziganti ('Giants') in Venetian before their *ab initio* gilding wore off in the course of the sixteenth century, is at the top of the unmistakable landmark that is the clock tower at the north end of St Mark's Square. The elegant structure of the Torre dell'Orologio, housing the intricate mechanism of its remarkable clock — originally functioning on a complex pulley system — stands over the entrance to the Venice's central thoroughfare, the *Mercerie* (Early/Middle Venetian, *Marzaria*), that winds its packed, shop-lined way to the Rialto.

The clock on the tower was commissioned by the Signoria in 1493 from Zuan Paolo Rainieri and his son Zuan Carlo, famous Emilian clockmakers from Reggio (Early/Middle Venetian, Rezo), to replace the only clock in the square, which had been housed for centuries at the side of the St Alypius portal of the Basilica. Rainieri senior had previously been responsible for building the public clock in Reggio. The beautiful blue and gold clock-face on the Torre dell'Orologio, with its hours and zodiac signs, may well have been influenced in design by the handsome and rather similar fifteenth-century clock face on the tower of the Piazza dei Signori in nearby Padua. The decision to knock down a portion of the Procuratie to house the Venice clock in a tower over the entrance to the Mercerie was actually taken only at the end of 1495, with building starting in 1496, and documents have yet to be found identifying the architect(s) of the tower itself. The whole structure was completed and unveiled in February 1499, the year recorded in the Latin inscription in monumental capitals (albeit with two unorthodox ligatures) on the marble architrave under the clock face and over the archway into the Mercerie: *Io · P$\widehat{au}$ · $\widehat{et}$ · Io · Caroli · fil · regien · op · M·ID* ('The work of Zuan Paolo and Zuan Carlo, his son, from Reggio. 1499'). On the construction and structure of the clock tower and clock, with documentation, see PUPPI and OLIVATO PUPPI (1977: 208–12) and GOY (2006: 234–38).

LETTERING: Roman square capitals, *c.* 2.3 cm high, bronze-cast and raised, with the raised-rosette word divisions giving the writing the appearance, at first sight, of *scriptio continua*. This is a fine piece of inscriptional work, and the perfectly raised letters are undamaged, clear and eminently readable. Simion managed to give his *capitalis* lettering all its characteristic features of squareness, balance, stroke contrast and serifing. This can be seen to particular effect on <a>, <d>, <m>, <p>, <r> and <v> as well as on the numeral <x>.

LANGUAGE: Partly in Latin, partly in Venetian, with the IHS Christogram between them. *Opus Simeonus fecit* '(This) work was done by Simion' reads like a trademark. For Simion to use his first name alone suggests that he and his Campanato brand needed no further advertisement. For the characteristic Venetian *-brio* ending on *decembrio* (December) see CI 79.

RECENT STUDIES: None. The inscription is mentioned in passing in a range of publications, starting with ERIZZO (1866), but has always been rendered inaccurately in spite of its perfect clarity, even by Cicogna who recorded but did not publish the inscription. This has undoubtedly contributed to the confusion over the dating of the bell.

Corpus Inscription 81

S(R) IAC(OMO) DE SIMON S(R) ANT(ONIO) DI UARISCHO S(R) IAC(OMO) BEUILAQUA S(R) FELIPO ₁| DE BELTRAME S(R) ZUANE DE ZORZI S(R) ALBERTO DARIN ₂| S(R) FERMO DI STEFANO S(R) NICHOLO DE MARCHO S(R) MICHIEL ₃| UERZO S(R) ALESIO DE ANDREA QUESTI SON LI ZUDEXI E LI PRO|UEDADORI || 1499 ADI 18. MAZO ₅

[Sr Iacomo de Simon, sr Antonio di Varischo, sr Iacomo Bevilaqua, sr Felipo de Beltrame, sr Zuane de Zorzi, sr Alberto Darin, sr Fermo di Stefano, sr Nicholò de Marcho, sr Michiel Verzo, sr Alesio de Andrea. Questi son li zudexi e li provedadori. 1499, adi 18 mazo.]

TRANSLATION: Mr Iacomo de Simon, Mr Antonio di Varischo, Mr Iacomo Bevilaqua, Mr Felipo de Beltrame, Mr Zuane de Zorzi, Mr Alberto Darin, Mr Fermo di Stefano, Mr Nicholò de Marcho, Mr Michiel Verzo, Mr Alesio de Andrea. These are the judges and superintendents. 1499, on the 18th of May.

DATE: May 1499.

LOCATION: Painted writing on a cartellino at the foot of the oil panel of the *Arrest of St Mark in the Synagogue* (164 × 146 cm) by Giovanni Mansueti (Early/Middle Venetian, Zuan di Mansueti). Since the late nineteenth century the painting has been in the Princes of Liechtenstein collection in Vienna. It was sold to count Johann II von Liechtenstein in 1890 by Vincenzo Favenza. The panel was originally in an apse chapel of the church of S. Maria dei Crosechieri (Italian, Crociferi), now the church of the Gesuiti in the *sestiere* of Cannaregio. The chapel belonged to the silk weavers' guild and confraternity, the *Scuola* of the *Testori de Pani de Seda* (Italian, *tessitori di panni di seta*). On the apse chapel of the *testori* in the Crosechieri and on its painting cycle dedicated to St Mark by Cima da Conegliano, Mansueti and Lattanzio da Rimini see FORTINI BROWN (1988: 286–87) and SHERMAN (2010: 173–81).

TYPE AND DESCRIPTION: Declarative and documentary. Painted message on a *trompe l'œil* cartellino mimicking the writing on an unfolded letter. The 'message' actually serves to list and publicise the names of the ten major officials of the confraternity-guild — the judges and superintendents — who commissioned the painting. As with the painted message at the foot of Carpaccio's *Annunciation* (CI 92), Mansueti's cartellino was probably placed in such a way as to be more or less directly at the eye level of the spectator. The names of the officials were, of course, well known to the many hundreds of members of the confraternity-guild. Above the *faux* letter is another smaller folded out cartellino 'letter' with Mansueti's signature painted in Latin in fine monumental capitals: *Ioanes de Ma/nsvetis / · P ·* .

Silk weaving was established in Venice from at least the thirteenth century. It was successful and complex enough by the fourteenth century to support two separate guilds. The earlier was that of the *samiteri*, named after the pattern-piled and sometimes brocaded silk velvet known as *samito* in Venetian, *sciamito* in Tuscan/

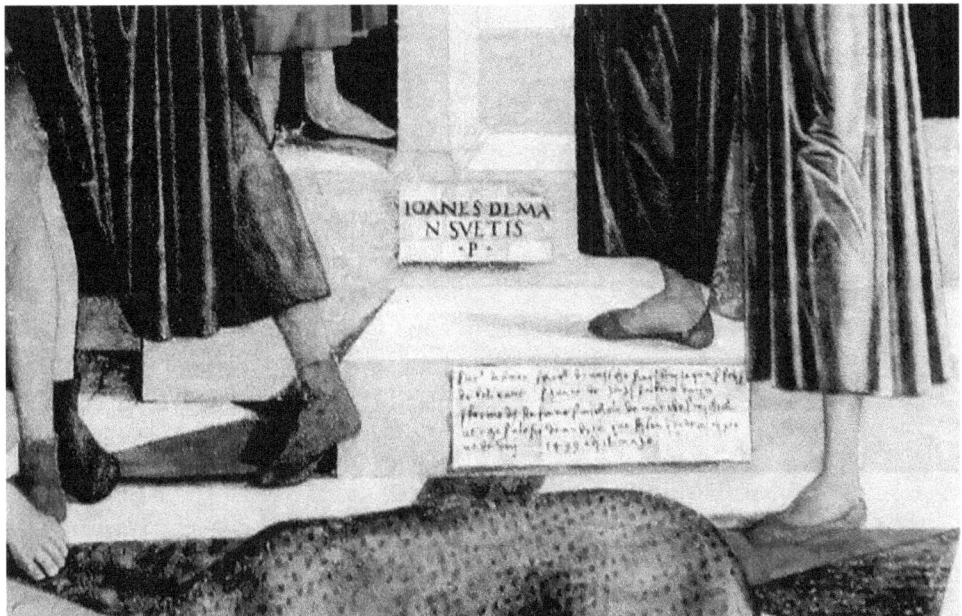

Fig. 3.88. CI 81 in context. © A. S. Ferguson.

Italian and *samite* in English (< Byzantine Greek ἑξάμιτον 'six threaded'). There were, in addition, the velvet makers proper, known as *veluderi* (Venetian, *veludo* 'velvet' < late Latin VILLŪTUM 'hairy'). On the two guilds, which were permitted to amalgamate in 1347, and on their *mariegole* see Rauch (2009). The rapid expansion of the silk industry in Venice from the mid-fifteenth century led in 1488 to the fusion into a single *scuola* of all the silk workers in the city, under the designation of *testori de pani de seda* 'weavers of silk cloth' (Venetian *seda* 'silk' < SĒTAM 'bristle, mane'). On this composite brotherhood — well-off, with a numerous body of craftsmen from a luxury trade, and with one of the most lavishly decorated guild chapels in Venice around 1500 — see G. Vio (2004: 584–85). Since the confraternity was dedicated both to the Virgin and to St Christopher it was naturally attracted to the Crosechieri where relics of that saint were worshipped. Although it retained down to the eighteenth century offices near the church, at what is now house no. 4877, it transferred its headquarters in the early seventeenth century to the much more comodious former meeting house of the Scuola Grande della Misericordia (see CI 93). These geographical locations are not coincidental. Workers in the industry clustered in the eastern parishes of Cannaregio, from S. Zuane Grisostomo and the SS. Apostoli northwards.

Mansueti's depiction of Mark's arrest is spectacularly exotic and anachronistic. The dark-haired and bearded saint — with hands bound and head yanked down by guards — is led away brusquely through a marble doorway on the spectator's left. The main picture space — foreground, background and, in part, middle ground — is an Eastern cityscape, evocative of Egypt or Syria, occupied by teeming scenes of conversing and gesticulating Mamluk figures with their flowing robes and billowing turbans. The sumptuousness of the garments on show reminds us that the commissioners of the painting were the ultimate connoisseurs of fine fabrics in Venice relating to the Muslim world which was both supplier of raw silk to Venice and major consumer of its finished products. The eye is also mesmerised by the complex multi-layered architecture of columns, arches, stairs, marble wall pannelling and inlaid flooring. The drama of the scene is enhanced by the intensity of the colour scheme, dominated by a palette of reds. The final touch of exoticism is the large leopard at the foot of the panel prowling before the spectator.

LETTERING: Cursive minuscule painted in imitation of handwriting. The longhand reproduced here is an example of the common medium of everyday writing and correspondence in Venice in the late Quattrocento and early Cinquecento. Less elegant and flourished than the Venetian chancery hand, it is broadly classifiable as *mercantesca* or mercantile, although in Venice it was not actually restricted to merchants and artisans. While already influenced, like chancery practice, by the new Humanist cursive norms elaborated in Padua and Venice itself, *marc(h)adantesc(h)a* or *merc(h)adantesc(h)a* (as it was called in Early Venetian) retained something of the feel of late Gothic and was very much an organic continuation of the non-chancery hand in use in Venice since the fourteenth century. The Mansueti cartellino features a more flowing version of the minuscule employed by Jacopo de' Barbari on his view of Venice of 1500 (CI 82–91). Mansueti's hand, with its natural looking mix of letter joining and pen lifting, its strongly looped <d> and <l> and its elongated <i> in the form of a <j>, even in internal positions, is also related to the varieties of *mercantesca* that cluster in the Marciana codex BNM Ital. XI 66 (6730). This is the most important surviving manuscript collection of early sixteenth-century Venetian and Veneto 'popular' literature, including versions of six Ruzante plays. On folio 173 the carefully written first page of Ruzante's *La Betia* — with its cast list, action summary and unique practitioner's sketch of the stage-set for the play — shows this cursive at its controlled handsomest. In calligraphic display form it appears on Carpaccio's *Annunciation* painted for the confraternity of the Albanians (CI 92). On the complex origins of Italian mercantile writing generally see CECCHERINI (2008). On the range of *mercantesca* realisations in the Veneto, with a corpus of examples, see VIGHY (1990).

LANGUAGE: The surnames on display show an interesting mix of both Tuscan and Venetian that probably reflects the aftermath of the strong input of originally Tuscan, and specifically Lucchese, silk weavers into the guild in the fourteenth century. This is most obvious on the patronymics with 'of' which sometimes show the north Italian *de* and sometimes the Tuscan or central Italian *di*. So *de Beltrame, de Zorzi, de Marcho, de Andrea* versus *di Varischo, di Stefano*. However, the possibility that some Tuscan names have been superficially Venetianised cannot be excluded. The surname *Darin* (l. 2), also now spelled Da Rin, is characteristic of the Belluno area of the northern Veneto. I have tentatively opted for *Antonio*, rather than the dipthongized *Antuonio*, in l. 1. There is no indication to allow the ten abbreviations for 'Mr' to be opened out as either *ser* or *sier*. The spelling tendencies of the inscription remain typical of Early Venetian, with the <ch> for the velar /k/ in *Varischo* (l. 1); the later-period <z> rather than the traditional <ç> in *Zuane* (l. 2), *Zorzi* (l. 2), *Verzo* (l. 4), *zudexi* (l. 4), *mazo* (l. 5); and the <x> for the voiced sibilant /z/ in *zudexi*. Of note are the dual nomenclature names of the top officials of the guild, different from those in almost every other *arte* in Venice: *zudexi* and *provedadori* 'judges' and 'superintendents'. The 1489 *mariegola* of the confraternity stipulated that four judges should be elected among the masters of the amalgamated crafts (two working in smooth cloths and two in raised fabrics), as well as six superintendents. The equivalent Tuscan/Italian terms are *giudici* and *provveditori*. Our inscription contains the ten names of these officials, with the four judges listed first. Slightly surprising is the maintenance of the traditional plural definite article *li* — probably chosen for its formality — which would be replaced by the variant *i* in the early sixteenth century. The Tuscanising *son* '(they) are' (l. 4) may have been preferred — as it was on the captions of Fra Mauro's *mappa mundi* (see CI 62–66) — in order to avoid the potential ambiguity between singular and plural inherent in the Venetian equivalent *xe* '(it) is, (they) are'.

RECENT STUDIES: MILLER (1978: 91); BAUMSTARK (1981: 49); FORTINI BROWN (1988: 287).

Corpus Inscriptions 82–91
[de' Barbari's view of Venice]

CI 82 [Mainland towns]

MARGERA $_1$ | | MESTRE $_2$ | | TERVIXIO $_3$ | | SERAVAL $_4$

CI 83 [Lagoon islands]

TORCELLO $_1$ | | MACORBO $_2$ | | BVRAN $_3$ | | S(ANCTVS) IAC^O $_4$ | | S. NICOLO $_5$ | | S. ZUL|IAN $_6$ | | S. SEGONDO $_7$ | | S. CRISTOFFOLO $_8$ | | [S.] MICHAHEL $_9$ | | MVRAN $_{10}$

CI 84 [Churches and religious houses on Murano]

S. M. DI ANZOLI $_1$ | | S. BERNHARDI $_2$ | | S. MARIA $_3$ | | S. CIPRIAN $_4$ | | S. STEFFANO . $_5$ | | S. DONA $_6$ | | S. CIARA $_7$ | | S. IACOB(US) $_8$

CI 85 [Landmarks and sights in Venice]

RIALTO $_1$ | | FONTICO · DALAMANI $_2$ | | DVANA DE· M $_3$ | | SA(NCTVS) | MAR|CVS $_4$ | | PA|LA|CI|VS $_5$ | | CA·DE DIO $_6$ | | ARSENAL $_7$ | | HOSPI|TALES | (S(ANCTUS) |. ANTONIUS) $_8$ | |, IVDECA , $_9$ | | REGA|TA $_{10}$

CI 86–92 [Churches and religious houses in Venice by *sestiere*]
CI 86 [Cannaregio]

CORPUS | DOMINI $_1$ | | S. LUCIA $_2$ | | S. GEREMIA $_3$ | | IOB $_4$ | | . S . LUNHAR^{DO} $_5$ | | S. IERONIMUS $_6$ | | S. MAR|COLA $_7$ | | SERVI $_8$ | | S. ALOVIXE $_9$ | | S(ANTA) FOS|CHA $_{10}$ | | S. | MA‹D›ALE|NA $_{11}$ | | S. M. DEL ORTO $_{12}$ | | MI|SERI|COR|‹D›IA $_{13}$ | | . S . | SOVIA $_{14}$ | | F[EL]|IXE $_{15}$ | | APOSTOLI $_{16}$ | | CROXECHIERI $_{17}$ | | S. IO. | GRISOS|TIMO $_{18}$ | | S. CANCIAN $_{19}$ | | S M | NOVA $_{20}$ | | MIRACULI $_{21}$

CI 87 [Castello]

S. IOHANES | ET PAULE $_1$ | | S. IUSTINA $_2$ | | FRANC(ESC)^O $_3$ | | TER|[NITA] $_4$ | | CELESTIA $_5$ | | LE VERGINE $_6$ | | . S(ANCTI) . PETRI IN CASTELLO . ◆ | S(ANCTUS) IO(HANES) N $_8$ | | S | PRO|VOLO $_9$ | | S(ANCTUS) | ZA|CA|RI|A|S $_{10}$ | | S. | IO. | BR^A $_{11}$ | | S(AN). | MARTIN $_{12}$ | | . S(AN) . BOR|T^O(LOMIO) $_{13}$ | | . S(ANCTUS) | DO|MI|NI|CUS $_{14}$ | | S(ANTA) . ANN|A $_{15}$ | | . S(ANTA) ELLENA . $_{16}$ | | S. LIO $_{17}$ | | S. MA|RI$_N$A $_{18}$ | | S. M. FORMOSA $_{19}$ | | . S(AN) | SOVERO $_{20}$ | | LORE(NZ)^O $_{21}$ | | S(ANCTUS) . IO(HANES) DEL TE(MPIO) $_{22}$ | | S(ANTO) | AN|TO|LIN $_{23}$ | | . S(AN) | DAN|IEL $_{24}$ | | S(ANCTUS) | . ANTONIUS $_{25}$

CI 88 [S. Marco and the island of S. Giorgio]

VIDAL $_1$ || S. S⟨A⟩MUEL $_2$ || S . MAURIC(I)O $_3$ | MAURI $_4$ || STEFF|[A]NO $_5$ ||
S. | ANZ|OLO $_6$ || S(AN) | BENETO $_7$ || S LUCA $_8$ || S PATE|RNOAN $_9$ || .
S(ANTA) . MAR(IA) | ZUBENIGO $_{10}$ || S | F⟨A⟩|NT|IN $_{11}$ || . S . MOISE $_{12}$ ||
. S . ZI$^\text{M}$I$^\text{N}$IA(N) $_{13}$ || S. BO|RTOLO|MIO $_{14}$ || . S . SALVATOR $_{15}$ ||
. S . ZULIAN $_{16}$ || S(ANCTI) | GEORGII . $_{17}$

CI 89 [Dorsoduro and the Giudecca]

S MARTHA $_1$ || . S . NIC[OLO] $_2$ || S . BASE $_3$ || CARITA $_4$ || S. G|EROL(IMI) $_5$ ||
S. SEBA|STIAN $_5$ || CAR|MI|NI $_6$ || S TROVA(SIO) $_7$ | S. TROVASIO $_8$ ||
S | ANZO $_9$ || IESUATI $_{10}$ || . S . ANGNESE $_{11}$ || . S. | VIDO $_{12}$ || . SPIRITI .
SAN(CTI) $_{13}$ || LATRINITA $_{14}$ || BARN|ABA $_{15}$ || S. PANTA|LON $_{16}$ ||
. S MARGARITA $_{17}$ || . S(ANCTUS) | IO(HANES) . BATISTA . $_{18}$ || S | + $_{19}$ || .
S . IACOB(US) $_{20}$

CI 90 [S. Crose]

S. CIARA . $_1$ || S. ANDREA . $_2$ || S | + $_3$ || S . | SIMO$^\text{N}$ | PICOLO $_4$ ||
. S IO(HANES) . ⟨D⟩EGO $_5$ || S . IACOB(US) $_6$ || S | STAI $_7$ || S M M. DOM. $_8$ ||
. S . | BOL⟨D⟩O $_9$ || S | CASSA|N $_{10}$

CI 91 [S. Polo]

S. RO|CHO $_1$ || . F . | MI|NO|RES $_2$ || TOMA $_3$ || . S . IO(HANES) .
VAN|GELISTA $_4$ || S. AUGOSTIN $_5$ || STIN | SAN $_6$ || . S . POLO $_7$ ||
S APONAL $_8$ || . S . IACOBUS $_9$

DATE: Explicitly dated 1500 on the map title itself. According to the written declaration of the German merchant Anton Kolb, who financed the project and successfully petitioned the Signoria for copyright protection and duty exemption for the map, it was some three years in the making.

LOCATION: At present the six original oblong blocks from which the map was printed are on display in the Museo Correr along with a first-state print of 1500 (Correr 1830, Inv. XLIV, no. 00098). Until 1830 this first print was in the Venetian collection of Teodoro Correr in his *palazzo* at S. Zan Degolà. It was bequeathed to the city with the rest of his collection when the aristocrat died. The blocks were in the Correr collection in the 1830s but their whereabouts previously are unknown. Twelve copies of the 1500 printing, showing the top of St Mark's bell tower in its temporary flat-roofed state following lightning damage (1489) and repair, are still extant. This is an exceptional survival rate for an early modern map where the sale of print runs of 200–300 was probably required to break even financially. Two copies are in the Correr, one is at the Fondazione Querini Stampalia and another is in the Museo Storico Navale. Outside of Venice imprints are held in Berlin (Kupferstichkabinett); Boston (Museum of Fine Arts); Cleveland (Museum of Art); Hamburg (Kunsthalle); London (British Museum); Nuremberg

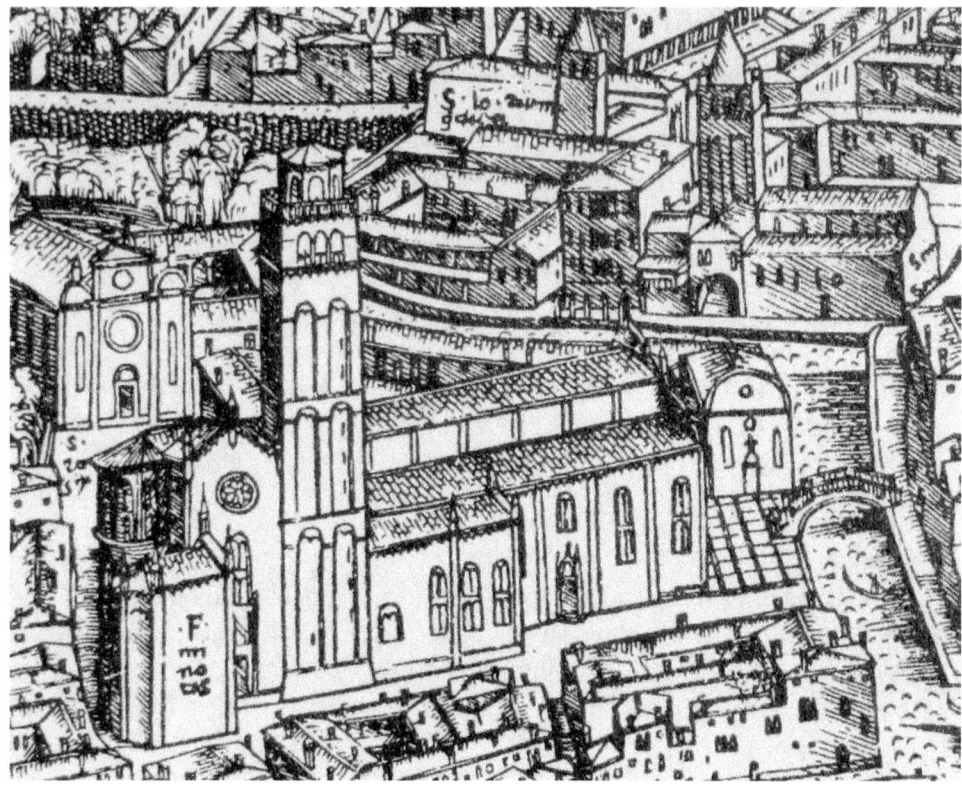

Fig. 3.89. CI 91 (1, 2, 4, 6). © A. S. Ferguson.

(Germanisches Nationalmuseum); Minneapolis (Institute of Art); and Paris (Bibliothèque Nationale). A second series of prints, showing the *campanile* with spire restored, was drawn off *c.* 1514.

TYPE AND DESCRIPTION: Toponyms in black ink on the anonymous woodcut print of Venice attributed to the Venetian painter and printmaker Jacopo de' Barbari (*c.* 1460/1475-*c.* 1516). The huge bird's-eye view, the first of its kind of Venice, is like no other of its time in terms of ambition and mapping technique. It is some 4 m square, measuring *c.* 282 × *c.* 135 cm, and the original six sheets comprising it, at roughly 99 × 66 cm, were the largest ever made. The six rectangular inked blocks themselves consist of butterfly-mortised pearwood planks cut along the grain and stabilised at the back with metal cross-pieces.

The attribution to de' Barbari is underpinned by limited material evidence but the circumstantial and stylistic evidence is strong and has long achieved critical consensus. The commissioner was the Nuremberg merchant Anton Kolb (or Colb/Cholb) who had strong links with Venice and had documented contacts with de' Barbari. Kolb's successful petition of October 1500 to the Signoria for copyright and for duty exemption has survived in early copied form (ASV, *Collegio, Notatorio*, reg. 15, fol. 28r). The view, which according to Kolb's testimony had to retail for at least three ducats to cover costs, was a luxury item meant for wall display. It sold well in Venice, to judge by the number of surviving copies there, and according to Kolb's petition was meant for shipping abroad too.

The map is an exquisite object of exceptional significance, authoritatively recording the city's enduring topography, at micro- and macro-level, as well as its toponymy. It frames Venice's centrality with a ring of carefully documented lagoon settlements (particularly rich in detail for Murano) and strategic points on the immediate mainland, including the Seraval (Italian, Serravalle) Dolomite fortress. Its restrained choice of signed Venetian landmarks is significant too: the key centres of political, religious and military power at S. Marco and the Arsenal, the mercantile focal points of the Rialto, the Fontego dei Todeschi and the Dogana da Mar, and also the city's assistential vocation, with two important state-sponsored hospitals at the eastern end of Castello: the Ca' de Dio and the hospital of St Anthony (the latter depicted alongside the captioned church of S. Antonio Abate whose foundation epigraph we examined in CI 13). The map thereby reproduced and simultaneously created a unique 'image' of Venice at a pivotal moment in the city's history. It straddled the boundary between private and public display, between art and science, and between Venetian and international exposure. It is all the more surprising that the linguistic and palaeographic aspects of its unassuming vernacular writing have hitherto been almost completely ignored.

On the map, its cartographical conception and its cultural context see SCHULZ (1978); FALCHETTA (1991); BALISTRERI-TRINCANATO and ZANVERDIANI (2000). On its potential Venetian and international audience see HOWARD (1997). On de' Barbari's life and œuvre see FERRARI (2006), reviewed by LEVENSON (2008), and BÖCKEM (2016).

LETTERING: Mainly cursive minuscule with some larger titling in Roman square capitals. The outlines of the view were first drawn on to the six woodblock matrices. The captions and other lettering were then added in the appropriate places by de' Barbari himself or by his assistant(s). The captions, drawn in reverse, were then inscribed in relief. The blocks were finally inked over before the large paper impressions were drawn from them and the prints subsequently collated.

The almost exclusively toponymic captions are discrete, terse and modest for an obvious practical reason. The astonishingly accurate rendering of Venice, down to house and street level, meant that except on blank lagoon or canal space the legends had to adapt ingeniously to whatever spaces were available on the map, however awkward. We therefore come across them jotted (sometimes scrawled) unobtrusively in the built-up areas on fronts, walls, *campi*, roofs, domes and towers in diminutive, cramped or almost cryptic captions that required particular deftness of touch. Some churches, like S. Marcilian in Cannaregio, S. Zuane at the Rialto and S. Maria in Broglio near S. Marco went unlabelled for lack of room. Other designations were necessarily allusive — for example, *Iob* (= S. Giobbe), *Franc͞o* (= S. Francesco della Vigna) and the S. Ziminian caption spelled out using the structure of the *campanile* to suggest the <m> and first <n>. Also amusingly impudent is the use of the far-right arched window on the church of S. Antonin in Castello (CI 87, l. 23) to stand in for the final <n> in *Antolin* (a trick also adopted for the <l> of *Samuel* on CI 88, l. 2), and the co-opting of a bell-tower roof line to stand for the <l> in *S. M. di Anzoli* (CI 84, l. 1). One suspects, in any case, that few if any purchasers or viewers of de' Barbari's splendid and expensive artefact would have been total strangers to the city. For this reason obvious landmarks like St Mark's Square or the Rialto bridge are not even labelled, the city being largely its own explanation.

It is instructive to compare de' Barbari's captions with those on the undated woodcut view of Venice produced by the Vavassore workshop in Venice in the early to mid-sixteenth century (LUSSEY 2015: 152–53) and with the woodcut view of Venice by Erwin Reuwich from 1486. The Vavassore map is clearly influenced, as all subsequent views were for centuries, by de' Barbari's example, but in all respects it is more conventional and less demanding of the viewer, even providing a long explanatory insert about the city in its bottom right-hand corner. The numerous captions are noticeably larger and easier to read than on de' Barbari. This is not only because they employ a more regular, well-formed minuscule but rather because the conventionality of building representation generally allows for their simpler, and more unrealistically prominent, insertion into the fabric of the city. This has the advantage of allowing the naming of churches which were unlabelled by de' Barbari, such as S. Marcilian in Cannaregio, S. Zuane at the Rialto, and S. Greguol (Italian, S. Gregorio) in Dorsoduro. It also permits more landmark labelling such as the Riva del Carbon at the Rialto, the Bari district in S. Crose, *la piaza d(e) .S. Marco* itself, and the Colleoni monument signed as *Bartolomeo / da Bergamo*, as well as the occasional explanatory observation such as *dove sta ./ el patriarcha* 'where the Patriarch lives' after the S. Piero de Castello caption. Erwin Reuwich's beautifully coloured woodcut view of Venice published in Breydenbach's *Peregrinatio ad Terram Sanctam* of 1486 also uses captions, though few compared to de' Barbari or Vavassore. These legends, in a minuscule still unmistakably influenced by Gothic, may possibly have given de' Barbari the idea of using building fronts to inscribe them on to, but he did not follow Reuwich in placing them on decorative cartouches and banderoles.

On the de' Barbari view *capitalis* is employed for the main title (VENETIE | MD), for the large-scale Latin motto above it under the figure of Mercury; for the smaller Latin motto on the caduceus held by Neptune in St Mark's basin; and for the designations of the eight personified winds on the surrounds. Among the map captions capitals are reserved for vernacular names of the larger lagoon islands in CI 83 (Torcello, Burano, Mazzorbo, Murano), for the four mainland towns (Marghera, Mestre, Treviso, Seravalle) in CI 82 and for six of the Venice landmarks/sights: the Dogana (CI 85, l. 3), the Arsenal (CI 85, l. 7), the Giudecca (CI 85, l. 9) and the *regata* (CI 85, l. 10), all four in Venetian, the basilica of St Mark and the Doge's Palace, both in Latin (CI 85, ll. 4, 5). The title, mottoes and surrounds are in impeccable Roman square capitals, beautifully balanced and serifed. The smaller map captions in capitals sometimes display heavier serifing. Indeed the central *Palativs* caption across the façade of the Palazzo Ducale actually leans towards Gothic decorativeness in this respect: a tendency also appearing occasionally in the minuscule captions, as on the *S. Iohanes et paule* inscription over S. Zanipolo, *S(ancti) Petri in Castello* over the church of S. Piero de Castello and *S(ancti) Georgii* over S. Giorgio.

The overwhelming majority of the map captions are in the *mercantesca* cursive minuscule, in common use in Venice in the late fifteenth and early sixteenth centuries and described in CI 81. The casual de' Barbari hand is necessarily less flowing than is normal in this longhand style because of the constraints imposed by the reverse writing and relief raising involved in the woodcut process. Nevertheless it is not unlike that employed by Marin Sanudo in his diaries, although Sanudo tended to place his <f> and <s> higher and to close his <g>.

The overall aspect of the de' Barbari hand is conditioned by the use of a thick nib on the woodcut block. The resulting stroke contrast produces a 'Gothic' look. Typical of his script are the long <f> and <s> dropping well below the baseline; the alternation of regular <r> with the rounded 2 type and of majuscule and minuscule <z> in initial positions; mostly cursive rather than uncial <a>; the distinction (in most but not all cases) of <u> from <v>; and <d> with generally straight ascender. In some contexts <m> can appear to have four minims and <n> to have three. The descender on <g> is seldom fully looped and closed, and the <l> is rarely joined and never looped. Very characteristic are the toponym word-ends on our map which are frequently closed with downward rounding. This occurs not just on final <i>, <m> and <n>, as might be expected, but even on <o>. On the vernacular captions abbreviation is mostly limited to a period — on the baseline next to the letter or mid high — on S. 'saint' and M. 'Maria'. Occasionally a suspension line over <s> indicates 'san(to)' or 'santa' more explicitly. The ending on a toponym is sometimes abbreviated with a superscript letter as in *Iac^o* (CI 83, l. 4) for *Iacobus* or else simply dropped as in *S. Anzo* for S. Anzolo Rafael (CI 89, l. 9). Apostrophes and accents are never present, so *dalamani* (CI 85, l. 2) for *d'alamani*, *ca de dio* (CI 85, l. 6) for *Ca' de Dio*, and *carita* (CI 89, l. 4) for *Carità*. The initial reversing of the lettering on the block has led to some recurring errors or potential confusions in the finished product. *San Stin* is reversed as *Stin san* on the church wall (CI 91, l. 6). Sporadically <d> (and on one occasion <b>) appears in print as <g>, so *Misericorgia* for *Misericordia* (CI 86, l. 13), *Gego[la]* for *Dego[la]* (CI 90, l. 5), *Magalena* for *Madalena* (CI 86, l. 11) and *Barnaga*, visibly corrected to *Barnaba* (CI 89, l. 15), while <g> and minuscule <z> are sometimes confusable, as on *S. M. di Anzoli* (CI 83, l. 1). The realisations of <a> and <o> can occasionally overlap in form, so that *S. Samuel* looks at first glance like *S. Somuel* (CI 88, l. 2) and *S. Fantin* could be taken for *S. Fontin* (CI 88, l. 11). I have restored what is plausibly the intended letter within angled brackets in the transcription. Abrasion or printing defects have led to the loss on some prints from 1500 of a letter or word part — for example, the *S.* on *S. Michahel* (CI 83, l. 9) or the last three letters of *S. Nicolo* (CI 89, l. 2). I have restored what is missing within square brackets.

LANGUAGE: Even if one did not know that the printmaker was born and brought up in Venice, one would receive that impression strongly from the captions which, apart from the Latin or Latin-influenced ones, mostly reproduce traditional Venetian pronunciations.

In de' Barbari's spellings one notes that the <ç> for the palato-dental affricate sounds, common in the corpus and prominent in Fra Mauro's *mappa mundi*, is now totally absent, replaced by <z> as in *Zulian* (CI 88, l. 16) or by <c> as in *Macorbo* (CI 83, l. 2). A sign that the traditional Venetian orthographic system was under pressure is the presence of <ci> to indicate the unvoiced palato-alveolar affricate [tʃ] where <chi> would have been employed previously, and still is on *Croxechieri* (CI 86, l. 17). Tuscan/Italian spelling intrusion is also perhaps indicated by the presence of what looks like the voiced palato-alveolar affricate [dʒ] on *S. Geremia* (CI 86, l. 3), where initial <i> might have been expected as in *Iesuati* (CI 89, l. 10). Other Venetian traditions appear but seem weakened, so that *Santa Foscha* (CI 86, l. 10) and *S. Rocho* (CI 91, l. 1), with <ch> representing velar /k/, stand alongside multiple instances of <c> alone. The voiced sibilant /z/ is alternately rendered by <x> and <s>, so *Tervixio* for Treviso (CI 82, l. 3) and *S. Alovixe* (CI 86, l. 9) but *S. Angnese* (CI 89, l. 11) and *S. Moise* (CI 88, l. 12). The velar /g/ is represented once by freestanding <g> on *Margera* (CI 82, l. 1).

Much of de' Barbari's parish nomenclature, constant from Early to Contemporary Venetian, is preserved in its familiar and highly characteristic native form — for example, *S. Anzolo* (Italian, S. Angelo), *S. Aponal* (Italian, S. Apollinare), *S. Beneto* (Italian, S. Benedetto), *S. Boldo* (Italian, S. Ubaldo), *S. Bortolomio* (Italian, S. Bartolomeo), *S. Fantin* (Italian, S. Fantino), *S. Lio* (Italian, S. Leo), *S. Lun(h)ardo* (Italian, S. Leonardo), *S. Margarita* (Italian, S. Margherita), *S. Martin* (Italian, S. Martino), *S. Pantalon* (Italian, S. Pantaleone), *S. Polo* (Italian, S. Paolo), *S. Provolo* (Italian, S. Procolo), *S. Samuel* (Italian, S. Samuele), *S. Simon Picolo* (Italian, S. Simeone Piccolo), *S. Stae* (Italian, S. Eustachio), *S. Stin* (Italian, S. Stefano confessore), *S. Ternita* (Italian, S. Trinità), *S. Tomà* (Italian, S. Tommaso), *S. Vidal* (Italian, S. Vitale). Other captions preserve forms which are now obsolete, have rarely been documented or are even unique — for example, *S. Alovixe* (Contemporary Venetian, S. Alvise), *S. Antolin* (Contemporary Venetian, S. Antonin), *S. Marcola* (Contemporary Venetian, S. Marcuola), *S. Sovero* (Contemporary Venetian, S. Severo), *S. Trovasio* (Contemporary Venetian, S. Trovaso), *S. Vido* (Contemporary Venetian, S. Vio), *S. Maria Zubenigo* (Modern Venetian, S. Maria Zobenigo), and the striking pronunciation variant *S. Sovia* (CI 86, l. 14) for the usual Early Venetian written forms S. Sophia ~ S. Sofia, designating the church of S. Sofia in Cannaregio. The latter are learned outcomes whereas the former is the kind of popular rendering of intervocalic PH (from Greek phi) seen in Venice in our period in sequences such as the forename Stephano ~ Stefano ~ Stevano (Stephen). For PH > /v/ in Early Venetian and other northern Italian dialects, see ROHLFS (1949–54, I: 359–61) and CORTELAZZO (1970: lx).

Regata 'boat race' (CI 85, l. 10) is an early use of this characteristic Venetian term — related to Early/Middle Venetian *regatar* 'to compete' — which would be exported to English where it is first recorded in 1613. The captioned flotilla of racing boats surges out of the bottom right-hand corner of the view.

RECENT STUDIES: SCHULZ (1978: 473).

Corpus Inscription 92

IN TEMPO DE ZUAN DE NICOLO ZIMADOR E SOI COMPAGNI
~ M CCCCC IIII ~ DEL MESE DAPRIL ~ X

[In tempo de Zuan de Nicolò Zimador e soi compagni. Mccccciiii, del mese d'april.]

TRANSLATION: In the time (of office) of Zuan, son of Nicolò Zimador, and his colleagues. 1504, in the month of April.

DATE: April 1504. The *Annunciation* with our inscription is the most impressive painting of the *Life of the Virgin* cycle undertaken by Carpaccio and his workshop. Intriguingly, it is the only one of the cycle to record commissioners and date even though the whole series was not finished until around four years later. One suspects strongly that it was the first to be completed.

LOCATION: Painted along the bottom of Carpaccio's *Annunciation* displayed in the Galleria Franchetti at the Ca' d'Oro. The picture was originally executed as one of a set of six on the *Life of the Virgin* for the newly built meeting hall of the confraternity of the Albanian nation — Scuola degli Albanesi (Middle Venetian, Scola d(e)i Albanesi) — at S. Maurizio in the *sestiere* of S. Marco. It is documented as being in the *scuola* until the end of the eighteenth century. After the Napoleonic suppressions it became Venetian state property for a time before being taken by the Austrian authorities to the Academy in Vienna. It was restored to Venice in 1918 after the Austrian defeat in the First World War and has been at the Ca' d'Oro ever since. Two of the other paintings in the cycle, the *Visitation* and the *Death of the Virgin*, are also now at the Ca' d'Oro. Of the remainder, two (the *Presentation* and the *Marriage*) are at the Brera in Milan and one (the *Birth*) is at the Accademia Carrara in Bergamo.

TYPE AND DESCRIPTION: Commemorative of a painting commission, the *trompe l'œil* epigraph painted in black runs along the bottom of Carpaccio's oil. It is meant to resemble inked writing on a strip of paper stuck to the front edge of the pink marble plinth at the foot of the scene. The message, which specifies the date of the painting and its confraternity commissioners (the named alderman and his fellow board members), is deliberately centred and visible. It was clearly meant to be seen and read. Both painting and inscription are undamaged and in remarkably good condition. It is curious that, contrary to his habit, Carpaccio did not sign either the *Annunciation* or any of the other paintings in the Albanian cycle.

On the *Life of the Virgin* paintings in the Scuola degli Albanesi, including source documents and reconstructions, see FORTINI BROWN (1988: 290–91). On the historical vicissitudes of the series see ZORZI (1984: 359–61). The Scuola degli Albanesi had been founded at the church of S. Severo (*sestiere* of Castello) in 1442 by a community of Albanian immigrants. Dedicated to the Virgin Mary and to St Gall the confraternity was allowed to move in 1448 to an altar at S. Maurizio. After the fall of the Venetian stronghold of Scutari in Albania to the Ottoman Turks in

FIG. 3.90. CI 92. © A. S. Ferguson.

1479 the confraternity was reinforced by an influx of Albanian refugees to Venice who received assistance from the Venetian government. After acquiring land near the church of S. Maurizio the *scuola* built its independent meeting house and small hospital in the parish at the turn of the century. It was upon completion of its upper floor that Carpaccio and his *bottega* were commissioned to paint the *Virgin* cycle. The façade of the building was decorated with relief sculptures and inscriptions, mostly but not exclusively from around 1530.

Carpaccio's *Annunciation* is a painting remarkable for the tension within it of apparent opposites: spirituality and sensuality, interior and exterior, dynamism and stillness, the dramatic and the everyday. Mary reading at her desk turns her head as if in response to the sign of the blond angel with its striking pointed wings, just as God the Father sends the dove of the Holy Ghost in a ray of light to her. The movement towards her from outside to inside is underlined by the contrast between the interior of her dwelling, receding towards the half-open curtain of her bed chamber, and the outdoor walled garden with birds, trees and sky beyond. The turn of Mary's head is mirrored by the measured gesture of the liminal angel. The crystalline clarity, delicacy and unity of the scene is enhanced by Carpaccio's exquisite tonalities dominated by shades of pink offset by greys, greens and black. The architecture framing the Virgin — with twin arches in the style of Codussi and two pillars with beautifully etched and painted motifs in the Lombardo style — is both solid and ethereal.

LETTERING: Display minuscule. Carpaccio's script, averaging 1.5 cm in height, is a high-grade version of the eclectic everyday Venetian *mercantesca* cursive hand that we have seen exemplified by Mansueti (CI 81) and de' Barbari (CI 82–91). Elegant and decorative, with the letters more often than not detached and deftly finished, it has a touch of the Gothic about it. This is particularly apparent in the carefully tapered minims of <m> <n> and <i>; in the curved-over ascender of <d>; in the shape and hairstroking of <r>; in the serifed <e>; in the multi-stroked <p>; and in the thick-thin contrast on <g>. The aspect of this lettering marries perfectly with the aesthetically refined, slightly archaic style of the *Annunciation*.

LANGUAGE: A brief but fully consistent example of Middle Venetian. As in CI 23 *zimador* is a tradename or proto-surname meaning 'cloth-shearer'. It was most often spelled with initial <ç> rather than <z> in Early Venetian. As we noted in CI 23 it is a derivative of medieval Latin CIMATOR, from CIMAM 'top part'. *April* < APRĪLIS shows the Latinising or Tuscanising restitution of <p>, as against the native *avril* which dominated most Early Venetian writing, including the inscriptions in our corpus, until the latter part of the fifteenth century (see CI 9, CI 79). The elision on *dapril* (= *d'april*) mirrors that on the same month in CI 23. On *soi* 'his' and other masculine possessive adjective forms see CI 94.

RECENT STUDIES: FORTINI BROWN (1988: 291); GEYMONAT (2014: 74).

Corpus Inscription 93

DEL ▲ 1505 ▲ FORONO ▲ PRINCIPIATE ▲ ET ▲ COMPIVṬ[E] ▲ QVESTE CASE ▲ PER ▲ ABITATION ▲ ₁| DE ▲ NOSTRI ▲ POVERI ▲ FRATELI ▲ AD LAVDE ▲ DE ▲ DIO ▲ [E]T ▲ DE ▲ L[A] ▲ VIRGINE ▲ MARIA ▲ ET ▲ ₂| DEL ▲ SERENISSIMO ▲ PRINCIPE ▲ MISIER ▲ LEONARDO ▲ LOVREDANO ▲ ET ▲ DE ▲ TVTO ▲ EL ▲ SVO ₃| GLORIOSO ▲ STATO ▲ CHE ▲ DIO ▲ FELICE ▲ LO ▲ CONSERV[I] ₄

[Del 1505 forono principiate et compiute queste case per abitation de nostri poveri frateli. *Ad laude* de Dio et de la Virgine Maria, et del serenissimo principe misier Leonardo Louredano, et de tuto el suo glorioso stato. Che Dio felice lo conservi.]

TRANSLATION: In the course of 1505 these houses for lodging our poor brothers were started and completed. *In praise* of God and of the Virgin Mary, and of the most serene prince Sir Leonardo Louredano, and of all his glorious state. May God keep him happy.

DATE: 1505.

LOCATION: Inscribed, in situ, on the architrave over the majestic gateway that leads into the Corte Nova courtyard in the northern part of the *sestiere* of Cannaregio. The out-of-the-way yard is located off the Fondamenta de l'Abazia beside the Rio de la Sensa canal as it approaches what remains of the original meeting house of the Scuola Grande di S. Maria del(l)a Misericordia (or *del(l)a Valverde*). Corte Nova with its charming little garden is the site of the cluster of twenty-two almshouses built by the *scuola* in 1505 that is the subject of the inscription. For a groundplan of the site as it is at present see SEMI (1983: 205–06). The original layout stretching back to the lagoon is reproduced in FABBRI (1999: 23–24). The gateway is depicted in Federico del Campo's oil painting of 1902 titled *Canal in Venice*.

TYPE AND DESCRIPTION: Commemorative and laudatory. The inscription records the founding date and purpose of the confraternity almshouses. It dedicates them to the heavenly authorities and, with fulsome praise, to the Venetian powers that be.

The inscribed Istrian stone architrave on which the epigraph is carved stands *c.* 316 cm off the ground and measures *c.* 212 × *c.* 25 cm. The slightly recessed inscription area itself is aligned with the opening of the portal in *pietra d'Istria* and is *c.* 160 × *c.* 20 cm. The remaining space on either side of the writing is filled with the emblem of the *scuola* in low relief. This consists of a roundel featuring the brotherhood's stylised initials SMV (= Santa Maria Valverde), with the decorative M topped by a crown: an emblem much in evidence in this part of Cannaregio. The inscription remains largely legible apart from the <e> on *compiute* (l. 1), the <e> on *et* (l. 2) and the <i> of *conservi* at the end of l. 4. In all three cases the culprit is the diagonal crack running down through the right-hand side of the inscription which has provoked slippage of surface stone and the large gape at the bottom of the plaque.

It is clear from the cement filling the cracks that the affected area has been repaired in relatively recent times. This is confirmed by the fact that when Cicogna saw and transcribed the inscription the illegible sections did not correspond exactly to the present situation. Through the gap caused by the damage to the plaque one can make out a large, strongly hairstroked <c> on the underlying architrave. This is part of an older inscription, not connected to the 1505 work. It probably refers instead to the confraternity's earlier almshouse cottages located across the Rio de la Sensa behind the Scuola's original *hospedal* building. Both the hospital (labelled *Misericor‹d›ia* at CI 86, l. 13) and the two rows of cottages behind can be seen prominently on de' Barbari's cityscape. The underlying architrave and the magnificent high relief above it — the latter also depicted by de' Barbari — seem to have been relocated to their present position over the entrance of the Corte Nova in 1505.

This superstructure above the architrave is a grandiose and complex Gothic relief in Istrian stone depicting the *platytera* Madonna flanked by the dignified bearded figures of two saints: John the Baptist on her right, St James the Greater on her left. The Madonna holds open her richly folded mantle beneath which the miniaturised figures of ten hooded confraternity brothers kneel in adoration. An ogival canopy, supported by a pair of spiral columns and topped by three prophets, frames the scene and is framed, in turn, by a larger ogival arch, intricately worked and sustained by two thicker spiral columns. This Gothic relief of the Madonna first decorated the façade of the Misericordia *scuola* building itself and is, in all likelihood, the *fegura della Nostra Donna* which the confraternity decided to move to the entrance portal of its earlier almshouse complex in a building campaign in the mid-fifteenth century (NEPI SCIRÈ 1978: 10). Its place on the meeting house frontage was taken by an early to mid-fifteenth-century tympanum relief (probably by Bartolomeo Bon, who was a brother of the confraternity) of the *platytera* Madonna, with confraternity brothers in adoration, ringed by prophets in the Tree of Jesse. This is the powerful, originally polychrome, *Virgin of Mercy* which — after spells on the subsequent *scuola* building then in the abbey church of the Misericordia — made its way in 1881 from the open market to what is now the Victoria and Albert Museum in London where it is still exhibited. That the *platytera* motif with the mandorla of the Christ child on the Virgin's chest, and with worshipping brothers in attendance, was the favourite leitmotiv of the *scuola* is further confirmed by its appearance, beautifully illuminated, in the confraternity's mid-fourteenth-century *mariegola* (HUMPHREY 2015: ill. XIIa).

As the inscription confirms, the building of the new hospital-hospice complex was completed in 1505. Its realisation was made possible by a concession of land to the confraternity, for an annual rent of fifty gold ducats, by the patrician Moro brothers. They were among the wealthiest residents of the neighbourhood and held the *jus patronatus* of the nearby Augustinian priory of the Misericordia. The *Abazia*, as it was known, had provided the concessionary space on which the first *scuola* building had been raised in 1310 and it maintained close links with the brotherhood. The ceding of real estate by the Moro family, with the say-so of the priory, allowed the confraternity to extend backwards towards the lagoon. The legal agreement

Fig. 3.91. CI 93 in context. © A. S. Ferguson.

Fig. 3.92. CI 93 (left-side detail). © A. S. Ferguson.

is in the ASV, *Procuratori di S. Marco, de Citra, commissaria Giorgio Baseggio*, 5 April 1505. The twenty-two almshouse cottages were given over free to infirm or needy brothers of the *scuola*, the *poveri frateli* (l. 2) of the inscription.

This is the only surviving vernacular inscription that has come down to us from the Misericordia, one of the four great *scuole grandi* founded in Venice in the thirteenth and early fourteenth centuries. The confraternity's original meeting house, much deteriorated, still stands at the end of the Fondamenta de la Misericordia in Cannaregio. After a long period of decline, followed by its sale in the early seventeenth century to the silk weavers' guild (see CI 81) and its dereliction in the modern period, it is now an official workshop for the restoration of Venetian works of art. The hugely popular and oversubscribed *scuola grande* became a victim of its own success, competitive ambition and financial mismanagement. The enormous, never finished, brickwork hulk of its subsequent sixteenth-century meeting house — the Scuola Nuova della Misericordia, situated just across the Rio de la Sensa and dominating the skyline of this quiet corner of Venice — is testimony to the brotherhood's overreach.

LETTERING: Roman square capitals cut in V-section. This is an impressive piece of inscriptional work. The sculptor was unquestionably provided with a master text to follow by the *scuola*, and the careful *ordinatio* of the epigraph suggests close collaboration between commissioner and stonemason. The inscription, justified on the left, is laid out with great care in terms of the spacing between letters and words, of interlinear distance, and of the deliberate centring of the shorter final line which is framed by leaf decorations in relief. Legibility is therefore high and is further increased by the good height of the letters at *c.* 2.5 cm, by large consistent interpuncts, by generous groove depth, and by the fine contrast between thick and thin strokes. The script, tendentially square in module and beautifully balanced, displays a confident understanding of *capitalis* lettering of the Roman imperial period. Abbreviations are conspicuous by their absence. This is not surprising on an inscription that was self-consciously aware of elite trends in script and language and, therefore, of correct usage with monumental capitals.

LANGUAGE: A unique example in the corpus of an inscription that deliberately attempts to express its message in a fully Tuscanising vernacular. It puts this apparently eccentric choice into perspective to note that ours is the only vernacular epigraph to have come down to us from a *scuola grande* after the elitist turn in Venice in the mid-fifteenth century. Within the confraternities this shift coincided with the full control by well-to-do merchants, civil servants and professionals of the management structures of these formerly more democratic institutions, and with Latin becoming their inscriptional language of choice. It may not be a coincidence that the *vardian grando* of the Misericordia in 1505 was the influential figure of Benedetto Fioravanti who held high office in the confraternity over decades and who was warden three times in the late fifteenth and early sixteenth centuries. Fioravanti's name and function suggest that he could have been a Venetian citizen *de intus et de extra* from a central Italian, possibly Tuscan, emigré background (ASV, *Scuola Grande della Misericordia*, busta 11). As *vardian* it is likely that he would have provided or overseen the written template for the sculptor to work from. The result shows, at the very least, an awareness of high-register writing trends in the peninsula in the direction of Tuscan, and a desire to emulate these. For emigré Tuscan influence on three other inscriptions in the corpus see CI 8, CI 26, CI 54. One cannot help but observe the somewhat fawning tone of the epigraphic message towards the Venetian authorities. This obsequiousness is unprecedented in the corpus among the inscriptions emanating from the *scuole grandi*.

Particularly noticeable on the inscription is the avoidance of Venetian voicing of intervocalic T > /d/ on *principiate* 'commenced' (l. 1), *compiute* 'completed' (l. 1), *frateli* 'brothers' (l. 2), and *stato* 'state' (l. 4). The Tuscan ending *-ono* on the 3rd plural past historic *forono* 'were' (l. 1) also stands out, although the intended verb form is imperfectly realised: with the stem of *forono* unintentionally based on Early/Middle Venetian *fo* rather than Tuscan *fu*. The *scriptor*'s underlying Venetian is also betrayed by the phonology of *abitation* 'lodging' (l. 1), with deletion of final /e/, by the consistent use of *de* 'of' rather than *di* (ll. 2, 3), by the definite article *el* (l. 3) for *il*, and by *misier* 'Sir' (l. 3). *Frateli* 'brothers', with absence of the double /l/, appears to stand midway between Tuscan *fratelli* and Venetian *fradeli*. The passive construction *forono principiate et compiute queste case* 'these houses were commenced and completed' (l. 1) — conforming to the pattern of passive agreement that dominates the numerous passive constructions in the corpus — is essentially Tuscan. Clearly motivated by Tuscan is the choice to give the doge's Christian name as *Leonardo* (l. 3) rather than the normal Venetian form Lunardo (CI 11, l. 2; CI 86, l. 5). There is a palpable effort to further elevate the language of the epigraph via a Latinising patina, with *et* 'and' (ll. 1, 2, 3), the etymological second /t/ in *abitation*, the phrase *ad laude* (in other words, *ad laudem*) 'in praise (of)' (l. 2), and the spelling *virgine* 'virgin' (l. 2) rather than *vergine*. *Louredano* (l. 3), the doge's family name, hybridises Venetian Loredan, its Latin equivalent Lauredanus and a Tuscan-type ending in *-o*. It probably mimics the spelling Lauredano often used for the name in Latin chancery practice.

RECENT STUDIES: WOLTERS (1976, I: 197). The Corte Nova inscription was first recorded in GREVEMBROCH (1754, II: 82). It was subsequently recorded, but not published, by Cicogna.

Corpus Inscription 94

M ⁕ CCCCC ⁕ V[⁕] II ⁕ DEL ⁕ MEXE ⁕ DE ⁕ MARZO ⁕ FV ⁕ FATA ⁕ QVE[S]TA ⁕
SCOLA $_I$ | [IN ⁕TE]MPO ⁕ DE ⁕ HI ⁕ DISCRETI ⁕ HOMENI ⁕ S(R) ⁕ ALEXANDRO ⁑ |
STRA[Ç]AROL ⁕ VARDIAN ⁕ ET ⁕ S(R) ⁕ BERNARDIN ⁕ DA◊LA ⁕ IVSTI | CIA ⁕
SPICIER ⁕ AVICHARIO ⁕ ET ⁕ DE ⁕ HI ⁕ SVI ⁕ COMPAGNI ❀❀ $_4$

[MCCCCCVII, del mexe de marzo, fu fata questa scola in tempo de hi discreti homeni sr Alexandro Straçarol, vardian, et sr Bernardin dala Iusticia, spicier, avichario, et de hi sui compagni.]

TRANSLATION: 1507, in the month of March, this confraternity house was built in the time (in office) of the prudent gentlemen Mr Alexandro Straçarol, warden, and Mr Bernardin dala Iusticia, druggist, (his) deputy, and of their colleagues.

DATE: March 1507.

LOCATION: In situ. The inscription is on the architrave over one of the two doors on the former meeting house of a devotional confraternity dedicated to the Virgin Mary, the *Sc(u)ola de l'Assunta*. The small two-storey meeting house stands immediately opposite the church of S. Maria Mazor (Italian, S. Maria Maggiore), in the parish of the Tolentini (*sestiere* of S. Crose) at no. 322. The isolated building is situated in the corner on the south side of the grassy Campo S. Maria Mazor where Rio de le Procuratie and Rio de S. Maria Mazor meet. Just along from it, at no. 324, is Venice's main prison centre, the Carcere di S. Maria Maggiore.

TYPE AND DESCRIPTION: Commemorative. The epigraph records the completion of the brotherhood's first meeting house, with the date and the names of the warden and his deputy. The inscription is carved on the Istrian stone architrave, measuring *c.* 194 × *c.* 30, over the main door of the building. It stands some 270 cm above ground level.

The *Scuola de l'Assunta*, dedicated to St Mary Major and attached to the Franciscan nun's church and convent of S. Maria Mazor standing immediately opposite, was a purely devotional *scuola piccola*. It was not linked to any trade guild and had an open membership that included women. The meeting house was built, like the church — whose elegant brick façade is often attributed to Tullio Lombardo — in the first decade of the sixteenth century in a secluded western corner of Venice overlooking the lagoon, a once beautiful site that has been largely disfigured by nineteenth and twentieth century developments. The original parallel strips of reclaimed land, the so-called *arzeri* (Italian, *argini*) *de S. Andrea*, on which it and the church were built can still be seen, largely uninhabited, on de' Barbari's woodcut map of 1500. Our confraternity was founded in 1502, with a membership of 100 men and women, and in 1505 it purchased two thousand wooden piles to consolidate the ground on which it intended to build its meeting house. In its *mariegola* (ASV, *Provveditori di Comun*, reg. S, fols 327–64) the brotherhood provided precious evidence of its own early patronage, and was unique among the confraternities in the corpus in explicitly naming the sculptor hired to build its inscriptional structure. A master

FIG. 3.93. CI 94. © A. S. Ferguson.

stonemason, Andrea de Zuan *taiapiera*, quite possibly the head of the well-known Buora family business at S. Stefano (see CI 106), was contracted on 27 December 1506 to construct the door and two windows for the meeting house. The impression emerges of a brotherhood that was comfortably off, in the early years of its existence at least. In 1511–12 it had its devotional cross fashioned by a goldsmith, master Sebastian de Bartolamio, while in 1515 it employed Tullio Lombardo himself to build its altar in the meeting house, paying him 100 ducats, and Palma il Vecchio to paint the accompanying altarpiece at a cost of 50 ducats. It must have had a strong processional presence, too, since by 1520 it had invested in 'bandiere numero 5 con la Madona dorada suso' (G. VIO 2004: 731).

On an identical Istrian stone lintel over the side door of the building there is an undated two-line Latin inscription, presumably slightly later than the vernacular one, by a different sculptor than the first to judge by the deftness of its lettering. It sets out in stone the spiritual ideology of the brotherhood in a way that, to my knowledge, has no precedent in *scuola* public statements. Carved in beautiful, large-size *capitalis* lettering — featuring a series of remarkable, elegant ligatures after the Romanesque manner and a low-relief crown over the <m> of Maria — it remains undamaged and legible: *Hec · est · vera · fraternitas · qvam · spretis · secli · vi/tiis · Sancta · Maria · Maior · perdvcit · ad celestia* ('This is a true brotherhood, which — since it scorns the vices of this world — Saint Mary Major leads to heaven'). This important inscription was missed by Cicogna who did record the vernacular one, although he was unable to identify the confraternity that it belonged to (CICOGNA 1824–53, III: 465).

The church and the meeting house opposite were used as barracks and storehouses following the Napoleonic suppressions before being allowed to fall, in the twentieth century, into a state of dilapidation. In recent times the former confraternity building, now in the charge of the prison authorities, has undergone restoration work. The church, which had been stripped of its many important artworks in the nineteenth century, was secured structurally around 1970. On the history and former contents of the church see ZORZI (1984: 349–51).

LETTERING: Roman square capitals cut in V-section, with the four lines filling up the area of the architrave. The large bold lettering, 4.5 cm in height, with ample spacing between letters and words, shows a good understanding of *capitalis* practice and must originally have stood out impressively over the entrance to the meeting house. As it is, the plaque has suffered generally from wear and tear, with flaking at its worst along the top line and particularly over the far left of the inscription where legibility is in part compromised. The epigraph is justified on the left and the mason has obviously made an effort to lay out his four lines of script evenly and fully across the tablet. To achieve this he has filled the gap at the end of the second line with a colon and the space at the end of the final line with a double flower-head device. More interestingly, he has increased word spacing on ll. 3 and 4, and even stretched the gaps between letters, as can be seen particularly clearly on *avichario* (l. 4). The letters show a good balance between forcefulness and elegance of ductus, with controlled stroke contrast. Their restrained smartness is emphasised by the delicate spiral interpuncts. Letter height and width are regular overall, although one notes some discrepancies, for example between the <h> of *avichario* (l. 4) and that of *hi* (l. 4), with the latter slightly compressed and featuring a higher cross stroke. Before the <l> of *dala* (l. 3) is another partly cancelled letter, realised almost like an <i> with an outsized wedge serif on top. It appears to be a mistake which the stonecutter may have attempted to erase.

LANGUAGE: In line with the majority of passives in the corpus *fu fata questa scola* 'this confraternity meeting house was built' (l. 1) is perfectly regular in its agreements. As on CI 60 of 1446 and CI 77 of *c.* 1482 the undiphthongised form *scola* 'meeting house, confraternity house' — eclipsed since the early fourteenth century — is preferred, with the previous uses of the variant *scuola* in our collection going back to the 1420s. However, as with *ser* (Mr) versus *sier* (see CI 95) the still variegated picture regarding diphthongisation of stressed mid-high vowels is suggested by the reappearance of *scuola* in CI 98 of 1518. On *avichario* 'deputy' (l. 4), pronounced [aviˈkario] and featuring an initial *a-*, see CI 50. Revealing of the spiritual status of our *scuola* is the designation of the confraternity head as *vardian* (like that of the *scuole grandi*) rather than as the *gastaldo* mostly associated with *scuole piccole* that were based on trade guilds. *Discreti* 'wise, prudent' (l. 2) is cognate with English *discreet*. Interestingly, three different letters are employed in the inscription to signify the unvoiced affricate of the /ts/ type. *Marzo* (March, l. 1) has the <z> which had become dominant in Venetian since the late fifteenth century. However, *Straçarol*, literally 'rag man' or 'rag merchant' (l. 3) — a surname already encountered on CI 13 — retains the <ç> which dominated most of Early Venetian. The relevant letter is much effaced but high resolution photographs unmistakably reveal the <c> with cedilla. Its retention is certainly down to the inherent conservatism of anthroponymy. The common term *spicier* (l. 4) is a variant form, with raised pretonic vowel, of Middle Venetian *specier* or *spezier* 'grocer, druggist' (see CI 41), itself from *specie* or *spezie* 'spices' (< SPECIES) in the sense of 'ingredients making up a drug or perfume'. On *mexe* (l. 1) the voiced sibilant /z/ is still represented by the traditional Venetian <x>. On the other hand, the <x> on *Alexandro* (l. 2) was probably pronounced as /s/.

Two particular features of morphosyntax stand out. Unique on a stone carved inscription in the corpus is the masculine plural form of the partitive *de hi* 'of the' (ll. 2, 4), where *deli*, *dei* or *di* would have been expected. This rare partitive type also appears repeatedly on the captions of Fra Mauro's *mappa mundi* (see CI 62–66 where the phenomenon is considered). Interesting is the 3rd person masculine possessive adjective *sui* 'his, her, their' (l. 4). The paradigm of unstressed masculine possessives as revealed by the evidence of the corpus — ranging across the fourteenth and fifteenth centuries — is: singular *so*, plural *suò* ~ *soi*. This distribution would stabilise and simplify out in Modern Venetian into singular *so*, plural *so*. The rarer plural form *sui* found in the present inscription would be assigned exclusively in Modern Venetian to the equivalent stressed possessive pronoun meaning 'his, hers, theirs'.

RECENT STUDIES: MOCELLIN (2016: 60–62). First published by CICOGNA (1824–53, III: 464).

Corpus Inscription 95

NEL ▲ TEMPO ▲ D(E) ▲ SER ▲ ZVANE ▲ DE LOVI(N) ▲ PISTOR ▲ A ▲ S(AN) ▲ APONAL ₁| GASTALDO ▲ E COMPAGNI ▼ M ▲ D ▲ VIII ▲ ADI ▲ II ▲ DE ▲ MARZO ₂|| [ᵀDE L]A ▲ PAR°|CHI̦[A] ▲ DE [▲] S(AN) ▲ ₄| SI[L]V[ESTRO] ₅

[Nel tempo de ser Zuane de Lovin, pistor a san Aponal, gastaldo e compagni*. MDVIII, adì 11 de marzo. *dela parochia de san Silvestro.]

TRANSLATION: In the time (in office) of Mr Zuane de Lovin — baker at S. Aponal — alderman, and (his) colleagues ★. 1508, on the 2nd of March. ★of the parish of S. Silvestro.

DATE: March 1508.

LOCATION: In situ on the architrave over the large ground-floor window of what is now a shop at S. Polo no. 1252. As one approaches the Rialto from S. Polo the store stands in Campo S. Aponal between the church and its bell tower, just as the square opens out into Calle del Campaniel.

TYPE AND DESCRIPTION: Commemorative. The inscription, without making it explicit, appears to celebrate the opening in 1508 of a meeting room on the ground floor of the building by a chapter of the brotherhood of German master bakers and bakery workers — the *pistori maistri e lavoranti todeschi* — in Venice. Given that 1508 marked the start of a major campaign by the Habsburg Holy Roman Empire against Venetian territory and that the War of the League of Cambrai was imminent, the bakers may have felt it imprudent to foreground their 'Germanness'. This concern may also explain the inscriptional addendum, discussed below, which emphasises the bakers' embeddedness in their local community. The Istrian stone window lintel on which it is carved measures *c.* 182 × *c.* 20 cm and is *c.* 292 cm above pavement level in the corner of the busy *campo*. From the inscription it is clear that the initiative was sponsored by the alderman of the brotherhood, Zuane de Lovin resident in the parish of S.Aponal, in conjunction with his fellow bakers operating out of the densely populated contiguous parish of S. Silvestro (VUILLEMIN 2018: 43–121). The second floor of the building in question had been occupied since 1394 by the confraternity-guild of wholesale druggists (Middle Venetian, *spezieri* or *specieri da grosso*: see CI 41, CI 94) while, as of 1514, the third floor would belong to the confraternity-guild of the stonemasons, the *Scola d(e)i Taiapiera* (later Middle Venetian and Modern Venetian, *tagiapiera*). The masons' splendid Istrian stone relief of the four crowned martyrs, the confraternity's patron saints, stands high up on the façade, with beneath it an inscription in square capitals from 1652: MDCLII // *Scola di tagiapiera*.

The brotherhood of the German bakers, dedicated like the German shoemakers in Venice (see CI 42) to the Virgin Conception, was founded in the early fourteenth century. After a series of peregrinations it eventually settled, like the shoemakers, in the S. Stefano-S. Samuel area. Like them it too founded an almshouse for its members, most of whom originated in the southern German lands. It was located

Fig. 3.94. CI 95. © A. S. Ferguson.

Fig. 3.95. CI 95 (right-side detail). © A. S. Ferguson.

in Calle dei Todeschi at S. Samuel which has retained, in its name, the memory of their presence. The *pistori* < PISTŌRII 'bread makers, grain grinders' did the baking but not the retailing of bread which was the prerogative of the *forneri* < FŬRNARII 'bakers, oven workers'. The *pistori* in Venice under the *ancien régime* were divided into the three nations of *pistori veneti*, *lombardi* and *todeschi*. Despite attempts by the authorities to amalgamate them into a single unit (SBRIZIOLO 1967–68: 427–28) the German bakers — who, from the names on the 1471 list of master bakers in the city in the *mariegola* of the bakers' *scuola* (BRAUNSTEIN 2016: 841–42), were a dominant presence — stubbornly retained their independence, at least as far as their devotional activities were concerned. This is strikingly proclaimed by their communal burial plot which was situated in front of the altar of the Virgin Conception in the church of S. Stefano. The accompanying vernacular inscription, transcribed by Cicogna but no longer extant, happened to carry the name of the same Zuane de Lovin as at S. Aponal. He had evidently been re-elected as alderman in 1511: *Sepoltura della fraternita / de pistori e / lavoranti germanici / in tempo de ser / Zuanne de Lovin / gastaldo e compagni /* MDXI.

LETTERING: Roman square capitals cut in V-section. A bold, consistent and sophisticated piece of inscriptional work. At around 5 cm high the letters on the main epigraph are eminently visible and still perfectly legible. The monumental capitals are impressively realised, with the contrast between thick and thin strokes both enhancing and softening the squareness of the module. This can be seen particularly well on <a>, <d>, <l>, <m>, <n>, <o>, <p>, <t> and <v>. The aesthetic attractiveness of the script is also enhanced by the understated serifing, seen to good effect on <e> and <g>, and by the clear, rational letter spacing emphasized by triangular interpuncts. There are only two uses of abbreviation, affecting the <n> on *Lovin* (l. 1) and the <an> of *san* (l. 1). In both cases the missing letters are indicated by a discreet horizontal line over the preceding letter. In this way the 'Roman-ness' of the lettering is minimally interfered with.

At first sight the spectator's focus is exclusively on the epigraph filling the lintel. Upon close inspection, though, one becomes aware of an area with smaller scale lettering carved on the right-hand surround of the window and level with the main plaque. The now faded and sporadically legible writing on it is not, as might be suspected, an inscription underlying the one on the architrave. It is, in fact, the continuation of it in the form of a codicil. The oversight is signalled on the main text by an omission-insertion sign after *compagni* (l. 2), consisting of a semicircle with a kind of 1 attached (of a type also used on CI 108 to insert a missing letter). It specifies that the colleagues involved were all, like the alderman Zuane de Lovin himself, bakers specifically from the parish of S. Silvestro and not from the city as a whole. This addendum was presumably inserted by the stonecutter, at some point after the completion of the original remit, at the behest of the commissioners who had realised their important oversight.

The main lintel inscription has been affected by dark staining over most of its surface, apart from the far left side, but this actually enhances rather than detracts from its present high legibility. On the other hand, the window surround with the follow-up writing has been badly scuffed up by what looks like plaster work. In addition, it has been disfigured by the intrusion of a rusty iron bar from the grating of the contiguous window which obliterates the end of *Silvestro* (l. 5). The result is that only snippets of the side writing can still be read. This additional inscriptional area, with its three short lines, is very roughly 22 × 20 cm and the letters are reduced-sized versions of those on the main tablet. The <o> on *parochia* (ll. 3–4) is in superscript because of space constraints at the edge of the surround.

LANGUAGE: On Venetian *pistor* 'baker' (l. 1) see above. *Aponal* (l. 1) is the traditional Venetian rendering of the name of St Apollinaris of Ravenna, known as Apollinare in Italian. *Lovin* in the alderman's surname *de Lovin* (l. 1) is Lübbenau in Brandenburg. *Parochia* 'parish' (ll. 3–4; Italian, *parrocchia*), from late Latin PARŌCHIAM, is the only example of the term in the corpus. *Ser* 'Mr' (l. 1) suggests the undoubted trend away from diphthongisation of mid vowels in the early Middle Venetian period, although the picture even with this exceedingly common word remained varied. Marin Sanudo, notably, retained the diphthongised variant *sier*.

RECENT STUDIES: The present is the first published edition with commentary of the full inscription. The inscription is reproduced in part in GRAMIGNA and PERISSA (2008: 86). First published by CICOGNA (1824–53, III: 271).

Corpus Inscriptions 96–99

CI 96

PAX · | TIBI · | MARC{E · | EVAN|GELISTA · MEVS ·₁ | | 1508 ⨳ADI ⨳25 ⨳
MAÇO ⨳S(R) CRISTOFALO ⨳DE ⨳ANBRVOXO ⨳GASTALD{O ⨳STA ⨳A SAN ⨳
MOIXE ⨳AVIC{HARIO S(R) ⨳DAMIAN ₂| DE [⨳] MICHIEL [⨳] STA ⨳A SAN ⨳NIC{HOLO
⨳SCRIVAN ⨳S(R) ANTONIO ⨳ DE ⨳VIVIAN NARANC{ER ⨳A SAN ⨳BENETO ⨳E ⨳
(CON)PAGNI ~✿ ₃| | C{EXERE | FAVE^TA | FAX^OLI | FAVA T{O(N)DA ₄

[*Pax tibi Marce, Evangelista meus.* 1508, adì 25 maço. Sr Cristofalo de Anbruoxo, gastaldo, sta a San Moixè; avichario sr Damian de Michiel, sta a San Nicholò; scrivan sr Antonio de Vivian, narancer a San Beneto, e conpagni. Cexere, faveta, faxoli, fava tonda.]

CI 97

⨳I ⨳D ⨳XVII ⨳IN ⨳ TENPO ⨳DE ⨳ MAISTRO ⨳NICHOLO ⨳ DE ⨳ MARCHO ⨳
MARCHOVICHIO ⨳ DITO ⨳DE ⨳ANDRONICHO ₁| GASTALDO ⨳ DE ⨳LARTE ⨳
DE ⨳ REMERI ⨳ E (CON) I SVO ⨳(CON)PAGNI ~✿ ₂

[IDXVII, in tenpo de maistro Nicholò de Marcho Marchovichio, dito de Andronicho, gastaldo de l'Arte de Remeri, e con i suò conpagni.]

CI 98

▲ 1518 ₁| ADI ▲ 12 MAZO ▲ IN ▲ TEMPO ▲ ₂| D(E) ▲ S(R) ▲ STEFANO ▲
D(E) ▲ PIERO ▲ ₃| CHASTALDO ▲ E CHOMPAGNI ▲ DE ▲ ₄|
LA ▲ SCVOLA ▲ DE ▲ BVTERI ▲ ₅

[1518, adì 12 mazo, in tempo de sr Stefano de Piero, chastaldo, e chompagni de la Scuola de Buteri.]

CI 99

⨳M ^O ⨳D ⨳XX ADÌ SETE ZENER PER LARTE DE SABIONERI

[MDXX, adì sete zener, per l'Arte de Sabioneri.]

TRANSLATIONS: CI 96: *Peace to you, Mark, my Evangelist.* 1508, on the 25th of May. Mr Cristofalo de Anbruoxo, alderman, residing at San Moixè; (his) deputy, Mr Damian de Michiel, residing at San Nicholò; (his) secretary, Mr Antonio de Vivian, orange merchant at San Beneto; and (their) colleagues. Chick peas. Cannellini bean. Kidney beans. Fava bean.

CI 97: 1517, in the time (in office) of master Nicholò de Marcho Marchovichio, known as 'de Andronicho', alderman of the Guild of Oar Makers, and with his colleagues.

CI 98: 1518, on the 12th of May, in the time (in office) of Mr Stefano de Piero, alderman, and (his) colleagues from the Confraternity of Coopers.

CI 99: 1520, on the 7th of January, for the Guild of Sand Suppliers.

FIG. 3.96. CI 96 in context. © A. S. Ferguson.

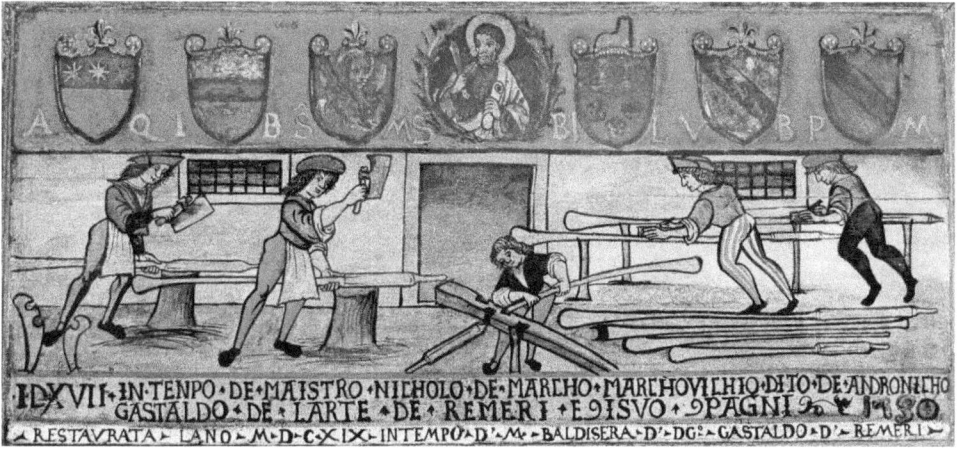

FIG. 3.97. CI 97 in context. © A. S. Ferguson.

DATE: CI 96: May 1508. CI 97: 1517. CI 98: May 1517. CI 99: January 1520.

LOCATION: Until the fall of the Venetian Republic these four, like all trade guild boards, were hung in the premises of the magistrates of the Giustizia Vecchia (Middle Venetian, Oficiali ala Iusticia Vechia) in the Palazzo dei Camerlenghi beside the Rialto bridge. After 1797 they were transferred to the Doge's Palace where they were held in storage until 1937. With all the other boards they were then moved to the Museo Correr where they are kept and displayed, on a selective basis, at present. They underwent restoration in 1980.

TYPE AND DESCRIPTION: Commemorative and documentary. The four boards, each with its oil-painted illustration, celebrate the presence and essence of their respective trade guild on a given date: the fruiterers, the oar makers, the coopers and the sand suppliers. The painted inscriptions on them have a similar, though not identical, format to one another. They record the name of the guild in question (but not in the case of CI 96, for reasons touched on below) and the date of the panel's completion. More often than not they provide the name of the guild's alderman and, sometimes, of other members of the governing board. The exception is the sand supplier's inscription (CI 99) which omits the names of the officials altogether. The layout of the four panels, while not completely standardised, always comprises three strata. At the top are featured the escutcheons of the Iusticia Vechia which oversaw the trade guilds in Venice. Sometimes also present are the painted initials of the magistrates in office at the time, along with the Venetian lion, and the coat of arms of the reigning doge. In three cases the inscription is laid out in a horizontal strip, either at the foot of the board (CI 97, CI 99) or across the middle (CI 96). In the case of CI 98, from the coopers' guild, it is 'inscribed' in *trompe l'œil* on to a desk structure painted at the bottom of the picture.

Altogether, the panels of forty-four Venetian trade guilds survive, spanning the sixteenth, seventeenth and eighteenth centuries. Earlier boards undoubtedly existed but have either been overpainted or lost. Our four, along with all the other early ones, are painted on wood, with canvas only appearing in the eighteenth century. While the names of some of the painters of the later examples are modestly well known, all the sixteenth-century boards are anonymous. They were shown in the Camerlenghi palace but their precise purpose has yet to be established for certain. Produced (or restored) at the periodic instigation of the Iusticieri Vechi in office at the time, it is believed that each would have been hung alongside a notice board in order to allow the guild to display its presence and to receive official communications (FOGOLARI 1928–29: 724). This supposition is plausible given that, according to Marin Sanudo writing at the time, the officials of the Iusticia Vechia — who micro-managed the implementation of guild statutes and membership rules — 'fanno sententie con cartoline come li Consoli' (CARACCIOLO ARICÒ 2011: 287). Hanging, as they did in the Iusticia premises, the boards were well and truly on public display: seen not just by the members of the other guilds but by the busy throng in the building where prices of staple commodities were set and where duties were paid.

Three of our panels appear to have survived intact and unaltered into the modern period. The fourth, that of the oar makers (CI 97), was restored twice under the Republic, with the restoration dates of 1619 and 1730 recorded on the panel. However, it is clear that the restoration work only involved cleaning and adding a supplementary inscription in 1619. Both painted scene and original inscription remain unmistakably early sixteenth century. After careful evaluation I have excluded other inscriptions which were originally executed pre-1525.

That of the fruiterers, measuring 105 × 45 cm, is arguably the most visually exuberant of the surviving guild boards, as well as being the most verbally informative. The illustration covering its lower half is a pictorial summary and sublimation of the fruiterers' and greengrocers' trade. The viewer is regaled with a festive cornucopia of produce, dominated by the colour red. Prominent are cherries, apples, pears, gourds, pea pods and a gorgeous outsized wedge of watermelon in the foreground, its rind bright green, its intense crimson flesh studded with black seeds. With it, along the foreground, are baskets, flasks and containers heaped with goods, including the four filled sacks with the names of different pulses painted on the outside. Hanging in the middle are weighing scales, barrels and other tools of the greengrocer's trade. The admirably balanced whole is held together by the peripheral figures in Renaissance costume, weighing on one side, picking on the other, and by the ribbons, festoons and cherubs running through the top part of the picture. In the centre of the upper section of the board, with its dark green background, the large official emblems stand out strongly. In the centre are the golden lion of St Mark, a figuration of Jehoshephat, the biblical king of Judah in whose reign God brought prosperity to the people 'in their basket and their store' and who was the guild patron, and the shield of the doge Lunardo Loredan (who is mentioned in CI 93). Flanking these are the colourful initialled family escutcheons of the Iusticieri Vechi in office at the time: Malipiero, Lion, Civran and Zorzi. The board of the fruiterers (Middle/Modern Venetian, *frutar(i)oli*) predates the great Rialto fire of 1514, so it is likely to have hung for six years in the Iusticia Vechia's previous premises over the meat market at the Rialto ('sora la Becharia' as Sanudo put it: CARACCIOLO ARICÒ 2011: 287). The *Sc(u)ola de S. Giosafat del Arte dei Frutaroli* dated officially from 1423. The fruiterers and greengrocers had an altar in the church of S. Maria Formosa and a confraternity-guild meeting house next to the church.

Apparently very different is the trade figuration chosen by the oar makers and their painter for a similar sized board (100 × 45 cm). However, although the depiction is superficially more down-to-earth, the same impulse towards balance and abstraction is evident. Of the four master oar makers depicted working with their sleeves rolled up, the two on the left, with hat, apron and hatchet, are each roughing out the top of an oar, while the two on the right are in the act of planing down oars. The left-to-right movement of the first group is answered by the right-to-left dynamic of the second. Between the two groups is a hatless apprentice running a finished oar through a gauge. Here, too, at the centre of the picture, the diagonals of tool and oar are in balance. All five craftsmen are dressed in jerkins and hose which are both similar and diverse. In particular, their tights — plain and partied, dark and light — set each other off. The layout of the background workshop is also deliberately balanced, with two grated windows on either side and a door in the middle. In the left foreground are two typical Venetian rowlocks (Venetian, *forcole*). On the right a selection of oars lies in the yard. The colours of the scene, in shades of brown and ochre enlivened by the red, white and black of the hose, is complemented by the dark red background of the frieze at the top, picked out in gold on both shields and initials. In a central wreath, indicated by the initials S(anctvs) B(artholomevs), with a notched abbreviation bar over the <s>, is the guild's patron St Bartholomew. He is flanked by a shielded Venetian lion *in moleca*, with the initials S(anctvs) M(arcvs), and by the escutcheon of doge Lunardo Loredan again. The four other initialled coats of arms are Querini, Barozzi, Barbarigo and Morosini. The *Sc(u)ola de S. Bortolamio del Arte dei Remeri*, of which the largest component were the oar makers of the

Arsenal, went back to the early fourteenth century. It was based in the church of its patron saint near the Rialto. The Slavic sounding name of the alderman listed on our guild board (*Marchovichio* = Marković) hints at the traditional importance of Venice's Dalmatian *schiavoni* community among the oar makers of the Arsenal. See ČORALIĆ (2011). The oar makers sourced their wood, mainly beech, from the great *bosco del Cansiglio* forest north of Belluno.

Altogether more prosaic and naive, although not without aesthetic interest, is the less well preserved board of the coopers' guild, measuring 98 × 97 cm. On the unusually large top frieze is painted the Lion of St Mark flanked by the bold escutcheons of the Lippomano, Barbarigo, Tron and Gradenigo. The scene below features the inside of a building belonging to the guild where three coopers display the three main stages of barrel making: the preparation of staves, their mounting within hoops, and the nailing and finishing. On the right, at a desk with a ledger on it, sit three soberly dressed officials of the guild. Most interesting are the two windows at the back providing a deep view into surrounding hilly countryside: this is possibly a visual reference to the areas of the northern Veneto where the coopers sourced their wood. The ancient *Arte dei Boteri* or *Buteri* (also *Butigleri* in Early Venetian) dedicated to the Virgin Purification was operational from 1271. It was originally based at the church of S. Agostin but sometime before 1486 it moved to the high altar at the church of the Crosechieri (now the Gesuiti: see CI 86, l. 17), opposite which it built its confraternity-guild meeting house, visible on de' Barbari's view of Venice. Although this building was cleared in the nineteenth century, three of the *scuola*'s inscriptions, including a Latin one of epigraphic importance from 1299, were saved and are embedded on a house front, corresponding to where the meeting house stood, at Cannaregio no. 4902. In the adjacent Calle de la Scuola dei Boteri an Istrian stone relief of a barrel is embedded in the wall at no. 4899.

The smallest of the boards, that of the sand suppliers, measuring 57 × 38 cm, is also affected by overall fading. Nevertheless, it retains a haunting atmosphere all its own. In the foreground a boat approaches a paved Venetian quayside. Its sail is furled and three men, one steering the boat, are about to land on the *fondamenta* and discharge a boatload of sand: an indispensable commodity in Venice for building and paving works, for the construction of wells, and for ballast in ships. In the middle ground a similar boat, this time with its sail billowing in the wind, departs the quay having already unloaded its cargo of sand. Although the colour has largely drained from the panel, the *fondamenta* and the houses on this extreme point of Venice are beautifully rendered, with an almost intarsia effect. The view selected by guild and artist is likely to represent schematically the edge of the *insula* of S. Pietro di Castello. From the sweep of the *fondamenta* — leading the eye to the expanse of the lagoon, and from there to the hills of the mainland — one can clearly discern the foreshortened outlines of Murano and Mazzorbo. The coats of arms painted at the top, against the sky, belong to the Vitturi, Orio, Diedo and Paruta. The ancient *Sc(u)ola de S. Andrea del Arte dei Sabioneri*, founded in the mid-thirteenth century, was dedicated to St Andrew and had an altar in the church of S. Zuane (in) Bragora in the *sestiere* of Castello.

LETTERING: Variations on *capitalis*, painted in black (CI 96, CI 97, CI 98) or white (CI 99). In two cases, the impressively vivid CI 96 and CI 97, the script is an eccentric take on classic Roman square capitals. Paradoxically, perhaps, it is the rather modest and subdued CI 98 and CI 99 which are more conventional in this respect. On both of the latter inscriptions the letters are sturdily square, with some stroke contrast. Modulation is visible on <a>, <b>, <e> and <x> of CI 99. It can also just be detected on the <e> and <s> of CI 98 although, in general, the letters on the four packed lines of writing tucked away on the front panel of the guild officials' desk are thickly monoline. On CI 99 there is balanced serifing, as on the three instances of <d> where the bowl is nicely tapered and extends beyond the perpendicular; on the six instances of <e> showing careful squaring off of the arms; on the <s> of *sete* and *sabioneri* where the ends are bowed off; on the <t> of *sete* and *Arte* with its longish pointed downstrokes; and on the <z> of *zener* with its contrastive diagonal flicks. On CI 98 serifing is most conspicuous on the head and foot of stems, on the crossbar wedges of the <t> of *Stefano* (l. 3), and on the <z> of *mazo* (l. 2). Overall, the lettering on CI 98 is too closely packed and the letters too small at *c.* 1 cm to be truly effective, whereas the single line of script at the bottom of CI 99, although not particularly tall at *c.* 1.5 cm, is bold and clear. An idiosyncratic touch on CI 98, employed only one other time in the corpus (on CI 71) and inappropriate on capitals, are the large triangular dots over <i> on *adi* and *sabioneri*, which the painter possibly had recourse to as a way of evening up the height differential caused by the superscript <o> over the <m> in the date. On neither inscription, however, is the lettering perfectly level in height.

More ambitious, complex and *sui generis* are the epigraphs on CI 96 and CI 97. Here the main inscription is set within parallel painted guidelines spread along the entire length of the panel: in the middle of the former, at the foot of the latter. In addition, and uniquely among our four boards, CI 96 features two areas of miniaturised writing. In the middle of the top layer of official insignia the winged lion of Venice holds open the bible exhibiting the well-known words in Latin said to have been spoken by the angel to St Mark. At the foot of the panel are the charming vernacular labels on four sacks of pulses. At first glance CI 96 and CI 97 appear different in their lettering. This impression comes from layout and height differences in the script: *c.* 2.5 cm on the main inscription of CI 96, with *c.* 1.2 cm on the pulse-sack words, versus 2 cm on the top line of CI 97 and 2.5 cm on the bottom line. It also results from the presence of a number of features of CI 96 not found on CI 97. In particular there is the conspicuous majuscular <ç> on *maço* (CI 96, l. 2); the <an> ligature on *Anbruoxo* (CI 96, l. 2) and the <ne> ligature on *Beneto* (CI 96, l. 3); the letter nesting of <o> within <d> on *gastaldo* (CI 96, l. 2), of <h> under <c> in *avichario* (CI 96, l. 2) and *Nicholo* (CI 96, l. 3), and of <e> under <c> on *narancer* (CI 96, l. 3). On CI 97 there is the unexpected capital <i> instead of capital <m> (for one thousand) at the start of the date. However, closer comparative inspection belies this series of accidental differences. The scripts on CI 96 and CI 97 reveal themselves as strikingly similar in their forcefulness and slightly compressed module; in their unusual combined use of the square <c> and the notched <i>; in the choice of the Gothic-type <a> with horizontal topstroke; in their employment of the Tironian 9 abbreviation for <con>; and in the use of prominent spiral interpuncts between words. Last but not least, the flower motif that rounds off the main inscription on both panels is identical, as well as being without parallel in the corpus. Either the painter of CI 97 consciously imitated CI 96 nine years later or else, and this seems more likely, we are in the presence of the same artist.

LANGUAGE: The guild boards were known in Early/Middle Venetian as *tolele* — in other words, little boards, from *tola* < TABŬLAM 'board, plank, table'. The relative homogeneity of the four *tolele* under consideration — in terms of social context, format and chronology — provides some useful information about the state of spelling trends and variants at the start of the Middle Venetian period. In addition, the panels introduce a series of interesting names of trades and, unexpectedly, of vegetables to the corpus.

Anbruoxo Ambrose (CI 96, l. 2), *Moixe* — in other words, *Moixè* Moses (CI 96, l. 2) —, *cexere* 'chick peas' (CI 96, l. 4) and *faxoli* 'kidney beans' (CI 96, l. 4) confirm the persistence of the traditional <x> spelling for the voiced sibilant /z/. The voiced affricate of the /dz/ type is represented by the traditional <ç> in the earliest of the four boards (*maço* 'May', CI 96, l. 2), whereas the innovative <z> spelling predominates elsewhere with *mazo* 'May' (CI 98, l. 2) and *zener* 'January' (CI 99). The formerly predominant <ç> spelling for the /ts/-type affricate is replaced by the simple <c> in *narancer* 'orange merchant' (CI 96, l. 3). The Venetian hesitation between <m> and <n> over the representation of nasalisation at syllable end is still present. CI 96 and CI 97 prefer <n>, with *Anbruoxo, conpagni* 'colleagues' (CI 96, l. 3), *tenpo* 'time' (CI 97, l. 1) and *conpagni* (CI 97, l. 2). On the other hand, CI 98 opts for *tempo* (CI 98, l. 2) and *chompagni* (CI 98, l. 4). The <ch> digraph, to represent velar /k/, seems to have remained anchored in Venetian practice with *avichario* 'deputy' (CI 96, l. 2), *Nicholo* (CI 96, l. 3), *Nicholo, Marcho* (Mark), *Marchovichio, Andronicho* (all CI 97, l. 1), *chastaldo* 'alderman' and *chompagni* (CI 98, l. 4). Only *Cristofalo* Christopher (CI 96, l. 2) bucks this trend. The variant *gastaldo* 'alderman', present twice (CI 96, l. 2, CI 97, l. 2), has ousted the older *gastoldo*, once dominant in Early Venetian. However, CI 98, l. 4 presents another variant, *chastaldo* (=/kastaldo/), only seen once before in the corpus (CI 22). This form, relatively common in Early Tuscan, was rare in Early Venetian. Rather than showing Tuscan influence it may be an example of the tendency in Venetian to devoice initial /g/.

Striking and slightly unexpected is the standardised formula used by the guilds to denote themselves on the boards. One would have expected the partitive *d(e)i* 'of the' to be present in their title. Instead, they all prefer the less definite *de* 'of': *arte de remeri* (CI 97, l. 2), *scuola de buteri* (CI 98, l, 5), *arte de sabioneri* (CI 99). The fruiterers did not bother to name themselves, presumably because both board illustration and inscriptional content made the guild concerned self evident. Uniquely, their board provided the Iusticieri Vechi with the address of the three guild officials mentioned on it. The hazy boundary in the nomenclature of these trade corporations, between *arte* and *scuola*, is evident in the three designations present here.

The four trade names on display — *narancer* 'orange merchant', *remeri* 'oar makers' (CI 97, l. 2), *buteri* 'coopers' (CI 98, l. 5) and *sabioneri* 'sand suppliers' (CI 99) — all show the archetypal Venetian agentive ending in *-er* < -ĀRIUS. *Narancer* derives from the Venetian for 'orange', historically spelled *naranca* or *naranza* < Arabic-Persian *nārang*. The orange depot in Venice was at the quayside of the Rialto, in the area still called Naranzaria today. *Remeri*, singular *remer* (as in the picturesque Corte del Remer near the Rialto), is of course from Early/Middle/Modern Venetian *remo* 'oar' < RĒMUS. The *buteri* or *boteri*, singular *boter*, derived their name from Early/Middle/Modern Venetian *bota* (Italian, *botte*) 'barrel'. The plural form *buteri* shows a Venetian tendency to raise pre-tonic /o/ to /u/. The *sabioneri*, singular *sabioner*, were literally the 'sand men' who transported and/or sold loads of sand. Their name is from Early/Middle/Modern Venetian *sabion* 'sand' (Italian, *sabbia*).

Two of the four inscribed pulse names, given in the collective singular (CI 96, l. 4), involve the key word *fava* 'bean' < FĂBAM: the diminutive *faveta*, for what would now be called Canellini beans, and *fava tonda*, literally 'round bean', for the fava or butter bean. *Faxoli* 'kidney beans', known in Modern/Contemporary Venetian as *fasioi* = [faˈzjɔi], are still an essential ingredient of the city's cooking. *Cexere* 'chick peas' on CI 96, l. 4 (Italian, *ceci*) is from CĬCER: see MUSSAFIA (1873, *s.v. césera*) and SALLACH (1993, *s.vv. ceseri, zexere*). In Modern Venetian the metaplasmic variant *cesara* = [ˈsezara], showing the /er/ to /ar/ shift, predominated (BOERIO 1865, *s.v. cèsara*).

RECENT STUDIES: FOGOLARI (1928–29: 726–27); ANZALONE (*c*. 1982: 19, 31, 81, 95).

Corpus Inscription 100

S(AN)C(TVS) · HO(MO)B(ONV)S · S(AN)C(TA) · B(ARBARA) · ~1~ | | M·D·XI· ~2~ | |
OSPEDAL ~ DEI ~~3~ | POVERI ~ S(AR)TORI ~4~

[*Sanctus Homobonus. Sancta Barbara.* MDXI. *Ospedal dei poveri sartori.*]

TRANSLATION: *Saint Homobonus. Saint Barbara.* 1511. Hospital of the poor tailors.

DATE: 1511.

LOCATION: In situ. The inscription is carved on a plaque embedded *c.* 310 cm off the ground on the wall of house no. 4838 on Fondamenta dei Sartori. The *fondamenta* is just south of Campo dei Gesuiti in the parish of the SS. Apostoli (*sestiere* of Cannaregio). Situated to the left of the doorway and immediately under a first-floor window, it marks the spot where the confraternity-guild of tailors, dedicated to St Homobonus and St Barbara, ran an almshouse with attached lodgings — in the attiguous, and no longer existent, Corte dei Sartori — for seventeen impoverished and infirm brothers and their families. A plan of the building and the site on the quayside, off which the tailors owned its series of properties, is in SEMI (1983: 206–07). The area is now given over to private ownership.

TYPE AND DESCRIPTION: Commemorative of the presence of the tailors' almshouse. The plaque in Istrian stone measures 115 × 58 cm, including its narrow border, and is an impressive piece of sculptural and inscriptional work that Hugh Douglas called 'a most perfect bas-relief' (DOUGLAS 1907: 156). Surrounded by a plain strip frame the tablet is deeply recessed and has angled sides. The relief sculptures within depict a complex scene, at once symbolic and strikingly realistic, that achieves a pleasing visual balance. On the spectator's left stands the tall bearded figure of St Homobonus, dressed like a well-to-do Renaissance tailor, with professional man's hat (topped by a halo) and long pleated robe. In his right hand he holds up a huge pair of tailor's shears, in his left a bag of money, derived from his business dealings, with which he will carry out good works for the poor. On the spectator's right stands the figure of the martyr St Barbara holding the two attributes associated with her: the tower where she was confined by her father and the thunderbolt (represented by a large arrow) which killed him after he beheaded her. Between them sit the Virgin and Child on an elaborate lion's-paw throne, her headdress and draperies rendered with exquisite contouring, her right hand lying across the sleeping baby's left leg. Beneath the throne lies a charming lapdog, with shaggy head and front paws visible, while kneeling in front of the throne and on its backrest are two miniature outline figures of tailor supplicants, both holding out a bolt of cloth. The throne and the Virgin have an oriental feel about them, perhaps suggested to commissioner or sculptor by the Greek St Barbara's reputed origins in the Middle East. On the frame side of each saint are depicted a church and a steep rocky landscape. On the escarpment to the left of the male saint three small figures of kneeling tailors can be seen, the larger one at the front again proffering a bolt of cloth. Above them, protruding from an outcrop, flutters a pennant bearing scissors,

Fig. 3.98. CI 100 in context. © A. S. Ferguson.

an arrow and an <h> followed by what appears to be the remainder of *Homobonus* or *Homobono*, although the tiny letters are so worn away as to be largely invisible.

That the twelfth-century Cremonese tailor-saint Homobonus ('Good man') should be the patron of our guild is no surprise. St Barbara had no direct connection to the *sartori*. However, her remains were kept in the Crosechieri (now the Gesuiti) church and had been in the safekeeping of the tailors since the late fifteenth century. There the confraternity venerated her at their altar. On St Barbara's relics in the Crosichieri and on the tailor's altar there see SHERMAN (2010: 183–88).

The tailors had their meeting house, which may have been founded as early as 1391, just to the right of the former Crosechieri church in Campo dei Gesuiti at what is now house no. 4881. There and in a number of locations in the vicinity one can still see their sculpted symbol, a roundel with a relief of the shears that were the characteristic tool of the trade. For the ground-floor altar in their meeting house the tailors' confraternity-guild, 'assai ricca et honorata' according to SANSOVINO (1581: 60v), had a fine altarpiece painted by Bonifacio Veronese in 1533. Like our inscription plaque the painting, now in the Accademia, depicts a *Madonna and Child with St Barbara and St Homobonus*.

LETTERING: Roman square capitals cut in V-section. The writing is carved on or within the plaque itself at three different levels, in a way that has no parallel in the corpus. The heavily abbreviated saints' names, in larger lettering measuring *c.* 3.5 cm, run along the recessed and angled strip between the heads of the holy figures. The date, *c.* 2.5 cm in height, is immediately beneath, lying between St Homobonus and the Virgin. The main epigraph, with letters also *c.* 2.5 cm high, is carved on the front of the raised plinth section on which the Virgin and her throne sit. As this feature is both centred and protruding the inscriptional message is highly visible and eminently legible.

The script itself is a poised and distinguished example of *capitalis*. Thanks to skilful modulation of stroke contrast and groove depth the sculptor has achieved the trick of making his lettering by turns bold and delicate. This is most apparent on the main two-line inscription on the plinth, especially in raking light. The three isolated perpendiculars of <i> stand out dark and clean, with classical wedge serifs top and bottom. On other letters with strong perpendiculars, such as <d>, <e>, <l>, <p> and <r>, this strong effect is echoed, but a play of light is set up between their thick stem and their lateral stroke or bowl. This is quite obvious on the three <e>s where the lateral lines are thin and end in small wedges. A similar contrast embellishes <p> and <r> which each appear twice. Here the curves are rendered with perfect touch, tapering almost to nothing on <r> and actually finishing with a gap between bowl and stem on <p>. On letters with no perpendicular, such as <a>, <o> and <s>, stroke depth and thickness is carefully and attractively varied. The diagonal swash through the <s> to represent the <ar> of *sartori* is light and airy. Words are given ample separations, quietly emphasized by spiral interpuncts.

A kinked abbreviation bar runs through the bottom section of the <s>, standing for 'saint', before the names of Homobonus and Barbara, and curves up to terminate on the <c> of *sanctus* and *sancta*. This type of hooked sign representing a group of letters was not unknown on Gothic inscriptions in the city (see CI 3, CI 23) but it is unique to my knowledge on monumental capitals in Venice. Homobonus is abbreviated by a short horizontal bar above the <h> and by a thin hooked line, ending in an <s>, through the bottom of <b>. *Barbara* is simply abbreviated by a horizontal line over the <b> which is now almost effaced.

The plaque is in good condition and is legible both aesthetically and epigraphically. The most serious damage it has sustained is in the wearing away of the facial traits of the Virgin and, to a lesser extent, St Barbara, and in the chipping away of the latter's right hand which holds the arrow. Abrasions affect the inclined upper frame with the saints' names, making the abbreviation strokes hard to make out.

LANGUAGE: On *ospedal* 'almshouse, hospital, hospice' (l. 3) see CI 4. Venetian *sartori* (l. 4) is the plural of *sartor* (pronounced [sarˈtor]) 'tailor', from the accusative case SARTŌREM. Tuscan/Italian *sarto*, on the other hand, is the reflex of the nominative SARTOR.

RECENT STUDIES: MONTICOLO (1896–1914, II: lxxxvi); RIZZI (1987: 295). The inscription was not recorded by Cicogna.

Corpus Inscriptions 101, 102

PER LA IVRIDICIOM DI ₁| BARBACANI ₂

[Per la iuridiciom di barbacani.]

LA IVRIḌICIOM DỊ ₁| BAR̩BACAN̩I ₂

[La iuridiciom di barbacani.]

TRANSLATIONS: CI 101: For (establishing) the legal extent of corbels.

CI 102: Legal extent of corbels.

DATE: Undated and undocumented. Lettering and language are compatible with a date in the last quarter of the fifteenth century or first quarter of the sixteenth century. It is possible that the inscribed model *barbacane* dates from the rebuilding period of the Rialto district immediately after the great fire of 10 January 1514 (1513, *more veneto*) that devastated the area. The conflagration is described vividly, as an eyewitness, by Marin Sanudo: FULIN (1879–1902, XVII: cols 458–62).

LOCATION: The inscriptions are carved on the sides of a freestanding stone corbel — in situ in Calle de la Madona off the Riva del Vin near the Rialto (*sestiere* of S. Polo, beside house no. 574) — at the rear of the well-known *Madonna* restaurant.

TYPE AND DESCRIPTION: Admonitory public notice. The corbel and its inscriptional message concretely define the legal dimensions of *barbacani* buttressing allowed in a long narrow street in the heart of the Rialto where the practice of extending buildings out in order to gain space was widespread. It is nowadays generally believed that our structure also served as a model for regulating the permitted size of all *barbacani* in Venice. While there is no documented proof of this assertion it is likely to be the case that the length of the Calle de la Madona *barbacane* made publicly explicit the officially authorised legal limit. This is likely, and particularly appropriate in that the street is lined with corbels on both sides and was actually called in our period *cale d(e)i barbac(h)ani*.

The model corbel is in Istrian stone. It stands *c.* 320 cm off the ground and is *c.* 104 cm long on the fully-exposed CI 101 side. It protrudes 73 cm in length on the shorter CI 102 side: the key length for determining how far jetty buttresses or brackets could be build out into the street. In height and width it measures *c.* 24 × *c.* 12 cm at its maximum extent and *c.* 12 × *c.* 12 cm at its minimum where it tapers at the nose. The legislation on buttress length was necessary to ensure that enough public space was left on narrow alleyways packed with shops, warehouses and inns, rather than residential housing, and that overhanging buildings did not encroach to such an extent that they obscured the natural light and created a fire hazard. Calle de la Madona itself and Calle del Paradiso at S. Lio (see CI 22) are perfect examples of how extra building room was contrived by the use of this picturesque technique.

The joint Trevisan-Gradenigo coat of arms on the pointed tip of the *barbacane*, replicated on the architrave of the nearby doorway, undoubtedly records the joint

Fig. 3.99. CI 101. © A. S. Ferguson.

initiative of these two patrician families to erect the artefact. The Gradenigo were major owners of warehouses in precisely this part of the Rialto, with the parallel street, now Calle Toscana, originally bearing their name (see CI 103, CI 104). The stone yardstick which delimits the width of that narrow alley also bears the arms of the Gradenigo. The Trevisan traditionally had interests in the parish of S. Zuane de Rialto, the church which the family had founded. It cannot be a coincidence that Paolo Trevisan was *Provedador sopra le fabriche* for Rialto in the immediate rebuilding period (CALABI and MORACHIELLO 1987: 71). It goes without saying that these objects were of public utility and that, given the acute fire risk in the densely packed and strategically central Rialto *insula*, they were put up with the blessing of the authorities.

LETTERING: Roman square capitals cut in V-section. Large, handsome and fit-for-purpose, the lettering is carved adroitly and confidently and shows an excellent understanding of the modular basis of square capitals. In addition, the stonemason subtly renders the contrast within letters in a way that is pleasing to the eye and enhances clarity. This can be seen to best effect on the <b> of *barbacani* (CI 101, l. 2), with its play of thick and thin strokes, and also on the two <d>s of l. 1. The <r> on *iuridiciom* (CI 101, l. 1) and on *barbacani* is elegantly balanced, as is the discrete serifing present throughout. The mason has striven for absolute regularity but occasionally he falls just short. This is apparent on the three <a>s of *barbacani* where the width of the arms and the height of the cross stroke are not quite consistent. The lettering is *c.* 3.8 cm high on CI 101 and *c.* 3.5 cm on the shorter CI 102 side. Tall, well-spaced and clear, it would have been eminently legible. CI 101, the longer of the two inscriptions, faces the entrance to the Riva del Vin. Although the grooving on it is a little worn down it remains intact and perfectly clear. CI 102, facing into the *calle*, has been drastically weathered down and apart from a few letters on the left, at the start of the message, it is no longer easy to read. The coat of arms on the tip would undoubtedly have been painted and the two epigraphs themselves would probably have been infilled to highlight their message, although no trace of this remains.

LANGUAGE: The blunt message was meant to be read and understood by all concerned and was therefore written in Venetian. In Early and Middle Venetian *iuridiciom* on CI 101 (l. 1), CI 102 (l. 1), like its variant *iurisdition* on the first line of CI 103 and CI 104 (and the form *jurisdicion* also found in documents of the period), had a range of related meanings: from 'jurisdiction' itself to 'right of way', 'right of use', 'legal authority' and, as here, 'legal extent'. Rather than deriving directly from IŪRISDICTIŌNEM, *iuridiciom* comes via Old French *juridicion*, and shows the common Early/Middle Venetian hesitation between /n/ and /m/ in rendering the nasal. *Di* 'of the', also found in CI 103, CI 104, is the contracted partitive form that we have encountered repeatedly in the corpus from the end of the fourteenth century onwards.

Barbacani (singular *barbacan*) are the tiered wooden (or occasionally stone) brackets typical of narrow streets in Venice. These protruding rows of supports allowed extra floor space to be gained on the upper floor(s) of buildings by extending outward into alleyways but their use had, as here, to be regulated so that streets did not become too dark and cramped. The term, cognate with English *barbican*, is usually connected with fortifications, especially a double tower erected on a gate or bridge and serving as a watch tower. More generally it referred to wall supports or buttresses, and in this sense it was applied in Venice to the recessed wooden supports between column and roof typically seen in fifteenth-century porticos in the city (see CI 58). Only Venetian, though, seems to have developed the special architectural meaning found in our inscriptions. The origins of the word are obscure, although it may possibly derive from Arabic-Persian *bāb-khānah* 'gate-house'. First attested in twelfth-century French, in the Latin of that period in Pisa and in the Latin of the thirteenth century in Venice, the *barbacane* type spread to most Romance languages. It was in English before 1300. It is worth remarking, though, that while corbels are referred to quite frequently in wills and ownership disputes in the Venetian documentation, both Latin and vernacular, they are often known in the former as *modilione(m)* — from an unattested late Latin *MUTILIŌNEM, a diminutuve of MŪTULUS 'shelf' applied to corbels in classical architecture — and in the latter by the Early/Middle Venetian reflex *modion* 'bracket' (Tuscan/Italian, *modiglione*, whence English *modillion*). *Barbacani* are specifically called *canes* in the Latin documentation.

RECENT STUDIES: None. Both inscriptions were first recorded, but not published, by Cicogna.

Corpus Inscriptions 103, 104

✦ PER ✦ IVRISDITION ✦ ₁| DE ✦ LA ✦ CALE ✦ DI GRADENIGI ₂
[Per iurisdition de la cale di Gradenigi.]

✦ PER ✦ IVRISDITION ✦ ₁| DE ✦ LA ✦ CALE ✦ [D]I ✦ GRADENIGI ✦ ₂
[Per iurisdition de la cale di Gradenigi.]

TRANSLATION: (Showing) the (minimum) legal extent of the street of the Gradenigos.

DATE: Undated and undocumented. Lettering and language are compatible with a date in the late fifteenth century or early sixteenth century. It is possible that, like the model *barbacane* in the parallel Calle de la Madona (CI 101, CI 102), this legal yardstick was erected immediately after January 1514, when the Rialto district was devastated by fire, in order to enforce a safe distance between buildings in the street.

LOCATION: The in situ yardstick spans the Calle Toscana (*sestiere* of S. Polo) between first and second floor levels. On one side (at S. Polo no. 554A) it touches the wall at the rear of the former meeting house of the confraternity-guild of goldsmiths, the *Sc(u)ola dei Oresi* (Italian, *degli orefici*), which fronts on to Campo Rialto Novo.

TYPE AND DESCRIPTION: Admonitory public notice. The thick Istrian stone separator measures approximately 185 cm in length × 20 cm in height (rising to 25 cm on its flared middle section) × 20 cm in width. It appears to be a yardstick set up across the formerly busy narrow alley in order to publicise the legal minimum for street width in the *calle* in the interests of health and safety. This was evidently felt to be necessary in order to prevent further encroachment into the already restricted street space in this densely built up, sought-after central location where valuable goods were stored in depots, some of whose derelict fronts can still be made out along the alleyway. Carved in relief in the centre of both inscriptions is the characteristic Gradenigo shield, with its single diagonal zigzag line, which was also present in CI 101, CI 102. The Gradenigo were the patrician family which owned and rented out the warehouses and outlets on the thoroughfare and had done so for at least three centuries (BUENGER ROBBERT 1999).

LETTERING: Roman square capitals carved in V-section. The prominent *capitalis* lettering averages some 7 cm in height on the two identical inscriptions. Well spaced, strongly square and elegantly carved it served its enforcement purpose effectively. Perched high above the alley, the epigraphic message's readability was enhanced by its effective symmetrical layout, by the regularity of its spacing, and by the wedge interpuncts between words. The lettering must originally have been picked out by black or coloured infilling and the Gradenigo escutcheon in relief which divides both epigraphs in the middle — separating *iuris-* from *-dition* on l. 1 and *di* and *Gradenigi* on l. 2 — is likely to have been painted.

FIG. 3.100. CI 104 in context. © A. S. Ferguson.

LANGUAGE: The message on both sides of the notice needed to be clear to all concerned and is consequently in Venetian. Like its variant *iuridiciom* (CI 101, CI 102), *iurisdition* 'jurisdiction' (l. 1) had the sense of 'legal extent' in the present context. The Latinising spelling here reflects its direct derivation from IŪRISDICTIŌNEM. *Di* 'of the' (l. 2) is the characteristic contracted partitive form repeatedly found in Venetian writing in the fifteenth and early sixteenth centuries and much in evidence in the corpus, including on the other public notices CI 101, CI 102. *Cale* (l. 2) is the only example in our collection of the iconic Venetian term for 'street', still very much in use and spelled *calle* in the city's street signage. Pronounced ['kae] in Contemporary Venetian it is derived, like the cognate term in Spanish and Old Tuscan, from CALLIS, CALLEM 'way, lane' which appears frequently in Venetian legal documents of the medieval period. The plural *Gradenigi* (l. 2) of the well-known patrician name Gradenigo is entirely typical of the Early/Middle Venetian practice of declining aristocratic surnames. It is found in particular in feminine forms such as Sanuda (from Sanudo) and Contarina (from Contarini) which could also be used as female first names. *Gradenigi* is pronounced [grade'nigi], with <g> — as was usual in Early Venetian — representing the hard velar sound even when followed by a front vowel. It would have been written 'Gradenighi' in later Venetian.

RECENT STUDIES: None. The present editions are the first to be published. Neither inscription was recorded by Cicogna.

Corpus Inscription 105

A BENE ₁| PLACI|TO ⁚ | ~ ₄|| DI · SI|GNORI · ₆| PR‹O›CV ·|RATORI ⁚ | ~ ₉||
PIERO · BRESA(N) · GAS|TALD{O · E CO(N)PAGNI · ₁₁| DEL · TRAGETO · A FA|TO
FAR · QVESTA · ₁₃| OPERA · M · D · XVI · ₁₄

[A bene placito di signori procuratori, Piero Bresan, gastaldo, e conpagni del trageto a fato far questa opera. MDXVI].

TRANSLATION: With the consent of the Lord Procurators, alderman Piero Bresan and colleagues of the gondola ferry had this work made. 1516.

DATE: 1516.

LOCATION: On a shrine in Campiello de la Crose no. 172D, parish of S. Eufemia, on the island of the Giudecca (*sestiere* of Dorsoduro). Tucked away in this secluded little square the shrine is next door to its original location on the nearby quayside of the Fondamenta de la Crose (Italian, *della Croce*) canal where the boatmen would have had their station. This is confirmed by the guild's *mariegola* which records a decision taken in 1559 to place a boat on what is called *nostra riva* ('our quayside') in order to illuminate the image of the Madonna set up on the gondola station itself (G. VIO 2004: 925).

TYPE AND DESCRIPTION: Commemorative. The inscription marks the commissioning and completion in 1516 of a devotional statue dedicated to the Virgin Mary and sponsored by the guild of gondoliers on the Giudecca. The epigraph is carved in part on the front plaque, and in part on the two narrower side facets, of an Istrian stone plinth that is 19 cm high and 56 cm long overall. The plinth supports an early sixteenth century half-length bust (92 cm tall) in Carrara marble of the Madonna and Child. This popular neighbourhood shrine is at present in a protective booth with white background and sides which are decorated with a painted garland of red flowers with green stems and leaves. On either side of the plinth are vases with flowers. The booth is protected by a metal grille that is opened during the day, and there is electric light on the inside.

The small corporation of ferryboatmen operating the main crossing on the Giudecca, the *trag(h)eto* of S. Eufemia, formed their *scuola* and began their *mariegola* in the late fifteenth century. They were dedicated to St Nicholas and they worshipped at the parish church of S. Eufemia on the Giudecca which exists to this day. Bringing together around thirty gondoliers at any one time, and a set number of boats which increased over the decades of the sixteenth century, they were licensed by the Provedadori di Comun and enjoyed the monopoly of ferrying paying passengers across the Giudecca canal. In our period their working perimeter stretched across the northern shore of the island from the monastery of S. Croce, near which their home base with our shrine stood, westward to the church of SS. Biagio e Cataldo. They had pick-up points at various locations along the way, including the *ponte longo* 'long bridge' that joins both halves of the island, and they delivered customers to the entrance point of the Rio S. Trovaso on what is now the Zattere. Their

Fig. 3.101. CI 105 (detail). © A. S. Ferguson.

target area was extended later in the century to a wide swathe on the Zattere side, stretching from S. Agnese to S. Basegio. Their normal fare seems to have been one *bagatin*, just like the regular *traghet(t)i* along the Grand Canal, although this could be quadrupled in bad weather, when two gondoliers had legally to be on board, or if a client wished to leave immediately without waiting for other fares. In *La città di Venetia (1493–1530)* Sanudo listed our service ('a San Trovaso, va alla Zuecca') as one of the fourteen *traghetti dove stanno barche per guadagnar* (CARACCIOLO ARICÒ 2011: 52).

LETTERING: Roman square capitals cut in V-section. This is a modest but competent piece of inscriptional work, with the stonecutter showing a good understanding of the nature of *capitalis*. The original grooving is now substantially reduced but looks to have been reasonably deep *ab initio* while stroke contrast, although limited, is present. The sturdy aspect of the *c.* 2 cm high lettering is unassuming but effective. The epigraph is justified on the left and words or syntagms are separated by interpuncts. Abbreviations are restricted to the simple horizontal suspension bar representing <n> placed over the <a> of *Bresan* (l. 10) and over the <o> of *conpagni* (l. 11). The main plaque is clean of irregularities except for the <o> of *gastaldo* (ll. 10–11) which has been miniaturised and nested within the preceding <d>. This is likely to be a correction, although it may possibly have been consciously chosen to allow for more room on the tablet later. The stonemason is at his least surefooted on the two side sections, where he has undoubtedly misjudged some of his spacing. It has led to his leaving awkward gaps filled with 'punctuation' and to some faulty letter alignments. In addition, he appears to have omitted the first <o> of *procuratori* (ll. 7–8). It is now hard to tell because of letter fading but it seems that to compensate he may have inserted a miniature <o> over the leg of the preceding <r>.

Overall, it is to the mason's credit that the inscription has remained relatively legible, in spite of half a millennium's exposure to the salt air of the lagoon. He also made intelligent use of the space available on the awkwardly facetted plinth by inscribing the main message on the large rectangular front plaque facing the spectator and by restricting the legal 'small print' to the less immediately visible sides. The sacrifice he made, though, was the less-than-ideal splitting of the permission statement into two detached sections, with the space problems that this entailed.

LANGUAGE: The contracted partitive *di* 'of the' (l. 5), for *dei* or *deli*, makes another appearance in this inscription, as does the familiar *gastaldo* 'alderman' (ll. 10–11). Noticeable is the presence of the Tuscanising or Latinising neologism *opera* 'work, piece of work' (l. 14) rather than the native form *ovra* encountered earlier in the corpus (CI 29). *A bene placito* 'with the blessing/permission' (ll. 1–3) is Latinising bureaucratic language. The warden's surname *Bresan* (l. 10), still relatively common in Venice and spelled Bressan, is an adjective meaning 'from Brescia' (*Bres(s)a* or *Bersa* in Venetian). *Trageto* 'boat crossing, ferry' (l. 12), pronounced even without the /h/ as [tra'geto] with velar /g/, is the first and only appearance in our collection of this quintessentially Venetian word — from TRĀJICĔRE 'to transport, ferry across' — still used in the city for short gondola crossings. It was adopted into written Italian as *traghetto* as early as 1581 (FERGUSON 2007: 283).

RECENT STUDIES: RIZZI (1987: 517). The inscription was not recorded by Cicogna.

Corpus Inscription 106

M ⁕D ⁕ XVIII ⁕ADI ⁕ XXVIII | ⁕ ZVGNO ⁕ IN ⁕ T(EMPO) ⁕ ₂| ⁕ DE ⁕ MA(DRE) ⁕ S(VPERIORA) ⁕ PACIFICA ⁕ ₃| ⁕ABBATESA⁕

[MDXVIII, adì XXVIII zugno, in tempo de madre superiora Pacifica, abbatesa.]

TRANSLATION: 1518, on the 28th of June, in the time of Mother Superior Pacifica, abbess.

DATE: June 1518.

LOCATION: The well head with its two inscriptions — one Roman, one Renaissance — is at present kept outside in the first courtyard of the Museo Nazionale Archeologico (Museo Correr, catalogue ref. Cl. XXV, 1075) off St Mark's Square where I was given permission to examine, measure and have it photographed.

In the CIL (V 2270) the artefact's original provenance, *qua* funerary urn, is plausibly suggested as Altino on the mainland off Torcello in the X Regio Venetia et Histria. This is confirmed by SCHIVO (2012: 59) in her study of inscriptions relating to the *gens Terentia* in Altino. Citing the anonymous mid-fifteenth-century Redianus manuscript in the Biblioteca Medicea Laurenziana in Florence, the CIL records the earliest historical reference to the whereabouts of the object's original Latin epitaph as being 'Venetiis ad S. Gervasium in quodam puteo'. In other words, at least half a century before having its new dated vernacular message cut on to it, the urn had already been converted for use as a well head: a practice far from unusual in Venice where early well heads and stoups often originated in *spolia* (see CI 31). Its Quattrocento location in Venice at S. Gervasius — in other words, in the *contrada* of S. Trovaso (= Saints Gervasius and Protasius) in the *sestiere* of Dorsoduro — provides the link to its eventual three-century sojourn as a well head with a Venetian inscription in the nearby Cistercian complex of the Ognissanti, not far from the church of S. Trovaso and just off the Zattere. It was probably sited in one of the convent cloisters at the Ognissanti. The Ognissanti papers in the Archivio di Stato record a payment of 18 *soldi* on 18 June 1518 by the mother superior Pacifica whose name appears on the inscription: 'Adi 18 [zugno], per barcha fachini che porto el fondi de pozo de piera viva dal taiapiera'. The local stonemason in question, who would have carved (or had carved) the new epigraph, is undoubtedly the 'maistro Andrea taiapiera fiolo fu de maistro Zan Buora' much employed by the convent between 1511 and 1521 for the major building work on its new cloister complex. The Buoras operated out of their workshop in Campo S. Stefano and were an important family of sculptors involved in many prestigious commissions in Venice and the mainland in our period (see MARKHAM SCHULZ 1983 and CI 94). A fortnight later, on 3 July, Pacifica paid a Master Gabriel, a specialised well maker (Middle Venetian, *pozer*), 11 ducats to install the well at the Ognissanti: 'Adi 3 dito contadi a maistro Chabriel pozer per far el pozo'. See ASV, *Ognissanti*, b. 3, *registro spese*, 1510 (*more veneto*)-1530, fols. 27v, 42r, 43v. It is highly

FIG. 3.102. CI 106. © A. S. Ferguson.

likely that the object came to the Archaeological Museum via the Museo Correr in the nineteenth century following the Napoleonic suppression of the Ognissanti church and convent in 1807.

TYPE AND DESCRIPTION: Commemorative of the installation of a well head. The inscription is on one side of an already inscribed Roman funerary box-urn in grey Aurisina marble (a type of limestone from near Trieste) which was converted in the late medieval period into a well head. The urn lid is now lost and part of the original base has clearly been refashioned. The artefact, measuring 91 × 63 × 88 cm, is the oldest example in the corpus of antique *spolia* being recycled for a different function from its original one. It is unique in preserving a Renaissance inscription in Venetian alongside its *ab origine* Latin epigraph. The commissioner of the inscription was Pacifica, the abbess of the recently founded convent of the Ognissanti. Real name Cassandra Barbarigo, she was the daughter of doge Marco Barbarigo (died 1486) and her father had placed her and her sister Guida (*sor* Vienna) in the convent which rapidly became a favourite filial repository for the Venetian nobility. The Barbarigo family in particular, whose main fiefdom was in the *contrada* of S. Trovaso, were so intimately connected with the convent that it became known popularly as *Ognissanti dei Barbarigo*.

The complex had had modest beginnings in the early 1470s with a legacy of some properties in Dorsoduro to a nun of the Cistercian convent of S. Margherita on Torcello. This led to a group of nuns obtaining permission to found a small monastic community and hospice in Dorsoduro, electing its first abbess in 1475 and quickly enlarging its foundation by the purchase of properties and vacant land in the vicinity via their influential patrician procurators. Its attractiveness was also enhanced by a miraculous image of the Virgin Mary associated with it. The first abbess, Eufrosina Berengo, is commemorated on an inscription in the site's earliest well head, which happens to be extant and in situ. It can be seen in the so-called Campo dei Ognissanti, one of the internal courtyards of the former Ognissanti complex which was partly converted in the twentieth century into the Giustinian hospital. Dating from 20 May 1488, and inscribed in a cruder Roman monumental capital script than ours, the epigraph reads: · O M · Sac^c / MCCCCLXX/XVIII · XX · maco / + S · Evphroxi/nae abbatissae / p(re) Zampiero · F(ara) · . Although in Latin the date is in Venetian, as is the name of the nun's chaplain and confessor *pre'* Zampiero (Italian, Giampiero or Gianpiero) Fara who may well have been involved in the moral laxness for which the convent was initially notorious. The nuns' original chapel, dedicated to the Virgin of Peace and to All Saints, can be seen on de' Barbari's bird's eye view of Venice just behind the church of S. Trovaso.

The building of the church and convent complex, soon called simply the Ognissanti, began in earnest in 1511 when Pacifica took over as mother superior. It is she who kept the detailed records of the payments to tradesmen which allow us to understand how, when and where the well head was re-inscribed and ended up where it did. She wrote a note in the accounts in Venetian upon taking office and assuming financial responsibility on 1 November 1511 (ASV, *Ognissanti*, cit., fol. 20r): 'In Christi nomine Amen. Io sor Pacifica, indegna abbadesa del monastier d'Ognissanti de Venezia, in questo presente zorno chomenzo a ministrar i danari di la fabricha nova'. On the history of the Ognissanti and its building programme see SANTOSTEFANO (1992–93).

LETTERING: Roman square capitals cut in V-section. This is a sophisticated example of inscriptional carving and *mise-en-page* that shows an impressive understanding of the *capitalis* system. There is a beautiful balance between thick and thin strokes and the serifing is quietly effective. The clear, well-spaced, impeccably regular letters stand some 7 cm high, with words separated by spiral interpuncts. In addition, the exceptionally skilled *taiapiera* has sought for a pleasing visual equilibrium by laying the text out symetrically across the whole rectangular surface of the side of the well rather than seeking to justify it. It is quite clear that he was acutely aware of the original Latin inscription on the adjacent side of the artefact and strove to stay as close as possible to his model. This is most obvious in the module and ductus of <a>, <e>, <m>, <n> and <s>. One can even see how he has reproduced the slight upswing on the bottom stroke of the <e> and has gone on to balance it with a slight downcurve on the middle stroke of the <f> of *Pacifica* (l. 3), though the Roman epitaph has no example of <f>. He has even abbreviated in the Roman fashion with *litterae singulares*, using T for *tempo* (l. 2), MA for *madre* (l. 3) and S for *superiora* (l. 3), in a way that was alien to Venetian epigraphic practice and is found nowhere else in our corpus. One wonders if such inscriptional sensitivity is purely down to the aesthetic taste of Buora (or his assistant) or else if Pacifica (or her proxy) was directly involved in the decision making. The fact that the convent obtained this particular well and replicated its lettering hints at the prestige, at this point in time, of antique artefacts and of neo-antique script for the Venetian elite. This cultural trend would spur the taste for collecting that led later in the century to the formation of Giovanni Grimani's great assemblage of antiquities in his palace at S. Maria Formosa: the basis of the Museo Archeologico at San Marco where the Ognissanti well head eventually ended up. The Latin original on the former funerary urn reads: *Terentia · C(ai) l(iberta) · Hicite / sibi · matri · patri · sorori / testamento · fieri · ivssit* ('Terentia Hicete, freedwoman of Caius, ordered by will that (this) be made for herself, her mother, her father and her sister').

LANGUAGE: It is interesting to note that on the eve of Bembo's linguistic reforms the patrician convent of the Ognissanti, led by the daughter of a doge, turned to its Venetian vernacular for a piece of formal inscriptional writing. On *zugno* (June; l. 2), see CI 79. *Abbatesa* 'abbess' (l. 4) is a Latinising form: a cross between late Latin ABBATISSA (found in the 1488 Ognissanti well-head inscription transcribed above) and the fully Venetian form *badesa* (pronounced with the unvoiced sibilant /s/) found on CI 35. An even fuller compromise is found, as we saw, in Pacifica's own handwritten *abbadesa*.

RECENT STUDIES: CALVELLI (2016: 466–67).

Corpus Inscription 107

EL ⁂ CHLARISIMO ⁂ M(ISR) ⁂ ANTONIO ₁|
TRO(N) ⁂ P(ER)CHOLATOR ⁂ DE ⁂ S(AN) ⁂ MARCHO ₂|
LASO ⁂ QVESTA ⁂ CHAXA ⁂ ALA S(C)H(O)LA ₃|
DE ⁂ S(ANTA) ⁂ MARIA ⁂ DI MARCHADANTI ₄|
ESENDO ⁂ VARDIAN M(ISR) ⁂ BERNARDO DE MARIN
⁂ FO ⁂ DE ⁂ M(ISR) ⁂ BORTOLAMIO ₅|
⁂ DEL ⁂ M · D · X · X · III ·

[El chlarisimo mis. Antonio Tron, percholator de San Marcho, lasò questa chaxa ala Schola de Santa Maria di Marchadanti, esendo vardian mis. Bernardo de Marin, fo de mis. Bortolamio. Del MDXXIII.]

TRANSLATION: The distinguished Sir Antonio Tron, Procurator of St Mark, left this house to the Confraternity of St Mary of the Merchants, when the warden was Mr Bernardo de Marin, son of the late Bortolamio. (Done) in the course of 1523.

DATE: 1523.

LOCATION: The artefact with its accompanying insignia is embedded in situ on the wall of house no. 4701 at the Ponte de le Balote (*sestiere* of S. Marco). The plaque is roughly 220 cm above the steps of the bridge beside the Rio S. Salvador canal.

TYPE AND DESCRIPTION: Commemorative. The plaque marks the legacy of a house — S. Marco no. 4701, in Calle dei Monti, at the foot of Ponte de le Balote — by Antonio Tron, a recently deceased Procurator of S. Mark, to the merchants' confraternity in the city. It also records the date as well as the name of the confraternity warden. The handsome Istrian stone plaque with its sober recessed frame measures 98 × 47 cm, the inscription surface itself being *c.* 93 × *c.* 42 cm and the frame *c.* 5 cm wide. Set into the wall above the plaque and touching it is a large circular disk in Istrian stone measuring 42 cm in diameter. Within it is a smaller disk, 23 cm in diameter and decorated entirely in mosaic, featuring in its centre the escutcheon of the Tron family flanked by spiral ribbons and topped by a star. The background mosaic is blue while the shield is in gold mosaic featuring three red diagonal stripes. The fringe decorations are also golden. The mosaic disk is itself surrounded by a circular *pietra d'Istria* relief which is in the form of a wreath of laurel leaves. Above the large disk and touching it is a second much smaller Istrian stone disk with the raised symbol of the merchants' confraternity: a downward pointing hand, in the act of blessing, fringed by stars. The entire ensemble, cleaned in recent years, is *sui generis* as well as being unique in the corpus in its use of mosaic in the vernacular inscription context. The mosaic was commissioned from the mosaicist Crisogono Novello, probably by Tron's son Marco who was procurator of the nearby church of S. Salvador where he had recently contracted Novello to carry out important decorative work (MERKEL 1994: 101–02).

The founding of the confraternity of *S. Maria e S. Francesco d(e)i Merc(h)adanti* or *Marc(h)adanti* went back to 1261 when in its ancient *mariegola* in Latin it was called

Fig. 3.103. CI 107 in context. © A. S. Ferguson.

the *Scola seu fraternitas Beate genetricis Dei et domini nostri Ihesu Christi gloriose Virginis Marie matris misericordie et beati Francisci*. Later the title would often be modified to *d(e)i Merc(h)adanti e Naviganti*. This fascinating confraternity is hard to classify. The nomenclature of its officials, with a *vardian* (l. 5) rather than a *gastaldo* in charge, may reflect this ambiguity, although in the early *mariegole* only the term *gastaldus* is used. It came into being at the same time as the earliest of the flagellant *scuole grandi* and it too practised flagellation in its processions although, as in the latter, the practice was soon restricted then abandoned. Nonetheless, it was never raised to the status of a *scuola grande* in the fifteenth century like the other flagellant brotherhoods in the city. Possibly because of its perceived professional basis it continued to be considered a *scola comunis*. However, while it was an association of merchants — Marco Polo was registered as a brother in 1310 (MONEGO 2012: 103) — it set out no guild regulations and operated an open admissions policy which also, at least in the early stages of its existence, welcomed women. Its numbers were high, often well over three hundred in the medieval and Renaissance periods, and it was undoubtedly wealthy. In spite of this it produced no great cycles of art. Its meeting house, after a spell within the Frari monastery complex itself, became established in the Campo dei Frari. From its inception the *scuola* had an altar within the great Franciscan basilica where it worshipped. On this intriguing brotherhood and its *mariegole*, see G. VIO (2004: 614–31); MONEGO (2012); HUMPHREY (2015: 138–45).

Antonio Tron, who bequeathed to the merchants' confraternity the property referred to in our inscription, had been one of the most interesting, active and influential politicians in Venice of his generation, during a watershed moment of commercial and political change and turbulence. This culminated in the War of the League of Cambrai when Venice came close to losing her mainland possessions and to being overrun by the Europe-wide alliance ranged against her. Tron occupied many of the great positions of state in this period, and in 1507 became a Procurator of St Mark. With Domenego Trevisan he was one of the main candidates for the dogeship when it fell vacant in 1523 following the deaths in rapid succession of the two previous incumbents, Lunardo Loredan and Antonio Grimani. Although he came third in the final ballot, achieving eighteen votes to Trevisan's twenty-one and Andrea Gritti's twenty-five, he was the favourite of the people. Suspicious like him of the ambitious, moralistic and despotic Gritti, the crowds chanted Tron's name and paraded the elderly statesman's effigy in St Mark's Square when the dogeship result was announced, according to Marin Sanudo (FULIN 1879–1902, XXXIV: col. 159). It is not surprising that Tron, who died shortly afterwards in 1523, should have left property to this particular confraternity, of which he may possibly have been a member. A traditionalist, he had always worked to enhance the city's mercantile vocation and infrastructure, supporting in particular the great seasonal convoys (Early/Middle Venetian, *le mude*) which were the city's commercial lifeblood. Many members of the brotherhood of *mercadanti* and *naviganti* would have been heavily involved in, or dependent on, overseas trade. Tron's patronage can therefore reasonably be interpreted as, in some sense, a political as well as a personal statement from beyond the grave, and we can assume that he left instructions for how his bequest should be publicised in stone. He reinforced his implicit message by the deliberate and, as far as I am aware, unheard of bringing together of his family crest — advertised colourfully in mosaic — and the confraternity's symbol, in the context of a highly visible inscription in Venetian. The classicising Gritti was himself not shy of advertising his own name epigraphically, albeit always in Latin.

LETTERING: Roman square capitals cut in V-section. An impressive piece of inscriptional work, notable for its balance, sobriety and clarity. The text with its proud announcement is likely to have been commissioned and drafted by the confraternity warden himself, possibly at the original behest or suggestion of the legatee Tron. The prominent letters, standing *c.* 3.6 cm high, are admirably consistent in cut, alignment and spacing, and the unobtrusive equilibrium between stroke modulation and precise squaring shows a restrained forcefulness. A touch of decorativeness is added by the spiral interpuncts and by a few stylish medieval suspension strokes not really consistent with Roman capital script. These are the sinuous line through <m> abbreviating, unusually drastically, *m(iser)* or *m(isier)* 'Sir, Mr' (ll. 1, 5); the keyhole overbars on <s> indicating *san* (l. 2) and *santa* (l. 4); and on the <o> of Tron to cover for <n>. Possible errors by the sculptor are the missing <c> and <o> in *schola* (l. 3) which are compensated for by a kinked overbar, incorporating a reduced <o>, on the <h>. However, given the impeccable layout of the inscription — justified on both sides, with a centred final line, and eschewing split words at line-end — it is perfectly possible that he deliberately opted for this expedient in order to maintain the pre-planned pagination. An unexpected blemish, though, is the enlarged initial 'capital' <b> on *Bernardo* (l. 5) not replicated on any of the other names on the inscription.

LANGUAGE: High-register Middle Venetian. The use of Venetian for such a distinguished piece of public writing at this late date merits reflection. It suggests that the confraternities, outside of the *scuole grandi*, were still firmly attached to the vernacular as their means of public communication. It implies, too, that a Procurator of St Mark was aware that maximum publicity for his generosity and for his choice of recipient would be achieved by having it recorded in *venexian*.

Immediately apparent is the maintenance of some traditional Early Venetian spelling norms, notably <ch> to represent /k/ in *chlarisimo* 'most distinguished' (l. 1), *percholator* 'procurator' (l. 2), *chaxa* 'house' (l. 3), *schola* 'confraternity' and *marchadanti* 'merchants' (l. 4). Also conservative are the use of <x> for the voiced sibilant /z/ in *chaxa*, and the single <s> for the unvoiced sibilant /s/ in *chlarisimo*. Most striking in this respect is the retention of the <l> in *chlarisimo* when the pronunciation had probably long evolved to the palatal [tʃ]. In line with gradual Venetian evolutions are: the absence of diphthongisation on *schola* and the choice of the 3rd singular past historic variant *laso* (= *lasò*) '(he) left' (l. 3) instead of the formerly dominant form *las(s)à*. Most notably, *esendo* 'being' (l. 5) also shows the regularisation of the gerund of *eser* 'to be' along the same lines as its Tuscan/Italian equivalent. In the six previous occurrences of the construction in the corpus (the last in 1424) the traditional Early Venetian metaplasmic form *siando* was used exclusively. See CI 13, CI 28, CI 29, CI 35, CI 38, CI 50. *Marc(h)adanti* 'merchants' (l. 4), with the characteristic Veneto raising of <er> to <ar>, co-existed in Early/Middle Venetian with the variant *merc(h)adanti*, more common elsewhere in the peninsula. *Di* 'of the' (l. 4) confirms the tenacity in early sixteenth-century Venice of the contracted variant partitive of *de(l)i* or *dei* found in such iconic constructions as *conseio di X* 'Council of (the)10' (see CI 41).

RECENT STUDIES: RIZZI (1987: 148–49). First published by B. GAMBA (1832: 19), probably from a manuscript copy given to him by Cicogna who recorded the inscription but did not publish it himself.

Corpus Inscription 108

S(ANCTVS) ▲ | ▲ M(ATHEVS) ▲ || IN TEMPO DE ₃| SER FRANCESC | HO DE
PIERO ₅| GVARDIAN ₆| E COMPA^GNII ₇| M·D·X·X·IIII

[*Sanctus Matheus*. In tempo de ser Francescho de Piero, guardian,
e compagnii. MDXXIIII.]

TRANSLATION: *Saint Matthew*. In the time (of office) of Mr Francescho de Piero, warden, and his colleagues. 1524.

DATE: 1524.

LOCATION: Since the early nineteenth century the inscription plaque has been housed in the Seminario Patriarcale at the Salute where it was seen and transcribed by MOSCHINI (1842: 91). According to Moschini and to Cicogna (PAZZI, II: 134) its previous location was on the bell tower of the church of S. Mattio in the heart of the Rialto district. Presumably it must have been embedded near the base to ensure legibility. The *campanile* was demolished in 1818 following the Napoleonic suppressions. The inscription is at present displayed indoors on the *piano nobile* of the Seminario. It is framed in its display area by two fascinating ancient scaled-down bell towers, each *c.* 120 cm high, presenting a now rare type of conical pinnacle reminiscent of that on the tower of the church of S. Barnaba. Since our plaque is itself linked to a *campanile* it is not unusual for the casual visitor to connect the displayed objects. The two miniature bell towers come, however, from an unrelated church. They are original scale models of the bell tower of S. Lucia, the church demolished in the nineteenth century to make way for the city's railway station which is itself named after the church.

TYPE AND DESCRIPTION: Commemorative. The epigraph may commemorate the completion of the plaque itself but is more likely to refer to a renovation of the fabric of the bell tower at the expense of the butchers' guild. Neither hypothesis is referred to on the inscription which limits itself to recording the date as well as the name of the confraternity warden. The handsome white marble plaque with its narrow, slightly raised, strip frame measures *c.* 116 × *c.* 63 cm. The top half features a relief of a bearded and stocky St Matthew, the Apostle and Evangelist, seated at his desk and writing out the gospel into an open book. His vigorously rendered cloaked legs protrude from under the desk, with his sandled feet resting on top of the slightly raised inscription plaque beneath him. The initials <SM> identify him, while the two large hatchets framing him identify the confraternity as that of the butchers' guild, the *Sc(u)ola del Arte d(e)i Becheri*, dedicated to St Michael the archangel and to St Matthew. The inscription tablet itself measures *c.* 45 × *c.* 45 cm. Its centrality and solidity are emphasized by the four diagonal stone crosspieces radiating in from the frame and appearing to support it. The whole object, as befits a butchers' guild, radiates no-nonsense muscularity. The recently cleaned artefact is in good shape, with damage limited to the bottom left of the frame and plaque. The marble inscriptional tablet has suffered some abrasion but no substantial deterioration, so that the relief has not lost its power and the inscription is easily read.

The ancient confraternity-guild of the butchers, who operated out of the Rialto market area and had a monopoly on the butchering of cows and sheep in Venice and

Fig. 3.104. CI 108 in context. © A. S. Ferguson.

on the selling of their meat, had been in existence since at least the thirteenth century. The butchers eventually based themselves in the church of S. Mat(t)io (or Maf(f)io) de Rialto, building their meeting house next to it. In 1436 they were, remarkably, accorded the *jus patronatus* of the church by Pope Eugene IV, himself a Venetian, with the right to appoint the parish priest: a status underlined by the use of warden rather than alderman for their head. The church was closed down in the early nineteenth century and destroyed soon thereafter. Nothing is left of either *scuola* or church which were situated in what is now Campiello S. Matio, in an area of the Rialto market surrounded by street designations featuring the term *becarie* 'slaughterhouses' from Early/Middle/Modern Venetian *becher* 'butcher', pronounced [beˈkɛr], itself derived from medieval Latin BECCARIUS 'butcher of male goats and sheep'.

LETTERING: Roman square capitals cut in V-section. The sculptor of the artefact undeniably produced an effective piece of work, more forceful than finessed, but serving its purpose well. The same can be said of his handling of the written message given to him to carve by the guild commissioner(s). His lettering is generous in size, averaging 3.8 cm in height. It is amply spaced, clear and eminently legible, with no abbreviations employed. He deals with the *capitalis* script solidly, achieving a good square module with effectively understated stroke contrast, and indulging in no frills or bravura work. However, his command of layout leaves something to be desired, with justification on the left abandoned after three lines, and the awkward splitting of *Francescho* between ll. 4–5. More seriously, he seems to have allowed his attention to slip at two points, leading him into a pair of necessary but inelegant corrections. The more interesting of the two is his attempt to rectify the error *guardin* (for *guardian*) on l. 6. By the time he realised his mistake there was no room to insert the missing <a>, and abandoning an expensive and labour intensive marble block would have been out of the question. His solution was to try to trick the eye with a lightly cut horizontal cross stroke between the left upright and the diagonal of the <n>: after the fashion, as it happens, of a type of <an> ligature not unknown on Roman inscriptions and present on the right-side architrave epigraph in Latin on the great Arsenal gate of 1460. He indicated the presence of this cross stroke with a small drop-down correction sign over the <n>, of the kind we noted on CI 95. In the second case, having originally missed out the <g> in *compagnii* (l. 7), he reinserted it in superscript.

LANGUAGE: While the inscription is in perfect Middle Venetian there is a noticeable tendency for forms to converge on native variants that happened to coincide with Tuscan/Italian. So we find *tempo* 'time' (l. 3) not *tenpo*, and the first syllable of *compagnii* 'colleagues, fellow executives' (l. 7) in *com-* rather than *con-*. In *Francescho* (ll. 4–5) the presumed affricate /ts/ is written with <c> rather than with <ç>, although the traditional Venetian spelling of <ch> for velar /k/ is maintained. Striking in this respect is the choice of *guardian* 'warden' (l. 6), where the dominant (but not exclusive) form in the corpus is *vardian*. Such spelling choices must have been down to the commissioner, as must the hypercorrected *compagnii* with <ii>. On the undiphthongised *ser* 'Mr' (l. 4) see CI 95.

RECENT STUDIES: None. Recorded, but not published, by Cicogna. First published by MOSCHINI (1842: 91).

Corpus Inscription 109

ALDA LA B | ELA E GALAN | TA 3
[Alda, la bela e galanta.]

TRANSLATION: Alda, beautiful and courteous.

DATE: Undated, but stylistically attributable to the 1520s. The Museo Correr dates it 1520–1530.

LOCATION: The inscribed dish was part of the collection of Renaissance ceramics owned by Teodoro Correr (1780–1830) and bequeathed to the city upon his death. It has been in the Correr since then. Its original owner is unknown. Some pieces in the collection were commissioned by Venetians from the great centres of maiolica production in Umbria, especially Casteldurante, although in the present case Venetian manufacture cannot be ruled out. The language of the inscription strongly suggests a Venetian commissioner.

TYPE AND DESCRIPTION: Dedicatory. Maiolica dish with painted inscription on a ribbon. The banderole swirls on either side of the portrait of the young woman to whom the message is dedicated. The handsome tin-glazed earthenware plate is 22 cm in diameter and 4 cm tall, including the base. The background of the dish is painted deep blue, the same colour as the inscriptional letters, as the lady's eyes and as most of the elaborate stitching on her high-necked dress. Alda's complexion is suffused with the warmth of the golden colouring which dominates her beautiful brocaded headdress, tinges the background of the swirling ribbon and is echoed by the gold thread in her dress and by the simple gold link-necklace she wears. Her plaited hair is a rich brown. The artefact is in remarkably good condition.

The inscribed plate belongs to a Renaissance genre called the *coppa amatoria* in Italian and sometimes known as *belle donne* in English. It refers to maiolica dishes featuring the bust of a lady and carrying a name label or, like ours, a brief legend with the lady's name. Central Italian examples can be found in a number of museums, with captions such as *Elena bella*, *Elisabetta bella*, *Lucrezia bella* and *Livia bella*. As their Italian designation suggests they were a gift by a man to his woman friend. The peak period of their production was the first half of the sixteenth century, although Luigi Conton's ceramics collection, now in the Galleria Franchetti at the Ca' d'Oro, contains some fragmentary late fifteenth-century examples found in the Venice lagoon. The most notable of these features a profile portrait of a woman ('Catherine the beautiful') with an elaborate hairstyle. She is surrounded by rosettes and a banderole bearing an inscription in capital lettering that reads: *Chatarina B.*

> Mass produced, many of these valentines might have been readily available as pre-made dishes with standardised features already depicted on the surface. Cheap variants would thus be ready to pick up after a short inscription of a name was added to match the recipient. More fanciful lovers could have brought their lady to the workshop for a posing session, to create a more personalised representation. (STANCIOIU 2010: 141)

Fig. 3.105. CI 109 in context. © A. S. Ferguson.

The quality of the Correr dish suggests that it was not mass produced and that the portrait of the unknown Alda, with her clear skin, slight smile and melancholy gaze, was a commissioned likeness. Hovering, as it did, between the personal and the conventional such a gift article straddled the boundary between private token and object of display.

LETTERING: Decorative capitals painted in blue on to an illusionistic banderole. The *capitalis*-type lettering is attractively stylish, as befits both the message of the inscription and the elegant lady depicted on the plate. Letter stems and bow ends have been given slightly tapered serifs, sometimes straight, sometimes curved, as can be seen respectively on <a> and <d>. Stroke contrast is deliberately emphasized, as on <n>; the bowls of <b> are clearly differentiated; and the <l>, present on four of the five words of the inscription, has been given a wavy horizontal stroke. Blank spaces on the ribbon are filled with a light-blue bow motif. The cumulative effect on the eye is pleasingly calligraphic.

LANGUAGE: The brief vernacular message contains two un-Tuscan traits characteristically found in Venetian. *Bela* 'beautiful' (ll. 1–2) is spelled with a single <l>, and *galanta* (ll. 2–3), rather than Tuscan/Italian *galante*, shows a metaplasmic shift from 3rd to 1st conjugation. The use of *galanta* — in other words, gallant in the sense of 'courteous' — evokes the mood of Castiglione's *Cortegiano* (written 1518–24), the Renaissance book of manners *par excellence*.

RECENT STUDIES: None.

Corpus Inscription 110

*The present inscription has been inserted out of sequence in the
Corpus. Its existence only came to light after the first edition of*
Venetian Inscriptions *was published.*

MCCCCLXXVII · ADÌ · XVI · ZVGNO · FO [F]ATO · QVES|[T]O LAVORIER ·
I(N) [·] TENPO · DE · S(R) IACOMO · DE ANGE[LI D]A 2|
TR(EVIXO) · GVARDIAN · GRANDO · E · S(R) LORENZO · DE [A]NT[O|N]IO ·
GVARDIAN · DA · MATIN · (CON) I SVO · CONPAGNI ~

[MCCCCLXXVII, adì XVI zugno, fo fato questo lavorier in tenpo de s(r) Iacomo
de Angeli da Trevixo, guardian grando, e s(r) Lorenzo de Antonio, guardian
da matin, con i suò conpagni.]

FIG. 3.106. S. Paternian well inscription lines 1 and 3. © R. Ferguson
FIG. 3.107. S. Paternian well inscription lines 2 and 4. © R. Ferguson

TRANSLATION: 1477, on June 16th, this work was completed in the time in office of Mr Iacomo de Angeli from Treviso, warden, and Mr Lorenzo de Antonio, finance officer, with their colleagues.

DATE: June 16, 1477. This makes it comfortably the latest Gothic inscription, vernacular or Latin, to survive in Venice, superseding CI 70 of 1463.

LOCATION: Formerly in situ in Campo S. Paternian (now Campo Manin), *sestiere* of S. Marco, the well head carrying the inscription was replaced in the eighteenth century. Its subsequent whereabouts are not documented. It is at present stored nearby in a private courtyard off Calle dei Fuseri (S. Marco 4278). Remarkably, the well head (Early Venetian, *pozal*) was clearly depicted in its original location, some twenty-three years after its installation, by Jacopo de' Barbari in his bird's eye view of Venice. The whole area was redeveloped in the nineteenth century when the ancient church of S. Paternian was demolished.

TYPE AND DESCRIPTION: Commemorative. The inscription, previously unrecorded, celebrates the completion of the well and wellcurb in Istrian stone commissioned by an unnamed confraternity. It is one of the few inscribed well heads to survive from medieval and Renaissance Venice (see CI 15, CI 16, CI 51,

FIG. 3.108. S. Paternian well head motif. © R. Ferguson

CI 106). The imposing object is 98 cm high × 123 cm at its widest point. The two-line inscription on it runs continuously along adjacent rims. The cross and crown of St Theodore sculpted in low relief on the sides of the artefact suggest strongly that the well complex was sponsored by the *scuola* of S. Teodoro (Modern Venetian, *San Todaro*), an originally flagellant confraternity (founded in 1261), with a prosperous membership, that was elevated to *scuola grande* status in 1552 and has been revived in modern times. The brotherhood has always been connected to the nearby church of S. Salvador, opposite which it built its splendid and still surviving headquarters. The provision of a well for the use of the general public would have been part of its mission to succour the poor. The *scuola* was probably too well known in the neighbourhood for its sponsorship to require explicit spelling out on the artefact. On another side of the object is a prominent inscription running across the body of the wellcurb, in Latin in forceful Roman capitals dated 1559, marking the renovation of the well by the confraternity executive: *Restavratvs ᴛ anno ᴛ domini ᴛ M ᴛ D ᴛ LVIIII / indvstria ᴛ et ᴛ diligentia ᴛ gvbernatorvm ᴛ.*

LETTERING: The large, elegant and remarkably late Gothic lettering, damaged or abrased on some parts of the upper lines but still mostly readable, is *c.* 4 cm high. Although groove depth has been worn away and fissuring affects both rims it is still possible to appreciate the sharply-cut lettering, with the stonemason achieving

Fig. 3.109. S. Paternian well head in situ in 1500. From De' Barbari's view of Venice.

a fine balance between rigour and decorativeness. Most eye-catching are the <n> with its right leg curled and suspended above the baseline, the strongly uncial <m>, the neat <g> and <r>, the <s> with prominent serifs, and the minuscule <z> in majuscule format on *Lorenzo* (l. 3). With a height-to-width ratio on the letter <o> of *c*. 1.3 : 1, the inscription is entirely typical in its open aspect of Venetian Gothic practice. In its way this modest but handsome epigraphic artefact brings to a fitting end the inscriptional aesthetic that dominated Venice for some 150 years.

LANGUAGE: The language of the inscription is fully and regularly Venetian, featuring terms such as *zugno* 'June' (l. 1), *lavorier* '(piece of) work, artefact' (l. 2) and *guardian grando* 'warden' (l. 3) that recur in the Corpus, and *guardian da matin* 'finance officer, master of ceremonies' (l. 4) which appears here for the only time (see CI 3). On the possessive *suò* 'their' (l. 4) see CI 94. I opted for the spelling *Trevixo* rather than *Treviso* on l. 3 as <x> for /z/ was commoner in Venetian practice at this date. There is no indication to allow the abbreviations for 'Mr' to be opened out as either *ser* or *sier*.

RECENT STUDIES: None. I am grateful to Dr Franco Benucci of Padua University who brought the inscription to my attention in May 2023.

INDEX

(1) Inscriptional Persons

Albaregno, Françesco (parish priest) CI 29
Alda (gift recipient) CI 109
Antonio de Muran = Antonio Vivarin(i) (painter) CI 59
(Arian), Antuoni(i)o (merchant) CI 15, CI 16
Arian, Marcho (merchant sponsor of community well) CI 15, CI 16
Aristotile = Aristotle CI 54
Badoer, Albertin (patrician landowner) CI 17
Badoer, Çanin 'da Peraga' (patrician landowner) CI 17
Badoer, Felipo (patrician landowner) CI 17
Badoer, Iacomo 'da Perega' (patrician landowner and site prior) CI 17
Badoer, Marcho (patrician landowner and site prior) CI 18
Badoer, Marin 'de sen Iacomo de Lorio' (patrician landowner) CI 17
Badoer, Marin 'de sento Stina' (patrician landowner) CI 17
Badoer, Nic(h)olò (patrician landowner and almshouse prior) CI 18, CI 48
Becin, Çane (proctor) CI 13
Bereter, Nicolò (confraternity officer) CI 23
Bevilaqua, Iacomo (confraternity-guild officer) CI 81
Bianco, Çorçi (confraternity-guild alderman) CI 70
Bisuol, Mafio (confraternity warden) CI 9
Bon, Iacomo (confraternity warden) CI 14
Bonaza, maistro (confraternity-guild officer) CI 76
Bon dal Fero, Piero (confraternity officer) CI 23
Bortolamio 'Maçuco' (prior's deputy) CI 17
Bresan, Piero (guild alderman) CI 105
Bruto, Piero (confraternity-guild officer) CI 70
Buxelo, Çan (confraternity warden) CI 38
Caleger, Iacomelo (confraternity officer) CI 23
Chataiapiera, Polo di Iachomel (sculptor) CI 44
Chatapan, Marcho (proctor) CI 13
Chatarinus (painter) CI 40
Chavoduro, Ioane (confraternity officer) CI 38
Chorner, Piero (Procurator of St Mark) CI 39
Çimador, Piero (confraternity officer) CI 23
Çio, Anthonio (confraternity officer) CI 38

Climento sexsto [sic] = Clement VI (Pope) CI 20
Cristian, Natichlier (almshouse benefactor) CI 4
Çulian, Marcho (confraternity warden) CI 10
Da Bologna, Çuane (painter) CI 43
D'Acre, Andrea (confraternity-guild officer) CI 76
Da Ferara, Cristofol (woodcarver) CI 59
Da Gaio, Iacomelo (surgeon) CI 56
Dala Iusticia, Bernardin (grocer and confraternity officer) CI 94
Dala Sosa, Chatarina (confraternity officer) CI 23
Dale Store, Nicoleto (confraternity officer) CI 23
Dal Melon, Çechin (confraternity founder and sponsor) CI 41
Dal Soler, Nicholò (confraternity officer) CI 38
Da Modon, Antuonio (confraternity-guild alderman) CI 76
Da Molin, Iachomelo (confraternity officer) CI 38
Da Molten, Zorçi (confraternity head) CI 49
Dandolo, Andrea (Doge) CI 13
Dandolo, Felipo (Procurator of St Mark) CI 28
Dandolo, Simon (public figure) CI 25
Da Ponte, Alixe (monastery benefactress) CI 21
Darin, Alberto (confraternity-guild officer) CI 81
D'Arpo, Olivier (confraternity officer) CI 38
D'Astra, Menegelo (confraternity officer) CI 38
Da Tressaga, Çuane (confraternity warden) CI 3
De Anbruoxo, Cristofalo (confraternity-guild alderman) CI 96
De Andrea, Alesio (confraternity-guild officer) CI 81
De Angeli, Iacomo (confraternity warden) CI 110
De Antonio, Lorenzo (confraternity officer) CI 110
De Beltrame, Felipo (confraternity-guild officer) CI 81
De Bonomo, Çulian (confraternity warden) CI 46
De Cechin, Bortolamio (sponsor of inscribed stoup) CI 31
De Chandia, Agnolo (priest and sponsor of inscribed stoup) CI 31
De Chimento, Matio (confraternity-guild officer) CI 70
De Conteribus, Çane (steward and factor) CI 22
De Fiorio, Marcho (builder) CI 78
De Francischi, Francischo (notary) CI 49
De Greguol, Nicholeto (confraternity officer) CI 38
De Griguol, Polo (confraternity-guild alderman) CI 75
Deli Abati, Gioto (man of religion) CI 13
De li Amadi, Michiel (dyer and confraternity warden) CI 26
Deli Nevodi, Girardo (proctor) CI 13
De Lovin, Zuane (guild alderman) CI 95
De Marcho, Nicholò (confraternity-guild officer) CI 81
De Marcho Marchovichio, Nicholò (confraternity-guild alderman) CI 97
De Marin, Bernardo (confraternity warden) CI 107

De Marin, Bortolamio (father of Bernardo, above) CI 107
De Michiel, Damian (confraternity-guild officer) CI 96
De Michiel, Valentin (confraternity-guild officer) CI 70
De Muran, Antonio = Antonio Vivarin(i) (painter) CI 59
De Piero, Francescho (confraternity-guild alderman) CI 108
De Piero, Stefano (confraternity-guild alderman) CI 98
De Simon, Iacomo (confraternity-guild officer) CI 81
De Simon, Nicolò (confraternity-guild officer) CI 70
De Varischo, Antonio (confraternity-guild officer) CI 81
De Vivian, Antonio (orange merchant and confraternity-guild officer) CI 96
De Zorzi, Zuane (confraternity-guild officer) CI 81
De Zuane, Lucha (confraternity-guild officer) CI 75
Di Stefano, Fermo (confraternity-guild officer) CI 81
Dolphin, Beta (abbess of S. Caterina, Mazzorbo) CI 35
Dolze, maistro (confraternity-guild officer) CI 76
Dominus frater Antonius (Bishop of Como) CI 49
Donado, Iachomo (mayor of Murano) CI 51
Don Andrea (abbot of Pomposa) CI 22
Dona Nicolota (confraternity alderwoman) CI 23
Foscari, Francesco (Doge) CI 50
Gabriel, Çacharia (mayor of Murano) CI 38
Galeder, Antonio (confraternity officer) CI 23
Galeder, Piero (confraternity officer) CI 23
Gradenigi = Gredenigo family CI 103, CI 104
Iachomo da Venexia (painter) CI 55
Isipione = Scipio Africanus CI 54
Istrigo, Christofalo (proctor) CI 13
Lorenco (painter) CI 24
Lorenço da Venexia (painter) CI 55
Loto, Bortolamio (confraternity alderman) CI 50
Louredano, Leonardo = Lunardo Loredan (Doge) CI 93
Magno, Nicholò (proctor) CI 13
Marcante, Alvise (confraternity officer) CI 38
Maser, Piero (sponsor of devotional image with inscription) CI 29
Memo, Donato (mayor of Murano) CI 2
Michiel, Çane (nuns' procurator) CI 35
Minio, Lorencio (proctor) CI 13
Minoto, Marcho (Prior of S. Andrea de Lido) CI 21
Moise = Moses CI 54
Moresini, Michiel (Procurator of St Mark) CI 39
Morexini, Nicolò (Bishop of Castello) CI 13
Nadal, Felipo (confraternity officer) CI 23
Nadal, Mafio (confraternity alderman) CI 23
Negro, Antonio (confraternity-guild officer) CI 76

Orexe, Andrea (confraternity officer) CI 23
Pacifica (abbess of the Ognissanti convent) CI 106
Piarini, Angelo (church and almshouse benefactor) CI 8
Piarini, Tunina (testamentary executor, wife of Angelo, above) CI 8
Pistor, Benvegnù (confraternity officer) CI 38
Polo, Piero (confraternity officer) CI 50
Ponpilio, Numa = Numa Pompilius CI 54
Posca, Christofalo (father of Francisco Posca) CI 49
Posca, Francisco (Milanese merchant and confraternity head) CI 49
Roso, Mafio (confraternity officer) CI 38
Salon = Solon the lawgiver CI 54
Santo, Marcho (confraternity officer) CI 38
Sartor, Paris (confraternity officer) CI 38
Simeonus (bell maker) CI 80
Straçarol, Alexandro (confraternity warden) CI 94
Straçarol, Vielmo (proctor) CI 13
Taiapiera, Girardo (sculptor) CI 47
Tataro, Iachomo (confraternity warden) CI 18
Tentor, Lorenço (confraternity officer) CI 23
(Tiepolo), Baiamonte (patrician conspirator) CI 32
Traiano = Trajan CI 54
Trivisan, Piero (confraternity warden) CI 14
Trivixan, Lunardo (confraternity officer) CI 50
Tron, Antonio (Procurator of St Mark and confraternity benefactor) CI 107
Urban vescovo = Urban V (Pope) CI 30
Venier, Anthonio (Doge) CI 41
Verier, Francesco (confraternity officer) CI 23
Verzo, Michiel (confraternity-guild officer) CI 81
Zimador, Zuan de Nicolò (confraternity alderman) CI 92
Zuhane de Muran = Giovanni d'Alemagna (painter) CI 59

INDEX

(2) By Present Location

Arsenal (Castello) CI 67, CI 68, CI 69
Basilica of the Frari = S. Maria Gloriosa dei Frari (S. Polo):
interior CI 25, CI 49
cloister CI 58
Basilica of St Mark (S. Marco):
exterior CI 1, CI 79
treasury CI 36, CI 39, CI 52
Basilica of S. Zanipolo = SS. Giovanni e Paolo (Castello):
interior CI 44, CI 73, CI 74
exterior CI 57
Ca' Da Lezze, exterior (Lista de Spagna, S. Geremia, Cannaregio) CI 61
Calle de le Boteghe (S. Stefano, S. Marco) CI 42
Calle de la Laca (S. Giovanni Evangelista, S. Polo) CI 48
Calle de la Madona (Rialto, S. Polo) CI 101, CI 102
Calle dei Fuseri, in private courtyard (S. Luca, S. Marco 4278) CI 110
Calle del Morion (S. Ternita = S. Trinità, Castello) CI 4
Calle Toscana (Rialto, S. Polo) CI 103, CI 104
Calle Zancani / Fondamenta Moro (S. Marcilian = S. Marziale, Cannaregio) CI 72
Campiello de la Crose (S. Eufemia, Giudecca) CI 105
Campiello del Piovan (S. Tomà, S. Polo) CI 23
Campo del Anzolo Rafael (S. Anzolo Rafael = S. Angelo Raffaele, Dorsoduro) CI 15, CI 16
Campo S. Aponal (S. Aponal, S. Polo) CI 95
Campo S. Marcilian (S. Marcilian = S. Marziale, Cannaregio) CI 50, CI 71
Campo S. Maria Mazor (= S. Maria Maggiore, S. Crose) CI 94
Campo dei Santi Apostoli (SS. Apostoli, Cannaregio) CI 19
Campo S. Stefano (Murano) CI 51
Campo S. Tomà (S. Tomà, S. Polo) CI 60, CI 75
Church of S. Caterina, exterior (Mazzorbo) CI 35
Church of S. Fosca, exterior (Torcello) CI 46, CI 56
Church of S. Francesco della Vigna, cloisters (Castello) CI 78
Church of S. Martin, exterior (S. Martin = S. Martino, Castello) CI 29
Church of S. Pantalon, interior (Dorsoduro) CI 59

Church of S. Polo, *campanile* (S. Polo) CI 28
Corte Nova (Fondamenta de l'Abazia, S. Marcilian = S. Marziale, Cannaregio) CI 93
Corte S. Andrea (S. Luca, S. Marco) CI 21
Doge's Palace:
capitals CI 53, CI 54
loggia CI 30
storage CI 32
Fondamenta dei Sartori (Gesuiti, Cannaregio) CI 100
Museums and galleries:
Accademia, Venice:
interior CI 24, CI 40, CI 43
courtyard CI 14
façade CI 10, CI 11, CI 12
Biblioteca Nazionale Marciana (Venice) CI 62–66
Ca' d'Oro, Galleria Franchetti (Venice) CI 92
Ca' Rezzonico, garden (Venice) CI 70
Fondazione Giorgio Cini (Venice) CI 55
Glienicke Park (Potsdam) CI 38
Metropolitan Museum of Art (New York) CI 47
Museo Archeologico Nazionale (Venice) CI 106
Museo Correr (Venice) CI 5, CI 6, CI 7, CI 31, CI 82–91, CI 96–99, CI 109
Museo del Vetro, cloister (Murano) CI 8, CI 26
Museo Diocesano (Venice) CI 2
Museo Provinciale (Torcello) CI 33, CI 34
Palazzo Cini Collection (S. Vio, Venice) CI 37
Princes of Liechtenstein Collection (Vienna) CI 81
Seminario Patriarcale (Venice):
cloisters CI 9, CI 13
interior CI 27, CI 108
Villa Contarini-Camerini (Piazzola sul Brenta, Padua) CI 41
Ponte dei Frati (S. Anzolo = S. Angelo, S. Marco) CI 20
Ponte de le Balote (S. Salvador, S. Marco) CI 107
Salizzada S. Lio (S. Lio, Castello) CI 22
Salizzada S. Samuel (S. Samuel = S. Samuele, S. Marco) CI 76, CI 77
Scuola Grande di San Giovanni Evangelista, interior (S. Polo) CI 3, CI 17, CI 18, CI 45
Torre dell'Orologio (Piazza S. Marco, S. Marco) CI 80

INDEX

(3) Commented Words, Constructions and Linguistic Features

abado 'abbot' CI 22
abbatesa 'abbess' CI 106
a bene placito 'with the blessing/permission' CI 105
abitation 'lodging' CI 93
absence of gemination CI 33, CI 34, CI 39, CI 62, CI 63, CI 65, CI 66, CI 70, CI 93
abstract nouns CI 5, CI 6, CI 7, CI 30
accomplir ~ complir 'to carry out, accomplish, complete' CI 8
accusative vs nominative derivation CI 100
acrese 'to increase' CI 25
ad laude 'in praise (of)' CI 93
adverbial endings CI 14, CI 30
a fato '(he) did, (he) made' CI 55
affirmative particle *si* CI 21
affricates CI 5, CI 6, CI 7, CI 9, CI 12, CI 34, CI 38, CI 40, CI 47, CI 55, CI 57, CI 58, CI 62, CI 63, CI 71, CI 72, CI 76, CI 79, CI 81, CI 83, CI 86, CI 88, CI 92, CI 94, CI 96, CI 97, CI 98, CI 99, CI 108
agosto 'August' CI 55, CI 79
a hi 'to the' CI 66
aida 'help' CI 17
aidadi 'helped' CI 30
/al/ → /ol/ CI 9, CI 14, CI 30, CI 41
albergo 'confraternity meeting room or hall' CI 18, CI 38
alguna 'any' CI 8
alguni 'some (people)' CI 14
alla 'to the' CI 54
Alovixe (Louis) CI 86
altare 'altar' CI 49
altaro 'altar' CI 41
altrui 'others, other people' CI 32
Alvise (Louis) CI 38
/an/ → /en/ CI 30
analogy CI 17, CI 79

Anbruoxo (element of patronymic) CI 96
ancona 'icon, devotional image' CI 2, CI 24
Angnese (Agnes) CI 89
anno 'year' CI 8, CI 20
Anthonio (Anthony) CI 41
anthroponymy CI 94
Antiopia (Ethiopia) CI 37
Antonio (Anthony) CI 76
Antuoniio (Anthony) CI 15
Antuonio (Anthony) CI 16, CI 76
aotoritade 'authority' CI 30
aphaeresis CI 20, CI 30
apocope CI 1, CI 2, CI 12, CI 25, CI 27, CI 38, CI 44, CI 63, CI 70
Aponal (Apollinaris) CI 95
apopulata 'peopled, populated' CI 62
april 'April' CI 79, CI 92
archa 'sarcophagus, tomb' CI 37
Aristotile (Aristotle) CI 54
-ĀRIUS > -*er* CI 41, CI 97, CI 98, CI 99
arte 'guild' CI 60
-ĀTEM reflexes CI 2, CI 9, CI 30
-ĀTUM reflexes CI 2, CI 30, CI 60, CI 62, CI 63, CI 66
avanti dei 'before, ahead of' CI 67
ave '(they) had' CI 14
avicario 'deputy' CI 50
avichario 'deputy' CI 94, CI 96
avolio 'ivory' CI 63
avosto 'August' CI 33, CI 34
avril 'April' CI 9, CI 27
badesa 'abbess' CI 35
barbacani 'corbels, recessed supports' CI 101, CI 102
Barbaria (toponym) CI 14
batudo 'beaten' CI 39
bela 'beautiful' CI 109
benedicta 'blessed' CI 49
beni 'goods' CI 48
bereter 'hatter' CI 23
Bertuçi (forename) CI 41
besporo 'evening' CI 14
Beta (Betty, Liz) CI 35
biatisima 'most blessed' CI 9
Bonaza (surname) CI 76
Bonomo (surname element) CI 46
borgi 'suburbs' CI 62

Bresan (surname) CI 105
-brio ending on months CI 60, CI 69, CI 79
buono 'good' CI 8
Buran da mar (Burano) CI 8
bureaucratic language CI 30, CI 49, CI 105
buteri 'coopers' CI 98
C + front vowel CI 71, CI 72
çaçe = *caçé* '(they) fell' CI 14
caleger 'shoemaker, cobbler' CI 23
calegeri 'shoemakers, cobblers' CI 42, CI 60
Çane (John) CI 3, CI 22
Çane vangelista (John the Evangelist) CI 17
canpanili 'bell towers' CI 14
canton 'corner' CI 63
capitelli 'capitals' CI 64
caro 'carriage' CI 63
carta 'paper' CI 8
casa 'house' CI 58
Castelo (toponym) CI 20
castoldo 'steward' CI 22
catch-all relative *che* CI 39
cavi 'heads' CI 17
Cavoduro (surname) CI 38
caxe 'houses' CI 22, CI 71, CI 72
Cechin (element of patronymic) CI 31
Çechin (forename) CI 41
celebradi 'celebrated' CI 30
celestial 'celestial' CI 47
çener 'January' CI 12, CI 14
çentileçe 'delights' CI 63
çerchera = *çercherà* 'will seek' CI 8
çerexis 'cherries' CI 53
cexere 'chick peas' CI 96
<ch> = /k/ CI 4, CI 5, CI 6, CI 19, CI 28, CI 30, CI 37, CI 38, CI 39, CI 40, CI 44, CI 53, CI 55, CI 75, CI 81, CI 86, CI 91, CI 96, CI 97, CI 98, CI 107, CI 108
cha 'house, family, palace' CI 4
Chandia (Heraklion, Crete) CI 31
cha nome 'who is called' CI 44
chanpanil 'bell tower' CI 28
chapel(l)a 'chapel' CI 30
charcere 'prisons' CI 30
charitade 'charity' CI 9
chasion 'occasion' CI 30
chastaldo 'alderman' CI 98

chastita = *chastità* 'chastity' CI 54
Chataiapiera (surname) CI 44
Chatapan (surname) CI 13
Chatarinus (forename) CI 40
chaxa 'house, meeting house' CI 19, CI 107
chiese 'churches' CI 54
chlarisimo 'most distinguished' CI 107
chognosie = *chognosié* 'know!' CI 61
cholona 'column' CI 39
chomençada 'begun' CI 9
chompagni 'colleagues, fellow executives' CI 98
chomum 'common' CI 25
chomun 'common' CI 32
chonpagni 'colleagues, fellow executives' CI 50
chonstancia 'constancy' CI 6
chosa 'thing' CI 30
Christofol (Christopher) CI 59
chucumeris 'cucumbers' CI 53
churches and religious houses in Venice CI 86, CI 87, CI 88, CI 89, CI 90, CI 91
churches and religious houses on Murano CI 84
çiascuno 'each' CI 8
çimador 'cloth shearer' CI 23
ciroico 'surgeon' CI 56
cita = *cità* 'city' CI 62
claritade 'clarity' CI 30
clementissimo 'most clement' CI 30
co 'like' CI 6
co 'with' CI 6
code mixing CI 8, CI 26, CI 54
code switching CI 8, CI 54
çoie 'jewels' CI 63
collone 'columns' CI 64
colmo e fito 'roof and rent/owned and rented out' CI 8
colonial Venetian CI 5, CI 6, CI 7
començа = *començà* 'it began' CI 14
comencado 'begun' CI 22
comesaria 'executor' CI 8
como çio sia 'to this effect' CI 49
compagnii 'colleagues, fellow executives' CI 108
complida 'carried out, accomplished, completed' CI 48
comuna mentre 'commonly' CI 14
conceduda 'conceded' CI 30
conçero 'upkeep, maintenance' CI 8
concession 'concession' CI 48

concesso 'conceded' CI 41
condam '(son of) the late' CI 41
conpagni 'colleagues, fellow executives' CI 17, CI 18, CI 46, CI 96, CI 97
conparse 'appeared' CI 23
conpido 'carried out, accomplished, completed' CI 18
conplida 'carried out, accomplished, completed' CI 19
conplio 'carried out, accomplished, completed' CI 8
conprado 'bought' CI 60
conputade 'counted, computed' CI 62
consecrato 'consecrated' CI 49
conseio 'council' CI 41
consonant + L CI 18, CI 19, CI 29, CI 41, CI 48, CI 49, CI 107
continuada 'continued' CI 30
continuamente 'continually' CI 30
contrada 'district' CI 8
convecini 'neighbourhood association' CI 72
convexini 'neighbourhood association' CI 71
corando 'during, in the course of' CI 2
Çorçi (George) CI 70
Cristofalo (Christopher) CI 96
Croxechieri (church in Cannaregio) CI 86
Çuane (John) CI 36, CI 43
Çuane evançelista (John the Evangelist) CI 18
Çuane evangelista (John the Evangelist) CI 48
çuche 'gourds' CI 53
Çudecha (Giudecca) CI 14
cugno 'June' CI 22
çugno 'June' CI 21
cum ço sia chosa che 'in consideration of the fact that' CI 30
dacre = *d'Acre* (surname) CI 76
dadriedo 'behind' CI 63
da Modon (surname) CI 76
Darin (surname) CI 81
data 'given' CI 8
de 'of' CI 93
decembrio 'December' CI 60, CI 79, CI 80
decenbrio 'December' CI 28
declined surnames CI 103, CI 104
definite articles CI 14, CI 30, CI 35, CI 37, CI 41, CI 49, CI 63, CI 64, CI 81, CI 93
degan 'dean, deacon, counsellor' CI 23
degana 'female dean, deacon, counsellor' CI 23
de hi 'of the' CI 94
deictics CI 9, CI 19
de Lovin (surname) CI 95

deputada 'reserved, allocated' CI 66
derota 'rout' CI 14
destribuida 'distributed' CI 8
destro 'opportunity, advantage' CI 9
detegnudi 'held, detained' CI 30
devini 'divine' CI 30
de-voicing of initial /g/ CI 98
di 'of' CI 49
di [sic] 'gave' CI 20
di 'on the day of' CI 58
di ~ *de* 'of' CI 8
diasystem CI 35
dico 'I say' CI 62
die 'must' CI 1, CI 27
die = *dié* '(he) gave' CI 54
die 'on the day of' CI 22
die primo 'on the first day' CI 35
diexe 'ten' CI 41
diphthongisation CI 1, CI 3, CI 11, CI 13, CI 15, CI 16, CI 17, CI 18, CI 22, CI 24, CI 26, CI 27, CI 28, CI 30, CI 31, CI 35, CI 38, CI 39, CI 41, CI 45, CI 47, CI 49, CI 50, CI 56, CI 57, CI 62, CI 63, CI 75, CI 76, CI 77, CI 94, CI 95, CI 107, CI 108
di piu nobili 'of the most noble' CI 63
discreti 'wise, prudent' CI 94
disiroso 'desirous' CI 25
dissimilation CI 1, CI 17, CI 39, CI 45, CI 75
dita '(the) said' CI 8, CI 48
dito '(the) said' CI 21, CI 48
dito 'called, known as' CI 66
doctor 'doctor' CI 49
dodexe 'twelve' CI 19
dolce 'sweet' CI 9
Dolphin (surname) CI 35
Dolze (surname) CI 76
Domenedio 'God' CI 47
domina 'lady, mistress' CI 8
domini 'of lord' CI 25
don 'Sir, Lord' CI 22
Donado (surname) CI 51
Donado ~ *Donato* (forename) CI 2
donna e domina 'lady and mistress' CI 8
doxe 'doge' CI 13, CI 41
drio 'behind, after' CI 8
dura = *durà* '(it) lasted' CI 14
durar 'to last, endure' CI 27

edifichador 'builder' CI 54
Efienia (Ephigenia) CI 37
ego sum lus mondi [sic] 'I am the light of the world' CI 35
egregia 'esteemed, distinguished, eminent' CI 35
egregio 'esteemed, distinguished, eminent' CI 48
elision CI 23
el senta 'he sits' CI 63
el va a spaso 'he goes out and about' CI 63
emphatic pronouns CI 6, CI 67
epenthesis CI 33, CI 34
<er> vs <ar> CI 7, CI 96, CI 107
eredi 'heirs' CI 8
eriedi 'heirs' CI 56, CI 78
esendo 'being' CI 107
et 'and' CI 93
exhortative present subjunctive CI 1
explicit 3rd plural verb endings CI 62, CI 63
facta fo 'was made' CI 2
fameie 'families' CI 62
fano '(they) make' CI 62
fantolini 'little children, infants, babies' CI 20
far 'to do, make, act' CI 1
fato 'made' CI 33, CI 34
fatto 'made' CI 44
fava 'bean' CI 96
faxoli 'kidney beans' CI 96
fe = fé '(he) made, gave' CI 54
fe far = fé far 'had made' CI 21, CI 39
Felipo (Philip) CI 28
Ferara (Ferrara) CI 59
fermeça 'firmness' CI 8
fevraro 'February' CI 24
fevrer 'February' CI 41
fexe '(he) made' CI 47
fia 'daughter' CI 37, CI 54
fici 'figs' CI 53
fio 'son' CI 15
fiio 'son' CI 16
fiol 'son' CI 14
fo '(there) was' CI 14
fo '(it) was' CI 68
fo fato far 'was ordered to be made' CI 45
fondadore 'founder' CI 13
fontego 'warehouse' CI 74

fontigo 'warehouse' CI 73
fora 'out' CI 8
forono '(they) were' CI 93
Foscha (Fusca) CI 86
fradeli 'brothers' CI 18
fradelitade 'brotherhood' CI 42
fra menori 'friars minor' CI 49
Francescho (Francis) CI 108
franchado '(completed and) released for use' CI 38
Francisc(h)o (Francis) CI 49
frar 'brother' CI 17
frari 'brothers' CI 9
frateli 'brothers' CI 93
fratirnitade 'brotherhood' CI 11
fu '(it) was' CI 60
fui 'I was' CI 67
fuogo 'fire, hearth' CI 62
fuogi 'fires, hearths' CI 62
future stem CI 7, CI 30
future tense CI 5, CI 7
G + front vowel CI 57
galanta 'courteous' CI 109
galeder 'wooden pail or bucket cooper' CI 23
Gallo-Italian dialects CI 59
garcia 'grace' CI 14
gastaldo 'alderman' CI 96, CI 97, CI 105
gastolda 'alderwoman' CI 23
gastoldo 'alderman' CI 23, CI 46, CI 50, CI 70
gemination of /l/ CI 8, CI 30, CI 64
generation 'offspring' CI 66
Geremia (Jeremy) CI 86
Germanic W > /v/ CI 9
gerunds CI 2, CI 8, CI 28, CI 35, CI 107
Gioto (forename) CI 13
Girardo (Gerald, Gerard) CI 47
glanduxe 'lymph nodes, bubos' CI 14
glexia 'church' CI 8, CI 41, CI 49
gliesia 'church' CI 27
gliexia 'church' CI 13
Gradenigi (plural surname) CI 103, CI 104
grandemente 'greatly' CI 30
grando 'great, big' CI 18
Greçia (Greece) CI 54
Griguol (element of patronymic) CI 75

guardian 'warden' CI 3, CI 108, CI 110
gubernadori 'governors' CI 49
hapax CI 8, CI 54
helemuosena 'alms' CI 30
homeni 'men' CI 63
homo 'man' CI 2, CI 48, CI 51, CI 61
honorado 'honoured' CI 2
honorevele '(right) honourable' CI 51
hospedal 'almshouse, hospital, hospice' CI 4, CI 48
humilitade 'humility' CI 30
huva 'grapes' CI 53
hybrid forms CI 8, CI 93
hypercorrection CI 44, CI 69, CI 79, CI 108
hypotaxis CI 30
Iachomel (forename) CI 44
Iachomelo (forename) CI 56
identical 3rd singular/plural verb forms CI 39, CI 55, CI 59
iera 'was' CI 45, CI 48
Iesuati (Gesuati church in Dorsoduro) CI 89
imagine 'images' CI 64
imperative CI 61
imperfect tense CI 14
impersonal constructions CI 63, CI 64
inchontrar 'to befall' CI 1
indicion 'indiction' CI 2
indirect object pronouns CI 1, CI 5
ineffabele 'ineffable' CI 30
inextimabile 'inestimable' CI 63
initial /g/ → /k/ CI 22
in la 'in the' CI 8
inlumina ' illuminates' CI 30
inperador 'emperor' CI 54, CI 63
intaia = *intaià* '(he) engraved' CI 59
intendudo 'heard, understood' CI 30
Iohane (John) CI 3
i quali 'which' CI 8
Irtachus (Hirtacus) CI 37
iselerita 'Israelite' CI 54
Isipione (Scipio Africanus) CI 54
Istrigo (surname) CI 13
Italo-Romance vernaculars CI 78
iuridiciom 'jurisdiction, legal extent' CI 101, CI 102
iurisdition 'jurisdiction, legal extent' CI 103, CI 104
iustitia 'justice' CI 54

koineisation CI 25
L + yod CI 41, CI 62
la fe = la fé 'made it' CI 44
lagoon islands CI 83
landmarks and sights in Venice CI 85
laqual 'which' CI 23
lasemo 'we leave' CI 30
laso = lasò '(he) left' CI 107
late 'milk' CI 52
Latinisms and Latin influence CI 22, CI 30, CI 41, CI 47, CI 48, CI 49, CI 51, CI 53, CI 58, CI 61, CI 62, CI 63, CI 64, CI 65, CI 93, CI 94, CI 105
la toa 'your' CI 7
lavorenti 'journeymen, workers' CI 42
lavorer 'work, piece of work, artefact' CI 10
lavorier 'work, piece of work, artefact' CI 11, CI 12, CI 41, CI 110
lavoriero 'work, piece of work, artefact' CI 35
lavoro 'work, piece of work, artefact' CI 57
le 'of her' CI 5
leçce 'laws' CI 54
legalli 'legal' CI 8
lege 'law(s)' CI 54
le mie posesione 'my possessions' CI 8
lemusena 'alms' CI 20
lençene 'groin' CI 14
lenition/voicing CI 2, CI 4, CI 8, CI 9, CI 13, CI 14, CI 17, CI 21, CI 23, CI 27, CI 29, CI 30, CI 33, CI 34, CI 37, CI 39, CI 48, CI 63, CI 64, CI 93
Leonardo (Leonard) CI 93
levar 'to raise, to build' CI 13
li 'to him' CI 1
lido 'shore' CI 21, CI 37
liera 'was' CI 14
ligador 'packer(s)' CI 74
ligadori 'packers' CI 73
linguistic latitude CI 25, CI 35
lioni 'lions' CI 64
li soi 'his' CI 3
logo 'place' CI 17, CI 35
lonipotente 'the omnipotent' CI 57
Louredano (surname) CI 93
Lucha (Luke) CI 75
luio 'July' CI 15, CI 16, CI 19, CI 78, CI 79
Lunardo (Leonard) CI 11, CI 50
luntan 'far' CI 62
luogo 'place' CI 13, CI 18, CI 30, CI 48

maçius 'May' CI 79
maço 'May' CI 23, CI 45, CI 96
maçor 'greater, bigger' CI 62
Macorbo (Mazzorbo) CI 83
Mafeus (Matthew) CI 37
Mafio (Matthew) CI 23, CI 38, CI 41
magnificentie 'luxury, luxuries' CI 62
maiestade 'majesty' CI 30
mainland towns CI 82
maistro 'master' CI 55, CI 56, CI 76, CI 78
mal del carbon 'carbuncles' CI 14
Marcante (surname) CI 38
marchadanti 'merchants' CI 107
Marcho (element of patronymic) CI 97
Marchovichio (surname) CI 97
marçius 'March' CI 79
marco 'March' CI 57
março 'March' CI 18, CI 40, CI 58
Margera (Marghera) CI 82
mariegola 'confraternity statute and membership book' CI 23
martore 'martyr' CI 57
marzo 'March' CI 76, CI 79, CI 94
maser 'administrator, treasurer' CI 75
Maser (surname) CI 29
mazo 'May' CI 79, CI 81
Mazzorban features CI 35
meço 'middle' CI 62
me fecit 'made me' CI 15, CI 16
memuoria 'memory' CI 11
menado 'pulled, drawn' CI 63
mese 'month' CI 23
metaphony CI 53
metaplasms CI 18, CI 22, CI 35, CI 41, CI 96, CI 109
metathesis CI 13, CI 14, CI 17, CI 28, CI 35, CI 39, CI 44
metuda 'laid, put, placed' CI 13, CI 30
mexe 'month' CI 19, CI 40, CI 94
mi 'me' CI 67
mia 'miles' CI 62
Michiel (Michael) CI 39
mie 'my' CI 67
mieriti 'merits' CI 30
Milano (Milan) CI 49
milia 'miles' CI 64
mirabile 'marvellous' CI 66

miser 'Sir, Mr' CI 2, CI 14, CI 17, CI 22, CI 38, CI 49
miserichordievolemente 'mercifully' CI 30
misier 'Sir, Mr' CI 17, CI 28, CI 31, CI 41, CI 47, CI 50, CI 57, CI 93
mistro 'master' CI 70, CI 75
mo 'now' CI 30, CI 32
modal verbs CI 1
Moise (Moses) CI 54, CI 88
Moixe (Moses) CI 96
moloni 'melons' CI 53
monestiero 'monastery' CI 21
monte 'bank account, government bonds' CI 8
Moresini (surname) CI 39
moria '(they) died' CI 14
morte 'death' CI 8
mortilitade 'death rate' CI 14
muiere 'wife' CI 8
Muran (Murano) CI 2
Muranese features CI 8, CI 26
murer 'builder' CI 78
mureri 'builders' CI 77
Nadal (surname) CI 23
narancer 'orange merchant' CI 96
nasalisation CI 17, CI 18, CI 22, CI 28, CI 31, CI 32, CI 35, CI 50, CI 63, CI 96, CI 97, CI 98, CI 101, CI 102
nasion 'nation(s)' CI 14
Natichlier (forename) CI 4
nativitade 'nativity' CI 30
nato di 'born of' CI 44
Negro (surname) CI 76
Nicholo = *Nicholò* (Nicholas) CI 30, CI 96, CI 97
Nicolota (forename) CI 23
nientemeno 'no less' CI 8
nobele 'noble' CI 17, CI 18, CI 28
nobel e savio 'noble and wise' CI 38
noder 'notary, lawyer' CI 49
nonçolo 'caretaker, undertaker' CI 23
non-standard features CI 25, CI 35
northern dialects CI 63
novembrio 'November' CI 51, CI 79
novenbrio 'November' CI 35
Numa Ponpilio (Numa Pompilius) CI 54
obligatory 3rd person subject pronoun CI 63
obsequious language CI 93
oficiali 'board officials, officers' CI 3, CI 38

ogno 'each, every' CI 8
oltisimo 'most high' CI 9
oltro 'other' CI 14
olturio 'help' CI 30
om 'man' CI 1
opera 'work, piece of work' CI 105
opus Simeonus fecit '(this) work was done by Simion' CI 80
orexe 'goldsmith' CI 23
organo 'organ' CI 45
ornado 'adorned, decorated' CI 63
ospedal 'almshouse, hospital, hospice' CI 100
otobrio 'October' CI 8, CI 79
otubrio 'October' CI 47
ovra 'work, piece of work, object' CI 29
palaçi 'palaces' CI 62
palatal approximant CI 14, CI 15, CI 66, CI 68
palatal lateral CI 44
paratactic syntax CI 14
pare 'father' CI 13
parochia 'parish' CI 95
parte 'share' CI 8
partitive articles CI 17, CI 18, CI 38, CI 41, CI 45, CI 48, CI 60, CI 63, CI 66, CI 71, CI 72, CI 73, CI 74, CI 77, CI 94, CI 97, CI 98, CI 99, CI 101, CI 102, CI 103, CI 104, CI 105, CI 107
passives CI 2, CI 5, CI 9, CI 10, CI 11, CI 12, CI 18, CI 19, CI 22, CI 23, CI 24, CI 28, CI 33, CI 34, CI 41, CI 48, CI 50, CI 58, CI 60, CI 63, CI 70, CI 93, CI 94
past historic tense CI 14, CI 59, CI 60, CI 67, CI 68, CI 93, CI 107
past participle endings CI 8, CI 62, CI 63, CI 66
patriacha [sic] 'patriarch' CI 20
patroni 'patrons, holders of a *jus patronatus*' CI 17
patronymics CI 81
penelo 'banner' CI 33, CI 34
penetencie 'penances' CI 30
pense '(he) painted' CI 43
pense '(they) painted' CI 59
pentidi 'repented' CI 30
pentor 'painter' CI 24
Peraga (locality) CI 17
percholator 'procurator' CI 107
perchurador 'procurator' CI 28
percolator 'stand-in, deputy' CI 17
percolatori 'procurators' CI 39
perdon 'pardon' CI 20
pergolo 'pulpit' CI 45

permanga e duri 'survive and endure' CI 8
per mano 'by the hand' CI 8
persici 'peaches' CI 53
PH > /v/ CI 86
phoneme CI 44
Piatade ~ Pietate (La Pietà foundling hospital) CI 20
piera 'stone' CI 13, CI 39, CI 44
Piero (Peter) CI 30, CI 39, CI 47, CI 57
pilastro 'pillar, pier' CI 67, CI 68
piri 'pears' CI 53
pistor 'baker' CI 38, CI 95
plovan 'parish priest, rector' CI 29
po 'can' CI 1
podesta = podestà 'mayor' CI 2, CI 38
podestade 'mayor' CI 51
Polo (Paul) CI 44
Ponpoxa (locality) CI 22
pontifichado 'pontificate' CI 30
popular pronunciation CI 15, CI 16, CI 18, CI 54
porce 'offers, proffers' CI 20
posando 'being able' CI 8
Posca (surname) CI 49
posesion 'property' CI 9, CI 21
posi 'may' CI 8
possa 'can, may' CI 41
possessives CI 3, CI 7, CI 67, CI 92, CI 94, CI 110
post-tonic vowels CI 13, CI 17, CI 18, CI 28, CI 29, CI 30, CI 51,
poveri '(the) poor' CI 8, CI 17, CI 18
povolo 'people' CI 54
pre = pre' 'priest, reverend' CI 29
precioxo 'precious' CI 57
prencipiada 'begun' CI 58
present subjunctive forms CI 30
present tense forms CI 30
presentia 'presence' CI 49
pretiosa 'precious' CI 66
pre-tonic vowels CI 2, CI 5, CI 8, CI 9, CI 14, CI 20, CI 25, CI 28, CI 30, CI 47, CI 50, CI 62, CI 64, CI 75, CI 98
priegi 'prayers' CI 30
priesio 'price' CI 63
principiada 'begun' CI 48
principo 'prince' CI 50
prior 'prior' CI 17, CI 18, CI 48
priori 'confraternity heads' CI 49

prochuradori 'proctors' CI 13
procoratori 'administrators' CI 8
procurator 'procurator, administrator' CI 35
pronunciation of <x> CI 41
propia 'the very' CI 39
proponimento 'proposal' CI 8
proprii 'own, personal' CI 45
prosthetic vowels CI 50, CI 54
proto-surnames CI 23, CI 29, CI 92
provedadori 'superintendents' CI 81
puoveri 'poor' CI 30
queli 'those (people)' CI 62
questa 'this' CI 9
questopera dintalglio = *quest'opera d'intaglio* 'this sculpted work' CI 44
re 'king' CI 37
recevera = *receverà* 'will receive' CI 30
redur 'to restore, return, bring back, draw up' CI 27
regata 'boat race' CI 85
regeno '(they) support, escort' CI 63
register CI 41, CI 93
religiliosa [sic] 'religious' CI 35
remeri 'oar makers' CI 97
reverentia 'reverence' CI 47
reze '(they) support' CI 64
riceve = *ricevé* 'he received' CI 54
roborada 'supported, strengthened, firmed up, confirmed' CI 9
Rocho (Roch) CI 91
rogata 'drawn up' CI 49
ronpere o speçar 'break or split' CI 8
sabioneri 'sand suppliers' CI 99
sacho 'sack, common fund' CI 9
saludemo 'we greet' CI 30
san 'saint' CI 36, CI 41, CI 57
sancta 'saint' CI 9, CI 49
sancto 'saint' CI 49
santo ~ *santa* 'saint' CI 11
sartor 'tailor' CI 38
sartori 'tailors' CI 100
scaii 'armpits' CI 14
schola 'confraternity' CI 107
schuola 'confraternity' CI 11, CI 18, CI 49
scientia 'science' CI 62
scola 'confraternity' CI 3, CI 14, CI 17, CI 77
scola 'confraternity building/meeting house' CI 94

scolla 'confraternity building/meeting house' CI 60
scomençada 'begun' CI 9
scripta CI 5, CI 6, CI 7
scrivan 'clerk, secretary, scrivener' CI 23, CI 50
scuola 'confraternity' CI 9, CI 19, CI 26, CI 38, CI 41, CI 48, CI 49, CI 50
se 'it is' CI 32
semi-learned forms CI 25, CI 30, CI 49
sen 'saint' CI 11, CI 14, CI 17, CI 26, CI 27, CI 30
sen Baseio (toponym) CI 14
sen Bortolamio (toponym) CI 27
sen Iacomo de Lorio (toponym) CI 17
sen Polo (St Paul) CI 30
s-n Rafiel (toponym) CI 15, CI 16
sen Salvador (toponym) CI 27
seno 'wisdom, good sense' CI 32
senpre 'always' CI 32
sento 'saint' CI 17
sento Stina (toponym) CI 17
senti 'saints' CI 30
se piase 'were caught' CI 14
sepoltura 'burial place, tomb' CI 78
sepultura 'burial place, tomb' CI 25
ser 'Mr' CI 3, CI 4, CI 22, CI 49, CI 95, CI 108
sera = *serà* 'will be' CI 30
sera e vera = *serà e verà* 'will be and will come' CI 8
setenbrio 'September' CI 46, CI 69, CI 75
se traversa 'one crosses' CI 64
se trova = *se trovà* 'found himself' CI 14
sette 'seven' CI 54
se vega 'see themselves' CI 30
sexsto 'sixth' CI 20
sia 'be' CI 30
siando 'being' CI 28, CI 29, CI 35
sibilants CI 19, CI 23, CI 40, CI 41, CI 47, CI 58, CI 63, CI 64, CI 71, CI 72, CI 75, CI 81, CI 82, CI 86, CI 88, CI 89, CI 94, CI 96, CI 107
si e = *si è* '(it) is' CI 42
sier 'Mr' CI 26, CI 31, CI 38, CI 41, CI 47, CI 50
singular-plural in *-n* CI 21
sira = *sirà* 'will be' CI 5
sociesori 'successors' CI 8
soi 'his' CI 92
soler 'floor, storey, platform' CI 50
son '(they) are' CI 81
sono '(they/there) are' CI 62, CI 63

soto 'under' CI 63
Sovia (Sophia) CI 86
sovratuto 'above all' CI 8
speech community CI 17
spelling conventions CI 71, CI 72
spicier 'grocer, druggist' CI 94
splandor 'splendour' CI 30
spoken inflections CI 67
Sprachmischung CI 8, CI 54
ssta 'this' CI 19
sta 'this' CI 24
stabele e mobele 'fixed and moveable' CI 8
stabilitate 'stability' CI 6
stado 'state' CI 23
stete '(it) ceased' CI 14
Straçarol (surname) CI 13, CI 94
studio 'study, diligence' CI 62
stue 'stoves' CI 62
suma 'sum (total)' CI 20
suoi 'his' CI 26
sui 'their' CI 94, CI 110
supra-regional features CI 49
syncope CI 29
syntactic recurrence CI 13, CI 23, CI 30, CI 63, CI 64
syntagmic amalgamation CI 44, CI 57
Taiapiera (surname) CI 47
taramoto 'earthquake' CI 14
Tataro (nickname) CI 18
tempo 'time' CI 2, CI 41, CI 50, CI 98, CI 108
temprara = *temprarà* 'will temper' CI 7
tenpo 'time' CI 31, CI 35, CI 46, CI 70, CI 75
tenpi 'temples' CI 54
tentor 'dyer' CI 23
teren '(plot) of land' CI 70
tereno 'plot, land' CI 32
Tervixio (Treviso) CI 82
testamento 'will' CI 8
ti 'you' CI 6
tintore 'dyer' CI 26
todesci 'Germans' CI 42
todeshi 'Germans' CI 74
Toma = *Tomà* 'Thomas' CI 23
Tomado 'Thomas' CI 23
Torçelo (Torcello) CI 34

trade names CI 96, CI 97, CI 98, CI 99
traditional Venetian parish designations CI 86, CI 87, CI 88, CI 89, CI 90, CI 91
tragando 'drawing' CI 8
trageto 'boat crossing, ferry' CI 105
Traiano (Trajan) CI 54
tresento 'three hundred' CI 64
Trevixo (Treviso) CI 110
triumpho 'triumph' CI 65
Trivisan (surname) CI 14
Trivixan (surname) CI 50
Tunina (forename) CI 8
Tuscan features CI 8, CI 13, CI 26, CI 44, CI 54, CI 62, CI 63, CI 64, CI 66, CI 81, CI 93, CI 107, CI 108
tuti officiali 'all the officials' CI 49
ubertosamente 'fruitfully' CI 30
uno 'one' CI 20
vada 'go' CI 30
vano '(they) go' CI 63
vardian 'warden' CI 9, CI 38, CI 94
variation CI 17, CI 18, CI 25, CI 26, CI 30, CI 32, CI 35, CI 41, CI 60, CI 71, CI 72, CI 78, CI 94, CI 107
Varischo (surname) CI 81
vedera = *vederà* 'will see' CI 30
vedova 'widow' CI 54
vega '(let him) see/consider' CI 1
vegnir 'to come' as auxiliary CI 63
vegniva ~ *vegnia* 'came' CI 14
velar <g> CI 42, CI 60, CI 62, CI 82, CI 103, CI 104, CI 105
Venexia (Venice) CI 13
venician '(a) Venetian' CI 44
Veniesia (Venice) CI 30
Veniexia (Venice) CI 13, CI 41, CI 62
venire 'to come' CI 8
verbal prefix *in-* CI 1, CI 30
vergene 'virgin' CI 30
verier 'glazier' CI 23
vernacular pronunciation and spelling CI 79
Verzo (surname) CI 81
vescodo [sic] 'bishop' CI 20
vicario 'deputy' CI 23
Vielmo (William) CI 13
vien menado 'it is led/it gets led' CI 63
Vignon (Avignon) CI 30
virgine 'virgin' CI 93

vive = *vivé* '(he) lived' CI 14
voio e ordino 'I wish and order' CI 8
volenta = *volentà* 'will' CI 17
written standard CI 30
<x> = /z/ CI 13, CI 22, CI 41, CI 96
zenaro 'January' CI 79
zener 'January' CI 67, CI 99
zimador 'cloth-shearer' CI 92
Zorzi (element of patronymic) CI 81
Zuane (John) CI 81
zudesi 'judges' CI 81
zugno 'June' CI 49, CI 79, CI 106, CI 110
Zulian (Julian) CI 88

BIBLIOGRAPHY

AGAZZI, MICHELA. 1991. *Platea Sancti Marci: i luoghi marciani dall'XI al XIII secolo e la formazione della piazza* (Venice: Comune di Venezia/Università di Venezia)
—— 2005. 'Sarcofagi altomedievali nel territorio del Dogado veneziano', in *Medioevo: immagini e ideologia*, ed. by Arturo Carlo Quintavalle (Milan: Electa), pp. 565–75
—— 2019. 'Questioni marciane: architettura e scultura', in *San Marco, la Basilica di Venezia: arte, storia, conservazione*, ed. by Ettore Vio, 2 vols (Venice: Marsilio), I, pp. 91–109
ALINEI, MARIO. 1984. 'La grafia veneziana delle origini', in his *Lingua e dialetti: struttura, storia e geografia* (Bologna: Il Mulino), pp. 225–56
AMMANATI, GIULIA. 2017. *'Pinxit industria docte mentis'. Le iscrizioni delle allegorie di Virtù e Vizi dipinte da Giotto nella Cappella degli Scrovegni* (Pisa: Edizioni della Normale)
ANZALONE, MARIA SANTINA, ET AL. c. 1982. *Le insegne delle arti veneziane al Museo Correr* (Venice: Stamperia di Venezia)
BAGLIONI, DANIELE. 2016. 'Sulle sorti di [ɔ] in veneziano', in *Actes du XXVIIe Congrès international de linguistique et de philologie romanes (Nancy, 15–20 juillet 2013)*, ed. by Eva Buchi, Jean-Paul Chauveau and Jean-Marie Pierrel (Strasbourg: Société de linguistique romane/ÉliPhi), I, pp. 353–65
BALISTRERI-TRINCANATO, CORRADO, and DARIO ZANVERDIANI. 2000. *Jacopo de Barbari. Il racconto di una città* (Venice: Edizioni Stamperia Cetid)
BANTI, OTTAVIO (ed.). 1996. *Le epigrafi e le scritte obituarie del Duomo di Pisa* (Pisa: Pacini)
—— 2000. 'Dall'epigrafica romanica alla pre-umanistica: la scrittura epigrafica dal XII alla fine del XV secolo a Pisa', *Scrittura e Civiltà*, 24: 61–101
BARBERI, CLAUDIO (ed.). 2000. *Psalterium Egberti: facsimile del ms. CXXXVI del Museo Archeologico Nazionale di Cividale del Friuli* (Rome and Trieste: Ministero per i Beni e le Attività Culturali/Archivio di Stato/Soprintendenza del Friuli-Venezia Giulia)
BARTOLI LANGELI, ATTILIO. 2000. *La scrittura dell'italiano* (Florence: Il Mulino)
—— 2006. *Notai. Scrivere documenti nell'Italia medievale* (Rome: Viella)
BARTOLINI, DONATELLA. 2015. 'On the Borders. Surgeons and their Activities in the Venetian State (1540–1640)', *Medical History*, 59.1: 83–100
BASSI, ELENA. 1997. *Tracce di chiese veneziane distrutte: ricostruzioni dai disegni di Antonio Visentini* (Venice: Istituto Veneto di Scienze, Lettere ed Arti)
BATTAGLINI, NICOLÒ. 1871. *Torcello antico e moderno. Studii* (Venice: Marco Visentini)
BAUMSTARK, REINHOLD. 1981. *Masterpieces from the Collection of the Princes of Liechtenstein* (New York: Hudson Hills Press)
BEMBO, PIETRO. 1525. *Prose [...] nelle quali si ragiona della volgar lingua* (Venice: Tacuino)
BENESCH, OTTO. 1969. 'The Ancient and the Gothic Revival in French Art and Literature', in *French Humanism, 1470–1600*, ed. by Werner Gundersheimer (London: Macmillan), pp. 209–28
BENUCCI, FRANCO. 2009A. 'Costruzioni passive negli antichi volgari italiani', *Padua Working Papers in Linguistics*, 3: 70–102
—— 2009B. 'Latino e volgare nell'epigrafia medievale padovana', in *Dialetto: usi, funzioni, forme*, ed. by Gianna Marcato (Padua: Unipress), pp. 307–12

—— (ed.). 2015. Corpus *dell'epigrafia medievale di Padova 1. Le iscrizioni medievali dei Musei Civici di Padova. Museo d'arte medievale e moderna* (Verona: Cierre)

BERTANZA, ENRICO, and VITTORIO LAZZARINI. 1891. *Il dialetto veneziano fino alla morte di Dante Alighieri, 1321. Notizie e documenti editi e inediti* (Venice: Tipografia Editrice di M. S. fra Compositori Tipografi)

BERTOLI, BRUNO. 2002. *La soppressione di monasteri e conventi a Venezia dal 1797 al 1810* (Venice: Deputazione di Storia Patria per le Venezie)

BETTIO, PIETRO. 1829. *Commentari della Guerra di Ferrara tra li Veneziani ed il Duca Ercole d'Este, di Marin Sanuto* (Venice: Giuseppe Picotti)

BISCHOFF, BERNHARD. 1990. *Latin Palaeography: Antiquity and the Middle Ages* (Cambridge: Cambridge University Press)

BÖCKEM, BEATE. 2016. *Jacopo de' Barbari:Künstlerschaft und Hofkultur um 1500* (Cologne: Böhlau)

BOELHOWER, WILLIAM. 2018. 'Framing anew Ocean Genealogy: The Case of Cartography in the Early Modern Period', *Atlantic Studies*, 15.2: 279–97

BOERIO, GIUSEPPE. 1829. *Dizionario del dialetto veneziano* (Venice: Andrea Santini e figlio)

—— 1865. *Dizionario del dialetto veneziano* (Venice: Cecchetti)

BÖNINGER, LORENZ (ed.). 2002. *La 'Regula' bilingue della Scuola dei Calzolai Tedeschi a Venezia del 1383* (Venice: Il Comitato Editore)

BORNSCHLEGEL, FRANZ-ALBRECHT. 2010. 'Die gotische Majuskel im deutschen Sprachraum', in *Las inscripciones góticas. II coloquio internacional de epigrafía medieval*, ed. by María Encarnación Martín López and Vicente García Lobo (Leon: Corpus Inscriptionum Hispaniae Medievalum), pp. 202–29

BOTTAZZI, MARIALUISA. 2008. 'Fonditori di campane: dalla bottega medievale alla produzione industriale nell'ambiente del Rinascimento veneziano', in *L'industria artistica del bronzo del Rinascimento a Venezia e nell'Italia settentrionale*, ed. by Matteo Ceriana and Victoria Avery (Verona: Scripta), pp. 363–74

—— 2012. *Italia medievale epigrafica. L'alto medioevo attraverso le scritture incise (secc. IX-XI)* (Trieste: Centro Europeo Ricerche Medievali)

BRAUNSTEIN, PHILIPPE. 2016. *Les allemands à Venise (1380–1520)* (Rome: École Française de Rome)

BRECK, JOSEPH. 1912. 'Una scultura ascritta a Gerardo di Mainardo', *L'arte*, 15: 202–04

BREVEGLIERI, BRUNO. 1997. 'Il volgare nelle scritture esposte bolognesi. Memorie di costruzioni e opere d'arte', in *'Visibile parlare'. Le scritture esposte nei volgari italiani dal Medioevo al Rinascimento*, ed. Claudio Ciociola (Naples: Edizioni Scientifiche Italiane), pp. 73–100

BUCKTON, DAVID, ET AL. 1984. *The Treasury of San Marco, Venice* (Milan: Olivetti)

BUENGER ROBBERT, LOUISE. 1999. 'Domenico Gradenigo: a Thirteenth-Century Venetian Merchant', in *Medieval and Renaissance Venice*, ed. by Donald Queller, Ellen Kittell and Thomas Madden (Urbana: University of Illinois Press), pp. 27–48

BUONOPANE, ALFREDO. 2014. 'Marin Sanudo e gli "antiquissimi epitaphii"', in Marin Sanudo, *Itinerario per la terraferma veneziana*, ed. by Gian Maria Varanini (Rome: Viella), pp. 95–104

CACCHIOLI, LUNA, and ALESSANDRA TIBURZI. 2014. 'Lingua e forme dell'epigrafia in volgare (secc. IX-XV)', *Studj Romanzi*, 10: 311–52

—— 2015. 'Contributi e fonti per lo studio del volgare esposto in Italia', *Critica del Testo*, 18.2: 103–08

CACCHIOLI, LUNA, NADIA CANNATA and ALESSANDRA TIBURZI. 2016. 'EDV. Italian Medieval Epigraphy in the Vernacular (9th-15th Century). A New Database', in *Off the Beaten Track. Epigraphy at the Borders*, ed. by Antonio Felle and Anita Rocco (Oxford: Archaeopress), pp. 91–129

CALABI, DONATELLA, and PAOLO MORACHIELLO. 1987. *Rialto. Le fabbriche e il ponte* (Turin: Einaudi)

CALLEGARI, ADOLFO. 1930. *Il Museo Provinciale di Torcello* (Venice: Stamperia Zanetti)

CALVELLI, LORENZO. 2015. 'Reimpieghi epigrafici datati da Venezia e dalla laguna veneta', in *Pietre di Venezia. Spolia in se, spolia in re*, ed. by Monica Centanni and Luigi Sperti (Rome: L'Erma di Bretschneider), pp. 113–34

—— 2016. 'Iscrizioni esposte in contesti di reimpiego: l'esempio veneziano', in *L'iscrizione esposta. Atti del Convegno Borghesi 2015*, ed. by Angela Donati (Faenza: Fratelli Lega), pp. 457–90

CAMPANA, AUGUSTO. 1968. 'Tutela dei beni epigrafici', *Epigraphica*, 30: 5–19

—— 1976. 'Le iscrizioni medievali di San Gemini', in *San Gemini e Carsulae*, ed. by Umberto Ciotti, et al. (Milan and Rome: Bestetti), pp. 83–132

—— 1984. 'La testimonianza delle iscrizioni', in *Lanfranco e Wiligelmo. Il Duomo di Modena*, ed. by Marina Armandi, et al. (Modena: Panini), pp. 365–404

CANIATO, GIOVANNI, and MICHELA DAL BORGO. 1990. *Le arti edili a Venezia* (Rome: Edilstampa)

CANNATA, NADIA. 2020. 'Le scritture esposte e il latino in Italia fra XIV e XV secolo', in *Acta Conventus Neo-Latini Albasitensis*, ed. by Florian Schaffenrath and María Teresa Santamaría Hernández (Leiden: Brill), pp. 189–201

CANTÙ, CESARE. 1856. *Scorsa di un Lombardo negli archivj di Venezia* (Milan and Verona: Civelli)

CAPPELLI, ADRIANO. 1928. *Lexicon Abbreviaturum. Wörterbuch lateinischer und italienischer Abkürzungen* (Leipzig: Weber)

CARACCIOLO ARICÒ, ANGELA (ed.). 2007–09. *Giorgio Dolfin, Cronicha dela Nobil Città de Venetia et dela sua Provintia et Destretto*, 2 vols (Venice: Centro di Studi Medievali e Rinascimentali)

—— (ed.). 2011. *Marin Sanudo il giovane, De Origine, Situ et Magistratibus Urbis Venetae, ovvero La Città di Venetia (1493–1530)* (Venice: Centro di Studi Medievali e Rinascimentali)

CARLEVARIJS, LUCA. 1703. *Le fabriche e vedute di Venetia, disegnate, poste in prospettiva e intagliate* (Venice: Giovanni Battista Finazzi)

CASONI, GIOVANNI. 1829. *Guida per l'Arsenale di Venezia* (Venice: Giuseppe Antonelli)

CASTELNUOVO-TEDESCO, LISBETH, and JACK SOULTANIAN. 2010. *Italian Medieval Sculpture in the Metropolitan Museum of Art and the Cloisters* (New York and New Haven: Metropolitan Museum of Art/Yale University Press)

CATTANEO, ANGELO. 2011. *Fra Mauro's Mappa Mundi and Fifteenth-Century Venice* (Turnhout: Brepols)

CECCHERINI, IRENE. 2008. 'La genesi della scrittura mercantesca', in *Régionalisme et internationalisme. Problèmes de paléographie et de codicologie au Moyen Âge*, ed. by Otto Kresten and Franz Lackner (Vienna: Österreichische Akademie der Wissenschaften), pp. 123–37

CECCHETTI, BARTOLOMEO. 1869–70. 'Dei primordi della lingua italiana e del dialetto in Venezia', *Atti del Reale Istituto Veneto di Scienze, Lettere ed Arti*, 15: 1585–1626

—— 1887A. 'Funerali e sepulture dei Veneziani antichi', *Archivio Veneto*, 34.2: 265–84

—— 1887B. 'Nomi di pittori e lapicidi antichi', *Archivio Veneto*, 33: 45–65

CECCHETTI, BARTOLOMEO, ET AL. (eds). 1886. *Documenti per la storia dell'augusta ducale basilica di San Marco in Venezia dal nono secolo al secolo decimo ottavo* (Venice: Ferdinando Ongania)

CECCHINI, ISABELLA. 2015. 'I Fiorentini ai Frari: uso pubblico dello spazio religioso in età moderna', in *Santa Maria Gloriosa dei Frari. Immagini di devozione, spazi di fede*, ed. by Carlo Corsato and Deborah Howard (Padua: Centro Studi Antoniani), pp. 127–38

CICOGNA, EMMANUELE ANTONIO. 1824–53. *Delle inscrizioni veneziane*, 6 vols (Venice: Orlandelli, vol. I/the Author, vols II-VI)

—— 1844. *I due gruppi di porfido sull'angolo del Tesoro della Basilica di S. Marco esaminati e descritti* (Venice: Tipografia Merlo)

—— 1855. *Breve notizia intorno alla origine della confraternita di S. Giovanni Evangelista in Venezia* (Venice: Tipografia Merlo)

CICOGNARA, LEOPOLDO. 1813–18. *Storia della scultura italiana dal suo risorgimento in Italia fino al secolo di Canova*, 8 vols (Prato: Fratelli Giachetti)

CIOCIOLA, CLAUDIO. 1995. 'Scrittura per l'arte, arte per la scrittura', in *Storia della letteratura italiana*, ed. by Enrico Malato, vol. II (Rome: Salerno), pp. 531–80

—— (ed.). 1997. *'Visibile parlare'. Le scritture esposte nei volgari italiani dal Medioevo al Rinascimento* (Naples: Edizioni Scientifiche Italiane)

CLARKE, PAULA, ELISABETTA BARILE, and GIORGIA NORDIO. 2006. *Cittadini veneziani del Quattrocento: i due Giovanni Marcanova, il mercante e l'umanista* (Venice: Istituto Veneto di Scienze, Lettere ed Arti)

COLLINGWOOD, ROBIN GEORGE. 1930. *The Archaeology of Roman Britain* (London: Methuen)

COLONNA, FRANCESCO. 1499. *Hypnerotomachia Poliphili* (Venice: Aldo Manuzio)

CONNELL, SUSAN. 1988. *The Employment of Sculptors and Stonemasons in Venice in the Fifteenth Century* (New York and London: Garland)

—— 1993. 'Gli artigiani dell'edilizia', *Ricerche Venete*, 2: 31–92

CONTON, LUIGI. 1927. *Torcello: il suo estuario e i suoi monumenti* (Venice: U. Bortoli)

ČORALIĆ, LAVORKA. 2011. 'Compagni e gastaldi della Scuola dei remèri: hrvatski veslari u Mlecima (XV.-XVII. stoljeće)', *Povijesni Prilozi*, 40: 161–75

CORNER [CORNARO], FLAMINIO. 1749. *Ecclesiæ Venetæ antiquis monumentis, nunc primum editis, illustratæ ac in decades distributæ*, 13 vols (Venice: Pasquali)

—— 1758. *Notizie storiche delle chiese e monasteri di Venezia e di Torcello* (Padua: Giovanni Manfrè)

CORTELAZZO, MANLIO. 1970. *L'influsso linguistico greco a Venezia* (Bologna: Pàtron)

—— 2007. *Dizionario veneziano della lingua e della cultura popolare nel XVI secolo* (Limena: La Lina)

CORTELAZZO, MANLIO, and CARLA MARCATO. 1998. *I dialetti italiani. Dizionario etimologico* (Turin: UTET)

CORTELAZZO, MANLIO, and PAOLO ZOLLI. 1979–88. *Dizionario etimologico della lingua italiana*, 5 vols (Bologna: Zanichelli)

CRIFÒ, FRANCESCO. 2016. *I 'Diarii' di Marin Sanudo (1496–1533): sondaggi filologici e linguistici* (Berlin and Boston: De Gruyter)

CROUZET-PAVAN, ELISABETH. 2015. *Le Moyen Âge de Venise. Des eaux salées au miracle de pierres* (Paris: Albin Michel)

—— 2017. *La mort lente de Torcello: histoire d'une cité disparue* (Paris: Albin Michel)

D'ACHILLE, PAOLO. 2017. 'Cronache, scritture esposte, testi semicolti', in *Le cronache volgari in Italia*, ed. by Giampaolo Francesconi and Massimo Miglio (Rome: Istituto Storico Italiano per il Medio Evo)

D'AMBROSIO, SILVIA. 2012A. 'Monumento funebre di Jacopo Cavalli', in *La Basilica dei Santi Giovanni e Paolo. Pantheon della Serenissima*, ed. by Giuseppe Pavanello (Venice: Marcianum/Fondazione Giorgio Cini), pp. 106–10

—— 2012B. 'Portalino. Lapicida veneziano', in *La Basilica dei Santi Giovanni e Paolo. Pantheon della Serenissima*, ed. by Giuseppe Pavanello (Venice: Marcianum/Fondazione Giorgio Cini), p. 119

D'ANDREA, DAVID. 2013. 'Charities and Confraternities', in *A Companion to Venetian History, 1400–1797*, ed. by Eric Dursteler (Leiden: Brill), pp. 421–48

DAVANZO POLI, DORA. 2000. 'Reperti tessili del Museo Provinciale di Torcello', *Venezia Arti*, 14: 113–18

DA VILLA URBANI, MARIA. 1991. 'Le iscrizioni', in *Basilica patriarcale in Venezia*, ed. by Maria da Villa Urbani, et al. (Milan: Fabbri), pp. 17–218

DAY, WILLIAM R., MICHAEL MATZKE and Andrea SACCOCCI (eds). 2016. *Medieval European Coinage, with a Catalogue of the Coins in the Fitzwilliam Museum Cambridge: 12 Italy (I) (Northern Italy)* (Cambridge: Cambridge University Press)

DEBIAIS, VINCENT. 2009. *Messages de pierre: la lecture des inscriptions dans la communication médiévale* (Turnhout: Brepols)

―― 2015. 'Des figures et des lettres. Note méthodologique sur les inscriptions dans la peinture murale romane de Catalogne', *Summa*, 6: 48–66

DEBIAIS, VINCENT, ROBERT FAVREAU and CÉCILE TREFFORT. 2007. 'L'évolution de l'écriture épigraphique en France au Moyen Âge et ses enjeux historiques', *Bibliothèque de l'École des Chartes*, 165: 101–37

DE FRANCESCHI, ENZO. 2005. 'I mosaici della cappella di Sant'Isidoro nella basilica di San Marco', *Arte Veneta*, 30: 6–29

DEHMER, ANDREAS. 2004. *Italienische Bruderschaftsbanner des Mittelalters und der Renaissance* (Munich and Berlin: Deutscher Kunstverlag)

DELORENZI, PAOLO. 2016. 'Guglielmo Veneziano', in *Capolavori ritrovati della Collezione di Vittorio Cini. Crivelli, Tiziano, Lotto, Canaletto, Guardi, Tiepolo*, ed. by Luca Massimo Barbero (Venice: Marsilio), pp. 21–23

DE LUCIA, GIUSEPPE. 1908. *La Sala d'Armi nel Museo dell'Arsenale di Venezia* (Rome: Rivista Marittima)

DE MARCHI, ANDREA. 2003. '*Lorenzo e Jachomo da Venexia*: un percorso da Zanino a Jacopo Bellini e un enigma da risolvere', *Saggi e Memorie di Storia dell'Arte*, 27: 71–100

DE MAURO, TULLIO. 2000. *Grande dizionario italiano dell'uso* (Turin: UTET)

DEMUS, OTTO. 1960. *The Church of San Marco in Venice. History, Architecture, Sculpture* (Washington: Dumbarton Oaks)

DE RUBEIS, FLAVIA. 2002. 'Epigraphs', in *Italy in the Early Middle Ages*, ed. by Cristina La Rocca (Oxford: Oxford University Press), pp. 220–27

―― 2008. 'La capitale romanica e la gotica epigrafica: una relazione difficile', *Scripta*, 1: 33–43

―― (ed.). 2010. *Inscriptiones Medii Ævi Italiæ: (saec. VI-XII): 3 Veneto — Belluno, Treviso, Vicenza* (Spoleto: Fondazione Centro Italiano di Studi sull'Alto Medioevo)

DESCHAMPS, PAUL. 1929. *Étude sur la paléographie des inscriptions lapidaires de la fin de l'époque mérovingienne aux dernières années du XIIe siècle* (Paris: Société Générale d'Imprimerie et d'Édition)

DI LENARDO, LORENZO (ed.). 2014. *La collezione epigrafica del Seminario Patriarcale di Venezia. Catalogo (secoli XII-XV)* (Venice: Marcianum)

DI STEFANO MANZELLA, IVAN. 1987. *Mestiere di epigrafista* (Rome: Quasar)

DORIGO, WLADIMIRO. 2003. *Venezia romanica. La formazione della città medioevale fino all'età gotica*, 2 vols (Venice: Istituto Veneto di Scienze, Lettere ed Arti/Cierre/Regione del Veneto)

DOTTO, DIEGO. 2008. *Scriptae venezianeggianti a Ragusa nel XIV secolo. Edizione e commento di testi volgari dell'Archivio di Stato di Dubrovnik* (Rome: Viella)

DOUGLAS, HUGH. 1907. *Venice on Foot, with the Itinerary of the Grand Canal and Several Direct Routes to Important Places* (London: Methuen)

EAMON, WILLIAM. 2013. 'Science and Medicine in Early Modern Venice', in *A Companion to Venetian History, 1400–1797*, ed. by Eric Dursteler (Leiden: Brill), pp. 701–42

EDMONDSON, JONATHAN. 2014. 'Inscribing Roman texts: *Officinæ*, Layout, and Carving Techniques', in *The Oxford Handbook of Roman Epigraphy*, ed. by Christer Bruun and Jonathan Edmondson (Oxford: Oxford University Press), pp. 111–30

ENZO, ANDREA. 2005. 'Il Lapidario del Seminario Patriarcale di Venezia. Problemi della conservazione e percorsi per la ricerca', *Ateneo Veneto*, 163: 91–112
ERIZZO, NICOLÒ. 1866. *Relazione storico-artistica della Torre dell'Orologio di S. Marco in Venezia: colla descrizione del meccanismo dell'orologio e relativi documenti autentici* (Venice: Tipografia del Commercio)
FABBRI, GIANNI. 1999. *La Scuola Grande della Misericordia. Storia e progetto* (Milan: Skira)
FALCHETTA, PIERO. 1991. 'La misura dipinta: rilettura tecnica e semantica della veduta di Venezia di Jacopo de' Barbari', *Ateneo Veneto*, 29: 273–305
—— 2006. *Fra Mauro's World Map: With a Commentary and Translation of the Inscriptions* (Turnhout and Venice: Brepols/Biblioteca Nazionale Marciana)
—— 2013. *Fra Mauro's World Map: A History* (Rimini and Bologna: Imago)
FAVREAU, ROBERT. 1997. *Épigraphie médiévale* (Turnhout: Brepols)
FERGUSON, RONNIE. 2000. *The Theatre of Angelo Beolco. Text, Context and Performance* (Ravenna: Longo)
—— 2003. 'The Formation of the Dialect of Venice', *Forum for Modern Language Studies*, 39.4: 450–64
—— 2005. 'Alle origini del veneziano: una koiné lagunare?', *Zeitschrift für Romanische Philologie*, 121.3: 476–509
—— 2007. *A Linguistic History of Venice* (Florence: Olschki)
—— 2013A. 'Dinamiche contrastive di mutamento linguistico in veneziano', in Ronnie Ferguson, *Saggi di lingua e cultura veneta*, (Padua: Cleup), pp. 197–235
—— 2013B. 'La formazione del veneziano', in Ronnie Ferguson, *Saggi di lingua e cultura veneta* (Padua: Cleup), pp. 13–65
—— 2013C. 'Le pubbliche iscrizioni in volgare antico a Venezia', in Ronnie Ferguson, *Saggi di lingua e cultura veneta* (Padua: Cleup), pp. 67–134
—— 2013D. 'Venetian Language', in *A Companion to Venetian History*, ed. by Eric Dursteler (Leiden: Brill), pp. 928–58
—— 2015A. 'Un'iscrizione in veneziano trecentesco su reliquiario marciano', *Quaderni Veneti*, 4.1: 1–10
—— 2015B. 'Torcello 1366: le scritte in volgare ricamate sul gonfalone di Santa Fosca', *Lingua e Stile*, 50.2: 193–207
—— 2015C (ed.). *Le iscrizioni in antico volgare delle confraternite laiche veneziane. Edizione e commento* (Venice: Marcianum)
—— 2017. 'Dating the Vernacular Inscription on the Wall of St Mark's Treasury in Venice. A Case Study in Medieval Epigraphic Philology', *Italian Studies*, 72.3: 222–37
FERRARI, SIMONE. 2006. *Jacopo de' Barbari: un protagonista del Rinascimento tra Venezia e Dürer* (Milan: Mondadori)
FERRO, GIOVANNI. 1889. 'Antiche iscrizioni veneziane', *Il Propugnatore*, 2: 444–53
FOGOLARI, GINO. 1928–29. 'Le tavolette delle arti veneziane', *Dedalo*, 3: 724–41
FOLADORE, GIULIA. 2009. 'Il racconto della vita e la memoria della morte nelle iscrizioni del corpus epigrafico della basilica di Sant'Antonio di Padova (secoli XIII-XV)' (unpublished doctoral thesis, University of Padua)
—— 2010. *Parole di pietra: le epigrafi quattrocentesche del Santo* (Padua: Centro Studi Antoniani)
FOLIN, MARCO. 1990. 'Procedure testamentarie e alfabetismo a Venezia nel Quattrocento', *Scrittura e Civiltà*, 14: 243–70
FONTANELLA, LUCIA. 2000. *Un volgarizzamento tardo duecentesco dell' 'Antidotarium Nicolai'* (Alessandria: Edizioni dell'Orso)
FORMENTIN, VITTORIO. 2014. 'Rendiconti duecenteschi in volgare dall'archivio dei Procuratori di San Marco', *Lingua e Stile*, 49: 5–41
—— 2015. 'Volgare o latino? Le "didascalie identificative" d'età romanica tra grammatica e storia', *Studi di Grammatica Italiana*, 34: 1–20

―― 2017. *Baruffe muranesi. Una fonte giudiziaria medievale tra letteratura e storia della lingua* (Rome: Edizioni di Storia e Letteratura)
FORTINI BROWN, PATRICIA. 1988. *Venetian Narrative Painting in the Age of Carpaccio* (New Haven and London: Yale University Press)
―― 1996A. 'Le *Scuole*', in *Storia di Venezia. Dalle Origini alla caduta della Serenissima*, vol. V, ed. by Alberto Tenenti and Ugo Tucci (Rome: Istituto della Enciclopedia Italiana), pp. 307–54
―― 1996B. *Venice & Antiquity. The Venetian Sense of the Past* (New Haven and London: Yale University Press)
―― 2006. 'The Venetian *casa*', in *At Home in Renaissance Italy*, ed. by Marta Ajmar-Wollheim and Flora Dennis (London: V&A Publications), pp. 50–65
FULIN, RENATO, ET AL. (eds). 1879–1902. *Marino Sanuto: i Diarii*, 58 vols (Venice: Visentini)
GALLO, RODOLFO. 1967. *Il tesoro di S. Marco* (Venice and Rome: Istituto per la Collaborazione Culturale)
GAMBA, BARTOLOMEO. 1832. *Serie degli scritti impressi in dialetto veneziano* (Venice: Alvisopoli)
GAMBA, GIULIANA. 2015. 'La gotica epigrafica tra XIII e XIV secolo da Carrara Santo Stefano alla Scodosia' (Tesi di Laurea, University of Venice Ca' Foscari)
GARDNER, JULIAN. 2010. 'The Placement of Inscriptions on Painting and Sculpture in Italy *c.* 1250–*c.* 1350: Contexts and Status', in *Las inscripciones góticas. II coloquio internacional de epigrafía medieval*, ed. by María Encarnación Martín López and Vicente García Lobo (Leon: Corpus Inscriptionum Hispaniae Medievalum), pp. 351–65
GASPARRINI LEPORACE, TULLIA. 1956. *Il mappamondo di Fra Mauro* (Rome: Istituto Poligrafico dello Stato)
GEREVINI, STEFANIA. 2019. 'Inscribing History, (Over)Writing Politics: Word and Image in the Chapel of Sant'Isodoro at San Marco, Venice', in *Sacred Scripture/Sacred Space: the Interlacing of Real Places and Conceptual Spaces in Medieval Art and Architecture*, ed. by Tobias Frese, Wilfried E. Keil and Kristina Krüger (Berlin and Boston: De Gruyter), pp. 323–50
GEYMONAT, FRANCESCA. 2014. 'Scritture esposte', in *Storia dell'italiano scritto: 3 Italiano dell'uso*, ed. by Giuseppe Antonelli, et al. (Rome: Carocci), pp. 57–100
GIOVÈ MARCHIOLI, NICOLETTA. 1994. 'L'epigrafia comunale cittadina', in *Le forme della propaganda politica nel Due e nel Trecento*, ed. by Paolo Cammarosano (Rome: École Française de Rome), pp. 263–68
―― 2015. 'Le iscrizioni medievali dei Musei Civici di Padova. Note paleografiche', in *Corpus dell'epigrafia medievale di Padova: 1 Le iscrizioni medievali dei Musei Civici di Padova. Museo d'arte medievale e moderna*, ed. by Franco Benucci (Verona: Cierre), pp. 25–36
GIULIANI, GIAMBATTISTA. 1865. *Sul vivente linguaggio della Toscana* (Florence: Le Monnier)
GLIXON, JONATHAN. 2003. *Honoring God and the City. Music in the Venetian Confraternities, 1260–1807* (Oxford: Oxford University Press)
GODEFROY, FRÉDÉRIC. 1881–1902. *Dictionnaire de l'ancienne langue française et de tous ses dialectes du IX*[e] *au XV*[e] *siècle*, 10 vols (Paris: Vieweg)
GOY, RICHARD. 2006. *Building Renaissance Venice: Patrons, Architects and Builders, c. 1439–1500* (New Haven and London: Yale University Press)
GRAEVIUS, JOHANN GEORG. 1722. *Thesaurus antiquitatum et historiarum Italiæ*, V (Leiden: Petrus van der Aa)
GRAMIGNA, SILVIA, and ANNALISA PERISSA. 1981. *Scuole di arti, mestiere e devozione a Venezia* (Venice: Arsenale Editrice)
―― 2008. *Scuole grandi e piccole a Venezia tra arte e storia. Confraternite di mestieri e devozione in sei itinerari* (Venice: Scuola Grande di San Teodoro)
GRAMIGNI, TOMMASO. 2012. *Iscrizioni medievali nel territorio fiorentino fino al XIII secolo* (Florence: Florence University Press)
GRAY, NICOLETE. 1948. 'The Palaeography of Latin Inscriptions in the Eighth, Ninth and Tenth Centuries in Italy', *Papers of the British School at Rome*, 16: 38–171

GRAZIANI, FEDERICO. 2013. 'Epigrafi volgari venete' (Tesi di Laurea, University of Venice Ca' Foscari)
GREVEMBROCH, JAN [GIOVANNI]. 1754. *Monumenta veneta ex antiquis ruderibus, Templorum, aliorumq. Ædium vetustate collapsarum collecta studio, et cura Petri Gradonici Jacobi Sen. F. anno MDCCLIV*, 4 vols (Venice: Museo Civico Correr, ms Gradenigo-Dolfin 228)
GUARNIERI, CRISTINA. 2006. 'Per un corpus della pittura veneziana del Trecento al tempo di Lorenzo', *Saggi e Memorie di Storia dell'Arte*, 30: 1–132
—— 2011. 'Lorenzo Veneziano e l'ordine dei predicatori: nuove riflessioni critiche attorno alle tre tele con la *Madonna dell'umiltà*', in *Lorenzo Veneziano, Le Virgines humilitatis. Tre Madonne 'de panno lineo'. Indagini, tecnica, iconografia*, ed. by Chiara Rigoni and Chiara Scardellato (Milan: Silvana), pp. 19–41
—— 2015. 'Il monumento funebre di Francesco Dandolo nella sala del capitolo ai Frari', in *Santa Maria Gloriosa dei Frari. Immagini di devozione, spazi della fede*, ed. by Carlo Corsato and Deborah Howard (Padua: Centro Studi Antoniani), pp. 151–62
GUARNIERI, CRISTINA, and ANDREA DE MARCHI. 2016. *Lorenzo di Nicolò detto Lorenzo Veneziano. San Giovanni Battista* (Maastricht: Altomani)
GULLINO, GIUSEPPE. 2010. 'Quando la Terraferma volle conquistare Venezia: la congiura di Baiamonte Tiepolo', *Archivio Veneto*, 209: 5–11
GUZZETTI, LINDA, and ANTJE ZIEMANN. 2002. 'Women in the Fifteenth-Century Venetian *Scuola*', *Renaissance Quarterly*, 55: 1151–95
HAHNLOSER, HANS ROBERT. 1971. *Il tesoro di San Marco, vol. II (il tesoro e il museo)* (Florence: Sansoni)
HEMPEL, GIULIA, and JÜRGEN JULIER. 1979. 'Katalog der Skulpturen', in *Die Skulpturen von San Marco in Venedig: die figurlichen Skulpturen der Aussenfassaden bis zum 14. Jahrhundert*, ed. by Wolfgang Wolters (Munich and Berlin: Deutscher Kunstverlag), pp. 17–55
HOWARD, DEBORAH. 1997. 'Venice as a Dolphin: Further Investigations into Jacopo de' Barbari's View', *Artibus et Historiae*, 18.35: 101–11
HUMFREY, PETER. 1980. 'Cima da Conegliano, Sebastiano Mariani and Alvise Vivarini at the East End of S. Giovanni in Bragora in Venice', *The Art Bulletin*, 62.3: 350–63
—— 1988. 'Competitive Devotions: the Venetian *Scuole Piccole* as Donors of Altarpieces in the Years around 1500', *The Art Bulletin*, 70.3: 401–23
HUMFREY, PETER, and RICHARD S. MACKENNY. 1986. 'The Venetian Trade Guilds as Patrons of Art in the Renaissance', *The Burlington Magazine*, 128: 317–30
HUMPHREY, LYLE. 2007. 'The Illumination of Confraternity and Guild Statutes in Venice, ca. 1260–1500: Mariegola Production, Iconography, and Use' (unpublished doctoral thesis, New York University)
—— 2015. *La miniatura per le confraternite e le arti veneziane. Mariegole dal 1260 al 1460* (Verona and Venice: Cierre/Fondazione Giorgio Cini)
INGRAND-VARENNE, ESTELLE, 2016. 'Trois petits points. L'interponctuation dans les inscriptions médiévales', in *Ponctuer l'œuvre médiévale: des signes au sens*, ed. by Valérie Fasseur and Cécile Rochelois (Geneva: Droz), pp. 215–33
—— 2017. *Langues de bois, de pierre et de verre: latin et français dans les inscriptions médiévales* (Paris: Garnier)
KLOOS, RUDOLF. 1980. *Einführung in die Epigraphik der frühen Neuzeit* (Darmstadt: Wissenschaftliche Buchgesellschaft)
—— 1984. 'The Palaeography of San Marco', in Otto Demus, *The Mosaics of San Marco in Venice* (Chicago: Chicago University Press), I, pp. 295–307
KOCH, WALTER. 1995. 'Spezialfragen der Inschriftenpaläographie', in *Epigrafia medievale greca e latina. Ideologia e funzione*, ed. by Guglielmo Cavallo and Cyril Mango (Spoleto: Centro Italiano di Studi sull'Alto Medioevo), pp. 267–91
—— 1999. 'Auf dem Wege zur Gotischen Majuskel. Anmerkungen zur epigraphischen Schrift in romanischer Zeit', in *Inschrift und Material. Inschrift und Buchschrift*, ed. by Walter

Koch and Christine Steininger (Munich: Bayerische Akademie der Wissenschaften), pp. 225–47

—— 2010. 'Epigraphy', in *Handbook of Medieval Studies: Terms-Methods-Trends*, ed. by Albrecht Classen (Berlin and New York: De Gruyter), pp. 489–505

KÖSTER, GABRIELE. 2008. *Künstler und ihre Brüder. Maler, Bildhauer und Architekten in den venezianischen Scuole grandi* (Berlin: Mann)

LAZZARINI, VITTORIO. 1923. 'Il Mausoleo di Raffaello Fulgosio nella Basilica del Santo', *Archivio Veneto Tridentino*, 4: 147–53

LEPSCHY, ANNA LAURA. 1996. 'La lingua dei *Diarii* di Sanudo', in her *Varietà linguistiche e pluralità di codici nel Rinascimento* (Florence: Olschki), pp. 33–51

LEVANTINO, LAURA. 2011. *La Scuola Grande di San Giovanni Evangelista: inventario dell'archivio storico* (Venice: Marsilio)

LEVENSON, JAY A. 2008. REVIEW OF SIMONE FERRARI, *Jacopo de' Barbari: un protagonista del Rinascimento tra Venezie e Dürer*, in *Print Quarterly*, 25.2: 207–09

LONGHI, ROBERTO. 1978. *Ricerche sulla pittura veneta, 1946–1949*, in *Edizione delle opere complete di Roberto Longhi* (Sansoni: Florence), X, pp. 3–63

LORENZETTI, GIULIO. 2010. *Venezia e il suo estuario* (Padua: Edizioni Erredici)

LOWE, ELIAS AVERY. 1924. *Codices Lugdunenses Antiquissimi. Le scriptorium de Lyon* (Lyon: Bibliothèque de la Ville de Lyon)

LUCCO, MAURO. 1989. 'Venezia, 1400–1430', in *La pittura nel Veneto. Il Quattrocento*, ed. by Mauro Lucco (Milan: Electa), pp. 13–48

LUCIANI, TOMASO. 1876. 'Accuse contra ser Nicolaum Zeno olim comitem', *Archivio Veneto*, 11.2: 231–57

LUSSEY, NATALIE. 2015. 'Giovanni Andrea Vavassore and the Business of Print in Early Modern Venice' (unpublished doctoral thesis, University of Edinburgh)

MACKENNY, RICHARD. 1987. *Tradesmen and Traders. The World of the Guilds in Venice and Europe, c. 1250-c. 1650* (London and Sidney: Croom Helm)

—— 1997. 'The Guilds of Venice: State and Society in the *longue durée*', *Studi Veneziani*, 34: 15–43

—— 2000. 'The *scuole piccole* of Venice: Formations and Transformations', in *The Politics of Ritual Kinship. Confraternities and Social Order in Early Modern Italy*, ed. by Nicholas Terpstra (Cambridge: Cambridge University Press)

—— 2018. *Venice as the Polity of Mercy: Guilds, Confraternities and the Social Order, c. 1250-c. 1650* (Toronto: Toronto University Press)

MCKITTERICK, ROSAMUND. 1990. 'Carolingian Uncial: A Context for the Lothar Psalter', *The British Library Journal*, 16: 1–15

MACMULLEN, RAMSEY. 1982. 'The Epigraphic Habit in the Roman Empire', *The American Journal of Philology*, 103.3: 233–46

MALAGNINI, FRANCESCA. 2017. *Il Lazzaretto Nuovo di Venezia. Le scritture parietali* (Florence: Franco Cesati)

—— 2018. *Il Lazzaretto Vecchio di Venezia. Scritture epigrafiche* (Venice: Marcianum)

MANNO, ANTONIO. 1992. 'Pietre filosofali. I capitelli del Palazzo Ducale di Venezia: catalogo delle iscrizioni', *Studi Veneziani*, 23: 15–100

—— 1995. *I mestieri di Venezia: storia, arte e devozione delle corporazioni dal XIII al XVIII secolo* (Cittadella: Biblos)

—— 1999. *Il poema del tempo. I capitelli del Palazzo Ducale di Venezia: storia e iconografia* (Venice: Canal & Stamperia Editrice)

MARDERSTEIG, GIOVANNI. 1959. 'Leon Battista Alberti e la rinascita del carattere lapidario romano del Quattrocento', *Italia Medioevale e Umanistica*, 2: 285–312

MARETTO, PAOLO. 1992. *La casa veneziana nella storia della città dalle origini all'Ottocento* (Venice: Marsilio)

MARIACHER, GIOVANNI. 1957. *Il Museo Correr di Venezia: dipinti dal XIV al XVI secolo* (Venice: Neri Pozza)
MARIN, ŞERBAN V. (ed.). 2008–12. *Giovanni Giacomo Caroldo, Istorii Veneţiene*, 5 vols (Bucharest: Arhivele Naţionale ale României)
MARKHAM SCHULZ, Anne. 1983. 'Giovanni Buora lapicida', *Arte Lombarda*, 65.2: 49–72
—— 2004. 'Antonio Bonvicino and Venetian crucifixes of the early Quattrocento', *Mitteilungen des Kunsthistorisches Institutes in Florenz*, 48.3: 283–332
—— 2011. 'Due scultori fiorentini a Venezia: Andrea Pisano e Niccolò Lamberti', *Arte Veneta*, 68: 34–55
—— 2012. 'Scultura del secondo Quattrocento e del primo Cinquecento. Il Rinascimento (1)', in *La Basilica dei Santi Giovanni e Paolo. Pantheon della Serenissima*, ed. by Giuseppe Pavanello (Venice: Marcianum/Fondazione Giorgio Cini), pp. 123–202
—— 2017. *The History of Venetian Renaissance Sculpture, ca 1400–1530*, 2 vols (London: Harvey Miller)
MARTINELLI, DOMENICO. 1684. *Il ritratto di Venezia diviso in due parti* (Venice: Hertz)
MARTÍN LÓPEZ, MARÍA ENCARNACIÓN, and VICENTE GARCÍA LOBO (eds). 2010. *Las inscripciones góticas. II coloquio internacional de epigrafía medieval* (Leon: Corpus Inscriptionum Hispaniae Medievalum)
MASCHIO, RUGGERO. 1981. 'Le scuole grandi a Venezia', in *Storia della cultura veneta*, vol. III/3, ed. by Girolamo Arnaldi and Manlio Pastore Stocchi (Vicenza: Neri Pozza), pp. 193–206
MEERSSEMAN, GILLES GÉRARD. 1977. *Ordo fraternitatis. Confraternite e pietà dei laici nel Medioevo*, 3 vols (Rome: Herder)
MEISS, MILLARD. 1960. 'Towards a More Comprehensive Renaissance Palaeography', *The Art Bulletin*, 42: 97–112
MENEGUOLO, ANTONIO. 2019. 'Le liturgie della settimana santa e della festa di San Marco', in *San Marco, la Basilica di Venezia: arte, storia, conservazione*, ed. by Ettore Vio, 2 vols (Venice: Marsilio), I, pp. 47–55
MERKEL, ETTORE. 1989. 'Venezia, 1430–1450', in *La pittura nel Veneto. Il Quattrocento*, ed. by Mauro Lucco (Milan: Electa), pp. 49–79
—— 1994. 'I mosaici del Cinquecento veneziano', *Saggi e Memorie di Storia dell'Arte*, 19: 73–140
MERLO, CLEMENTE. 1904. *I nomi romanzi delle stagioni e dei mesi studiati particolarmente nei dialetti ladini, italiani, franco-provenzali e provenzali. Saggio di onomasiologia* (Turin: Loescher)
MESCHINELLO, GIANNANTONIO. 1753. *La chiesa ducale di S. Marco: Spiegazione delli Mosaici, e delle Iscrizioni*, 3 vols (Venice: Bartolomeo Baronchelli)
MEYER, ELIZABETH A. 1990. 'Explaining the Epigraphic Habit in the Roman Empire: the Evidence of Epitaphs', *The Journal of Roman Studies*, 80: 74–96
MIGLIORINI, BRUNO, and GIANFRANCO FOLENA (eds). 1952. *Testi non toscani del Trecento* (Modena: Società Tipografica Modenese)
MILLER, SANDA. 1978. 'Giovanni Mansueti, a Little Master of the Venetian Quattrocento', *Revue Roumaine d'Histoire de l'Art*, 15: 77–115
MOCELLIN, MARCO. 2016. 'Epigrafi veneziane in volgare del XV secolo' (Tesi di Laurea, University of Venice Ca' Foscari)
MOLÀ, LUCA. 1994. *La comunità dei Lucchesi a Venezia: immigrazione e industria della seta nel tardo Medioevo* (Venice: Istituto Veneto di Scienze, Lettere ed Arti)
MONACI, ERNESTO. 1912. *Crestomazia italiana dei primi secoli* (Città di Castello: Lapi)
MONEGO, LUISA. 2012. 'Le mariegole latine della Scuola di Santa Maria e San Francesco dei Mercanti ai Frari' (Tesi di Laurea, University of Venice Ca' Foscari)
MONTICOLO, GIOVANNI (ed.). 1896–1914. *I capitolari delle Arti veneziane sottoposte alla Giustizia poi alla Giustizia Vecchia dalle Origini al MCCCXXX*, 3 vols (Rome: Forzani)

MORETTI, SILVIA, and MARIA TERESA TODESCO. 2008. 'Il cantiere della cappella di Sant'Alvise nella chiesa dei Santi Giovanni e Paolo a Venezia', *Annali di Architettura*, 20: 83–108

MORISON, STANLEY. 1972. *Politics and Script* (Oxford: Oxford University Press)

MOSCHINI, GIANNANTONIO. 1808. *Guida all'isola di Murano* (Venice: Palese)

—— 1815. *Guida per la città di Venezia all'amico delle belle arti*, 2 vols (Venice: Alvisopoli)

—— 1842. *La chiesa e il seminario di S.ta Maria della Salute in Venezia* (Venice: Giuseppe Antonelli)

MUELLER, REINHOLD C. 1997. *The Venetian Money Market: Banks, Panics and Public Debt, 1200–1500* (Baltimore and London: Johns Hopkins University Press)

MURARO, MICHELANGELO. 1985. *La vita nelle pietre. Sculture marciane e civiltà veneziana del Duecento* (Venice: Arsenale)

MUSSAFIA, ADOLFO. 1873. *Beitrag zur Kunde der norditalienischen Mundarten im XV. Jahrhunderte* (Vienna: Österreichische Akademie der Wissenschaften)

MUTINELLI, FABIO. 1841. *Annali urbani di Venezia dall'anno 810 al 12 maggio 1797* (Venice: Giambattista Merlo)

NANETTI, ANDREA (ed.). 2010. *Il Codice Morosini. Il mondo visto da Venezia*, 4 vols (Spoleto: Fondazione Centro Italiano di Studi sull'Alto Medioevo)

NEPI SCIRÈ, GIOVANNA. 1978. 'La Scuola Vecchia della Misericordia', *Quaderni della Soprintendenza ai Beni Artistici e Storici di Venezia*, 7: 9–29

NIERO, ANTONIO. 1965. 'Testimonianze epigrafiche sul convento di S. Antonio Abate di Castello. Nota sul culto del Santo', *Studi Veneziani*, 7: 347–62

—— 1993. 'Simbologia dotta e popolare nelle sculture esterne', in *La basilica di San Marco, arte e simbologia*, ed. by Bruno Bertoli (Venice: Studium Cattolico Veneziano), pp. 125–48

NYBERG, ULLA. 1978. 'Über inschriftliche Abkürzungen der gotischen und humanistischen Schriftperioden', *Arctos*, 12: 63–79

ONGANIA, FERDINANDO. 1881–85. *La Basilica di San Marco in Venezia. Portafogli 1–5* (Venice: Ferdinando Ongania)

ORTALLI, FRANCESCA. 2001. *'Per salute delle anime e delli corpi'. Scuole piccole a Venezia nel tardo Medioevo* (Venice: Marsilio)

PACCAGNELLA, IVANO. 2012. *Vocabolario del pavano (XIV-XVII secolo)* (Padua: Esedra)

PALLUCCHINI, RODOLFO. 1964. *La pittura veneziana del Trecento* (Venice and Rome: Istituto per la Collaborazione Culturale)

PAMATO, LORENZA. 1999. 'Le scuole dei battuti di Venezia (1260–ca. 1401): tra fonti e storia' (unpublished doctoral thesis, University of Padua)

—— 2001. *'De dominabus mundanis in istis nostris scolis*. La matricola femminile dei battuti di San Giovanni Evangelista (sec. XIV)', *Annali di Studi Religiosi*, 2: 439–501

PANZER, FRIEDRICH, ET AL. (eds). 1934-. *Die deutschen Inschriften des Mittelalters und der frühen Neuzeit* (Wiesbaden: Reichert)

PAOLETTI, PIETRO. 1893–97. *L'architettura e la scultura del Rinascimento in Venezia*, 2 vols (Venice: Ongania-Naya)

PARTRIDGE, LOREN. 2015. *Art of Renaissance Venice, 1400–1600* (Oakland, University of California Press)

PASINI, ANTONIO. 1887. *Il Tesoro di San Marco in Venezia* (Venice: Ongania)

PAZZI, PIERO (ed.). 2001. *Corpus delle iscrizioni di Venezia e delle isole della laguna veneta di Emmanuele Antonio Cicogna*, 3 vols (Venice: Biblioteca Orafa di Sant'Antonio Abate)

PEDROCCO, FILIPPO. 1981. 'Vicende della Scuola', in *Le Scuole di Venezia*, ed. by Terisio Pignatti (Milan: Electa), pp. 48–50

PERRY, MARILYN. 1977. 'St Mark's Trophies: Legend, Superstition and Archaeology in Renaissance Venice', *Journal of the Warburg and Courtauld Institutes*, 40: 27–49

PERTUSI, AGOSTINO. 1990. *Saggi veneto-bizantini* (Florence: Olschki)
PETRUCCI, ARMANDO. 1985. *Potere, spazi urbani, scritture esposte: proposte ed esempi* (Rome: École Française de Rome)
—— 1986. *La scrittura. Ideologia e rappresentazione* (Turin: Einaudi)
—— 1991. 'Scrivere "alla greca" nell'Italia del Quattrocento', in *Bisanzio fuori di Bisanzio*, ed. by Guglielmo Cavallo (Palermo: Sellerio), pp. 121–36
—— 1992. *Medioevo da leggere. Guida allo studio delle testimonianze scritte del Medioevo italiano* (Turin: Einaudi)
—— 1995. *Le scritture ultime: ideologia della morte e strategie dello scrivere nella cultura occidentale* (Turin: Einaudi)
—— 1997. 'Il volgare esposto: problemi e prospettive', in *'Visibile parlare'. Le scritture esposte nei volgari italiani dal Medioevo al Rinascimento*, ed. by Claudio Ciociola (Naples: Edizioni Scientifiche Italiane), pp. 45–58
PETRUCCI, ARMANDO, ET AL. 1981. 'Epigrafia e paleografia. Inchiesta sui rapporti fra due discipline', *Scrittura e Civiltà*, 5: 265–312
PETRUCCI, LIVIO. 2010. *Alle origini dell'epigrafia volgare. Iscrizioni italiane e romanze fino al 1275* (Pisa: Pisa University Press)
PIANA, MARIO. 1995. 'Il restauro del portale maggiore di San Marco', in *Le sculture esterne di San Marco*, ed. by Otto Demus, et al. (Milan: Electa), pp. 235–46
PICHI, SILVIA. 2013. 'I lavoranti del Fondaco dei Tedeschi. Mestiere, corporazione e devozione a Venezia', in *La chiesa di San Bartolomeo e la comunità tedesca a Venezia*, ed. by Natalino Bonazza, Isabella di Lenardo and Gianmario Guidarelli (Venice: Marcianum), pp. 231–74
PIEGADI, ALESSANDRO. 1847. *Leggende sopra Santa Fosca Vergine e Martire di Ravenna e sopra la chiesa di Santa Fosca in Venezia* (Venice: Gaspari)
PIGNATTI, TERISIO (ed.). 1981. *Le Scuole di Venezia* (Milan: Electa)
PINCUS, DEBRA. 2000. *The Tombs of the Doges of Venice* (Cambridge: Cambridge University Press)
—— 2016. 'Venetian Ducal Tomb Epitaphs: The Stones of History', in *The Tombs of the Doges of Venice. From the Beginning of the Serenissima to 1907*, ed. by Benjamin Paul (Rome: Viella), pp. 243–66
—— 2017. 'Calligraphy, Epigraphy and the Paduan-Venetian Culture of Letters in the Early Renaissance', in *Padua and Venice. Transcultural Exchange in the Early Modern Age*, ed. by Birgit Blass-Simmen and Stefan Weppelmann (Berlin and Boston: De Gruyter)
—— 2019. 'The Beginning of Gothic Lettering at the Basilica of San Marco: the Contribution of Doge Andrea Dandolo', in *San Marco, la Basilica di Venezia: arte, storia, conservazione*, ed. by Ettore Vio, 2 vols (Venice: Marsilio), I, pp. 319–30
PIVATI, GIOVANNI FRANCESCO. 1746–51. *Nuovo dizionario scientifico e curioso sacro-profano*, 10 vols (Venice: Benedetto Milocco)
POLACCO, RENATO, GIOVANNA NEPI SCIRÈ and GUIDO ZATTERA. 1978. *Museo di Torcello. Sezione medioevale e moderna* (Venice: Provincia di Venezia)
POTTER, DAVID S. 2014. 'Inscriptions and the Narrative of Roman History', in *The Oxford Handbook of Roman Epigraphy*, ed. by Christer Bruun and Jonathan Edmondson (Oxford: Oxford University Press), pp. 345–63
POZZA, MARCO. 1982. *I Badoer: una famiglia veneziana dal X al XIII secolo* (Abano Terme: Francisci)
PRATI, ANGELICO. 1968. *Etimologie venete*, ed. by Gianfranco Folena and Giambattista Pellegrini (Venice and Rome: Istituto per la Collaborazione Culturale)
PREVITALI, GIOVANNI. 1979. 'La periodizzazione della storia dell'arte italiana', in *Storia dell'arte italiana. Parte prima (materiali e problemi), I: Questioni e metodi*, ed. by Giovanni Previtali (Turin: Einaudi)

PULLAN, BRIAN. 1971. *Rich and Poor in Renaissance Venice: The Social Institutions of a Catholic State, to 1620* (Cambridge, Massachusetts: Harvard University Press)
—— 1981. 'Natura e carattere delle Scuole', in *Le Scuole di Venezia*, ed. by Teresio Pignatti (Milan: Electa), pp. 9–26
PUPPI, LIONELLO, and LOREDANA OLIVATO PUPPI. 1977. *Mauro Codussi* (Milan: Electa)
RACKHAM, OLIVER, and JENNIFER MOODY. 1996. *The Making of the Cretan Landscape* (Manchester and New York: Manchester University Press)
RAUCH, SIMONE (ed.). 2009. *Le mariegole delle arti dei tessitori di seta: i* veluderi *(1347–1474) e i* samiteri *(1370–1475)* (Venice: Il Comitato Editore)
REDON, ODILE, ET AL. 2002. *Les langues de l'Italie médiévale* (Turnhout: Brepols)
REMACLE, LOUIS. 1948. *Le problème de l'ancien wallon* (Liège: Faculté de Philosophie et Lettres)
REYNOLDS, JOYCE. 1960. 'Inscriptions and Roman Studies 1910–1960', *The Journal of Roman Studies*, 50: 204–09
RICCIONI, STEFANO. 2017. 'Per un progetto sui dipinti firmati di Venezia in età gotica e tardogotica', *Venezia Arti*, 26: 65–69
RIGONI, CHIARA, and CHIARA SCARDELLATO. 2011. *Lorenzo Veneziano. Le* Virgines humilitatis. *Tre madonne 'de panno lineo'. Indagini, tecnica, iconografia* (Milan: Silvana)
RIZZARDI, CLEMENTINA (ed.). 2005. *Venezia e Bisanzio. Aspetti della cultura artistica bizantina da Ravenna a Venezia (V-XIV secolo)*
RIZZI, ALBERTO. 1976. *Le vere da pozzo pubbliche di Venezia e del suo estuario* (Venice: Bollettino dei Musei Civici di Venezia)
—— 1981. *Vere da pozzo: i puteali pubblici di Venezia e della sua laguna* (Venice: Stamperia di Venezia)
—— 1987. *Scultura esterna a Venezia. Corpus delle sculture erratiche di Venezia e della laguna* (Venice: Stamperia di Venezia)
ROHLFS, GERHARD. 1949–54. *Historische Grammatik der italienischen Sprache und ihrer Mundarten*, 3 vols (Bern: Francke)
ROMANIN, SAMUELE. 1853–61. *Storia documentata di Venezia*, 10 vols (Venice: Pietro Naratovich)
ROSSI, GINO, and GIOVANNI SALERNI. 1952. *I capitelli del Palazzo Ducale di Venezia* (Venice: Ongania)
ROVERSI, GIANCARLO (ed.). 1982. *Iscrizioni medievali bolognesi* (Bologna: Istituto per la Storia di Bologna)
RUSKIN, JOHN. 1851–53. *The Stones of Venice*, 3 vols (London: Smith, Elder and Co.)
—— 1886. *The Stones of Venice*, 3 vols (Orpington: George Allen)
SACCARDO, GIOVANNI. 1888–92. 'Sculture simboliche', in *La Basilica di San Marco in Venezia: illustrata nella storia e nell'arte da scrittori veneziani*, ed. by Camillo Boito (Venice: Ongania), II, pp. 245–65
SAGREDO, AGOSTINO. 1856. *Sulle consorterie delle arti edificative. Studi storici* (Venice: Pietro Naratovich)
SALLACH, ELKE. 1993. *Studien zum venezianischen Wortschatz des 15. und 16. Jahrhunderts* (Tübingen: Niemeyer)
SALSI, ANDREA. 1837. *De' pievani della chiesa di S. Pantaleone in Venezia. Cenni storico-critici illustrati con note, ritratti, iscrizioni* (Venice: Merlo)
SANSOVINO, FRANCESCO. 1581. *Venetia città nobilissima et singolare* (Venice: Sansovino)
SANSOVINO, FRANCESCO, and GIOVANNI STRINGA. 1604. *Venetia città nobilissima et singolare* (Venice: Altobello Salicato)
SANTOSTEFANO, PIERO. 1992–93. 'Tagliapietra e proti nel monastero e nella chiesa di Ognissanti in Venezia (Giovanni e Andrea Buora, Francesco Smeraldi, Francesco Contin, Giovanni Scalfarotto)', *Atti dell'Istituto Veneto di Scienze, Lettere ed Arti*, 151: 141–219

Sapienza, Valentina. 2013. 'Il cammino del tredicesimo apostolo: Leonardo Corona e "gli huomeni facinorosi" della Scuola di San Mattia', in *La chiesa di San Bartolomeo e la comunità tedesca a Venezia*, ed. by Natalino Bonazza, Isabella di Lenardo and Gianmario Guidarelli (Venice: Marcianum), pp. 155–70

Sartori, Antonio. 1949. *Guida storico-artistica della Basilica di S. M. Gloriosa dei Frari in Venezia* (Padua: Il Messaggero di Sant'Antonio)

—— 1983–89. *Archivio Sartori. Documenti di storia e arte francescana*, ed. by Giovanni Luisetto, 4 vols (Padua: Biblioteca Antoniana)

Sattin, Antonella. 1986. 'Ricerche sul veneziano del sec. XV (con edizione di testi)', *L'Italia Dialettale*, 49: 1–172

Sbriziolo, Lia. 1967. 'Le confraternite veneziane di devozione: saggio bibliografico e premesse storiografiche (dal particolare esame dello statuto della scuola mestrina di San Rocco)', *Rivista della Storia della Chiesa in Italia*, 21: 167–97, 502–42

—— 1967–68. 'Per la storia delle confraternite veneziane: dalle deliberazioni miste del Consiglio dei Dieci. *Scolae comunes*, artigiane e nazionali', *Atti dell'Istituto Veneto di Scienze, Lettere ed Arti*, 126: 405–52

—— 1970. 'Per la storia delle confraternite veneziane: dalle deliberazioni miste (1310–1476) del Consiglio dei Dieci. Le scuole dei battuti', in Cinzio Violante, et al., *Miscellanea Gilles Gérard Meersseman* (Padua: Antenore), II, pp. 715–63

Schivo, Sarah. 2012. 'La gens Terentia ad Altinum e nella decima regio: le evidenze epigrafiche' (Tesi di Laurea, University of Venice Ca' Foscari)

Schrader, Lorenz. 1592. *Monumentorum Italiæ, quæ hoc nostro sæculo & à Christianis posita sunt* (Saxone Helmaestadii: Iacobi Luceij Transylvani)

Schreiner, Peter. 2019. 'I "Tetrarchi" tra Basilica e Palazzo Ducale: simbolo tra religione e potere', in *San Marco, la Basilica di Venezia: arte, storia, conservazione*, ed. by Ettore Vio, 2 vols (Venice: Marsilio), II, pp. 87–98

Schulz, Juergen. 1978. 'Jacopo de' Barbari's View of Venice: Map Making, City Views, and Moralized Geography before the Year 1500', *The Art Bulletin*, 60.3: 425–74

—— 1993. 'The Houses of the Dandolo. A Family Compound in Medieval Venice', *Journal of the Society of Architectural Historians*, 52.4: 391–415

Semi, Franca. 1983. *Gli 'Ospizi' di Venezia* (Venice: Helvetia)

Sherman, Allison. 2010. 'The Lost Venetian Church of Santa Maria Assunta dei Crociferi: Form, Decoration and Patronage' (unpublished doctoral thesis, University of St Andrews)

Simeone, Gian Andrea (ed.). 2003. *La mariegola della Scuola Grande di San Giovanni Evangelista a Venezia (1261–1457)* (Venice: Scuola Grande di San Giovanni Evangelista)

Simonsfeld, Henry. 1887. *Der Fondaco dei Tedeschi in Venedig und die Deutsch-Venetianischen Handelsbeziehungen. Quellen und Forschungen*, 2 vols (Stuttgart: Verlag der J. G. Cotta'schen Buchhandlung)

Sohm, Phillip Lindsay. 1982. *The Scuola Grande di San Marco, 1437–1550. The Architecture of a Venetian Lay Confraternity* (New York and London: Garland)

Soravia, Giovanni Battista. 1822–24. *Le chiese di Venezia descritte ed illustrate*, 3 vols (Venice: Andreola)

Spinazzi, Alberto. 2003. 'La Scuola Grande di San Giovanni Evangelista a Venezia (1340–1515)' (Tesi di Laurea, University of Venice IUAV)

Stancioiu, Cristina. 2010. '*... I ever loved thee lady muse, and yet my love increases*: Rhodian Portrait Ceramics and Cultural Dialogue in the Mediterranean', *Al-Masāq: Journal of the Medieval Mediterranean*, 22: 129–50

Stirnemann, Patricia, and Marc H. Smith. 2007. 'Forme et fonction des écritures d'apparat dans les manuscrits latins (VIIIe-XVe siècle)', *Bibliothèque de l'École des Chartes*, 165: 67–100

STUSSI, ALFREDO. 1965. *Testi veneziani del Duecento e dei primi del Trecento* (Pisa: Nistri-Lischi)

—— 1980A. 'Antichi testi dialettali veneti', in *Guida ai dialetti veneti*, ed. by Manlio Cortelazzo, 15 vols (Padua: Cleup), II, pp. 85–100

—— (ed.). 1980B. *Epigrafe veneziana in volgare (1310)* (Pisa: Cursi)

—— 1995A. 'La carta lapidaria di Urbano V', in *Scritti filologici e linguistici in onore di Tristano Bolelli*, ed. by Roberto Ajello and Saverio Sani (Pisa: Pacini), pp. 483–91

—— 1995B. 'Due epigrafi della Scuola Grande di San Giovanni Evangelista in Venezia', in *Da una riva all'altra. Studi in onore di Antonio d'Andrea*, ed. by Dante della Terza (Fiesole: Il Calamo), II, pp. 189–96

—— 1997A. 'Epigrafi medievali in volgare dell'Italia settentrionale e della Toscana', in *'Visibile parlare'. Le scritture esposte nei volgari italiani dal Medioevo al Rinascimento*, ed. by Claudio Ciociola (Napoli: Edizioni Scientifiche Italiane), pp. 149–76

—— 1997B. 'La lingua', in *Storia di Venezia dalle Origini alla caduta della Serenissima, III: La formazione dello stato patrizio*, ed. by Girolamo Arnaldi, Giorgio Cracco and Alberto Tenenti (Rome: Istituto della Enciclopedia Italiana), pp. 911–32

—— 2005. 'Medioevo volgare veneziano', in Alfredo Stussi, *Storia linguistica e storia letteraria* (Bologna: Il Mulino), pp. 23–80

ŚWIECHOWSKI, ZYGMUNT. 1977. 'Venetobyzantinische Fassadenreliefs im Klosterhof zu Berlin-Glienicke', in *Festschrift für Otto von Simson zum 65. Geburtstag*, ed. by Lucius Grisebach and Konrad Renger (Frankfurt am Mein: Propyläen), pp. 62–71

TASSINI, GIUSEPPE. 1863. *Curiosità Veneziane, ovvero origini delle denominazioni stradali di Venezia* (Venice: Cecchini)

—— 1876. 'Iscrizioni dell'ex chiesa, convento e confraternita di S. Maria della Carità', *Archivio Veneto*, 12.1: 357–92 and 12.2: 112–29

—— 1879. *Alcuni palazzi ed antichi edificii di Venezia storicamente illustrati con annotazioni* (Venice: Tipografia M. Fontana)

TESTI, LAUDEDEO. 1909. *La storia della pittura veneziana*, I (Bergamo: Istituto Italiano di Arti Grafiche)

THOMAS, GEORG MARTIN. 1874. *Capitolare dei Visdomini del Fontego dei Todeschi in Venezia* (Berlin: A. Asher)

TIGLER, GUIDO. 1993. 'Le fonti teologiche del programma iconografico negli arconi del portale maggiore', in *La Basilica di San Marco: arte e simbologia*, ed. by Bruno Bertoli (Venice: Edizioni Studium Cattolico Veneziano), pp. 149–66

—— 1995A. 'Catalogo delle sculture', in *Le sculture esterne di San Marco*, ed. by Otto Demus, et al. (Milan: Electa), pp. 25–227

—— 1995B. *Il portale maggiore di San Marco a Venezia. Aspetti iconografici e stilistici dei rilievi duecenteschi* (Venice: Istituto Veneto di Scienze, Lettere ed Arti)

—— 1999. 'The Arches of the Central Portal', in *The Basilica of St Mark in Venice*, ed. by Ettore Vio (New York: Riverside), p. 68

—— 2019. 'Trofei della quarta Crociata? Punti fermi per la datazione delle facciate marmoree di San Marco', in *San Marco, la Basilica di Venezia: arte, storia, conservazione*, ed. by Ettore Vio, 2 vols (Venice: Marsilio), I, pp. 131–50

TOMASIN, LORENZO. 2001A. 'La lapide veneziana di S. Gottardo a Piazzola sul Brenta (1384)', *L'Italia Dialettale*, 62: 173–77

—— 2001B. *Il volgare e la legge. Storia linguistica del diritto veneziano (secoli XIII-XVIII)* (Padua: Esedra)

—— 2007. 'Il volgare nella cancelleria veneziana fra Tre e Quattrocento', *Medioevo Letterario d'Italia*, 4: 69–89

—— 2012A. 'Epigrafi trecentesche in volgare nei dintorni di Venezia', *Lingua e Stile*, 47: 23–44

—— 2012B. '*Minima muralia*: esercizio di epigrafia volgare medievale', *Vox Romanica*, 71: 1–12

―― 2013. 'Quindici testi veneziani 1300–1310', *Lingua e Stile*, 48: 3–48
―― 2014. 'Venezia', in *Città italiane, storie di lingue e culture*, ed. by Pietro Trifone (Rome: Carocci), pp. 157–202
―― 2016. 'Su filologia romanza e epigrafia medievale', *Zeitschrift für Romanische Philologie*, 132.2: 493–526
Toso Borella, Marco. 2009. *I dossali di San Zuanne '...a percorrer la meraviglia'* (Murano: Isolainvisibile/Unità Pastorale di Murano)
Troncarelli, Fabio. 1991. 'Il medico', in *Condizione umana e ruoli sociali nel Mezzogiorno normanno-svevo*, ed. by Giosuè Musca (Bari: Dedalo), pp. 337–57
Unrau, John. 1984. *Ruskin and St Mark's* (Wisbech: Thames and Hudson)
Van Marle, Raimond. 1924. *The Development of the Italian Schools of Painting*, IV (The Hague: Nijhoff).
Vazzoler, Chiara. 2005. *La Scuola Grande di San Giovanni Evangelista* (Venice: Marsilio)
Vecchi, Maurizia. 1982. *Torcello: nuove ricerche* (Rome: L'Erma di Bretschneider)
―― 1993. *Chiese e monasteri medioevali scomparsi della laguna superiore di Venezia: ricerche storico-archeologiche* (Rome: L'Erma di Bretschneider)
Videsott, Paul. 2009. *Padania scrittologica: analisi scrittologiche e scrittometriche di testi in italiano settentrionale dalle origini al 1525* (Tübingen: Niemeyer)
Vighy, Francesca. 1990. 'La scrittura mercantesca in area veneta' (Tesi di Laurea, University of Padua)
Vio, Ettore. 1999. *The Basilica of St Mark in Venice* (New York: Riverside)
Vio, Gastone. 2004. *Le Scuole Piccole nella Venezia dei Dogi. Note d'archivio per la storia delle confraternite veneziane* (Vicenza: Angelo Colla)
Vuillemin, Pascal. 2018. *Parochiæ Venetiarum. Les paroisses de Venise au Moyen Âge* (Paris: Garnier)
Wixom, William D. 1984. 'Western Metalwork', in *The Treasury of San Marco, Venice*, ed. by David Buckton, et al. (Milan: Olivetti), pp. 306–09
Wolters, Wolfgang. 1976. *La scultura veneziana gotica (1300-1460)*, 2 vols (Venice: Alfieri)
―― 2008. 'Una storia dei bronzi veneziani senza le campane?', in *L'industria artistica del bronzo del Rinascimento a Venezia e nell'Italia settentrionale*, ed. by Matteo Ceriana and Victoria Avery (Verona: Scripta), pp. 375–86
Woolf, Greg. 1996. 'Monumental Writing and the Experience of Roman Society in the Early Empire', *The Journal of Roman Studies*, 86: 22–39
Wurthmann, William. 1989. 'The Council of Ten and the *Scuole Grandi* in Early Renaissance Venice', *Studi Veneziani*, 18: 15–66
Zabbia, Marino. 2009. 'Circolazione di persone e diffusione di modelli in ambito notarile (secoli XIII-XIV)', in *Cultura cittadina e documentazione. Formazione e circolazione di modelli*, ed. by Anna Laura Trombetti Budriesi (Bologna: Cleub), pp. 23–39
Zamponi, Stefano. 2006. 'La metamorfosi dell'antico: la tradizione antiquaria veneta', in *I luoghi dello scrivere da Francesco Petrarca agli albori dell'età moderna*, ed. by Caterina Tristano, Marta Calleri and Leonardo Magionami (Spoleto: Centro Italiano di Studi sull'Alto Medioevo), pp. 37–67
Zanetti, Vincenzo. 1881. *Il Museo civico-vetrario di Murano* (Venice: Gaetano Longo)
Zanotto, Francesco. 1842–58. *Il Palazzo ducale di Venezia illustrato da Francesco Zanotto*, 4 vols (Venice: Giuseppe Antonelli)
Zorzi, Alvise. 1984. *Venezia scomparsa* (Milan: Electa)
Zovatto, Paolo Lino. 1971. *Grado. Antichi monumenti* (Bologna: Calderini)
Zuchold, Gerd-H. 1993. *Der 'Klosterhof' des Prinzen Karl von Preussen im Park von Schloss Glienicke in Berlin* (Berlin: Mann)
Zurla, Placido. 1806. *Il mappamondo di Fra Mauro Camaldolese* (Venice: n. pub.)

www.ingramcontent.com/pod-product-compliance
Lightning Source LLC
Chambersburg PA
CBHW080833230426
43665CB00021B/2827